BALTINGLASS AND THE PREHISTORIC HILLFORTS OF IRELAND

Baltinglass and the Prehistoric Hillforts of Ireland

James O'Driscoll, Alan Hawkes and William O'Brien
with contributions from Nick Hogan and Kevin Kearney

Wordwell

For Barry Cunliffe, who showed the way.

First published in 2024
Wordwell Ltd
Unit 9, 78 Furze Road, Sandyford Industrial Estate,
Dublin 18
www.wordwellbooks.com

Cover: Aerial photograph of the large enclosure of Rathcoran on Baltinglass Hill, with excavation of inner enclosure in progress

ISBN 978-1-916742-08-6

British Library Cataloguing-in-Publication Data.
A catalogue record for this book is available from the British Library.

Typeset in Ireland by Wordwell Ltd
Copy-editor: Helena King
Cover design by Wordwell Ltd
Printed by SprintBooks

CONTENTS

LIST OF FIGURES

All illustrations provided by the authors unless stated otherwise.

Chapter 4

Chapter 5

Chapter 6

FOREWORD

The significance of the Baltinglass Hillfort Cluster was highlighted some 25 years ago by Tom Condit of the National Monuments Service, who called it 'Ireland's Hillfort Capital'. Since that time, thanks to the ongoing research by University College Cork, our knowledge of this fascinating landscape has only expanded.

The hillforts in the Baltinglass area include some of the largest examples known in Ireland, and collectively, with numerous other monument types, they form a unique and fascinating prehistoric landscape. This publication represents the culmination of extensive archaeological research in recent years, and I would like to commend the authors for their dedication, and for producing such a fine resource for County Wicklow. I would also like to acknowledge the role of our Heritage Officer, Deirdre Burns, who has worked with the authors and the local community over the last number of years to ensure that the archaeological heritage of this part of county Wicklow gets the recognition it truly deserves.

Paul O'Brien, Cathaoirleach, Wicklow County Council

I am delighted to welcome this important and timely new publication, which sheds light on the remarkable archaeological landscape of the Baltinglass area of West Wicklow.

Wicklow County Council has been pleased to support the authors on their journey of investigation over the last number for years, from the discretionary funding provided by the Baltinglass Municipal district members in 2020, to funds co-ordinated by our Heritage Officer through the National Monuments Service's Community Monuments Fund in 2021 and 2022.

We look forward to working in partnership with the local community to continue to protect and promote this remarkable heritage, and to support heritage-led regeneration for the benefit of Baltinglass and the surrounding area.

Emer O'Gorman, Chief Executive, Wicklow County Council.

PREFACE

The Baltinglass area of south-west Wicklow has a remarkable concentration of prehistoric hillforts, with as many as thirteen large enclosures on hills overlooking the modern town. This book presents the results of an archaeological investigation that examined these sites in their cultural landscape setting. The study began in 2011 with an Irish Research Council-funded project on 'Hillforts, Warfare and Society in Bronze Age Ireland', based in the Department of Archaeology, University College Cork. This five-year project, directed by William O'Brien, examined the archaeology of warfare and inter-regional conflict during the Bronze Age, with a focus on multiple-enclosure hillforts. Scientific survey and sample excavation were undertaken at several hillforts across southern Ireland, including five examples at Baltinglass. One of the aims was to examine the prehistoric landscape of the Baltinglass hillforts in detail, a project undertaken by James O'Driscoll as a doctoral study (O'Driscoll 2016). This first phase of research was published as a monograph (O'Brien and O'Driscoll 2017), along with other publications in the same period.

A second phase of research at Baltinglass began with a LiDAR aerial survey commissioned by Dr James O'Driscoll, with the support of Wicklow County Council through the NMS Community Monuments Fund. One of the project team, Dr Alan Hawkes, was funded in 2017–21 by the Royal Irish Academy, Wicklow County Council and University College Cork to excavate Rathcoran, one the best known of the Baltinglass hillforts. University College Cork also funded a palaeoecological study of a local bog by Dr Kevin Kearney. The results of those efforts are brought together in this publication, to shed new light on some of the most impressive ancient monuments in Ireland. The earliest hill-top enclosures at Baltinglass date back five-and-a-half-thousand years, to the first farmers of the Neolithic age. Large hillforts built on those same hills *c.*1400–800 BC attest to an important centre of regional power during the Middle and Late Bronze Age. This landscape certainly deserves the label it has carried ever since its importance was highlighted by Tom Condit 30 years ago—'Ireland's Hillfort Capital'.

I wish to thank my colleagues and former students, James O'Driscoll, Alan Hawkes, Kevin Kearney and Nick Hogan for their essential contribution to this project. Nick Hogan assisted with the production of this book. Funding was gratefully received from the Irish Research Council, Royal Irish Academy and University College Cork, with support from Wicklow County Council and their heritage officer, Deirdre Burns. I also wish to thank the National Museum of Ireland for assistance in archival research. Thanks also to the landowners in Baltinglass who gave permission for fieldwork, and the UCC students who assisted with excavation work. The book was produced under the expert eye of Nick Maxwell, Una McConville and Ronan Colgan at Wordwell, with editing by Madeline O'Brien and Helena King.

William O'Brien
University College Cork

1. HILLFORTS IN EARLY IRELAND

William O'Brien

Hillforts are the largest prehistoric monuments in Ireland. They are broadly defined as large, built enclosures that take advantage of topography to create a defendable position in a prominent part of the landscape. The building of hillforts was not a specific historical phenomenon, as different types of these structures, of varying age and cultural associations, are recorded in Ireland and in many other parts of Europe. Hillfort sites share two essential features: a prominent location and the physical demarcation of an exceptionally large space to which access was controlled by both the topography and artificial means. The latter involved the building of one or more lines of earthworks, stone walls or timber palisades to take advantage of elevation and slope. Visual impact was important in the siting of these monuments, which were often regarded as strategic in relation to a specific territory, resources and routeways. Most Irish hillforts are large enclosures sited on a prominent hill, low mountain, ridge, plateau, inland promontory, spur or cliff, at elevations of 100–300m OD; there are a few examples in higher mountain settings (Fig. 1.1). This positioning ensures panoramic views over broad expanses of lowland, from which the hillforts are visible across great distances.

Landform is always a significant part of hillfort design, however, and topography and artificial barriers generally combine to create an enclosure so large that its full extent is generally not visible from any one point in the landscape. Small examples, of <1–5ha, are common, but many hillforts enclose an area up to 20ha; larger variants in some parts of Europe can reach as much as 100–300ha. Their imposing presence speaks to the significance they held for early societies. The scale and logistics of hillfort construction are considerable, requiring the clearance of large areas of land and the creation of large perimeters of artificial defences.

Fig. 1.1 Brusselstown Ring hillfort at Baltinglass, with Keadeen Mountain in background.

In most cases this was well beyond the capabilities of small communities, thus requiring the mobilisation of labour in larger population groups. What special significance these enclosures had for these groups, in economic, political and other terms, is one of the key questions of hillfort research.

STUDYING HILLFORTS

The number of hillforts in Ireland is not certain. While not all examples have survived or been discovered, determining their number also depends on the criteria used to define these sites. Barry Raftery (1972) estimated 40 hillforts in Ireland, later increasing this number to 60–80 (Raftery 1994). Grogan (2005b) identified 74 examples, while a more recent review increased this to around 108 (O'Brien and O'Driscoll 2017, 22). These figures for Ireland compare to an estimate of some 3,200 confirmed examples in Britain, a figure that includes coastal promontory forts (Lock and Ralston 2022, table 2.1). The building of hillforts was a wider phenomenon, and one estimate for mainland Europe is of 30,000 examples, mostly of Bronze Age and Iron Age date (Ralston 2006).

There was little investigation of hillforts in Ireland prior to the twentieth century, and there is no record of antiquarian digging. The basic identification of these monuments owes much to the surveys of Thomas Westropp in the early twentieth century. His publication on *The Ancient Forts of Ireland* (1902) was the first significant attempt to classify early enclosures in Ireland, even if he did not identify hillforts as a separate category. Westropp included at least ten hillforts in his publication, including a number of the Baltinglass hillforts in Wicklow. He regarded the majority of so-called ringforts as early Medieval structures, suggesting that larger hilltop and cliff forts, such as at Mooghaun, Co. Clare, and Dún Aonghasa, Co. Galway, were built as early as 1200 BC. He rejected

Fig. 1.2 Class I hillfort excavated by Gerhard Bersu at Freestone Hill, Co. Kilkenny.

Fig. 1.3 Class 2a hillfort at Rathgall, Co. Wicklow, with nearby Class I hillfort at Knockeen (far-right).

mythological origins, such as the view that Dún Aonghasa was the last stronghold of the mythical Fir Bolg (O'Donovan 1839; Petrie and O'Malley 1972). Westropp considered these large forts as part of a series of monuments stretching throughout Europe, also recognising their ritual and ceremonial significance (Ashe FitzGerald 2000, 56; Westropp 1911, 347).

One of the earliest hillfort investigations in Ireland was a study by the antiquarian Goddard Orpen, of the hillforts at Rathgall and Knockeen, Co. Wicklow. He was the first to record the design of Rathgall hillfort, comparing it to Dún Aonghasa and other large stone forts in the west of Ireland (Orpen 1911, 143). Orpen interpreted Rathgall as a centre of political power in south Leinster, connected to early kings of Okinselagh. In a later paper, Orpen (1916, 42) tentatively identified Rathgall as the Dun Galion marked on Ptolemy's map of Ireland, describing the hillfort as an *oppidum munitum* or fortified town.

The first scientific excavation of an Irish hillfort/hilltop enclosure was undertaken in 1948–9 by the German archaeologist Gerhard Bersu, at Freestone Hill, Co. Kilkenny (Fig. 1.2). This was followed by excavations at Downpatrick, Co. Down (Proudfoot 1954; 1955) and Lyles Hill, Co. Antrim (Evans 1953; Simpson and Gibson 1989). The Freestone Hill work was published in 1969 by Barry Raftery, a leading researcher of the Irish Iron Age. He proposed an Iron Age date based on the presence of Roman material in a central enclosure, though Late Bronze Age pottery associated with the enclosing elements may date the hillfort to that period (Ó Floinn 2000). That same year, Raftery commenced excavation at Rathgall hillfort in south-west Wicklow (Fig. 1.3). The project was undertaken at a time when Irish hillforts were regarded as Iron Age constructions; this view was influenced by research in Britain where hillforts, such as Maiden Castle in Dorset, are classic monuments of the period. Rathgall was to change that perception, however, as excavations there over the next five years uncovered a settlement complex of the Middle to Late Bronze Age. Evidence of high-status residence, specialist craft-working and funerary ritual was found, as were exotic items indicative of long-distance trade (Raftery 1970a; 1971; 1973; 1976; Raftery and Becker forthcoming).

There have been many other hillfort excavations in the years since Rathgall was excavated. These include at Clogher, Co. Tyrone (Warner 2009); Haughey's Fort, Co. Armagh (Mallory 1995); Knockacarrigeen Hill, Co. Galway (Carey 2002); Rahally, Co. Galway (Mullins 2008); Knockdhu, Co. Antrim (MacDonald 2016); and the Hill of Ward (Davis and Moore 2024) and Faughan Hill (Dowling and Schot 2023) in Co. Meath. In addition, there has been some rescue excavation at Knockanacuig, Co. Kerry (Dunne and Bartlett 2009) and the Commons of Lloyd, Co. Meath (Neary 2004), among other sites. Also of note are excavations conducted by the Discovery Programme at Mooghaun, Co. Clare (Grogan 2005a) and Dún Aonghasa, Inis Mór, Co. Galway (Cotter 2012; see also Doody 2008). These were among the first studies to consider hillforts as part of a wider cultural landscape, broadening our understanding of their importance for regional societies of the Irish Bronze Age.

This book is based on a more recent project, in which survey and excavation were conducted at ten hillforts across southern Ireland (O'Brien and O'Driscoll 2017). These include examples in counties Cork, Kerry, Limerick, Clare and Kilkenny, as well as survey and excavation in the Baltinglass cluster in Co. Wicklow. The findings provide new insights into the design and chronology of these immense sites, as well as details of their occupation and abandonment. On a wider level, the project examined the connection between hillforts, warfare, social complexity and the political climate of late prehistoric Ireland.

TYPES OF HILLFORT

It was Barry Raftery who proposed the first classification of Irish hillforts, separating some forty known examples into three groups (1972, 39). Class 1 hillforts are univallate sites with a single enclosure; Class 2 examples have widely spaced, multiple enclosures, located on hills (class 2a) or cliffs (class 2b); Class 3 refers to inland promontory forts at high elevations. All three classes occur widely throughout Ireland, with gaps in their distribution in areas of extensive lowland. Coastal promontory forts were excluded from this classification, as were other types of smaller hill-top enclosure.

The wide distribution of Irish hillforts suggests to many that these were focal places in regional territories (Grogan 2005a, 87–99). Class 1 (univallate) hillforts have a wider distribution than their Class 2 multiple-enclosure counterparts, which are mostly found in southern Ireland, particularly in north Munster and south Leinster (Fig. 1.4). Whereas topography explains why there are relatively few examples of hillforts in the Central Plain of the Irish Midlands, topography was not a determining factor in their distribution. For example, their absence in the hilly and mountainous terrain of western Galway, Mayo and Donegal is notable. Irish hillforts typically occur in isolation, although there are a few instances where two examples are in close proximity, such as the Rathgall and Knockeen hillforts in south-west Wicklow (O'Driscoll and Becker 2022). The largest concentration is the cluster of twelve or so examples in an area of approximately 50 square kilometres at Baltinglass, Co. Wicklow.

An estimated 55% of Irish hillforts are univallate (Class 1), 40% have multiple enclosures (Class 2a), and the remainder are inland promontory forts (Class 3). Class 1 and 2 hillforts are sited in similar topographical positions, typically at elevations of 167–178m OD. Only three hillforts lie above 410m OD: Claragh, Co. Cork (446m OD) and two sites on the Dingle Peninsula in Kerry, at Caherconree (659m OD) and Faha (777m OD) respectively. Grogan (2005b, 121) observed that elevation on its own was not a significant factor in hillfort location; extensive views over parts of the local landscape were more important. An estimated 69% of Class 1 hillforts have panoramic views (360°), with a further 20% having extensive (approximately 270°) visibility of the surrounding landscape (O'Brien and O'Driscoll 2017). Class 2 hillforts generally have more extensive viewsheds, with approximately 80% having panoramic views and 15% with extensive visibility. Irrespective of classification, many Irish hillforts tend to be located at the interface between upland and lower terrain. Very few are in lowland settings, an example being Rathgall (130–139m OD).

Size is the main distinction between Class 1 and Class 2 hillforts. The latter average 7.82ha, around twice the size of Class 1 examples. Approximately half Class 1 hillforts are under 2ha, with 20% being over 5ha. In comparison, 16% of Class 2 sites are under 2ha, while 20% are over 10ha. Some examples can be much larger, with Tinoran in the Baltinglass cluster potentially as large as 84ha. Even larger is the contour enclosure at Spinans Hill 2, also at Baltinglass,

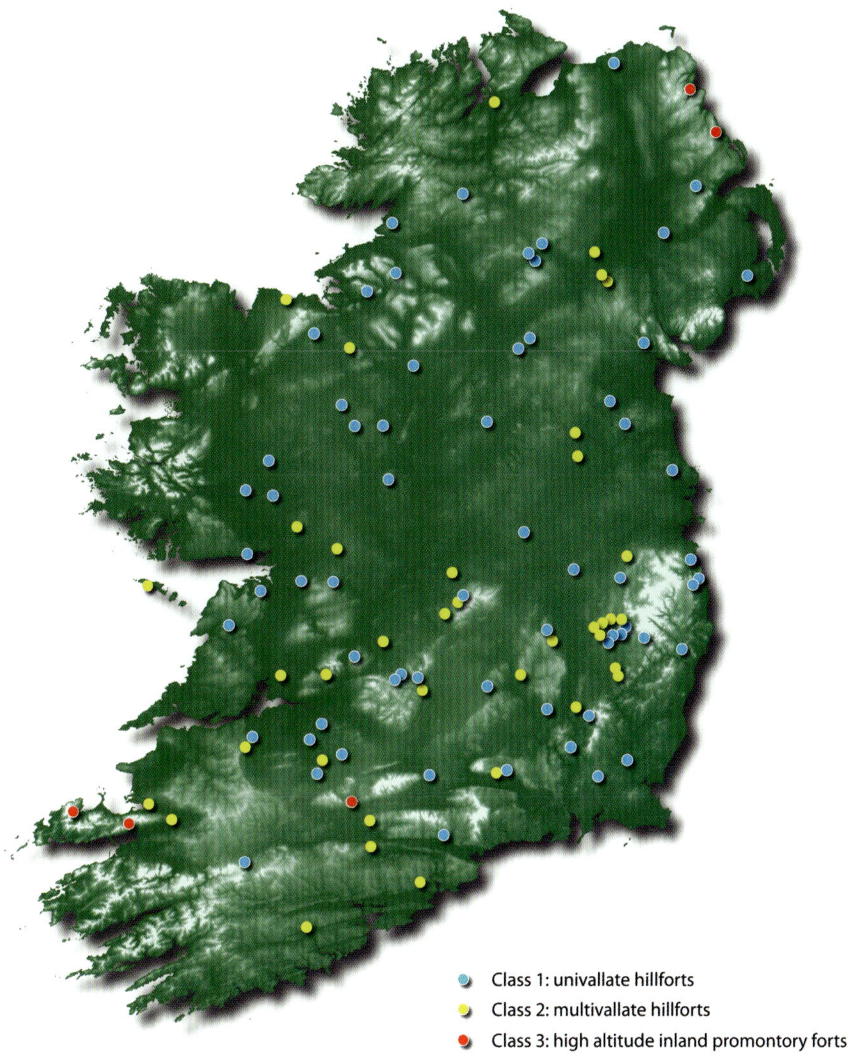

Fig. 1.4 Distribution of hillforts in Ireland, by Raftery (1972) classification.

where a single earthwork surrounds an area of 131ha.

There is also morphological variation within the hillfort types recognised by Raftery. Approximately 55% of the Class 2(a) type have enclosing elements spaced 55m or more apart, an example being Kill Hill, Co. Kildare. About 30% have more closely spaced enclosing features, separated by 20–30m, as at Rathgall, Co. Wicklow and Haughey's Fort, Co. Armagh. The remaining Class 2a hillforts have closely spaced multivallation, with no significant space between the enclosing elements, an example being Ballinkillin, Co. Carlow. The significance of the multiple enclosures in Class 2 hillforts is much debated, with interpretations ranging from the practical (separation of human residence from animal stockades), to the military (layered defence) and the symbolic (restricted elite residence and ceremonial/ritual space). This will be discussed later in the chapter when the use and meaning of hillforts is explored.

Class 3 hillforts in Ireland are inland promontory forts, of which there are fewer than a dozen examples. These typically occur at higher elevations, where artificial defences protect the landward approach on narrow mountain spurs protected by steep slopes (Fig. 1.5). They include the impressive sites at Caherconree (659m OD) and Faha (777m OD) on the Dingle Peninsula of Co. Kerry; Castle Gale, Co. Limerick (319m OD); and Lurigethan (343m OD) and Knockdhu (362m OD) on the Antrim Plateau in north-east Ireland. Knockdhu is the only excavated example. There, a narrow promontory is defended by three closely spaced banks and ditches, with as many as 100 hut circles in the interior. Excavation of two of these huts confirms occupation of this site during the later Bronze Age (MacDonald 2016).

Fig. 1.5 Class 3 inland promontory fort at Lurigethan, Co. Antrim.

The identification of hillforts in Ireland depends on the criteria chosen, with size and landscape setting being to the fore. The most common definition places these sites at over 1ha in area. Smaller examples in similar settings are classified as 'hilltop enclosures' (Grogan 2005b, 116–17). The Archaeological Survey of Ireland has recorded 124 of the latter, while Grogan lists some 200 examples (2005b, tables 7.6 and 7.7). A recent review, however, identified only 73 examples that might be termed hilltop enclosures (O'Brien and O'Driscoll 2017). While it has been suggested these smaller sites were contemporary with Bronze Age hillforts (Grogan 2005a, 247), there is no evidence to support this view. Excavation of a hilltop enclosure at Clenagh, Co. Clare, did not recover information on the dating or use of this site (Grogan 2005a, 253).

Without excavation, it can be difficult to distinguish 'hilltop enclosures' from medieval ringforts in similar landscape settings. The latter are small enclosures of earth and/or stone construction, usually under 0.2ha in size, occasionally found on prominent hills. They were an important part of the rural settlement landscape of early medieval Ireland (*c.*AD 400–1100). While most were protected, single-family farmsteads, a small number had special significance as centres of political power and elite residence, and were associated with specialised crafts. A good example is the minor royal site at Garranes, Co. Cork, dated to the fifth and sixth centuries AD (O'Brien and Hogan 2021). Ringforts are the most common archaeological site from the early medieval period (Stout 1997). Originally there may have been as many as 60,000 examples in Ireland, with less than half that number extant today. Excavation confirms they were built from as early as the fifth century until perhaps the twelfth century, with some later occupation, but there is little evidence of prehistoric origins (O'Sullivan *et al.* 2013). They are not chronologically or culturally associated with hillforts, though there are later associations, as in the stone-built examples (cashels) inside Mooghaun, Co. Clare and Rathgall, Co. Wicklow.

Reference can also be made to large hilltop enclosures at 'royal sites' of the developed Iron Age. These include Ráth na Ríogh on the Hill of Tara, Co. Meath (Roche 2002); Dún Ailinne in Co. Kildare (Wailes 1990; Johnston and Wailes 2007); and Navan Fort in Co. Armagh (Mallory 2000; Lynn 2003), all places of very special significance in myth and legend. While those univallate enclosures have a prominent hilltop setting, their earthworks differ from hillforts in having substantial internal ditches. This suggests a ceremonial enclosure rather than a fortification, with the inner ditch considered by some to represent protection against Otherworldly powers in the interior (see Warner 2000). This morphological difference, combined with their later date, raises questions about whether Iron Age 'royal enclosures' are hillforts. This depends on the criteria applied, as the latter also had ceremonial significance as places of assembly and ritual power.

Finally, the coastal promontory fort — where the neck of a small headland, promontory or cliff is blocked by a stone wall and/or earthwork defences — is related in design to the hillfort, particularly its inland equivalent (Raftery's Class 3). Some 300 examples are recorded in Ireland, though that number has not been confirmed by fieldwork. The enclosed area varies from 0.01 to 32ha, though many have been reduced in size by ongoing coastal erosion. What little excavation has been undertaken indicates that many coastal promontory forts are early- to late-medieval in date, with the oldest examples likely to be Iron Age. While coastal promontory forts and hillforts both take advantage of natural topography, the former is a separate class of monument in terms of chronology and cultural associations, which is why they were excluded from the Raftery hillfort classification.

UNDERSTANDING HILLFORTS

There are several notable features in the design and building of hillforts in Ireland. A considerable degree of planning was required in terms of time and resources, particularly as those involved were farmers, which would limit the pool of labour available at certain times of the year. There is evidence of coherent design in the layout of these enclosures over large areas of undulating ground, which suggests that basic principles of measurement and line of sight were followed. Without excavation it is difficult to know whether some hillforts are the result of a single design executed over one phase of construction, or if the monuments were instead created over a longer period, in a process involving repair and re-building, adjustments to size, enhanced fortification and other structural changes. Most Class 1 and Class 3 hillforts in Ireland were probably built as part of a single period design. This is less certain in the case of Class 2 hillforts, of which Dún Aonghasa is a good example of structural change over a long period (Fig. 1.6).

While the morphology of individual hillforts was adapted to specific topographic settings, there is evidence of purposeful design over a wide geographical area. This is true

Fig. 1.6 Class 2b cliff-edge hillfort at Dún Aonghasa, Inis Mór, Co. Galway. (Source: University of Galway collection.)

of Class 2 (multiple enclosure) hillforts in Ireland, where consistency of form suggests their builders worked to some template. Why hillforts vary in size is unclear. It may be connected in some way to the size of the hillfort's population, in terms of the capacity to build such large enclosures, but it is not simply about accommodating a large number of people. Some design features of Class 2 hillforts in Ireland also require explanation, such as the division of the spaces created by their wide concentric enclosures.

The logistics of hillfort construction were considerable, involving the clearance of large areas of land and the building of great lengths of artificial defences. The creation of rock-cut ditches, earthen banks, stone walls and timber palisades over such distances required a massive commitment of resources and time. Why particular enclosing elements were chosen, individually or in combination, is not always clear. In some instances environmental constraints, including geology, soil cover and the presence of local woodland, influenced the decision to build stone walls or wooden palisades, or to dig ditches. The size of those enclosing elements was also quite variable. Some hillforts are surrounded by enclosing elements less than 2m in height; others had impressive earthwork defences. The inner enclosure of a Class 2 hillfort at Clashanimud, Co Cork, for instance, was protected by the 6–7m high barrier of a stone-faced palisaded bank inside a rock-cut ditch (O'Brien 2016).

Unlike their Iron Age counterparts in Britain, Irish hillforts do not have elaborate entrances. Most have a single opening in an enclosing bank or wall, with a causeway across an accompanying ditch. Recent excavation at Clashanimud, Co. Cork, and Ballylin, Co. Limerick, confirms that wooden gates were used at these openings, connected in some instances to palisades in the adjacent banks (O'Brien and O'Driscoll 2017, figs 3.46 and 4.25).

Approximately one-quarter of Irish hillforts enclose ancient cairns or mounds, often located at the hill summit. While only a few are excavated, these are generally interpreted as prehistoric burial mounds, and three examples are confirmed as megalithic tombs. This incorporation of older burial monuments within hillforts may have been in part

Fig. 1.7 Class 3 inland promontory fort at Knockdhu, Co. Antrim.

religious, and designed to legitimise social control through a highly visible appropriation of the past. A good example is Freestone Hill, Co. Kilkenny, where hillfort builders during the Late Bronze Age avoided an earlier cairn that was subsequently destroyed by Iron Age occupation of the site (Raftery 1969; Ó Floinn 2000). Later in this book we will examine the significance of the Baltinglass passage tomb located inside Rathcoran hillfort at the summit of Tuckmill Hill.

Our knowledge of hillfort occupation depends very much on the excavation strategy applied at individual sites. There is evidence of intensive occupation over a long period at some sites, notably Rathgall, Haughey's Fort and Dún Aonghasa. Against this, some extensively excavated hillforts have yielded little evidence of occupation, including Rahally, Co. Galway (Mullins 2008) and Clashanimud. Much depends on the history of individual sites, with Clashanimud, for example, having been destroyed in an act of war.

Where hillforts are not excavated, there can be surface evidence of habitation, though the relationship with the enclosure is generally unclear. Approximately 31 hillforts in Ireland have visible hut circles, most of which have not been excavated. These range from locations where there are only a few examples of hut circles, to nine hillforts that have more than ten hut sites visible. The accessibility of hillforts did not limit their occupation. For example, at Caherconree, an inland promontory fort sited at 659m OD in the Slieve Mish mountain range on the Dingle Peninsula, Co. Kerry, there are 22 hut structures visible. As already noted, there may be as many as 100 hut circles at the inland promontory fort at Knockdhu, Co. Antrim (Fig. 1.7).

How old are hillforts?

As outlined above, the classification of Irish hillforts is complicated by a long history of enclosure across the island, with the result that sites of different age and use may have similar surface features today. While certain standardised types of hillfort can be identified, there may be no chronologically specific form, and smaller hillforts are easily confused with other types of hill-top enclosure. The chronology of Class 2 (multiple enclosure) hillforts is now reasonably well understood, though many examples remain undated. This lack of dating is even more the case for the Class 1 (univallate hillforts) and Class 3 (inland promontory forts) types, while the chronology of hilltop enclosures and coastal promontory forts remains very unclear (O'Brien 2017).

In the early years of research, Irish hillforts were dated to the 'Celtic' Iron Age by comparison with similar sites in Britain and mainland Europe. An example is the Class 1 hillfort on Freestone Hill, initially regarded as

> *...a product of an indigenous Celtic group having close contacts with the Roman world, but continuing a tradition of hillfort building, which had been going on unbroken in Ireland for some considerable period beforehand (Raftery 1969, 102).*

Some uncertainty was created by earlier dates for hilltop enclosures at Lyles Hill, Co. Antrim (Evans 1953; also O'Kelly 1956), and Downpatrick, Co. Down (Proudfoot 1954). The possibility of pre-Iron Age origins was raised by Westropp (1902), who with some prescience speculated that hillforts may date as early as 1200 BC, and also by Macalister, who proposed an association between Mooghaun and a great hoard of Late Bronze Age gold found in 1854 in the vicinity of that hillfort (Macalister 1928, 82, fn 5).

As in many parts of Europe, there is a Neolithic background to the hillfort phenomenon in Ireland. This centres on a small number of hilltop enclosures of early- to mid-fourth millennium BC date. Excavated examples include Donegore, Co. Antrim (Mallory *et al.* 2011), Thornhill, Co. Derry (Logue 2003), and Knocknarea, Co. Sligo (Bergh 2002), among others. While these are univallate sites, multiple enclosures of Early Neolithic date have also been identified, including Faughan Hill, Co. Meath (Dowling and Schot 2023) and Hughstown and Rathcoran at Baltinglass. This points to there being more than one tradition of enclosure during the earlier Neolithic (Sheridan 2001; Cooney 2002).

Some of these Irish sites have been compared to causewayed enclosures, sometimes called interrupted ditch enclosures, in southern Britain. These are not generally considered permanent settlements, but more places of assembly, ceremony, agriculture and trade. This may apply to some Neolithic enclosures in Ireland, such as Donegore and a recent discovery at Magheraboy, Co. Sligo (Danaher 2007). There is evidence in other sites that security is what was important, with evidence of combinations of ditches, banks, stone walls and timber palisades, creating what is essentially a Neolithic hillfort.

The realisation that many Irish hillforts are Bronze Age came as a result of the Rathgall excavation, which revealed a high-status occupation with specialised metalworking

Fig. 1.8 Iron Age 'royal site' at Navan Fort, Co. Armagh.

activity and funerary ritual of the Middle to Late Bronze Age, *c.*1400–1000 BC (Raftery 1976; Becker 2010). There are similar findings from large-scale excavations at Haughey's Fort, Moogaun, Dún Aonghasa and Rahally, among others. These excavations highlight the difficulty of obtaining secure dates for the construction and abandonment of hillfort defences, as many radiocarbon results obtained relate to episodes of occupation. This was addressed by an investigation of Class 2 hillforts in southern Ireland, where radiocarbon samples were obtained from defensive elements at Ballylin, Co. Limerick; Clashanimud, Co. Cork; Formoyle, Co. Clare; Glanbane, Co. Kerry; Toor More, Co. Kilkenny; as well as at Rathnagree and Tinoran in the Baltinglass complex (O'Brien and O'Driscoll 2017).

There is evidence of Late Bronze Age activity at other hillfort types in Ireland. This was revealed through the recent excavation of a triple-ramparted inland promontory fort at Knockdhu, Co. Antrim, where radiocarbon results indicate occupation during the tenth and ninth centuries BC (McNeary 2014). This is the only securely dated Class 3 hillfort in Ireland. In the case of Class I (univallate) hillforts, Late Bronze Age pottery is recorded at Freestone Hill, Co. Kilkenny (Raftery 1969; Ó Floinn 2000); Downpatrick (Cathedral Hill), Co. Down (Proudfoot 1954; Raftery 1976); and Clogher, Co. Tyrone (Warner 2009). In each instance the hillfort defences cannot be closely dated, and there is evidence of significant occupation from the Iron Age to medieval times. The excavation of two other Class 1 hillforts, at Knockacarrigeen Hill, Co. Galway (Carey 2002) and at Clenagh, Co. Clare (Grogan and Daly 2005), did not secure any dating evidence.

Taken together, these results establish the Bishopsland phase of the Middle Bronze Age (*c.*1400–1150 BC), equivalent to the Taunton (1400–1275 BC) and Penard phases (1275–1140 BC) in southern Britain, as an important period in the emergence of the Bronze Age hillforts in Ireland. The building of Class 2 multiple-enclosure hillforts intensified in the early part of the Roscommon phase (1150–1000 BC), which marks the beginning of the Late Bronze Age in Ireland and is equivalent to the Wilburton (1140–1020 BC) phase of metalworking in Britain. There is evidence for continued construction of these hillforts in the tenth and ninth centuries BC, during the transition from the Roscommon to the Dowris phase of the Late Bronze Age.

The occupation of hillforts in Ireland declined

significantly around the eighth century BC, with no examples built during the Iron Age (600 BC–AD 400). Whether large, internally ditched enclosures at 'royal sites' of the Iron Age should be considered hillforts is questionable (Fig. 1.8). Harding (2012, 284) suggests these sites may lie at the end of the hillfort spectrum, as their importance to Iron Age groups was such that they would have been actively defended when threatened. Iron Age occupation is recorded at a few Bronze Age hillforts, notably Rathgall (Becker 2010), Dún Aonghasa (Cotter 2012), and Haughey's Fort (Mallory and Baban 2014). There is also evidence of re-occupation of older hillforts during the early medieval period, with the building of ringfort-type enclosures at some sites (for instance Mooghaun, Rahally and Rathgall). The large stone ringforts of that period, including Cahercommaun and Ballykinvarga in Co. Clare; the Grianán of Aileach, Co. Donegal; and Staigue Fort, Co. Kerry, might be considered a later expression of the hillfort phenomenon in terms of their defensive features and socio-political significance.

It is now apparent there was more than one hillfort tradition in prehistoric Ireland, such that there is no chronological basis to Raftery's (1972) classification. Recent excavation reveals that sites with similar enclosing features can date to either the early Neolithic or the later Bronze Age. The earliest examples were of univallate and multiple-enclosure design, built by early Neolithic farming communities, *c.*3700/3600–3400 BC, with defensive and other considerations in mind. Similar types of large enclosure were developed two thousand years later during the Bishopsland phase of the Middle Bronze Age *c.*1400–1150 BC, and in increasing numbers during the ensuing Roscommon phase (1150–1000 BC) of the Late Bronze Age. A smaller number of hillforts were built and occupied during the Dowris phase of the Late Bronze Age, with their use declining sharply after 800 BC for reasons connected to some re-configuration of that highly complex Bronze Age society. What constitutes a hillfort after that is partly a matter of definition, with internally ditched 'royal enclosures' of the Iron Age and large stone forts of the early medieval period having certain elements in common with their Bronze Age predecessors. That said, the absence of classic hillforts and a significant number of coastal promontory forts continues to distinguish the aceramic Iron Age in Ireland from other parts of Atlantic Europe.

The origins of the Irish hillfort remain uncertain. Once regarded as being connected to invading hordes of Celts, the emphasis in recent research has shifted to understanding these monuments in the context of internal processes in the regional societies of the Middle to Late Bronze Age. While comparisons can be made with smaller enclosed settlements of the Middle Bronze Age, the Irish hillfort represents an entirely different scale of construction and intent. Furthermore, not all settlements in Ireland during the later Bronze Age were enclosed, as revealed by the 'village' discovered at Corrstown, Co. Derry (Ginn and Rathbone 2011). In light of parallel developments in Britain and mainland Europe (Harding 2006; Primas 2002), external influences cannot be discounted, particularly given the extensive trade and other connections among hillfort groups in Ireland during the second millennium BC.

Why build a hillfort?

The purpose of hillforts is much debated by prehistorians, with opinion divided between researchers who regard them as defensive strongholds and those who argue for wider meaning in economic, social and ideological terms. These views need not be in opposition, as excavation evidence confirms hillforts served many different roles in their respective communities (O'Brien and O'Driscoll 2017; O'Driscoll 2017a). The intention was to create an enclosed space that would serve as a central place in the society. The physical barriers represent a control of access to a space that could be defended if necessary, but that does not tell us what the space was used for in times of peace (Fig. 1.9). The function of hillforts was highly variable over time and space, and the form had different expressions in diverse cultural contexts. The significance of an individual hillfort changed over time through habitual use and changing associations, and in response to changing historical and other circumstances, which means 'there may be no such thing as a typical hillfort' (Cunliffe 2006).

As the name suggests, military and defensive considerations loom large in any discussion of hillforts. The basic and widely held definition of a hillfort is 'a site fortified so as to be defensible against human attack' (Avery 1976, 30). This was achieved by the creation of physical barriers, such as the types listed above, and by the tactical use of natural terrain at locations that enjoyed a commanding position in the landscape. Despite these important features of hillfort design, the defensibility of many sites can be questioned. The defensive potential of each hillfort has to be assessed on its own merits, taking into account topographical location, the size and layout of the enclosure(s), the strength

Fig. 1.9 Stone bank at Mooghaun hillfort, Co. Clare, with project team members Alan Hawkes (left), James O'Driscoll (centre) and Nick Hogan (right).

of the enclosing element(s), and the form of the entrance(s). The overall size and extended perimeters of hillforts, restricted visibility from within, availability of water supply and position in exposed locations were also factors affecting the potential to defend them. The 'refuge' theory of hillfort use is problematic for the same reasons. This is only relevant if we consider hillfort design in terms of passive defence, when it is unlikely that siege warfare was ever conducted at these sites.

Furthermore, there is the uncertainty of what constituted the active force of defenders, and the possibility that the real defensive value of a hillfort was one of deterrence. Understanding the nature of hillfort warfare is further complicated by the likelihood that many confrontations likely took place some distance away from these sites. Depending on the outcome, the hillfort itself may have become a strategic target: a place of final resistance and refuge, a store of wealth that could be pillaged, and a symbol of group identity chosen for punitive destruction.

In a broader sense, the purpose of hillfort enclosure was to define and segregate space in a place of significance. As Harding observed, the purpose of enclosure may have been less to underline the distinction between 'them' and 'us', and more to emphasise something that was special for the group in question (Harding 2012, 6). In Ireland the idea of retaining dangerous supernatural forces can be applied to henge enclosures of the later Neolithic, or to internally ditched 'royal' enclosures of the Iron Age. Hillforts with a record of permanent occupation are not directly comparable to these ceremonial centres, even if many do have defined areas of 'ritual space' in their interiors. Some Irish hillforts were built on hills that already had older burial mounds; an explicit referencing of the past tied up with religious belief, identity and the legitimisation of power.

Who lived in these hillforts is a major question. The scale of construction, strategic location and imposing design points to the powerful in society. Hillforts are often considered places of elite residence, distinguished from other settlements by their monumentality and prominence in the landscape. These were also locations for the accumulation and conspicuous consumption of wealth, which is consistent with their role as places of assembly and ceremony. The source of the chiefly power is contentious, often connected to military strength, but also to core economic functions of hillforts, such as the centralised storage and redistribution of commodities, trade in raw materials and exotica, and patronage of specialist crafts such as metalworking. Each hillfort has to be assessed individually in this regard, as excavation evidence reveals considerable variability in their economy.

In recent research, hillforts are often placed at the apex of a settlement hierarchy that extends far into the surrounding landscape. This perspective is based on the imposing nature of these central places, the evidence of elite residence, and the highly visible concentration of wealth under the control of a particular individual or group. The 'rise of the privileged' is a broad social phenomenon with origins in the Chalcolithic and which has its strongest expression in the chiefdom societies of the European Bronze Age (Kristiansen 1999; Kristiansen and Larsson 2005). This power paradigm has been criticised in recent years (for example by Brück and Fontijn 2013), with greater emphasis placed instead on the use of hillforts as community assembly locations having a range of communal functions and religious associations.

Many researchers believe siting and visibility was central to the significance of hillforts in the landscape. This suggests that hillforts were located in the most visible positions in order to control territories and routeways through visibility, and, by extension, this indicates the occupants' ability to trade high-status goods. The hillforts at Ballylin, Co. Limerick and Toor More, Co. Kilkenny are good examples of prominent siting based on a need to control territory and routeways through visibility. This was particularly important in circumstances in which Bronze Age elites created and maintained positions of social dominance by controlling the population and the supply of prestige goods and metal (O'Brien 2022; Kristiansen, 1999; Kristiansen and Larsson, 2005).

Though often considered as discrete monuments, these great enclosures were connected to a wider cultural landscape of farms and fields, routeways and settlements, and places of religious significance. The first hilltop enclosures were part of a wider enclosure of land, and of settlement and ritual space that dates back in Ireland some 6000 years, to the earliest Neolithic farmers. The creation of fields and animal enclosures was important in agricultural intensification, and an assertion of land ownership. The building of hillforts was a further affirmation of territorial rights for an identity group. Farming was also a critical practice during the later Bronze Age, when many hillforts were part of a wider landscape of agricultural settlement. They may have been important in the stockading of cattle; this is particularly true of Class 2 hillforts, where the outer enclosure(s) could have been used for that purpose. The significance of cattle and cattle-raiding is well attested in Irish epic literature (Lucas 1989), which may preserve oral tradition that extends back to the Bronze Age.

The ceremonial aspects of hillfort use must also be considered. Given their prominence in the landscape, it is likely these locations were important places of assembly. Harding (2012, 282) makes a distinction between different types of assembly for the related or dependent community. These include social (seasonal festivals, marriages, etc.), economic (markets, craft centres), political (inauguration, alliances), and ritual (funerals, votive displays) assembly, many of which were mutually embedded with multiple meanings for the group in question. Such roles are not well understood in the Irish record, partly because of a lack of large-scale excavation of hillforts, but also because such gatherings may have left little archaeological evidence.

Where excavation has taken place, it confirms that many hillforts contained areas of ritual space and religious observance. The elevated locations may have had liminal significance, as places where the world of the living met the supernatural. In many sites this was given added significance by the presence of older burial mounds. The high status of their occupancy is suggested by the presence of elite funerary complexes and the ritual deposition of material culture within or close to the hillfort. These associations added significantly to the importance of hillforts over time, and were an important resource in the exercise of social power.

While often considered collectively as distinct 'types', each hillfort had its own unique history of occupation and abandonment, the details of which were contingent on local and wider historical and environmental circumstances. The occupation of hillforts was affected by many inter-linked variables, such as environmental change, population pressure, cycles of economic expansion and decline, religious prescription, and social relations within and outside of the group in question. Changes in social organisation may explain the increase in the amount of hillfort building during the Middle Bronze Age, through to the 'collapse' of their society around the eighth century BC.

The building of a hillfort had a significant symbolic impact in terms of the creation of an imposing presence in the landscape. This promoted a sense of group identity by controlling access to a central place and by the exclusion of outsiders. In that regard, the building of hillforts was important in the symbolic construction of community and was a striking physical affirmation of tribal power. This is not to suggest that the act of construction was more important than the intended use, as the significance of the latter is borne out by the evidence of prolonged occupation in many sites.

As mentioned above, narratives of competition and warfare have been to the fore in hillfort studies in most parts of Europe. This has been tempered in recent research by a consideration of other uses. On occasion, this has gone too far, when a military role is rejected in favour of symbolic meaning (see Armit 2007 and Lock 2011). That deliberate or unconscious 'pacification of the past' often ignores other indications of militarism and warrior culture in early societies. A middle ground is required, whereby the multi-layered meaning of these central places in different contexts is acknowledged, recognising that each hillfort had its own historically contingent and culture-specific story.

The excavation of hillforts confirms that many were centres of high-status residence, specialist crafts and trade, with a connection to a local and wider agricultural economy. They also had a significance in terms of fortification and the visible projection of military strength. They were places of assembly, ritual and ceremony, central to a symbolic construction of community and to the formation of a political economy. Their prominent siting was strategic, connected in some instances to control of routeways, but mostly part of a highly visible display of political power and identity in the landscape.

THIS BOOK

It is now possible to advance our understanding of Irish hillforts by looking in detail at the Baltinglass area of south-west Wicklow, a place often referred to as 'Ireland's hillfort capital' (Condit 1992). The following chapter introduces the physical and cultural landscape of Baltinglass and the remarkable concentration of hillforts and enclosures across its many hills. Chapters 3 and 4 examine the recent discovery and excavation of three Neolithic enclosures in that landscape, looking also at an older excavation of a large passage tomb on Baltinglass Hill. The chronological thread continues in Chapter 5, which presents the results from recent excavation of three Bronze Age hillforts in the area. Chapter 6 examines other hillforts and large enclosures at Baltinglass that have not been excavated.

The environmental context of this early settlement at Baltinglass is explored in Chapter 7, through the results of a palynological study undertaken for this book. This provides a vegetational history of the area, along with details of human impacts on the environment connected to agriculture and possibly the building of hillforts. The wider significance of the Baltinglass hillforts is then considered, in terms of both their cultural landscape setting (Chapter 8) and the wider Irish and international context (Chapter 9). The final chapter looks at Baltinglass as a unique hillfort landscape in Ireland, and at how this heritage can be protected and presented today.

2. THE BALTINGLASS HILLFORT LANDSCAPE

James O'Driscoll

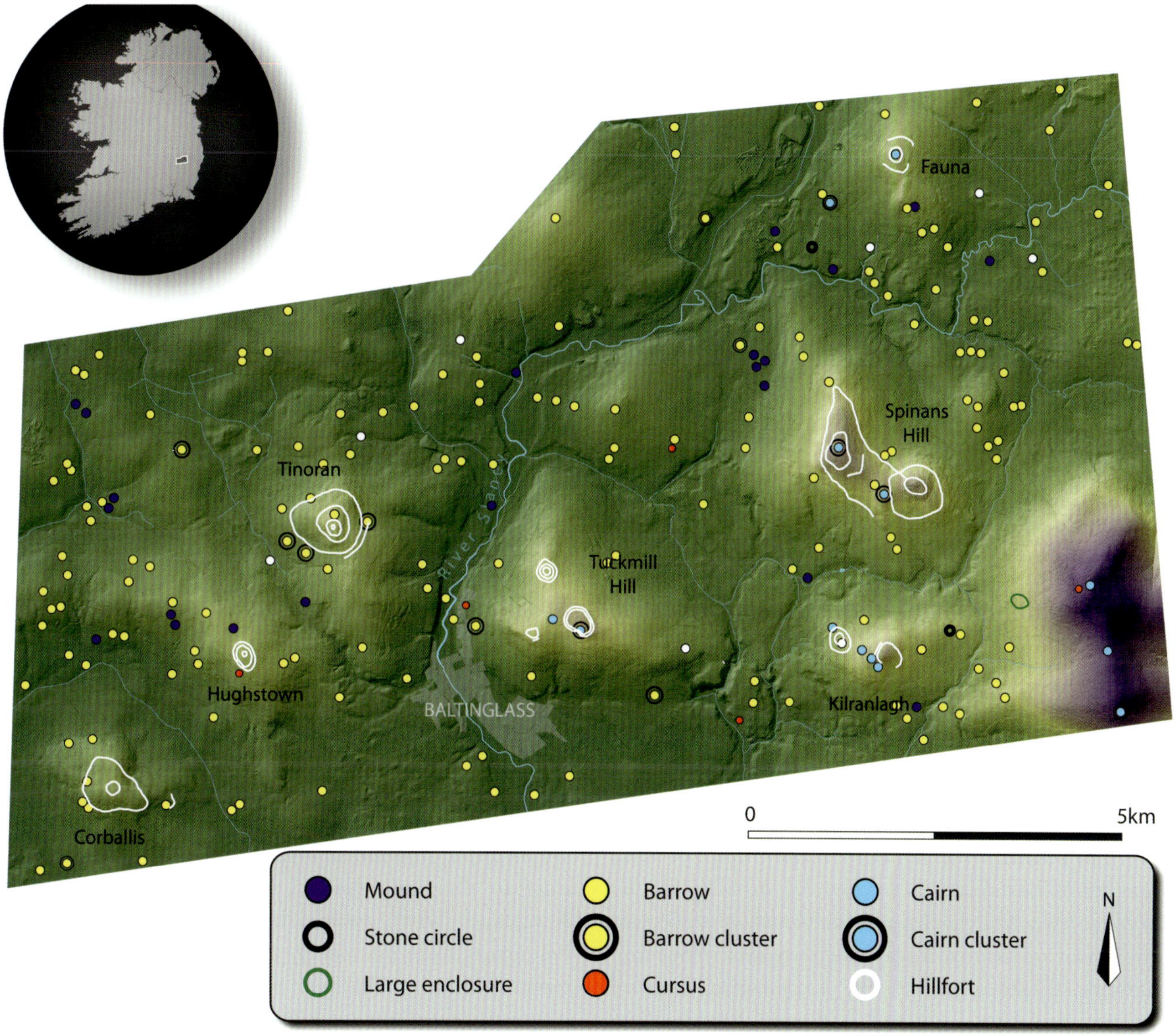

Fig. 2.1 Hillforts, large hilltop enclosures and other prehistoric monuments in the Baltinglass area.

The modern town of Baltinglass is located in south-west Wicklow, close to the boundaries of counties Carlow and Kildare. The town straddles the River Slaney, which rises in the western Wicklow Mountains to the north, flowing south-east to the coast at Wexford Harbour. Those mountains are a striking backdrop to the east of Baltinglass, while several prominent hills border the town on its northern and western sides, with a broad expanse of lowland to the south. The imposing summit of Baltinglass Hill overlooks the town on its northern side. To the immediate west are Corballis Hill, Carrigeen Hill and Tinoran Hill, while Spinans Hill, Kilranelagh Hill and Fauna Hill are to the east (Fig. 2.1).

Baltinglass is first mentioned in medieval sources, such as the eleventh century *Bórama Laigen* (Stokes 1892; see also Price 1949a, 128). This was probably the name of the area,

Fig. 2.2 Rathcoran on Baltinglass Hill, overlooking the modern town of Baltinglass.

as opposed to a settlement, with *Bealach Conglais* translating as 'the way of Cúglas', a route probably associated with the River Slaney. Others suggest the name derives from *Belach Con Glais* ('The road of the hound of Glas'), while a more fanciful antiquarian translation connects *Beal-tinne-glas* ('The fire of Beal's mysteries') to druid sun worship (Marsh 2007). The origins of the modern town lie in the Cistercian monastery of Baltinglass Abbey founded in AD 1148 by Diarmuid Mac Murchadha, around which a settlement formed in later centuries. Today, the town has a population of around 2,000 people, with a nineteenth-century courthouse and church, as well as a monument to Sam McAllister, who fought in the 1798 Rebellion (Fig. 2.2).

This chapter provides an overview of the physical landscapes of the Baltinglass region, detailing how the distinct landforms visible today were created in geological times. The topography of this landscape is examined to understand the physical setting of its many hillforts. The history of research on these sites is outlined, as are details of recent projects that form the basis of this book.

PHYSICAL ENVIRONMENT

Irish archaeologists know Baltinglass as 'Ireland's hillfort capital'; as many as thirteen large hill-top enclosures have been identified in the area, by far the largest concentration of such sites in Ireland. These are located on the highest points of the aforementioned hills near the modern town, close to the south-western edge of the West Wicklow Mountains. While dwarfed by that mountain range, the Baltinglass hills are highly visible against the low-lying terrain to the north, west and south. They divide this landscape of fertile agricultural land on either side of the meandering Slaney River (Fig. 2.3).

Two distinct landforms are apparent in the Baltinglass landscape, namely the Wicklow Mountains to the east and north-east, and the flat plains to the south and west. The Wicklow Mountains are part of the Leinster Granite, the largest mass of this type of igneous rock in north-western Europe. Other rocks in the area include diorite formations, with slates, mudstones and siltstones of Ordovician age to the south (Fig. 2.4). These extend into the largely flat landscape of Co. Carlow, which is surrounded by a thin

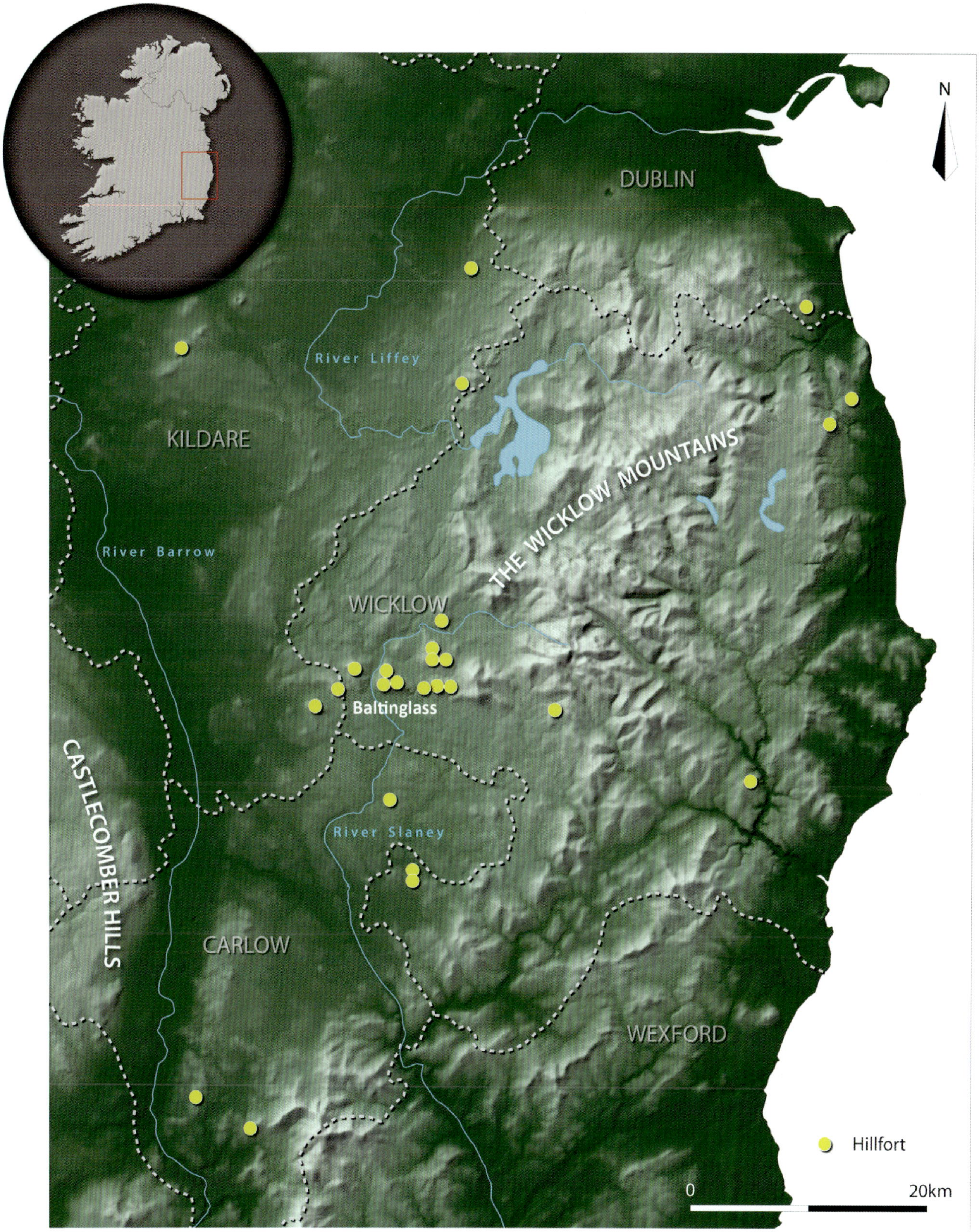

Fig. 2.3 Hillforts and the topography of eastern Ireland.

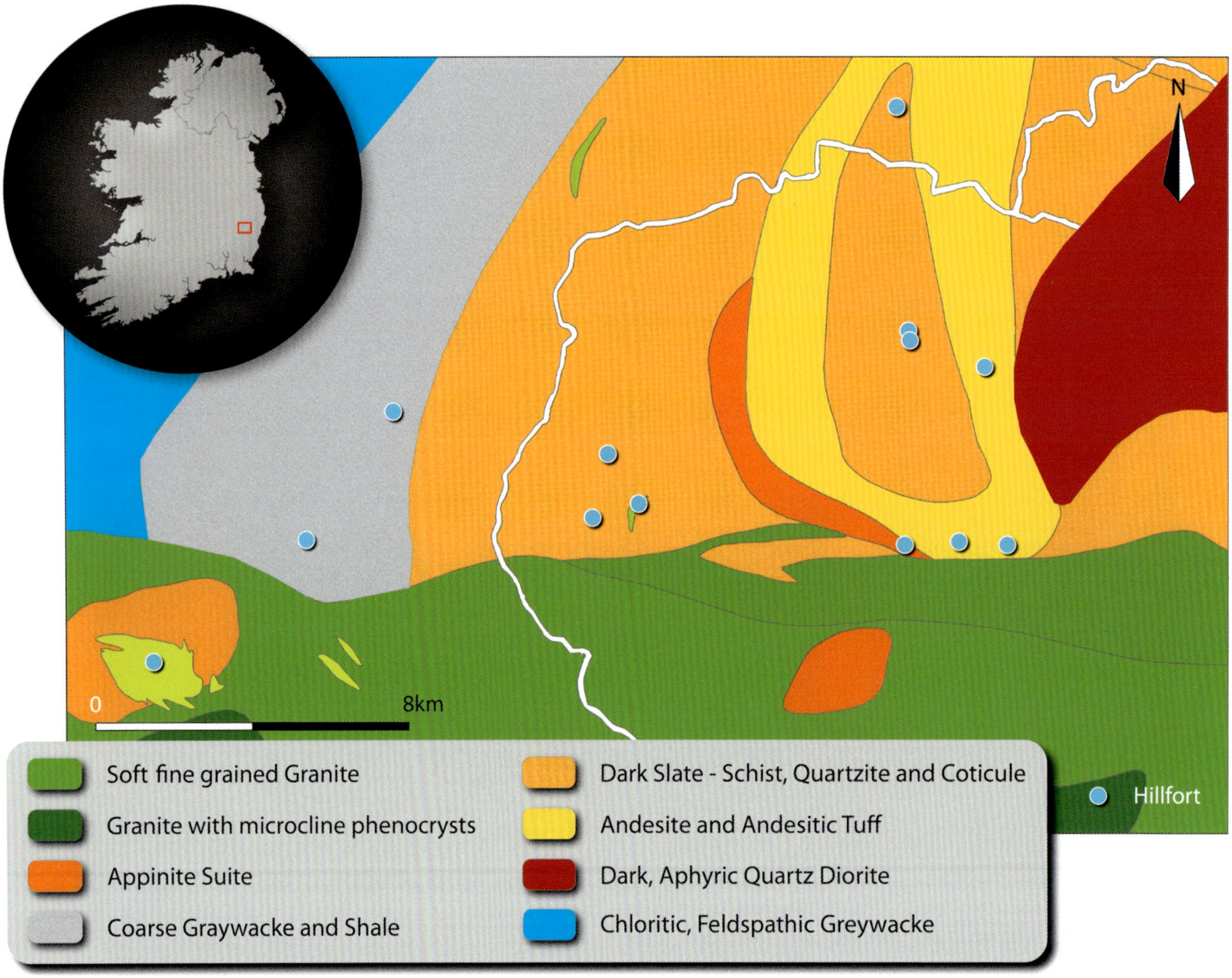

Fig. 2.4 Geology (1 : 500,000 scale) of the Baltinglass study area (data from www.gsi.ie).

band of Cambrian metasediments (Jackson *et al.* 2010; Parkes *et al.* 2022, 16). This mica-schist and other rocks were formed over millions of years, when large amounts of mud, silt and sand accumulating on the floor of the ancient 'Iapetus Ocean' were compressed into rock. The mountains began to be formed at the end of the Silurian period 443–415 million years ago, when the Iapetus Suture closed as the North American and European plates collided, eventually forcing those rocks out of the Iapetus Ocean at the start of the Devonian period around 415–358 million years ago (Williams and Harper 1999, 23–28). The heat from the collision metamorphosed the mudstone and sandstone into schists, creating one of Ireland's most significant metalliferous belts (Whittow 1975, 261). Underlying this, the molten layer of the earth's crust was also raised, and this subsequently cooled to form granite (Holland 2003, 29).

Approximately 2.6 million–11,700 years ago, Pleistocene glaciation removed much of the overlying metamorphic rock in this part of Wicklow to expose the underlying granite (Holland 2003, 29). The passage of ice re-deposited this broken rock as till over much of the lowland around these hills and mountains. The many episodes of glaciation created deep valleys with lakes, such as those found at Blessington and Glendalough, and moulded the higher ground to its present state (Parkes *et al.* 2022, 15; Sleeman *et al.* 2004, 111).

The Baltinglass hills lie just off the northern edge of the Leinster Granite mass, which extends into the southern plain over most of Co. Carlow. Several different rock types of Lower Palaeozoic age occur in the area. The hillforts at Hughstown and Tinoran are located on a large formation of Silurian sandstone, greywacke and shale that extends

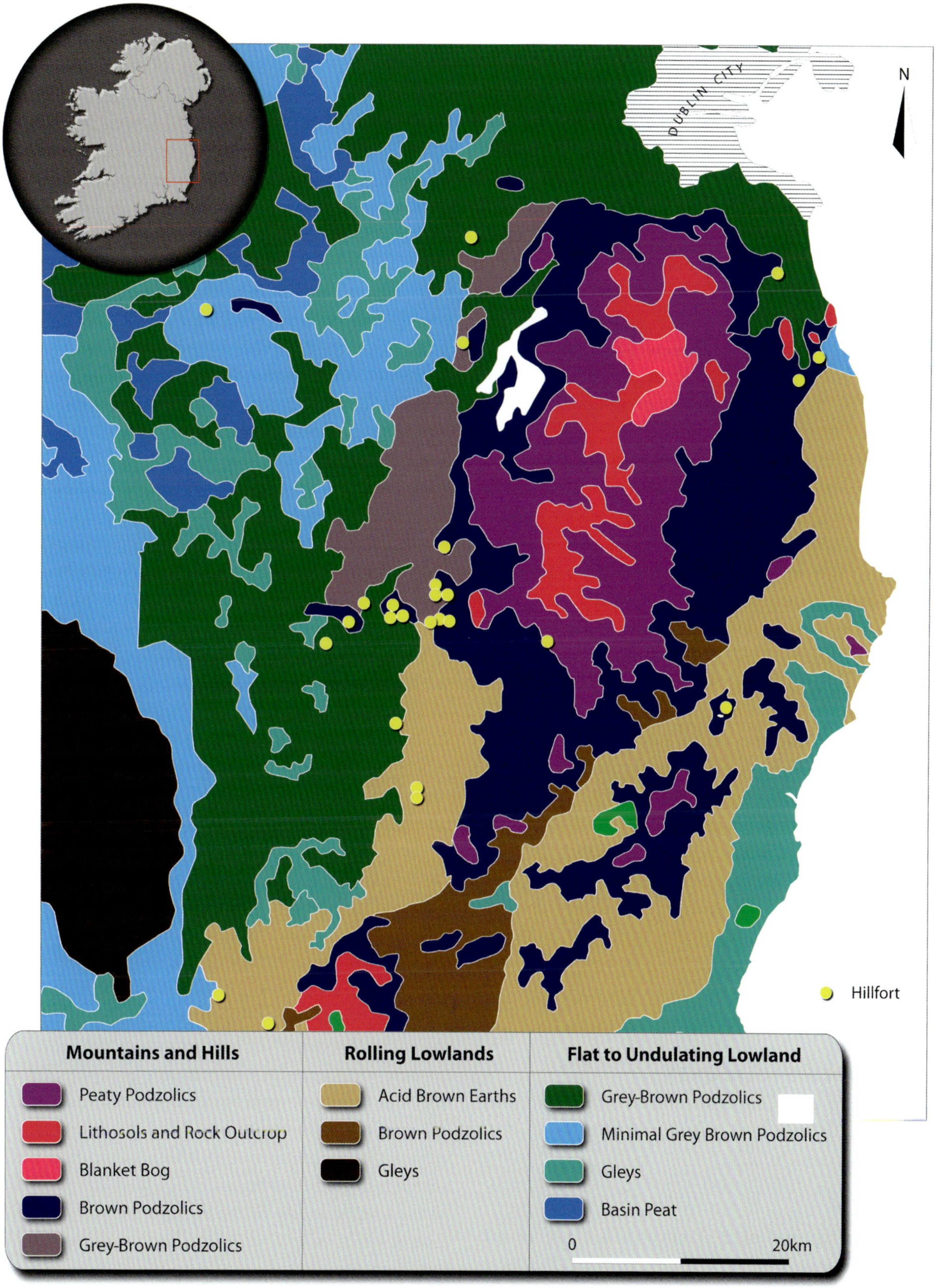

Fig. 2.5 Soils (1 : 575,000 scale) of the Baltinglass area (data from second edition 'General Soils Map').

northwards to the southern edge of Dublin City. The three forts on Baltinglass Hill (Rathnagree, Rathcoran and Sruhaun) are on a Lower/Middle Ordovician slate formation that extends 14km to the north-east, although the central portion of Rathcoran is on a small ridge of granite. To the east, the Spinans Hill 1 enclosure and the northern and western portions of Spinans Hill 2 are on the same formation. Brusselstown Ring and the southern and eastern portion of Spinans Hill 2 are on a small formation of andesite and andesitic tuff, a consolidated volcanic rock of the Lower/Middle Ordovician period. The newly discovered hillfort on Corballis Hill is on an island of Silurian sandstone, greywacke and shale surrounded by granite, while the enclosure on Fauna Hill and the two examples on Kilranelagh Hill are on a narrow ridge of Lower/Middle Ordovician volcanics.

The majority of soil types in Wicklow are brown earths at lower elevations and brown podsols with peat, blanket bog and lithosols on higher ground where the hillforts are located (Fig. 2.5). The lowland soils of Baltinglass are a mixture of brown earths and brown podzols overlying a bedrock geology of slates, shales, schists and igneous rock. These well-drained soils support intensive farming today and were also farmed in ancient times. This is one of many reasons why the area was intensively settled during the Neolithic and Bronze Age.

The Wicklow Mountains are the source of several major river systems, including the Liffey, Slaney and Avoca, which flow through glaciated valleys (Parkes *et al.* 2022, 20). The Slaney flows westward from Lugnaquilla Mountain towards Baltinglass town, where it bends to run south into the Irish Sea at Wexford. The Avoca River valley to the south of Baltinglass is famous for the discovery of alluvial gold in 1795, a source believed to have been significant in earlier times. Copper was also mined at Avoca between 1720 and 1983, with a total output of 16 million tons of copper ore (Sleeman *et al.* 2004, 36).

THE BALTINGLASS HILLFORTS

A total of thirteen large enclosures have now been identified across seven hills within a radius of 10km or less of Baltinglass town (see Fig. 2.1).

Baltinglass Hill

There are three large enclosures (Rathcoran, Rathnagree and Sruhaun) on the three summits of Baltinglass Hill (Fig. 2.6). The highest point, known as the Pinnacle, is on the south-eastern side (382m OD) where a large Neolithic passage tomb is located. The northern spur is known as Tuckmill Hill, while that on the southern side is historically known as Carr's Rock (FitzGerald 1908a). The southern slopes are particularly steep, rising some 240m over the course of a 900m ascent, while more gradual slopes on the northern and eastern sides provide easier access to the summit. The upper slopes of the hill are used today for extensive cattle and sheep grazing, with little sub-division of land; the lower slopes have smaller field patterns with improved land. The River Slaney and its tributaries meander around the northern and western base of the hill, which rises some 240m above the surrounding landscape, peaking at 378m OD.

At just over 10 hectares in extent, Rathcoran is the largest of the three enclosures on Baltinglass Hill, listed as site WI027-026001 in the *Record of Monuments and Places* inventory of archaeological sites in Wicklow (www.archaeology.ie). This pear-shaped hillfort lies on the south-eastern summit (the Pinnacle), enclosed by two concentric banks spaced from 10 to 28m apart (Fig. 2.7). The interior slopes gently to a slightly domed summit, from which nearly all of the hillfort is visible. A number of circular platforms may represent internal areas of occupation. The summit has two cairns, one of which was excavated in the 1930s, and there is a third example on the southern side of the hillfort. From the summit there is an unobstructed view of the Carlow lowlands, extending as far as Mount Leinster some 40km to the south. The northern and southern spurs of Baltinglass Hill limit visibility of its lower slopes, while views to the east and west are interrupted by Spinans Hill, Carrigeen Hill and Tinoran Hill.

The second hillfort on Baltinglass Hill is Rathnagree (WI027-027010), a 5.78ha multiple enclosure on the spur of Tuckmill Hill (327m OD), 400m north-west of Rathcoran (Fig. 2.8). The inner and outer enclosures are surrounded by low banks of stone, while the middle enclosure has a more substantial bank-and-ditch earthwork. The location of the monument is unusual, as its roughly circular outline does not follow the contours of the hill, but rather drapes over a narrow north/south ridge, with steeply sloping ground on the western side. The latter is covered by recent conifer plantation, which has encroached on the outer enclosure of the hillfort. The views from Rathnagree are excellent, particularly across the northern slopes of Baltinglass Hill. The hillfort is overlooked on the south-east side by the Pinnacle summit, with views to the east impacted by Spinans Hill and to the west by Tinoran and Carrigeen Hill.

Using aerial LiDAR survey, the project reported on in this book discovered a third enclosure on Baltinglass Hill,

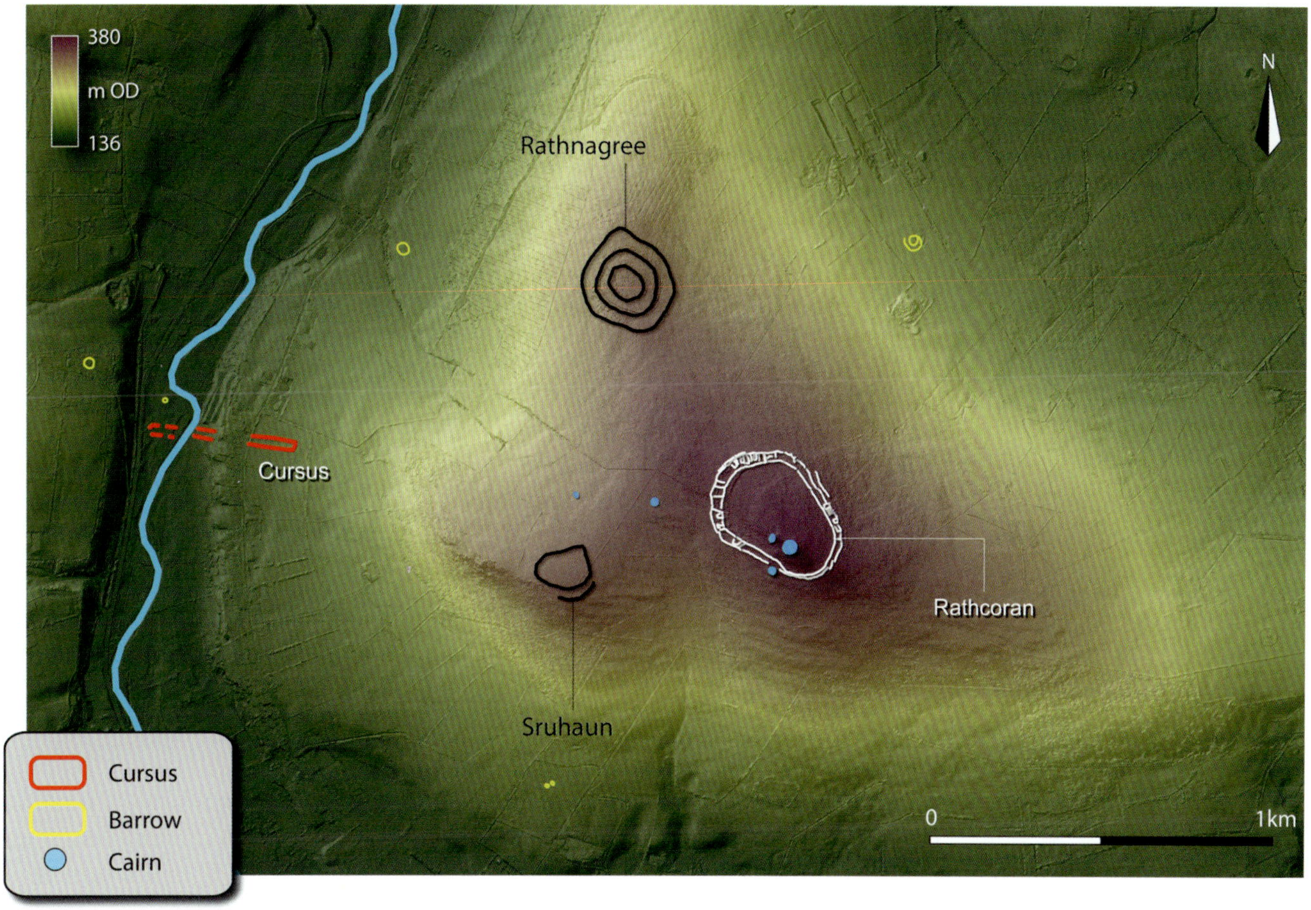

Fig. 2.6 The archaeology of Baltinglass Hill, Co. Wicklow.

located in Sruhaun townland on its southern (Carr's Rock) spur (327m OD). This 1.43ha enclosure (WI027-090) is on a level terrace, with steep slopes to the south and east, in an open area of reclaimed land used today for animal grazing. The enclosure has a single, low bank with no archaeological features visible in the interior. There are excellent views of the lower slopes of the hill on its north-western, western and southern sides, as well as unrestricted views of the Baltinglass lowlands. Visibility to the east and north is impacted by the ridge of high ground that connects the Pinnacle and Tuckmill Hill summits of Baltinglass Hill. The nearby hills of Tinoran and Carrigeen interrupt views of lowland areas to the north-west and west.

Spinans Hill

Three large enclosures have been discovered on the twin summits of Spinans Hill (highest point 410m OD), to the east of Baltinglass town. These include Brusselstown Ring and Spinans Hill 1 on the south-eastern and north-western summits respectively, while the entire ridge is surrounded by a massive enclosure named Spinans Hill 2 (Figs 2.9 and 2.10). The ridge has a curved north-west/south-east orientation, with steep slopes, particularly on the western and north-eastern sides. The surrounding lowland has good land, farmed today with cattle and tillage. The north-western summit of Spinans Hill is covered by a thin blanket bog, with open grazing of cattle and sheep on rough ground. Large parts of Spinans Hill are under commercial forestry, mostly on the saddle between the two summits.

Brusselstown Hill is the best known of the ancient enclosures on Spinans Hill, located on its prominent south-east summit (400m OD) (Fig. 2.11). This 37.81ha bivallate hillfort (WI027-018) is very visible from the Glen of Imaal lowlands to the north-east and the lowlands to the south-west, with nearby Kilranelagh Hill restricting visibility to the south-west. The flat summit area of Brusselstown Ring has numerous rock outcrops, around which there is a dense concentration of circular house platforms. This settlement

Fig. 2.7 Aerial photograph of the large enclosure of Rathcoran on Baltinglass Hill, with excavation of inner enclosure in progress (bottom-centre).

occurs within the partly collapsed stone bank of the inner enclosure. Some 200m downslope, another large stone bank forms an outer enclosure, with many more house platforms.

A large, pear-shaped enclosure known as Spinans Hill 1 (WI027-078002) is recorded on the north-western summit (408m OD) of this ridge (Fig. 2.12). This univallate enclosure is approximately 11.11ha in extent, defined by a low bank on its northern, western and southern sides, and a more substantial bank-and-ditch earthwork on the eastern side. Inside this enclosure, there is a large, robbed-out cairn surrounded by smaller mounds, which some have suggested may be a passage tomb cemetery. Spinans Hill 1 has much more extensive views than Brusselstown Ring, towards the Glen of Imaal and the northern and western lowlands, while Kilranelagh Hill and Baltinglass Hill impede views to the south and west respectively.

The third ancient enclosure on this ridge is the largest, namely the contour fort of Spinans Hill 2 (see Fig. 2.9).

Fig. 2.8 Aerial photograph of the large hillfort of Rathnagree on Baltinglass Hill.

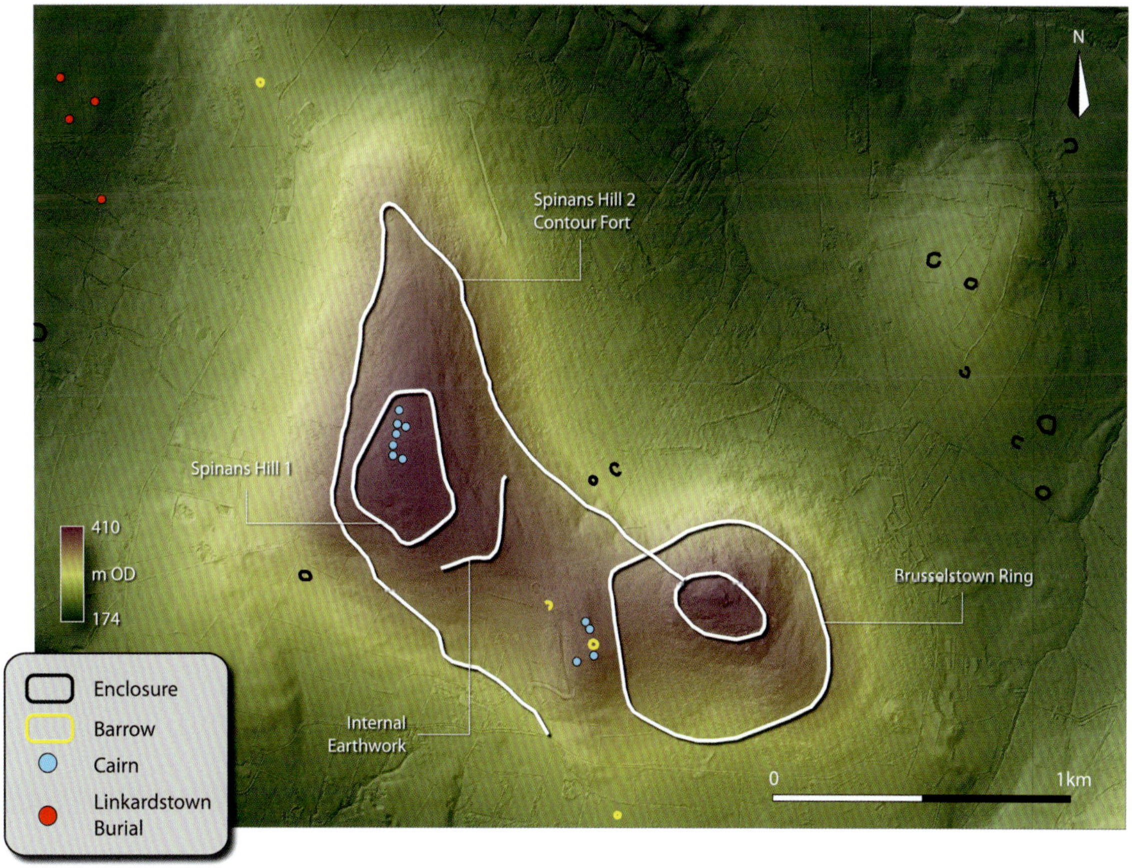

Fig. 2.9 The archaeology of Spinans Hill, Co. Wicklow.

Fig. 2.10 Spinans Hill, viewed from the south, with the enclosures of Brusselstown Ring on the south-eastern summit (right) and Spinans Hill 1 on the north-western summit (left).

Fig. 2.11 Aerial photograph of Brusselstown Ring on Spinans Hill.

Fig. 2.12 Aerial photograph of the large enclosure of Spinans Hill 1 on Spinans Hill.

This banana-shaped enclosure is 131ha in extent, representing the largest prehistoric hillfort in Ireland. The enclosing element is a massive bank-and-ditch earthwork that continues in large parts unbroken for some five kilometres. The south-eastern section seems to partly overlie and incorporate the outer enclosing elements of Brusselstown Ring, indicating that Spinans Hill 2 was broadly contemporary with, or possibly later than, that hillfort. Given the size of the monument, there are many questions regarding its age and function. Was this a Bronze Age fortification? Could it be practically defended? Was it a ritual/ceremonial enclosure? Is it the location of an early medieval royal caput known as Dun Bólg?

Kilranelagh Hill

A large enclosure has been identified on the rounded summit of Kilranelagh Hill, with another on its eastern ridge and a third on the western slopes (Fig. 2.13). This hill, 5.5km east of Baltinglass town, is surrounded on all sides, apart from the south, by tributaries of the River Slaney, and is directly overlooked by Keadeen Mountain to the east. The northern and southern sides of the hill are the steepest, with the terrain rising 125m over the course of 500m. The western slopes are also steep, but fall more gradually towards the lowlands. There is a small spur on the eastern slope. Almost the entire hill has been planted by commercial forestry in recent decades, with small pockets of open land on the summit and the south-western slopes covered by scrub vegetation with thin blanket bog (Fig. 2.14). From the summit there are excellent views of the southern lowlands of Wicklow and Carlow, with the Barrow River valley and the Castlecomer Hills to the west. Visibility to the east and north, however, is restricted by surrounding hills and mountains.

There is a pear-shaped enclosure (WI027-097), 7.76ha in extent, in Colvinstown Upper townland on the summit of Kilranelagh Hill (380m OD). This is defined by a single stone bank, with traces of a second bank on its north-western side. There are few visible features in the interior, because of vegetation and bog cover. Three large cairns (WI027-035, -036 and -037) are recorded on the western side of the enclosure. The presence of prehistoric cairns is known from many Irish hillforts, including Rathcoran and possibly Spinans Hill 1 at Baltinglass.

Another large enclosure has recently been identified in Ballinroan Upper townland, on the lower north-western

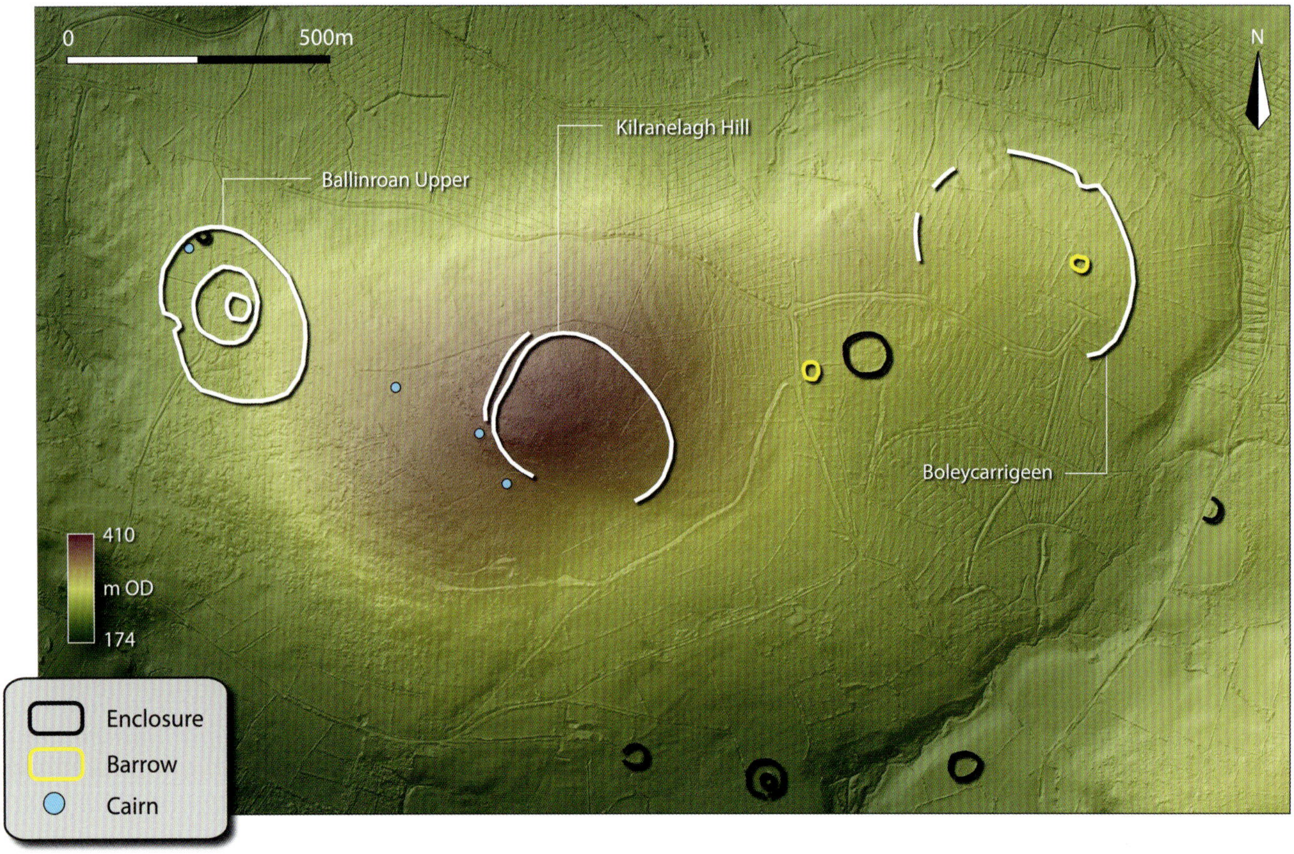

Fig. 2.13 The archaeology of Kilranelagh Hill, Co. Wicklow.

Fig. 2.14 The heavily forested Kilranelagh Hill.

slopes of Kilranelagh Hill in an area of conifer plantation. The highest point of this enclosure (306m OD) is some 50m higher than the lowest (256m OD). There are three partly concentric circular enclosures over an area of 6.64ha. The inner enclosure (WI027-034005) is associated with a church (WI027-034001) and is probably an ecclesiastical boundary. Surrounding this and defining the limits of an extensive graveyard is another enclosure that, again, likely relates to the ecclesiastical elements on the hill (Fig. 2.15). The significance of a third outer enclosing element is unclear. Was it part of an early monastic settlement mentioned in medieval sources, or an older enclosure re-used for that purpose? Ballinroan Upper has similar views of the landscape to Kilranelagh Hill, though they are more restricted to the west.

Recent LiDAR survey has identified a third enclosure in this area, located on the eastern spur off Kilranelagh Hill (291m OD) in the townland of Boleycarrigeen. This unrecorded univallate enclosure has been significantly damaged by commercial forestry. It surrounds the embanked stone circle known as 'the Griddle Stones' (Fig. 2.16), as well as a possible mound barrow of prehistoric date. Visibility is more restricted at this location, as the summit of Kilranelagh Hill obstructs views to the west and south-west, with other hills limiting visibility to the north and east.

Corballis Hill

This small prominent hill (259m OD) is located just inside Co. Kildare, midway between the towns of Baltinglass and Castledermot on the western limits of the Baltinglass landscape (Fig. 2.17). The southern hillslopes are particularly steep, rising nearly 100m over the course of a 500m ascent. The other slopes have a more gradual incline, with the western approach the most accessible. Much of the hill and the large enclosure on its summit is covered with dense commercial forestry. The summit of the hill and its western slopes are divided by field boundaries — now used for cattle and sheep grazing — which largely pre-date the Ordnance Survey mapping of the 1840s.

LiDAR survey undertaken for this project identified a large bivallate hillfort (KD038-081), 41.23ha in extent, on the summit and upper slopes of Corballis Hill. The enclosing elements have been significantly levelled by commercial forestry but are still visible as low relief features, allowing us to record the size and shape of this new enclosure. The inner enclosure on the summit comprises a

Fig. 2.15 The graveyard in Ballinroan Upper on Kilranelagh Hill, with the large, unrecorded enclosure partially visible in the foreground (lower-left).

Fig. 2.16 The embanked stone circle known as 'the Griddle Stones' within a large unrecorded enclosure on Boleycarrigeen.

circular bank. A second enclosure, *c.*200m outside that bank, largely follows the contours of the hill. There are no archaeological features in the interior, but that may be as a result of the forestry. While Corballis Hill is not as high as other hilltops at Baltinglass, there are panoramic views from the summit, with visibility restricted only to the north-east by Carrigeen Hill.

Carrigeen Hill

This north-west/south-east ridge, with a broad relatively flat summit, is located on the western side of the Baltinglass landscape, just inside Co. Kildare. There is a large, multiple enclosure hillfort (KD038-025001) on its highest point in the townland of Hughstown (Fig. 2.18). The hill peaks on the south-east side, with a gently rounded summit (298m OD). While it is prominent in the landscape, the slopes are not as steep as other hills in the area. This lower elevation and better soil make this land more suited to agriculture, with the ridge divided today into large fields used for cattle grazing. There is a small conifer plantation on the south-western side of the hill.

The enclosure on Hughstown is almost completely levelled, with the exception of its innermost enclosure. LiDAR and geophysical survey undertaken for the project reported here identified four, broadly concentric, oval enclosures over an area of about 8.22ha. The central enclosure is defined by a low bank of uncertain date (Fig. 2.19). The three outer enclosures are visible on the ground as low-relief depressions, better viewed on aerial photographs. Their full extent was mapped by magnetic gradiometry survey, with details of construction revealed by excavation. There are no visible features in the interior of the

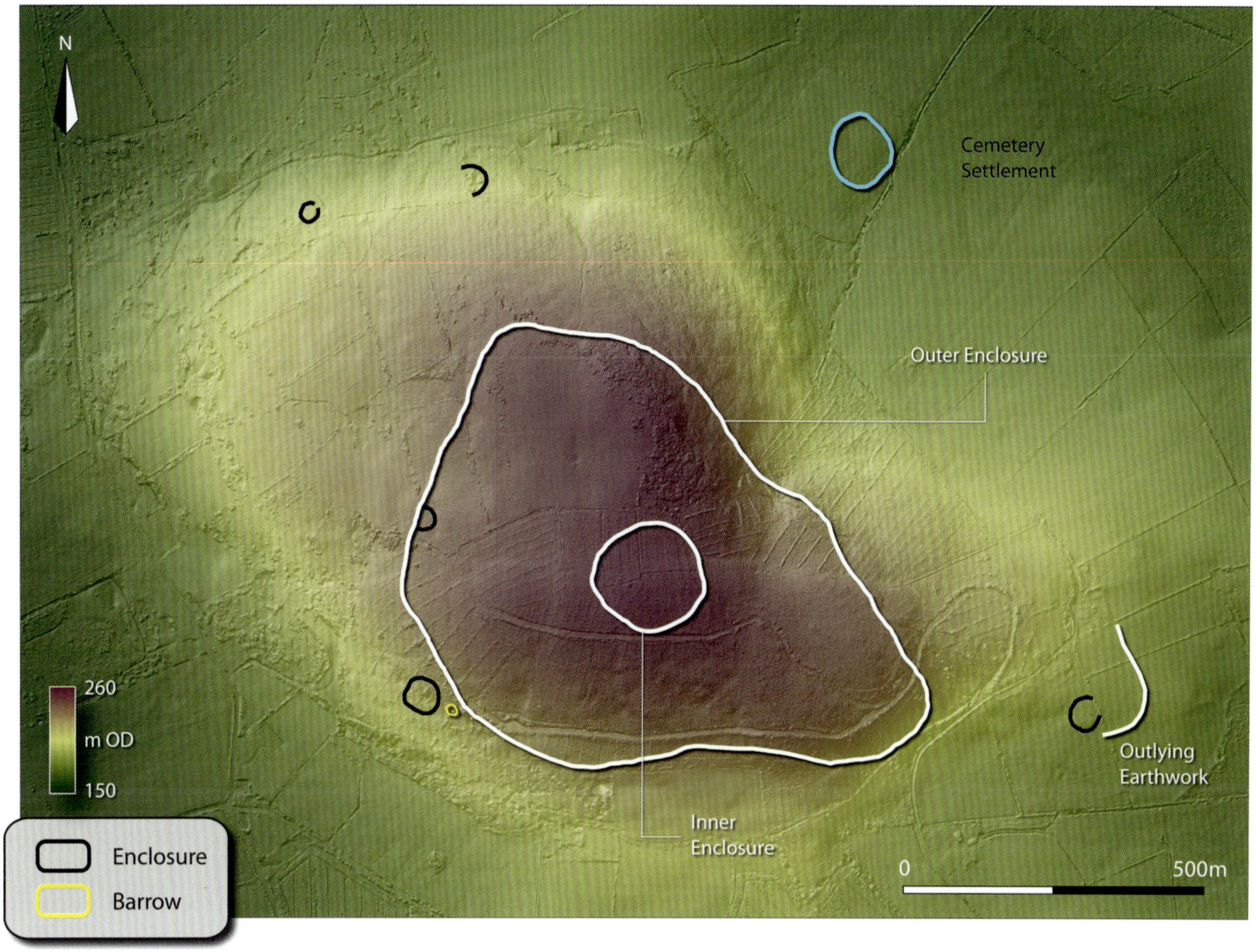

Fig. 2.17 The archaeology of Corballis Hill, Co. Kildare, showing hillfort, cemetery settlement and other features.

hillfort, though a mound, a possible cursus monument, an embanked pond and a ring-barrow are recorded on the hill (see Fig. 2.18). The summit of the hill offers excellent views, which are limited only to the north-east and south-west by the presence of Tinoran Hill and Corballis Hill respectively.

Tinoran Hill

One of the most impressive hillforts at Baltinglass lies on Tinoran Hill, just inside Co. Wicklow, 2km north/north-west of the modern town. This is a prominent hill (312m OD) on the northern edge of a broad north/south ridge (Fig. 2.20). The aforementioned enclosure at Hughstown is directly south-west of Tinoran, with these two ridges separated by a narrow valley carrying a tributary of the River Slaney. The main river separates Tinoran Hill from the hillforts on Baltinglass Hill to the south-east. Tinoran has steep slopes on the western, northern and eastern sides, which rise some 110m over a 500m ascent. The southern slopes incorporate the north/south running ridge and, as such, are more gradual, making this the easiest approach to the summit. Unfortunately, a large portion of the hillfort, including the summit and upper slopes, are covered with commercial forestry, which is regularly harvested and replanted, resulting in extensive damage to the interior and enclosing elements of the hillfort (Fig. 2.21). Most of the outer enclosures lie just outside this forestry, in fields given over to sheep and cattle grazing. This agricultural land is sub-divided by a series of rectangular fields, many of which pre-date Ordnance Survey mapping of the mid nineteenth century.

With four definite, widely spaced enclosures, and a possible fifth example to be confirmed, Tinoran (WI026-004) has a potential area of 84ha, making this one of the largest hillforts in Ireland. The enclosing elements variously comprise bank-and-ditch earthworks and stone banks, large sections of which have been levelled by recent forestry work

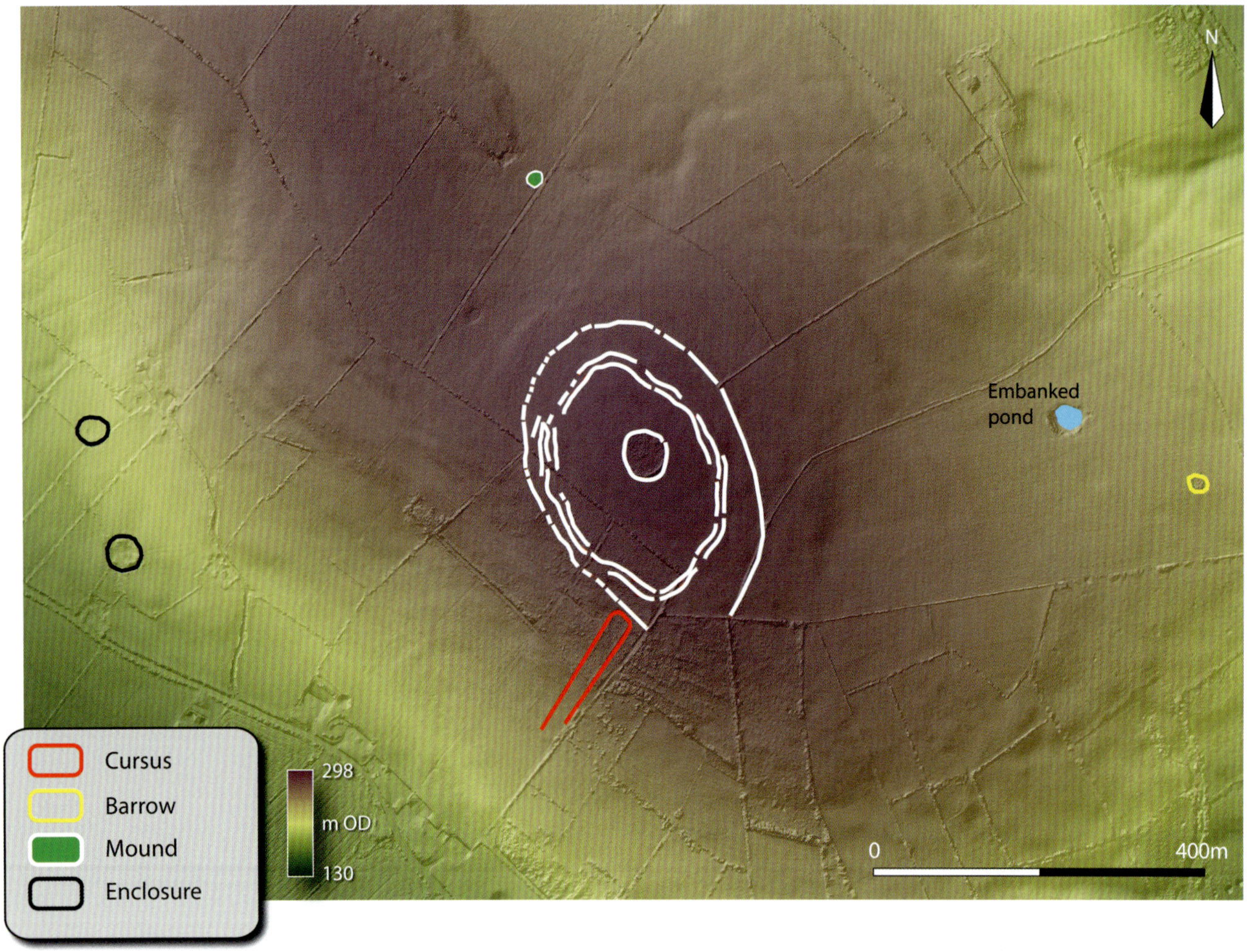

Fig. 2.18 The archaeology of Carrigeen Hill, Co. Kildare, showing Hughstown hillfort, embanked pond and possible cursus monument.

and early modern agriculture. The smaller summit enclosure, known as the 'Round O', survives in a good condition, and, like that at Hughstown, may be more recent than the larger enclosures that surround it. The only recorded archaeological monument inside this exceptionally large hillfort is a hut site (WI026-004001). A large ring-barrow (WI026-005) is recorded next to the outer enclosure on the eastern side of the hillfort. Given its prominence in the landscape, Tinoran Hill offers near panoramic views that are obstructed only to the south-west by Hughstown and to the south-east by Baltinglass Hill.

Fauna Hill

Another potential hillfort was recently identified in Fauna townland on the northern side of the River Slaney, 8.5km north-east of Baltinglass town. This prominent hill (314m OD) has steep western slopes, rising some 120m over the course of a 700m ascent, with the other slopes more gradual. Most of the hill, including all of the newly discovered hillfort, is covered by commercial forestry (Fig. 2.22), with the result that there is significant damage to the monument.

The outline of a widely spaced, bivallate enclosure, some 15.91ha in extent, can be identified. The slight remains of a circular bank enclosing the summit are surrounded by a broadly concentric enclosure 120m downslope. There is a possible unrecorded cairn topping the summit, but no other visible features inside the hillfort. Given its prominent location on the south-western side of the West Wicklow Mountains, there are good views to the north-west and west as far as the Castlecomer Hills, and to the south as far as the Baltinglass Hills.

Fig. 2.19 Aerial photo of Hughstown enclosure, Co. Kildare, July 1966 (reproduced with permission of the Cambridge Collection of Aerial Photography; © copyright reserved).

HISTORY OF RESEARCH

As noted previously, the study of Irish hillforts essentially began with the work of antiquarian Thomas Westropp in the early twentieth century. A prolific scholar, Westropp published many papers on the early fortifications of Ireland (Ashe FitzGerald 2000). His book, *The Ancient Forts of Ireland* (1902), was the first significant attempt to classify the many different types of fort, including the sites of Brusselstown Ring, Rathnagree and Rathcoran at Baltinglass. These were previously recorded on the first edition of the Ordnance Survey six inch mapping published in 1838, with the following description of Brusselstown Ring:

> *An ancient stone wall or Ring (made without mortar) at top of hill in Brusselstown townland. Supposed to be of Druidical origin. The ring encloses an area of about ten and a half acres. It is formed of large unhewn blocks of stones piled up several feet high. The North,*

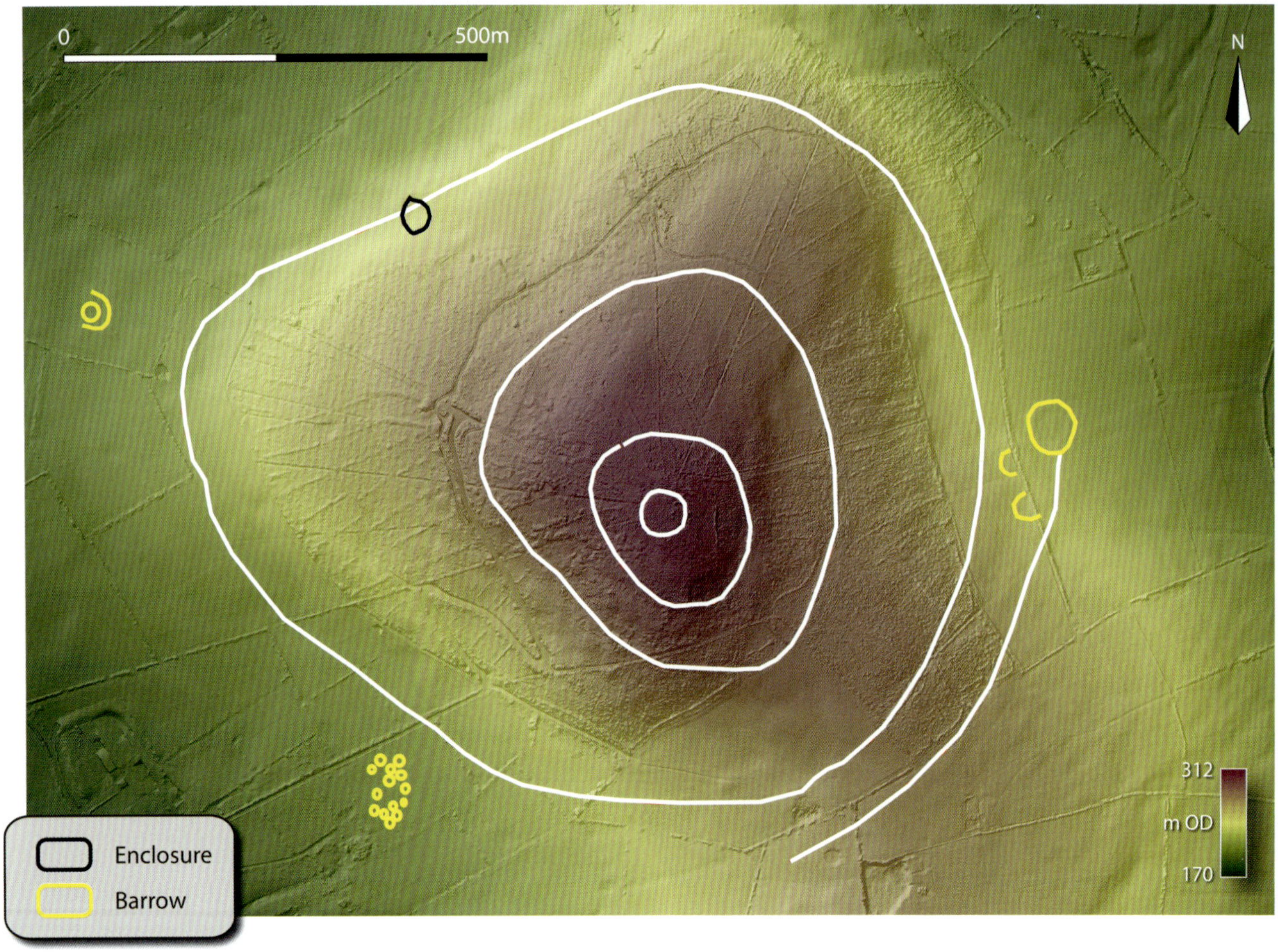

Fig. 2.20 Tinoran hillfort, Co. Wicklow.

> *East and South sides of the hill are very steep, there being a difference of 618 feet in half a mile on the North side, 484 feet in half a mile on the east side and 405 feet in a quarter of a mile on the south side. Tradition says that formerly a boar was kept in the Ring, that it was so large that it filled the whole area, that when it required water it would stretch its neck down to the stream in the hollow a distance of three fourths of a mile. It is also said that the hill took its name (Brusselstown) from this extraordinary Boar.* Ordnance Survey Name Books for Co. Wicklow (vol. 2, 103).

A revision of Ordnance Survey maps (25-inch scale) at the beginning of the twentieth century provided more accurate plans of Brusselstown Ring, Rathnagree and Rathcoran at Baltinglass. Westropp provided a sketch for Rathcoran with the following description:

> *This fine earthwork girds a lofty hill, 1256 feet high, overlooking Baltinglass. It consists of a small circular fort on the very summit, and a large irregular ring of two mounds and a fosse about 80 feet lower, and running nearly on a level (1181 to 1187 feet) round the hill. This encloses a space, 1400 feet north and south, and 900 feet east and west. In the upper fort is a kistvaen, or 'cave', which, when opened, contained pottery and human bones. The upper fort is reduced to a cairn-like heap of stones.*
>
> *Near this rath, on a slope to the north lies Rathnagree, another large fort of two ring mounds, the inner 400 feet in diameter, and the outer 600 feet; in it, early in the late century, was found a hoard of golden coins* (Westropp 1902, 107, 114).

Westropp differentiated these monuments, along with other large hilltop sites such as Mooghaun, Co. Clare and Dún Aonghasa, Co. Galway, from the much smaller lowland

Fig. 2.21 View of Tinoran from Hughstown hillfort.

ringforts of the early medieval period. Half a century before the invention of absolute dating techniques, Westropp argued that smaller ringforts were likely an early medieval phenomenon, while the larger hilltop sites were prehistoric. Although cautious when considering the chronology of these large forts, using documentary sources and evidence from stray finds, Westropp (1902, 725) concluded that they 'originate at least 1200 years before our era' (that is, 1200 BC), a view consistent with the dating of many Irish hillforts today to the Middle and Late Bronze Age.

It was not until the 1920s that these forts would pique the interest of another notable scholar of Wicklow history and antiquities. Liam Price was a barrister by profession, who devoted much of his life to historical research, visiting the Baltinglass landscape on many occasions during the early to mid-twentieth century, often in the company of distinguished archaeologists. His copious field notes, published by Corlett and Weaver (2002), are an important source of site information. Price was the first to identify and record the cairns at the summit of Spinans Hill (Corlett and Weaver 2002, vol. 2, 539) and the inner enclosure of the hillfort of Fauna (487–8), the latter recently re-discovered by LiDAR survey. Other sites he noted, such as a large, unrecorded enclosure and cairn at the base of Kilranelagh Hill (Corlett and Weaver 2002, 540), are an important record of monuments that no longer exist.

The mid twentieth century was a period of renewed interest in Irish hillforts. The first scientific excavation was undertaken at Freestone Hill, Co. Kilkenny by Gerard Bersu (Raftery 1969), followed by investigations at Downpatrick, Co. Down (Proudfoot 1954; 1955) and Rathgall, Co. Wicklow (Raftery 1970a; 1970b; 1972). No research was undertaken at Baltinglass in those years, though many of the hilltop sites (Brusselstown Ring, Rathcoran, Rathnagree and Hughstown) were recorded in the 1960s by the Cambridge University aerial survey. The potential of aerial survey to inform our understanding of the Baltinglass sites was first realised by the archaeologist Tom Condit, who discovered

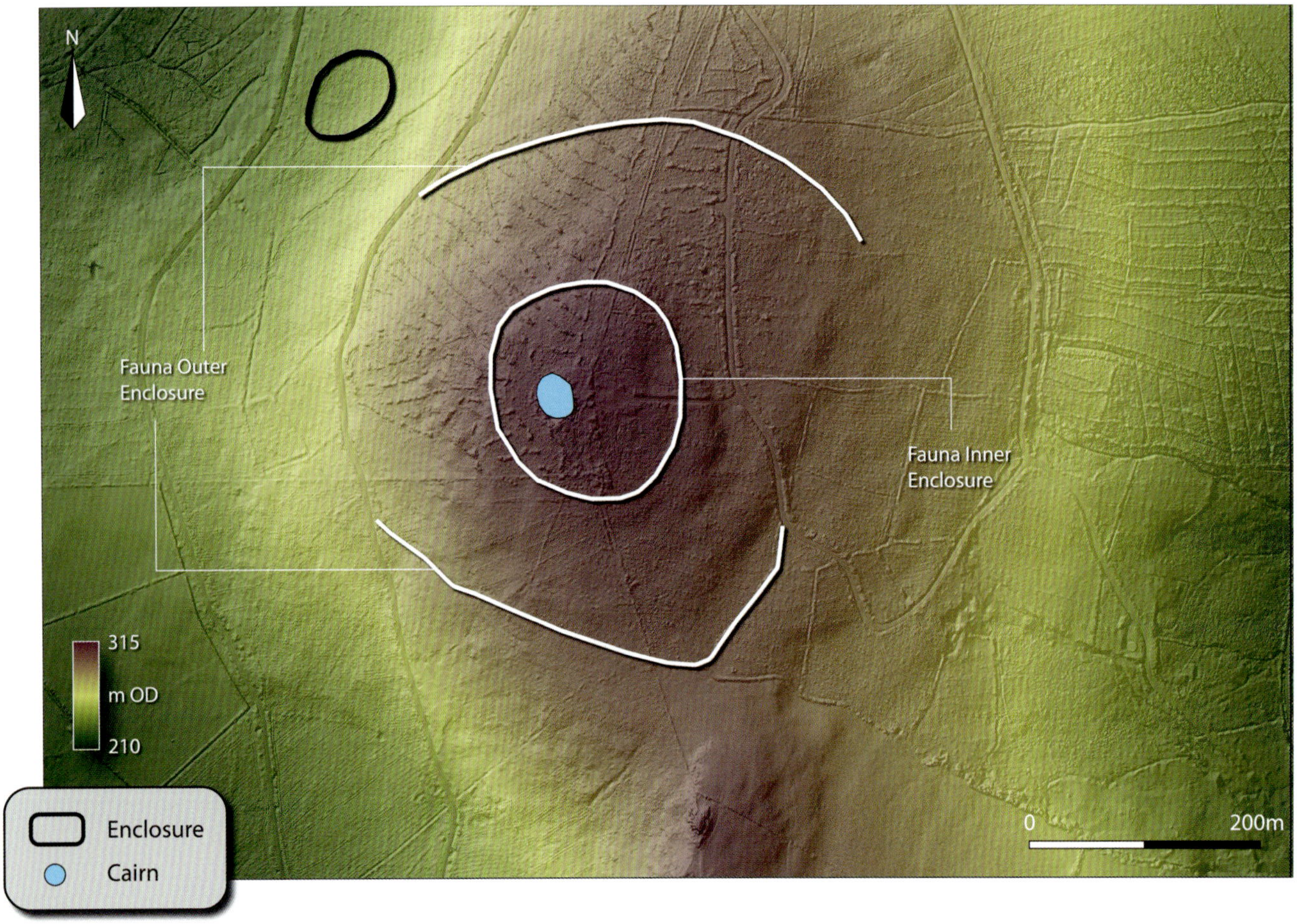

Fig. 2.22 The archaeology of Fauna Hill, Co. Wicklow.

the massive Spinans Hill 2 contour fort and the multiple enclosure hillfort at Tinoran in the 1990s using Irish Army Air Corp photographs (Condit 1992; 1998). Condit published a brief description with basic ground plans of the then known sites at Baltinglass, which included Hughstown, Rathnagree, Rathcoran, Tinoran, Brusselstown Ring, Spinans Hill 1 and Spinans Hill 2, drawing comparisons to other Irish hillforts. Based on this work, these Baltinglass sites were added to the national database of archaeological monuments in Ireland (Grogan and Kilfeather 1997), affording them some protection by the state in the longer term.

Condit's work brought the Baltinglass landscape to wider academic attention, with public interest sparked by his 1992 article in *Archaeology Ireland*, and by a feature article in a leading Irish newspaper written by the scholar Liam De Paor ('The Folks on the Hill', *Irish Times*, 30th January 1993). This prompted many years of speculation on the significance of this unique cluster of hillforts. Frank Mitchell and Michael Ryan offered two explanations, the first being that these hillforts were assembly places or fortifications on either side of the Slaney River erected by two opposing polities, the hillforts being 'rival works inspired by competitive emulation between political groups whose areas of influence bordered each other' (1997, 240). A second model viewed these hillforts as evidence of the movement over time of a tribal centre belonging to a single polity. John Waddell favoured the latter interpretation, suggesting the hillforts represented 'a sequence of activity over a long period of time' (1998, 356). Eoin Grogan supported the former view, stating 'their location is suggestive of the confrontational siting of forts belonging to rival neighbouring territories' (2005b, 124). These interesting ideas could not be tested in the absence of dating evidence for the Baltinglass sites, in a period when the *longue durée* of hillforts and hill-top enclosures in Ireland was not yet fully appreciated.

Following Condit's discovery, much of the discussion on Baltinglass focused on Spinans Hill 2, regarded by many as

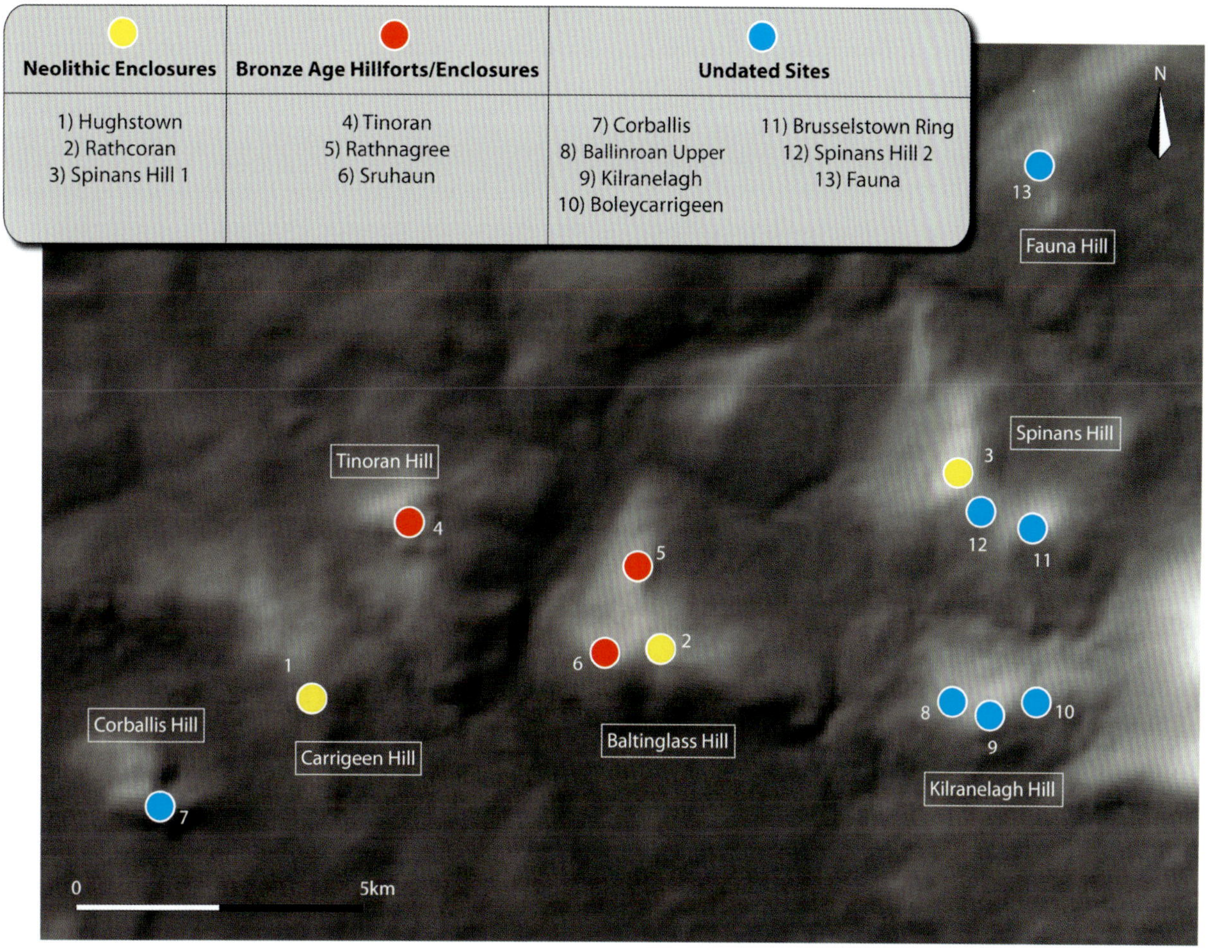

Fig. 2.23 Distribution of hillforts and hill-top enclosures at Baltinglass, with locations of dated and undated sites.

the largest hillfort in Ireland. Barry Raftery (1994, 63) speculated this massive enclosure may have delimited an area of tribal assembly, or that it may be comparable to the Dorsey 'enclosure' in Co. Armagh. While they might compare in size, Condit (1998, 23) pointed out that Spinans Hill 2 encloses a hilltop, whereas the Dorsey and the Dun of Drumsna in Co. Roscommon were defensive dykes protecting river fords (Condit 1998, 22; Condit and Buckley 1998). In his unpublished thesis, Flood (2009, 83), drew a comparison between Spinans Hill 2 and Knocknarea Mountain in Co. Sligo, where Bergh (2000) discovered a system of discontinuous banks on the eastern upper slopes of the mountain, with Neolithic passage tombs.

Until recently, there has been little consideration of possible parallels for the Spinans Hill 2 contour fort outside of Ireland. Was it an invasion base, an assembly place, a trading centre, or a densely populated settlement? These are interpretations that have been advanced for the 114ha hillfort at Bindon Hill in Dorset (Hogg 1975, 36). Raftery (1994, 63) argued that its size meant Spinans Hill 2 could not have been a defended settlement, but he was unable to offer an alternative explanation. He did note, however, that regardless of function, its massive size represented a considerable effort by a large number of people, confirming Spinans Hill was a place of exceptional importance (Raftery 1994, 63).

The level of speculation regarding the Baltinglass hillforts was mainly due to an absence of detailed fieldwork, particularly excavation and scientific dating. While many sites were recorded by aerial photography and brief visits, a lot of them are located in difficult upland terrain, often covered by dense conifer forestry. Despite much damage caused by the latter, no rescue excavation was ever undertaken at these hillforts; because of their location, they have not been impacted by infrastructural projects such as road building and pipeline laying. In terms of broad interpretation, there has been a focus on individual hillforts at Baltinglass, but up to now a cultural landscape perspective has not been considered on these sites.

The recent phase of research at Baltinglass, as detailed in this book, began in 2011, when the Irish Research Council funded a project, based at University College Cork, on 'Hillforts, Warfare and Society in Bronze Age Ireland'. This five-year project, directed by William O'Brien, examined the archaeology of warfare and inter-regional conflict during the Bronze Age, with a focus on multiple-enclosure hillforts. Scientific survey and sample excavation was undertaken at many hillforts across southern Ireland, including five examples at Baltinglass. One of the aims of that element of the project, the subject of a doctoral study by James O'Driscoll (2016; see also O'Driscoll 2017c), was to examine the landscape context of the Baltinglass hillforts. The overall research was published in a 2017 monograph (O'Brien and O'Driscoll 2017), and other publications on Irish hillforts by those authors have also appeared in recent years (see *References*).

The outcomes of that project provide much of the content of this book, including evidence from topographical and geophysical surveys undertaken at Hughstown, Tinoran, Rathnagree, Rathcoran, Sruhaun, Brusselstown Ring, Kilranelagh and Spinans Hill 1, along with excavations at Hughstown, Tinoran, Rathnagree, Sruhaun and Spinans Hill 1. New work has also been undertaken, notably Alan Hawkes's five seasons of excavation at Rathcoran in 2017–21, funded by the Royal Irish Academy. A palaeoecological study was completed by Kevin Kearney in University College Cork; new work was undertaken by James O'Driscoll, including a drone-based topographical model of the Spinans Hill complex, funded by the Royal Irish Academy, and a high-resolution LiDAR survey of the entire landscape, funded by the National Monuments Service's Community Monuments Fund. These studies are published here for the first time, and are combined with the results of the 2011–17 project.

The chapters that follow, therefore, present the results of this Baltinglass research programme, beginning with the results of excavation undertaken at six hillforts, three of which date to the Neolithic and three others to the Bronze Age (Fig. 2.23). These investigations reveal an intensive use of the region, from the introduction of farming communities in Ireland around 3800 BC to the rise of chiefdom societies in the Bronze Age, and the emergence of regional kingdoms during the early medieval period. Why Baltinglass was chosen at different times for such impressive feats of construction is an interesting question. The farmers of the earlier Neolithic may have been drawn by the diverse ecozones and natural resources of the landscape, which had significant potential for agriculture in the fertile lowland around the Baltinglass Hills. The Bronze Age elites who built some of these hillforts had similar concerns, but they also may have used this landscape to control trade between the central midlands and the Leinster coastline, a significance possibly captured in the name *Bealach Conglais*. This long prehistory of settlement at Baltinglass had become mythologised by the early medieval period, with those establishing new power centres drawing legitimacy from the ancient hilltop fortifications. The residence of a king of Leinster at Baltinglass in the sixth century AD continued a story of power and place thousands of years after this landscape had first been settled.

3. RATHCORAN AND NEOLITHIC BALTINGLASS

Alan Hawkes

Rathcoran hillfort is located on the south-eastern side of Baltinglass Hill, at its highest point, known as The Pinnacle (382m OD). Two concentric banks, spaced 24–30m apart, enclose an area of 10ha on the upper slopes of this prominent hill, and the interior rises to a large passage tomb at the summit (Fig. 3.1). Several field walls meet at this tomb, to divide the hillfort area into the townlands of Coolinarrig Upper, Pinnacle and Tuckmill Hill. Steep-to-moderate slopes are recorded outside the monument on the southern and south-eastern sides, with more level terrain to the west and north-west, where the Bronze Age enclosures of Sruhaun and Rathnagree are situated on opposing spurs (see Chapter 5).

The earliest record of the site is the first edition (1842) of the Ordnance Survey six-inch mapping. This depicts two concentric oval enclosures, shown as hachured banks, with the name 'Rathcoran'. There is some uncertainty around the name, which Price (1949a, 135) translated as *Rath Cuaráin* ('Coran's fort') or *Ráth Chárnáin* ('fort of the cairn'). The six-inch map also records a 'cave' at this summit of the hill. This refers to one of the chambers of the passage tomb that was accessed via a small entrance to the north-west. A smaller cairn on this hill is shown as a circular enclosure abutting the outer bank on the south/south-western side of the hillfort.

The earliest description of the hillfort comes from a visit in the early 1900s by the well-known antiquarian Thomas J. Westropp. Along with providing a rough sketch plan of the site, he described the enclosure as

> *a large irregular ring of two mounds and a fosse about 80 feet lower, and running nearly on a level (1181 to 1187 feet) round the hill. This encloses a space, 1400 feet north and south, and 900 feet east and west.*

He labelled the large passage tomb as the 'upper fort' with a 'kistvaen, or cave, which, when opened, contained pottery and human bones' (Westropp 1902, 620). Lord Walter FitzGerald, writing in the early 1900s, would also remark briefly on the enclosing ramparts. He observed that 'around the carn, and enclosing a very large amount of heathery ground, is a double rampart of turf, now much levelled by time' (FitzGerald 1908a, 353).

There is no record of any antiquarian digging at the hillfort, apart from the vague reference to the discovery of human bones and pottery in the summit passage tomb (Westropp 1902a, 620). This reference may, however, explain the absence of finds in the main chamber when the tomb was excavated in 1934–6 by Patrick T. Walshe. The cairn removed at that time was not replaced; the stones were used to construct a 5.5m-wide wall around the exposed burial chambers. Walshe uncovered a multi-phased Neolithic burial monument with four chambers, and a cist of possible Bronze Age date (Walshe 1941, 221). Recent radiocarbon dating of human bone from that excavation indicates at least five phases of activity during the fourth millennium BC (Schulting *et al.* 2017, 317–18). The story of this passage tomb will be examined later in the chapter.

The significance of Rathcoran hillfort was highlighted in two short publications by Tom Condit of the National Monuments Service (Condit 1992; 1998). No detailed study was undertaken, and only brief mention was made of Rathcoran in subsequent publications (Raftery 1994; Mitchell and Ryan 1997; Waddell 1998; Cooney 2002; Grogan 2005b). The enclosure was recorded by the Archaeological Survey of Ireland (Grogan and Kilfeather 1997), with an entry in the *Record of Monuments and Places* for Co. Wicklow (RMP WI027-026001). The site is a National Monument in guardianship of the state.

Several archaeologists have suggested that Rathcoran is an 'unfinished' hillfort of the Late Bronze Age or Iron Age (Raftery 1994, 44; Condit 1992, 17; Waddell 1998, 356). This idea that the hillfort was abandoned during construction was based on the presence of many large depressions and rubble piles — interpreted as quarry pits — on the north-western side of the outer enclosure. This theory was explored by O'Driscoll (2016, 274), who cited examples from England, including Rybury Camp in Wiltshire (Brown, G. *et al.* 2005), and Crickley Hill in Gloucestershire (Dixon 1994, 134–9). The existence of these parallels has reinforced the idea that Rathcoran is a late prehistoric hillfort, though comparisons have also been made between its irregular design, featuring many small entrance gaps, and the Neolithic causewayed

Fig. 3.1 Aerial photo of Rathcoran hillfort *c.*1967, looking south-east (reproduced with permission of the Cambridge Collection of Aerial Photography; © copyright reserved).

Fig. 3.2 LiDAR survey of Rathcoran hillfort, clearly showing 'quarry hollows' between the two enclosing elements.

enclosures of southern Britain (Cooney 2002, 75).

Today, the hillfort at Rathcoran comprises two concentric banks, measuring 413m (NW–SE) by 282m (NE–SW), defining a pear-shaped monument with an overall area of 10.04ha. Including the enclosing elements, the inner enclosure is 347m (NW–SE) by 221m (NE–SW) over an area of 7.18ha. The inner bank is 7–12m in thickness, with an average internal height of 1.2m (range 0.6–1.9m), and an external height of 1.5m (range 1.2–2.1m). Inside this bank is a *c.*8m wide shallow depression, marking the location of an infilled ditch.

The outer enclosure extends *c.*24–30m from the inner bank and is widest on the north-western side, where the ground is relatively flat; it narrows to 5–10m at the south-eastern side with a noticeable terrace. The outer bank is almost imperceptible on that side due to the fall of the slope. The varied distance between the two banks is probably due to the hill slope on the south-western and south-eastern sides. The outer bank has a stone facing on the north-western side, visible only in areas where the growth of heather is reduced. It has an average width of 5m (range 4–6m), an internal height of 1.2m (range 0.4–1.7m), and an external height of 2.1m (range 0.4–2.1m). The external ditch is entirely infilled along the enclosure perimeter, except on the west/north-western side where there is a *c.*4m-wide by *c.*0.5m-deep depression, with a small counterscarp bank visible in places.

O'Driscoll (2016, 172) recorded 39 breaks along the inner and outer circuits of both enclosing elements. These are mostly simple gaps in both banks, averaging 2m in width, which are most obvious along the north western side where there are many hollows, interpreted as 'quarry scoops'. Although they are not clearly defined, O'Driscoll notes corresponding *c.*3.2m-wide gaps in both the inner and outer banks on the northern side of the hillfort, which he interprets as an original entrance (2016, 172). This is not certain, as the openings may be of more recent date, created to allow cattle access the interior.

Fig. 3.3 Aerial photo of Rathcoran hillfort, July 2017, looking south-east; annotated with location of internal features.

The 'quarry scoops' described by Raftery (1994, 44) occur in the north-western, northern and south-eastern sides of the outer enclosure. They comprise large, shallow depressions that mostly abut the inner side of the outer bank (Fig. 3.2), with a small number on the outside of the inner bank. O'Driscoll (2016, 172) noted that their size and depth seem to correspond to the size of the adjacent rampart, suggesting they were quarry pits for construction of the banks. Some of these hollows, particularly those on the north-western side, are surrounded on three sides by low banks.

There are a number of other recorded features at Rathcoran (Fig. 3.3), including the passage tomb (WI027-026003) at the summit and a smaller unexcavated cairn (WI027-076) outside the outer enclosure on the southern slope. The significance of a small cairn with an Ordnance Survey trigonometrical station, to the north-west of the passage tomb, is not known. The *Record of Monuments and Places* lists four possible hut sites in the interior of Rathcoran. Two rectangular structures (WI027-026005 and -026006) between the ramparts on the north-eastern side are defined by low banks of earth and stone, *c.*15m in length, with a sunken interior (Grogan and Kilfeather 1997). A hut-site in the inner enclosure (WI027-026002) is recorded as a circular raised area, 8m in diameter, defined by low, overgrown, stony banks. There is a possible hut-site (WI027-026004) of similar size in the outer enclosure on the north-eastern side. Other features include a large enclosure (WI027-026007) near the centre of the hillfort,

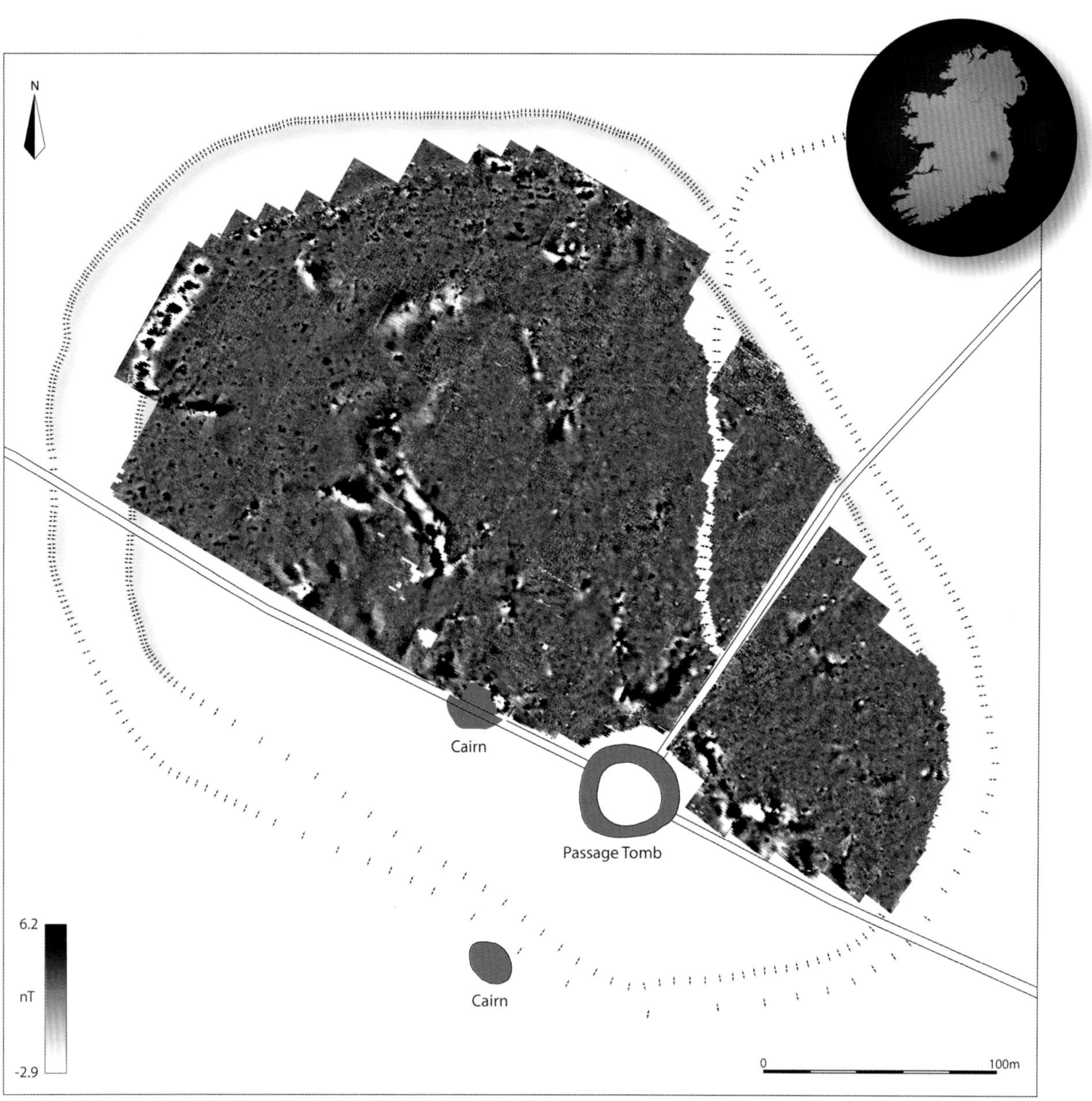

Fig. 3.4 Geophysical survey of interior and inner rampart of Rathcoran, clearly showing high magnetic readings along the crest of the bank on the north-western side.

discovered by aerial photography in 2014. This is visible as a circular setting of large boulders, *c.*14m in diameter. A short distance to the south-east is a possible standing stone, *c.*1.4m high and 1m wide at the base, which may be a natural erratic raised upright.

ARCHAEOLOGICAL EXCAVATION

The 'Rathcoran Hillfort Project' was established by the author (AH) in 2017, building on an earlier study of the Baltinglass landscape by University College Cork (O'Driscoll 2016; O'Brien and O'Driscoll 2017). Although Rathcoran was not chosen for excavation in that project, it was however, surveyed by geophysical prospection and LiDAR (O'Brien and O'Driscoll 2017, 208–9). A gradiometry survey over two-thirds or so of the inner enclosure did not identify definite traces of built structures. When the geophysical data was combined with LiDAR, GNSS and photogrammetry data, however, it suggested that there may be up to 124 possible hut-sites inside the hillfort (O'Driscoll 2023, 23). The gradiometry survey also detected high magnetic readings along the crest of the inner bank (Fig. 3.4), interpreted as the remains of a possible burnt timber palisade (O'Brien and O'Driscoll 2017, 209).

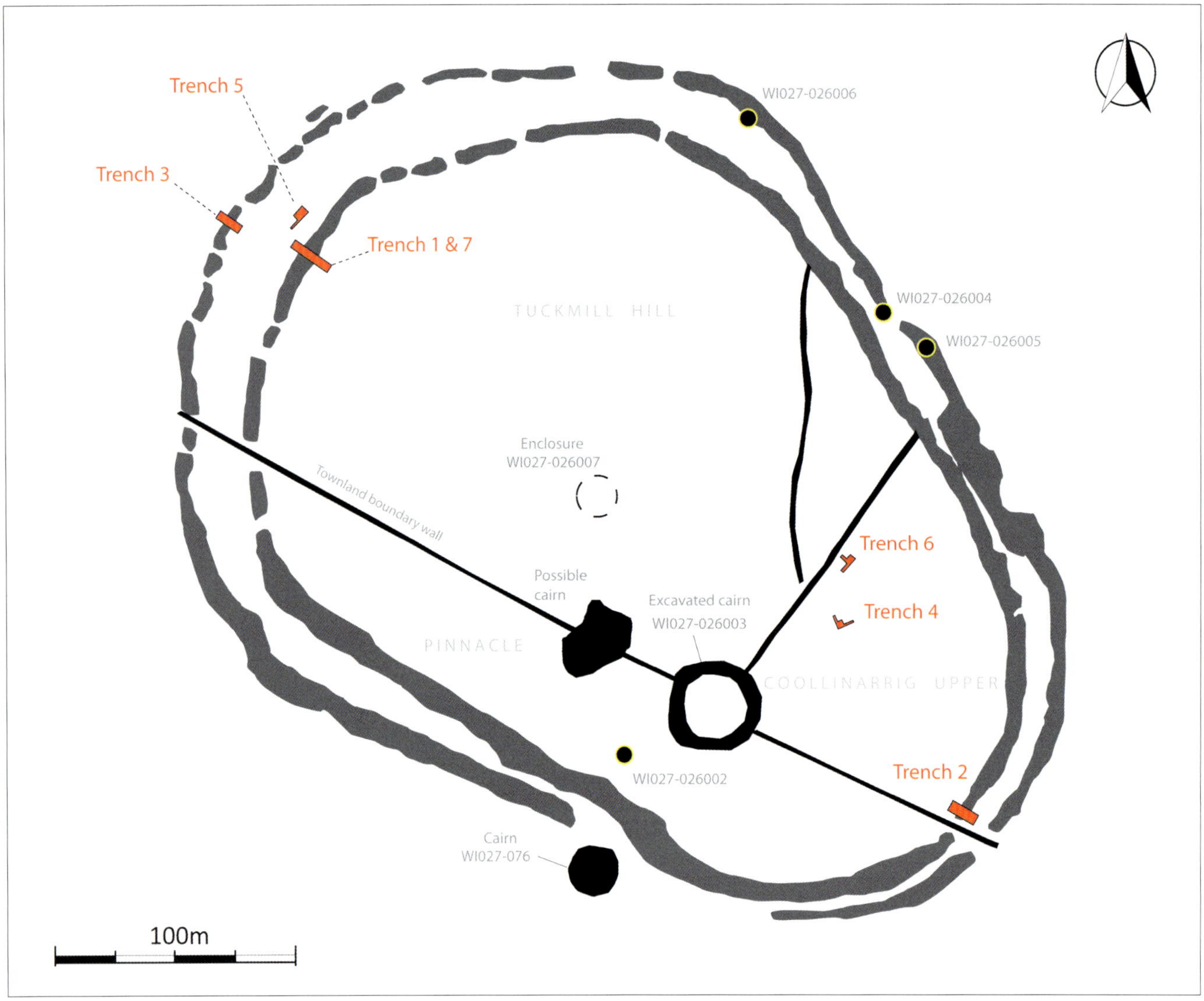

Fig. 3.5 Location of excavation trenches at Rathcoran (2017–2021).

The aim of the 2017 project was to obtain dating evidence for construction and abandonment of the hillfort, through sample excavation and radiocarbon dating of the enclosing elements. The intention was to examine how the banks were built and whether they represent a single phase or a longer period of construction. To examine the 'unfinished hillfort' theory, it was decided to excavate one of the quarry hollows in the outer enclosure to confirm their purpose and use history. A final objective of the excavation was to investigate some of the internal terrace features identified by O'Driscoll (2016, 175; 2023; 23) as potential hut sites.

Seven trenches were excavated at Rathcoran over five short seasons in 2017–21, under the direction of the author, with ministerial consent (C817; E004867) issued by the Department of Housing, Local Government and Heritage. Funding was provided by the Royal Irish Academy, with additional support from Wicklow County Council and the Department of Archaeology, University College Cork. Four trenches examined the enclosing elements (Trench 1, 2, 3 and 7); one was dug over a possible 'quarry scoop' (Trench 5); while two others (Trench 4 and 6) targeted possible internal hut sites (Fig. 3.5). The excavation results are summarised here; additional detail on the site stratigraphy and finds will be provided in future publications.

The defences at Rathcoran

The enclosing elements were investigated in three areas. These included the north-western (Trench 1 and 7) and

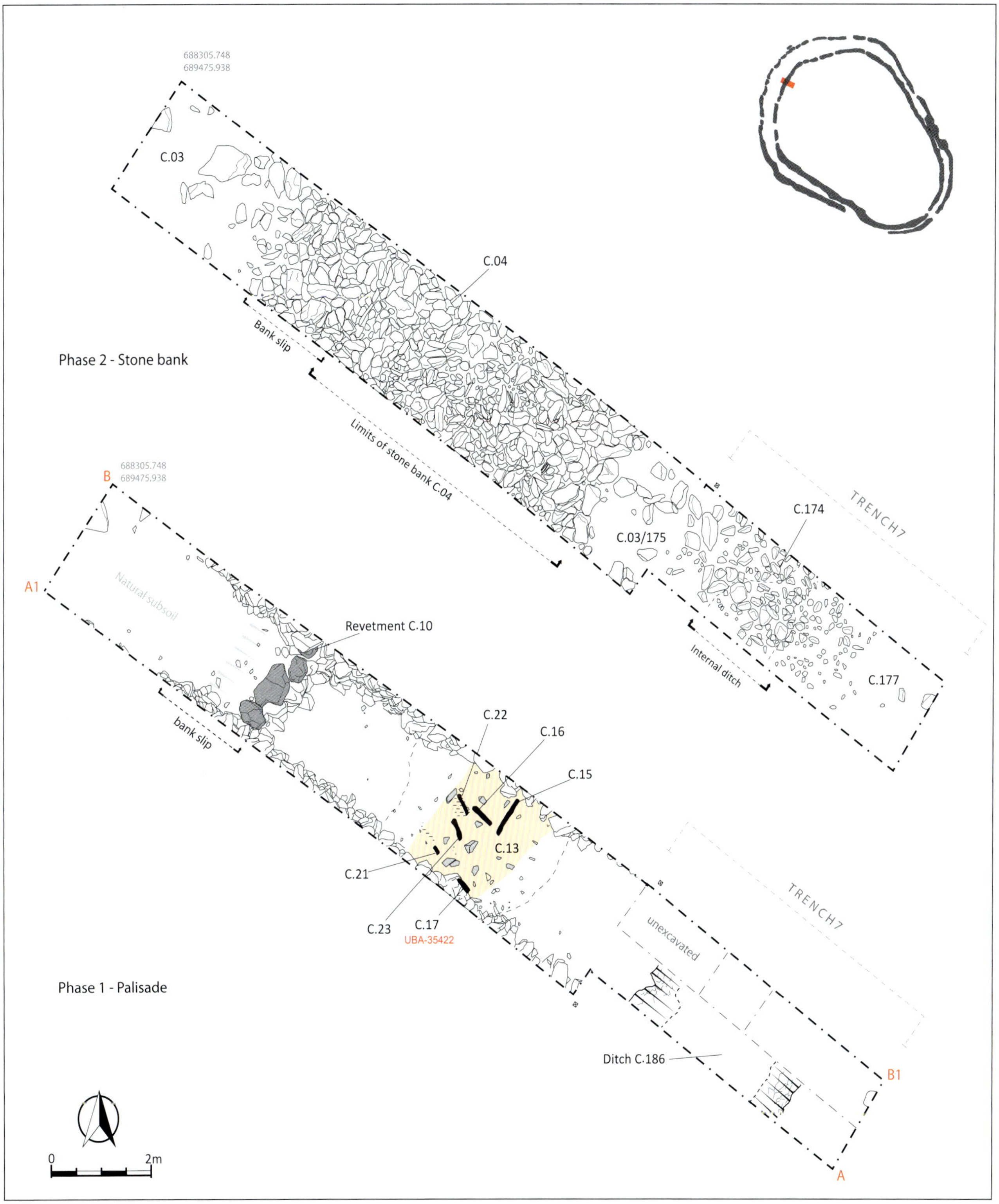

Fig. 3.6 Trench 1 and 7, Rathcoran, showing Phase 1 timber palisade/ditch (bottom), and Phase 2 stone bank (top).

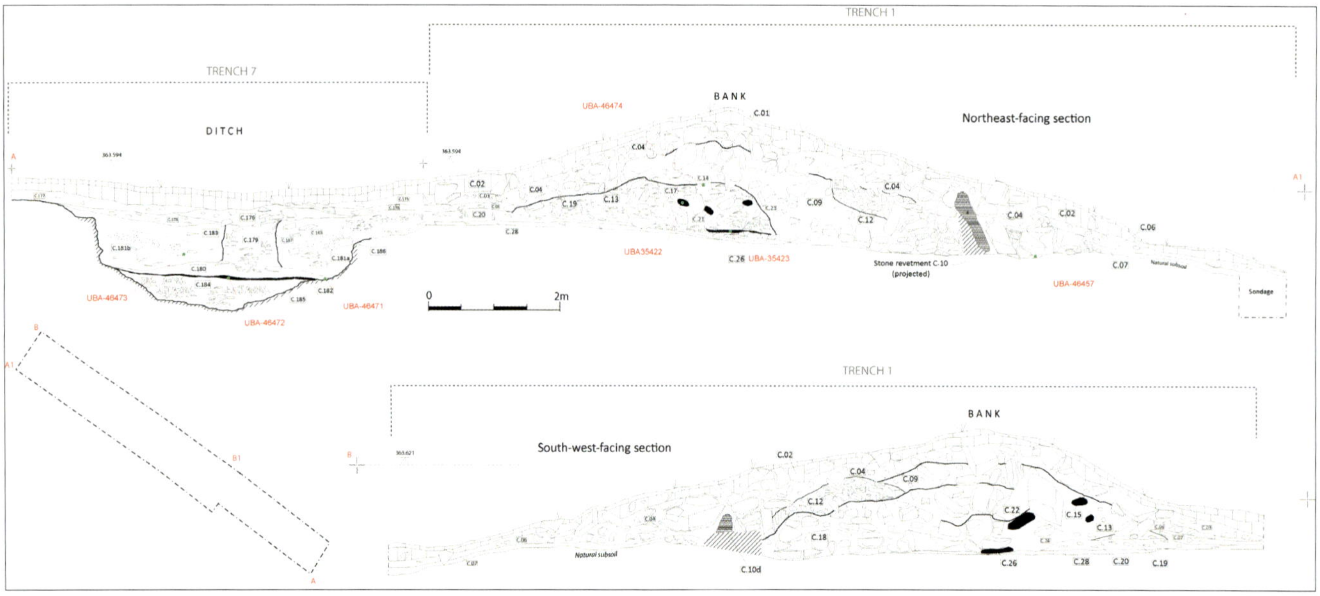

Fig. 3.7 Section drawings of Trench 1 and 7, Rathcoran.

south-eastern sides (Trench 2) of the inner enclosure, as well as the north-western side of the outer enclosure (Trench 3).

TRENCH 1/TRENCH 7

A 13m (E–W) by 2m (N–S) trench, with an 8m (E–W) by 1.5m (N–S) extension, was excavated across the inner bank and ditch on the north-western side of the enclosure. The bank was constructed in two phases, interrupted by a considerable episode of burning (Fig. 3.6). The first phase comprised a low stone and earthen bank, supporting either a light wooden fence or braced internally by horizontal roundwood or planking. This structure was subsequently burned, destroying the wooden elements. A lens of burnt material with charred cereals and Neolithic pottery found near the base of the associated ditch was contemporary with this burning event. Following this fire, construction of the bank resumed with additional layers of earth and stone, reinforced with a stone mantle. This bank was supported by a series of large stones on the northern side.

Phase 1 bank and palisade: The construction of the primary bank was preceded by a burning event, represented by a spread of charcoal-enriched silt on the old ground surface. The deposit contained charred wood, dominated by young hazel, which would suggest the remains of wattling. A sample of this hazel charcoal is dated 3626–3372 BC (4705±32 BP; UBA-35423). This burnt spread was overlain by the primary bank, made up of deposits of loose stony sediments dug out of an internal ditch (Fig. 3.7). These sediments were concentrated at the crest of the ditch on the south-eastern side, much of which seems to have slipped or been deliberately backfilled into the ditch. The main body of the primary bank comprised a red/orange stony subsoil that was entirely oxidised from an intense fire. Some larger boulders were also apparent in the make-up of this bank, which was *c.*2.9m wide, with a central height of 0.9–1m.

Several charcoal features were identified within the oxidised bank, including six pieces of carbonised wood lying on the crest and north-eastern side of the bank (Fig. 3.8). Some of the carbonised wood fragments had curved surfaces, which suggests the use of complete roundwood. Most were found lying horizontally in a NE/SW direction within the outer side of the bank. The alignment of these charcoal fragments indicated some type of wooden structure. They were identified as oak from mature heartwood, with one example likely to be the remains of a burnt plank. A sample from one of these charred oak branches is dated 3767–3637 BC (4905±32 BP; UBA-35422). The date is slightly earlier than others from this trench, possibly because of an 'old wood effect' in the sample analysed. A deposit of soft, grey, silty clay with charcoal was exposed in the top of the primary bank. Charcoal from this deposit was identified as hazel and dated 3635–3385 BC (4761±25 BP; UBA-46474). This result is probably a more accurate date for the construction of the Phase 1 bank and is consistent with the dated charcoal spread beneath the bank.

Fig. 3.8 Phase 1 bank at Rathcoran (Trench 1), showing charred remnants of palisade and oxidised soil from intense burning.

The charred posts probably formed part of a light fence on the outer crest of the bank, braced between larger posts that lie outside the limits of the excavation. It is also plausible that the wooden elements were part of a timber lacing, for which horizontal planks were laid within the core of the bank rather than set vertically. When the bank caught fire, the timbers subsequently oxidised. None of the timbers was associated with a palisade trench and there were no post-holes on the subsoil surface beneath the bank. Instead, it seems likely that these posts were either supported by the bank or driven into it.

Phase 2 bank: Construction of the bank continued after the fire event; deposits of small, medium and large angular stones in grey, stony silt with no charcoal, were dumped in a space between the oxidised bank and a new stone revetment (Fig. 3.9). Those stones were tabular to blocky in shape, indicative of quarried rock. This material was overlain by another layer of re-deposited subsoil and some large stones on the top and outer slopes of the oxidised bank. This, in turn, was overlain by a deposit of medium–large stones, piled in a loose fashion with numerous voids, partly filled with black humic silt. Some of that stone had the angular profile of quarried rock, but mostly these were sub-rounded clasts from the glacial drift. There was also a deposit of soft, dark-brown silt in the lower part of the bank, possibly the result of rain-wash through the loose stones.

The stone component of this bank had an overall width of *c.*8.19m, with a maximum thickness of 0.42m on the south-western side and 0.6m on the northern side. Stone slip from the bank continued north, for *c.*1.52m beyond the stone revetment. The original height of the overall bank is unlikely to have exceeded 2.5m, based on the amount of slip excavated beyond the line of the revetment stones. The

Fig. 3.9 North-east facing section of Trench 1, showing Phase 1 burning overlain by later stone bank relating to second phase of building.

width can be estimated at 6.2m. There was no stone facing on the inner side of the bank.

The north-eastern side of the bank was supported by four large, granite slabs on edge, aligned NE–SW and leaning 70–80° to the south-west (Fig. 3.10). These were irregular/sub-rectangular in shape, 0.45–1m in length, 0.36–0.7m in width, and 0.10–0.15m thick. These stones are interpreted as a revetment for the bank. All appeared to be set within a shallow depression, 2.5m long by 0.92m wide by 0.05m deep, adjacent to a 0.08–0.15m-high ledge. The depression was filled by a compact deposit of small-to-medium sized stones in a mid-brown silty clay with charcoal flecks, which contained a number of large stones as packing material. A sample of oak charcoal from this deposit is dated 3706–3537 BC (4865±26 BP; UBA-46457). It is possible, however, that the charcoal from this context is related to the Phase 1 burning event, and became mixed within the backfilled material of the shallow trench for the revetment stones.

The internal ditch: Excavation on the inside of the bank revealed a large ditch that seemed contemporary with the Phase 1 bank and palisade. The upper part was cut through a thin layer of subsoil into the softer Ordovician (slate, schist and minor greywacke) bedrock (Fig. 3.11 and Fig. 3.12). The sides of the ditch were vertical to steeply sloping, with an irregularly rounded base that exposed ribs of bedrock separated by pockets of compact sterile silt. The upper width of the ditch was 4.04–4.26m, with a 2.2m-wide base and a central depth of 1.4m from the top of the bedrock cut (1.6m to the modern surface).

The infilling of this ditch commenced with a soft, thin deposit of organic silt on its north-western side. This was overlain by an influx of large stones in brown, silty clay into the base of the ditch. A single body sherd from a Neolithic carinated pot was recovered from this deposit (National Museum of Ireland number E4867:83). It was overlain by a lens of burnt material, comprised of charcoal-enriched silt in a gritty soil, probably resulting from burning of the Phase 1

Fig. 3.10 Stone revetment related to the second phase of building, designed to retain the stone bank; Trench 1, looking south-east.

palisade. The deposit contained charred hazelnut shells, charcoal (oak, hazel, pine and ash), and charred grains identified as emmer wheat (*Triticum dicoccum*), one of which is dated 3508–3351 BC (4620±25 BP; UBA-46472). Prehistoric pottery was also recovered from this layer, in the form of sherds from two Early to Middle Neolithic carinated vessels (E4867:82a-b and E4867:85). There are burnt accretions on several sherds, suggestive of cooking. A heavily worn object (E4867:87), interpreted as a possible burnishing stone, was also found.

This lens of burnt material was overlain by a dark-brown clay with frequent stone, concentrated along the north-western slope of the ditch. This deposit was rich in charcoal (hazel, holly and oak) and contained sherds from two other vessels of carinated ware (E4867:79a-h, E4867:80a-i, E4867:81a-d and E4867:84), with evidence of burnishing and decoration in the form of applied lugs (Grogan 2021) Hazel charcoal from this deposit is dated 3633–3378 BC (4737±31 BP; UBA-46471). These layers containing Neolithic cultural material were overlain by re-deposited subsoil. This brown silt with broken shale was a deliberate backfill into the ditch, sealing the charcoal-rich layers below. A charred hazelnut from the base of one of these backfilled deposits is dated 3515–3198 BC (4613±32 BP; UBA-46473).

Excavation also revealed a 0.7–0.8m-wide by 0.73m-deep cut through the upper fill of the ditch. This slot-like feature extended across the full width of Trench 1 and was filled by dark-grey silt with small-to-medium sized fragments of shale. The significance of this feature is unclear, but it certainly post-dates the burning and related occupation. A gleyed, stony deposit overlying the top of this trench represents a water-lain sediment that accumulated

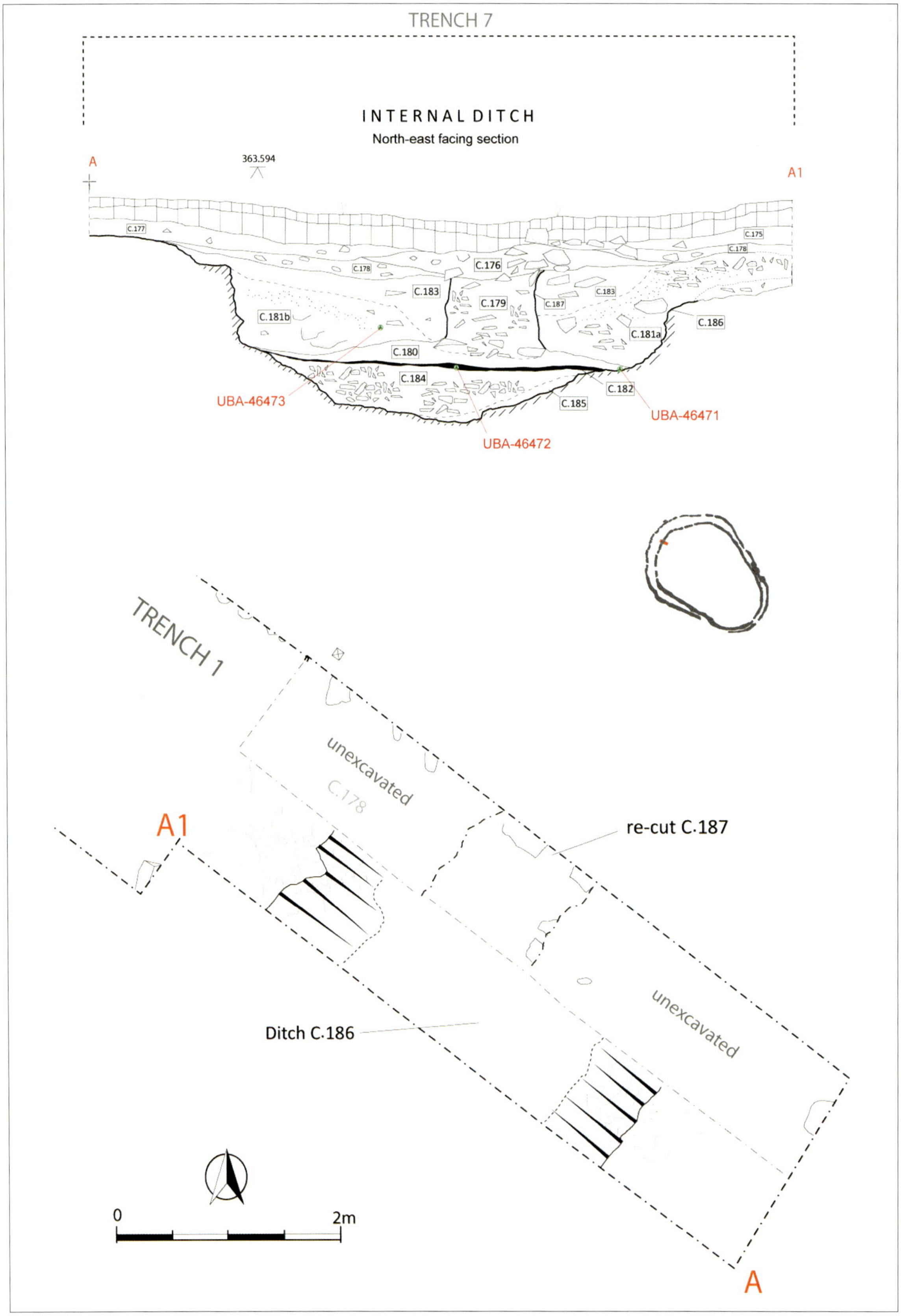

Fig. 3.11 Plan drawing (bottom) and section (top) of Trench 7, inner ditch, Rathcoran.

Fig. 3.12 The inner ditch at Rathcoran, post-excavation, looking south-east.

(Below) Fig. 3.13 Trench 2, Rathcoran, during excavation of the inner enclosure at the south-eastern side; looking north-west.

Fig. 3.14 Trench 2, Rathcoran, showing post-holes of Phase 1 palisade fence (bottom), and Phase 2 stone bank (top).

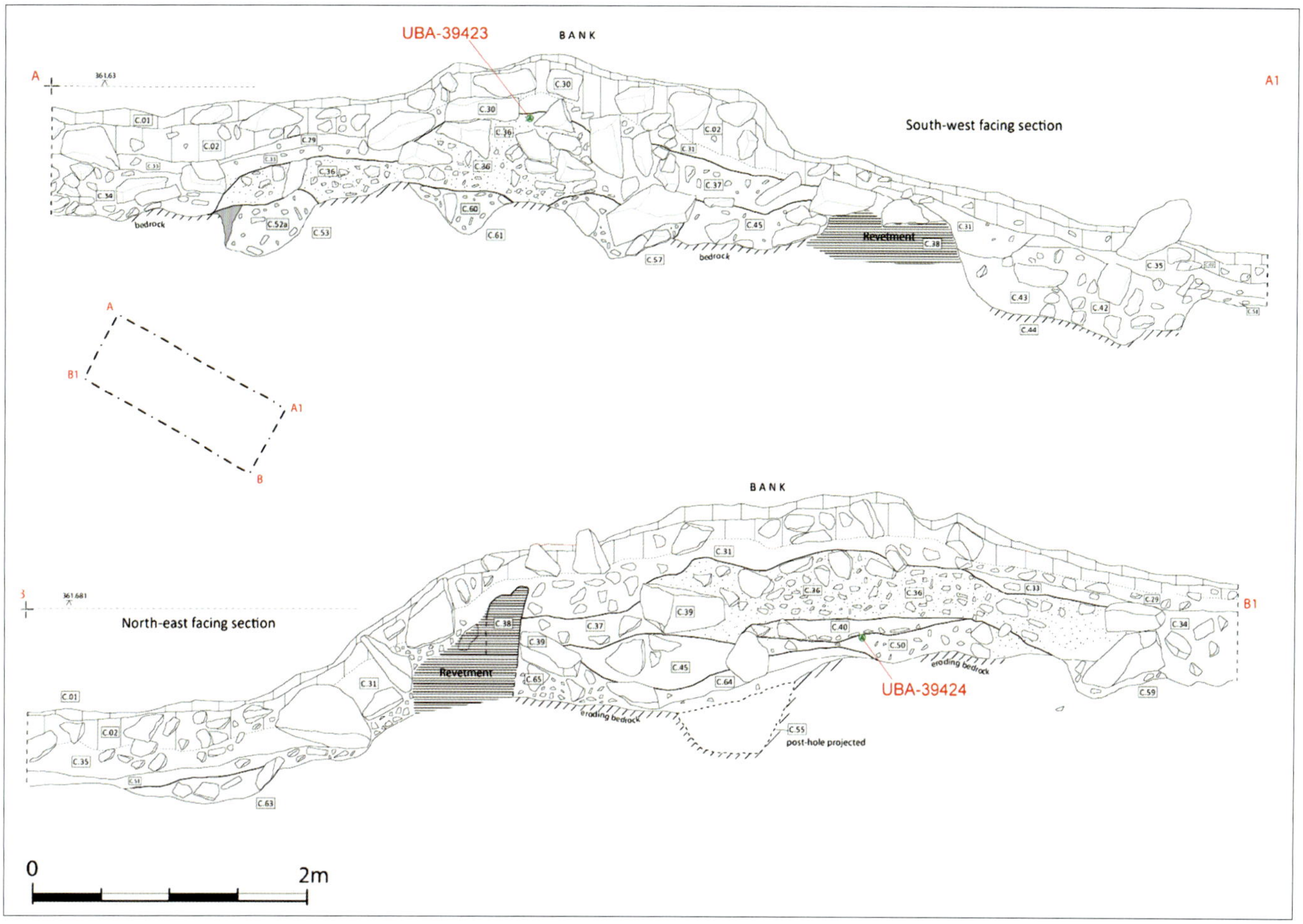

Fig. 3.15 Section drawings of Trench 2, Rathcoran.

gradually in the central area of the partially infilled ditch. Some larger stones representing tumble from the Phase 2 bank were found over this gleyed surface.

TRENCH 2

A 9m (NW–SE) by 3.5m (NE–SW) trench was excavated across the inner enclosure on the south-eastern side of the hill (Fig. 3.13). The investigation focused primarily on the bank and did not extend over the location of the inner ditch. Prior to excavation, this section of the rampart comprised a low bank *c*.6–7m wide, with an internal height of 0.6–0.8m and an external height of 1.2–1.4m. As with Trench 1, the bank was constructed in two phases. The first phase consisted of a double palisade supported by a low bank. After a short period, the posts were removed and the bank was widened and consolidated using a large amount of soil and stone, retained by a revetment on the south-eastern side.

Phase 1 bank and palisade: The earliest features in Trench 2 were four or possibly five pits, exposed in both section faces at a depth of 1.3m under the top of the existing bank (Figs 3.14 and 3.15). It is not entirely clear whether these all represent post-holes, but they were certainly part of a wooden fence. Their relative depths indicate that this may have been a light structure. The pits were cut into the subsoil and granite bedrock that slopes steeply to the east. The post-holes were arranged in opposing pairs to form two parallel rows, 1.8–2m apart, along two sides of the bank. The post-holes on each side appeared to form a NE–SW line, with each post 1.5–2m apart. There was no evidence of decay or burning *in situ*, with the pit fills indicating the original posts had been removed.

Only one post-hole was fully exposed within the trench. It was sub-circular in plan with a steeply sloping side to the west and a gradually sloped side to the east (Fig. 3.16). The shallower profile on the eastern side could represent a ramp

Fig. 3.16 Post-holes at the base of Trench 2, cut into the granite bedrock; looking south-east.

used to raise a post. This pit was 0.8m (N–S) by 0.5m (E–W) by 0.45m deep, with a single fill of loose, dark-grey silt with angular pieces of stone. Two large stones in the eastern half are likely to be packing stones. The largest was 0.59m by 0.16m by 0.11m, and was found in a vertical position, reaching to the base of the post-hole. The other definite post-holes were exposed along the south-west facing section of the trench. These were sub-circular/sub-oval in plan and extended north outside the limits of the trench. They measured 0.65m to 0.82m (NE–SW), by 0.30 to 0.48m (NW–SW), with depths of 0.31–0.4m. Each had a similar fill of grey, silty clay with stone inclusions; one post-hole contained several packing stones.

The primary bank was made up of loose, stony sediments, most likely derived from an internal ditch. Construction began with a deposit of light-brown, stony silt that was overlain with stone mixed with brown, silty clay. A small deposit of charcoal in this sediment was identified mostly as hazel, with small amounts of oak, willow and birch. A sample of the hazel charcoal is dated 3643–3528 BC (4807±29 BP; UBA-39424). The main component of the bank was a deposit of iron-enriched stony silt with small, broken stones (Fig. 3.17). This is probably subsoil and quarried stone extracted from an internal ditch that was not investigated. The bank was 2.8m wide with a central height of 0.4m. Charcoal identified as hazel, with small amounts of willow, heather and alder, was recovered from the top of this bank. The dating of this hazel charcoal to 1202–1007 BC (2898±25 BP; UBA-39423) probably represents the burning of scrub on the bank during the Late Bronze Age.

A 0.8–1m space between the primary bank and a stone revetment was filled with large boulders and soft, silty

Fig. 3.17 South-west facing section of Trench 2, Rathcoran, showing post-holes and natural granite bedrock surface.

sediments relating to a renewed period of bank construction (Fig. 3.18). The infilling of this space began with a stony gravel, possibly washed through the bank material, accompanied by a deposit of large stones with black, fibrous silt. This was overlain by dark-brown, sandy silt with roots, possibly representing turves placed in this space along with the stones. These deposits were then overlain by a layer of loosely piled large stones with a matrix of black, humic silt. This stone mantle had an overall width of *c.*4.7m, with a maximum thickness of 0.42m on the south-western side and 0.6m on the northern side. Stony slip from this bank continued east for *c.*4m beyond the stone revetment. The bank stone was mostly sub-rounded, indicating the use of gathered drift stone. The original height of the stone bank is unlikely to have exceeded 1.5m, based on the width of the bank and the amount of slip beyond the line of the revetment stones.

The south-eastern side of the bank was supported by a NE–SW line of large granite stones, interpreted as a revetment for the Phase 2 bank (Fig. 3.19). The excavated portion comprised 8–9 contiguous granite boulders overlying a foundation of small packing stones. The most southerly of these boulders were the largest, with one tabular block of granite, 1m by 0.25m and with an exposed height of 0.65m, extending from the section face. Another large, rounded stone immediately to the east was probably part of the same revetment. Abutting the northern side of this stone was a large, triangular stone set upright within the packing stones and underlying brown sediment. This tabular granite block was 0.28m by 0.18m, with an exposed height of 0.72m. The remaining stones had an angular, blocky appearance and were an average size of 0.4m by 0.35m by 0.3m.

External bank area (south-eastern side)

The removal of topsoil and underlying stone tumble and silt deposits revealed an iron-panned subsoil on which two pits

Fig. 3.18 Stone deposit filling a space on the inside of the revetment, relating to the second phase of building; Trench 2 looking north-west.

were recorded. The larger was an irregular feature cut into the granite bedrock on the south-eastern side of the trench. This pit was 0.5–1.35m wide, with an excavated length of 2.52m and an average depth of 0.35m, increasing to 0.52m at the eastern end. There was a lower fill of grey-to-brown sandy silt with occasional small stones, overlain by a red-brown silt with numerous stones. The purpose of this feature is unclear, but it may have been used to extract soil and stone for the bank. A second pit extended from the southern section of the trench. This was sub-circular in plan, with exposed dimensions of 0.35m (N–S) by 0.27m (E–W) cut into the subsoil. The base was not determined, because of the presence of a large number of stones projecting from the trench section, but its depth can be estimated at 0.12m. This pit was filled with a single deposit of grey silt that contained some small stones.

TRENCH 3

The outer bank of Rathcoran was investigated on the north-western side of the hill. An 11m (NW/SE) by 2.5m (NE/SW) wide trench was excavated across a 3.5–4m-wide by 1.2–1.3m-high bank over an infilled outer ditch (Fig. 3.20). Excavation revealed a carefully built bank and ditch earthwork, with no evidence of wooden structures (Fig. 3.21). The bank was composed of several deposits,

Opposite page
(Above) Fig 3.19 Stone revetment of Trench 2, comprised mostly of large boulders; looking north-west.

(Below) Fig. 3.20 Aerial view of Trench 3 on outer enclosure during excavation; looking south-east.

RATHCORAN
CO. WICKLOW

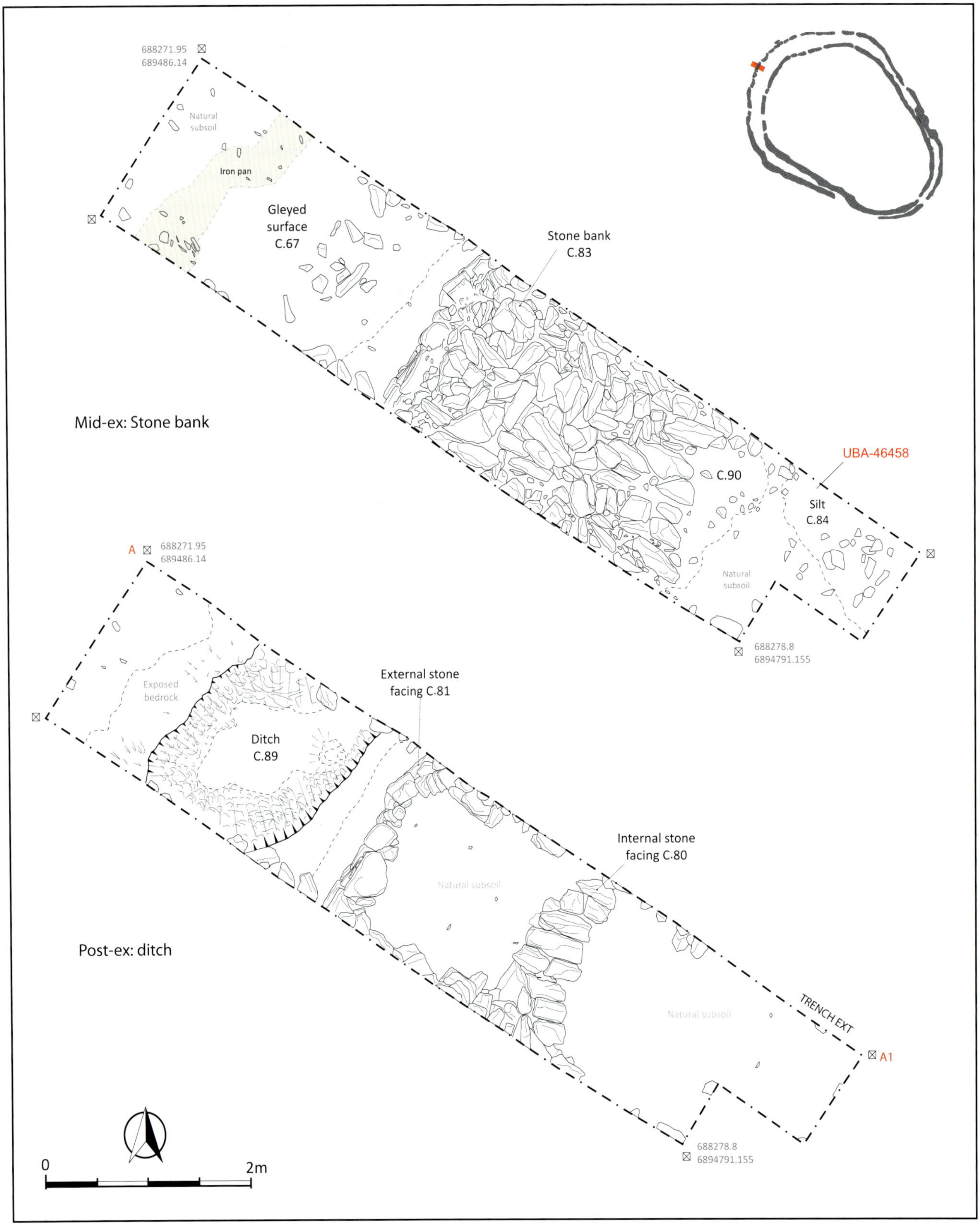

Fig. 3.21 Trench 3, Rathcoran, showing ditch/bank combination post-excavation (bottom), and stone bank/infilled ditch pre-excavation (top).

the earliest of which was a light-brown silt with small, broken stone overlying an old turf layer on subsoil. Fragments of elm charcoal from this old ground surface are dated 3954–3796 BC (5069±26 BP; UBA-46459), providing a *terminus post quem* for the bank (Fig. 3.22). The initial bank deposit was c.2.6m in width, retained by large stones forming roughly coursed inner and outer revetments. It seems that turves were also placed within this soil bank, in particular close to the outer stone facing (Fig. 3.23).

The lower soil in this bank was overlain by large stones, mostly angular shale suggestive of quarried material (Fig. 3.24). Two large stones (E4867:24 and E4867:31) recovered from the top of the bank are possible grinding or saddle querns, though many granite drift boulders on this hill do have naturally rounded surfaces. Additional soil seems to have been added to this stone bank, either from intermittent cleaning of the ditch or re-building at a later stage. This included a layer of stony, grey–brown, root-matted silt, with some medium sized angular stone. The exterior of the bank was supported by stone walling built of roughly hewn rectangular blocks of shale, with smaller stones filling spaces between the courses. This revetment was exposed across the entire width of the excavation trench, with 2–3 courses surviving.

Excavation revealed the terminal of a curving length of ditch extending NW/SE across Trench 3 for an exposed length of 2.3m (Fig. 3.25). The upper southern part of this ditch cut through a thin layer of subsoil, with the lower two-thirds quarried into the Ordovician bedrock. The upper part of this rock is heavily weathered and laminated with vertical fracture planes. The ditch had an irregularly rounded profile, with exposed ribs of bedrock separated by pockets of compact sterile silt. The upper width of the ditch was 1.85–1.95m, with a lower width of 1.23m, and a central depth of 1.02m from the top of the bedrock cut. The ditch was well drained, which explains the absence of waterlogged sediments. There were no visible tool marks on the sides or base of the ditch.

The filling of the ditch commenced with a series of stony sediments at the base and along the inner sides. These may

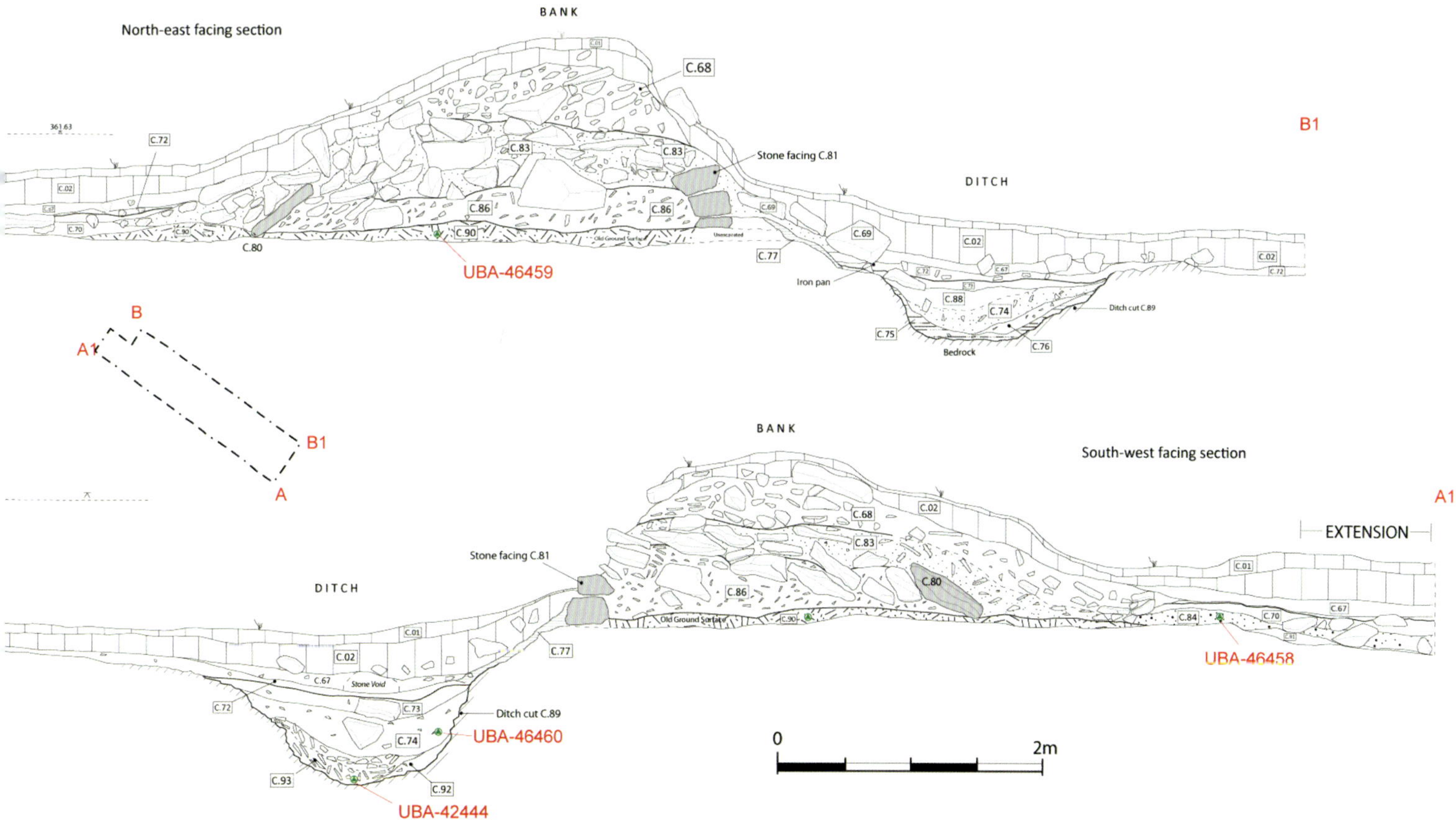

Fig. 3.22 Section drawings of Trench 3, Rathcoran.

(Above) Fig. 3.23 North-east facing section of outer bank in Trench 3, Rathcoran, showing stone component overlying deposit of subsoil/broken stone and old sod horizon (grey band).

(Left) Fig. 3.24 Stone bank of outer enclosure after the removal of peaty sod horizon; Trench 3, Rathcoran, looking north-west.

Fig. 3.25 External ditch of Trench 3, Rathcoran, cut into natural shale bedrock; looking north-west.

have formed from the weathering of the friable shale bedrock. The lower ditch sediments were mostly sterile, apart from a dark, stony silt with a small concentration of charcoal (alder) at the base. A sample of this charcoal is radiocarbon dated 3634–3378 BC (4738±37 BP; UBA-42444). A possible hammerstone (E4867:28) was recovered from the ditch here.

These layers were covered by an influx of soft, grey to light-brown, stony sediment with lighter and darker fractions of the same sediment. This represents the main fill of the ditch and was accompanied by a small number of larger stones that may have collapsed from the wall retaining the adjacent bank. There were occasional 0.02m-thick lenses of grey silt containing charcoal identified as hazel, willow and some minor oak. A sample of this hazel charcoal is dated 3650–3528 BC (4825±26 BP; UBA-46460).

The entire upper part of the ditch was filled by two deposits of orange–brown, stony silt. This subsoil-like sediment may derive from a former counterscarp bank along the outer edge of the ditch, indications of which are visible elsewhere. An iron-panned surface overlay these layers, the removal of which exposed a 0.26m by 0.23m post-hole cut into the upper ditch fills. The represents a post driven into the ditch after it was backfilled. The post-hole was subsequently covered by the partial collapse inwards of the stone facing and bank material.

Activity inside the bank

Excavation at the north-western end of Trench 3 exposed stony silt deposits that were mostly sealed by an iron pan and a leached layer. The latter overlay a compact surface of light-brown/orange, stony silt, with small angular stones and angular shale slabs, many of which appeared to be placed horizontally. A small number of lithic finds from this deposit include flint and chert scrapers and retouched flakes (E4867:13–20). The presence of white quartz fragments in this deposit is notable, as this material was not found elsewhere in the trench.

The removal of this deposit exposed a spread of soft, grey silt with charcoal at the south-eastern corner of the trench. This also contained a small number of charred hazelnut fragments and a number of flint and chert lithics (E4867:25;

Fig. 3.26 Aerial view of the quarry hollow (Trench 5, Rathcoran), after excavation; looking southwards.

E4867:29–36), the butt end of a broken stone axe (E4867:27), and a hone or polishing stone (E4867:26). The charcoal includes fragments of willow, pomaceous woods and hazel, with a sample of the latter dated 3636–3521 BC (4775±26 BP; UBA-46458). The archaeological layers are interpreted as relating to occupation of some kind on the inside of the bank.

The quarry hollow in Trench 5

A 6m (NE/SW) by 4m cutting, with a 4.5m by 1.5m extension, was excavated across one of the quarry hollows in the outer enclosure on the north-western side of Rathcoran (Fig. 3.26). This feature was broadly sub-rectangular in shape, defined by two NW/SE trending radial banks that abut the outside of the inner rampart. Prior to excavation, it extended 11m north from the bank of the inner enclosure, as a 5m-wide depression between two low radial banks, each *c.*1m high on the inside and *c.*0.54m on the outside. The hollow was open on the northern side, where the radial banks ended with rounded terminals. The interior was a grassy, peat-filled depression that sloped southwards to a boggy area.

Excavation revealed an L-shaped section of this quarry pit cut into bedrock along the western and south-eastern sides of Trench 5 (Fig. 3.27). This had a rounded end that was 2.54m wide at the surface and 1.3m at the base, with a depth of 1.4m to the modern surface (1.2m to top of bedrock cut). It extended north-west for a distance of 2.55m at the surface (2.05m at the base). The entire feature had an exposed width of 3.2m. It is likely the quarry pit continues south-east outside the limits of the excavation trench towards the bank of the inner enclosure.

While the upper part of the excavated ditch is irregularly oval, the lower section has a sub-rectangular profile at a height of 0.4–0.58m from the base. This can be explained by the methods used to extract the unaltered bedrock at this depth.

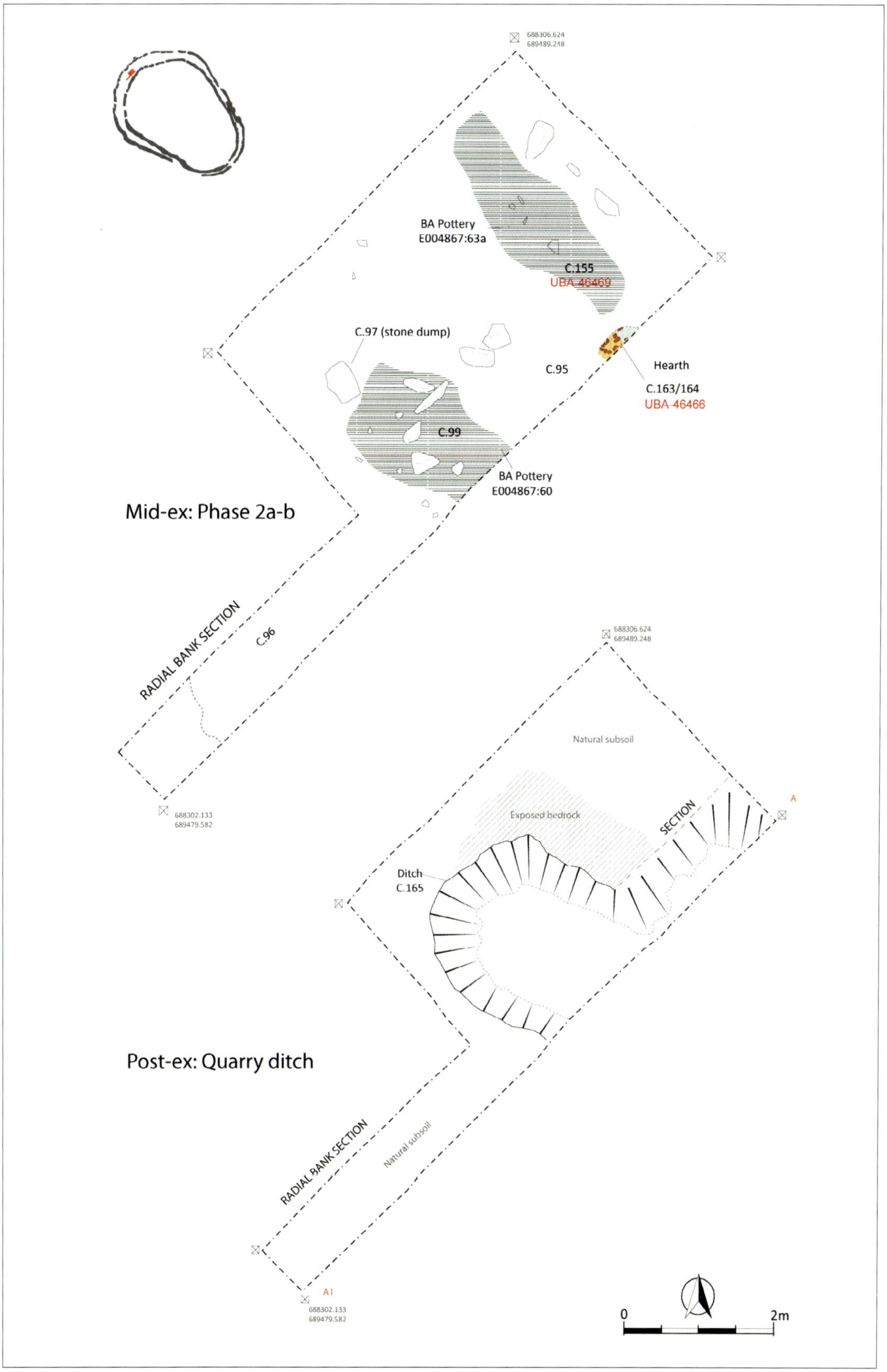

Fig. 3.27 Trench 5, Rathcoran, showing quarry hollow after excavation (bottom), and Early Bronze Age deposits during period of re-use when the hollow was infilled (top).

The upper part of the pit was dug through natural subsoil into the loosely-set weathered bedrock surface. This material was used to create the two adjacent radial banks. Quarrying continued into the unaltered Middle Ordovician slate, with extraction along bedding and joint planes, leaving no obvious tool marks. This stone was then used to build the main banks of the enclosure.

There were at least three phases in the infilling of this quarry hollow (Fig. 3.28 and Fig. 3.29). The first relates to some deliberate infilling during the Neolithic, after rock had been extracted. The second phase is associated with re-use during the Early Bronze Age, when the partly infilled hollow was the location of a fire where pottery was used. This hearth was later re-cut, during a third phase of activity. The hollow seems to have been open for a short period, as only a compact, sterile silt was visible at the base overlying the exposed bedrock surface. A triangular object of shale (E4867:76), with a crude hand grip, was found; it was possibly used as a wedge in the extraction of this rock.

Phase 1: The infilling of the quarry hollow commenced with a loose deposit of stone in soft, brown, silty clay with some charcoal. That latter is identified mainly as oak, with some willow and hazel. The hazel was dated 3339–3031 BC (4476±25 BP; UBA-46465). Fourteen sherds of prehistoric pottery (E4867:69a–x) recovered from the top of this deposit represent the remains of a single Neolithic carinated bowl. This stony deposit was followed by an influx of light-grey silt from the eastern and western sides of the ditch. The tip lines indicate infilling of the ditch from the western side with several deposits of light-brown, stony sediments similar in composition, albeit with varying stone and natural iron content in the soil.

Phase 2a: Following a long period of abandonment, the partly infilled quarry was re-used for shelter. Excavation exposed charcoal-flecked silt across the north-eastern part of Trench 5, overlying the uppermost fill of the quarry (Fig. 3.30). This contained some twenty sherds of prehistoric pottery (E4867:63a-s), identified as a single ribbed vessel of Early Bronze Age date. A sample of hazel from this silt is dated 2136–1935 BC (3649±30 BP; UBA-46469). A similar deposit was noted in patches along the western slope of the trench, where an additional sherd of pottery (E4867:60) from the same vessel was found, along with a flint flake (E4867:68).

Phase 2b: A possible hearth was discovered extending from the south-eastern section of Trench 5 (see Fig. 3.27). This comprised a layer of heat-altered stone overlain by a soft, reddish-brown clay with charcoal. The latter was identified as hazel, willow and pomaceous woods, with a sample of hazel dated 1887–1698 BC (3482±29 BP; UBA-46466). The deposit was abutted to the east by a lens of soft silt with flecks of charcoal. Both this silt and the hearth deposit

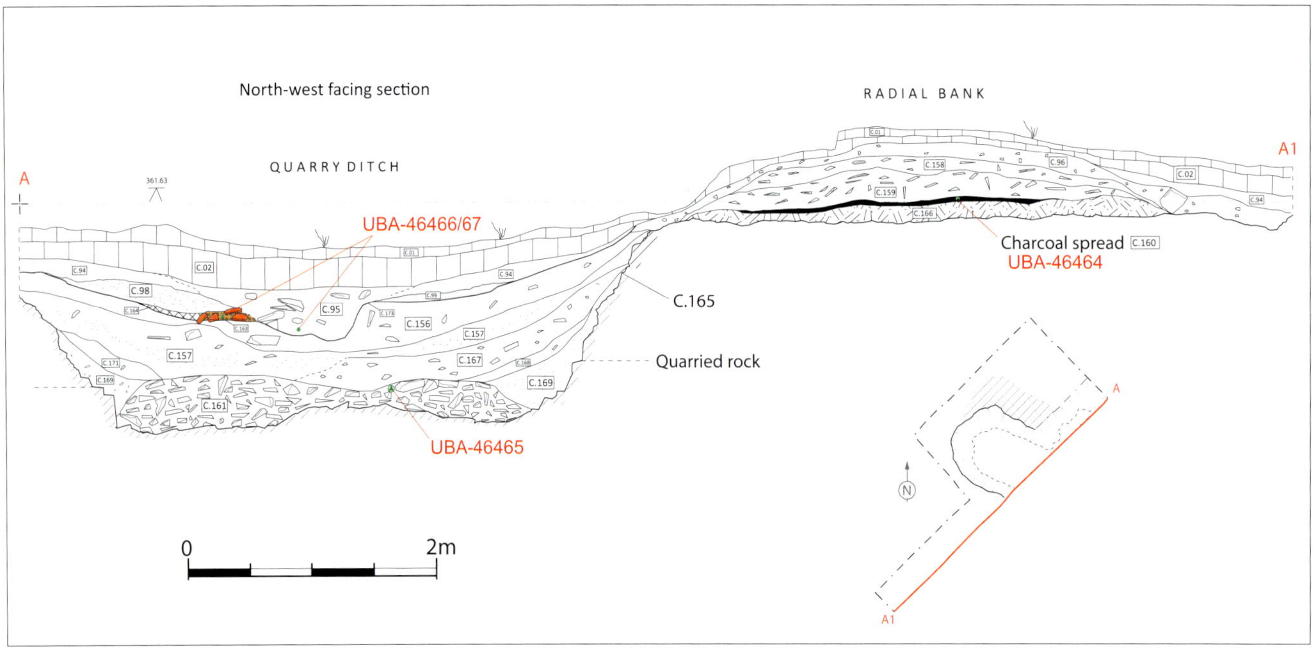

Fig. 3.28 North-west facing section of quarry hollow and radial bank, Trench 5 Rathcoran.

(Above) Fig. 3.29 Quarry hollow in Trench 5 after excavation, showing quarried bedrock surface and north-west-facing section.

(Left) Fig. 3.30 Layer of grey silt that contained sherds of Early Bronze Age pottery. This deposit overlay backfilled layers of natural subsoil that filled the quarry hollow in Trench 5.

occurred within a shallow depression in the upper fill of the ditch. The hearth was also overlain by soft, charcoal-flecked silt, containing five sherds of pottery (E4867:61a–e) from the same ribbed vessel from Phase 2a.

Phase 3: The final event recorded in this quarry hollow was the digging of a small pit through the aforementioned hearth and upper fill of the ditch. This feature was *c.*1.2m wide and 0.3m deep, extending 0.24m from the southern section of Trench 5. It was filled with a laminated clay sediment that contained charcoal, which included hazel dated 1876–1639 BC (3438±23 BP; UBA-46467). That result is similar to a date for the hearth deposit, meaning either that this pit was dug soon after the latter was abandoned or that the charcoal is residual from that feature

Radial bank

A 1.2m-wide extension cutting was excavated south-west from Trench 5 across one of the radial banks adjacent to the quarry hollow. The bank was built on an old ground surface that comprised a layer of grey silt with occasional small stones. A thin charcoal lens overlying this surface represents a burning event that pre-dates the overlying bank (Fig. 3.31). The charcoal was identified as mature oak, with a sample dated to 4317–4052 BC (5336±27 BP; UBA-46467). While this provides a useful *terminus post quem* for the digging of the quarry, it must be viewed with caution given the possible 'own age' of the sample. The charcoal lens was overlain by two successive layers of broken stone extracted from the quarry hollow and intermixed with silt sediments. The upper part of the bank was partially gleyed, creating a firm surface of dark-brown, stony silt with small angular stones that slipped eastwards over the inner edge of the ditch

The inner enclosure

O'Driscoll (2023) identified some 100 possible hut-sites in the interior of Rathcoran, using mainly LiDAR and geophysical survey techniques. Two areas of the interior

Fig. 3.31 Radial bank after excavation in Trench 5, Rathcoran, showing layers of broken shale and subsoil extracted from quarry hollow. It overlies a charcoal lens dating to later fifth millennium BC and an old ground surface.

(Trench 4 and Trench 6), located 20m apart on the south-eastern side of the enclosure, were selected for excavation. They are small terrraces on a gentle, east-facing slope, where roughly circular depressions, 5–8m in diameter, are outlined by boulders (referred to here as a stone 'kerb').

THE 'HUT-SITE' IN TRENCH 4

The first of these depressions was excavated in Trench 4—a 3m (NW/SE) by 3m (NE/SW) cutting with a 3m by 1m extension cutting across the 'kerb' on the northern side, and a 4m by 1m extension running downslope across the eastern side (Fig. 3.32 and Fig. 3.33). The earliest features in the trench were two pits. The smaller example was partially exposed in the northern corner. This was sub-oval in plan, 1.32m long by 0.45m wide in a NE/SW alignment, dug to a depth of 0.63m through subsoil into bedrock. It was filled with loose, grey/dark-brown silt with small stones and some lump charcoal. A sample of the latter identified as hazel is dated 3768–3643 BC (4925±26 BP; UBA-46463).

The larger pit was partially exposed along the southern side of Trench 4 (Fig. 3.34) and seemed to continue further to the south-west. This feature was linear in plan, 4.48m long (NE/SW), 1.2m wide at the top, narrowing to 0.55m at the base, with a depth of 1.2m dug through subsoil into granite bedrock. The pit seemed to be lined with stones, collapsed in places, though this was difficult to confirm due to the large amount of natural stone in the subsoil. The lower part of the pit was filled with soft, light-grey, silty sand, with frequent stones and occasional charcoal (Fig. 3.35). A sample of willow charcoal from the base is dated 3368–3101 BC (4537±37 BP; UBA-42443). A sherd from the body of a Middle Neolithic round-based vessel

Fig. 3.32 Aerial view of 'hut site' (Trench 4, Rathcoran), during excavation, a short distance to the south-east of the passage tomb, top-left.

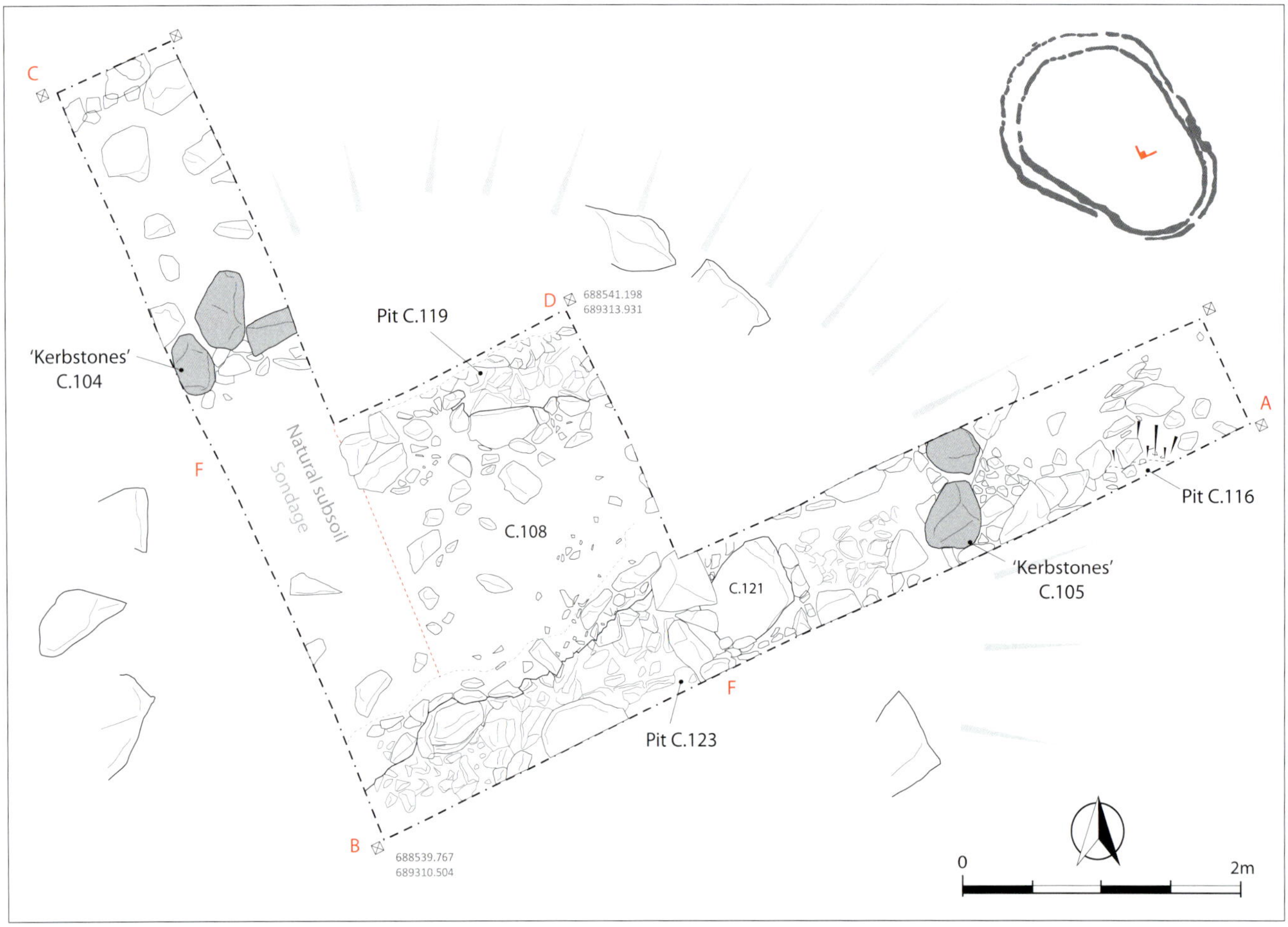

Fig. 3.33 'Hut site' (Trench 4, Rathcoran), post-excavation.

(Right) Fig. 3.34 Larger of two pits discovered in Trench 4, Rathcoran, cut into the stony subsoil with *in situ* stone slabs and boulders; looking north-east.

(E4867:54) was also found here.

A square granite slab, 0.86m long by 0.6m wide by 0.18m thick, was found leaning slightly to the east near the eastern end of the pit. This may have originally been in an upright position, placed deliberately to divide the pit in some way, though it could also be a natural stone. Close examination revealed a small motif on the upper edge, consisting of a rounded rectangle with two lower horizontal lines. This motif is somewhat similar to one carved on a basin stone of Chamber I (J on the plan) of the passage tomb on the summit of Baltinglass Hill (see below). Three large stones near this upright slab were square to triangular in shape and inclined inwards, suggesting they were deliberately deposited in the pit. The upper fill was composed of dark-grey, sandy silt with small angular stone,

Fig. 3.35 Section drawings of Trench 4, Rathcoran.

Fig. 3.36 Iron-rich stony subsoil, containing re-deposited soil from the excavation of the associated pits in Trench 4, Rathcoran.

probably a water-lain sediment that formed when the pit was abandoned and filled with stone. This sediment contained a flint bipolar core (E4867:51).

The north-eastern extension of Trench 4 extended 4m downslope on the outer side of the boulder 'kerb'. The removal of some stones and slope wash sediment revealed part of another pit in the stony subsoil. This sub-circular feature extended 0.61m from the southern baulk. It was 1.4m long and 0.4m deep, with gently sloping sides and a stony subsoil base. A lower fill of brown, clayey silt with small stones was overlain by a light-brown, silty clay in the western half of the pit, with a brown, stony silt on the northern side formed through slope wash. A quartz crystal point was recovered from this deposit (E4867:50).

Excavation across the central area of Trench 4 revealed a compact surface of brown, clayey silt with large, sub-angular stones (Fig. 3.36). This iron-panned surface probably represents subsoil re-deposited from the aforementioned pits. It was overlain by a grey silt with charcoal flecks confined to the space inside the boulder 'kerb'. That silt contained several flint flakes (E4867:49; E4867:52) and a retouched blade (E4867:53). Some lump charcoal identified as hazel from this context is dated 1200–933 BC (2882±32 BP; UBA-46461). The origin of this charcoal is unknown, as there was no evidence of a hearth in that area. Two layers of dark organic silt over this charcoal-flecked surface contained a retouched flint flake (E4867:48) and a possible burin (E4867:46).

The boulders outlining the circular space of the terrace are referred to here as 'kerb stones', even though they do not necessarily retain any material. This was initially interpreted as the wall of a hut-site, but that was not confirmed by excavation. Prior to excavation, seven partially exposed granite boulders enclosed a space approximately 8m in diameter. These were exposed by excavation on the north-eastern and north-western sides. The kerb in the eastern extension of the trench consisted of three sub-rounded, granite boulders aligned NE–SW, resting on a dark, stony silt. The central stone was inclined, but may have been upright originally.

While the significance of the two pits and the boulder 'kerb' is unclear, their stratigraphic relationship was confirmed by excavation. Both pits were overlain by stony sediment on which the large boulders of the 'kerb' were positioned. The latter represents a line of large, irregular boulders on an underlying stony surface, which is not connected in any way to the earlier pits. This, together with the absence of roof supports, an entrance or internal features, such as a hearth, makes it very unlikely this was a hut structure.

The 'hut-site' in Trench 6

A second of these terrace features was investigated inside the inner enclosure 20m to the south-east of Trench 4. A 4m (N/E) by 4m (N/W) trench was excavated, with a 4m by 1m extension on the south-western side and a 2m by 1m extension on the north-western side (Fig. 3.37). Prior to excavation, the 'kerb' on this terrace comprised three partially exposed granite boulders defining a circular space approximately 5m in diameter. There was one particularly large rounded boulder on the north-eastern side. The stone kerb was exposed in two trench extensions on the north-western and south-western sides respectively. All of these 'kerb' boulders overlay a stony sediment at the base of the surface peat. The stones delimited layers of re-deposited natural subsoil in this area. The significance of these boulders is unclear, but they were not part of a wall structure, and some may be of natural origin.

The earliest feature in Trench 6 was a large pit along the entire length of the cutting (Fig. 3.38 and Fig. 3.39). This was exposed for a length of 4.68m, a width of 1.93m at the wider north-eastern end, narrowing to 1.15m further to the south-west, and a maximum depth of 0.8m (Fig. 3.40). The pit sloped from south-west to north-east and was filled by a heavily compacted stone deposit (Fig. 3.39). There were some pockets of softer sediments on the north-eastern side, around some larger boulders. Some of the upper fills are possibly hill-wash sediments that accumulated in this pit

Fig. 3.37 Aerial view of Trench 6, Rathcoran, after excavation; looking northwards.

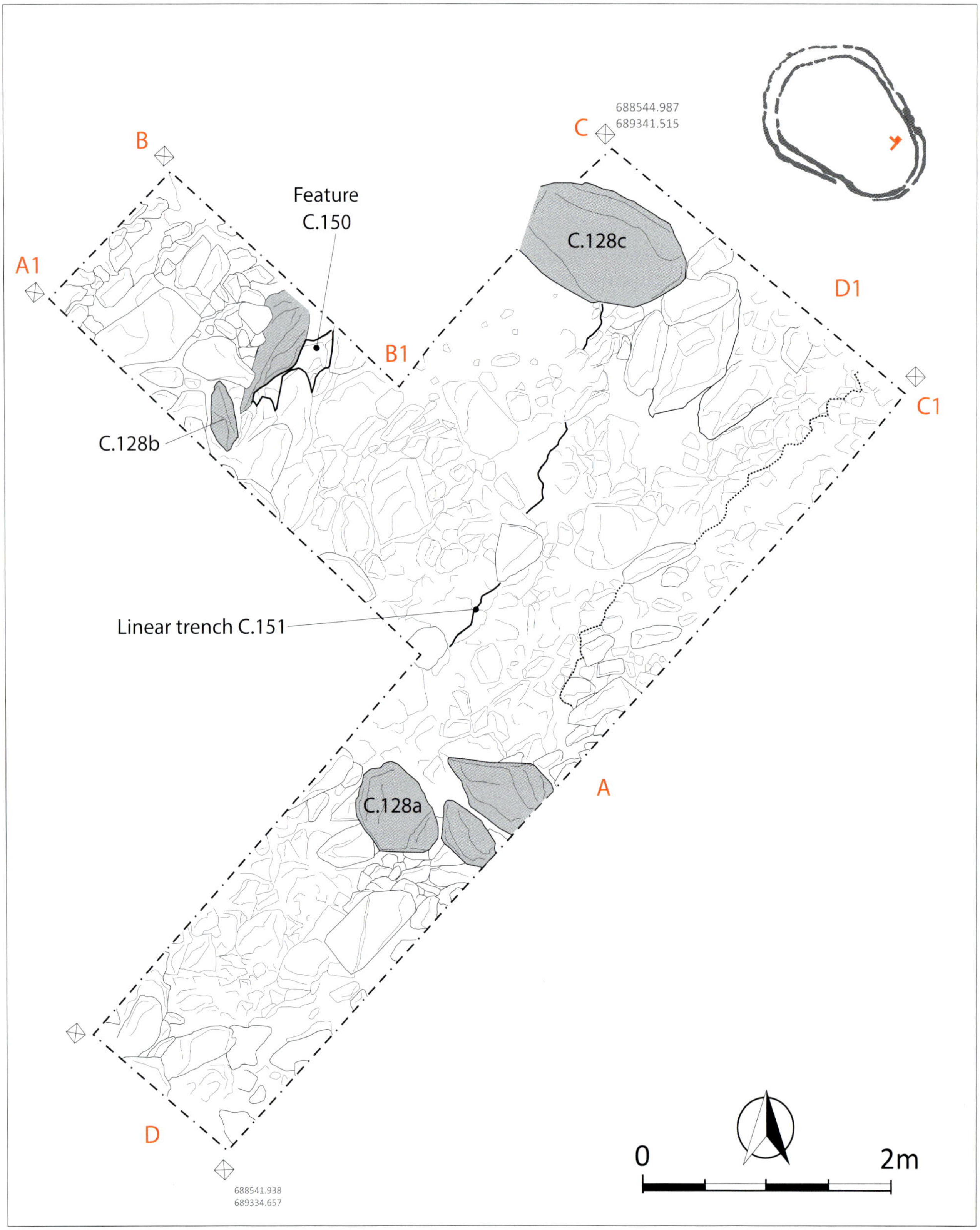

Fig. 3.38 Post-excavation plan of Trench 6, Rathcoran, showing linear pit trench.

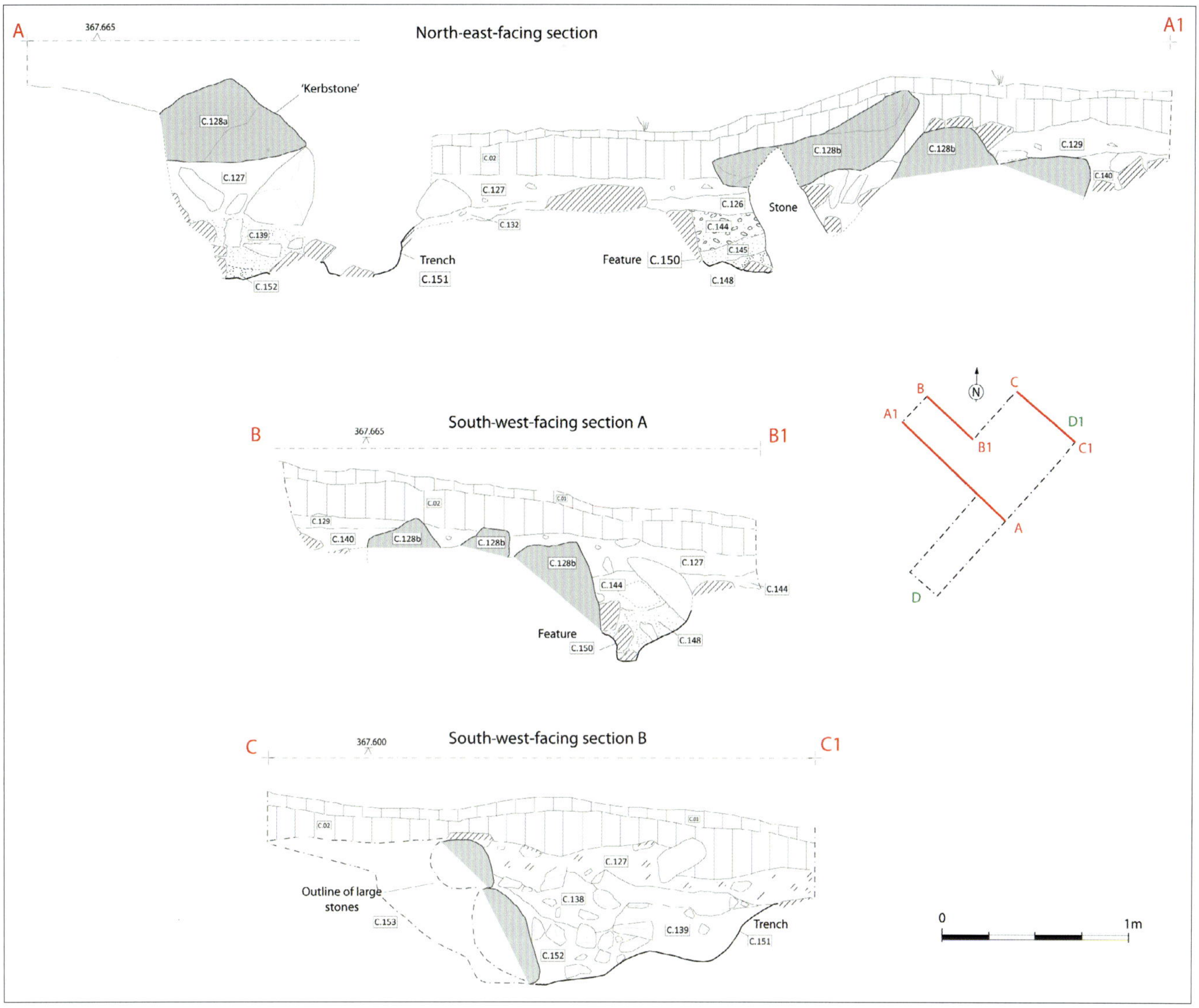

Fig. 3.39 Section drawings of Trench 6, Rathcoran.

over time (Fig. 3.41). The full length of the pit was not determined, as it continued outside the excavation trench to the north-east.

Excavation revealed a series of stony, silty sand sediments with large angular slabs infilling this pit. These were deliberately deposited, with many of the stones resting at an angle. There were no finds or material for radiocarbon dating from the pit. A group of large stones adjacent to a large kerb boulder on the north-western side of the trench had a large void. Full excavation of this feature proved difficult, due to a large stone at the base which was pinned in place by other large slabs. The cut was not well defined, with sloping stones creating a 1.6m (NE/SW) by 0.7m (NW/SE) space with an excavated depth of 0.4–0.5m. This was filled with red/dark-brown silt at the base, overlain by a stony, light-brown, sandy clay and three larger boulders. These deposits were overlain by a light-brown, silty clay that formed a layer of re-deposited subsoil over this part of the trench. There was a rounded quartz pebble (E4867:91) in this layer, with the layer being cut by a sub-circular pit, 0.3m (NE/SW) by 0.27m (NW/SE) by 0.18m deep, that had steeply sloping sides and a rounded base. This was filled with firm, dark-grey, silty sand overlain by a loose, grey/black layer derived from silting of organic soil in this area.

The central space within the 'kerb' of boulders in the north-eastern part of the trench was covered by light-brown, silty clay. This represents subsoil upcast from the large pit. There was a layer of dark-grey, clayey silt over much of the

Fig. 3.40 View of north-eastern end of Trench 6, Rathcoran, where linear pit curves to the east and west. Note large boulders in the natural subsoil.

south-eastern half of the trench, part of the final fill of the large pit. This probably represents a final silting of the linear feature, accumulating around the large stones pitched at steep angles. A similar deposit, darker in colour and with small stones, was recorded at the base of the peat in the north-western extension. This overlay a soft-brown, humic silt that accumulated over a pocket of larger stones. These layers of silt and redeposited subsoil in the central space were in turn overlain by a dark-grey, stony silt, with degraded stone under the surface peat. This silt extended across the centre of the trench to a maximum thickness of 0.16m. There were similar deposits with fine sand outside the kerb stones in both trench extensions, probably representing natural silting or a weathering of the surface prior to the growth of peat. Finds from this surface included several chert flakes (E4867:39-40; E4867:90 and E4867:92), and a worn pebble that resembles a toggle (E4867:78).

The results from Trench 6 are similar to those for Trench 4, with no evidence of a built structure. No features connected to roof supports or walling were uncovered, nor was any hearth or occupation surface. As in Trench 4, the boulders defining the southern side of the 'kerb' in Trench 6 were stratigraphically later than the underlying features.

FINDS FROM RATHCORAN

A small number of artefacts were recovered from the excavations at Rathcoran. These include sherds of Neolithic and Bronze Age pottery, three of which were submitted for residue analysis. A total of 61 items of worked flint and chert were found, along with a broken stone axe, a stone wedge and three coarse stone tools. Some additional stone items registered as artefacts may be natural in origin. No faunal remains were recovered during the excavations, most likely as a result of the acidic soil conditions.

Pottery

The excavations produced 78 sherds (plus 23 fragments and 22 crumbs, total weight 859g), of prehistoric pottery, representing six Neolithic carinated bowls, one Middle

Fig. 3.41 Stony fill within the upper horizon of the linear pit Trench 6, Rathcoran; looking south-west.

Neolithic bowl and a single Early Bronze Age bowl. One sherd was identified by Elaine Lynch (2019), with the remainder examined by Eoin Grogan (2021; 2022).

Fourteen sherds (E4867:69a–x) of pottery were found at the base of the quarry pit (Trench 5). These come from a single pot (Vessel 1) with a broad, sharply everted rim, a gently convex neck, stepped shoulder and a gently rounded body with thick walls (Fig. 3.42). It is well-fired, with a slip of fine clay applied to the upper external surface. The heavy rim is unusual, though wide, everted rims with pronounced shoulders are known in other Neolithic ceramic assemblages.

The internal ditch produced 36 sherds of pottery (E4867:79a–h; E4867:80a–i; E4867:81a–d; E4867:82a–b; E4867:83; E4867:84; E4867:85). These represent five carinated bowls (Vessels 3–7). The vessels have broad, sharply everted rims, with high, upright, gently concave necks, simple rounded or slight stepped shoulders and deep rounded body profiles. On Vessel 3, the rim is rounded with a broad horizontal top. Vessels 1 and 3 have wide, gently convex tops. Vessel 4 is a particularly fine example, with carefully executed decoration in the form of closely spaced lines; there is also an applied oval lug immediately beneath the shoulder. These are carefully made, coil-built vessels, with crushed quartzite present in all examples. While there may have been quartzite in the clay used, the presence of angular crushed grains suggests some of this material was added as temper. The vessels were evenly made, with smooth walls of consistent thickness, and some evidence of burnishing in the case of Vessels 3 and 4.

One lower body sherd (E4867:54) from a well-made pot (Vessel 8) of Middle Neolithic date was recovered from Trench 4. The sherd represents a thin-walled, round-bottomed vessel that was sparsely tempered with small pieces of crushed granite. The external surface was burnished, probably using a polished stone, piece of leather, bone or wood. A single sherd from the nearby hillfort at Hughstown,

Fig. 3.42 Sherds of Neolithic carinated bowl (Vessel 1) from quarry hollow, Trench 5, Rathcoran.

Co. Kildare was identified as having parallels to burnished wares of the Early/Middle Neolithic (Cleary in O'Brien and O'Driscoll 2017, 316). The fabric and treatment of the surface is similar to the sherd from Rathcoran, both having a burnished external surface and made from a similar mica-rich clay with granitic temper.

Twenty-six sherds of pottery (E4867:57; E4867:60; E4867:61a–e and E4867:63a–s) and eleven fragments (160g), were recovered from two layers overlying the uppermost fill of the quarry pit in Trench 5. The pottery was from the upper part of a single ribbed, round-bottomed vessel (Vessel 2) of Early Bronze Age date. The pot had a pointed rim with a flat, steep internal bevel, an upright or slightly in-turned neck and a single surviving horizontal rib at the junction with the body. The preserved sherds indicate a sparsely decorated vessel with simple, elongated, oval whipped cord ('maggot') impressions along the rib. There is also evidence for the application of a fine clay slip on this vessel.

Residue analysis was carried out on three sherds of Neolithic pottery (a rim and two body sherds from Vessel 1), found at the base of the quarry pit (Trench 5). This analysis was conducted at the University of Bristol (Dunne, Gillard and Evershed 2021). A summary of these results is presented here. All three potsherds had lipid profiles, with indications of free fatty acids — palmitic (C16) and stearic (C18) — typical of a degraded animal fat. Also present in low concentration were a series of long-chain fatty acids containing C20 to C26 acyl carbon atoms. These are thought to originate directly from animal fats, incorporated from a ruminant animal's plant diet. Significantly, odd carbon number ketones were present in one sherd. Experimental analysis has shown these ketones originate from the pyrolysis of acyl lipids and ketonic decarboxylation reactions, which occur in unglazed ceramic vessels during cooking when the temperature exceeds 300°C. These ketones are thought to accumulate gradually with repeated use, suggesting that the Rathcoran vessel was used for the sustained processing of animal products at high temperatures.

Two sherds plot within the dairy reference ellipse, while the other sherds plot just on the border. This indicates that the vessel was used to process dairy products, such as milk, butter and cheese. The largest accumulation of lipids was in the rim area, suggesting the heating of milk in this vessel, possibly to make cheese. The presence of ketones further indicates the vessel was used for the sustained processing of dairy products at high temperatures.

Stone tools

A total of 61 flaked stone objects were recovered across six excavation trenches at Rathcoran. Fifty three were identified by Martha Revell (2023), and a further eight by Seán Sharpe (2018). Of these, 20 proved to be natural, while the remaining 41 were struck flakes, cores or split pebbles, and there was one indeterminate piece. Of these, 23 are of flint and 13 of chert, one is a piece of struck quartz, and there are four items of siliceous material similar to flint or chert. One natural rock crystal may have been brought to the site from outside the local area. The majority of the flaked stone tools were recovered from inside the bank of the inner enclosure (Trench 3) and from the central area of Trench 4.

Two flint bipolar cores (E4867:35 and E4867:51) were recovered from Trench 3 and Trench 4 respectively, while a chert platform core (E4867:5) was found within the bank in Trench 2. Of 36 flakes examined, retouch was present on only nine examples, all but one of which was flint (Fig. 3.43). There is indeterminate retouch on two pieces, obscured due to burning, breakage or heavy edge damage. The retouched forms include four concave scrapers (E4867:13; E4867:18, E4867:25 and E4867:29) produced on regular tertiary and secondary flint and chert flakes, as well as three edge-retouched flakes, including one blade (E4867:17; E4867:45 and E4867:53), a possible burin (E4867:46), and an indeterminate retouched flake

Fig. 3.43 Retouched flint from Rathcoran excavation.

(4867:48). The latter was one of the pieces with heavy burning.

A small number of coarse stone tools were recovered at Rathcoran, all coming from secure Neolithic contexts with radiocarbon dates. These include part of a stone axe (E4867:27) from Trench 3, found in charcoal-flecked silt on the inside of the outer bank, along with a hone stone (E4867:26) and several flint flakes. The axe fragment is 125mm long by 64mm wide, narrowing to 26mm at the butt, and 40mm thick, and made of fine-grained sandstone. It is irregularly trapezoidal, with a heavily flaked narrow end. One side appears to be ground flat, while the other has a rounded and partly polished profile. It can be identified as the butt of a polished stone axe, broken at the mid-point leaving a sharp, triangular scar.

A long triangular stone (E4867:76) of local shale was found at the base of the quarry hollow in Trench 5. This is 240mm long by 62mm wide, narrowing to 23mm at the point, and is 38mm thick. One side has a triangular profile, while the other is flat. There is some flaking mid-way along the edges, particularly on one side, allowing the object to fit neatly in the hand. It may have been used as a wedge in quarrying, where it would have been inserted into the joints of the bedrock and driven in possibly with a wooden mallet.

A possible hone stone (E4867:26) was found with the broken stone axe (E4867:27) in the same charcoal-flecked silt on the inside of the bank (Trench 3). This object is rectangular in shape, 130mm long by 50mm wide, narrowing to 30mm. It has a rounded profile on one side, flat surfaces on the other three sides, and one particularly smooth face with obvious wear related to polishing or sharpening. The lithology is a coarse-grained, micaceous sandstone. A broadly hexagonal-shaped stone (E4867:28), possibly a hammer or grinding stone, was found in the base of the outer ditch (Trench 3). This is 80mm by 65mm by 38mm and is made of local granite. The surfaces are smooth and mostly flat, with one slightly concave face that has traces of pecking. A water-rolled piece of quartz (E4867:87) was also found. This object is sub-rectangular in shape, 49mm by 50mm by 23m, with an oval cross-section and a broad, flat face, smooth from use. This possible polishing or grinding stone comes from a charcoal-rich layer in the internal ditch of the inner enclosure (Trench 7), found in association with Neolithic pottery and charred cereals.

Three water-rolled stones were recovered from the excavations; two from the radial bank in Trench 5, and one from Trench 6. The latter (E4867:91) was an oval quartz pebble, 41mm long by 30mm wide by 24mm thick. The other two include a circular stone of local coarse granite (E4867:73), 42mm long by 39mm wide by 29mm thick, and a triangular stone of fine granite (E04867:74), 56mm long by 56mm wide by 40mm thick, with a smooth face possibly from use wear. Finally, a small stone (E4867:78) with two 10mm-wide grooves on both sides was found. This 23mm long by 21mm wide by 21mm thick object has an oval, rounded surface at the top and a flat, triangular base with a broken corner. It resembles a small toggle, but is probably a natural stone used expediently for some purpose.

Environmental remains

Charcoal and other plant remains were recovered during the Rathcoran excavation. These were analysed by Susan Lyons (2022); a short summary is provided here. A total of 47 soil samples were selected for flotation analysis. Some 1,363 charcoal fragments, weighing 237.2 grams and representing 11 wood taxa, were identified from these samples. Oak (*Quercus* sp.) dominated, followed by hazel (*Corylus avellana*) and willow (*Salix* sp.). Pomaceous woods (*Maloideae* spp.) were next most common, with gorse (*Ulex europeaus*), holly (*Ilex aquifolium*), birch (*Betula* sp.), pine (*Pinus* cf. *sylvestris*), alder (*Alnus glutinosa*), and heather (*Calluna*) present in smaller amounts.

The wood used at Rathcoran shows morphological characteristics that reveal that both large oak timbers and younger roundwood branches of various taxa, oak included, were utilised. The dominant wood species at Rathcoran was oak. The dominance of oak charcoal from bank deposits in Trench 1 and Trench 5 suggests the charred remains of timbers; many of the charcoal fragments were large chunks of mature oakwood. This provides an insight into wood selection, showing that the builders of Rathcoran knew the structural value of oak timber. Some of the oak samples displayed narrow (<2mm) and evenly spaced annual growth rings, which indicates these oak trees grew in dense woodland, but within favourable edaphic conditions. The absence of any insect channels and fungal spores indicates this wood was used when fresh, probably soon after cutting. The presence of hazel and willow charcoal in the excavation of the enclosing banks is notable, particularly since both taxa are recorded in deposits where oak charcoal was lower. Much of this material was also young-diameter roundwood (<11 years), suggesting the remains of wattling used between the larger oak timbers.

Examination of annual growth rings suggests this wood

was cut in Spring, an uncommon practice, since wood felling would normally occur in Autumn when trees are dormant, causing less damage to the tree. Sap and nutrient levels are highest in Spring each year, for the production of leaves and fruits, and this increase in moisture means wood is more pliable. The use of branches cut in Spring may indicate that flexible and easy to bend rods of suitable size were needed for the creation wattle structures. This shows the hillfort builders were skilled woodworkers who understood the properties of different wood species and the best season to gather supplies. It may also indicate the time of year the hillfort was built, though that would have taken many months over several years.

Other wood species at Rathcoran include elm (Trench 3) and, to a lesser extent, pine (Trench 7). Both of these wood taxa decline significantly in charcoal assemblages from the Late Neolithic and Bronze Age in Ireland (O'Donnell 2007; 2011, O'Carroll 2012). Pomaceous woods, gorse, birch, holly, ash and alder were also present in the Rathcoran samples, albeit in very low amounts. This reveals the use of tree species as fuel, in construction and for other purposes. Heather charcoal is less frequent from archaeological sites, possibly due to its scrubby nature — it tends to burn to ash easily. While the diversity of wood taxa from Rathcoran is high, the relative proportion of species used signals that a specific wood management strategy was at play, whereby the main supply of timber was provided by oak, hazel and willow. Oak was selected for heavy building, while hazel and willow were used for lighter structures.

In addition to charcoal, carbonised cereal grain of Neolithic date is also recorded at Rathcoran. There was a high occurrence of charred cereal grains in a charcoal-rich layer within the internal ditch of the inner enclosure (Trench 7). Emmer wheat (*Triticum dicoccum*) was the main grain present, accounting for over 65% of the cereal remains in that context. Wheat grains of indeterminate species accounted for 11%, while indeterminate barley grains (*Hordeum* sp.) comprised just 2%. Other abraded cereal grain of unidentified species made up the remaining 22% of the cereals recorded. Fragments of charred hazelnut shells were found in small quantities at the base of the quarry hollow (Trench 5), the internal ditch (Trench 7) and the charcoal-flecked silt on the inside of the outer bank (Trench 3).

Although the number of samples analysed is relatively low for the size of Rathcoran, the cereal grains recorded are a significant archaeobotanical assemblage. Despite the ubiquity of cereal grains from Neolithic and Bronze Age sites, they tend to be recovered in very low numbers (<100 grains) and associated with structural deposits or features located close to or within structures themselves. The high emmer content from Rathcoran is therefore an important find. Large cereal assemblages (having more than 100 grains) are rare from prehistoric contexts and have been identified at fewer than ten sites, the majority of which date to the Neolithic period (McClatchie *et al.* 2014). It is possible the Rathcoran cereal remains represent food waste, possibly a single deposit based on the single-species representation. The absence of any weed seeds or cereal chaff confirms this cereal cache was well threshed and sieved prior to arriving at Rathcoran. This usually indicates the cereal was intended for direct use in food preparation or to be milled for baking.

INTERPRETING RATHCORAN

Radiocarbon dating confirms that Rathcoran was built between the thirty-sixth and thirty-fourth centuries BC. This is one of a growing number of Neolithic enclosures recorded in Ireland (see Chapter 9). The site emphasises that this part of south-west Wicklow was intensively settled by early farmers during the early to mid-fourth millennium BC (see O'Brien 2017; O'Brien and O'Driscoll 2017). Rathcoran is one of three Early Neolithic enclosures in the Baltinglass landscape, the others being Hughstown *c.*4km to the west and Spinans Hill I, the same distance to the north-east (see Chapter 4).

Excavation has revealed three main periods of archaeological activity at Rathcoran, namely the Early to Middle Neolithic, the Early Bronze Age and the Late Bronze Age. While the stratigraphic evidence indicates two main phases of construction in the Neolithic, only one primary episode of building is represented in the radiocarbon chronology. This indicates that the building of the large stone banks *c.*3600–3400 BC (Phase 3b) immediately followed a burning event (Phase 3a) on the hill. A total of 21 radiocarbon dates are available for securely stratified contexts at Rathcoran. Thirteen of these relate to the enclosing elements, with the remaining eight are associated with contemporary occupation in the interior, or with later activity. Whereas some charcoal dates are problematic, due to an 'old wood' effect, the Rathcoran results reveal the following sequence of construction:

Period 1 (Neolithic)

Phase 1 – Pre-enclosure fires during the early fourth millennium BC. These are indicated by a pre-bank charcoal spread in Trench 5 (4317–4052 BC; UBA-46467) and lump charcoal from the old ground surface in Trench 3 (3954–3796 BC; UBA-46459). Even allowing for 'old wood', the dates indicate fires on site or in the immediate vicinity during a period that largely pre-dates model 2 of Cooney *et al.* (2011, 663) for the beginning of the Irish Neolithic at 3750–3680 BC.

Phase 2 – A date of 3768–3643 BC (UBA-46463) from a pit in Trench 4 indicates activity in the interior of Rathcoran. This is broadly contemporary with the suggested date of construction and use of Chamber III of the passage tomb (Schulting *et al.* 2017, 13) on the summit of this hill.

Phase 3a – Seven dates spanning the period 3600–3300 BC, from the inner ditch/bank and pre-bank of Trenches 1 and 2, indicate an early construction phase and burning event followed by a rebuilding soon after. These are consistent with the pre-tomb burning event and immediate covering of clay and rubble (Phase 2), followed by construction of the first chambered cairn on Baltinglass Hill (Phase 2/3; Schulting *et al.* 2017, 14).

Phase 3b – Widening and consolidation of the inner bank, backfilling of the inner ditch and possible building of the outer enclosure. This construction directly followed the burning event of Phase 3a. It is contemporary with the building of Chamber II and the first kerbed cairn in the passage tomb (Schulting *et al.* 2017, 14), which also followed the pre-tomb purification and preparation activities without an interval.

Phase 4 – Some other evidence of quarrying within the interior of the site, closer to the tomb in Trench 4 (and possibly Trench 6) during the period 3368–3101 BC (UBA-42443). This appears to be related to the construction of Chamber I, the larger, second cairn and to the deposition of bone in Chamber II of the passage tomb (Schulting *et al.* 2017, 14).

Period 2 (Early Bronze Age)

Phase 1 – Early Bronze Age activity *c.*2136–1935 BC (UBA-46469), represented by the temporary occupation of a quarry hollow in the outer enclosure, with a small fire and deposition of Early Bronze Age pottery.

Phase 2 – A second phase of activity in the same location during the Early-to-Middle Bronze Age *c.*1887–1698 BC (UBA-46466 and 1876–1639 BC; UBA-46467), indicated by a pit in the excavated quarry hollow. This phase may be contemporary with an undated cist inserted into the cairn of the passage tomb (Schulting *et al.* 2017, 14).

Period 3 (Late Bronze Age)

Late Bronze Age activity is represented by two radiocarbon dates from Trench 2 (1202–1007 BC: UBA-39423) and Trench 4 (1200–933 BC; UBA-46461) in the south-east quadrant of the enclosures. Both dates are for lump charcoal from below the surface and relate to fires in the vicinity during the Late Bronze Age.

The Rathcoran enclosures

The radiocarbon results reveal that a number of fires occurred on this hill prior to the building of the Rathcoran enclosures. Possible explanations include the clearing of scrub or the ritual preparation of the ground prior to construction. They include a spread of mature oak charcoal beneath the radial bank of the quarry hollow (Trench 5), which has a date of 4316–4052 BC (UBA-46467). Even factoring in an 'old-wood' effect, the date still represents activity at the site at the end of the fifth millennium BC, or more likely during the early years of the fourth millennium BC. There is also a date of 3953–3796 BC (UBA-46459) for young elm charcoal from the old ground surface beneath the bank of the outer enclosure (Trench 3). The origin of that charcoal is unknown, but it does indicate some burning in the vicinity during the early fourth millennium BC prior to construction of the enclosure. Interestingly, this date is contemporary with one obtained for cremated human bone from Chamber II of the passage tomb, assuming the latter result has not been affected by the use of old wood in the cremation pyre.

The construction of Rathcoran began with the inner enclosure and the building of a palisaded bank with an internal ditch. Four radiocarbon dates from charcoal contexts in this bank, and three from the ditch, place this activity in the Middle Neolithic *c.*3600–3300 BC, a time of considerable environmental, landscape, settlement and economic change in Ireland (Whitehouse *et al.* 2014, 20). The bank was composed of subsoil and stone excavated from an internal ditch, cut into the subsoil and underlying bedrock. The size of the inner ditch, 4.2m wide by 1.4m deep, at least along the north-eastern side, indicates the removal of a considerable quantity of soil, even if we cannot be certain the ditch was of a similar size around its entire perimeter. It is also unclear whether the ditch was dug as a continuous, uninterrupted feature; the geophysical results do not offer any useful insights there due to the peat cover. Excavation did confirm the ditch was not open for an extended period of time, being deliberately backfilled soon after it was dug.

Evidence of a wooden palisade along the inner bank was first suggested by the geophysical survey (O'Brien and O'Driscoll 2017, Fig. 5.20). Unlike some other Neolithic enclosures in Ireland, the palisade at Rathcoran was not set within a narrow foundation trench. Instead, the posts were placed within shallow, but well-defined, post-holes, with the evidence from Trench 2 indicating two parallel rows of posts on each side of a 3m-wide by 1m-high primary bank. These post-holes were not discovered in Trench 1, where lengths of charred oakwood were instead found along the top of the primary bank, which itself was oxidised by extreme heat. All of this wood is oak, likely to represent bracing elements between the larger posts that probably fell onto the crest of the bank when the fence was burnt. One of these charred timbers is dated 3767–3637 BC (UBA-35422), although a slightly younger age is possible due to an 'old wood' effect. A date of 3635–3385 BC (UBA-46474) from hazel charcoal overlying the burnt timber horizon in Trench 1 is probably a more accurate date range for the destruction of the fence. This is supported by a similar date of 3643–3528 BC (UBA-39424) obtained from Trench 2.

The outer enclosing element at Rathcoran did not incorporate a timber palisade, with the primary bank instead built with subsoil extracted from an external ditch. This soil and loose stone was retained by a stone revetment, preventing it from slipping into the ditch. Two radiocarbon dates from the ditch indicate this section of the enclosure was built *c.*3650–3378 BC (UBA-46460 and UBA-42444), broadly contemporary with the defences of the inner enclosure. This is supported by a possible occupation layer on the inside of the external bank that contained charred hazelnut shells, flaked stone tools and a broken polished stone axe, found with charcoal dated 3636–3521 BC (UBA-46458).

The burning and re-building of Rathcoran

Shortly after this initial stage of construction, or possibly during the building phase, a large section of the wooden palisade on the north-western side of the inner enclosure was burnt down, in what seems to have been a single, deliberate act. The evidence comes from the high magnetic gradiometry readings and from the excavation of Trench 1/7, where charcoal deposits and charred timbers were found collapsed on the primary bank. A discrete layer of burnt material within the lower fill of the internal ditch is further evidence of this intense fire. The ditch deposit contained a relatively large assemblage of charred emmer wheat, with some charred hazelnut shells. There was also carinated pottery, with some sherds from freshly broken vessels, while others had worn edges suggesting deposition of older pottery into the ditch (Grogan 2022). Two radiocarbon dates from this layer place the deposition of this material to 3633–3351 BC (UBA-46471; UBA-46473), contemporary with the palisade fence.

The soil of the primary bank of the inner enclosure was intensely oxidised by fire-reddened stones. This indicates an intense and prolonged fire that must have taken a considerable amount of tinder and brushwood to ignite and maintain. There was no evidence, however, that the wooden fence on the south-eastern side of the inner enclosure was burnt down (Trench 2), with the geophysical survey indicating a more localised event on the northern side of the inner enclosure, over a distance of approximately 250m. There is no evidence the outer enclosure was ever burnt, though, of course, there is no wooden component in those defences.

Excavation confirmed that immediately after this burning event, building recommenced along the inner circuit. This is supported by the absence of an old sod layer over the charred timbers in Trench 1. Additional layers of soil, but particularly large amounts of stone, were added to the primary bank, which were retained by a large stone revetment. This resulted in a widening of the bank to *c.*5–6m, with an estimated original height of 1.8–2.5m. There is no evidence to suggest the palisade was rebuilt or a new one created. From the Trench 2 evidence, it seems the original posts may have been removed along the southern section of the enclosure and the internal ditch backfilled, at least along the north-western section of the enclosure. A vertical *c.*1m-wide trench was dug in the upper fill of the inner ditch. This may have been used for some type of fence, but no evidence for posts or dating material was obtained.

Similar to Trench 1, the evidence from Trench 3 indicates that a considerable amount of stone was added to the outer enclosing element. There is little to indicate any break in the construction sequence there, suggesting it was built during a single phase. The stone used in both banks did not originate from their adjacent ditches, and so must have been obtained elsewhere. The most likely source is the large, sub-rectangular hollows in the outer enclosure, many of which extend from the inside of the outer bank. The findings from excavation of one of those hollows would seem to confirm this interpretration. In Trench 5, the softer upper layers of shattered shale bedrock were removed and stockpiled at either side of the quarry hollow to form two radial banks. It seems the lower, unaltered rock was then extracted to provide the large pieces of stone used in the inner and outer banks at Rathcoran.

A layer of stone containing Neolithic pottery found at the base of the quarry hollow in Trench 5 has charcoal dated 3339–3031 BC (UBA-46465). The charcoal cannot be connected to any burning event at this location. While the result does not date the rebuilding of the inner bank after the burning of the palisade, it does indicate when the quarry pit was infilled, as that deposit was sealed by an influx of re-deposited natural subsoil. The date can be compared to a charcoal result from one of the large linear pits in Trench 4 (3368–3101 BC; UBA-42443). It is also consistent with two dates (3331–2931 BC and 3011–2887 BC) obtained from burnt human bone found outside Chamber II of the passage tomb on this hill. Taken together, this indicates some additional activity at Rathcoran when the latest chambered tomb and cairn was being constructed.

The occupation of Rathcoran

The excavation of two small terraces in the south-eastern quadrant of the inner enclosure did not provide any evidence of roofed structures used for habitation. There are no definite external walls, post-holes or other internal roof supports, central hearths or any occupation floors at these locations. Added to this is an absence of domestic material culture that might be expected from a 'lived-in' space. Excavation at both sites revealed large linear pits, over 4m in length, which were probably created by the extraction of large granite blocks from the subsoil. The re-deposited soil from the digging of those pits contained a small proportion of retouched lithics of Neolithic technology (Revell 2023). It is significant that the boulders defining the circular space on both terraces are late in the stratigraphic sequence, with several examples directly overlying the upper fills of the linear pits. This suggests they were not related to the Neolithic activity and were placed there at a later time. Another possibility is that these are displaced natural boulders, part of the glacial drift on this hillside.

The terraces were previously interpreted as possible hut sites of Late Bronze Age date, representing a later occupation of an earlier Neolithic site, in what O'Driscoll (2023, 38) described as a nucleated hilltop settlement. While some circular anomalies in the geophysical survey may be built structures, the two examples excavated in the south-eastern quadrant are not hut sites. As discussed below, the two Late Bronze Age radiocarbon dates from Trench 4 and Trench 2 are not connected to any later occupation of the hillfort, with the charcoal probably originating from fires on this hill.

Other evidence of Neolithic occupation includes a small number of finds and plant remains uncovered from the ditches and on the inside of the outer enclosure. Among these are a broken polished stone axe, several retouched flint and chert lithics, carinated Neolithic pottery with burnt accretions, carbonised hazelnut shells and cereals identified as emmer wheat. This material alone does not identify Rathcoran as a place of permanent habitation, but instead suggests that the immediate landscape was occupied by domestic settlements engaged in arable farming. Residue analysis of Vessel 1 indicates the repeated use of the pot in heating milk, possibly in the production of cheese (Dunne *et al.* 2021). Various foodstuffs, including pots that contained milk or cheese, may have been brought to the enclosure for ceremonial feasting, with those vessels subsequently deposited in the ditches in a ritual act. A more mundane explanation is that the material in the ditches may be refuse left by the builders of the hillfort. The former interpretation is supported by evidence of ritual deposition in the excavated ditch deposits at other Neolithic enclosures in Britain and Ireland (see Whittle *et al.* 2011; Last 2022).

The evidence for later activity at Rathcoran is rather sparse, largely confined to deposits in one of the backfilled Neolithic quarry hollows. This includes a possible hearth and the deposition of pottery dating to the Early Bronze Age. Another phase of activity is related to the truncation of that hearth a few centuries later. Both may represent temporary occupation of a sheltered area on the hill, protected by the large internal bank and two smaller radial banks of the quarry pit. While the re-use of Neolithic enclosures by Grooved Ware and Beaker pottery cultures is known in Britain (Oswald *et al.* 2001, 137–9), Rathcoran is a rare example with activity connected to food vessel pottery. The vessel from Rathcoran is a ribbed bowl, belonging to the earliest phase of the Irish Bronze Age (Brindley 2007). While most such pottery comes from burial contexts, there are other examples from settlement sites (Grogan 2021, 4).

There may have been some activity at Rathcoran during the later Bronze Age, when the nearby Rathnagree hillfort and Sruhaun enclosure were occupied, and again possibly when Tinoran hillfort was occupied a few centuries later. Excavation revealed that an episode of burning occurred in the south-eastern quadrant of the enclosure, evidenced by charcoal found at the top of the inner bank in Trench 2, and below the peat horizon in Trench 4. Some of the charcoal from the bank included heather, indicating the burning of scrub at the site during the period 1200–900 BC.

In regard to the original form of the enclosure, we can be confident that during the primary phase of use, Rathcoran was protected by two substantial banks with stone revetments and/or stone walling. The outer bank had an external ditch, while a ditch inside the inner bank was backfilled at that time. It is not certain whether the monument fits the classification of what is termed a 'causewayed enclosure', as the excavation did not investigate extended lengths or gaps in those banks. A possible terminal to the outer ditch was uncovered in Trench 3, but more excavation would be required to establish if such openings were accompanied by causeways.

THE PASSAGE TOMB ON BALTINGLASS HILL

We turn now to the passage tomb inside Rathcoran, on the summit of Baltinglass Hill (382m OD). This multi-chambered passage tomb (WI027-026003) is located at the south-eastern side of the hillfort, at the junction of the townlands of Coolinarrig Upper, Tuckmill Hill and Pinnacle (Fig. 3.44). The monument is surrounded today by a circular drystone wall, *c.*5.5m thick and *c.*1.4m high, built with cairn material when the site was excavated in the 1930s. This wall encloses a space *c.*28.5m in diameter where three

Fig. 3.44 Aerial view of the Baltinglass Hill passage tomb (WI027-026003), as it looks today, showing internal chambers and stone kerbs, surrounded by a thick stone wall constructed after the 1930s excavation using stone from the overlying cairn.

(Above) Fig. 3.45 Chamber I of Baltinglass passage tomb, part of the second kerbed cairn dating to the period *c.*3300/3200–2900 BC.

(Below) Fig. 3.46 Mound with nineteenth-century trigonometrical station, located a short distance to the north-west of the main passage tomb on Baltinglass Hill. This is not a recorded monument.

Fig. 3.47 Smaller cairn (WI027-076) located on the outer southern slope of the Rathcoran hillfort.

burial chambers and the kerb of the passage tomb are exposed (Fig. 3.45; see also Fig. 10.4 in Chapter 10).

Some 45m north-west of this passage tomb is a smaller mound with an Ordnance Survey trigonometrical station on slightly elevated ground. This 11m (E/W) by 10m (N/S) by 1.2m mound is not a recorded monument. A number of small boulders on the northern side might indicate a kerb, suggesting a smaller satellite tomb to the main monument (Fig. 3.46). This cannot be confirmed without excavation. There is a second cairn (WI027-076), *c.*23m in diameter and 1.5m high, just outside the outer bank of the hillfort on the south-western side (Fig. 3.47). It is unclear from survey images if the bank of the hillfort turns slightly inwards to avoid the cairn or if the latter is a later feature that cuts across those defences. Condit (1998, 14), suggested the cairn predates the hillfort, whereas a recent LiDAR survey indicates the cairn is a later addition, possibly overlying an external ditch of the hillfort. Again, excavation is required to establish the significance of this feature.

As noted previously, there are two published accounts of the passage tomb on Baltinglass Hill before it was excavated. The antiquarian Thomas J. Westropp described the cairn as the 'upper fort', with a 'kistvaen' that 'when opened, contained pottery and human bones' (1902, 620). This suggests early disturbance of the passage tomb chambers. A short time later, Lord Walter FitzGerald described the monument as a 'vast pile of stones and boulders, more or less covered with sod' (1908a, 353). Accompanying his account are two photographs, one showing a general view of the cairn taken from the north-east with two stone boundary walls meeting at the summit (Fig. 3.48). Fitzgerald also noted the use of cairn stones in those walls. Prior to his excavation, Walshe (1941, 222) suggested large roof slabs had been removed from the burial chambers. Adding to this disturbance was the presence of a circular stone and mortar on the cairn used as a 'shooting box' up to early modern times. The foundations of the structure were at least 1.2m deep, with mortar from its construction found at the base of the cairn floor during excavation (Walshe 1941, 223).

The 1930s excavation

Baltinglass passage tomb was excavated by Patrick T. Walshe, assisted by Matthew J. Byrne and Liam Price, over three seasons from 1934 to 1936 (Fig. 3.49). The cairn was 25.6m (N/S) by 27.7m (E/W) in diameter and overlay two stone kerbs. The outer kerb was a continuous ring of large

Fig. 3.48 The Baltinglass passage tomb cairn, prior to excavation during the early 1900s. Source: W. FitzGerald, 1908a.

stones, each 1–2.4m in length. An inner kerb of large stones joined the outer at the south-east and south-west, leaving only one kerb on the south side. When the kerb stones were uncovered it was discovered that three examples had incised ornamentation on their outer faces (E, G, and H on the plan). While Walshe gave the height of the cairn as 15 feet (4.57m), the pre-excavation height was probably closer to 3m, as indicated by his profile drawing.

Prior to excavation, a chamber was noted at the base of the cairn on the northern side where the roofing stones were collapsed. This is probably the remains of Chamber I, noted by Westropp (1902) as once containing pottery and bones. Nothing was found in this chamber during the 1930s excavation. It consisted of an entrance passage, *c.*1m wide and 3.6m long, leading to a hexagonal chamber 2.4m in diameter, built with large upright stones. The back of the chamber has a single large slab, in front of which is a large basin stone. On the northern face of this stone is a 'curious design', comprising a rounded rectangular motif with a central vertical line, and two upper horizontal cross-bars (J on plan). As mentioned previously, this has some similarities to a motif found on a stone excavated at one of the terraced platforms (Trench 4) in the hillfort.

At the opposite side of the cairn, Walshe interpreted several large slabs as the remains of another burial compartment (Chamber II). This structure was in poor preservation, originally consisting of a central space 1.5m in length and 1.2m wide. It had five recesses or side chambers and was probably entered via a 3m-long passage on the south-western side (Walshe 1941, 224). Several uprights of the side chambers survived, two of which are decorated with spiral designs (K and L in Fig. 3.49). Each of the side chambers was separated from the central space by a low slab or sill-stone, while a similar sill-stone separated the central chamber from the passage. Chamber II contained fragments of cremated bone and a sherd of Carrowkeel Ware pottery.

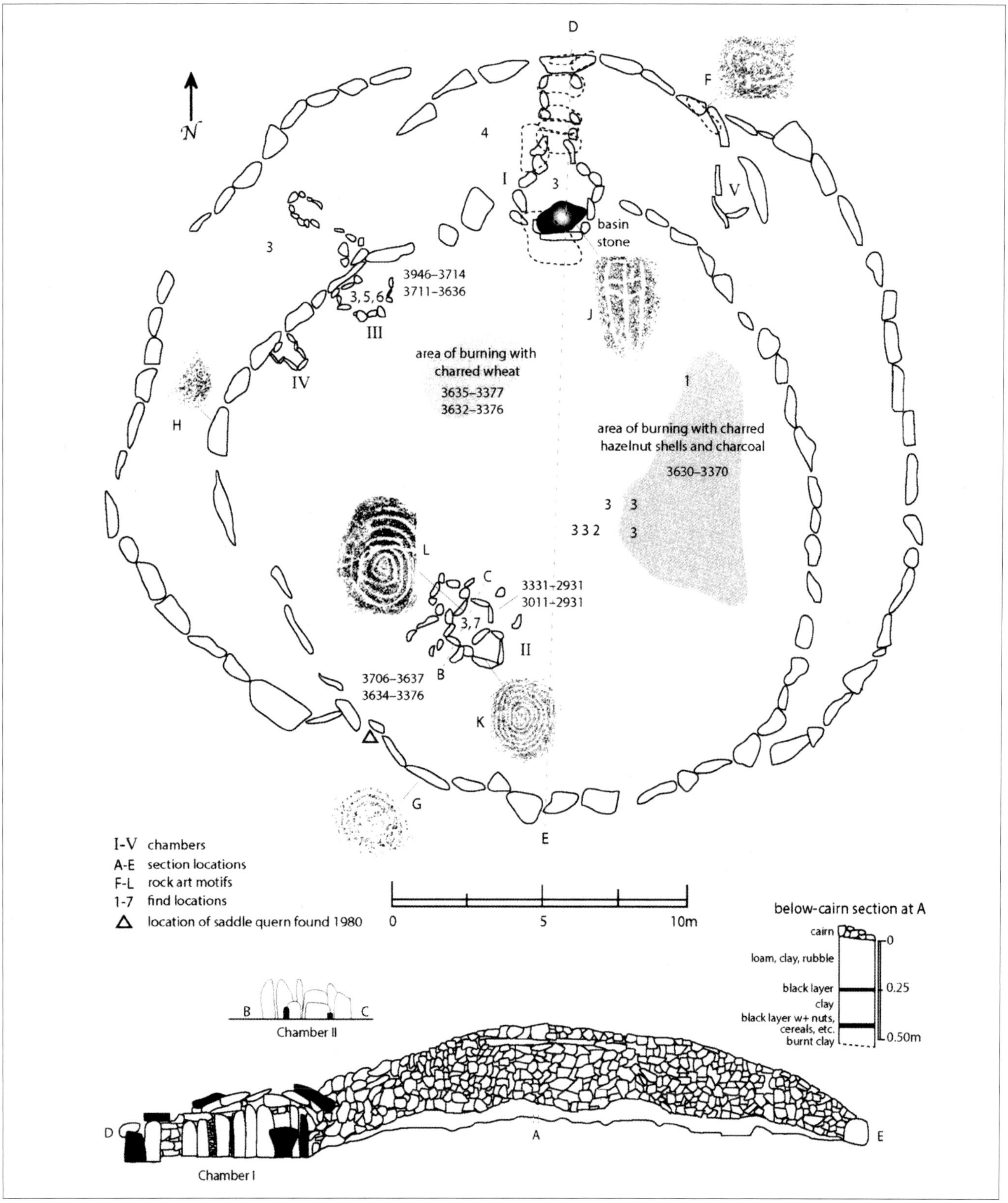

Fig. 3.49 Plan and section of the Baltinglass passage tomb (after Walshe 1941, pl. xviii, with overlain rock art rubbings from figs 8 and 9, not to scale), showing ^{14}C dates; approximate locations of main finds: 1) polished stone axe; 2) flint javelin head; 3) flint scrapers; 4) oval white pebble; 5) calcined bone pin and needle; 6) Carrowkeel sherds; 7) coarse sherd. Source: Schulting *et al.* 2017, fig. 4.

The bone was found in the central chamber area and in the side-chambers.

A third structure was identified on the north-western side of the cairn. Chamber III consisted of small upright slabs, 0.05–0.12m in height, forming an irregular passage 2.7m in length and 0.6m wide. Its identification as a burial chamber is questionable, given its ephemeral nature, though Walshe believed the passage was divided into four compartments by three small slabs. Cremated bone was found in the passage, chamber and inner recess, along with three flint scrapers, some worn pottery sherds and burnt bone pin fragments (1941, 225). A small basin stone also contained some cremated bone.

A fourth chamber was found a short distance to the west of Chamber III, on the inside of the inner kerb. Described as a small 'bee-hive hut', Chamber IV was rectangular in plan, *c.*1m wide and 1.5m high, roofed at the top by a single slab. Nothing was found in the excavation of this chamber, little of which survives today. A fifth chamber, described as a possible cist, was discovered between the two kerbs on the north-eastern side of the cairn. Four upright slabs formed a 1.8m by 0.9m space; there were no finds apart from a lump of clay the excavator suggested might be decayed pottery (Walshe 1941, 226).

Walshe identified two main phases of construction, based on the stratigraphic evidence. The building of the passage tomb was preceded by open fires, represented by burnt surfaces and spreads of charcoal with two concentrations of charred hazelnut shells and a number of flaked stone objects, including a polished stone axe and five flint scrapers. These were all found beneath the cairn and the layers of introduced soil. According to Walshe (1941, 235), this was most likely a 'ritual fire' to prepare the ground before the tomb was constructed. A bifacially-flaked flint javelin head with a broken tip was found near that area of burning.

The 1934–6 excavation revealed five definite or possible burial chambers of various design, size and construction. The earliest is likely to be Chamber II, with five side chambers around a central compartment, surrounded by a ring of kerb stones and covered by a cairn (Walshe 1941, 231). Chamber I was regarded as a 'secondary' chamber, evident from the 'joining on of the outer ring of kerb stones to the inner one', effectively enlarging the whole cairn into one monument. As for the beehive chamber (Chamber IV), this was regarded as a 'minor chamber' probably built at the same time as the original cairn. The excavation was unable to place Chamber III in the sequence, as the 'passage lies outside the kerb of the smaller cairn … and could hardly have been made after the larger cairn had been constructed' (Walshe 1941).

Radiocarbon dating

In 2017 samples of cremated human bone retained from Walshe's excavation were submitted for radiocarbon dating. The results provide an absolute chronology for the sequence of construction, spanning at least six centuries (Schulting *et al.* 2017). Five or six phases were identified, beginning with the construction of a rather simple tomb (Chamber III) and the deposition of cremated remains without an overlying cairn (Phase 1), prior to 3600 BC but possibly as early as *c.*3900 BC. There is some uncertainty as to the dating of activity at the site prior to *c.*3700 BC.

This first phase was followed by a burning event, interpreted as a ritual preparation of the ground, involving fires and the deposition of cereal grains and other cultural material *c.*3600–3400 BC (Phase 2). This cultural layer was rapidly and intentionally sealed by a layer of clay, and this activity was followed by the construction of Chamber II and the first kerbed cairn (Phase 3), the latter also covering part of Chamber III. Schulting *et al.* (2017, 14) suggested that because of its position within the first cairn, the beehive Chamber IV structure might be assigned to this period. The dating evidence suggests this episode of construction occurred soon after the 'purification and preparation' activities of Phase 2 (Schulting *et al.* 2017). A granite saddle quern found just inside the inner kerb on its southern side (Cooney 1981) cannot be connected to either pre-tomb activity or the use of this monument.

A fourth phase is associated with the continued deposition of cremated remains in Chamber II (the older remains being cast out of the chamber), and the execution of circular motifs on several uprights and kerb stones *c.*3300/3200–2900 BC. The cruciform Chamber I (complete with basin stone), with a second kerbed cairn, was added at that time (Phase 5). According to Schulting *et al.* (2017, 14), the passage tomb art on the outer kerb and the unusual motif on the basin stone of Chamber I may also have been added then, but these could also be re-used stones associated with Phase 4. Finally, a tentative sixth phase of activity might be connected to the construction of a cist (Chamber V) during the Early Bronze Age and the possible enlargement of the cairn.

The detailed chronology of the passage tomb provided by these radiocarbon results can be compared to the dating of

Rathcoran. This suggests that the initial tomb construction and the building of the hillfort were broadly contemporary. Common to both building phases are two burning events and the deposition of cultural remains. The burning of the palisade on the north-western side of Rathcoran was followed soon after by the rebuilding of its banks in stone. This occurred around the same time as the pre-tomb burning event and the subsequent construction of first kerbed cairn and burial chamber (Chamber II) *c.*3600–3400 BC. In both cases, little time appears to have lapsed between the fires and main construction phases.

Combining the chronology of the hillfort and passage tomb, the following sequence of events can be proposed. In the early centuries of the fourth millennium BC, there may have been an initial clearance phase on Baltinglass Hill. For Rathcoran, this would explain the charcoal dated from the old ground surface in Trench 3 (3953–3796 BC; UBA-46459) and the charcoal spread beneath the radial bank in Trench 5 (4316–4052 BC; UBA-46467), pre-dating the hillfort enclosures by several centuries or more. These early dates, particularly from Trench 3, add some support to a very early date (3946–3715 BC; UBA-14759) from the passage tomb, if one accepts that bone sample was not affected by old wood in the funerary pyre. That bone sample was recovered from the small Chamber III structure, the significance of which is uncertain. The early radiocarbon date remains controversial, although two statistically identical results within the range *c.*3700–3640 BC on calcined bone found within Chamber III and outside Chamber II indicate an early phase of funerary activity on this hill prior to construction of the hillfort ramparts.

During the period *c.*3600–3400 BC, a palisaded bank with an internal ditch was built around the upper slopes of the hill. Soon after, the palisade was destroyed by fire on the north-western side and cultural remains were deposited in the inner ditch, which was then backfilled. The fire may have occurred during or soon after construction, and was quickly followed by the re-building of the bank in stone. At the same time, a pre-cairn fire occurred at the summit of the hilltop, which was quickly covered over by the construction of Chamber II and the first kerbed cairn. Significant quarrying of stone occurred at that time, for the construction of the hillfort ramparts and the building of the passage tomb cairn. It is possible this extraction of stone continued at the site until *c.*3100 BC, for the building of additional chambers and the second kerbed cairn. Although it is not known whether the outer enclosure of Rathcoran was built at the same time as the inner palisade, it is possible that construction of the former commenced with re-building of the inner enclosure soon after the fire event. This is supported by the absence of any burning in Trench 3, and the location of many of the quarry hollows abutting the inside of the outer enclosure, providing stone for both banks.

The extent of occupation in such a large enclosed space as Rathcoran is unclear as so little of the interior has been excavated. The purpose of the monument must be viewed in the context of its passage tomb (or tombs) and the wider cultural landscape. While the Rathcoran banks are defensive in nature, they may have also helped to define a ritual space. They may have served to restrict access to the monuments and movement within the enclosed area, possibly to emphasise a division between the ancestral space inside the enclosure and the lived-in space outside.

Rathcoran is one of a large number of Irish hillforts with prehistoric stone cairns. Raftery (1976) suggested that approximately one-third of these enclosures have cairns or mounds, an estimate confirmed by a recent study (O'Driscoll 2016, 45). Examples include the hillforts at Corrin Hill (Carn Tigherna), Co. Cork; Knigh and Ballinacurra, Co. Tipperary; and Clomantagh, Co. Kilkenny. These cairns are typically sited at the summit of the enclosed hill, while some hillforts have several examples both inside and outside their ramparts (Condit 1998, 20). While dating evidence is generally lacking, the general view is that the cairns and mounds represent earlier funerary sites enclosed by Late Bronze Age hillforts. The reasons for incorporating older burial sites are debated, with some suggesting this was a way of connecting communities to past generations, with implications for land ownership (Raftery 1994, 41; Bradley 2002, 47; O'Driscoll 2016, 243).

While this may be the case for some hillforts, the evidence from Rathcoran indicates the tomb and the hillforts were broadly contemporary *c.*3600–3400 BC. Rathcoran is not the only hillfort in the Baltinglass landscape with burial monuments. On the northern summit of Spinans Hill are the remains of five smaller cairns, surrounding a larger example, all located within a small Neolithic enclosure (see Chapter 4). This raises the possibility that other hilltop enclosures in Ireland may be Neolithic in origin, with some functioning not as places for high-status occupation, but as social arenas for venerating the ancestral dead.

Rathcoran is the only confirmed Early Neolithic enclosure in Ireland with a funerary monument of similar construction date. The closest parallel is Knocknarea, Co. Sligo, a prominent mountain with up to five passage tombs, including the massive Maeve's Cairn, enclosed by a complex system of banks on the eastern side. Limited excavations at that site have confirmed those banks were built in two phases during the Middle Neolithic. The enclosure of sacred ground in this way 'represents another aspect of controlling space, as the banks make a physical as well as symbolic statement concerning the actual demarcation of space' (Bergh 2002, 150).

4. OTHER NEOLITHIC ENCLOSURES AT BALTINGLASS

William O'Brien and Nick Hogan

Fig. 4.1 Aerial photograph of the Hughstown enclosures. Note a probable circular house structure inside the small enclosure at the centre of this hillfort (Undated photograph, Irish Air Corps; from Condit 1992, plate 7).

The discoveries at Rathcoran provide important evidence of the first farming communities in the Baltinglass area. The scale of construction and imposing siting of the passage tomb and enclosure on Baltinglass Hill indicate an important settlement location during the fourth millennium BC. That Neolithic settlement extended to other hills at Baltinglass, and probably across its fertile lowlands. Recent investigations on Carrigeen Hill to the west of Baltinglass Hill, and at Spinans Hill to the north-east, identified enclosures of similar date, though different design, to Rathcoran.

HUGHSTOWN

This townland is located 2km west of Baltinglass town, just inside the border of Co. Kildare (see Fig. 2.23). There are four concentric, widely spaced enclosures on the upper part of Carrigeen Hill, where steep to moderate slopes lead to a rounded summit (298m OD). The latter is on the south-eastern side of a 2.5km-long (NW/SE) by 1.4km-wide ridge above the 200m OD contour (Fig. 4.1). The views from Carrigeen Hill are panoramic, apart from at the north-eastern side where the summit of Tinoran Hill (312m OD) lies 2km away. Both hills are prominent in the landscape,

Fig 4.2 Aerial photograph of the Hughstown enclosures, July 1966 (reproduced with permission of the Cambridge Collection of Aerial Photography; ©copyright reserved).

separated by a narrow valley carrying a tributary of the Slaney River.

Hughstown was first recorded as a hillfort by Condit (1992; 1998), with a subsequent listing in the *Record of Monuments and Places* for Co. Kildare (KD038-025001). None of its four enclosures is depicted on the first edition of the six-inch Ordnance Survey mapping (1842). The innermost enclosure is shown as a sub-circular hachured feature on later revisions of that mapping. It is apparent from the field pattern on those maps that the hillfort was substantially levelled by the mid nineteenth century. There are no antiquarian records for the site, nor any known discoveries or local folklore traditions.

Most of the hillfort lies today within a large, L-shaped field of managed pasture, approximately 500m (NW/SE) by 300m in extent. The L-shaped field is broadly similar to that depicted on the nineteenth-century Ordnance Survey mapping, except that a field bank photographed in 1966 by the Cambridge Aerial Survey has been removed (Fig. 4.2). The outer enclosure of the hillfort extends into smaller fields of managed pasture on the northern and north-eastern sides, and into two fields on the south-western side that are recently planted with conifers.

In 2012 a geophysical survey was undertaken across the entire site apart from that south-western side (O'Brien and O'Driscoll 2017, 219–23). When combined with aerial photographs and LiDAR data, the magnetic gradiometry recorded a multiple enclosure hillfort, *c.*356m (NW/SE) by *c.*261m (NE/SW) in overall extent (Fig. 4.3). There are four widely spaced enclosing elements over an area of 8.22ha. The only extant example is a small sub-circular enclosure at the summit, measuring 54m (NW/SE) by 50m (NE/SW).

Fig. 4.3 Magnetic gradiometry survey of Hughstown, showing location of three excavation trenches.

The other three enclosing elements were levelled by agriculture and are barely visible on the surface today.

The summit (first) enclosure is surrounded by a stony bank, with no accompanying ditch (see Fig. 4.1). The location of the original entrance to this first enclosure is not known. There is a modern gated entrance on the northern side, providing access to a memorial garden created in 2000, when an inscribed 'Jubilee Stone' was erected in a fenced area inside the early enclosure. There is a circular feature, 17m in diameter, near the centre of the enclosure, with no internal features. This is the base of a wall of large stones, 0.6m wide and up to 0.4m high; the northern side of the feature is now overlain by the memorial garden. High magnetic gradiometry readings on the eastern side of this circular feature may indicate the foundation of a large building. This remains to be confirmed by excavation.

Aerial photographs taken by Cambridge University in 1966–68 (APA039-042; AVL093-094; ASU052-053) record two concentric parch-marks 55–85m outside the inner enclosure (see Figs 2.19 and 4.2). These represent the

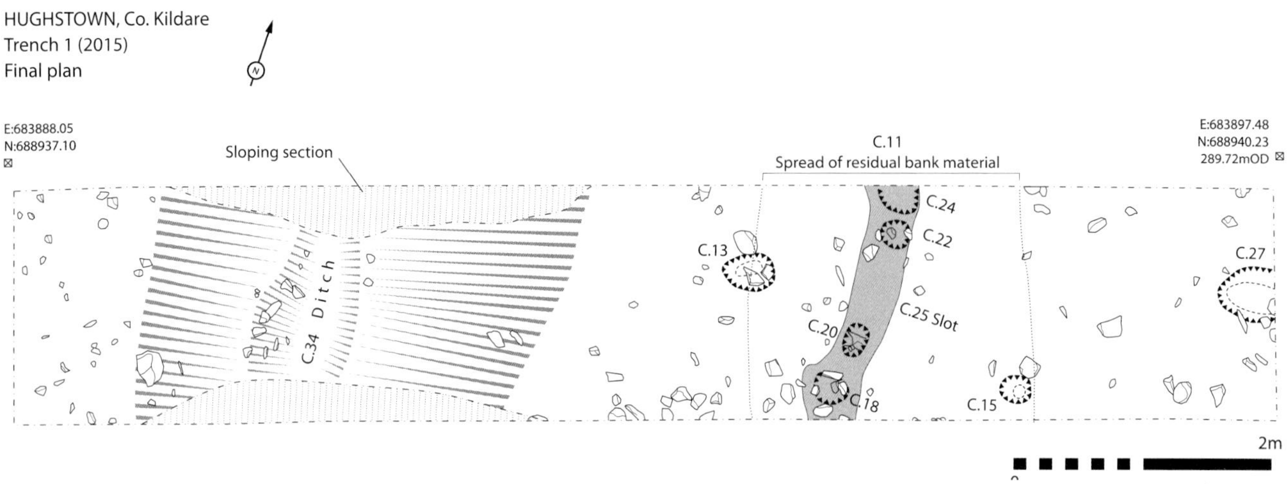

Fig. 4.4 Post-excavation plan, with rectified photograph, of Trench 1, Hughstown.

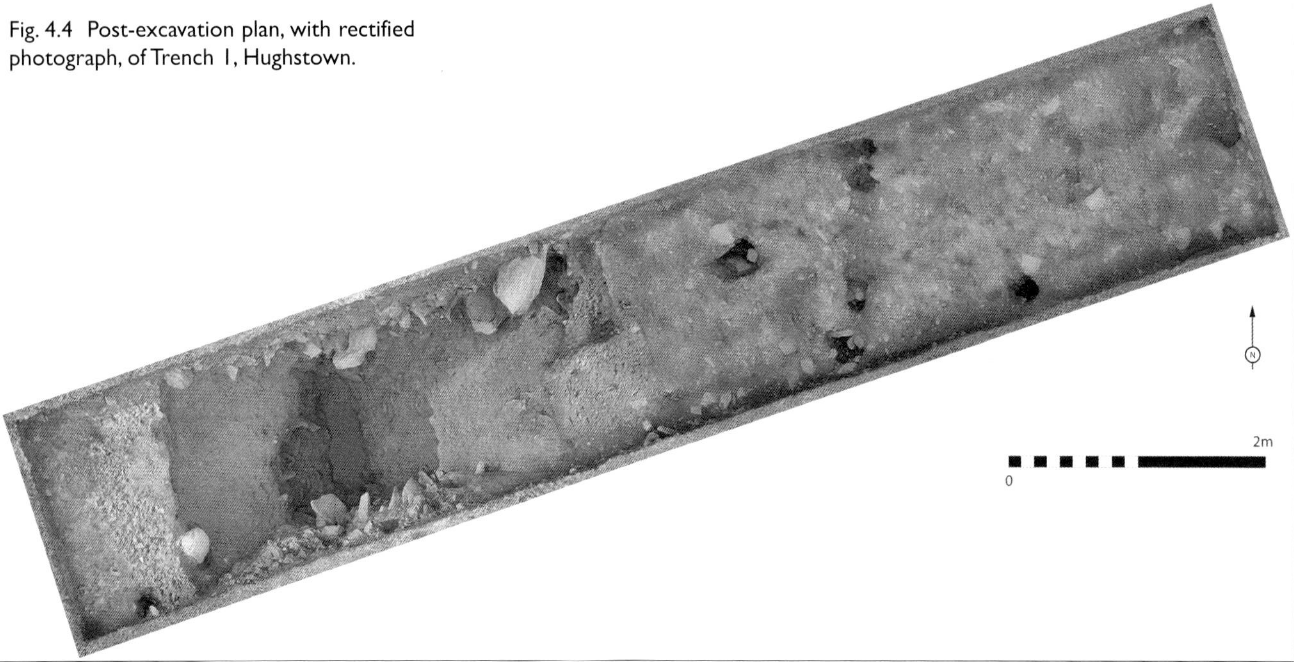

second and third enclosures of the hillfort, separated by a distance of only 23–48m, following the contours of the hill at 274–292m OD. These enclosures are not recorded on the Ordnance Survey historic mapping and are barely visible on the ground today. They are imaged in more detail by the geophysical survey. Magnetic gradiometry for the second enclosure indicates at least two enclosing elements, with similar, but lower, magnetic readings for the third enclosure (Fig. 4.3).

The second enclosure has a sub-oval plan, 248m (NW/SE) by 197m (NE/SW), with a low-relief bank visible in places. The third enclosure is 23–48m farther out and concentric with the second enclosure, measuring 290m (NW/SE) by 228m (NE/SW). The geophysical survey also indicated a fourth enclosure, represented by a band of low magnetic readings. This outer enclosure of the hillfort is 356m (NW/SE) by 261m (NE/SW) in extent and mostly levelled, with the north-eastern side represented by a curving field bank of later date.

There are numerous small openings across those three enclosures, but no clear indication of the location or number of original entrances, as there has been extensive land clearance and agriculture on the hill in modern times. The geophysical survey identified many faint circular magnetic anomalies, 6m to 17m in diameter, in the interior of the hillfort (O'Brien and O'Driscoll 2017, fig. 5.41). While some may be archaeological features such as hut-sites, this cannot be confirmed without excavation.

There are several confirmed or possible monuments in the immediate vicinity of the hillfort. The *Record of Monuments and Places* (RMP) records a tumulus (KD038-025002), 9m in diameter by 0.5–2m high, on the line of the inner enclosure near the summit. This is not visible today and it is possible the entry refers to the circular feature in the interior. There is an unrecorded, 1.5m-high earthen mound, 12m in diameter, *c.*180m north of the hillfort (O'Brien and O'Driscoll 2017, 220). An embanked pond, 350m to the east, is also unrecorded, but is shown on the Ordnance Survey historic mapping. There is an unrecorded ring-barrow 150m south-east of the hillfort, *c.*18m in diameter, surrounded by a 4m-wide by 0.3m-high band of stone with a low central mound.

The RMP lists a possible habitation site (KD038-026) close to the southern side of the outer enclosure. This is described as a 4m-wide ring of seven small boulders of uncertain date There is a suggestion of a cursus-type monument in the same area, represented by two parallel field banks, *c.*25m apart, approaching the outer enclosure of the hillfort. These now lie within a recently planted conifer plantation. These banks are shown on early aerial photographs (Fig. 4.1), but not on Ordnance Survey historic mapping. They are larger than the modern field banks on this hill, 9–12m in width and extending NE/SW for *c.*155m. This may suggest some antiquity, though any identification of a cursus or ceremonial avenue leading to the hillfort cannot be confirmed without excavation.

Excavation

Sample excavation was conducted at Hughstown in August 2015 and July 2016 (results summarised here, with detail in O'Brien and O'Driscoll 2017, 299–319). The aim was to obtain information about the three outer enclosures, all of which are substantially levelled. A single trench was excavated across each of these enclosing elements on the western side of the hillfort, with their position indicated by the geophysical and GNSS survey (Fig. 4.3).

Trench 1

This 10m by 2m trench was aligned east–west across the line of the second enclosure (Fig. 4.3). The magnetic gradiometry indicated two closely spaced, concentric lines of positive magnetic anomaly, with intervening weaker readings. The removal of topsoil by hand revealed a large earth-cut ditch in the western half of the trench, inside which the base of an earthen bank with a stake foundation trench were found.

Ditch

This feature had a V-shaped profile cut into compact, iron-enriched subsoil. The top of the ditch was 2.8–3m wide, narrowing to 0.5–0.6m at the base, with a central depth of 1.5–1.6m (Fig. 4.4). The smooth sides had a 45° slope, with a sharp break 0.4m above the base creating a narrow channel at the bottom of the ditch. There were four significant events in the infilling of this ditch (Fig. 4.5). These include charcoal from an early fire near the ditch, followed by erosion of the adjacent bank. A break in the fill sequence is represented by a sod layer, after which there was an influx of soil when the remaining bank was levelled.

Excavation exposed a thin deposit of charcoal at the base of the ditch. A radiocarbon date of 3661–3521 BC (4815±35 BP; GrA-64434) for a sample of alder charcoal should be close in time to the digging of the ditch. The source of that charcoal is uncertain, as it does not derive from any burning event in the ditch or adjacent bank. Neither the ditch cut nor the stones directly overlying the charcoal were fire-reddened. Thin pockets of red/brown silt containing charcoal were found along the mid outer slope of the ditch. This points to a fire outside the ditch, rather than in the internal bank area.

Following that influx of charcoal, the ditch continued to fill with a yellow/brown silt along the inner base and lower slope. Excavation of the inner slope of the ditch exposed a grey/brown silt with large, inclined slabs of grey sandstone. This represents a collapsed stone facing from the exterior of the adjacent bank (see Fig. 4.16 below). The majority were 0.1–0.25m in length, with some larger examples up to 0.3–0.45m, as well as five examples 0.6–0.7m (the largest was 0.81m by 0.43m by 0.14m). These revetment stones were mostly angular to sub-angular in shape, with many broken surfaces, but no obvious fire-reddening. Some had a slightly rolled appearance to indicate a drift source.

The collapse of the bank revetment resulted in a significant influx of soil into the open ditch, represented by large stones and dark-brown silt with numerous voids. None of those stones was fire-reddened, and so cannot be linked to any deliberate destruction of the bank. There was also an influx of orange, gravelly sediment from outside the ditch, which might represent the erosion of a low counterscarp bank.

The infilling of the ditch slowed considerably following

Fig. 4.5 Stratification of ditch, Trench 1, Hughstown (north-west facing section).

the collapse of the adjacent bank. This was marked by a thin sod layer in the half-filled ditch, visible as a thin lens of organic silt overlying stones in the centre of the ditch, which continued up to its outer edge (Fig. 4.5). Information from the landowner confirms the remaining bank had been levelled some 20–30 years previously, during agricultural land reclamation. This is recorded in the upper ditch stratification as a layer of bright-orange, stony silt, overlain by a layer of brown/orange, stony silt. Those sediments represent redeposited subsoil originally dug from the ditch to form the core of an adjacent bank. The subsequent levelling of that bank into the half-filled ditch was followed by an accumulation of mid-brown, organic silt with small reddened stones, overlain by topsoil.

The evidence from the ditch confirms the former presence of an inner bank with a stone facing. Though it had been substantially removed by modern agriculture, excavation uncovered a spread of residual bank material, 1.9–2.5m wide by 0.05–0.1m thick, extending 2m inside the ditch (Fig. 4.4). This compact deposit of yellow/brown silt contained broken stones, 0.04–0.1m in length, many of which had a reddened appearance. The latter is probably due to iron oxide weathering rather than heat-reddening, as there was no significant occurrence of charcoal in the bank spread.

Excavation identified a deposit of larger stones at the base of topsoil between the western margin of the bank spread and the inner edge of the ditch. These loose stones were 0.15–0.35m in length, mostly sub-angular clasts with a slightly rolled appearance. They represent the remaining lower stones of the collapsed bank revetment. Excavation recorded a thin spread of fine, black silt beneath that deposit, representing a buried sod layer under the former bank. This old ground surface contained a few flecks of charcoal, but nothing to indicate pre-enclosure activity.

Further excavation exposed small features cut into subsoil within or adjacent to the former bank (Fig. 4.4). These

Fig. 4.6 Post-excavation view of bank area, Trench 1, Hughstown, showing slot with stake setting (centre-right), and adjacent small pits.

include a possible post-hole, a slot trench with four possible stake settings, a large stake-hole and a small pit. The possible post-hole was a D-shaped pit, 0.38m (east–west) by 0.3m (north–south) by 0.27m deep, close to the original exterior of the bank. There were two large stones along its western side, 0.21m by 0.16m by 0.05m and 0.15m by 0.09m by 0.09m respectively. The sides were near-vertical to an irregularly flat base with a central depth of 0.27m. The upper fill was with a mid-brown, sandy silt, with similar reddened angular stone as the bank material. The lower fill was a grey/brown, sandy silt containing alder charcoal radiocarbon dated 3704–3533 BC (4850±35 BP; GrA-64436).

Excavation of the residual bank material exposed a narrow curving band of dark-brown silt. This was the fill of a narrow slot trench cut through the old ground surface into subsoil (Fig. 4.6). This feature had a slight curve, 0.25–0.36m in upper width and 0.1–0.14m at base, with a depth of 0.07–0.11m. It was filled with a compact, dark-brown silt that contained small, angular and reddened stones similar to the residual bank deposit. The upper fill of the slot also contained a small amount of willow charcoal, radiocarbon dated 3694–3523 BC (4825±35 BP; GrA-64437).

Four possible stake settings were identified along the excavated base of this slot trench. These were 0.23–0.35m in maximum length and 0.14–0.21m in depth, filled with light-brown, sandy silt, and contained no charcoal. One of the stake-holes had two large packing stones on the upper sides, leaving a 0.13m by 0.07m space for an upright stake. The upper fill of the slot trench was stony sediment, similar to the residual bank spread, which suggests these stakes stood within the original bank. The diameter of the stake settings indicates a light, roundwood fence.

Excavation on the inner side of the bank identified a large stake-hole, 0.27m in diameter and 0.34m deep, close to the southern side of Trench 1 (see Fig. 4.4). The fill consisted of a yellow/brown silt with occasional angular and

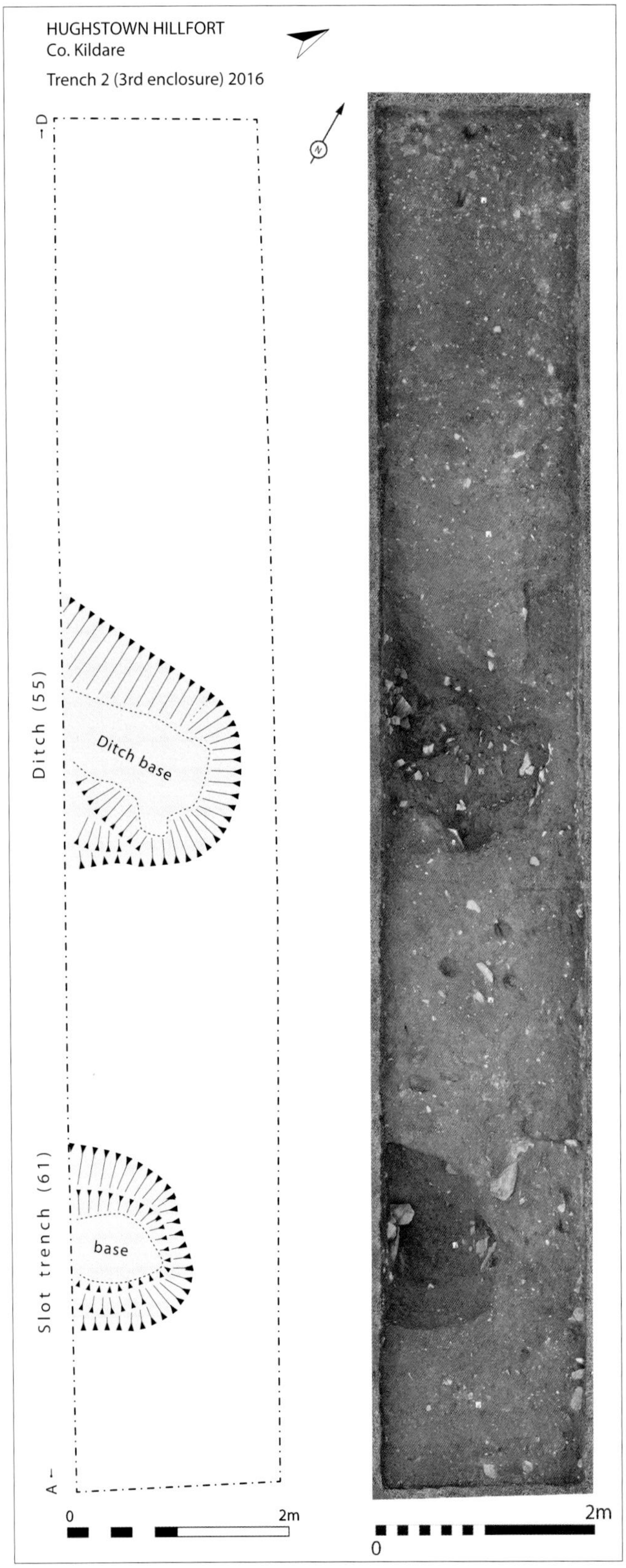

Fig. 4.7 Post-excavation plan, with rectified photograph, of Trench 2, Hughstown.

reddened stones in the 0.04–0.13m range, again similar to material in the residual bank spread. Finally, a small pit was found at the eastern end of the trench. This irregular cut was 0.41m long by at least 0.4m wide, with an irregularly flat base at a depth of 0.09–0.13m. It was filled with mid-brown silt with occasional small stones and flecks of charcoal. The significance of this feature is not known, as it cannot be stratigraphically linked to the bank or ditch.

TRENCH 2

This 12m by 2m east–west trench was excavated across the line of the third enclosure on the western side of the hillfort (see Fig. 4.3). The ground surface is managed pasture, with a gentle westerly slope. There are no surface features to indicate the now levelled enclosure. For that reason, the trench location was determined by magnetic gradiometry survey. This indicated a positive linear anomaly, alongside traces of a weaker anomaly.

The sod layer was removed by spade, followed by coarse trowelling of the organic soil, with fine trowelling to a subsoil surface. As in Trench 1, the natural soil is a brown podzol, with organic topsoil overlying a thin layer of hard iron pan on compact subsoil. Excavation recorded closely spaced plough furrows cut into that surface. These criss-crossed the western half of the trench in a N/S and NW/SE direction.

There were two significant features in Trench 2 (Fig. 4.7). The terminal of a small earth-cut ditch was discovered in the central area, with the end of a slot trench 2.6m inside that feature. The slot trench contained large amounts of charcoal and heat-shattered packing stones, probably connected to the burning of a wooden fence or palisade. There was no trace of any accompanying bank, though it is likely one did exist in the space between the ditch and the palisade trench.

The ditch was first exposed on removal of a thin layer of iron pan in the central area of the trench. Further excavation revealed the terminal of a shallow ditch, exposed to a length of 1.55m from the southern side of the trench (Fig. 4.7). This had an irregular U-shaped profile, with a straight northern end. The upper part had a maximum width of 2.35m on the southern side, narrowing to 1.8m in the centre, and 0.95m at the flattened northern end of the trench. There were corresponding depths of 0.72m, 0.54m and 0.44m from the subsoil surface, with a maximum depth of 1.03m from modern ground level. The irregular eastern side was steeply sloping in places; the western side had a

Fig. 4.8 Post-excavation view of ditch terminal, Trench 2 Hughstown.

uniform 45° slope; while the northern end was near-vertical. The base of the ditch was 0.5–0.55m wide and irregularly flat, except on the south-eastern side where the cut was narrower (Fig. 4.8). The ditch was cut into subsoil, with some ribs of bedrock exposed at the base. It is unlikely, however, that much bedrock was removed in that process.

There were two significant fills in the ditch terminal, along with a large number of stones. The upper fill was a loose deposit of orange/mid-brown silt with frequent small to medium stones, and only rare charcoal. The lower fill was a compact, yellow/light-brown silt with a large number of broken stones and frequent flecks of charcoal. The former probably represents the levelling of a low bank inside the ditch in the modern era. The lower fill and its stones derive from erosion of that bank over a long period, as well as from an influx of small amounts of charcoal from the burning of an adjacent wooden fence. A sample of alder charcoal is radiocarbon dated 3362–3373 BC (4710±35 BP; GrA-67384).

The foundation for that fence was first exposed as a 0.15–0.25m wide band of dark silt and charcoal. That was excavated to reveal the terminal of a small trench, 2.6m east of the ditch (Fig. 4.7). The cut had a U-shaped profile, with sides sloping steeply to an irregularly flat base (Fig. 4.9). The lower, northern side was interrupted by a small exposure of broken bedrock. The cut had an excavated length of 1.15m from the southern side of Trench 2, narrowing from 1.58m wide on the southern side to <1.1m at the rounded northern end. The maximum depth from the modern ground level is 0.94m, or 0.68m from the subsoil cut.

Excavation identified four fill deposits in this slot trench. The earliest was a burnt deposit of loose, dark-brown/black, fine silt on the western upper side of the slot trench. This burnt layer extended under the upper fills, covering the lower western sides and base of the cut to a thickness of 0.2–0.27m. The deposit was very rich in charcoal, both finely divided and small to large lumps. Radiocarbon dates of 3635–3376 BC (4725±35 BP; GrA-67382) and 3629–3369

Fig. 4.9 Post-excavation view of slot trench, east end of Trench 2, Hughstown.

BC (4690±35 BP; GrA-67383) for samples of alder and willow charcoal respectively from this context indicate when the fence was built. The deposit contained numerous small to large stones, many of which were fire-reddened and heat-shattered. These were mostly sub-rectangular to sub-triangular in shape, from 0.1–0.18m (30%), 0.18–0.25m (45%), 0.25–0.3m (20%) and 0.3–0.4m (5%) in length.

The presence of numerous fragments of alder charcoal, along with large stones probably used as packing, points to the burning of a light wooden fence in this slot trench. The possibility of a gate post cannot be dismissed, given the limited extent of excavation. The burnt deposit at the base and western side of the slot suggests a burning structure may have collapsed in that direction. While the slot itself was not obviously fire-reddened, the presence of some lenses of red oxidised sediment at the base indicates *in situ* burning of wood. This probably represents the firing of an upright post secured with packing stones.

TRENCH 3

This 12m by 2m trench was excavated east–west across the levelled defences of the fourth enclosure at Hughstown. This is in the same field as Trench 2, consisting of a large area of managed pasture on a gentle westerly slope. There are no surface features, apart from a slight 3–4m-wide depression suggestive of an infilled ditch. The position of Trench 3 was determined by imaging of the buried ditch using magnetic gradiometry (see Fig. 4.3). This recorded a linear response across the trench, consisting of a band of low magnetic readings with high readings on either side. The excavation trench was aligned across this anomaly, with a 3m-wide space on either side.

The trench was deturfed by spade, and coarse trowelling of organic soil was followed by fine trowelling to expose the underlying subsoil surface and any archaeological features therein. The latter included closely spaced cultivation furrows at the eastern end of the trench, with one such example at the western end. These parallel furrows were

(Above) Fig. 4.10 General post-excavation view of ditch in Trench 3, Hughstown.

0.12–0.18m wide and 0.1–0.15m apart. They followed a NW/SE direction, but swung sharply to the south-west as they approached the ditch.

The removal of topsoil exposed a *c*.3m wide band of dark-brown/black soil across the central area of the trench. This was excavated to expose a large rock-cut ditch, inside which there were faint traces of a bank (Fig. 4.10). The ditch was excavated to reveal a deep parallel-sided cut, dug through subsoil with the lower part in bedrock (Fig. 4.11). The ditch had a U-shaped profile, with an irregularly rounded base on broken bedrock (Fig. 4.12). The eastern side had a 45° slope, with projecting ribs of bedrock in the lower part. The western (outer) side was near vertical to steeply sloping in the upper part, rounding towards the base. The ditch was 3.08m wide on the southern side, 3.18m on the northern side, with a width of 1.08m and 0.96m respectively at the base. It had a central depth of 1.58m from the subsoil surface, or 1.75m from modern ground level.

Prior to excavation the ditch was entirely infilled, with

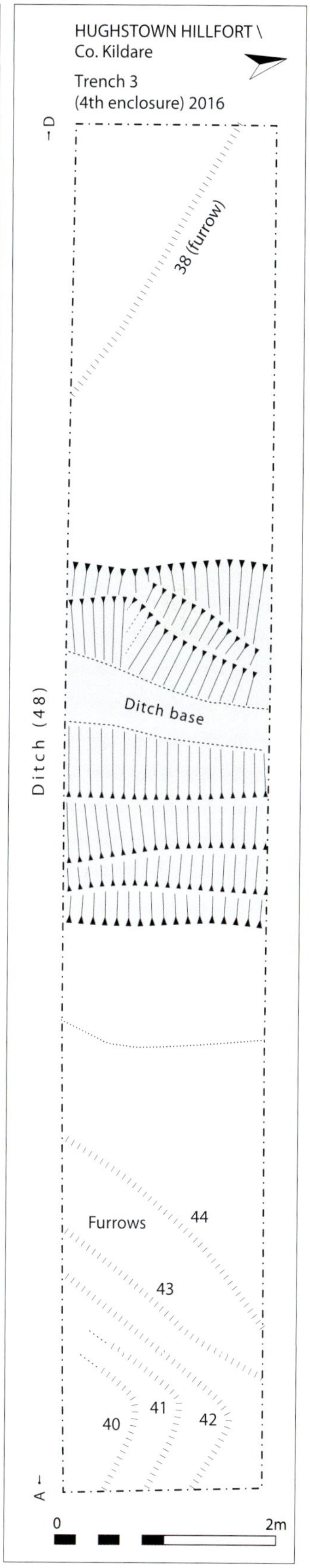

(Right) Fig. 4.11 Post-excavation plan of Trench 3, Hughstown.

Fig. 4.12 Post-excavation view of ditch, Trench 3, Hughstown.

only a slight depression visible on the surface. The removal of a thin layer of iron pan at the base of the organic soil exposed the upper fill of the ditch (Fig. 4.13). This comprised a 0.6–0.68m thick deposit of orange/brown silt with some stones, but no charcoal. The lower fill was a compact deposit of grey/light-brown, sandy silt with a central thickness of 0.55m. This sediment contained many small angular fragments of weathered shale, as well as larger stones in the 0.12–0.55m range. The latter were not fire-reddened or broken. This lower fill contained a small amount of charcoal radiocarbon dated 3627–3369 BC (4685±35 BP; GrA-67386). A 3–5cm thick lens of charcoal at the interface of the two main fills of the ditch is radiocarbon dated 3636–3376 BC (4730±40 BP; GrA-67385).

Neolithic pottery at Hughstown

The only early artifact find from Hughstown is a single sherd (15E322:01) of prehistoric pottery from the second enclosure (Trench 1). This is a well-preserved body sherd (12.2g), found in cultivated topsoil over the bank area. The ceramic parallels are with burnished wares of the Early/Middle Neolithic (Cleary in O'Brien and O'Driscoll 2017, 316), an identification consistent with the radiocarbon results from Trench 1 (see below).

The sherd has a slight convex curvature, suggesting it is probably from the neck area of a Neolithic carinated bowl (Fig. 4.14). The sherd thickness (*c.*9mm) suggests a fairly sturdy vessel of coil construction, made of mica-rich clay with a granitic temper sourced in a region of igneous geology. The external surface is burnished, which is a characteristic feature of Early Neolithic pottery. The evenness of firing indicates some control over the kiln temperature. The absence of any weathering suggests the sherd was buried soon after discard.

How old is Hughstown hillfort?

Radiocarbon dating of charcoal suggests that construction and/or use of the second enclosure at Hughstown occurred during the Early Neolithic, *c.*3694–3533 BC (Fig. 4.15; see also Appendix 1). A result of 3661–3521 BC (GrA-64434)

Fig. 4.13 Stratification of outer enclosure ditch, Trench 3, Hughstown.

Fig. 4.14 Sherd of Neolithic pottery (15E322:01) from Trench 1, Hughstown.

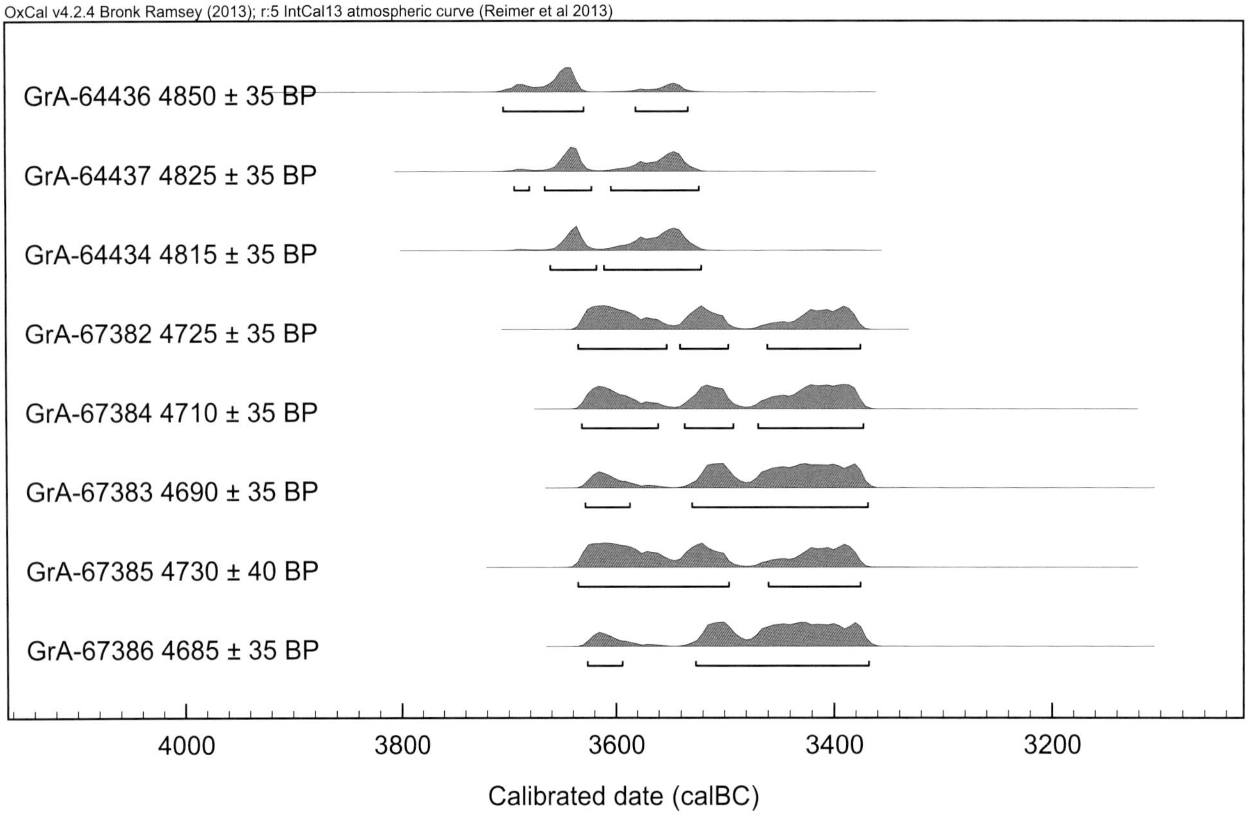

Fig. 4.15 Radiocarbon dates for Hughstown hillfort (calibration after OxCal v.4.2.4).

provides a *terminus ante quem* for the digging of the enclosure ditch, while a similar date range of 3694–3523 BC (GrA-64437) for charcoal in the slot trench is probably (but not certainly) part of the same construction event, as is the result of 3704–3533 BC (GrA-64436) for an adjacent pit (post-hole?). This is supported by the discovery of a sherd of pottery with parallels to burnished wares of the Early/Middle Neolithic.

Radiocarbon dating of charcoal from the slot trench (GrA-67382 and GrA-67383) suggests the third enclosure at Hughstown was built *c.* 3629–3376 BC. This is supported by a date range of 3632–3373 BC (GrA-67384) for charcoal from the lower fill of the adjacent ditch. In the case of the fourth enclosure, radiocarbon dating of charcoal from the lower ditch (GrA-67385 and GrN-67386) suggests this ditch was dug during or before 3627–3376 BC. Bayesian modelling of these dates returned a date range of 3780–3530 BC (95% probability), 3690–3550 BC (68% probability) for construction of the second and third enclosures (O'Brien and O'Driscoll 2017, 336, fig. 7.15).

Discussion

The Hughstown excavation provides important detail on the design and construction of this hillfort. The construction of the defences of the second enclosure involved the digging of a substantial ditch, soil from which was piled on the inside to form a bank. The discovery of numerous large stones in the ditch fill indicates the bank was faced with drystone walling (Fig. 4.16). Based on the depth of the ditch (1.5–1.6m below modern ground), the original height of this earthwork defence is estimated at 3m.

Outside this, the building of the third enclosure required the digging of a small ditch, soil from which was possibly piled on the inside to form a bank. A slot trench on the inside of that putative bank contained the burnt remains of a wooden fence. The corresponding terminals of the ditch and slot trench indicate the southern side of an original entrance or gap to access the third enclosure (Fig. 4.17).

Excavation of the fourth enclosure identified a substantial rock-cut ditch, approximately 3m wide and 1.75m deep. The soil and broken rock from this ditch seem to have been piled on the inside to form a bank. As with the

Fig. 4.16 Reconstructed appearance of exterior stone facing in bank of the second enclosure at Hughstown, using original stones excavated from the ditch in Trench 1.

Fig. 4.17 Possible entrance to third enclosure at Hughstown, after excavation of terminals of ditch (top) and slot trench (centre) in Trench 2.

former banks of the second and third enclosures, that feature was probably levelled in the early modern era, with its soil and stone used to infill the adjacent ditch. There is no evidence of wooden fencing in or near this bank.

Given the excavation strategy and recent levelling of the interior, it is not surprising there is little evidence for occupation of this hillfort. The discovery of charcoal at the base of the ditches of the second and fourth enclosures may be connected to an early occupation, but no details are available. A sherd of prehistoric pottery from Trench 1 hints at Neolithic occupation. Further excavation is required to investigate the interior of these enclosures, including examination of potential structures identified by geophysical survey.

The excavation did not yield information about the abandonment of Hughstown hillfort, or about any subsequent occupation into historic times. Geophysical survey did record high magnetic gradiometry readings along the defences of both the second and third enclosures. Subsequent excavation did not confirm deliberate destruction by fire of the defences of the second enclosure. There is a broad correspondence between the higher gradiometry readings and both the ditch and palisade slot trench, but neither can be associated with definite burning events. Excavation did confirm geophysical indicators of a fire in the slot trench of the third enclosure, which may be connected to the burning of those defences. No such evidence was found for the fourth enclosure.

SPINANS HILL 1

As discussed in Chapter 2, this univallate enclosure lies at the north-western summit of Spinans Hill (410m OD), on a broad shelf of blanket bog terrain in the townlands of Ballyhubbock Upper and Spinans Hill (see Fig. 4.1; ITM 691957, 691590). This is a sub-quadrangular enclosure, *c.*550m (north–south) by 320m (east–west), covering an area of 11.1ha (Fig. 4.18). An east–west field bank across the centre forms a boundary between Spinans Hill and Ballyhubbock Upper townlands. There are panoramic views from the summit, with Brusselstown Ring visible on a prominent hill (402m OD) to the south-east.

The Spinans Hill 1 enclosure has a perimeter of 1.29km, first identified by aerial photography (Condit 1992, 20). The bank is best preserved on the northern and eastern sides and is a low relief feature over the remainder of its circuit (Condit 1998, fig. 2; Grogan and Kilfeather 1997, 40–41). It is not shown on the historic mapping of the Ordnance Survey. The enclosing elements on the eastern side include a bank with outer ditch and low counterscarp bank (O'Brien and O'Driscoll 2017, 201–03). The bank is 7–9m in width and is 2.8m above the base of the 7–9m-wide ditch. It has an internal height of 0.8m, and an external stone facing. This eastern side of the enclosure is straight and follows the contours of the hill. The northern side is defined by a bank, 7–10m wide and up to 0.4m in height, with no indication of a ditch. The grass on that bank contrasts with the lush growth of heather across the boggy interior of the enclosure. The same vegetation pattern continues around to the west and south-west, where the bank is a low scarp following the contour of the hill. On the southern side, there is a 1.1m-high by 2.1m-wide earthen bank, with no obvious ditch. That section may have been re-built as a later field boundary.

There are a number of small gaps across the enclosing bank at Spinans Hill 1, but no clear original entrance. There are no visible hut-sites in the interior, though peat cover and heather growth make identification of ground features difficult. The Archaeological Survey of Ireland lists six cairns recorded inside the enclosure (Fig. 4.19; Grogan and Kilfeather 1997, 22, no. 128). These include a large cairn (WI021-080004) at the summit and up to six smaller examples in the vicinity (WI021-080003, WI021-080006, WI021-080007, WI021-080008, WI021-080009, with another not recorded in the RMP). Their significance will be considered later in the chapter.

Excavation

In July 2016 a single trench was excavated across the northern side of the enclosure (Fig. 4.19). This is the location of a low bank, with an external height of 0.95m and inner height less than 0.2m (Fig. 4.20). The 11m by 2m trench was excavated to a depth of 0.4–0.85m across the line of that bank (results summarised here, with detail in O'Brien and O'Driscoll 2017, 243–9). The natural soil is blanket peat on stony glacial till. The peat was 0.24–0.32m in thickness at the southern end of the trench, 0.25–0.3m at the northern end, and 0.09–0.15m over the centre of the bank. This overlay a compact layer of mid-brown humic silt with numerous small to large stones, including collapsed stones from both sides of the bank. The peat and those stones were removed to expose a thin layer of iron pan overlying the subsoil.

The bank was the only archaeological feature in this trench, visible as a 7.15m-wide spread of large stones piled

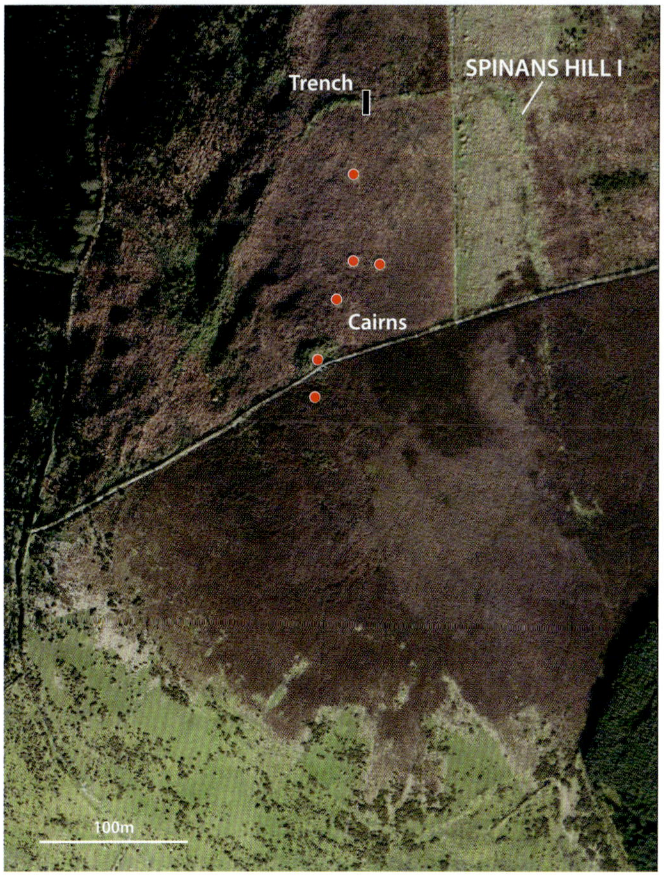

(Above) Fig. 4.18 Aerial view of Spinans Hill, north-western side, showing enclosures Spinans Hill 1 and Spinans Hill 2.

(Left) Fig. 4.19 Aerial view of Spinans Hill 1 hillfort, with location of excavation trench and cairns. Source: www.archaeology.ie.

Fig. 4.20 Location of excavation trench, Spinans Hill 1, looking west to other hillforts in Baltinglass (Tinoran at top-left).

loosely along a gentle slope (Fig. 4.21). The original width is estimated at 2.8m, with a 2.1m-wide tumble on the inner (south) side and 2.25m-wide on the outer side (Fig. 4.22). The excavated bank had a maximum thickness of 0.75m on the western side of the trench, and 0.66m on the eastern side. Based on the quantity of stone present, the original height of the bank probably did not exceed 1–1.5m.

The stones of the bank were 0.15–0.55m in length, with larger examples (0.25–0.4m) as well as smaller stones present. These were tabular to blocky in shape, with water-rolled surfaces indicative of a drift rather than a quarried source. The majority were intact, with only a few broken examples. There was no obvious structure in the bank, with no coursing or wall revetment (Fig. 4.23). Excavation recorded some vertical stones on the inner side, and small boulders on the outer side, which helped to retain the loose core of the bank. The eastern side of the original bank was piled between a 0.8m (north–south) by 0.45m (projecting west) outcrop of bedrock on the outside, and a subsoil boulder on the inside. In general, the bank stones were piled in a loose fashion with numerous voids, some of which were subsequently filled with humic silt and root matting. There was a deposit of compact, dark-brown silt with small amounts of charcoal in the lower part of the bank, probably the result of rain-wash through the loose stones.

The bank was built on an old ground surface that survives today as a thin layer of compact, blue-grey silt with occasional flecks of charcoal (Fig. 4.24). This was removed to an iron-rich subsoil, with no identified archaeological features. Excavation revealed a sub-circular cut, 0.16m by 0.15m by 0.21m deep, under the centre of the bank. This was filled with dark-brown silt with numerous small to large stones. It was irregular in shape, and may be a natural stone socket rather than a post-hole. The former seems likely, as the fill was overlain by silt of the pre-bank surface.

How old is Spinans Hill 1?

In the absence of dateable artifacts, such as pottery, the

(Above) Fig. 4.21 Stone bank of Spinans Hill 1 enclosure after removal of blanket peat.

dating of this enclosure relies on three radiocarbon results from the 2016 excavation (Fig. 4.25). A sample of peat taken on top of collapsed stones of the bank is dated to the modern era (102.13±0.35 BP; GrA-67391). This suggests the blanket peat is surprisingly recent, or that the sample was contaminated by modern roots. Whatever the explanation, the result does not help to date the enclosure. More important are identical radiocarbon dates for two samples of alder charcoal from the bank excavation. These include charcoal from the lower part of the bank (4835±35 BP; GrA-67387) and a sample from the underlying old ground surface (4835±35 BP; GrA-67389). Together, these indicate a date range of 3697–3527 BC for those contexts. While the charcoal under the bank either pre-dates or is contemporary with the building of this enclosure, the radiocarbon result for charcoal from the lower bank stones suggests the same period for construction. While both samples could derive from earlier activity, there is no evidence of digging in the bank construction that would account for residual charcoal in that feature. While further excavation and radiocarbon dating are required to confirm these two charcoal results, they do indicate an Early Neolithic enclosure.

Though limited in extent, the Spinans Hill 1 excavation provides important information about the enclosing element. This was built by piling stones, gathered probably from the surrounding hillside, to create a bank not exceeding 1.5m in height. This can hardly be described as a fortification, but more excavation is required to clarify the function and occupation history of the site. While the site chronology remains to be confirmed, a date range of 3697–3527 BC is suggested for the building of this enclosure. Whether this indicates that the cairns in the interior of Spinans Hill 1 are also Neolithic is uncertain. The relationship of Spinans Hill 1 to the larger Spinans Hill 2 enclosure and to the nearby hillfort of Brusselstown Ring is also unknown.

The Spinans Hill cairns

As already mentioned, six cairns are recorded inside the Spinans Hill 1 enclosure (see Fig. 4.19), none of which is shown on Ordnance Survey historic mapping. The earliest record is from a visit in July 1951 by the archaeologist Liam Price. He noted the location and size of a large summit cairn, as well as four smaller cairns with what seem to be robbed burial cists (in Corlett and Weaver 2002, 539). Condit (1998, 20) records the same number of cairns, speculating that these are megalithic tombs, possibly even a passage tomb cemetery.

The Spinans Hill 1 cairns were surveyed for this study (O'Driscoll 2016, 159–61), but have not been excavated. The large cairn (WI021-080004; O'Driscoll C1) at the summit is circular, measuring 30m (east-west) by 27m (north-south) and 1.1–2.3m in height. Some of the stone may have been removed to build an adjacent field wall that forms the boundary of Ballyhubbock Upper and Spinans Hill townlands. There is a circular depression, 14m in diameter at the centre, where a burial chamber may have existed. Price noted 'half a dozen kerbstones of the cairn still in position' on a visit in 1951.

There are four smaller cairns within 100m to the north of the large cairn. These have a general north–south distribution and are visible today as low, grassed-over circular to sub-circular spreads of loose stone. One of these

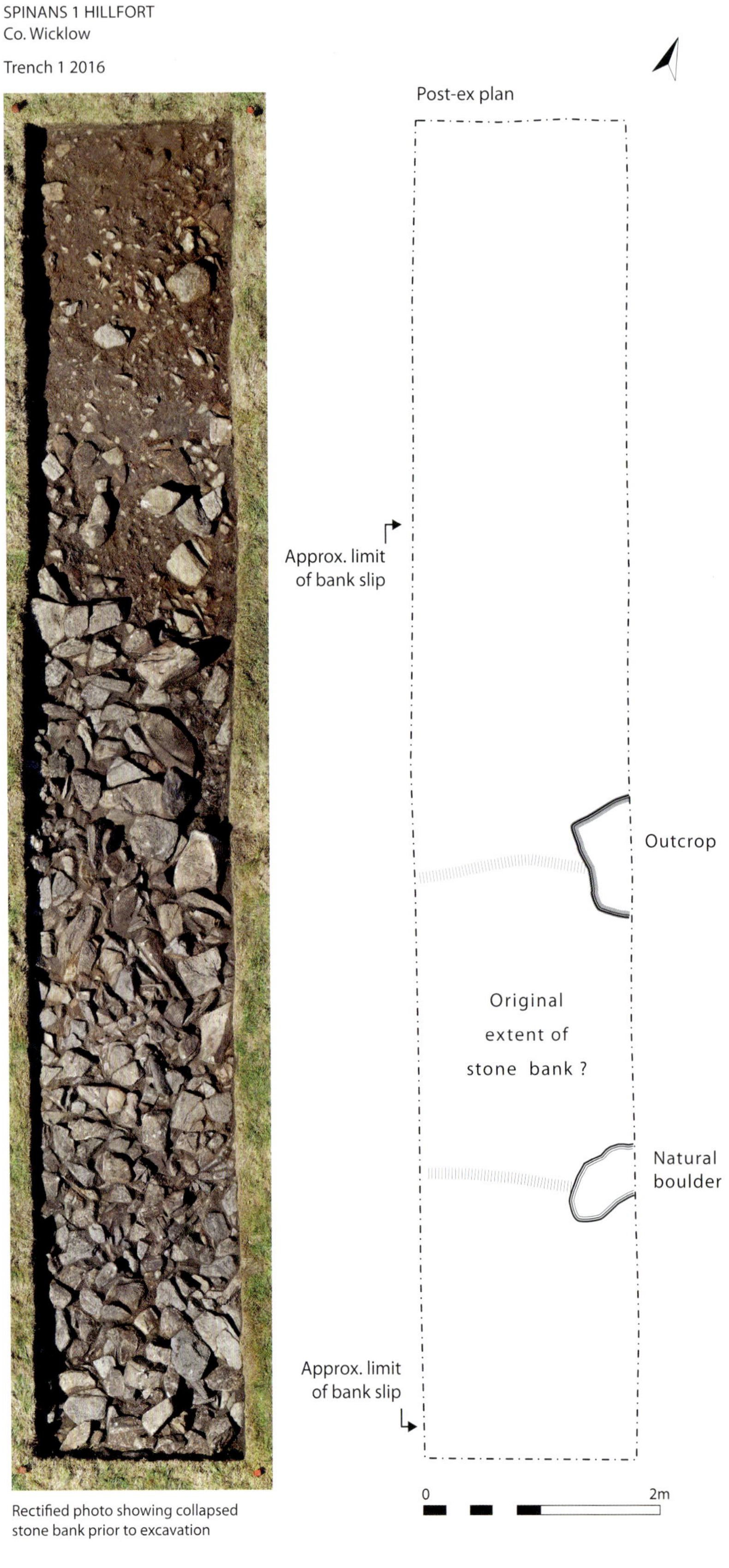

Fig. 4.22 Plan of excavated features with rectified photograph, Trench 1, Spinans Hill 1.

Fig. 4.23 Collapsed stones on outer side of bank after removal of peat, Spinans Hill 1.

(WI021-080006; O'Driscoll C2), 22m north/north-east of the large cairn, is 7.5m in diameter by 0.3m high. A rectangular depression at the centre, 1.8m by 1.2m by 0.6m deep, was interpreted by Price as a cist that 'was evidently dug out and rifled long ago' (Price 1951 in Corlett and Weaver 2002, 539). The next cairn (WI021-080007; O'Driscoll C3) is *c.*50m north of the large summit cairn, measuring 8.9m in diameter and 0.4m high (Fig. 4.26). A rectangular depression at the centre, 2m by 1.1m by 0.2m deep, may also be a robbed cist. The same is true of an adjacent cairn (WI021 080008; O'Driscoll C4) *c.*11m to the east, and *c.*55m north-east of the summit cairn; it has a rectangular depression 2.4m by 1.6m by 0.4m deep at the centre. The northernmost cairn (WI021-080009; O'Driscoll C5) is 8m wide and 0.2m high with no visible features. There are two small cairns south of the large summit cairn. The closest of these (WI021-080003; O'Driscoll C6) is a low, circular spread of stones, 6.5m in diameter, with no visible features. An unrecorded cairn (O'Driscoll C7) *c.*43m south of the summit cairn is 9.2m in diameter and 0.3m high, again with no features.

ENCLOSING THE LANDSCAPE

Radiocarbon dates from Hughstown indicate that three of its enclosures were built *c.*3700/3600–3400 BC. Whether they were part of a single design is unclear, as the dating evidence is not precise enough to rule out more than one phase of construction. The Hughstown occupation overlapped with nearby Rathcoran, *c.*3600–3400 BC. That Early Neolithic time-frame was a period of expanding farm settlement in Ireland, represented in the archaeological record by a distinctive 'house horizon', early megalithic tombs, single burials, as well as distinctive ceramic and stone tool production (see Waddell 1998). Farming was the basis of that economy, and there is a palaeoecological record of

(Above) Fig. 4.24 Spread of blue-grey silt representing an old ground surface under bank.
(Below) Fig. 4.25 Radiocarbon dates for Spinans Hill I (calibration after OxCal v.4.2.4).

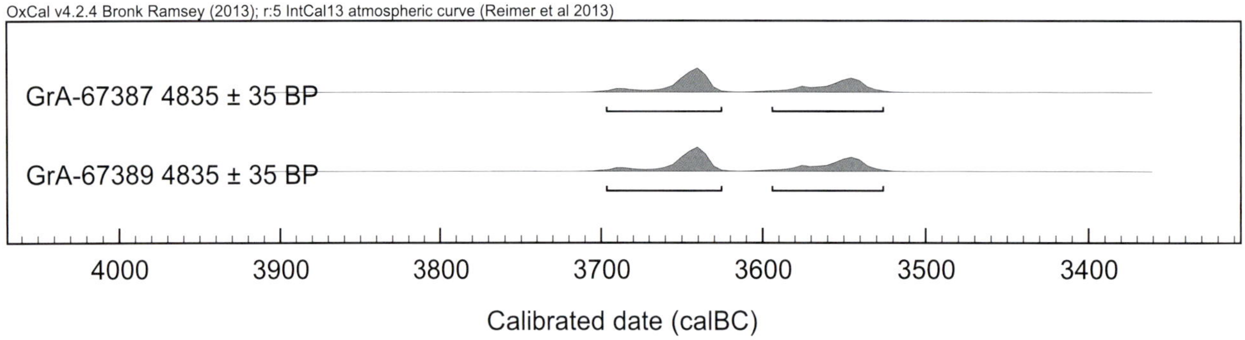

emerging farmscapes in many parts of Ireland from the early fourth millennium BC. Whether that record exists in the Baltinglass area will be examined in Chapter 7, when the results of a recent study at Holdenstown Upper bog are presented.

Hughstown and Rathcoran represent two different forms of hilltop settlement from that period. The former employed widely spaced enclosures on a broad ridge of what was probably well-drained agricultural land at a lower elevation (280–298m OD). It is possible animals were stockaded inside the second or fourth enclosures at Hughstown, in addition to it being a place of residential use and its other significance as a central place in the Early Neolithic landscape. The closer spacing of its second and third enclosures is more similar to the design of Rathcoran, except the latter has large, rock-cut trenches over much of the outer

Fig. 4.26 One of the small cairns inside the Spinans Hill I enclosure.

enclosure where it might be difficult to contain animals, so the inner enclosure was possibly used for that purpose. Rathcoran is also at a higher elevation (340–380m OD), with rougher, boggy ground more suitable for coarse grazing, though there was also direct access to grazing on the better-drained upper slopes of Tuckmill Hill.

As well as protection for animal stock, the Hughstown enclosures were defensive barriers for human occupants. There is evidence of fairly substantial bank-and-ditch earthworks reinforced by wood fencing. While there is no clear evidence these were destroyed by violence, the fencing of the third enclosure at Hughstown was burnt down. Moreover, the design of that site exceeds the practical requirements of animal enclosure. There is some indication from the geophysical survey of multiple small openings across the second and third enclosures. The excavation of one example identified fencing inside a narrow ditch causeway. Whether this indicates the type of Neolithic settlement called a causewayed enclosure needs to be confirmed by future investigation at the site.

Spinans Hill 1 is another variant of an Early Neolithic enclosure, surrounded by a single bank or a bank with ditch, on a small plateau at a high elevation (390–410m OD) on that prominent ridge. The agricultural use of that terrain may have been limited to rough grazing, suggesting the site was not used specifically for animals. The significance of the enclosure may be explained by its relationship to the five or more cairns in the interior. These have not been excavated, but could be prehistoric burial mounds, possibly even passage tombs. While that is speculation, the presence of a cemetery of ancient burial cairns could make this a ritual enclosure. A comparison could be made with the larger enclosure at Rathcoran with its passage tomb, or the earthworks demarcating the passage tomb cemetery at Knocknarea, Co. Sligo (Bergh 2002).

The discovery of an important burial at nearby

Ballintruer More (Raftery, J. 1973) has significant implications for contemporary hilltop enclosures in the Baltinglass area. That site represents an overt display of power in the settled landscape. The same applies to the passage tomb on the summit of Baltinglass Hill, which is a place for 'special dead' and for religious ceremony within the Rathcoran enclosure. These high-status burial contexts reflect the authority and leadership required to undertake such major works of construction as the Hughstown and Rathcoran enclosures are. The design of the distinctive pottery of the Ballintruer More burial, as well as the architecture and art of the passage tomb on Baltinglass Hill, also illustrate strong cultural ties with other Early Neolithic groups in eastern Ireland.

The enclosures at Rathcoran, Hughstown and Spinans Hill 1 were an important part of a distinctive Neolithic landscape at Baltinglass. The building of those enclosures reveals a concern with the safety of the human residents and their animals, with agricultural practices on those hills, and probably with trade and social exchanges. There were other concerns, including a visual display of power and status in a core Neolithic territory, the symbolic construction of community, and a connection to a cosmic religion. These and other questions relating to the Neolithic settlement of Baltinglass during the fourth millennium BC will be explored in Chapter 8.

5: BRONZE AGE HILLFORTS AT BALTINGLASS

William O'Brien and Nick Hogan

The Bronze Age was the main period of hillfort construction in prehistoric Ireland. This is probably true for the Baltinglass complex, where at least three examples date to the later second millennium BC (see Fig. 2.23). This chapter presents a recent investigation of those three sites, to understand their significance for the prehistory of this landscape.

RATHNAGREE

This is one of three large enclosures on Baltinglass Hill, prominently sited on its northern spur (Tuckmill hill) at an elevation of 315m OD. There is a panoramic view of the Baltinglass lowlands, apart from at the south-eastern side that is overlooked by the Rathcoran summit *c.*500m in the distance. Views to the west are restricted today by dense conifer forestry that has encroached on the outer enclosure of the hillfort (WI027-010). The enclosure lies within the townlands of Tuckmill Hill and Tuckmill Upper, with the eastern side of the middle enclosure forming the townland boundary. The site is depicted in nineteenth-century mapping by the Ordnance Survey as two widely spaced, concentric enclosures, with the name Rathnagree (*Rath na nGroigheadh*), translated by some as the rath of 'the studs of horses or herds of cattle' (FitzGerald 1908a; Price 1949a, 143). Thomas Westropp noted the size of two of its enclosures, and also the reputed discovery there of 'a hoard of golden coins' in the early nineteenth century (Westropp 1902, 107, 114).

The first record of Rathnagree in the modern era was by the archaeologist Liam Price, who observed the following on a visit in May 1931:

Fig. 5.1 Aerial photograph of Rathnagree hillfort (reproduced with permission of the Cambridge Collection of Aerial Photography; © copyright reserved).

> *Rathnagree near Baltinglass. A large circular earthwork, consisting of an outer ditch and two banks, enclosing part of the hill. There is no central mound, or anything artificial except the ditch and banks; the rock outcrops in several places inside the rath. (The* Namebook *is wrong in saying it is 'much elevated in the centre'; it is not so now, and I do not think from its appearance that it ever was). The outer ditch is dug in the surface of the hill; there is no bank outside it, except for a very low piece in one or two places, which looks like an old field fence. Next [to] the ditch on the inside is a large bank of stones and earth. The ditch and bank together are 7 or 8 yds wide: the bottom of the ditch is in places 10 or 12ft, in other places about 6ft below the level of the top of the bank. The present average depth of the ditch below the surface of the ground is about 3 or 4ft. Inside this, about 40 paces away on the S and about 50 paces away on the north is an inner bank, smaller and more ruined than the other: it is also of stones and earth, and is complete all the way round — more like a continuous low heap of stones than a bank. This inner ring is about 95yds in diameter. The diameter of the whole earthwork is about 200yds, and its circumference about 700yds. It is shut off from the S by the top of Baltinglass Hill, on which the monument called 'Rathcoran' is situated, but the view to the E, N and W is very wide and commanding (in Corlett and Weaver 2002, 111–12).*

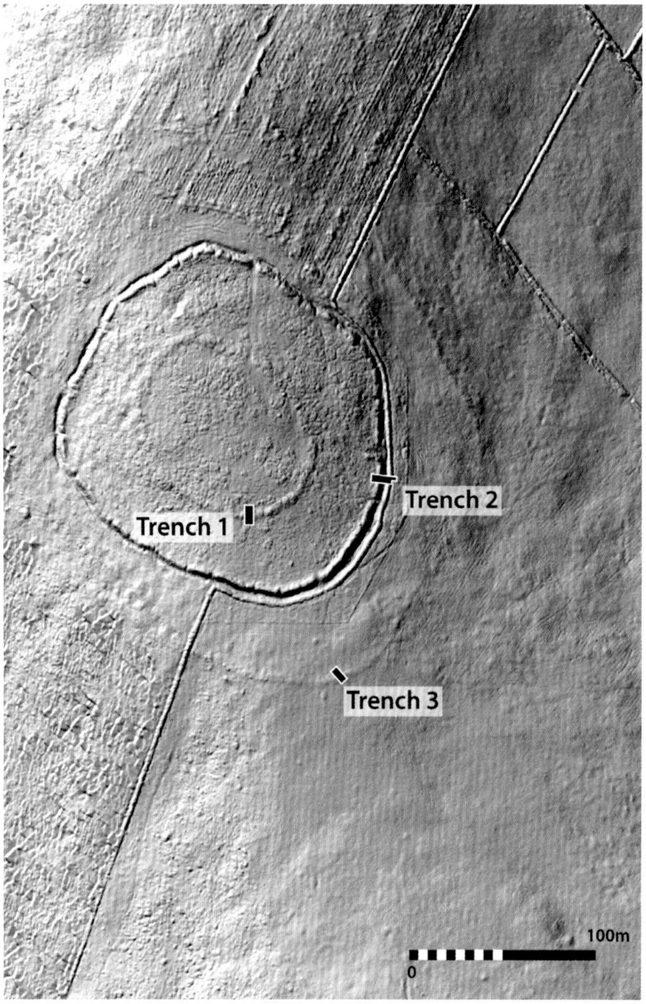

Fig. 5.2 LiDAR image of Rathnagree hillfort, showing location of three excavation trenches.

Price goes on to speculate as to the name of the hillfort and also mentions local legends of fairy associations. The hillfort was photographed by the Cambridge University Aerial Survey in July 1966 (Fig. 5.1), and subsequently recorded by the Archaeological Survey of Ireland (Condit 1992; 1998; Grogan and Kilfeather 1997, 43, no. 218), with an entry in the *Record of Monuments and Places* for Co. Wicklow (RMP WI027-010).

There are three concentric, sub-circular enclosures at Rathnagree, extending 294m by 273m over an area of 5.78ha (Fig. 5.2). The inner and middle enclosing elements are *c.*37m apart, with a 35m distance between the middle and outer defences. Unlike Rathcoran, these enclosures do not follow the contours of the hill. The inner and outer enclosures are each surrounded by a low stone bank, with no trace of an accompanying ditch. In contrast, the middle enclosure is protected by a more substantial earthwork, comprised of a bank with an external ditch and a counterscarp bank. Numerous small breaks along the perimeter of all three enclosures are probably the result of recent farming. There are two possible early entrances in the inner enclosure, located on the northern and north/north-eastern sides respectively. Four 2.8–6.1m wide openings in the bank of the middle enclosure, each with possible ditch causeways, may be original. They are positioned at the north, south, east and west of the perimeter respectively. The eastern example is the most substantial, with parallel lines of small boulders extending from the edge of the bank terminals. None of these openings has been excavated and so they cannot be confirmed as original entrances.

Where vegetation allowed, a gradiometry survey was conducted over parts of the interior of Rathnagree (O'Brien and O'Driscoll 2017, 212–15). This recorded strong magnetic anomalies along the perimeter of all three enclosing elements, suggestive of wooden fencing destroyed by fire (Figs 5.3 and 5.4). The geophysical survey did not identify definite traces of built structures inside the hillfort. There is a suggestion in the LiDAR survey of small circular

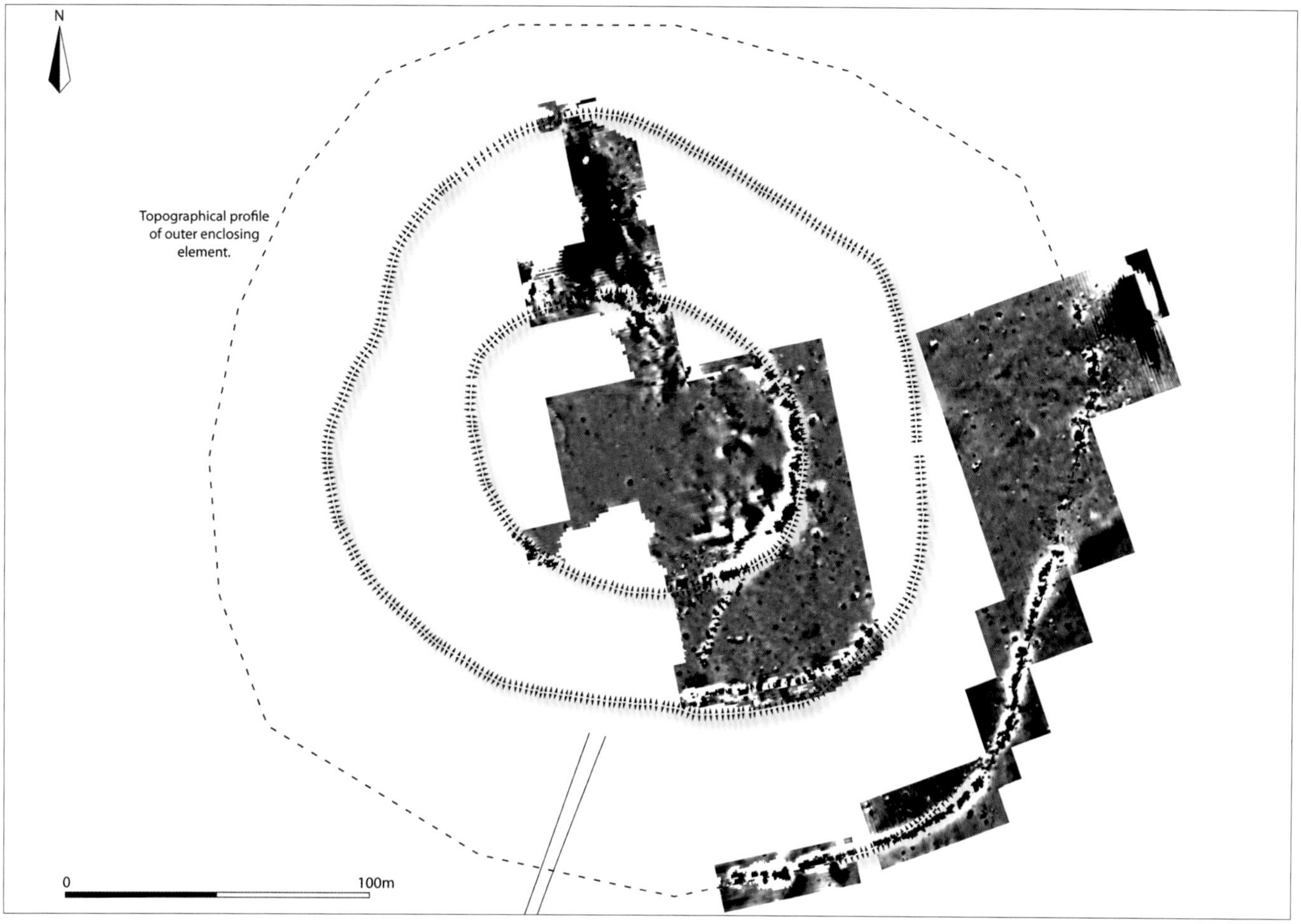

Fig. 5.3 Geophysical survey of Rathnagree hillfort.

terraces inside the middle enclosure on the western side, and in the outer enclosure on the south-western side (see Fig. 5.2). These have not been excavated, so it is not possible to confirm the presence of buildings inside the hillfort.

Excavation

Three cuttings were excavated at Rathnagree in July 2014 (results summarised here, with detail in O'Brien and O'Driscoll 2017, 249–71). Trench 1 was located across the line of the inner enclosure on its southern side; Trench 2 across the middle enclosure on the eastern side; Trench 3 was placed on the southern side of the outer enclosure (Fig. 5.2). Samples were recovered for radiocarbon dating from all three cuttings, and there was an important find of Bronze Age pottery from Trench 2.

INNER ENCLOSURE (TRENCH 1)

The inner enclosure at Rathnagree is 104m (N/S) by 93m (E/W) in extent, with a perimeter of 296m and a total area of 0.63ha. It is surrounded by a low bank of what appears to be loose stones, some of which are exposed. The bank averages 6m in width and 0.2m in height, with no indications of an accompanying ditch. An 8m (N/S) by 2m (E/W) trench was excavated across this bank (Fig. 5.5). This revealed a thin growth of peat, 0.08–0.23m in thickness, in a podzolised soil profile. A flint flake was found near the base of the organic soil at the northern end of the trench. This is a primary flake, 23mm by 13mm, with no cortex or obvious retouch, possibly struck with a bipolar technique. The flake cannot be dated or connected to flint-working at the site.

The removal of this organic soil exposed a 2.8m-wide bank of loose stones across the central part of the trench. These stones were mostly 0.1–0.2m in length, angular, with light-to-strong fire-reddening. This layer of heat-shattered stone on the bank surface overlay a tightly packed arrangement of large stones, set vertically or steeply inclined

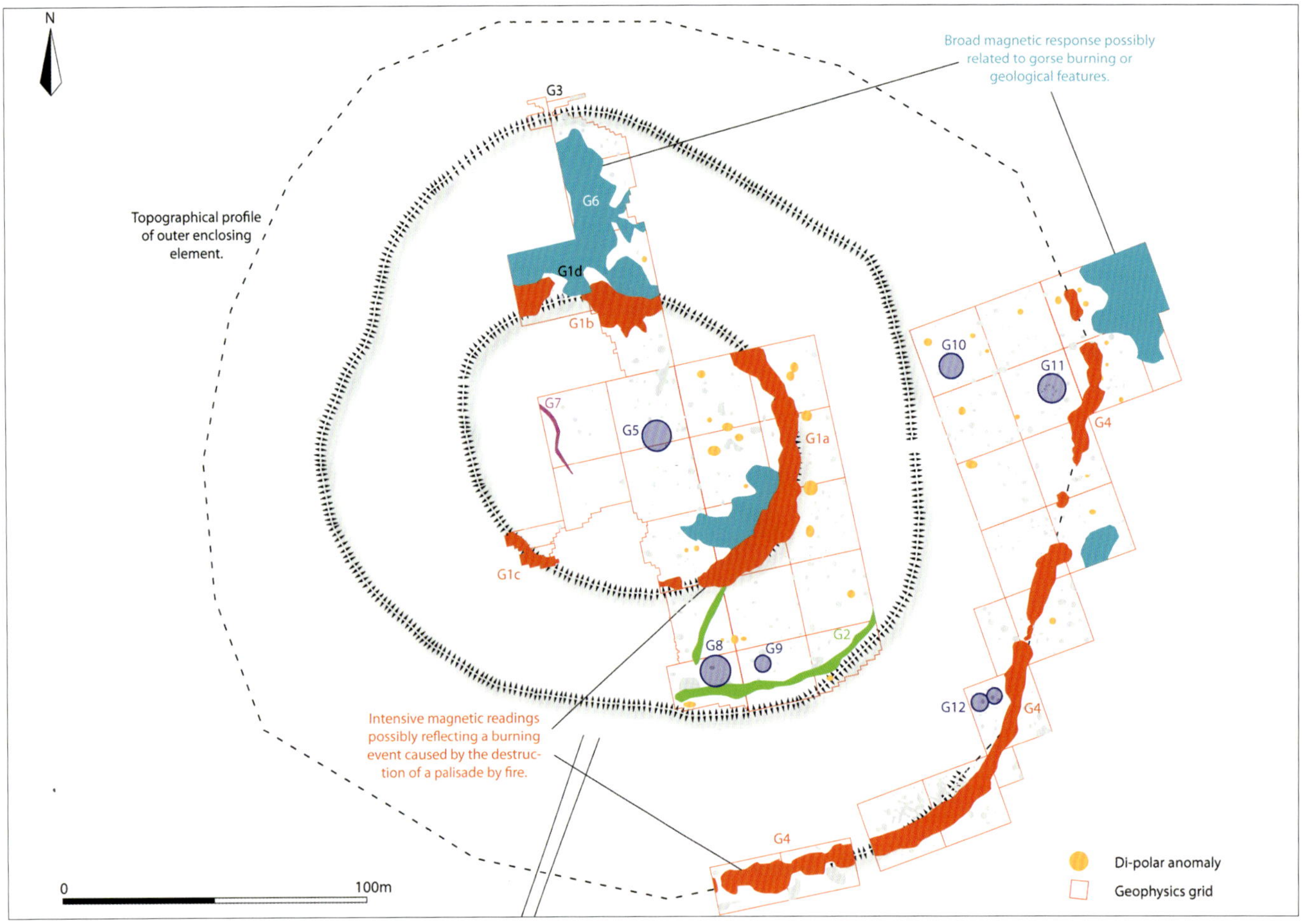

Fig. 5.4 Interpretation of magnetic gradiometry survey at Rathnagree.

along the outer (southern) side of the bank. Those stones were 0.18–0.4m in size, blocky in shape with some fire-reddening. They were placed on the natural subsoil to form an exterior facing to the bank.

The excavation of this stone bank exposed two large post-holes 0.5m apart on the subsoil surface (Figs 5.6 and 5.7). These originally held vertical posts secured with packing stones. The eastern post-hole was 0.59m (E/W) by 0.56m (N/S), narrowing to 0.28m (E/W) by 0.25m (N/S) at the base, with a depth of 0.71m. There was a rim of intense fire-reddening on the northern side of this post-hole (Fig. 5.8). Several large stones in the lower fill represent displaced packing. The western post-hole was 0.58m (E/W) by 0.54m (N/S), narrowing to 0.25m (E/W) by 0.34m (N/S) at base, with a depth of 0.77m. There were several large packing stones around the upper edges, including a rectangular slab, 0.31m by 0.17m by 0.11m, set on edge against the western side.

A spread of charcoal-rich sediment was discovered on the northern (inner) side of this bank. The underlying subsoil surface was fire-reddened in places, indicating a large fire at this location. Two lengths of burnt branch were recovered, one of which was sampled for radiocarbon dating. This was a single piece of burnt wood, at least 0.43m in length and 0.12m in diameter, identified as ash. Oak charcoal was found in one of the post-holes, suggesting the palisade was built with that wood.

These findings from Trench 1 confirm the inner enclosure of the hillfort was originally surrounded by a wooden palisade. This was built using large, roundwood posts of 0.2–0.25m diameter, set upright and secured with stone packing in individual pits dug to a depth of 0.7–0.8m. Further support was provided by a low stone bank, built against the front of this palisade (Fig. 5.9). With a post-hole spacing of *c.*0.5m, some 592 main posts were potentially used in the perimeter of this palisade, which was then

Fig. 5.5 Stony bank beneath peat, Trench 1, Rathnagree.

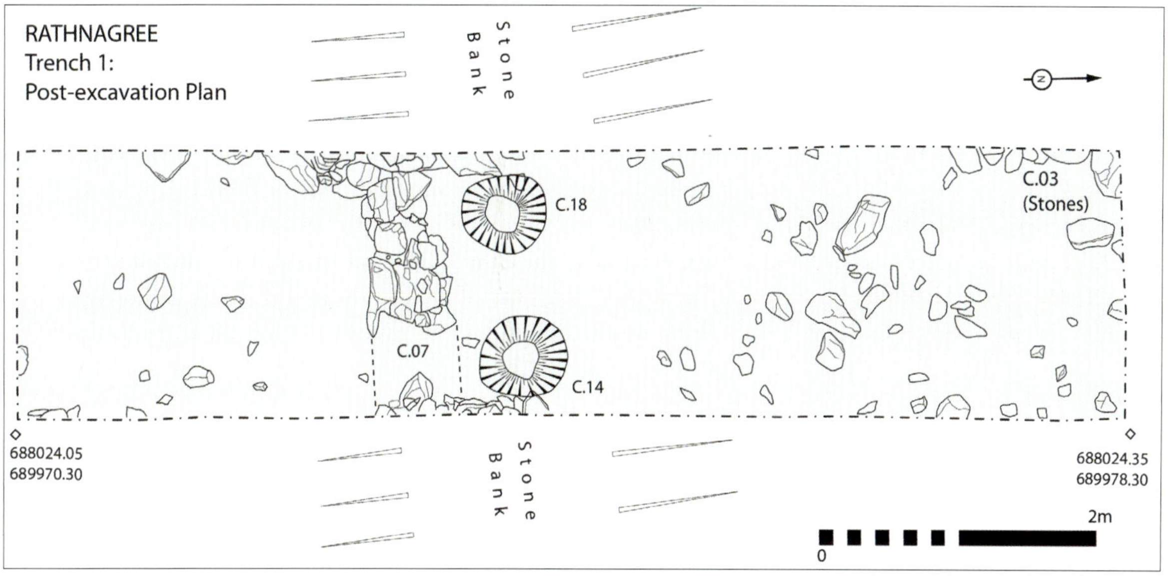

(Left) Fig. 5.6 Post-excavation plan of Trench 1, Rathnagree.

(Below) Fig. 5.7 Post-excavation rectified photograph, Trench 1, Rathnagree.

(Bottom-left) Fig. 5.8 Two post-holes with burnt surfaces, Trench 1, Rathnagree.

(Bottom-right) Fig. 5.9 Reconstruction of stone bank around post-hole, Trench 1, Rathnagree.

completed with numerous smaller posts. There was no indication of a slot trench or other post-/stake-holes between the main posts. This suggests the intervening posts were set into the surface of the stone bank and lashed together to the main posts to complete the fence.

The evidence of intense burning in this bank, in the form of charcoal spreads, heat-shattered stone and reddened subsoil, confirms the palisade was burnt down some time after construction. This is consistent with high magnetic readings along the bank (see Fig. 5.3). The burnt rim around each post-hole (Fig. 5.8) indicates the wooden uprights were burnt *in situ*. There was no attempt to re-build the palisade following its destruction.

Middle enclosure (Trench 2)

The middle enclosure at Rathnagree is 198m (N/S) by 182m (E/W), extending over 2.27ha with an outer perimeter of 549m (see Fig. 5.2). The enclosing element comprises a large bank with an external ditch, outside which there is a low counterscarp bank (Fig. 5.10). Today, the main bank is 3–5m wide, with an internal height of 0.1–0.3m and an external height of *c.*2m to the adjacent ditch. The inner side is gently sloping to a rounded top, while the exterior falls steeply into the round-bottomed ditch, which has a maximum width of 2.9–3.1m. The ditch is substantially infilled today, with an exposed central depth of 0.8m. The counterscarp bank has an external height of *c.*1m, with a flat-topped profile. A drystone facing on the exterior suggests this bank was re-built in modern times, probably to keep animals out of the ditch.

A 9m (E/W) by 2.5m (N/S) trench, with a 3m (E–W) by 1m (N/S) extension, was excavated across these defences on the eastern side of the middle enclosure (Fig. 5.11). This exposed a podzolised soil similar to that in Trench 1, with a thin, peaty soil overlying iron-enriched glacial till. Bedrock was exposed at the base of the ditch at a depth of 0.3–0.4m. There were five areas of excavation in Trench 2, including (from west to east) a flat area inside the main bank; the bank

Fig. 5.10 Bank-and-ditch defences of middle enclosure (Trench 2 location), Rathnagree.

Fig. 5.11 Plan of excavated features, Trench 2, Rathnagree.

itself; the external ditch; a counterscarp bank on the edge of that ditch; and finally, the area outside that bank. The excavation revealed three separate periods of construction:

Period 1 (Bronze Age): post palisade with stone revetment; possible timber structure on inside, destroyed by fire.

Period 2 (Bronze Age): earth/stone bank with stone walling, an external ditch and a counterscarp bank.

Period 3 (early modern): Rebuilding of the counterscarp bank.

Excavation of the main bank commenced with the removal of a thin sod and peaty soil. This exposed a deposit of orange/brown, stony silt, representing redeposited subsoil from the adjacent ditch. That sediment overlay the top and inner slope of the bank to a maximum thickness of 0.5m. The removal of this orange soil exposed the core of the bank, composed mostly of medium to large stones with numerous voids, with some inwash of grey/brown, humic silt. These stones were sub-rounded, indicating gathered field stone rather than quarried material. They were not fire-reddened or heat-shattered, and no charcoal was found in the core of the bank. The outer (eastern) side of the bank was supported by a line of large boulders packed together with smaller stones. While the upper portion of this bank revetment had collapsed into the ditch, the lower part was largely intact.

Excavation beneath the bank revealed a thin spread of dark-brown/black silt with much charcoal on a fire-reddened surface. This charcoal spread represents a burning event that pre-dates the bank. It was more or less continuous, except where interrupted by large stones in the subsoil, extending to the outer edge of the bank where it was truncated by the ditch. The burnt layer thinned considerably on the western side of the bank, visible as a spread of charcoal-flecked silt in the south-west corner of Trench 2. Identification of charcoal in the layer revealed a mix of ash, hazel, willow and oak, possibly a mix of structural wood and fuel used to burn the palisade.

The removal of the pre-bank burnt layer exposed a thin layer of orange, sandy silt up to 0.1m in thickness. This was

Fig. 5.12 Post-excavation view of slot trench under bank. Four postholes to right of slot, Trench 2, Rathnagree.

excavated to reveal the stony fill of a foundation trench extending north–south beneath the centre of the later bank (Fig. 5.12). The upper fill of this slot feature was a loose deposit of grey/brown, sandy silt, containing many stones 0.05–036m in length. These were mostly sub-rounded field stones, some of which were broken, but not fire-reddened. The removal of this stony fill revealed a dark silt with a few flecks of charcoal at the base of the slot.

The slot trench itself was 0.5m (north end) to 0.55m (centre) to 0.65m (south end) wide, with corresponding depths of 0.3m, 0.45m and 0.68m. The western side was near-vertical to steeply inclined, whereas the eastern side consisted of large stones forming an exterior revetment. The southern end was V-shaped in profile, with some thin stones placed against the western side as post packing. Excavation at the northern end uncovered a small post-setting, filled with grey/brown, sandy silt with charcoal flecks. This contained a 0.18m-long thin slab, placed vertically as a packing stone against the southern edge of the post-hole. The central area of the slot trench had a rounded profile.

Excavation identified four small post-holes and a single stake-hole on the same pre-bank surface west of the slot (Fig. 5.12). Two of these post-holes held packing stones and were parallel to the slot trench, possibly part of the Period 1 palisade. The same may be true of a stake-hole on the western edge of the slot. Two other post-holes at the western end of Trench 2 were on a different orientation. These may have been part of a built structure, with all four post-holes, and possibly others outside the area of excavation, built on the inside of the Period 1 palisade. While the two western post-holes were covered by slip from the bank, their stratigraphic position is unclear due to an uncertain relationship to the spread of charcoal-flecked silt from the burning of the Period 1 palisade. The two easterly post-holes were both beneath the burnt spread, which in turn was overlain by the Period 2 bank. If all four post-holes were part

Fig. 5.13 Post-excavation view of ditch, with bedrock at base, Trench 2, Rathnagree.

of the same structure, this indicates that the two western examples also date to Period 1. This cannot be confirmed without further excavation.

Excavation of a large ditch outside the main bank began with the removal of a 0.12–0.2m-thick layer of organic soil. This revealed the collapse of walling from the Period 2 bank into the open ditch, represented by a 0.4m-thick deposit of large stones in dark-brown, sandy silt. Those stones, which had an angular blocky appearance, were 0.3–4m in length; there were also some slab-like stones 0.15–0.7m long. They have the same lithology as the bedrock exposed at the base of the ditch, which is the most likely source. Their position in the upper ditch fill suggests collapse of a stone wall that stood on top of the main bank or, more likely, a stone revetment from the exterior of that bank. Some stones on the eastern (outer) side of the ditch may derive from collapse of the inner facing of the counterscarp bank.

The removal of this revetment stone exposed a thin layer of dark-brown silt on the inner slope of the ditch. This overlay a deposit of orange silt, which was removed to reveal grey, mottled silt on broken bedrock. The stone deposit also overlay a thick layer of compact bright-orange silt, containing Bronze Age pottery, on the lower exterior slope of the ditch. This, in turn, overlay mid-brown/orange silt on top of mottled silt on bedrock. The base of the ditch has an irregularly rounded profile, with exposed ribs of bedrock separated by pockets of compact sterile silt with flecks of charcoal. The upper width of the excavated ditch is 2.6–2.7m, with a lower width of 1.1–1.2m, and a central depth of 0.7–0.8m below modern ground surface (Fig. 5.13).

The outer edge of the ditch is raised today by a counterscarp bank, 1.2m (top) to 1.7m (base) in width. The original bank was re-built in the modern era. The central height of the present flat-topped bank is 1.35m, while the original height was around 0.7m. The removal of a thin sod and peaty layer on the exterior of this bank revealed a deposit of large stones in the organic soil. This represents the collapse of a stone facing, the lower part of which survives in the bank. Those stones overlay a shallow trench filled with organic silt at the base of the bank, cut into subsoil with bedrock on the lower outer edge. This is probably a field drain, dug when the counterscarp bank was re-built in the early modern era.

The upper part of the re-built bank was composed of orange/brown, sandy silt, probably upcast from that drain. This is confirmed by the presence of a 0.04–0.15m-thick buried sod layer separating the original counterscarp bank from the recently added soil. The former was a loose deposit of bright-orange silt, 0.25m in thickness, probably sourced from the ditch. This was retained on both sides by large stones forming a roughly coursed revetment. These had an angular blocky appearance, similar to stones in the upper ditch fill, suggesting they were also quarried from the ditch. The orange soil overlay a deposit of broken stones with numerous voids, forming the base of the bank on a shattered bedrock surface created during digging of the ditch.

No dating material or artifacts were recovered from the primary counterscarp bank. The stratigraphy indicates it was built at the same time as the adjacent ditch. Its main purpose was to increase the depth of the ditch on its outer, eastern side where there is a natural slope.

The findings from Trench 2 can be summarised as follows:

Fig. 5.14 Surface of stone bank, central area of Trench 3, Rathnagree.

Period 1: Palisade

The discovery of a slot trench with post settings underneath the bank indicates an earlier line of defence on this side of the hillfort. This slot trench held upright posts, secured with packing stones and by a low revetment of large stones on the outside. The discovery of four post-holes on the western side of the slot trench may indicate a post-built structure on the inside of the palisade. It is also possible that two of these post-holes were part of the palisade.

This arrangement of a post-built fence supported by low stone walling is similar to that in the inner enclosure (Trench 1) and, as we will see, the outer enclosure. The main difference is the use of a slot trench rather than individual post-holes to hold the main posts. With a perimeter of 549m and a suggested 1.2m spacing between the main posts, the middle enclosure required as many as 458 such posts to construct this palisade, in addition to a considerable number of other posts necessary to complete the fencing. The destruction of the middle enclosure palisade by fire is also similar to what was observed in Trench 1, represented by a burnt layer beneath the later bank. This burning event probably included the destruction of the posts held in the four post-holes inside the slot trench. Radiocarbon dating of this destruction level indicates the Period 1 palisade was built and probably destroyed *c.*1535–1126 BC.

Period 2: Walled bank-and-ditch

Unlike the other two enclosures, the middle enclosure was restored probably soon after it was burnt. This took a different form to the earlier palisade, with the building of an earth and stone bank, on top of which there may have been a wall of coursed stone, or more likely an external revetment. The stone used came from bedrock quarried in the adjacent ditch, while the soil and stones in the bank core came from the upper part of the ditch. The position of this earthwork on a natural slope explains the building of a low counterscarp bank on the outside of the ditch.

The subsequent collapse of the bank wall or facing into the ditch does not seem to have been a deliberate act; there is no evidence of burning. A radiocarbon result of 1495–1415 BC for pottery found from the base of the ditch provides a broad indication of when those defences were built.

Period 3: Re-building the counterscarp bank.

Excavation confirmed that the eroded counterscarp bank was re-built for agricultural purposes sometime in the early

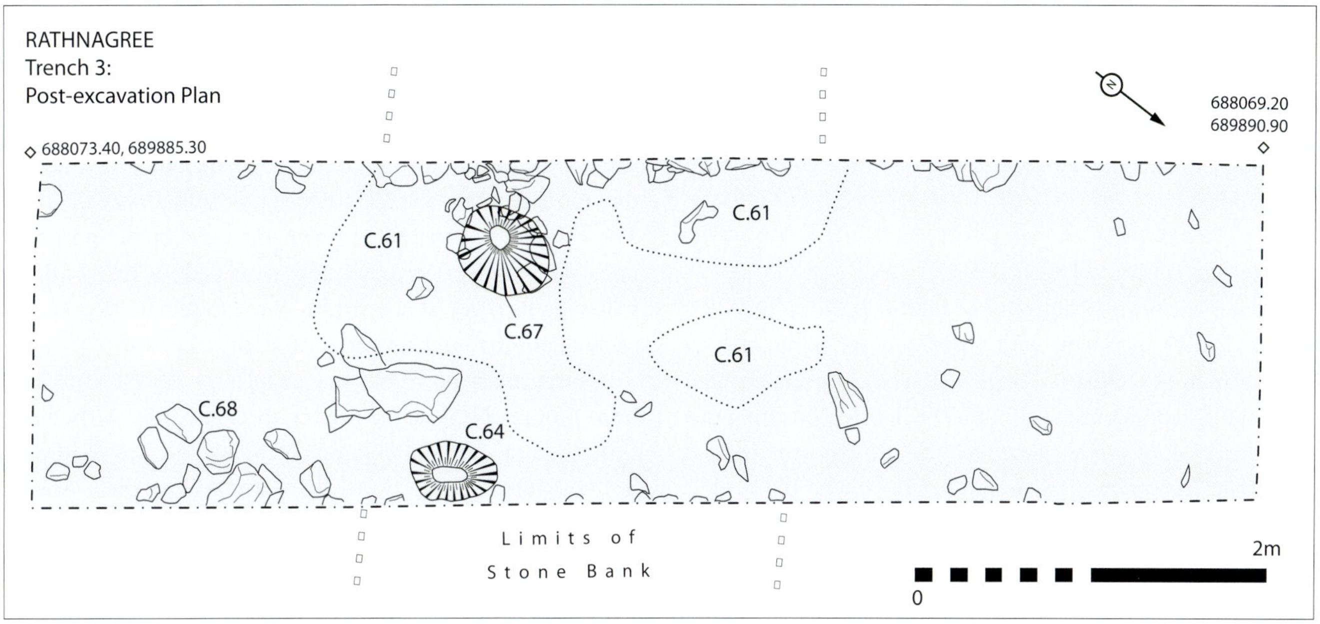

Fig. 5.15 Post-excavation plan of Trench 3, Rathnagree.

Fig. 5.16 Post-excavation rectified photograph of Trench 3, Rathnagree.

Fig. 5.17 Two post-holes with packing stones, Trench 3, Rathnagree.

modern era. This involved the digging of an external field drain, soil from which was piled to raise the Period 2 bank, with additional stones added to the external revetment. While there has been some collapse of the latter, this re-building explains the flat-topped profile of the counterscarp bank today.

Outer enclosure (Trench 3)

The outer enclosure of Rathnagree hillfort is 294m (N/S) by 273m (E–/W) in extent, with a perimeter of 873m and an internal area of 2.69ha (see Fig. 5.2). The enclosing element has a similar appearance to the inner enclosure, consisting of a denuded bank of stones, some of which are exposed. There is no surface indication of an accompanying ditch. The bank is most visible on the southern side of the enclosure, where it is 3m wide by 0.1–0.3m high.

A 7m (N/S) by 2m (E/W) trench was excavated across the line of the bank on that side. This revealed a low bank of stones with large post-holes, originally part of a wooden palisade. A number of large stones at the base of a thin, peaty topsoil represent tumble off the bank. The removal of this peat at the southern end of the trench exposed a compact layer of grey-brown, root-matted silt overlying a bright-orange, iron-rich, subsoil.

Excavation revealed a band of small to large stones across the centre of Trench 3 (Fig. 5.14). This had an overall width of 2.35–2.45m, with a maximum thickness of 0.3m on the eastern side and 0.35m on the western side. None of the bank stone had the angular profile of quarried rock, with the sub-rounded forms pointing to the use of gathered field stone. Most were in the 0.1–0.2m size range, with the largest up to 0.43m long and fewer intact stones under 0.1m. There was no obvious fire-reddening on the upper stones of this bank, possibly due to surface weathering. There were numerous heat-shattered stones in the lower part of the bank. This was particularly evident on the northern (inner) side of the bank, where those reddened stones overlay a spread of charcoal-rich sediment in which a burnt branch of oak was discovered (radiocarbon sample RNG2014-05). The presence of oak charcoal in one of the post-holes suggests the palisade was built with that wood, possibly similar to the palisade of the inner enclosure.

Excavation of that burnt surface revealed the position of two post-holes 0.7m apart on the outer side of the stone bank (Figs 5.15 and 5.16). The eastern post-hole was 0.51m (N/S) by 0.38m (E/W), with a vertical depth of 0.72m. This large pit was filled with stony silt; there was a small amount of charcoal, but not enough to indicate the burning of a post *in situ*. The overlying bank stone, some of which was fire-shattered and reddened, extended into the upper part of the post-hole. Excavation revealed large packing stones lining the sides of the post-hole (Fig. 5.17). These included six stones in the upper part, with at least eight other stones near the base. These stones were jammed down the sides of the post-hole once the post was erected, and remained in this position following its removal. The width of the lower cut suggests the original post had a diameter of *c.*0.25m.

The western post-hole was circular in shape, narrowing from 0.66m (N/S) at the surface to 0.34–0.4m at the base, with a central depth of 0.48m. The upper part was filled with heat-shattered bank stone, beneath which there was a red/dark-brown, silty fill containing charcoal. This became blacker towards the base, where there was a significant amount of charcoal. The removal of a horizontal stone, 0.33m by 0.28m by 0.13m, exposed a 0.1m-thick deposit of charcoal-rich silt at the base of the post-hole (radiocarbon sample RNG2014-06). There was not enough charcoal in the fill to indicate the original post was burnt *in situ*. Several large stones were found in a vertical position in the fill. The largest was 0.59m by 0.16m by 0.11m, and had been deliberately pointed for use as a packing stone. This was part of a tightly packed arrangement of five other stones, 0.19–0.29m in length.

The results from Trench 3 indicate that a wooden palisade, supported by a low bank of stones, delimited the outer enclosure of the hillfort. This consisted of upright posts, probably complete roundwood 0.2–0.25m in diameter, spaced 0.7m apart. With a perimeter of 873m, as many as 1,247 such posts were required to build this palisade, in addition to a large number of smaller roundwood poles to complete the structure. As with the inner enclosure, there is no evidence for a slot trench between the main posts, suggesting that any intervening posts were either set into the surface of the stone bank and/or lashed horizontally or obliquely to finish the palisade. The size of that fence is unknown, but given the depth of the excavated postholes (0.48m and 0.72m), it must have been at least 2–3m in height. The stone piled at the base of these posts probably did not exceed 1m in height, and so should be considered a revetment rather than a wall.

The discovery of reddened and heat-shattered stone in the lower bank deposit, together with charcoal overlying an oxidised surface around the post-holes, confirms the palisade was burnt down. There is no evidence that those defences were ever re-built.

How old is Rathnagree?

A total of eight radiocarbon dates are available from the 2014 excavation at Rathnagree hillfort (Appendix 1). These include two samples from the enclosing elements of the inner enclosure (Trench 1); four from those of the middle enclosure (Trench 2); and two from those of the outer enclosure (Trench 3).

Dates for the inner (1417–1135 BC), middle (1535–1126 BC), and outer (1411–1128 BC) palisaded enclosures confirm that Rathnagree hillfort was built between 1500 and 1200 BC and, most probably, around the fifteenth or fourteenth century BC (Fig. 5.18). The results do not clarify the history of hillfort occupation, except perhaps to indicate when the site may have been abandoned. There is no evidence of human activity pre-dating the hillfort, nor any information as to later activity on this hill before the early modern era.

The radiocarbon results from Trench 2 are supported by a find of coarse ware pottery of Bronze Age type in the ditch of the middle enclosure. While this is a Period 2 context connected to re-building of the defences, the pottery could be residual from Period 1 activity. This possibility is supported by the discovery of a sherd of similar pottery (14E227-20) in a burnt layer under the Period 2 bank. Also, a radiocarbon result of 1495–1415 BC (3170±35 BP; GrA-63008) for organic residue from one of the pot sherds overlaps with the earliest date (1535–1450 BC) from the same burnt layer. This suggests the interval between the burning of the Period 1 palisade and its re-building with a bank-and-ditch earthwork (Period 2) may have been brief, falling within the same tradition of ceramic use.

BRONZE AGE POTTERY AT RATHNAGREE

Seventeen sherds from a single pot were found near the base of the Period 2 ditch of the middle enclosure. Radiocarbon dating of carbonised residue on one of these sherds returned a Middle Bronze Age date (see above). A single sherd of a similar vessel was found in the burnt spread from the Period I defences. The sherds from the ditch are mostly body sherds, with two rims and a base fragment. The number of sherds makes it likely the vessel was broken when deposited in the ditch. Analysis revealed a small, squat, flat-based pot (Fig. 5.19), with a rim diameter of *c.*14cm, base diameter of 11cm and a height of *c.*14cm (Cleary in O'Brien and O'Driscoll 2017, 262–4). The rim is bevelled internally, which may indicate it had a cover of some type. The pot is well-made of coil-construction, typical of medium to large

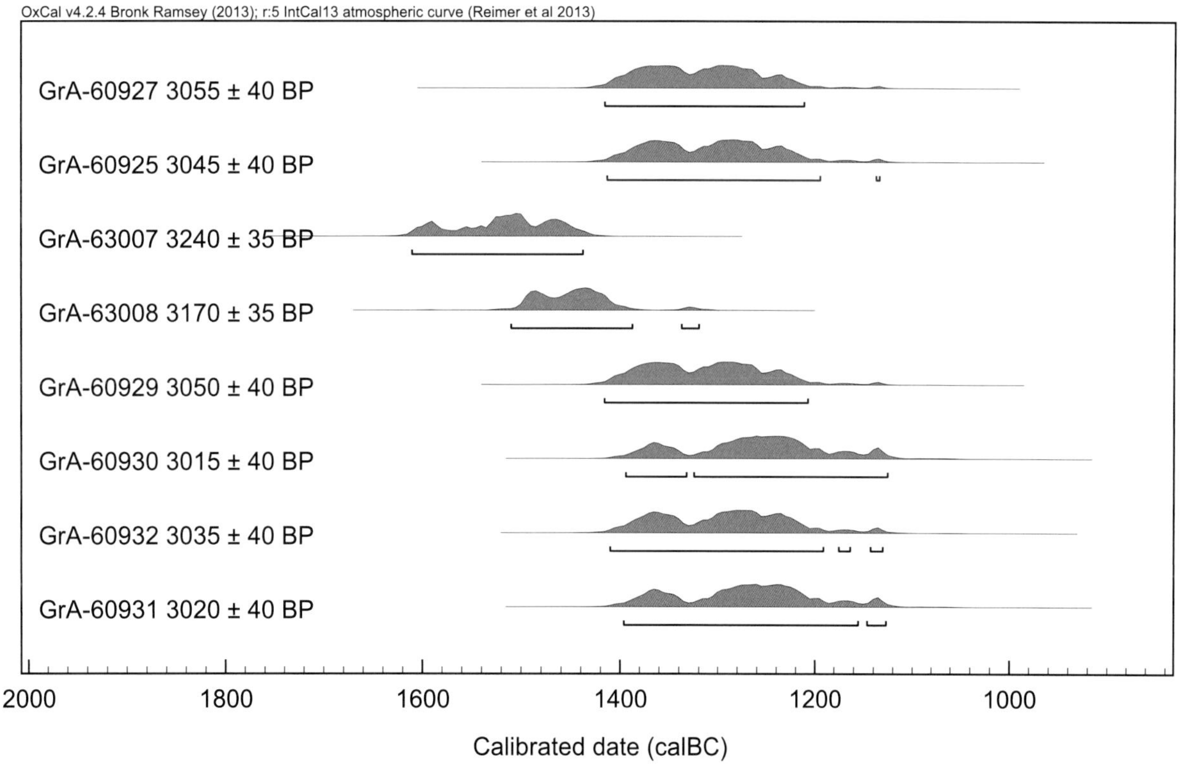

Fig. 5.18 Radiocarbon dates for Rathnagree hillfort (calibration after OxCal v.4.2.4).

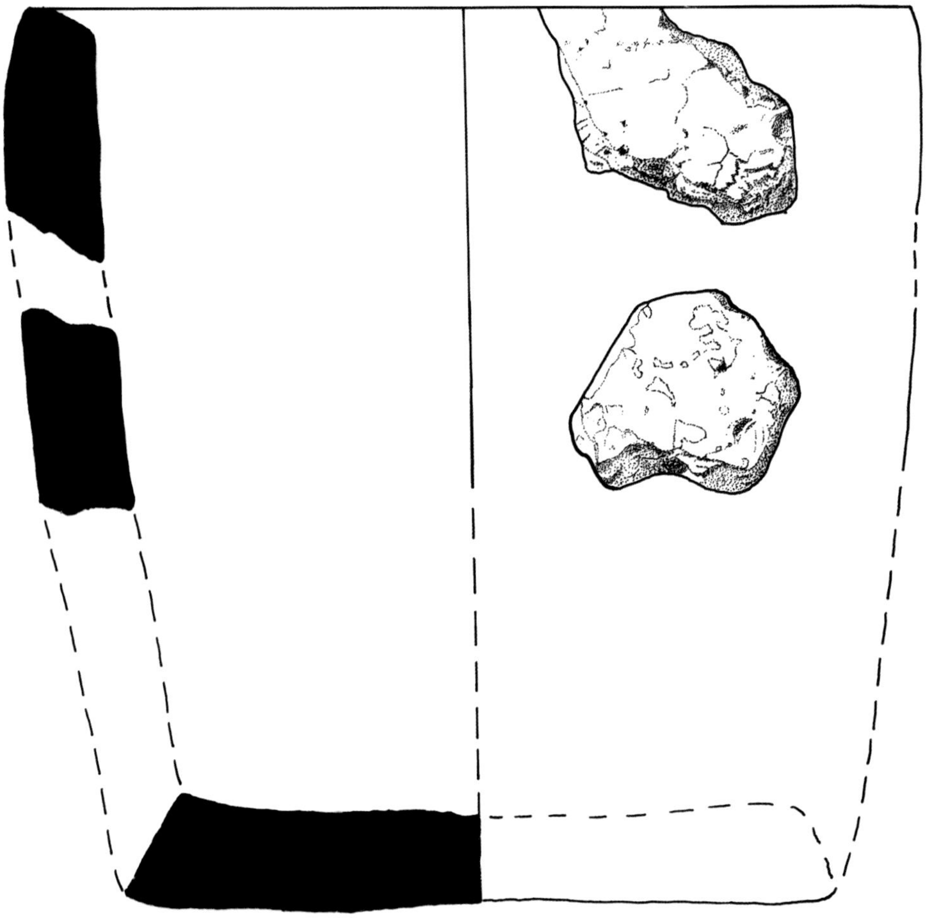

Fig. 5.19 Reconstruction of pottery from Trench 2, Rathnagree.

vessels from later prehistoric Ireland (Cleary 2000, 130). The fabric is mica-rich clay tempered with crushed granite. Evenness of colour indicates some control over the firing temperature, requiring some form of kiln rather than an open bonfire. As to use, soot accretion on the outside of some of the rims and body sherds suggests the vessel was heated over an open fire. The small size of the pot may have limited its use for bulk cooking.

The Rathnagree vessel is typical of Middle and Late Bronze Age domestic pottery in Ireland (Cleary 1995 and 2003; Grogan and Roche 2009). This includes the larger vessels of the so-called Class II ware from Lough Gur, Co. Limerick, which have rim diameters of *c.*20–26cm and heights of *c.*26–29cm (Ó Ríordáin 1954, 333). The difference may be related to domestic use, with the Rathnagree example representing tableware to contain rather than cook food. Several Middle and Late Bronze Age sites at Lough Gur have produced similar bucket-shaped vessels (Cleary 1995; 2003). Other examples include pottery from the Middle Bronze Age settlement at Chancellorsland, Co. Tipperary (Cleary 2008, fig. 2.5.2:12), and from a site of the same period at Carrigillihy, Co. Cork (O'Kelly 1951, fig. 8). This pottery is also recorded in Late Bronze Age levels at Dún Aonghasa, Inis Mór, Aran Islands (Cleary 2012, fig. 8.6). The Rathnagree vessel is therefore typical of domestic pottery used in Ireland during the later Bronze Age.

Discussion

While the extent of excavation at Rathnagree was limited to three trenches, there are significant findings in respect of the chronology, design and history of this hillfort.

The radiocarbon results suggest all three palisaded enclosures were broadly contemporary in the period *c.*1500–1300 BC. Their physical form is similar, as were the methods used in their construction. There were three widely spaced lines of strong, wooden palisade, the main posts of which were set in individual post-holes (inner and outer enclosures) or a slot trench (middle enclosure). This fencing was supported in each case by a low bank of stones. It is estimated that as many as 2,297 large, roundwood posts, mostly oak, were required for these three palisades, as well as several thousand smaller posts and lashing. That required a substantial effort in the clearance of woodland and preparation of the palisade timbers. This, together with the digging of post-holes and the gathering of stone for the supporting bank, represents a considerable investment of labour, organisation and leadership.

The excavation of the inner (Trench 1) and outer (Trench 3) defences did not uncover any evidence for occupation of this hillfort. No artifacts, food residues or structural remains were uncovered, apart from a single flint flake of uncertain date found in Trench 1. The paucity of occupation evidence can be explained by the limited extent of excavation. There is some evidence of occupation from Trench 2, where traces of a post structure were found inside the Period 1 palisade of the middle enclosure, with use of coarse ware pottery evident at the same location. Further excavation is required to clarify the occupation history of this hillfort

The evidence from Trench 2 confirms that the defences of the middle enclosure at Rathnagree were re-built after the early palisade was burnt down. While no radiocarbon dates are available for the Period 2 defences, this re-building probably occurred soon after the burning event. This is suggested by the preservation of a distinct destruction layer beneath the later bank, and by radiocarbon dating of pottery from that ditch. The date and circumstances of the final abandonment of this hillfort are not known, and there is no evidence of any occupation in historic times.

SRUHAUN

This is the second of three enclosures on Baltinglass Hill, prominently located on its southern spur (Carr's Rock) at an elevation of 310m OD. The site (WI027-090) is 600m south of Rathnagree in the townland of Sruhaun, partly extending into the adjacent townland of Pinnacle. This is an area of fairly level ground, with steep slopes to the south and east, giving panoramic views of the Baltinglass lowlands. The site is overlooked by rising ground on the northern side, which restricts visibility to Rathnagree, and also by Rathcoran on the Pinnacle summit of Baltinglass Hill, 375m to the north-east.

The Sruhaun enclosure is not recorded in Ordnance Survey historic mapping, nor is it visible in most aerial photographs. There is no history of research at the site, and no local folklore or recorded discoveries. The site was first identified by LiDAR survey undertaken for this project (Fig. 5.20), with further imagery provided by geophysical survey (Fig. 5.21). These surveys reveal a univallate enclosure of sub-ovoid shape, approximately 129m (NE/SW) by 152m (NW/SE) over an area of 1.43ha. The enclosing element is visible today as a low-relief bank, 4.5m wide and up to 0.2m high. The slight nature of the bank makes it difficult to identify at ground level. There are some indications of an internal ditch, visible in places as a shallow depression inside this bank. High magnetic readings along the bank indicate possible burning of the enclosing element. A 6m-wide break at the north-western side may represent an original entrance.

The eastern side of the enclosure is crossed by a modern field boundary, comprised of an older wall of smaller stones overlain by boulders from recent field clearance. There are no features in the interior, apart from a few large boulders and some outcrop. No internal features are visible in either the geophysical results or the LiDAR data. The landowner confirmed the site was cleared of most surface stone in modern times. As a consequence, the interior is mostly level, with a slight rise to the north. The enlarged field is used today for cattle and sheep grazing, part of an open pasture that extends across the southern slopes of Baltinglass Hill.

Excavation

A single, 8m by 2m trench was excavated in July 2015 (Fig. 5.22) across the enclosing elements on the southern side of the Sruhaun enclosure (the results are summarised here, with detail in O'Brien and O'Driscoll 2017, 271–81). The removal of a thin organic soil revealed a layer of yellow/brown, sandy silt representing redeposited subsoil across the entire trench. This material overlay an iron-enriched subsoil, with a thin layer of red/brown iron pan in the southern third of the trench. Excavation of the yellow/brown layer revealed two parallel ditches close together in the northern third of the trench (Fig. 5.23). The base of a stone bank/wall was exposed in the central part of the trench, along the line of the bank imaged by high magnetic readings and LiDAR survey. The bank overlay a slot trench connected to an earlier wooden fence.

Ditches

A ditch was cut into subsoil *c.*1.8m inside the enclosure bank (Fig. 5.23). It had a U-shaped profile, ranging in depth from 0.8m on the eastern side to only 0.2m on the western side (Fig. 5.24). The top of the ditch was 1.6–1.65m wide, narrowing to 1.3–1.4m at the base. This was irregularly

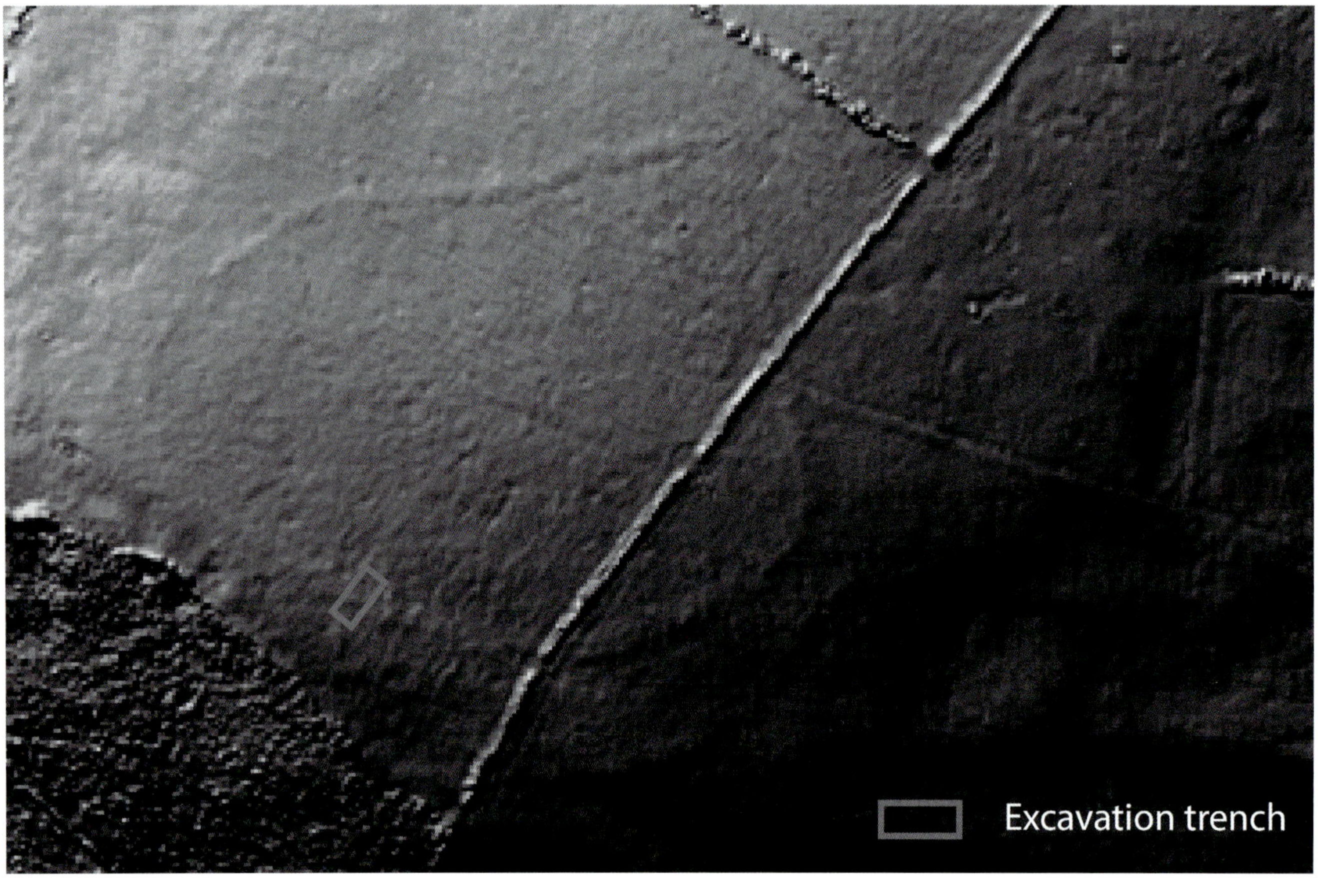

Fig. 5.20 LiDAR survey of Sruhaun enclosure, showing excavation trench.

Fig. 5.21 Magnetic gradiometry survey of Sruhaun.

Fig. 5.22 Post-excavation view of Sruhaun trench (looking north-west), showing piles of bank stones removed from the two ditches.

smooth and free of protruding stones, apart from three subsoil boulders, 0.4–0.7m in length, embedded in the base on the eastern side of the ditch.

The infilling of this ditch began with an accumulation of peat accompanied by large stones. A growth of black peat at the base varied from 0.55m in thickness on the eastern side to 0.08m on the western side. This contained numerous large stones that also filled the upper part of the ditch. Those stones were piled loosely, with no particular arrangement. They were mostly angular to sub-angular in shape, with only a few sub-rounded examples. The majority were 0.3–0.45m in length, with some examples as large as 0.6–0.7m or as small as 0.15–0.3m. Most were broken to some degree, with a few examples deliberately pointed. Approximately half of the stones had a reddened appearance, probably iron oxide staining caused by weathering.

These stones were apparently thrown into the open ditch, with heavier examples sinking into the lower peat formation. Peat continued to accumulate around the uppermost stones, with voids in several places. This stone/peat deposit in the inner ditch was overlain on the northern side by orange/brown silt that represents slip off the upper edge of the ditch cut. The entire ditch fill was then sealed by a 0.05–0.08m-thick layer of peaty silt. This represents a buried sod that formed in the ditch depression prior to the spread of redeposited subsoil across that area.

Excavation uncovered a parallel ditch on the southern side of the inner ditch, separated by a thin ridge of subsoil (Figs 5.23 and 5.24). This outer ditch was dug to a depth of 0.38–0.42m (0.58–0.74m from modern ground surface). It had a V-shaped profile, varying in upper width from 1.62m (east side), to 1.5m (centre) to 1.65m (west side). The sides were smooth, with few exposed stones.

Excavation revealed a similar fill sequence to that of the inner ditch. The primary fill was a well-humified peat, 0.2–0.4m in thickness and also slightly waterlogged at the base. As with the inner ditch, there were numerous large stones in this peat. These were mostly angular to sub-angular in shape, often fractured and reddened, averaging 0.15–0.25m in length, with some up to 0.3–0.45m. These stones were part of the same deposit as the stones in the inner ditch. Likewise, the stones and peat in the outer ditch were overlain by the spread of redeposited subsoil in this area.

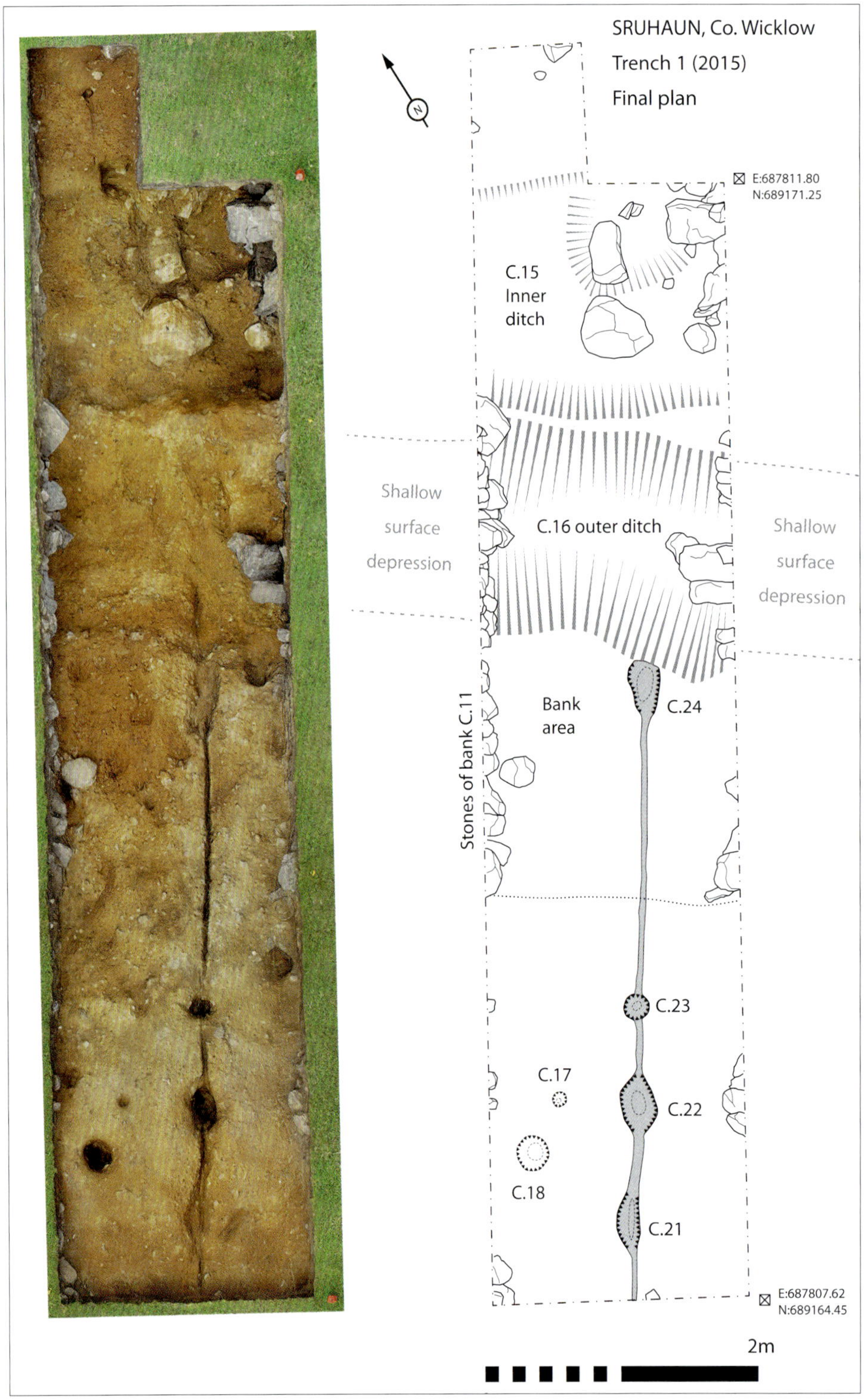

Fig. 5.23 Post-excavation plan, with rectified photograph, Sruhaun trench.

BANK

Prior to excavation this feature was visible as a low rise in the field. Even though the ground surface was levelled in modern times, the base of the original bank survived as a 2.6m-wide spread of large stones across the central area of the trench, extending south from the edge of the outer ditch (Fig. 5.23). These stones were arranged loosely, with no obvious coursing, though some examples were piled two or three high. While the surface stones were loose, the base of this deposit was compact. The individual stones were

Fig. 5.24 Post-excavation view of outer ditch and inner ditch, Sruhaun.

angular to sub-angular, with very few rounded examples. The majority were 0.15–0.25m in length, with some up to 0.3m, and many as small as 0.07–0.15m. The deposit was 0.12–0.18m in overall thickness, with the uppermost stones only 0.1m or less beneath the modern ground surface. A large proportion of these stones had reddened surfaces, which geological examination confirmed as iron oxide staining from weathering.

Excavation revealed a thin deposit of black silt, with lenses of granular quartz, between the lower stones in this bank. This represents rainwash through the stones, with no charcoal present. The removal of the silt revealed a spread of compact black silt, with few stones but much charcoal, overlying an iron-enriched subsoil (Fig. 5.25). This black silt extended over most of the bank area, and included several concentrations of oak charcoal. With no charcoal present in the overlying stones of the bank, this burnt layer seems to derive from an earlier wooden structure.

PRE-BANK FEATURE

Excavation of a thin layer of iron pan across the southern end of the trench exposed a narrow slot cut into subsoil. This straight feature extended 4.5m north-west (030–210°) from the southern end of the trench (Fig. 5.26). It continued under the spread of bank stones as far as the edge of the outer ditch, which truncated this feature. The slot was best preserved beneath the stone bank, where it averaged 4–5cm-wide and 6–9cm deep. The sides were vertical to a 1–2cm-wide, slightly pointed, base. It was not as well preserved south of the bank area. The fill consisted of tightly packed, reddened stones, many of which were set upright and had heat-shattered *in situ*.

The slot widened at four points to form stake settings. These had a similar fill to the slot, consisting of light-brown to dark-brown/black silt with fragments of burnt stone and some flecks of charcoal. The presence of these stake-holes suggests the slot is a foundation for a wooden fence structure that pre-dated the enclosing bank and ditches.

Dating

No artifacts were found in the Sruhaun excavation. The dating of this enclosure is based on the results of two samples

Fig. 5.25 Spread of charcoal-rich sediment under bank material, Sruhaun.

submitted for radiocarbon dating (see Appendix 1). The first of these is oak sapwood charcoal from a burnt layer under the enclosure bank, dated to 1375–1225 BC (3030± 50 BP; GrA-64430). The second is a sample of peat from the base of the inner ditch, dated to the modern era *c.*AD 1959–82 (126.73 ± 0.39 BP; GrA-64432).

In terms of absolute chronology, the charcoal result from the pre-bank layer is the only radiocarbon date available for the Sruhaun enclosure (Fig. 5.27). This charcoal derives from the burning of an earlier field fence and not a wooden feature in the bank. The stratigraphic evidence does not indicate a significant interval of time between the burning of that fence and the construction of the overlying bank, making it likely the enclosure was built *c.*1375–1225 BC. The second radiocarbon result indicates that peat growth in the inner ditch (and probably the outer ditch) commenced in the early modern era. It is likely that both ditches are of much later date than the adjacent bank, stone from which was thrown into these features during recent land clearance.

Discussion

Though limited in extent, the Sruhaun excavation provides important information about the construction history of this enclosure. The slot trench with stake settings under the enclosure bank represents a wooden fence connected to an animal stockade on that side of Tuckmill Hill, which was later replaced by a banked enclosure. The presence of fire-shattered stone in the slot indicates the fence was burnt down prior to construction of the enclosure bank. A spread of charcoal on either side of this slot may be connected to the burning and collapse of that fence. It is tempting to connect the burning of that fenced enclosure at Sruhaun to the destruction of the Period 1 defences at nearby Rathnagree. With the latter occuring *c.*1535–1126 BC, there is a significant overlap in the radiocarbon dating of both events. The rebuilding of the Sruhaun enclosure with a stone bank may also be linked to the rebuilding of the middle enclosure at Rathnagree, thus maintaining a functional relationship between the two sites.

The results from this excavation indicate four closely spaced enclosing elements at Sruhaun. These include:

1. A levelled *outer bank* of stones with no soil component. The base of this feature survives as a spread of broken stone. Some of the bank stones may be present in the adjacent ditches, but this is not certain.

Fig. 5.26 Narrow slot with stake settings, and small pit (bottom-centre), Sruhaun.

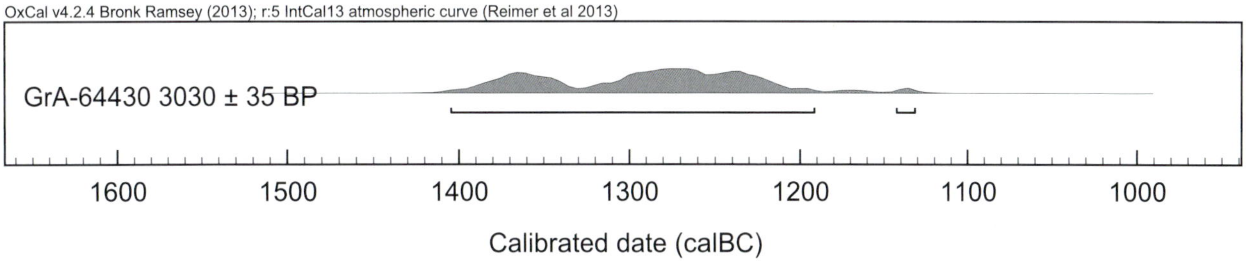

Fig. 5.27 Radiocarbon dates for the Sruhaun enclosure (calibration after OxCal v.4.2.4).

2. An *outer ditch* directly inside the bank.
3. An *inner ditch* directly inside the outer ditch.
4. A possible *inner bank* of earth and possibly some stone, now levelled, that may have been located on the inside of the inner ditch. The existence of such a bank, built with soil upcast from one or both ditches, is suggested by a spread of redeposited subsoil over the latter, likely placed there when this bank was levelled in modern times.

Radiocarbon dating confirms that these were not contemporary features, and so some rebuilding of the enclosure occurred on one or more occasions. The inner bank is likely to be contemporary with one or both of the ditches from where that bank material derived. The two ditches seem to be of much later date than the outer bank, as they do not contain any fine sediment derived from erosion of the latter. This possibility is supported by the late date for the commencement of peat growth in one of these ditches. The original height of the inner and outer banks is uncertain. Based on the amount of soil extracted from both ditches, and the amount of stone dumped there subsequently, neither bank/wall is likely to have exceeded a metre in height.

The excavation did not produce any evidence for occupation of the Sruhaun enclosure. The absence of material culture, food residues or structural remains could be explained by the limited nature of the excavation, but it is consistent with a geophysical survey that did not identify built structures inside the enclosure. This, together with the slight nature of the outer bank, means the site should not be regarded as a hillfort, particularly as there is no evidence of fortification. The likelihood that this enclosure was broadly contemporary with the nearby hillfort of Rathnagree does raise questions as to their relationship. One possibility is that Sruhaun was a livestock enclosure for the occupants of nearby Rathnagree hillfort.

The Sruhaun excavation did not yield much information on the final use of this enclosure. The geophysical survey records high magnetic gradiometry readings along the enclosing element, created by the stone bank and its underlying burnt layer. In the absence of post-holes or stake settings associated with the bank, there is no evidence of any wooden fencing that might have been destroyed by fire. The stones used to build the outer bank were subsequently dumped into both ditches, which must have been open when that levelling occurred. Radiocarbon dating of peat in the lower ditch suggests this occurred in the early modern era. The destruction of the putative inner bank is represented by soil levelled from that feature spread over both ditches, which were already partially infilled with peat and stone from the outer bank. This probably occurred during agricultural clearance in the modern era, which implies that the levelling of the outer bank must have been an earlier event.

TINORAN

This hillfort is located on the summit of a prominent hill (312m OD) 2km N/NW of Baltinglass town (see Fig. 2.23 and Fig. 5.28). Tinoran ('House of Odhrán') is one of the largest hillforts in Ireland, at least 56ha in extent and possibly as much as 84ha. The site is divided equally between the townlands of Tinoran Hill North and Tinoran Hill South, with panoramic views from the summit. Sadly, much of the hillfort is covered today by conifer forestry, which has destroyed large parts of the interior (Fig. 5.29). The site was first recorded by the Archaeological Survey of Ireland (Condit 1992) and subsequently listed in the *Record of Monuments and Places* for Co. Wicklow (WI026-004; Grogan and Kilfeather 1997). There is no earlier history of research on, nor any local traditions about, this hillfort.

There are four or possibly five widely spaced enclosing elements at Tinoran hillfort (Figs 5.30 and 5.31). The inner enclosure is a small, circular earthwork, 45–50m in diameter over 0.06ha, on the summit (312m OD) of this prominent hill. It is enclosed by a stone-faced bank, 2.2m wide and 0.9–1.2m high, with a mostly infilled outer ditch, 1.6m wide and 0.8m deep. There are traces of an internal ditch on the south-western side, though this needs to be confirmed. The interior of the enclosure is today planted with trees, and there are no visible archaeological features. This is the only enclosure at Tinoran hillfort recorded as an antiquity (labelled 'Round O') by the Ordnance Survey in its nineteenth-century mapping. Liam Price described the Round O as 'about 65 yards in diameter, surrounded by a single, much ruined, bank of stones and earth' (1949a, 150–1). A stone mortar of unknown date was found *c.*1939 in an 'old wall' at the Round O (National Museum of Ireland record).

The second enclosure is oval in shape, over an area of 4.67ha along the 300m contour (296–304m OD). The enclosing element is incorporated into modern field patterns, some of which are depicted on the Ordnance Survey historic mapping. This is best preserved at the south-west, where it survives as an 8m-wide by 2m-high bank of large stones, built on a steep slope, with no indication of an associated ditch. A hut structure (WI026-004001) is recorded inside the southern section of the bank. This is a D-shaped platform, 14m by 12m, cut into the hillslope, with a 1.2–1.3m-wide boulder wall on the northern and eastern slopes. Other occupation features are difficult to identity as most of the enclosure is covered by dense forestry, with significant damage caused by deep ploughing and recurring planting and harvesting of conifers.

The third enclosure is sub-oval, over an area of 14.46ha, surrounded by a 65–127m bank outside the second enclosure (Fig. 5.30). This bank follows the 280m contour (276–284m OD) along its 1.37km perimeter. The southern half of the bank is incorporated into a later field wall. The original bank survives best on the south-western side, where

Fig. 5.28 Aerial photograph of Tinoran hillfort prior to forestry (Irish Air Corps, unknown date; after Condit 1998, plate 6).

Fig. 5.29 Aerial photograph (*c.*2016) of Tinoran hillfort with forest cover, showing location of two excavation trenches. Source: Google Earth.

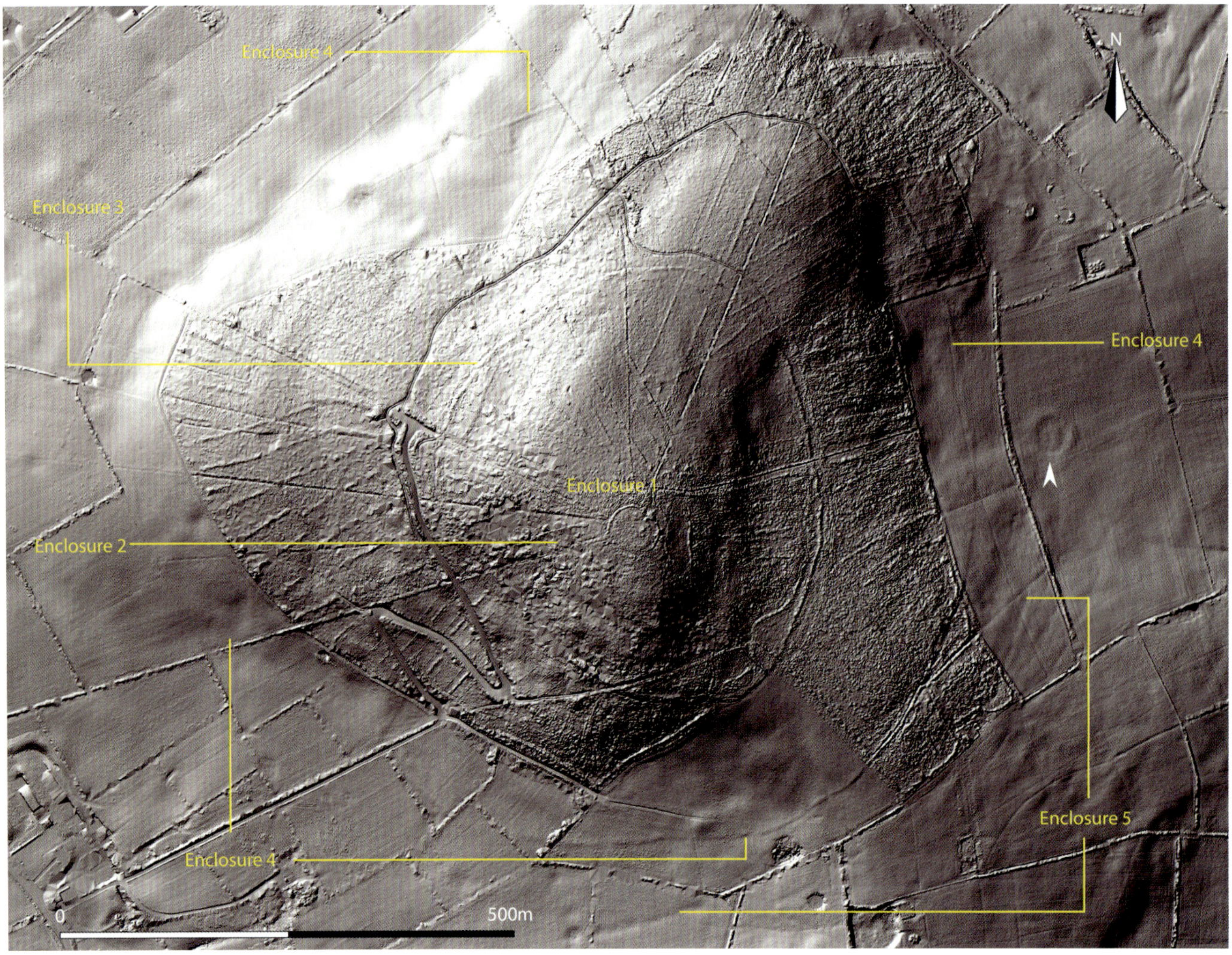

Fig. 5.30 Recent LiDAR image of Tinoran hillfort, showing location of widely spaced enclosures. Location of large ring-barrow (white arrow) outside eastern side of fourth enclosure.

it is under dense scrub and gorse growth. It is of similar construction to the second enclosure, consisting of a low-rise bank of boulders and large stones, 6m wide and 3.2m in external height. There is no indication of an associated ditch.

Examination of aerial photographs at Tinoran revealed a fourth enclosure covering an area of 55.74ha (Condit 1998, 15). The southern half of this enclosure survives as a low-rise bank in agricultural land at an elevation of 221–244m OD (Fig. 5.30). This bank is *c.*6m wide and up to 0.3m high, with a slight indication of an outer ditch. A large ring-barrow (WI026-005), 55m in diameter, abuts the enclosure on its eastern side. This has a low, domed interior, 16–22m in width and 0.4m in height, surrounded by a 7–9m-wide ditch, with an outer bank, 11–18m in width and 0.3m in average height.

LiDAR survey conducted for this project identified a possible fifth enclosure at Tinoran, 50–97m outside the previous example (Fig. 5.30). This is best preserved to the south, where it survives as a low-rise bank with an external ditch 8.2–11.6m wide and up to 1.2m deep. If confirmed, this extends the site area to *c.*84ha, making this one of the largest hillforts in Ireland, second only to the Spinans Hill 2 enclosure (131ha), also at Baltinglass.

Excavation

Due to dense forestry, most of Tinoran hillfort could not be surveyed with GNSS or geophysical techniques, while LiDAR survey obtained at 0.5m resolution is of limited value. Sample excavation was conducted at the hillfort in August 2015. Two trenches were excavated across the

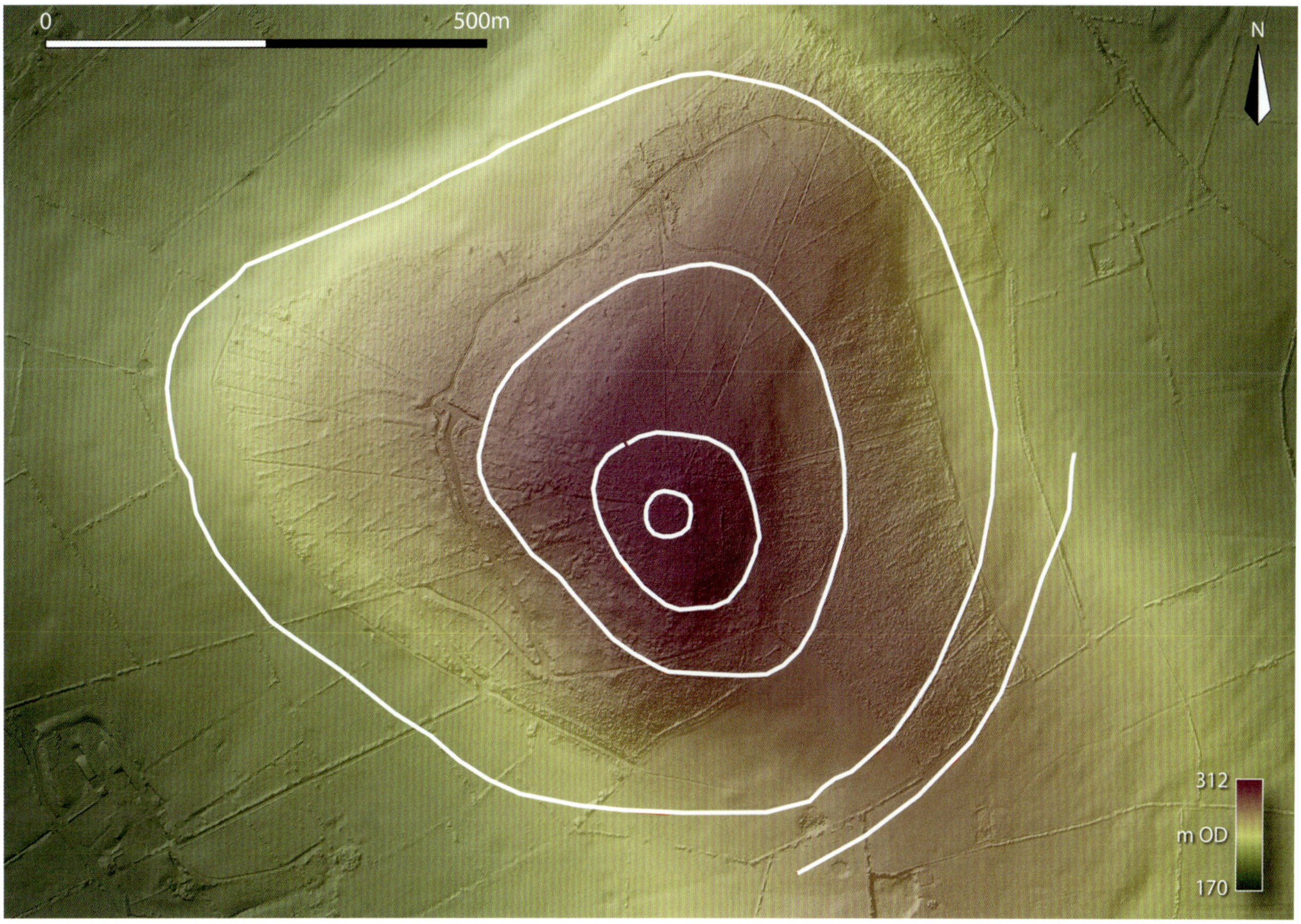

Fig. 5.31 Plan of Tinoran hillfort showing four confirmed enclosures, with a possible fifth example to be confirmed.

defences of the third and fourth enclosures respectively (the results are summarised here, with detail in O'Brien and O'Driscoll 2017, 281–99).

TRENCH 1 (FOURTH ENCLOSURE)

A single trench, measuring 10m by 2m, was excavated across the line of a levelled bank on the south-eastern side of the hillfort (Fig. 5.29). This trench was located on the eastern side of a large pasture field, which was cultivated at various times in the modern era. The bank is visible as a low slope over a distance of 4m, with no exposed stones or visible ditch (Fig. 5.32). The natural soil at this location is podzolised, with a dark-brown, organic silt overlying a thin layer of red/brown iron pan on bright-orange, stony silt subsoil. The absence of a leached layer in this podzol profile may be explained by recent cultivation.

Excavation uncovered a large, earth-cut ditch, inside which was the base of a levelled bank (Fig. 5.33). The ditch has a U-shaped profile, 1.7–1.8m wide, narrowing to 0.4–0.5m at the base, with a cut depth of 0.6–0.8m, or 0.9m from modern ground level (Fig. 5.34). The smooth sides of the ditch had a 45° slope dug into subsoil. The lower inner slope of the ditch was interrupted by a narrow ledge, 0.4–0.5m wide and 0.1–0.15m deep. This feature was part of the primary ditch cut, though its purpose is unknown. When this ledge is included, the overall width of the ditch is approximately 3.3m, with a central cut depth of 0.8m.

The filling of the ditch commenced with a thin deposit of bright-orange silt, derived from primary erosion of the cut. This basal sediment contained numerous flecks of charcoal and was overlain by a thin deposit of mottled, orange/brown silt, also with flecks of charcoal. This was covered by a deposit of compact, mid-brown silt, again with flecks of charcoal. The next layer was a compact grey silt containing lenses of red/orange iron pan, which was in turn overlain by a deposit of mid-brown silt with flecks of

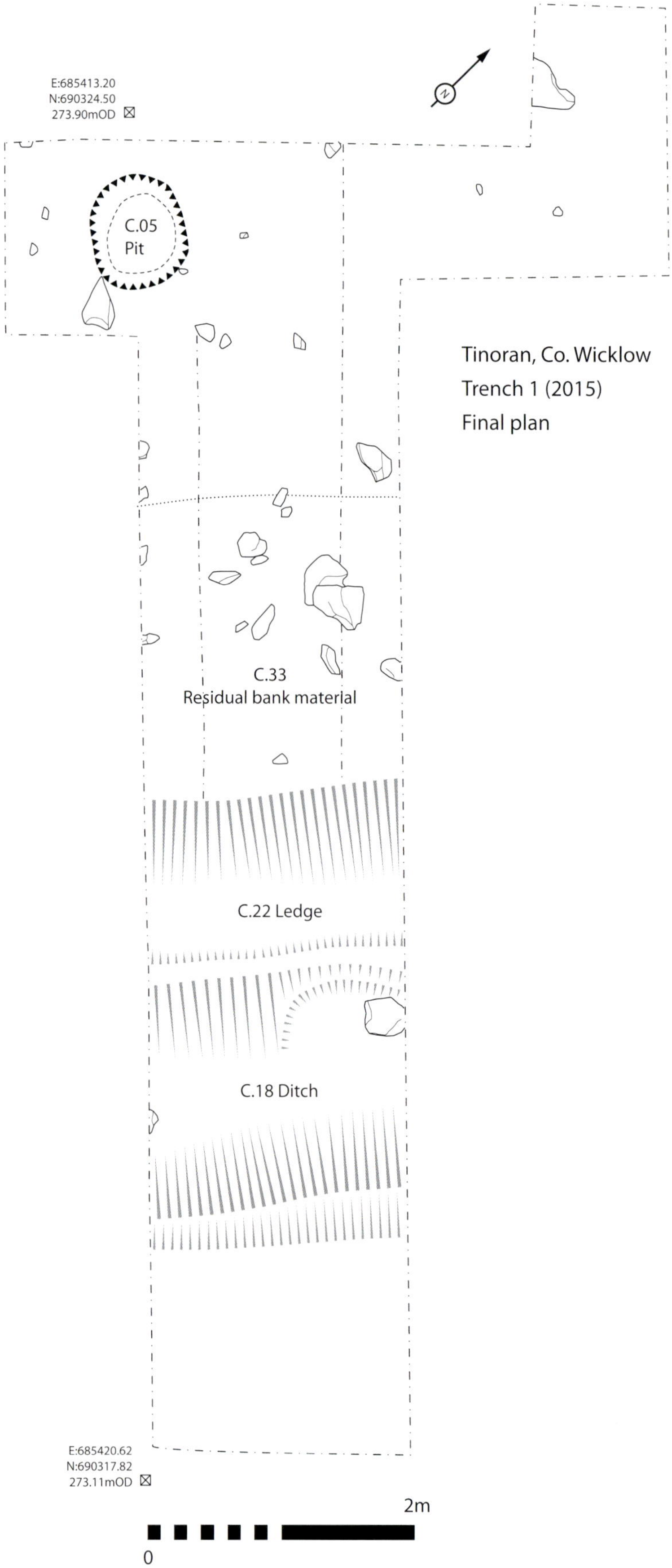
E:685413.20
N:690324.50
273.90mOD
C.05
Pit
Tinoran, Co. Wicklow
Trench 1 (2015)
Final plan
C.33
Residual bank material
C.22 Ledge
C.18 Ditch
E:685420.62
N:690317.82
273.11mOD
2m
0

Fig. 5.36 Bank of third enclosure, visible as a band of bracken growth across southern slope of Tinoran Hill. Trench 2 was located in centre of photograph.

charcoal forming the upper fill of the ditch. The latter included a lens of black, compact silt overlain by a small deposit of grey/brown silt on the western side of ditch. There are no artifact finds from these ditch sediments. Excavation also revealed a thin deposit of yellow/dark-brown mottled silt at the base of the narrow ledge on the lower, inner side of ditch. This sediment contained flecks and small lumps of charcoal. The upper fill of the ledge consisted of orange/brown, sandy silt, overlain on the eastern side by a lens of mid-brown silt.

The infilling of the main ditch was interrupted by a 0.05–0.09m-thick layer of grey/brown organic silt—a buried sod that separates the earlier fill from later deposits. This was overlain on the inner side of ditch by a spread of dark-brown, sandy silt, derived from levelling the adjacent bank. The landowner, Mr Victor O'Neill, recalled his father employed a local man *c.*1955 to level by spade a 'three-foot high bank' into the open ditch.

Excavation exposed a spread of residual bank material underneath the organic topsoil, 0.7m inside the ditch. This compact deposit of orange, sandy silt was 1.2–1.4m wide by 0.02–0.09m thick and contained only a few small stones. None of these was fire-reddened and there was no charcoal in this residual bank. That deposit overlay a 0.02–0.04m-thick layer of black, organic silt with few clasts, which extended 1.8–2.2m from the inner edge of the ditch. This represents an old ground surface beneath the former bank; it had a few flecks of charcoal present, but no archaeological material to indicate pre-enclosure activity.

Opposite page

(Top-left) Fig. 5.32 Excavation of Trench 1, Tinoran, looking north-west. The infilled ditch is visible as a dark band across centre of trench, beyond which the levelled bank is exposed as lighter soil with some large stones.

(Right) Fig. 5.33 Post-excavation plan, Trench 1, Tinoran.

(Left) Fig. 5.34 Post-excavation view of ditch, Trench 1 (looking south). Note ledge on inner slope of ditch (lower-centre).

(Bottom-left) Fig. 5.35 General view of pit (bottom-centre) in relation to excavated bank (top-centre) and ditch (top-right), Trench 1, Tinoran.

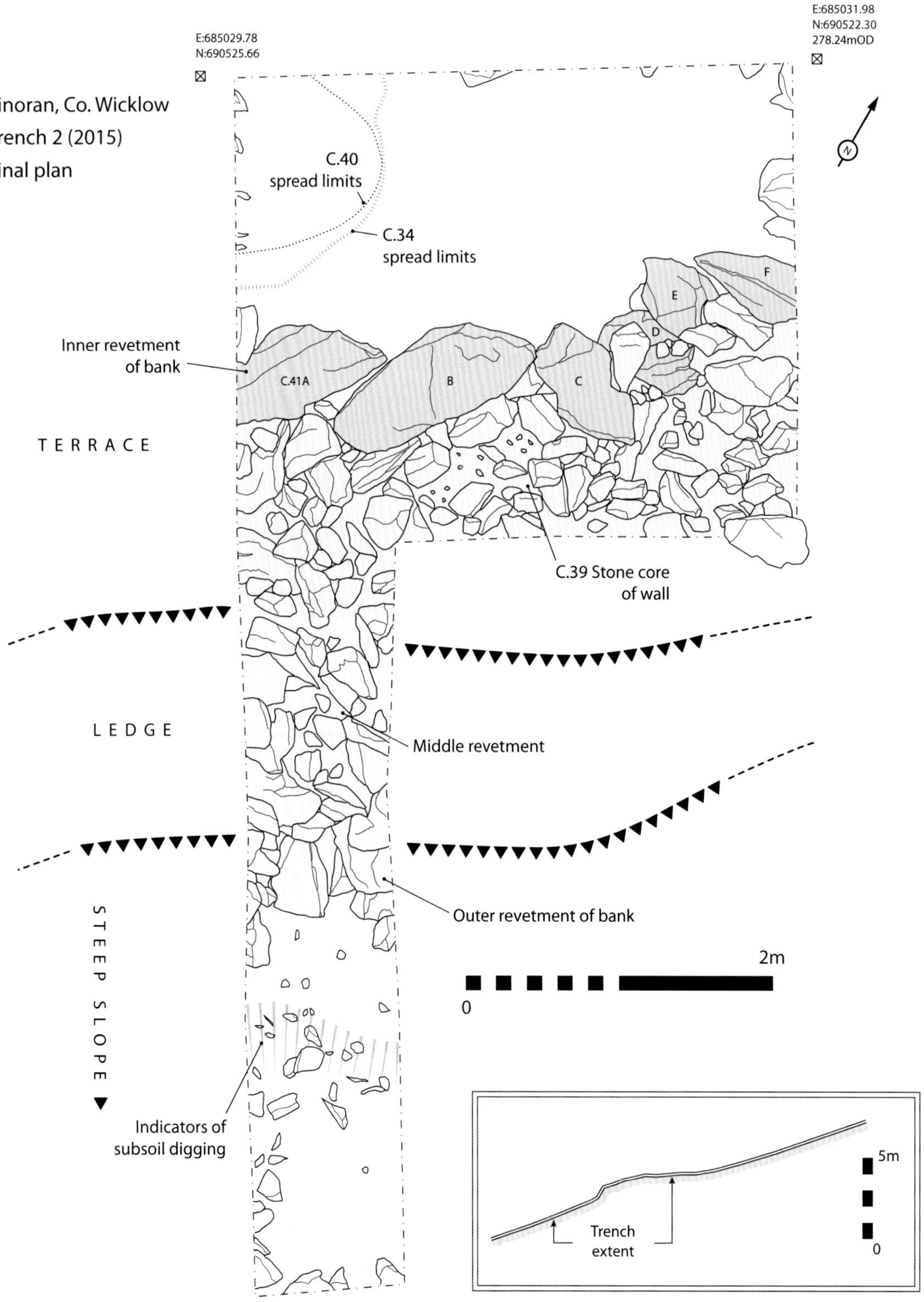

Fig. 5.37 Post-excavation plan, Trench 2, Tinoran.

A small, circular pit was discovered inside the bank in the north-western corner of Trench 1 (Fig. 5.33). The pit was 0.87m (N–S) by 0.85m (E–W) on top, and 0.6m (N–S) by 0.55m (E–W) at base, with sides sloping steeply to an irregularly flat base at a depth of 0.46m (Fig. 5.35). The upper fill was comprised of black, organic silt with some small stones and flecks of charcoal. A lower fill of grey/light-brown, sandy silt did not contain charcoal or other archaeological material.

No early artifacts were found in Trench 1. A sample of oak sapwood charcoal from the lower fill of the ditch was submitted for radiocarbon dating (see Appendix 1). This gave a result of 805–785 BC (2600 ± 30 BP; GrA-64438).

Trench 1 Discussion

Excavation confirmed that the fourth enclosure of this hillfort was surrounded by a single bank and ditch earthwork, which was levelled in the modern era. No evidence of pre-enclosure activity was found. The enclosing element consisted of a shallow, earth-cut ditch, the soil from which was dumped on the inside to form a low bank with no obvious revetment. No stone was used in the construction of this bank, nor is there any evidence of wooden fencing. Based on the ditch size, the original height of the bank is unlikely to have exceeded 1.5m, with a combined bank/ditch height of perhaps 2–2.5m. The ditch remained open for a long period, with primary erosion of the cut followed by an influx of organic silt, as well as eroded sediment from the bank. Radiocarbon dating of charcoal from the basal fill of the ditch suggests continued occupation of the hillfort into the Late Bronze Age. There is no evidence that the defences of the fourth enclosure were deliberately destroyed.

The only other feature discovered in Trench 1 was a large pit inside the bank. The excavation trench was extended one metre to the east to investigate the possibility of a line of post-holes connected to a wooden palisade inside the bank. No other pits were identified in the excavation of a 3m-wide space east of the pit. Magnetic gradiometry survey was also undertaken over a 20m distance to the west of this pit in search of similar examples. The results were negative, and so this remains an isolated feature.

TRENCH 2 (THIRD ENCLOSURE)

A single trench was excavated across the visible bank on the south-western side of the third enclosure at Tinoran hillfort (see Fig. 5.29). Prior to excavation the bank was visible as a 4–5m-wide band of ferns crossing an area of heavy gorse growth, with no trees in that area (Fig. 5.36). The excavation trench was 4m (NW/SE) by 3m (NE/SW), with a 5m by 1m extension on the southern side cutting across the bank (Figs 5.37 and 5.38).

Fig. 5.38 Post-excavation rectified photograph, Trench 2, Tinoran.

The removal of a thin sod and peaty soil revealed that two layers were deposited to create a level surface on which to build the bank. This began with a deposit of grey/light-brown silt that contained some charcoal radiocarbon dated

Fig. 5.39 Excavation of slope below stone bank, Trench 2, Tinoran. This slope was dug into at two levels (centre and top of photograph), to create a platform for the bank construction.

1110–980 BC (2865±35 BP; GrA-64439). This layer was 0.12m thick at the eastern end of the trench, thinning to 0.08m under the bank. A number of coarseware sherds (15E0321:02–106), probably from a single vessel, were trampled into the upper surface of this layer on the inner side of the bank. A whetstone (15E0321:01) was also discovered in the upper part of this deposit, close to where the pottery was found.

This grey/light-brown silt layer was overlain by a layer of orange/brown, stony sediment, which was also found on the inner side of and beneath the hillfort bank. This contained numerous small stones of slate-like form, possibly derived from soil dug from the slope below and outside the bank (Fig. 5.39). This material was spread on top of the grey/light-brown silt to further level the slope for bank construction.

The bank itself was built entirely of large boulders and smaller stones, with no soil component. The inner side comprised of a line of large boulders, mostly in a recumbent position, placed either contiguously or with a slight overlap (Fig. 5.40). The excavation area exposed six of these boulders on the pre-bank levelled surface. These were 0.72–1.47m in maximum length, sub-rectangular to sub-ovoid in cross-section, with a weathered appearance and no fractured surfaces. They were mostly horizontal, and in some cases were propped underneath by smaller stones.

The core of the bank consisted of grey sandstone clasts of weathered appearance, with an average size of 0.33m. These stones were piled loosely inside the boulder kerb, with no obvious coursing. They were retained by two possible settings of small boulders within the centre and outer side of the bank (see Fig. 5.38). This seems likely, but was difficult to confirm as the excavation trench was only one metre wide on that side. Excavation also revealed a small amount of redeposited subsoil against the lower exterior side of the bank, probably placed there as part of the construction process.

Occupation

Excavation uncovered a thin spread of dark-brown/black, fine silt inside the stone bank in the north-eastern corner of the trench (Fig. 5.41). This burnt sediment contained charcoal and fragments of burnt bone radiocarbon dated 899–803 BC (2685±30 BP; GrA-64571), which derived from a small hearth in the vicinity where some cooking probably occurred. The burnt sediment directly overlay a layer of orange/brown, stony sediment on which the bank was built. This in turn overlay a lower hearth deposit in the same corner of the excavation trench (Fig. 5.42). That 1–3cm-thick spread of dark-brown/black, fine silt had a similar high charcoal content with small fragments of burnt bone, radiocarbon dated 825–795 BC (2640±30 BP; GrA-64572).

These hearth fires were followed by a prolonged period of natural slopewash on the inner side of the hillfort bank. A layer of light-brown silt, overlain by mid-brown silt, was deposited to a combined thickness of 0.15–0.28m. There was no archaeological material in this sediment. This natural sedimentation continued with a build-up of organic silt on the inner side of the bank. This contained a number of large stones that represent tumble from the bank. A similar tumble of large stones was excavated in organic soil along the lower slope on the outer side of the bank.

The only artifacts from Tinoran Trench 2 are a

Fig. 5.40 Line of boulders forming inner kerb of stone bank, Trench 2, Tinoran.

whetstone and a small quantity of prehistoric pot sherds. The whetstone (15E0321:01) was found in a dark-brown/black, fine silt layer inside the hillfort bank. This is a cuboid, almost perfectly rectangular, stone, 127mm by 41mm by 38mm, with flat ends and very smooth surfaces (Fig. 5.43). The lithology is a grey, fine-grained, micaceous sandstone. Three of the four sides are slightly concave, with obvious wear related to use as a sharpening stone.

Bronze Age pottery at Tinoran

Fragments of a broken pot were recovered from the surface of the grey/light-brown silt construction layer inside the bank of the third enclosure. There are 108 sherds (605.2g) in the assemblage, mostly body fragments with some rim and base sherds, representing about 20% of a single vessel (Cleary in O'Brien and O'Driscoll 2017, 296–7). This is a relatively large, bucket-shaped vessel, with a flat rim and slightly footed base (Fig. 5.44). The rim diameter is estimated at 20cm, the base diameter at 14cm, with a vessel height of *c.*19cm. The wall thickness is 9–11mm, being thickest at the base. The vessel is coil-built and evenly fired, with a fine texture and some use of granite temper. The uniform colour suggests controlled temperatures in a kiln. The temper and mica-rich clay indicate a likely local manufacture. Radiocarbon dating of organic sediment on the inner surface of one of the sherds returned a date of 1155–1020 BC (2905 ± 35 BP; GrA-64440).

There is a row of perforations spaced 30mm apart, 7mm below the rim (Fig. 5.45). These perforations are punched through from the outside, and measure 3mm in external diameter tapering to 1mm internally. The holes may have been decorative or used to suspend the vessel, or perhaps to allow steam escape if the vessel was used as a lidded cooking pot (the absence of external soot or surface blackening suggests it was not used over an open fire). There are substantial charred residues on the inside of the vessel,

Fig. 5.41 Charcoal spread inside stone bank, Trench 2, Tinoran.

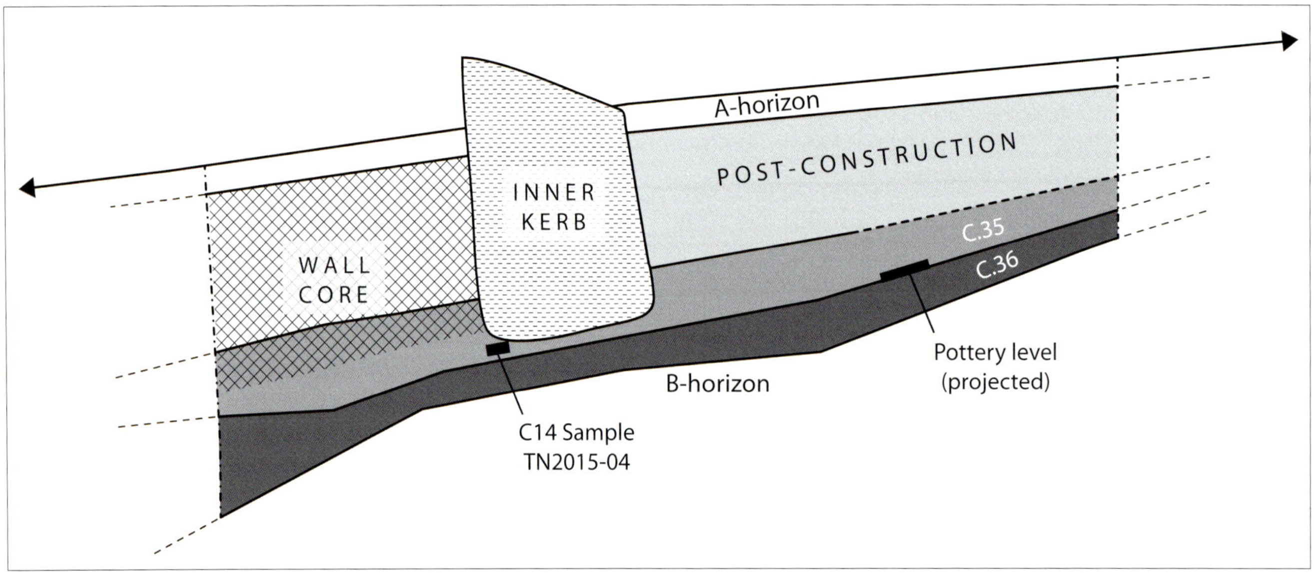

Fig. 5.42 Schematic section across hillfort bank, Trench 2, Tinoran.

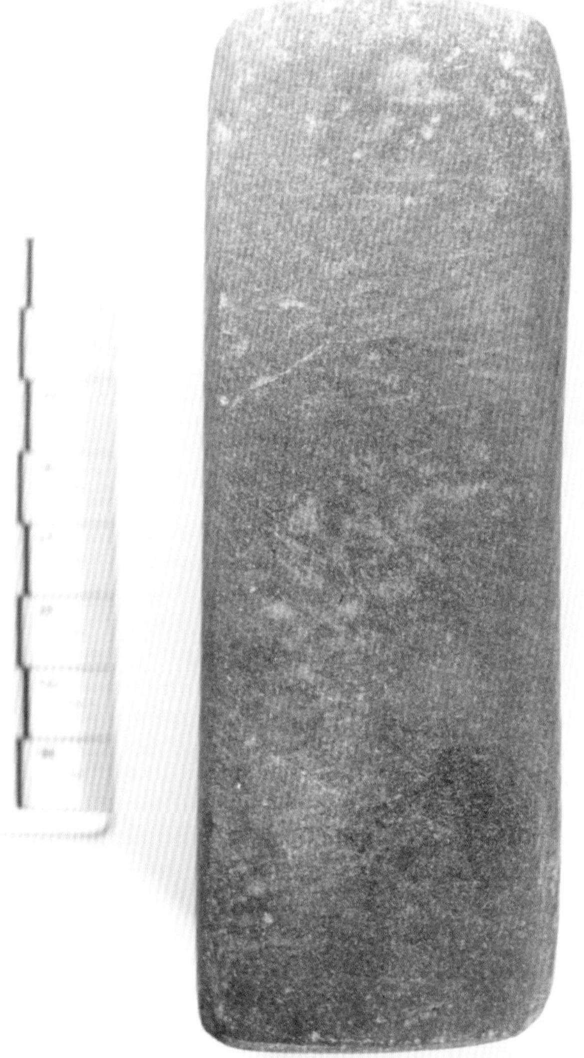

Fig. 5.43 Whetstone from Trench 2, Tinoran.

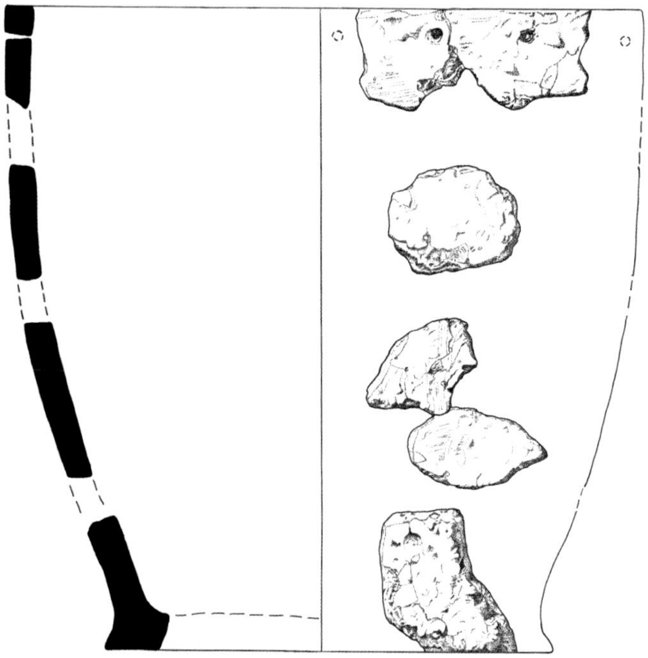

Fig. 5.44 Reconstruction of pot from Trench 2, Tinoran.

associated with use; these are mostly around the rim and upper body rather than the base.

Pottery of similar type is recorded from other Irish hillforts, including Freestone Hill, Co. Kilkenny; Rathgall, Co. Wicklow; and Navan Fort, Co. Armagh (Raftery 1969; McCorry 1997; Grogan and Roche 2009, 41). It is also well known within the Lough Gur Class II range of pottery from Late Bronze Age sites at Lough Gur, Co. Limerick (Cleary 2018). Pottery with perforations below the rim was recovered from the enclosures at Circle L and Circle K at Lough Gur, which were probably built during the Middle Bronze Age (Cleary 2003, 144–46). Similar pottery is recorded at an enclosed site on Knockadoon dated *c.*1400–1100 BC. (Cleary 2003, figs 20–21). These parallels confirm that the Tinoran vessel belongs to a widespread ceramic tradition in later Bronze Age Ireland.

Discussion

Radiocarbon dating indicates a date of 1155–980 BC for construction of the third enclosure of Tinoran hillfort (Fig. 5.46). This is based on the dating of pottery residues from the construction surface (GrA-64440) and charcoal from construction sediment directly below the stone bank (GrA-64439). There are no indications of activity at this location prior to construction of the hillfort bank.

The third enclosure at Tinoran was surrounded by a single substantial bank of stones, built on a slight break of slope along the steep southern side of the hill. This was achieved by digging into the slope to create a 1.3m-wide ledge. The soil, stones and broken rock removed in this way was piled on the upslope side of the ledge, to create a 3–4m-wide stretch of level ground. The wall was then built on this platform in the following sequence:

1. A contiguous line of massive boulders was arranged on top of the introduced layers on the platform. This formed

Fig. 5.45 Sherds of Bronze Age pottery with rim perforations, Trench 2, Tinoran.

the inner kerb of the bank, with the aim of reducing slopewash erosion of this structure.

2. A central line of large stones and some small boulders was stacked against the inner side of the ledge. This served to consolidate the loose, stony core of the bank.
3. A facing of similarly sized stones was stacked on the outside of the ledge to form the outer kerb of the bank. A small amount of redeposited subsoil was piled against the base of these facing stones.
4. The spaces between these three structures were then filled with medium to large stones. The stones were packed tightly together, but were not coursed. The end result was a stone bank measuring 3.5–3.7m in width, with an internal height of 0.6–0.8m; it was probably 1m or so originally. The stones used were surface drift material, probably gathered from the surrounding hill; there is no evidence of any quarried material. The large boulders of the inner kerb were probably rolled downslope into position, a process that required considerable effort. No soil was used in the bank, which is consistent with the absence of a ditch.

Occupation and abandonment

A small fire connected to the cooking of food was lit directly inside the stone bank during the early occupation of this enclosure. This is represented by two spreads of charcoal and burnt bone overlying each other in the northern corner of the trench. The lower deposit was directly on subsoil that was fire-reddened in places, suggesting an informal hearth. This burnt spread was overlain in the northern corner of the trench by a deposit of grey silt, covered in turn by a thin spread of orange-brown silt. The latter was then covered by a second deposit of charcoal and burnt bone. This overlay the entire hearth deposit, but was slightly wider in extent.

Initially, the two fire events were considered to have occurred separately in time, with a possible pre-bank hearth and a later example. The fact that the burnt spreads were similar in size and composition suggests another possibility.

Both fires may have been lit within a shallow pit, dug through the construction layers for a depth of 0.15–0.18m, down to the subsoil surface. The initial fire in this hearth pit was used for cooking, as indicated by the presence of burnt bone. This burnt sediment was subsequently covered by two spreads of sterile soil derived from the digging of the hearth pit. This explains why the sides of this hearth pit were not clearly visible in excavation, as the fill and cut material were very similar. A second cooking fire was lit soon afterwards at this location, represented by the charcoal and burnt bone in the overlying spread. Both fire events in this hearth pit are likely to have happened close together in time, possibly in the space of a matter of days. Radiocarbon dating of burnt bone from both hearth deposits (GrA-64571 and GrA-64572) indicate a date range of *c.*890–795 BC. This is significant, as it indicates continued occupation of the hillfort several centuries after it was built. There is no information available on the abandonment of this hillfort. Evidence for partial collapse and erosion of the bank exterior is consistent with natural erosion over a long period.

The defences of the third and fourth enclosures at Tinoran are markedly different in character. The former is a carefully built stone bank, while the fourth enclosure was protected by bank-and-ditch earthwork. This might indicate that the enclosures were built at different times, but it could also reflect topography at the respective locations. The stone bank of the third enclosure was built on a very steep slope, where an earthen bank and accompanying ditch would have been difficult to build. Such features were feasible on the more gentle slopes where the fourth enclosure is located, however. Other factors that may explain the different construction methods are the availability of stone, and the visual significance attached to different enclosures in this hillfort.

The Tinoran excavation did not produce much evidence for the occupation of this hillfort, mainly because the two trenches focused on the enclosing elements of the monument. The crushed pottery vessel and whetstone found in Trench 2 represent occupation during the construction of this stone bank enclosure, *c.*1155–980 BC. The small hearth inside that bank can be linked to continued occupation of the hillfort several centuries later, *c.*890–795 BC. There is no evidence from either trench for deliberate destruction connected to warfare.

BRONZE AGE HILLFORTS AT BALTINGLASS

This project has identified two hillforts (Rathnagree and Tinoran) and a hilltop enclosure (Sruhaun) of later Bronze Age date at Baltinglass. There may be other examples, possibly Brusselstown Ring, Kilranelagh or Corballis, but those sites are not dated. In the case of Rathnagree and Tinoran, radiocarbon dating indicates those two hillforts were not in contemporary use. The former was built and occupied during the fifteenth to thirteenth century BC, overlapping with use of the nearby Sruhaun enclosure.

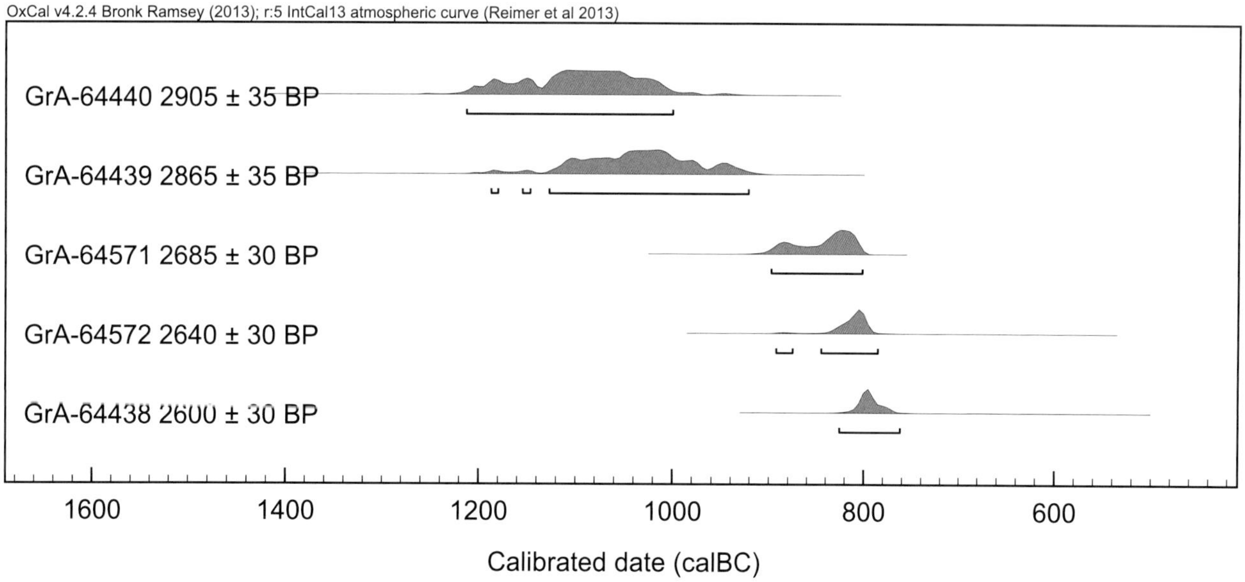

Fig. 5.46 Radiocarbon dates for Tinoran hillfort (calibration after OxCal v.4.2.4)

Tinoran hillfort is later in date and was probably built during the twelfth or eleventh century BC, with occupation to at least the ninth century BC. Together, these sites represent a hillfort presence at Baltinglass from the Middle to the Late Bronze Age. This occupation spanned the same ceramic tradition, as evidenced by the pots from Rathnagree and Tinoran, though whether that speaks to settlement continuity is unclear.

The two hillforts have a similar design, based on concentric, widely spaced, multiple enclosures: three in the case of Rathnagree and four, or possibly five, at Tinoran. There is variation in the respective enclosing elements, with wooden palisades at Rathnagree (Period 1) and stone banks at Tinoran (second and third enclosures). Both hillforts also employed earthworks in the form of a single bank-and-ditch defence (Rathnagree Period 2 middle enclosure and Tinoran fourth enclosure). All three Period 1 palisades at Rathnagree were broadly contemporary, whereas only two of the four–five enclosures at Tinoran are dated.

The contemporaneous use of the Rathnagree and Sruhaun enclosures on Tuckmill Hill raises the question of their functional relationship. With no evidence of occupation or fortification at Sruhaun, this site was possibly an animal stockade used by the residents of Rathnagree hillfort in the management of open pasture on the slopes on Tuckmill Hill. As to occupation evidence from Rathnagree or Tinoran, the record should be viewed against the limited amount of excavation undertaken at both sites. There is also poor archaeological visibility at Tinoran due to forestry, with the possibility that many hut sites similar to a recorded example (WI026-004001) remain to be discovered. The discovery of Bronze Age pottery in two small trenches at Rathnagree and Tinoran respectively is a strong indication of residential occupation of both hillforts.

Finally, one of the significant findings of these excavations is the deliberate destruction of Rathnagree hillfort and its subsequent rebuilding during the Middle Bronze Age. This event was broadly contemporary with the burning of the first enclosure at Sruhaun, which was also rebuilt in the same period as Rathnagree. The circumstances surrounding those events are unclear, as is the final abandonment of Tinoran hillfort, where no evidence of destruction was found. This is a subject we will return to in Chapter 9, when considering the hillfort wars of the later Bronze Age in Ireland

6. OTHER HILLFORTS AND ENCLOSURES IN BALTINGLASS

James O'Driscoll

Having looked at the excavation results from six hillforts at Baltinglass, we will now consider those sites that have not been excavated. Recent survey suggests there may be as many as thirteen large enclosures on the various hills of this landscape (see Fig. 2.23). There are distinct clusters on Baltinglass Hill, Spinans Hill and Kilranelagh Hill, along with isolated sites on a number of other hills. Other prehistoric monuments of interest include a number of cursus earthworks and embanked stones circles, part of a wider cultural landscape encompassing upland and lowland settlement in the Baltinglass area (Fig. 6.1).

SPINANS HILL

As discussed in Chapter 2, one of the most important clusters of hillforts at Baltinglass is on Spinans Hill, in the shadow of Keadeen Mountain to the east (Figs 6.2 and 6.3). The recorded sites are Brusselstown Ring, Spinans Hill 1 and the Spinans Hill 2 contour enclosure. All three lie on a prominent NE/SW ridge with two summits. The northern summit (410m OD) is the location of the Spinans Hill 1 enclosure examined in Chapter 4. The southern summit (400m OD) is surrounded by Brusselstown Ring, while the

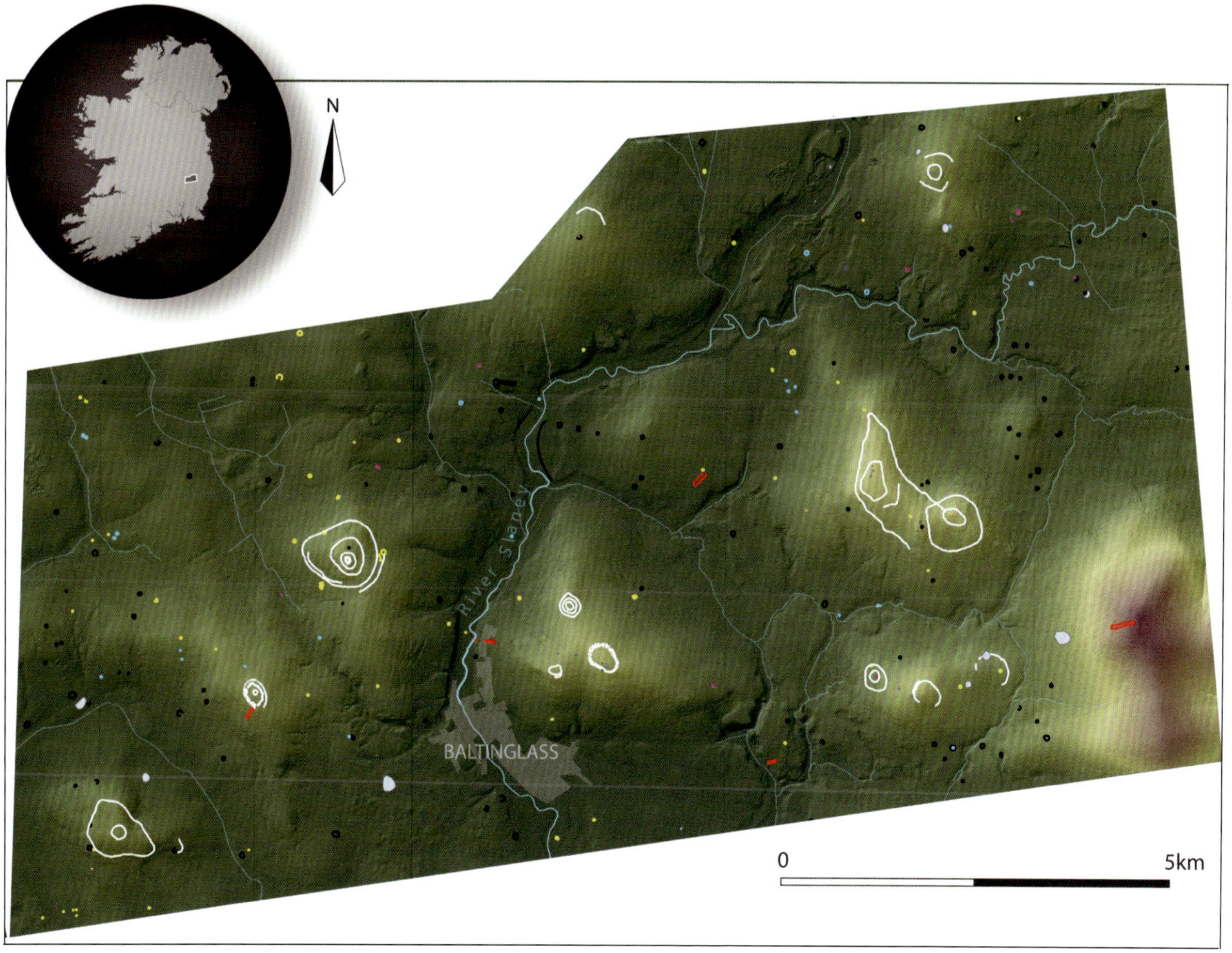

Fig. 6.1 Distribution of monuments in the Baltinglass landscape after LiDAR survey in this project, which has almost doubled the number of known archaeological sites.

Fig. 6.2 The Spinans Hill landscape with Brusselstown Ring (centre), viewed from the summit of Keadeen Mountain.

large enclosure of Spinans Hill 2 encloses the upper slopes of the entire ridge. While Spinans Hill 1 is tentatively dated to the Early Neolithic, the chronology of Brusselstown Ring and Spinans Hill 2 is not known, as neither site has been excavated.

Brusselstown Ring

This impressive monument (WI027-018) lies on a flat summit overlooking the Glen of Imaal to the north-east (Figs 6.4–6.6). There are two concentric, stone-walled enclosures, 124–305m apart, over an area of 37.81ha. The hillfort lies within the townlands of Brusselstown and Castlequarter, with the southern side of the inner stone enclosure forming the townland boundary. There are panoramic views from the site, only impeded on the northern side by the summit where Spinans Hill 1 is located.

The inner enclosure and the eastern side of the outer stone enclosure are depicted in the nineteenth-century mapping of the Ordnance Survey. The well-preserved nature of the inner stone enclosure drew the interest of the historian Liam Price, who visited the monument numerous times from the 1920s to 1940s, in the company of eminent scholars including the German archaeologists Gerhard Bersu and Adolf Mahr. Price made the following record of Brusselstown Ring during a visit in June 1947:

> *The total length of the wall is about 900 yrds, and it is in shape a fairly regular ellipse with the long axis lying ESE and WNW — about 300 yrds long and about 200 yrds wide. It follows (that is the wall) the contour of the hill at a fairly consistent level, about 1270 ft or so: it could not have been put at a lower level because it would have had to dip down at certain points where the slope below this level is very steep: so it was evidently built so as to take in as large a space as would be conveniently possible. The inside space is pretty tough, with big outcrops of rock especially at the highest*

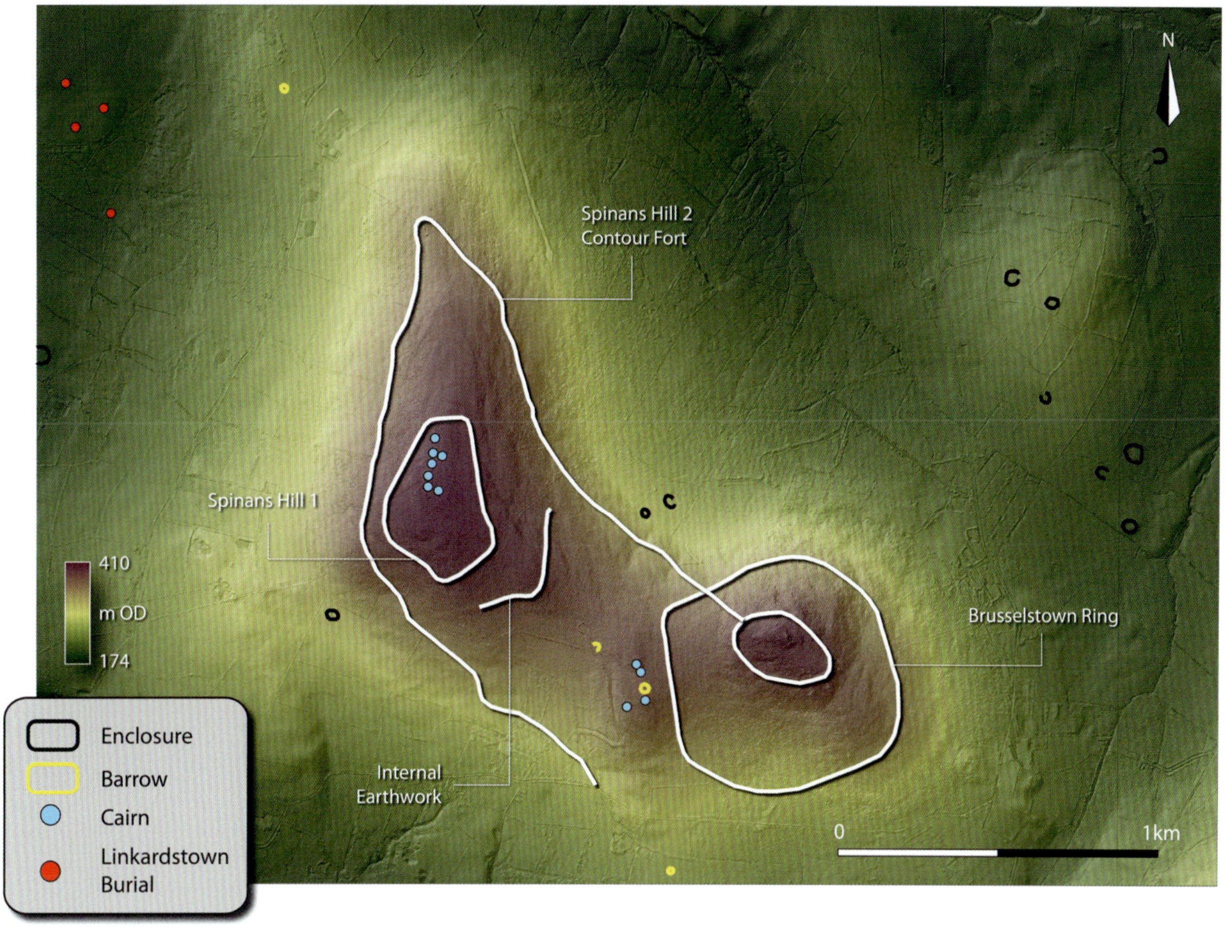

Fig. 6.3 The Spinans Hill complex on the eastern edge of the Baltinglass landscape.

point (1329 ft) but there is all the same a good deal of reasonably smooth ground inside the wall, even if not very level. I reckon that it would contain about 11 or 12 acres.

All along the S side where the wall of the ring is the boundary of Castlequater townland, the wall is from 4 ½ to 5 ½ ft high and 3 to 3 ½ ft thick. It is made of rough granite stones and boulders, none very big, i.e. two men could I think handle the biggest, with a bar.

The slope on this side is not steep, but gradual, from a point 50 yrds or so to the SE of the angle where I entered right round to the downward-running wall which is the boundary of Castlequarter and a bit further round, nearly to the next downward-running wall, which runs down to the E in Brusselstown townland. For all this distance, I suppose some 250 yrds or so, the slope is covered with boulders for a space of about 20 ft below the wall, that is boulders and stones similar to those in the wall. It is quite obvious that these are the scatter of the original wall, the stones of which have in the course of centuries slipped down the hill; and that none of the present wall is the original, but that it is merely a field or boundary wall built within, I suppose, the last 200 years or thereabouts. It is a good substantial dry wall, but the original wall must have been much larger, judging from the mass of stones: I should say that it must have been a wall of the same kind as those still to be seen in the big forts in the W, such as Staigue or Dun Beg, or Cahercommaun (the inner wall of Cahercommaun was roughly 25 ft wide and 14 ft high: this could never have been anything like so massive, but it could have been 10 ft wide and 10 ft high at any rate at this S side).

Continuing on round the wall, it is still 4 ½ to 5 ½ ft high and 3 to 3 ½ ft thick on the E and N sides, though no longer a townland boundary. Just N of the downward-running fence at the E, there is a scatter of fallen stones on the inside as well as on the outside. After passing the next downward running fence, the one which goes in a NE direction, one is at the place

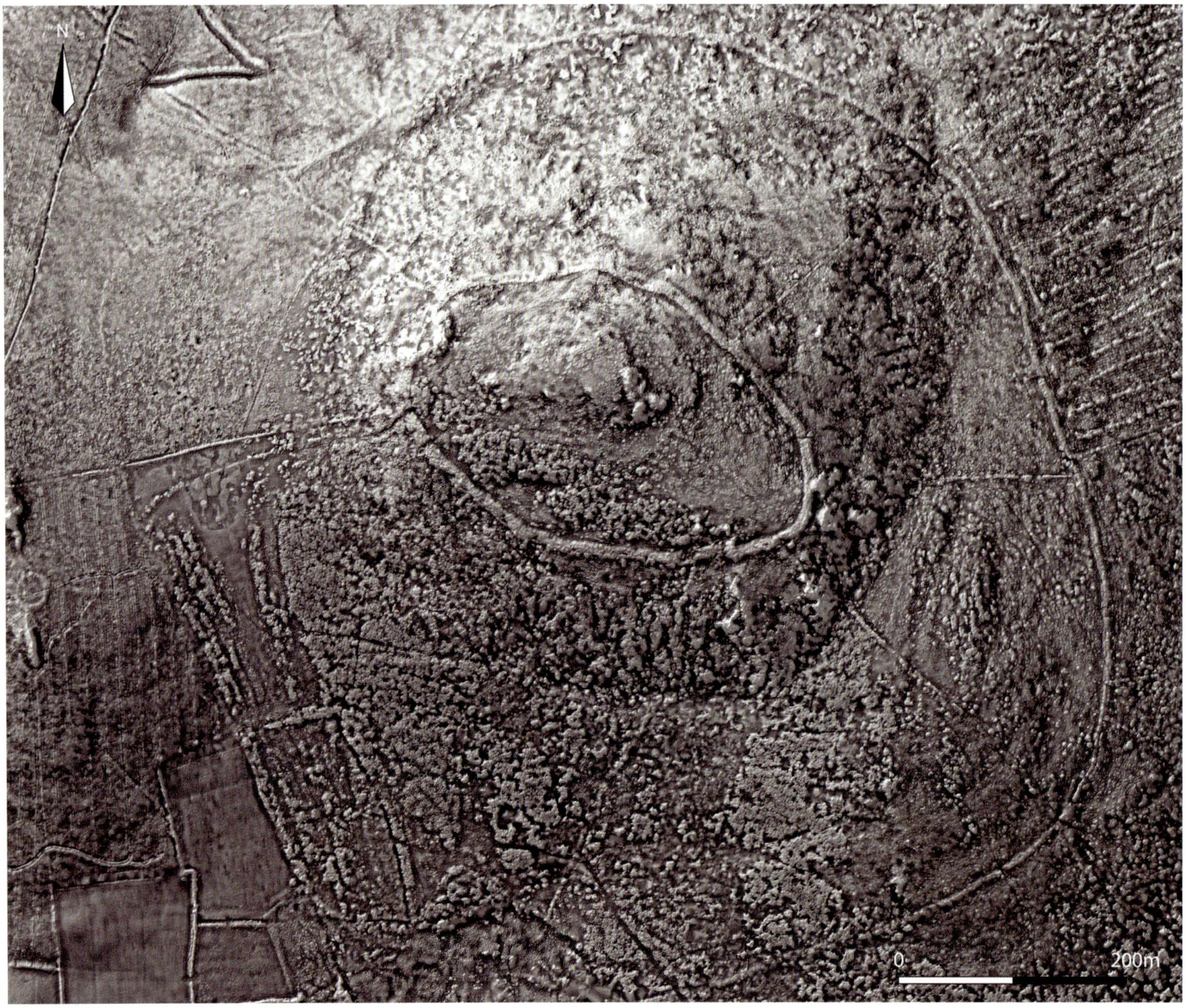
N
0
200m

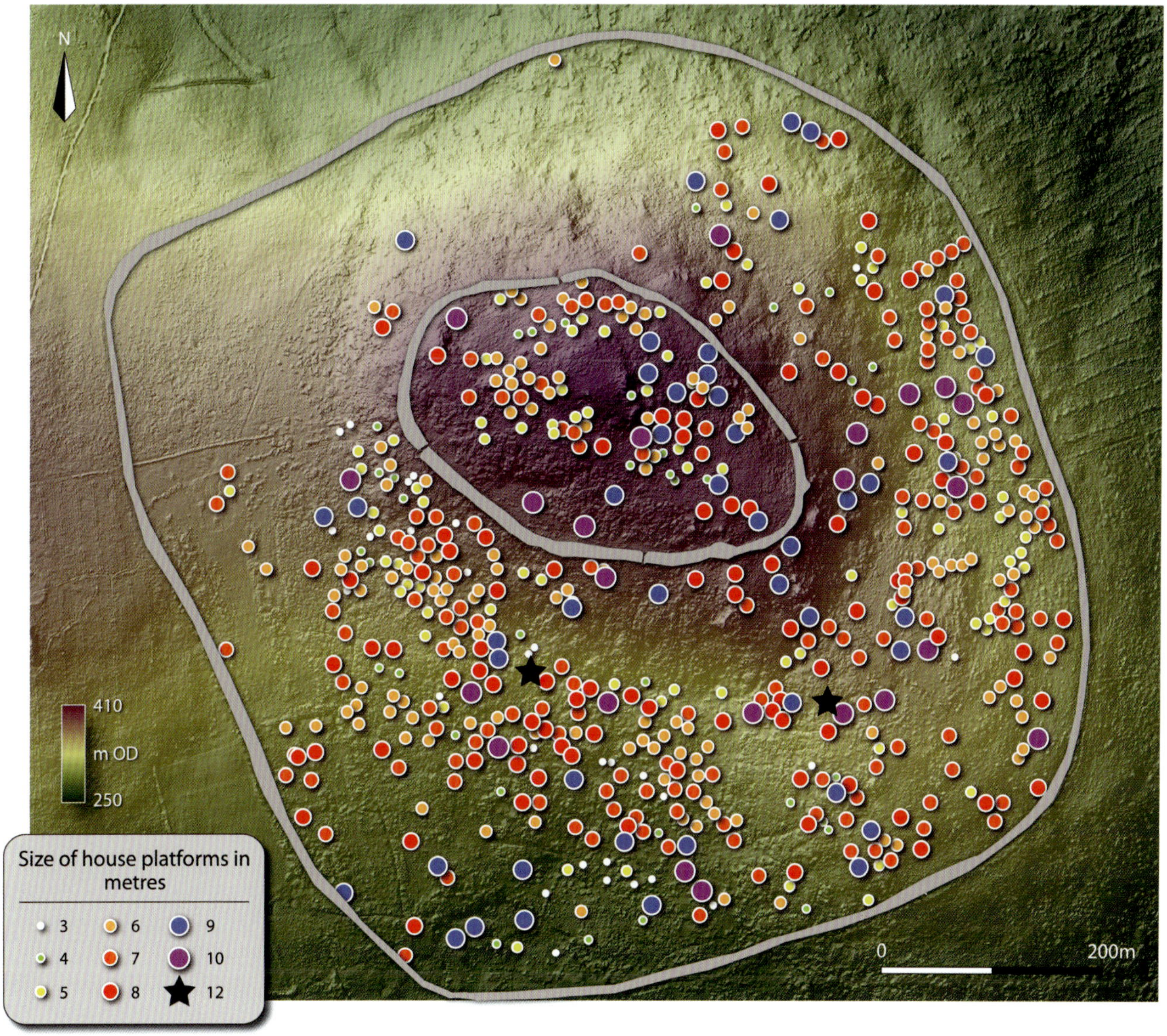

Opposite page
(Top) Fig. 6.4 Brusselstown Ring, viewed from the south.
(Bottom) Fig. 6.5 Multi-directional hillshade model of Brusselstown Ring.

Above
Fig. 6.6 Plan of Brusselstown Ring with house platforms, from GNSS, drone and LiDAR survey.

where the slope is very steep. Here the wall is on the outer side of the heaps of fallen stones, but the breadth of the area of scattered stones here is not so wide as on the S side, only some 8 or 10 ft. I should say that a lot of stones must have fallen right down the slope which descends very steeply for 100 ft or more, and these stones would have been removed, cleared away, in the course of time.

At a point about 40 yrds NW of this downward-running fence, some 6 ft inside the present wall, there are eleven or twelve fairly rectangular boulders, a foot or more, some 2 ft wide, lying in a line, which continues for 7 or 8 yards. This line of boulders looks like the foundation course of the face of the original wall. The wall having fallen and a lot of it having simply disappeared down slope here, the existing wall was built not on its inner face as on the S side but on its outer face leaving here a little but of the inner face remaining in position. At the NW side where the slope is still very steep, there is a good deal of scatter and the existing wall is only 3 to 3 ½ ft high and in places as thin as 1 ft. Here and on the little bit which runs N and S at the W side of the hill inside the wall rises very steeply up from it with a lot of irregular outcrops of rock, so that the interior space just here is very rough

Opposite page
(Top) Fig. 6.7 The southern side of the inner stone enclosure of Brusselstown Ring, looking west.

(Bottom) Fig. 6.8 Possible coursing of the external face of the inner bank at Brusselstown Ring.

> *and uneven. It does not look as If there could ever have been space here for a very thick wall. Just before reaching the angle where I got in the interior space gets much more smooth again and here again there is a lot of scattered stones inside the present wall, and again there are some boulders which look as if they might have been at the base of the interior face of the original wall; but they are not in as clear an arrangement as they are in the 7 or 8 yrd stretch already mentioned.*
>
> *In the whole interior there is only one place, so far as I could see, where remains are still in existence of a hut site: elsewhere the ground is grass-covered, mostly clear of boulders, but with outcrops of rock, large and small, occurring throughout* (in Corlett and Weaver 2002, 464–6).

Recent satellite and drone imagery, along with LiDAR and GNSS survey, now adds to Price's record of Brusselstown Ring. This is one of the few hillforts at Baltinglass that has not been disturbed by commercial forestry, allowing detailed examination of its interior. The inner enclosure closely follows the 370m OD contour, deviating by less than five metres along its 824m perimeter. A bank of stone encloses an area of 4.63ha on a natural oval terrace (Fig. 6.7). This is built of large, loose stones of andesite and andesitic tuff gathered from drift sources. The wall is 5.3–11.7m wide (average 9.5m) and up to 1.2m high, with a modern stone wall built into its inner face. Loose stone and boulders are scattered on the immediate lower slopes, suggesting that the bank was originally higher. A 98m length of stone facing, with up to three courses surviving, is exposed on the southern side of the outer stone enclosure (Fig. 6.8), with a similar facing identified by Price on the north-western side (in Corlett and Weaver 2002, 466). An estimated 61 small, circular depressions are also visible on top of the southern section of the inner stone bank. These are 1.5–2.7m in diameter and possibly represent large post-holes. In one part of the wall there are 17 such depressions, placed 0.7m apart in a continuous line. No such features are apparent in the outer enclosure, although that wall is more denuded and partially covered by vegetation.

Four possible entrances have been identified at the northern, southern, eastern and western sides of the inner enclosure, none of which corresponds with entrances to the outer enclosure. These openings are similar, 1.7–2.6m-wide breaks in the stone wall, each with a *c.*4m-long avenue of stones extending from the terminals. The latter may be an original feature identifying an entrance, but could also represent modern breaks in the wall associated with farming.

A second (outer) enclosure with a large number of probable house platforms has been identified (see Figs 6.5 and 6.6). The enclosing wall is 124–305m outside the inner wall, but unlike the latter does not follow the contours of the hill, with its position varying from 298–366m OD. It has a less substantial bank of loose, large andesite and andesitic tuff, the eastern and south-eastern sections of which are incorporated into modern field systems. This bank is best preserved to the north, where it averages 10.2m in width and 0.3m in height. The enclosure is sub-rectangular over an area of *c.*37.81ha (Fig. 6.6). There are no obvious entrances, though the western side is obscured by heavy gorse and commercial forestry. In that area, close to the outer enclosure, there are three circular cairns, one of which is recorded (WI027-078005), as well as an unusual long cairn and two small enclosures, one of which is recorded (WI027-078004). To the north-west, a settlement area (WI027-078003) comprised of hut sites and field walls was recorded by Condit (1992, 16–20).

The interior of Brusselstown Ring has numerous small outcrops of rock within a relatively level area that rises to 400m OD. The largest of these is at the centre of the hillfort, where it forms a prominent rise overlooking most of the interior. Grogan and Kilfeather (1997) recorded two structures inside the inner enclosure and 24 examples immediately outside to the south. Most of these are visible as small, circular platforms, 7–8m in diameter, with some larger examples, including one that is 20.8m by 18.6m. These structures were formed by digging into the hill and depositing that soil downslope to make a platform that was then outlined by roughly laid stones and boulders. Drone and LiDAR survey has identified as many as 607 possible platforms (Fig. 6.9). Some of these were noted by Gerhard Bersu during a visit to the site in August 1949 with Liam Price and Ruaidhrí de Valera (in Corlett and Weaver 2002, 504). The fact so few of these platforms overlap, with many occurring in rows, suggests that they could be contemporary with and connected to the hillfort within which they all occur. Similar large, densely occupied hillforts in Northern Britain were often considered to represent multi-period

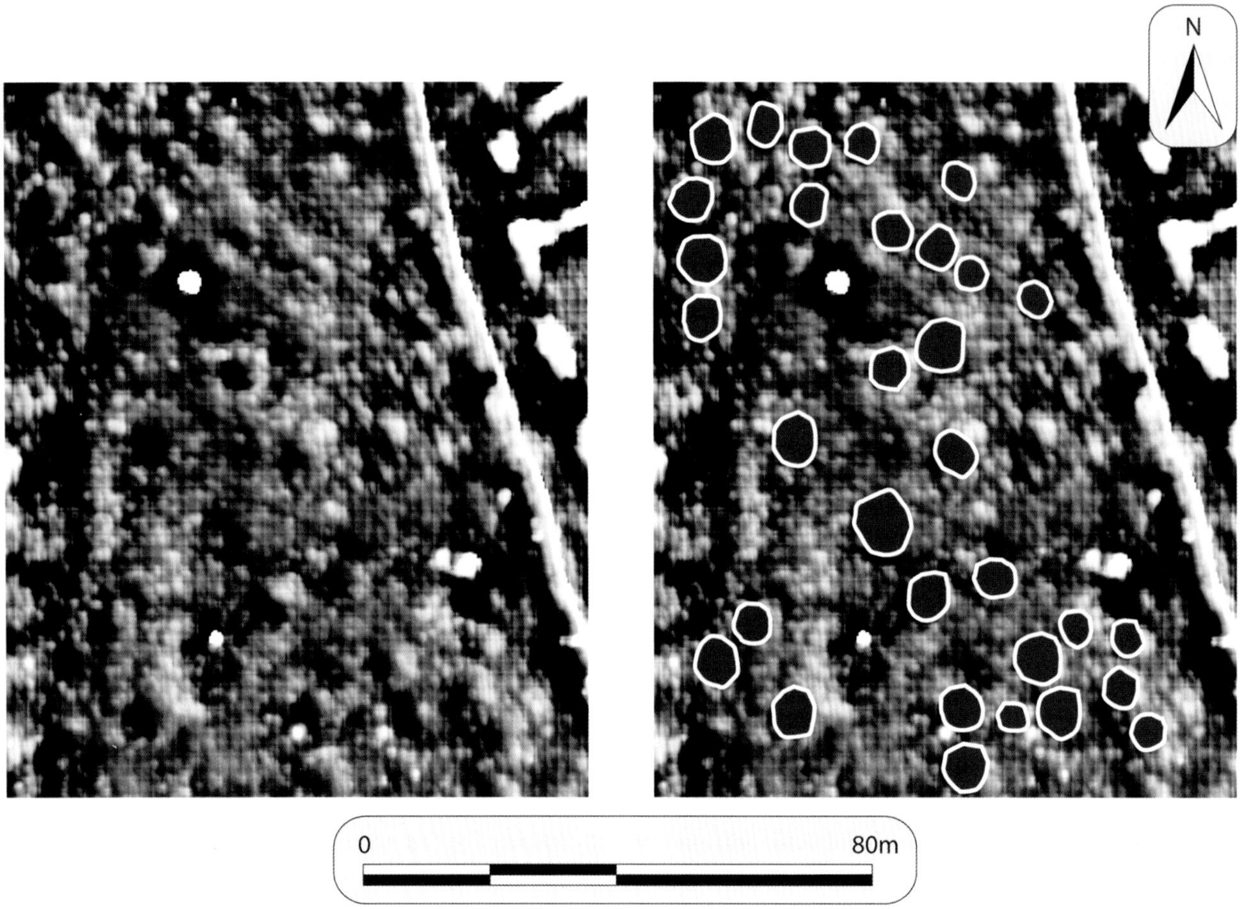

Fig. 6.9 Simple Local Relief Model from LiDAR data, showing some of the house platforms on the eastern side of Brusselstown Ring.

occupation (Halliday 1985, 238; Mercer and Tipping 1994, 5; Harding 2012, 96). Recent excavation of some of those sites suggests they formed large, contemporary settlements (Noble and O'Driscoll forthcoming).

The occupation represented by these structures inside Brusselstown Ring is more or less evenly spread along the southern and eastern slopes of the hillfort. The presence of dense scrub vegetation may obscure the identification of similar settlement on the northern and western sides. Generally, settlement was densely packed into every usable area, except where restricted by rock outcrop or steep slopes. Of the total number of platforms, 98 are located in the inner enclosure, and there are as many as 509 examples in the outer enclosure (see Fig. 6.6). These are flat, circular areas, ranging 3–12m in diameter, with a large number (64%) about 6–8m in diameter. In a study of Bronze Age houses in Ireland, Cleary (2007, 139) noted the majority were of similar size range. There is also a significant number (24%) of platforms in the 3–5m range at Brusselstown Ring, which like Bronze Age structures of similar size, may be ancillary buildings. Twenty-three (3.8%) of the Brusselstown Ring platforms are 10m in diameter, while only two structures here exceed 12m. The former are evenly distributed throughout the settlement, often occurring at the edge of dense clusters of smaller house platforms. While the two largest platforms are outside the inner enclosure, there is no clear distinction in the size of these platforms between the two enclosures.

At first glance, the difference between a structure built with an 8m diameter (the largest of the 'average' sized buildings) and one 12m in diameter (the largest identified structure) does not seem significant. The former would, however, have a total area of 50.27 m^2, which is less than half the 113.1m^2 footprint of the latter. Variation in the size of structures may reflect an element of social stratification, which cannot easily be identified when comparing isolated settlements dotted throughout the landscape. The largest cluster of house platforms at Brusselstown Ring is positioned immediately to the south of the west-facing entrance and forms a corridor for access to the hillfort interior. The terrain to the east and south falls away sharply, and this area remains largely clear of habitation. Similarly, the area immediately to the south, east and north of the inner enclosing elements has steep slopes, with large glacial erratics.

There are no platforms abutting or within 10m of the external face of the inner enclosing elements at Brusselstown Ring. The bank is positioned at the edge of a sharp drop in slope at the south-eastern, eastern, northern, and north-western sides, which probably influenced the distribution of platforms in those areas. More suitable terrain was available on the southern and south-western sides, but that area does not seem to have been occupied. The front of the enclosure wall may have been kept clear for defensive purposes or status display.

Some Irish hillforts have evidence for dense internal settlements, as outlined by O'Driscoll (2023). Survey at the large inland promontory fort at Knockdhu, Co. Antrim (MacDonald 2016; O'Driscoll 2023, 26–7) revealed up to 167 houses set out in clusters and rows within the interior (see Fig. 1.7). Four of five structures excavated by MacDonald (2016) date to the Late Bronze Age. Excavation at Haughey's Fort, Co. Armagh identified substantial Late Bronze Age occupation (Mallory 1995), with recent geophysical survey by the author suggesting a large settlement of over 100 houses. These findings, along with evidence at other hillforts, such as Freestone Hill, Co. Kilkenny (O'Driscoll 2023, 28–30), unenclosed hill settlements like Mullaghfarna, Co. Sligo and Turlough Hill, Co. Clare (Bergh 2015), and lowland sites including Corrstown, Co. Derry (Ginn and Rathbone 2011; Rathbone 2013), highlight the occurrence of Bronze Age nucleated settlement in Ireland.

Recent excavation by the author at some well-known hillforts in northern Britain has shed light on a previously unknown period of construction and use. The massive 16.2ha site known as Tap o'Noth in Aberdeenshire, Scotland is now dated to the fifth/sixth century AD (Noble and O'Driscoll forthcoming). Within the interior, an estimated 800 house platforms are positioned in rows along trackways, a layout that suggests contemporary use. This is supported by the excavation of nearly a dozen of the platforms, which has shown that the settlement was first established in the second century AD and grew to its full extent in the fifth/sixth century; evidence was found of houses that had multiple phases of rebuilding. A similar settlement history has been identified at Eildon Hill North hillfort in the Scottish Borders, and East Lomond in Fife (Noble and O'Driscoll forthcoming). Older excavations, such as those at Yeavering Bell in Northumberland (Miket 2013) and Traprain Law in East Lothian (Cree and Curle 1922), have major settlements associated with the building of these massive hillforts from the second to the sixth century AD. Historical sources refer to the importance of Dún Bolg in the Baltinglass region as a royal caput for some of the early kings of Leinster. This intriguing possibility will be discussed in Chapter 8.

Spinans Hill 2

This large earthwork (WI027-078001) encloses the upper slopes of the Spinans Hill ridge, encompassing Brusselstown Ring and Spinans Hill 1 (Fig. 6.10). The area enclosed is 131ha (the equivalent of 102 Croke Park-pitches), with a 5.46km-long perimeter, making this the largest hillfort in Ireland or Britain. Condit (1992) discovered the site through analysis of aerial photographs, with Barry Raftery describing the discovery as 'remarkable and dramatic' (1994, 62–4). Recent survey by the author, using GNSS mapping, drone photogrammetry and high-resolution LiDAR, has mapped the site and its environs in detail.

The enclosing elements of Spinans Hill 2 survive as a large bank-and-ditch with counterscarp bank along most of the perimeter (Figs 6.11 and 6.12), replaced on the south-eastern side by a stone bank that is also the outer enclosing element of Brusselstown Ring. On the northwestern side of Brusselstown Ring, however, the Spinans Hill 2 enclosure truncates the outer stone bank of Brusselstown Ring and extends eastward towards the inner stone enclosure. This relationship may indicate that Brusselstown Ring was constructed before Spinans Hill 2, but there is no absolute dating of either site. The Spinans Hill 2 enclosure broadly follows the outline of the hill, varying 295–368m OD in elevation as the ridge rises and falls, with the average elevation being 330m OD.

The enclosing earthwork was recorded by Condit (1992, 20), although not in detail. It is most visible on the northern side, where the internal bank ranges 5–8m in width and comprises mostly stone and boulders, capped in places with soil. Some sections are comprised of large boulders, possibly where the builders took advantage of natural erratics. The external ditch is 7–10m in width, with an outer depth of

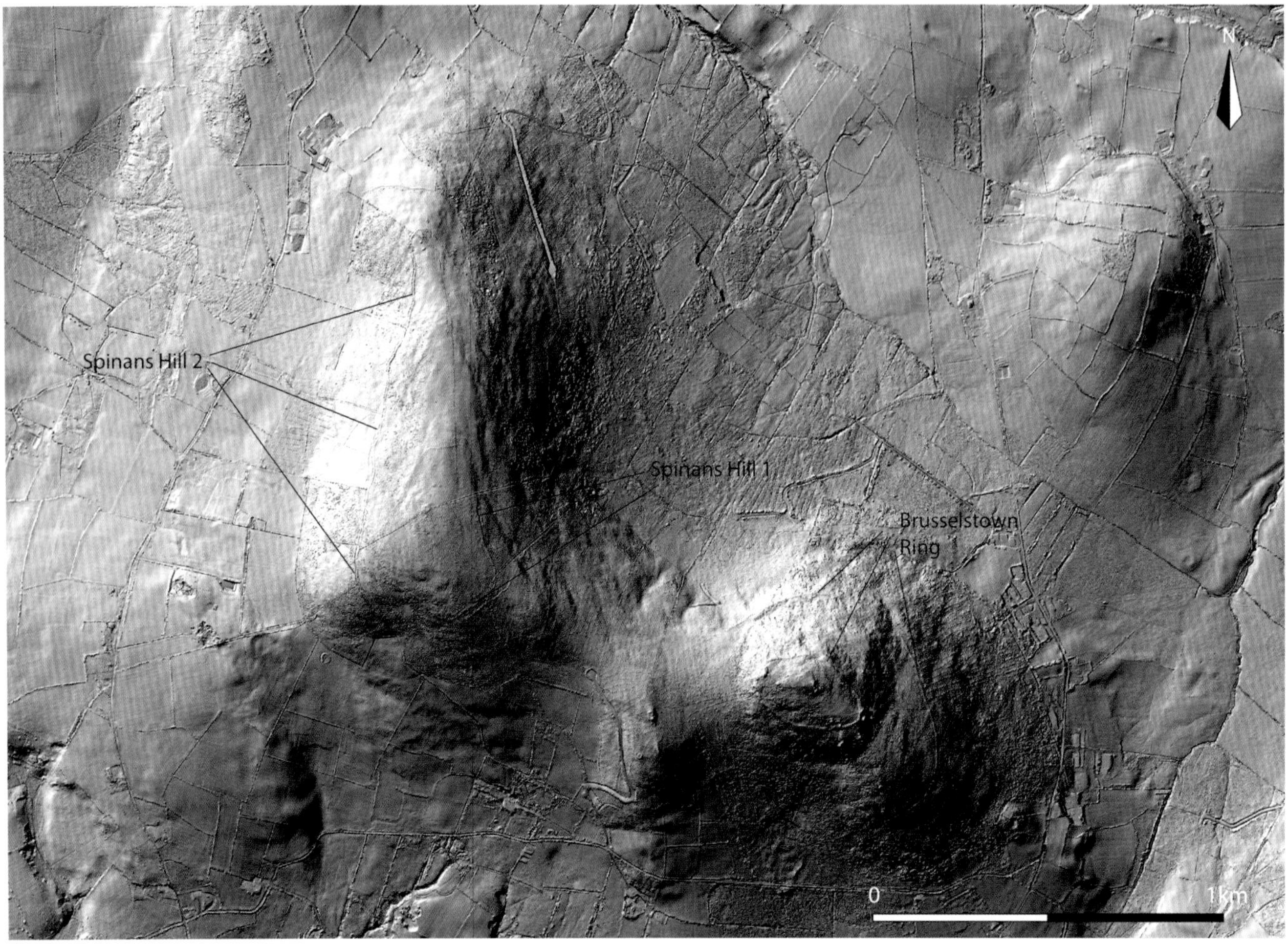

Fig. 6.10 Multi-directional hillshade model of Spinans Hill 2.

1.4m and an inner depth of 2.4m below the crest of the inner bank. The external counterscarp bank is 4–5m wide and up to 1.1m in height. In places, the total width of the defences is up to 23m. The builders of Spinans Hill 2 used the natural topography to enhance the effectiveness and visibility of this defensive earthwork. At the north-western side, for example, the external ditch was cut into the edge of a steep slope, up to 3.6m below the crest of the inner bank.

Condit (1992, 19) noted 'a number of breaches' on the northern limits of the Spinans Hill 2 earthwork, which he believes are original entrance features. Similarly, Bersu identified a 'roadway' to the hillfort at the south-west corner of Brusselstown Ring (in Corlett and Weaver 2002, 504), which he believed connected to an original entrance. Given the extent of the hillfort, there are remarkably few breaks in its perimeter. A 10.5m-wide break at the northern tip of the enclosure has the inner bank and counterscarp bank joining the ditch at both terminals. A number of smaller breaks on a steep slope along the western perimeter probably relate to later farming activity.

A newly identified earthwork in the interior of Spinans Hill 2 partly divides the hill (see Fig. 6.3). This is 5.8m wide and up to 0.58m high, but obscured and heavily damaged by commercial forestry. It is difficult to ascribe a date to this feature, as it does not connect to other archaeological monuments on the hill. The bank broadly mirrors the curve of the Spinans Hill 1 enclosure and so may be part of that monument.

The impact of commercial forestry, which covers a large portion of the interior of Spinans Hill 2, is also felt when trying to assess the function of this exceptionally large enclosure. Immediately outside Spinans Hill 2 to the east, Condit (1998, 12) recorded a 'settlement cluster' comprising enclosures, hut sites and field walls (WI027-078003), which

Fig. 6.11 The bank/ditch/counterscarp bank enclosing element on the north-western side of Spinans Hill 2.

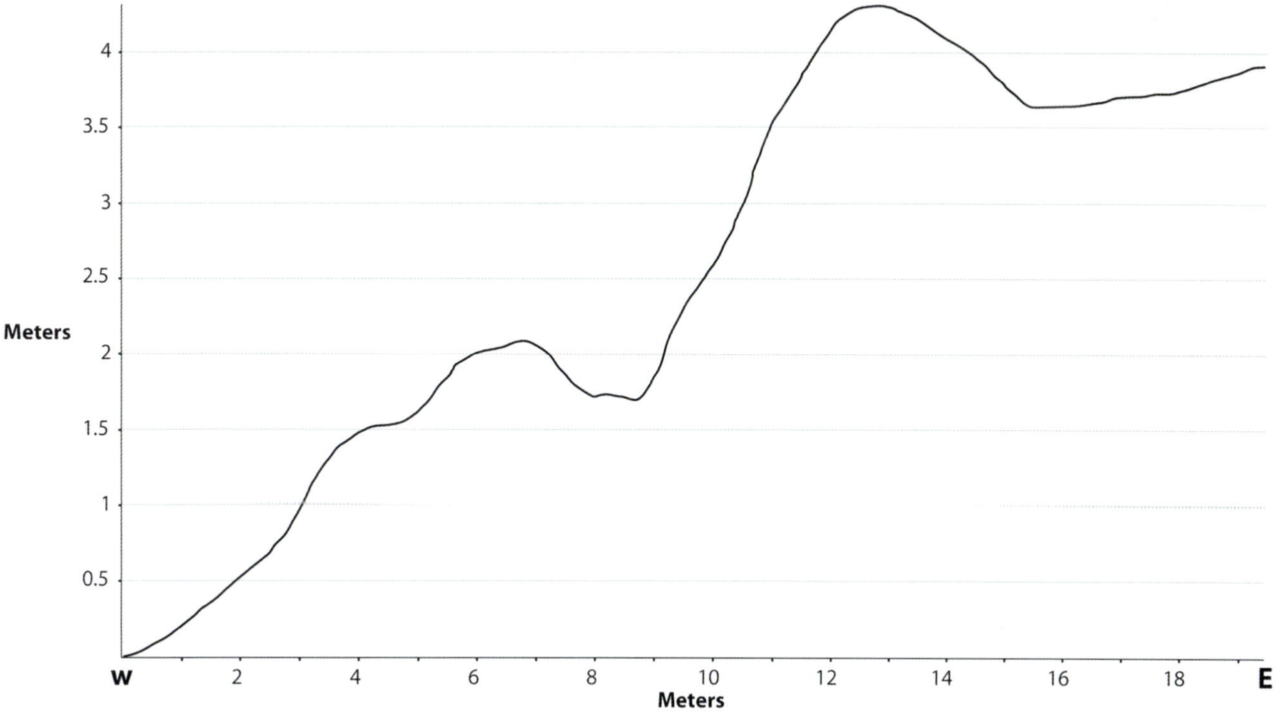

Fig. 6.12 Profile of enclosing elements on the western side of Spinans Hill 2.

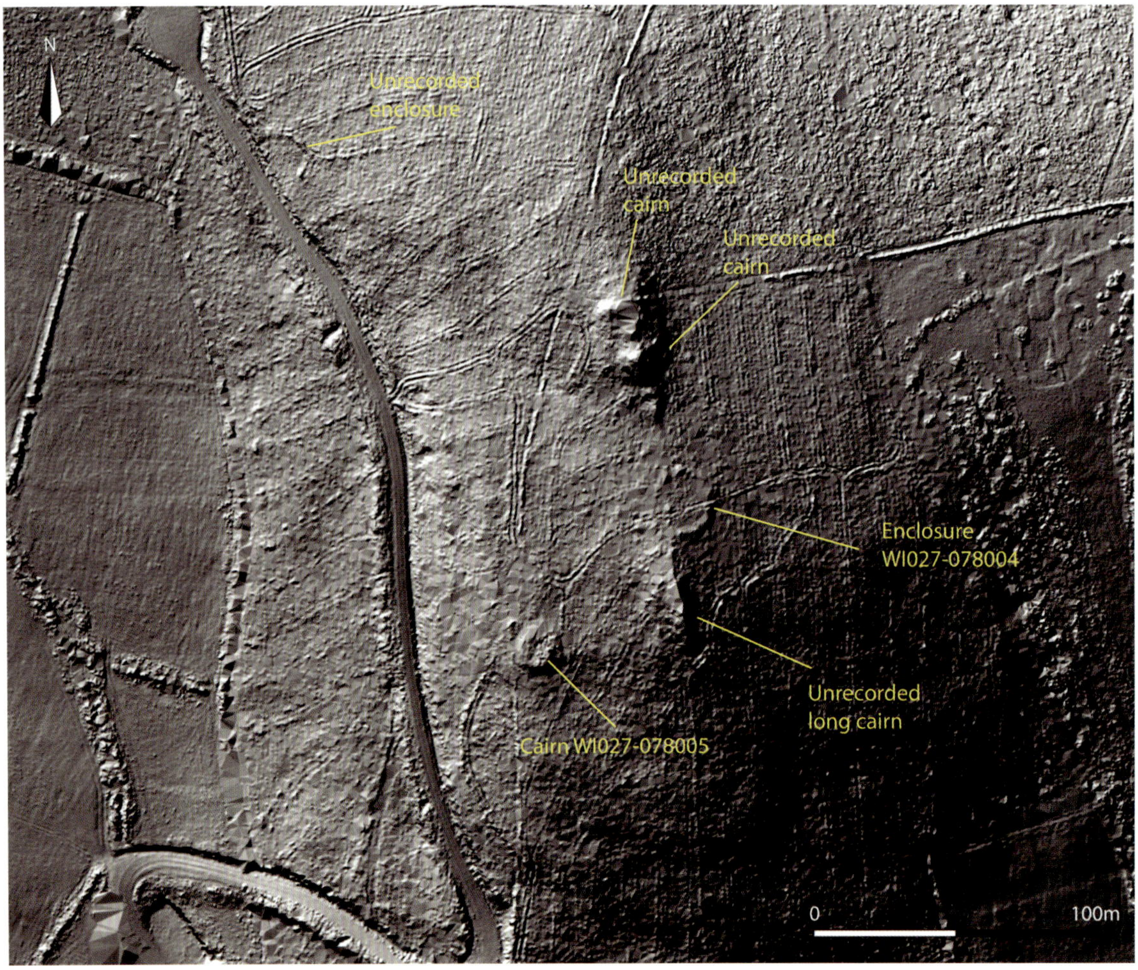

Fig. 6.13 Concentration of ritual monuments covered by forestry within Spinans Hill 2.

might suggest an ancillary settlement. This 'cluster' was identified through aerial photography, however, and its full extent is not recorded, and since Condit's discovery the area has been partly planted with forestry. GNSS and LiDAR survey has identified a less-extensive settlement zone, comprising enclosures, hut sites and field systems (O'Driscoll 2016, 163–4). The largest of these is a sub-rectangular enclosure, 38m (E/W) by 27m (N/S), with a single 2.4–3.2m wide by 0.4m high earthen bank with no ditch. There are three breaks in the bank, 1.2–2m wide, on the northern, southern and south-eastern sides respectively. There are two visible hut sites in the interior, 5m and 7m in diameter, abutting the north-eastern and western edge of the bank respectively. A sub-circular enclosure 61m to the south-west is 15m (E/W) by 17m (N/S), defined by a 2.1–3.2m-wide earthen bank with a 1.8m-wide opening on the north-western side. An unrecorded structure, 58m to the west, represents a 6.5m by 3.5m rectangular building cut into a steep slope, where it overlooks some unrecorded field patterns.

Apart from Brusselstown Ring and its large internal settlement, there are few indications of settlement features within Spinans Hill 2. There are, however, a number of possible burial monuments, similar to those in the Spinans Hill 1 enclosure, on its north-western summit. These include three cairns and two small enclosures on a narrow projection of higher ground along the ridge that connects Spinans Hill 1 and Brusselstown Ring (Fig. 6.13). Condit (1992, 20) identified a circular mound of stones (WI027-078005), *c.*10m in diameter and up to 0.12m high, and what he described as a ritual enclosure (WI027-078004). The latter is 24m in diameter with a slightly raised interior, surrounded by a 4.2m-wide by 0.3m-high earthen bank, with a 3m-wide entrance at its northern side. Recent survey has identified an unusually long cairn, 39m long by 23.5m wide, which seems to be orientated on a large sub-circular cairn, 41.4m by 32.5m and up to 4.1m high. A second circular enclosure, 18.9m in diameter, surrounded by a 3.2m-wide and 0.25m-high earthen bank, is located north-west of those cairns. This unrecorded feature has been significantly damaged by a forestry track. The significance of both 'enclosures' is unclear; the possibility is that they are a type of ring-barrow.

There is a notable distinction in the archaeological features within Spinans Hill 2. On the south-eastern side is the massive Brusselstown Ring, with its dense cluster of house platforms. Beyond this to the west and north-west is a concentration of cairns and possible ring-barrows, as well as the Spinans Hill 1 enclosure that may enclose a passage tomb cemetery. While this separation of burial and habitation may reflect different phases of activity on the hill, it is interesting to note that older monuments were seemingly not impacted by later monument building. Instead, it could be said they were deliberately incorporated into the Spinans Hill 2 enclosure and continued to be significant for later societies. Caution is required, in making such suggestions, however, as, with the exception of some limited investigation of Spinans Hill 1, none of these sites has been excavated and scientifically dated.

Flood (2009, 83) suggested that Knocknarea Mountain in Co. Sligo is the best comparator for the massive contour fort of Spinans Hill 2, although there are important differences that might suggest different dates and/or purposes for the two. The discontinuous banks across the upper eastern slopes of Knocknarea are dated to the Neolithic (Bergh 2000, 2002). Given its much larger size and the fact that it is an enclosure, Spinans Hill 2 may be of later date. One possibility, to be discussed in Chapter 8, is that this immense earthwork incorporating Brusselstown Ring was the Iron Age/early medieval royal site of Dún Bolg. Regardless of date, this enclosure represents an extraordinary construction project that required significant labour and other resources, all of which would have conveyed the power and prestige of the group responsible.

CORBALLIS HILL

Also known as Fraughan Hill (in Corlett and Weaver 2002, 4), this is the western-most hillfort in the Baltinglass cluster, located inside the Co. Kildare boundary, with panoramic views of the surrounding lowlands. Until recently, the location was conspicuous for being the only major hill at

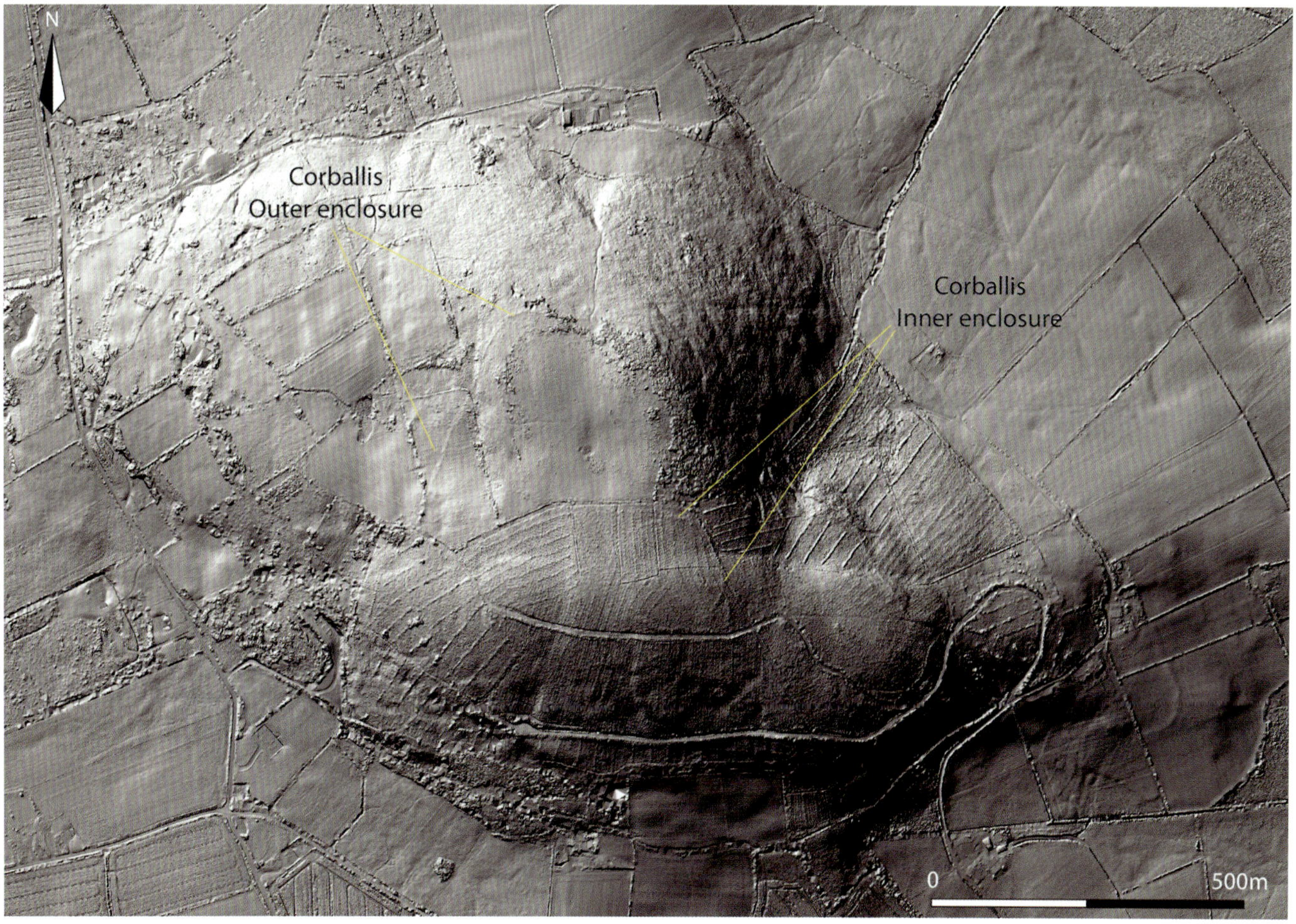

Fig. 6.14 Multi-directional hillshade model showing the newly discovered hillfort on Corballis Hill.

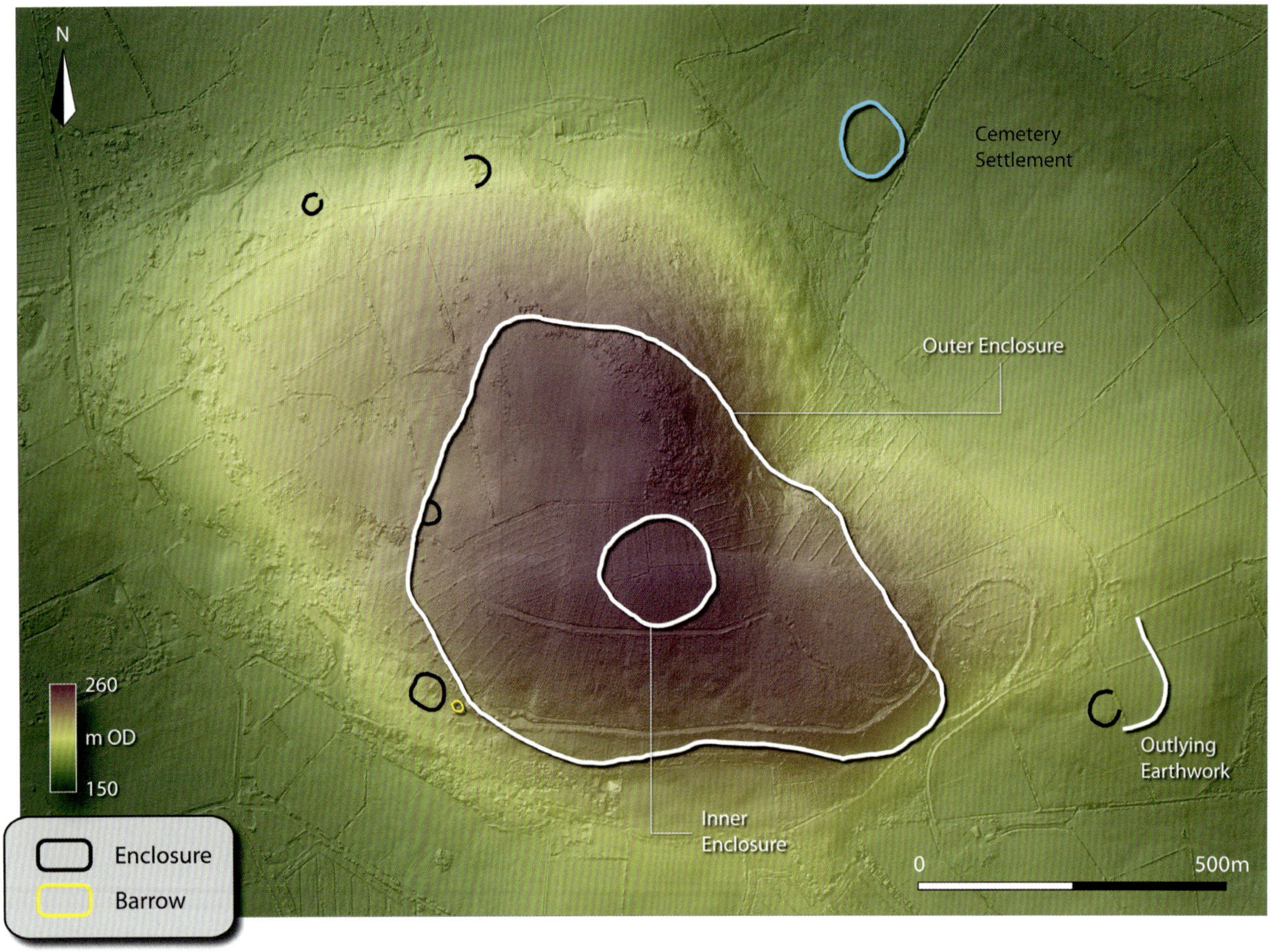

Fig. 6.15 Plan of Corballis Hill from LiDAR survey.

Baltinglass with no prehistoric enclosure on its summit. Liam Price visited the hill in August 1928, observing 'they used to have sports held on it, and they have been recently revived: they were on the second and third Sunday in July' (in Corlett and Weaver 2002, 4). The hill is planted in conifer forestry, making it difficult to identify archaeological features on the ground.

High-resolution LiDAR survey has recently been able to image through this tree cover to reveal a large, multiple-enclosure hillfort (KD038-081). This covers an area of 41.23ha in the townlands of Ballynacarrick Lower, Ballynacarrick Upper, Glowens, and Corballis (Figs 6.14 and 6.15). The inner enclosure of approximately 2.21ha takes in the irregular summit of Corballis Hill (259m OD), which is surrounded by a damaged earthen bank, up to 7.6m wide. There are no obvious breaks in this feature, though a slight in-turning of the earthwork at the south-east may indicate an original entrance. There are no visible features in the interior, where the ground surface has been heavily disturbed by forestry.

LiDAR identified a second earthen bank 205–410m outside the inner enclosure. The irregular shape of this outer enclosure reflects the contours of the hill, which the bank follows at an elevation of 210m OD. This feature survives best on the north-western side as a 3.9m wide by 0.2m high earthwork, which is mostly ploughed down to a 6.65m wide terrace. There is a slight indication of an external ditch in the LiDAR data, visible as a shallow dip directly outside the bank on the north-western side. There is only one obvious break in this bank, located on the northern side. This appears as a 2.35m-wide gap associated with a natural, dried-up watercourse that extends northwards towards the base of the hill. The LiDAR also shows a curving arc of bank, 242m in length, 360m outside the outer enclosure on the south-eastern side. This follows the curve of the outer enclosure and so could represent a third enclosure, or perhaps an additional defensive earthwork built on that side of the hill.

There are no visible features in the outer enclosure of the hillfort, though with 75% or so of that area covered by commercial forestry, it is possible that evidence of occupation has been destroyed. The hillfort overlooks a possible unrecorded barrow cemetery at the south-western side. There are a number of enclosures close to the hill, the most notable being the large example (KD038-041) at the north-eastern side, in Ballynacarrick Lower townland, that may represent an early medieval cemetery settlement. That site will be discussed below.

KILRANELAGH HILL COMPLEX

Another group of enclosures is recorded at Kilranelagh at the south-eastern side of the Baltinglass landscape (Fig. 6.16). The first of these lies on the summit of Kilranelagh Hill (380m OD), with a second example on its western slope (306m OD) in Ballinroan Upper, and a possible third enclosure at Boleycarrigeen on the lower eastern shoulder of the hill (291m OD). Like the examples on Spinans Hill to the north, these enclosures probably represent activity from different periods rather than contemporary sites.

Kilranelagh Hill

This pear-shaped enclosure (WI027-097) was recorded by aerial photography, GNSS survey and LiDAR survey over 5.33ha on the summit of Kilranelagh Hill in the townland of Colvinstown Upper (Fig. 6.17). The summit is largely covered in scrub and heather, while the surrounding slopes and the eastern side of the enclosure are planted in commercial forestry, making it difficult to identify the enclosure on the ground. Prior to the discovery of this enclosure, the hill was best known for a number of large cairns just off the summit on the western and north-western sides, and for a group of white quartz boulders, known as the Cows of Aife, one of the landmarks mentioned in the early historical text 'Fingal Rónáin' (see Chapter 8, Fig. 8.10).

The hillfort has two enclosures, separated by widely spaced stone banks. It encompasses the summit of

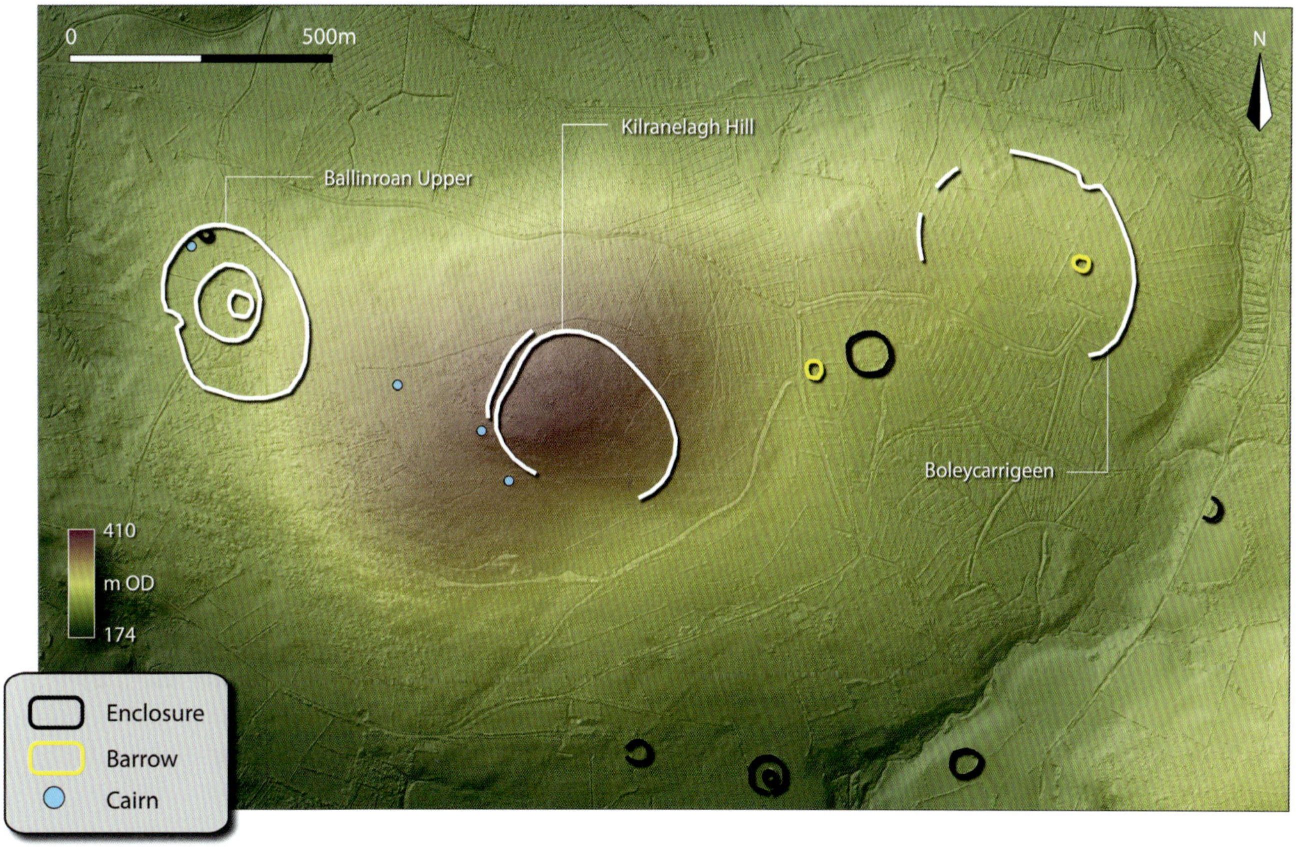

Fig. 6.16 Plan of the Kilranelagh Hill complex.

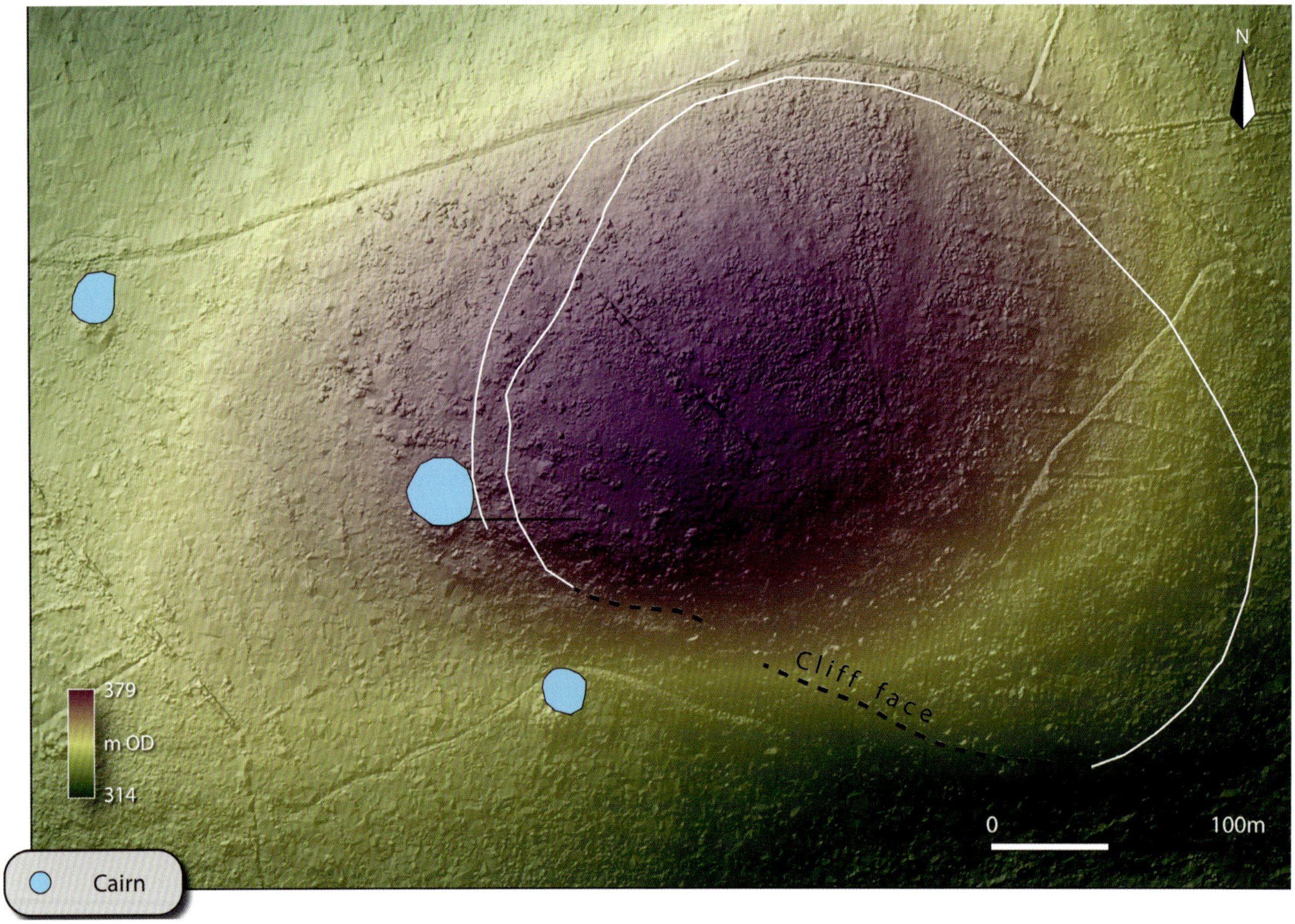

Fig. 6.17 Plan of Kilranelagh Hill from GNSS, drone and LiDAR survey.

Kilranelagh Hill and large parts of the south-east facing slopes, making it highly visible from the eastern lowlands. The inner enclosure covers an area of 7.76 hectares, surrounded by a 14m-wide by 0.6m-high stone bank, with a 6m-wide external ditch, best preserved at the western and north-western sides (Fig. 6.18). Large external facing slabs are evident along much of its perimeter. The eastern side of the enclosure was depicted in the 1840 Ordnance Survey mapping, but has since been ploughed down to a broad scarp. The southern edge of the enclosure incorporates a natural 3–6m-high cliff face, with no obvious built defence in that area. Curiously, the enclosure does not follow the contours of the hill, with its perimeter bank rising and falling between an elevation of 320–373m OD.

On the western and north-western sides of the enclosure, the remains of a second stone bank are apparent *c.*22m outside the inner enclosure. This 11.2m-wide by 0.4m-high bank extends for approximately 189m, but has no obvious facing or associated ditch. It is not certain whether this was a full enclosure or some elaboration of the western approach to the summit. The latter is suggested by the presence of two large cairns (WI027-036; WI027-037) immediately west of the outer enclosure, with a third example (WI027-035) 170m further west. The outer stone bank appears to abut the largest of those cairns (WI027-036). Whether the cairns influenced the location of the enclosure is unclear, as none of these sites is dated. A comparison can be made with Baltinglass Hill, where a passage tomb cairn was built around the same time as a Neolithic enclosure (Rathcoran) with large banks on the north-western side. While it is tempting to view Kilranelagh Hill in those terms, excavation is needed to date the enclosure and cairns on this hill.

Ballinroan Upper

An ecclesiastical enclosure (WI027-034005), with a church (WI027-034001) and graveyard (WI027-034002), has been

Fig. 6.18 Photograph of the wide inner stone rampart discovered surrounding the summit of Kilranelagh Hill.

Fig. 6.19 Simple Local Relief Model derived from LiDAR data, showing the newly identified enclosing elements at Ballinroan Upper.

Fig. 6.20 Plan of Ballinroan Upper from LiDAR survey.

identified on the north-western slopes of Kilranelagh Hill, 360m W/NW of the summit enclosure. These features occur in the townlands of Ballinroan Upper, Colvinstown Upper and Kilranelagh, in an area of dense commercial forestry on all sides, apart from the south. The ruins of a 15m by 4m stone church are centrally placed in a 57m by 44.5m sub-circular enclosure, surrounded by a 3.5m-wide by 0.5m-high earthen bank and a 3.7m-wide by 0.3m-deep external ditch, with a 1.5m-wide entrance on the western side.

Outside this, there is another enclosure over an area of 1.32ha, the southern and western sides of which are part of the boundary between Ballinroan Upper, Colvinstown Upper and Kilranelagh townlands (Figs 6.19 and 6.20). This was recorded by Liam Price during a visit in May 1928 as 'a low drystone fence, overgrown and undisturbed' (in Corlett and Weaver 2002, 2). Recent survey suggests several phases of construction along its perimeter. On the eastern side, the enclosing element is a 2.2m-wide earthen bank, faced on both sides with stone slabs. An external V-shaped ditch dug into the hill slope is 6.8m wide and up to 0.4m deep. The enclosing element on the south-western side is a 1.5m-wide, 0.7m-high drystone wall. There is an imposing earthwork on the north-western side, where an internal bank is 3.8m wide and 1m high, with a central V-shaped ditch, 2.5m wide by 1.1m deep, and an external bank 3.2m wide by 0.9m high. There is no obvious entrance to either enclosure, though they are truncated by a modern track on the southern side. This larger enclosure defines the limits of a disused graveyard of early modern date, with some use into the twentieth century (Price in Corlett and Weaver 2002, 2). There are two stone crosses (WI027-034004 and WI027-034006), and a holy well dedicated to St Bridget (WI027-034003), in the interior.

LiDAR survey recently identified a third enclosure 60–135m outside the ecclesiastical enclosure. This is oval in plan over 6.64ha, broadly concentric with the two other enclosures. The enclosing element is a 4.6m-wide by 0.3m-high earthen bank, with traces of an external ditch in places. There is a prominent in-turned entrance on its western side. The interior has a small unrecorded enclosure, 21m in diameter, on the northern side. This is possibly a ring-barrow, while a 5m-wide by 1m-high mound (WI027-033) in the same area is interpreted as a clearance cairn. Significant disturbance by forestry makes it difficult to identify other features in the interior.

It is possible this newly identified feature is a third ecclesiastical enclosure. Many early medieval churches in Ireland were surrounded by single or multiple enclosures. These are typically 90–120m in diameter, though more important sites have enclosures up to 500m wide (O'Sullivan *et al.* 2013, 147). The Kilranelagh site has features associated with an early medieval church, including a church building, curvilinear enclosures, a graveyard, a holy well and stone crosses, as well as the significance of the '*cill*' place-name. Also relevant are historic sources and saga literature, specifically the *Bórama Laigen*, in which *Cill Rannaireach* (Kilranelagh) features prominently (see Chapter 8). It is possible that these three enclosures were part of an important early ecclesiastical site.

Boleycarrigeen

LiDAR survey discovered the faint remains of a possible enclosure, some 12.46ha in extent, on the lower eastern shoulder of Kilranelagh Hill in the townland of Boleycarrigeen, (ITM: 693409, 689340). This is enclosed by a 7.7m-wide by 0.3m-high bank with no obvious ditch (Figs 6.21 and 6.22). The southern side is disturbed by a forestry road, with the entire monument being covered in the detritus of recent tree harvesting. There is a possible in-

Fig. 6.21 Simple Local Relief Model derived from LiDAR data, showing the possible hillfort at Boleycarrigeen.

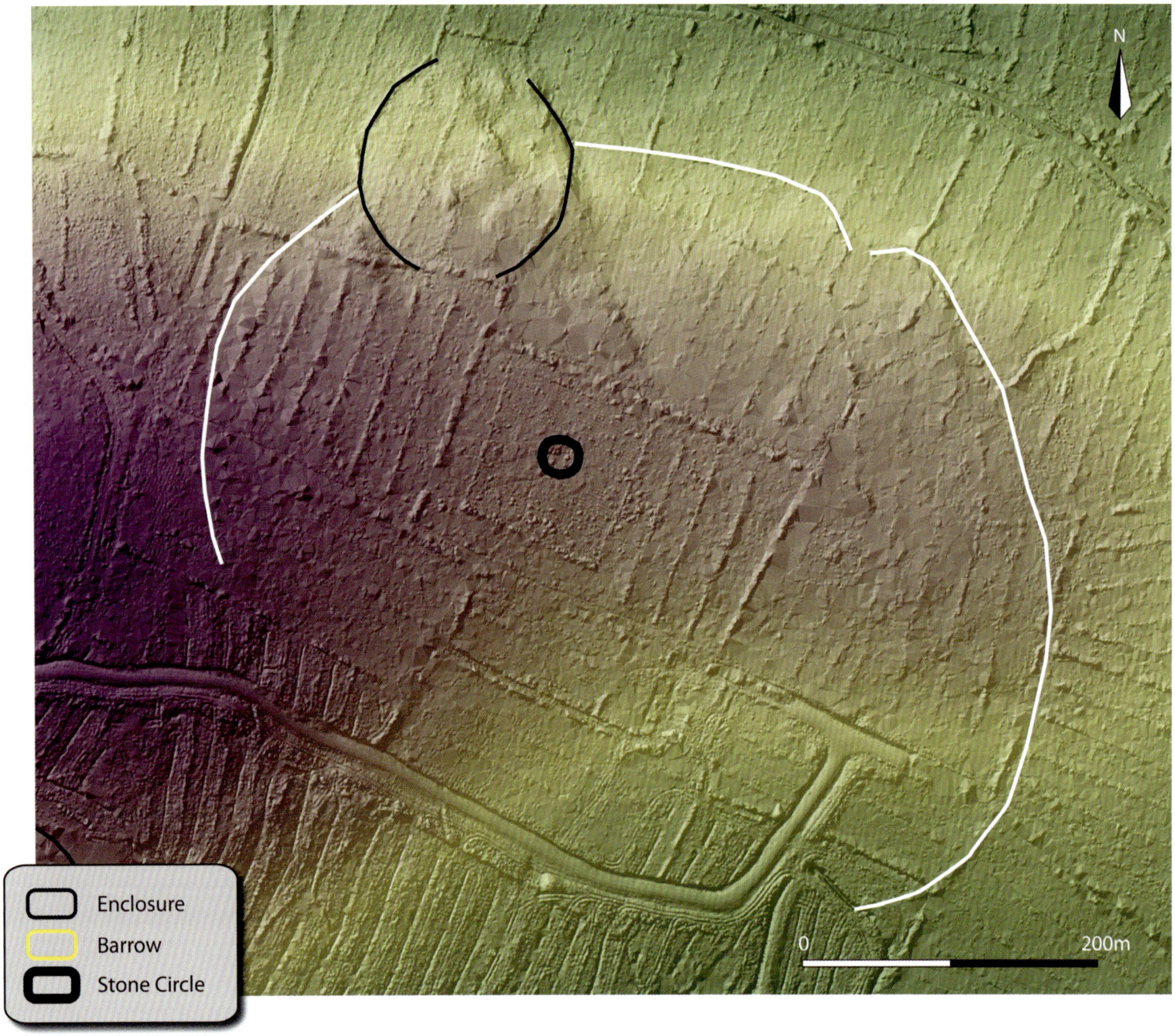

Fig. 6.22 Plan of Boleycarrigeen, from LiDAR survey.

turned entrance on the north-eastern side, while the northern side is truncated by a large univallate ringfort that was not previously recorded. The central area of this possible enclosure is free of trees around a prehistoric stone circle (WI027-039), known locally as 'the Griddle Stones'. Liam Price (1934, 40) identified a mound barrow (WI027-040) with a central cist 100m south-east of the stone circle. To the south-west of the possible enclosure is a univallate ringfort (WI027-038), 70m by 61m in size, with a bank-and-ditch enclosure. Price also discovered a weathered ogham stone (WI027-038002) in the bank, likely to be of early medieval date (Macalister 1945, 54). There are also two hut structures (WI027-038001 and -038003) in that ringfort.

Given the limited surface evidence and the damage caused by recent forestry, it is not possible to confirm whether there is another hillfort at this location. The date of any such enclosure is uncertain. While the presence of the stone circle confirms prehistoric activity on this ridge, the two ringforts at this location are likely to be of early medieval date.

FAUNA HILL

Another new enclosure has been discovered by LiDAR survey on a prominent hill in Fauna townland on the northern side of the River Slaney, 8.5km north-east of Baltinglass town (ITM: 692665, 695415). This site lies

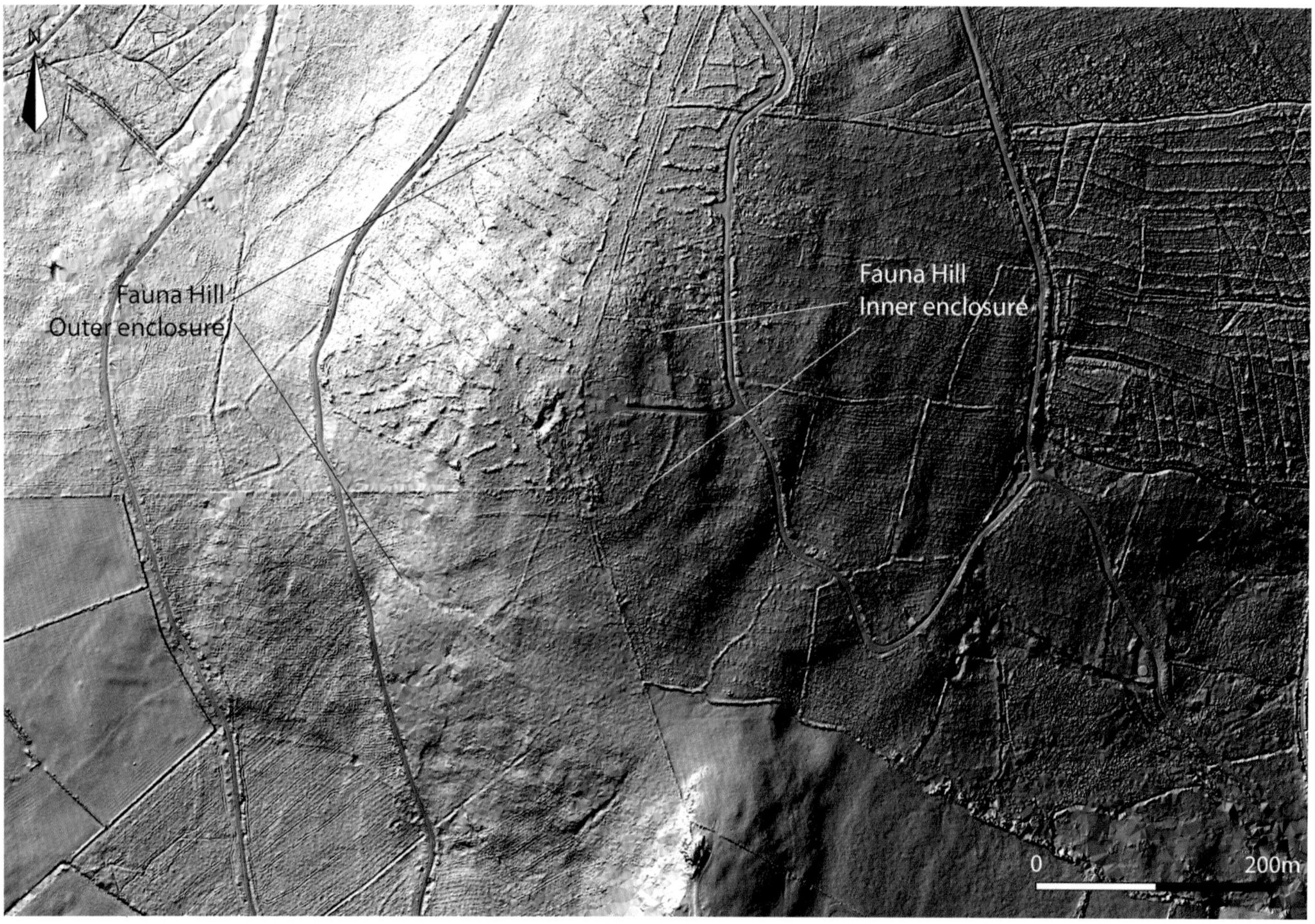

Fig. 6.23 Multi-directional hillshade model showing the two newly discovered enclosing elements on Fauna Hill.

within the townlands of Fauna, Donaghmore and Deerpark. The summit (314m OD) is surrounded by two widely spaced enclosures over an area of 15.91ha (Figs 6.23 and 6.24). The entire hill is covered by commercial forestry, with poor visibility of archaeological features.

The hillfort has two widely spaced enclosing elements. The inner enclosure is defined by a circular bank, 7.6m wide by 0.3m high, encircling an area of 2.47ha, with a large unrecorded cairn at its summit. The enclosure mostly follows the contours of the hill at 307m OD, with no obvious break in the perimeter. During a visit in May 1948, Price noted the remains of a large enclosure on this hill.

> *At the top of the hill in Fauna, where it meets Deerpark, just N of the wall of Castleruddery, there is what appears to be the ruins of a circumvallation: a very low bank, in places up to 2ft high, with a scatter of big stones. This is all in Fauna, i.e. on the E side of the boundary wall, and it is about 70 paces from the wall ... there is no sign of it in Deerpark* (Corlett and Weaver 2002, 487–8).

Price's mention of Deerpark townland suggests this enclosure corresponds with the inner earthwork of the newly identified hillfort.

The defences of the outer enclosure are 115–175m outside the inner bank. These survive as the partial remains of a circular bank, 7.1m wide by 0.2m high. The enclosure is visible at the northern, eastern and southern sides, with the western section destroyed by a forestry road. The outer enclosure mostly follows the 295m OD contour, though the western section partly descends the steep slopes on that side. This may have been an attempt to make the hillfort look more prominent when approaching from the western lowlands. Given its size, morphology and landscape setting, it is possible this new enclosure on Fauna Hill is a Bronze Age hillfort, but that remains to be confirmed by excavation.

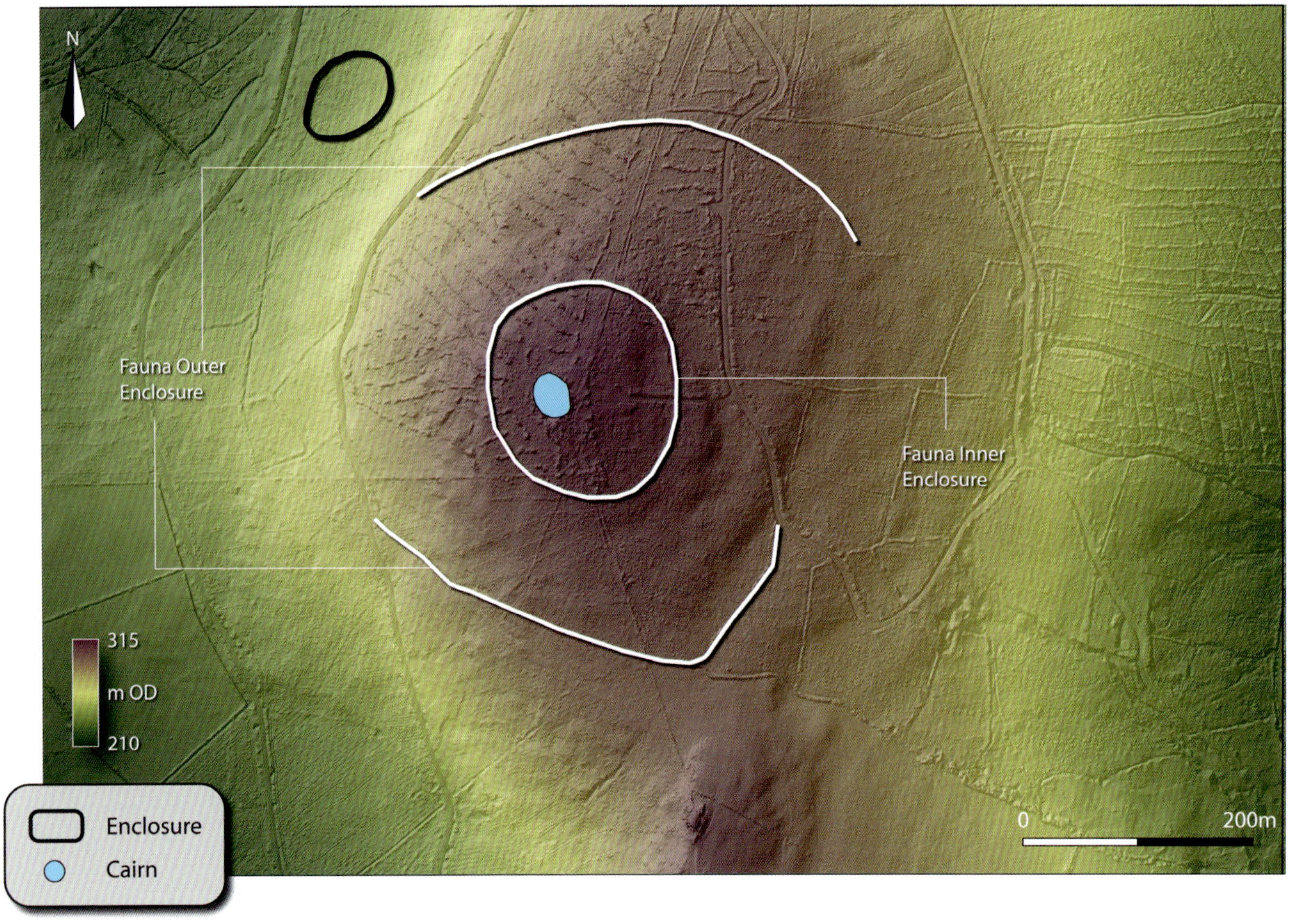

Fig. 6.24 Plan of Fauna Hill from LiDAR survey.

HILLS WITH NO ENCLOSURES

While many prominent hills near Baltinglass have one or more large enclosures of known or likely prehistoric date, some smaller hills have no such recorded features. Saundersgrove Hill, in Ballinacrow Upper townland, is a minor hill visible from all the other Baltinglass hills, 1.5km north-east of Baltinglass Hill and 2.2km west of Spinans Hill. As many as six small enclosures are recorded on the south-western slopes of the hill (WI021-048, WI021-049, WI021-050, WI021-052, WI021-053, WI027-013). While these are recorded as early medieval ringforts or enclosures, the fact that three are under 25m in diameter may be indicative of prehistoric barrows. Ballyhook Hill is another minor hill visible from all the Baltinglass hilltop enclosures. It is approximately 3.6km north-west of Spinans hill and 3.3km north of Tuckmill Hill. There are no early archaeological features at the site.

LARGE LOWLAND ENCLOSURES

A series of large enclosures has also been identified in the Baltinglass lowlands. While these are morphologically and topographically distinct from the hillforts, they may be an important part of an associated cultural landscape. There are four sites of particular interest, none of which has been excavated and so cannot be dated.

Rathmoon

The best recorded of these is a large enclosure in the townland of Rathmoon (WI026-009), to the south-west of Carrigeen Hill. The site was identified (Grogan and Kilfeather 1997; Grogan 2005b) as a hilltop enclosure, despite its low-lying location, and recorded as a 120m-diameter univallate enclosure. Aerial and satellite imagery suggest a more complex system of enclosure (Fig. 6.25), with geophysical survey in 2014 revealing at least four, somewhat concentric, enclosing elements.

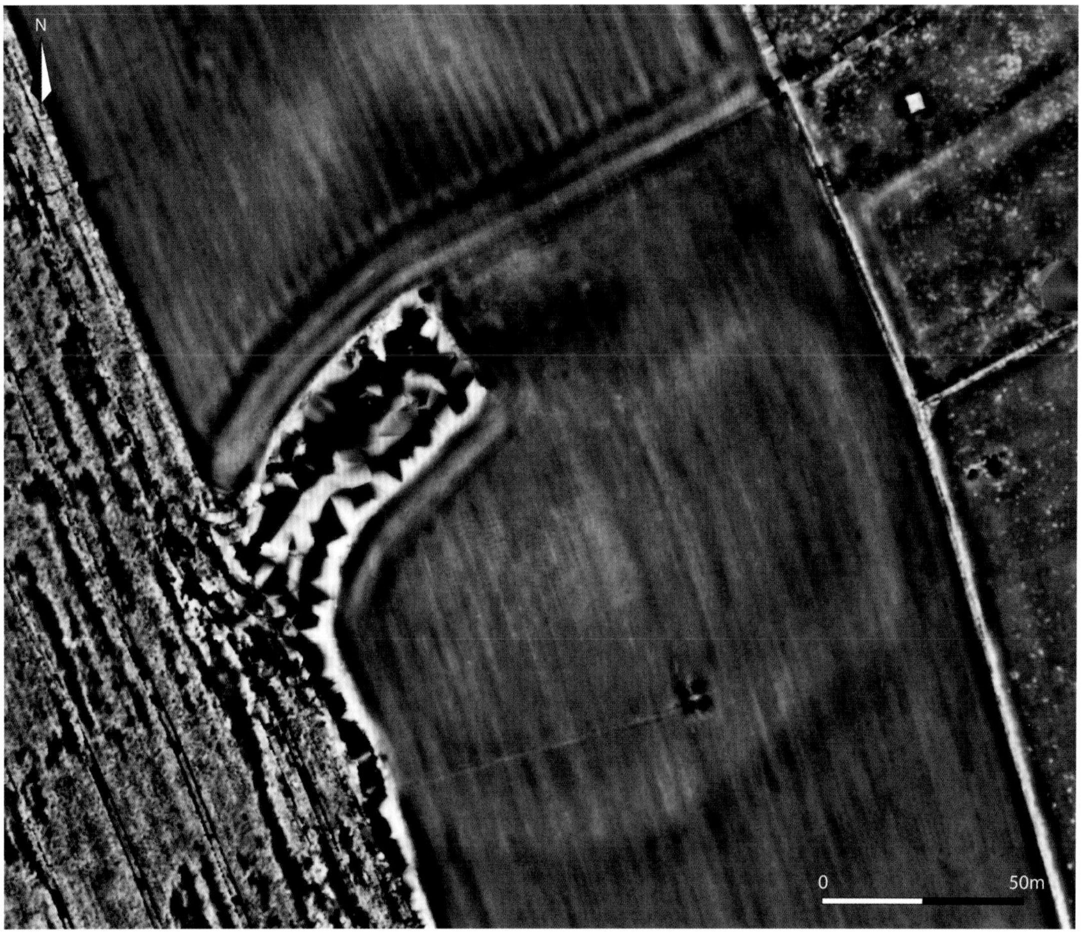

Fig. 6.25 Multi-directional hillshade model of Rathmoon cemetery settlement, from LiDAR survey.

That magnetic survey imaged a sub-rectangular enclosure, 160m (E/W) by 120m (N/S), with enclosing elements spaced 15–22m apart (Figs 6.26 and 6.27). The two outer enclosures do not form complete circuits and are appended to inner enclosures. The geophysical response suggests these are ditches, up to 8m wide, which originally may have had internal banks up to 9m in width. A series of radial banks between the outer two enclosures were probably created by farming in the early modern era. The two inner enclosures are defined by a series of high magnetic responses, 1.5–4m in width, which are likely to be ditches. The inner enclosure is sub-divided by a feature generating an annular band of magnetism, which probably indicates the presence of a shallow ditch.

On the eastern side where the enclosures overlap, there is a corresponding entrance in each of the enclosing elements. This suggests that all four enclosures were in use at the same time. These openings are 2.3–6m wide and together represent a formal entrance to the site. This is the only side of the enclosure where all four enclosing elements overlap. The entrance to the inner enclosure is slightly staggered, possibly designed to conceal the interior. There are also two other corresponding entrance breaks at the south.

Two faint, circular features are visible in the inner enclosure, and there are three 6–8m-wide features in the second enclosure that may represent hut structures. There is a concentration of pit-like features in the northern part of the inner enclosure, and immediately outside the entrance area, as well as a strong number of magnetic responses at its centre. These could be interpreted as burial features, though that cannot be confirmed without excavation. Considering the limited amount of habitation space available at the site, the monument could be regarded as a burial ground.

The size and layout of Rathmoon seems characteristic of an early medieval cemetery settlement. The average size of such monuments is 50–70m, though smaller examples are known, including a 25m-wide site at Westereave, Co. Dublin (O'Sullivan *et al.* 2008, 178). The cemeteries themselves can vary in size, with Mount Offaly in Co. Dublin producing 1,553 burials in total (Conway 2000, 36).

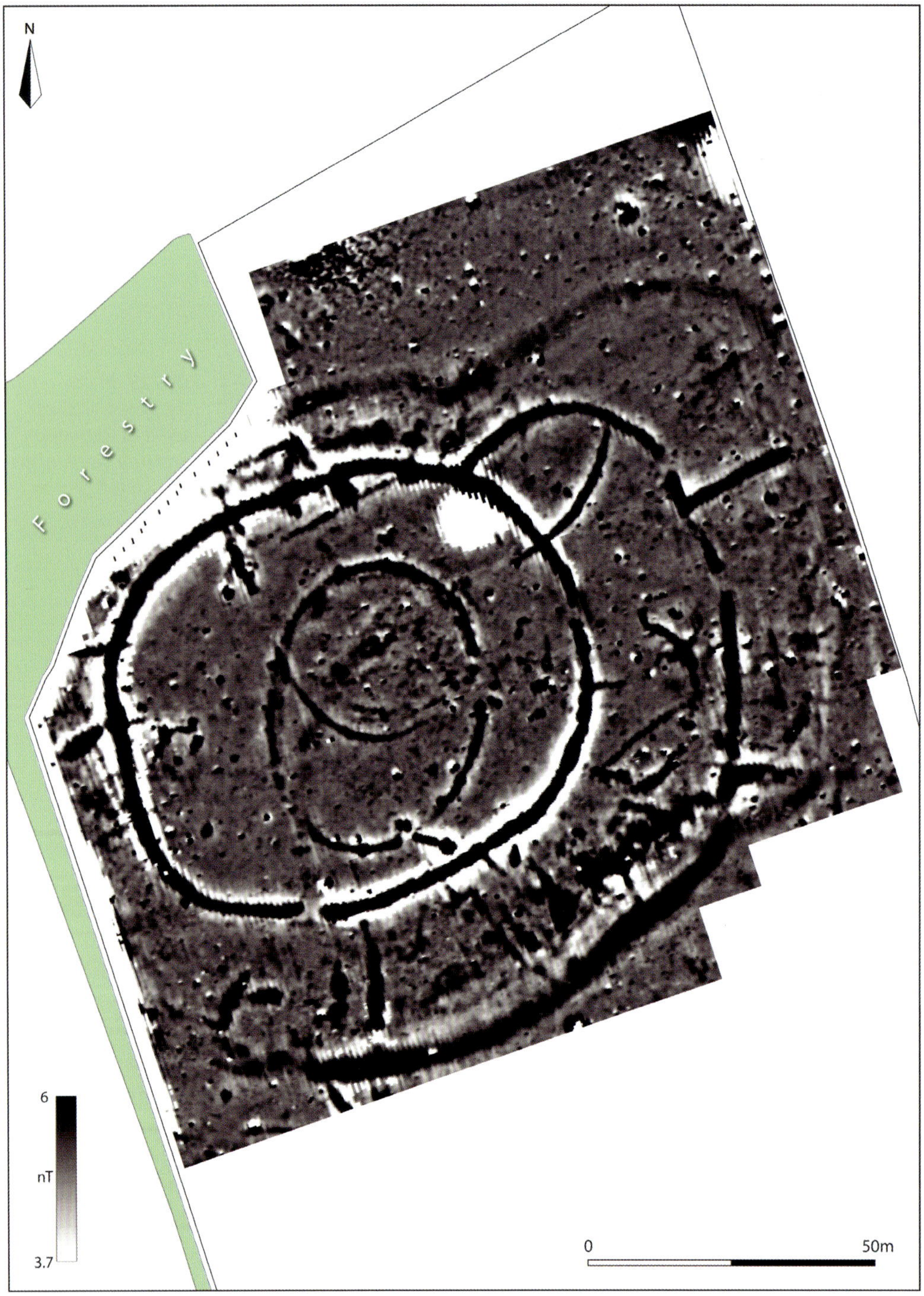

Fig. 6.26 Results of gradiometry survey at Rathmoon cemetery settlement.

Rathmoon is comparable in size to Site M at Knowth, Co. Meath (Stout and Stout 2008). As noted by O'Sullivan *et al.* (2008, 180), where soil conditions are favorable, these sites produce large quantities of animal bone, which has been connected with feasting as part of seasonal assemblies (Gleeson 2015, 40). A series of radial banks linking the outer two enclosures at Rathmoon was possibly created for cultivation and animal grazing, though without excavation we cannot be certain whether these were contemporary with the enclosures. At Site M, Knowth, early cultivation furrows both truncate and were truncated by early medieval burials (Stout and Stout 2008), indicating the site was connected with agricultural activity while being actively used as a cemetery.

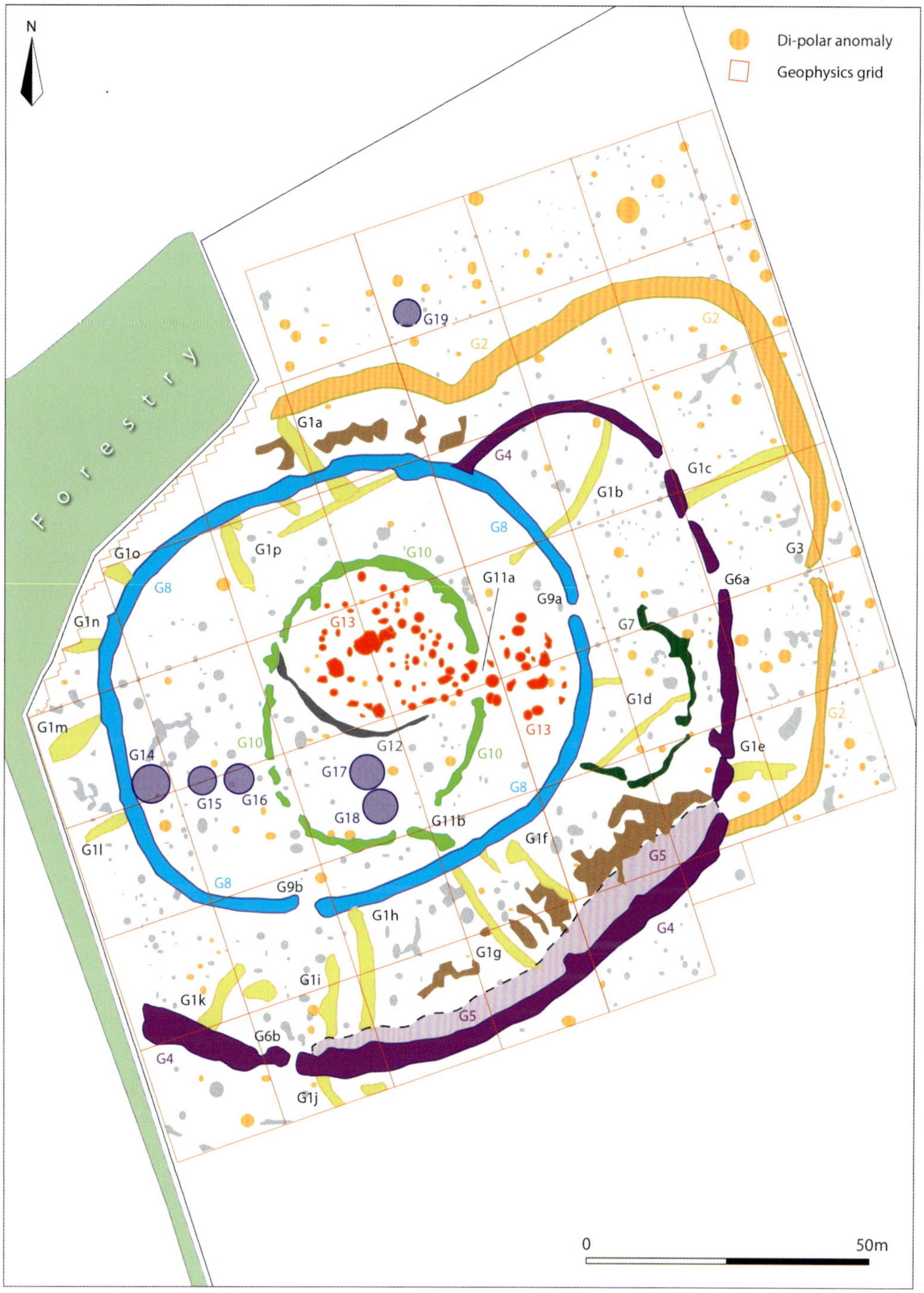

Fig. 6.27 Interpretation of results from gradiometry survey at Rathmoon cemetery settlement.

Geophysical survey identified five faint, circular features at Rathmoon that could represent hut structures or ring-ditches. Domestic structures are uncommon at cemetery settlements, though industrial activity in the form of craft- and iron-working often took place. The Rathmoon features may be associated with such activities, but again this cannot be confirmed without excavation. The focus of burial in some excavated cemetery settlements was within the northern part of the inner enclosure and immediately outside its entrance. This corresponds with Ó Carragáin's (2010, 217) observation that the burial precincts at these sites were well-defined and surrounded by much larger enclosing elements.

Ballynacarrick Lower
LiDAR survey has revealed a large lowland enclosure (KD038-041) close to the north-eastern side of Corballis Hill. This seems to be a sub-circular ditch enclosing and area of 1.05ha, with no obvious entrance or associated bank. The site is shown as a sub-circular enclosure on the most recent six-inch Ordnance Survey mapping. The site has not been investigated in detail and there is no indication of its date.

Keadeen
A large enclosure (WI027-043001) was identified by aerial photography in an area of overgrown scrub on the lower western slopes of Keadeen Mountain (Corlett 2004). This 2.81ha enclosure is defined by a partially collapsed stone wall, 1.5–1.8m wide and 0.5m in average height. There are up to eight stone-walled, circular structures in the interior (WI027-043003 to -043010), as well as a possible standing stone (WI027-043002) at the centre of the enclosure. The hut sites are 1.8–5m in diameter, and are noticeably different from the house platforms on nearby Brusselstown Ring. While Corlett (2004, 90) compared this large lowland enclosure to the larger hilltop enclosures at Baltinglass, its size, location and hut structures suggest it may be of later date.

Kilranelagh
Liam Price recorded a large enclosure in woodland at the northern base of Kilranelagh Hill (ITM: 691707, 689801). He describes a 10m-wide outer ditch, with an internal bank 'only a couple of feet high' (in Corlett and Weaver 2002, vol. 2, 539–40), and an inner ditch about 6m in width. He also recorded a small cairn, 6.6m in diameter and 0.6m high, speculating this may be the location where the landowner had previously discovered a 'Late Bronze Age urn'.

Recent aerial survey has identified an enclosure based on a circular vegetation mark, 172m in diameter encircling an area of 2.37ha. The enclosure and immediate surroundings are very overgrown, making identification of other features difficult. This vegetation mark does not correspond to any feature in the LiDAR survey. It is a different structure than that located further to the north and recently identified by Robert Hanbidge (see RMP record WI027-098 for detail). This represents the partial remains of an old field boundary, with a combination of well-built drystone walls, an earthen bank, and a bank with an external ditch. It is unlikely to be part of an early enclosure.

RELATED MONUMENTS

In the summer of 2022, the author commissioned a large-scale, high resolution, LiDAR survey of the Baltinglass landscape, undertaken by Bluesky International Ltd with funding from Wicklow County Council through the Community Monuments Fund. LiDAR (**Li**ght **D**etecting **a**nd **R**anging) is a remote sensing technique whereby laser light emitted from an aircraft scans the ground surface. The time it takes for the light to be reflected to the source is then measured, to calculate distances to objects. The technique allows for large areas to be rapidly scanned in three dimensions. For the Baltinglass survey, an area of 122 square kilometres was scanned, with data collected at 16 points per cubic metre. This led to the discovery of many new archaeological monuments, from small prehistoric burial monuments such as ring-barrows and mounds, to newly identified hilltop fortifications of considerable size.

Linkardstown burials
We have already seen the value of LiDAR survey to investigate large hilltop enclosures in forested environments. The technique can also be used to examine other monument types. There is one confirmed Linkardstown burial (WI021-057) in the Baltinglass area (Raftery, J. 1973), located in Ballintruer More townland at the north-western side of Spinans Hill, and a possible example in Rathmoon townland (WI026-006001). The Ballintruer More burial is close to at least four possible levelled ring-barrows (WI021-054001, -054002, -054003 and -054004), three cists (WI021-087, -088 and -089), a standing stone (WI021-079) and a recently discovered mound that may be another Linkardstown burial (WI021-091) (Fig. 6.28). LiDAR survey has identified a further two, unrecorded, circular mounds that measure 26.8m and 24.2m in diameter respectively. These are located less than 100m to the north and east of the Ballintruer More burial. Without excavation we can only speculate about these features, but they may have been part of a Neolithic burial ground in that area.

Cursus monuments
The LiDAR survey has also added to the number of possible cursus monuments recorded at Baltinglass. The best-known of these is on the upper western slopes of Keadeen Mountain, the summit of which has a possible passage tomb (WI027-044). The Keadeen cursus (WI027-089) is a 303m-long by 32–43m-wide rectangular enclosure, which rises

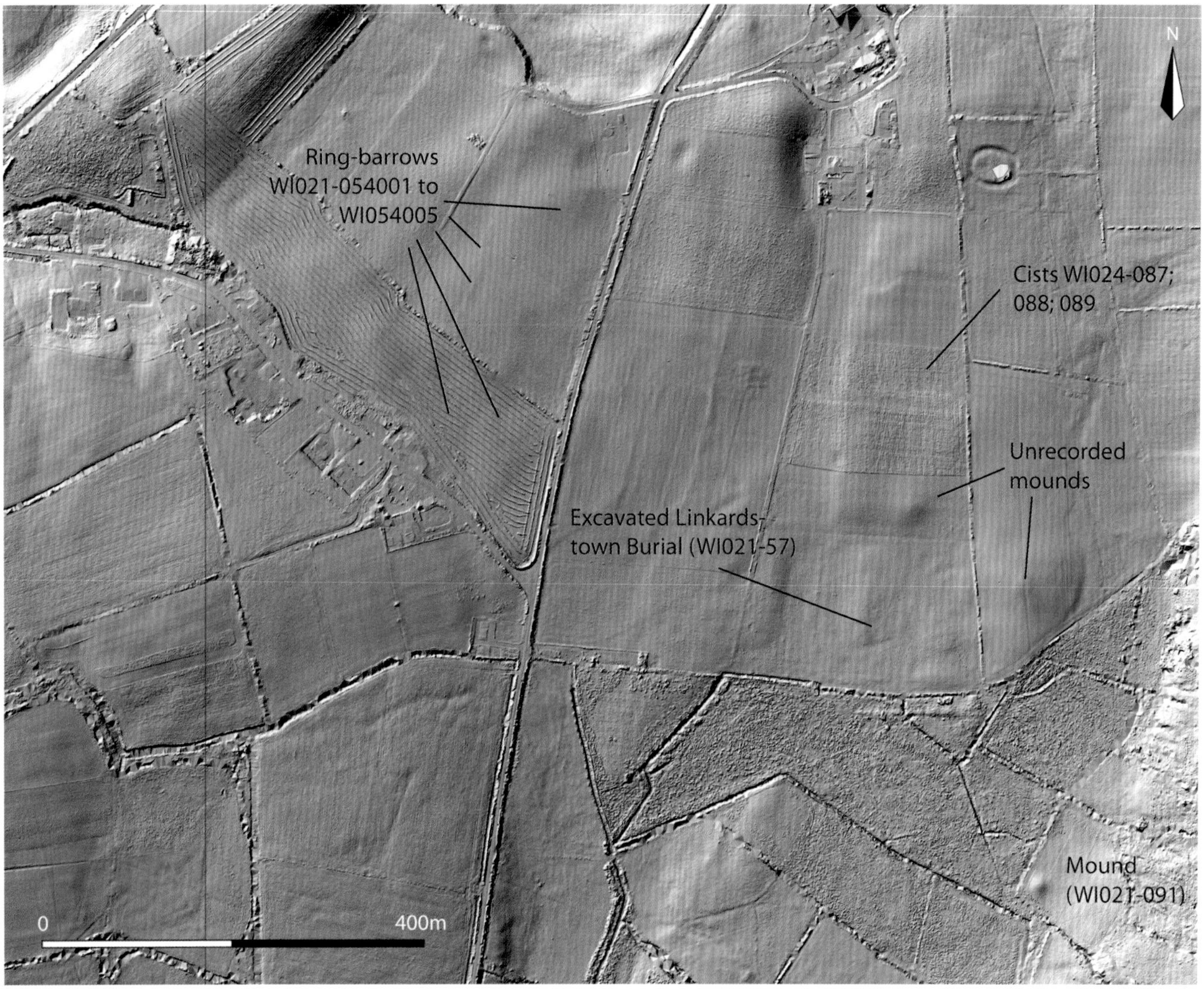

Fig. 6.28 Plan of the Ballintruer More burial complex.

131m in elevation along its length. There are two slightly curving parallel banks, averaging 4–5m wide by 0.3–0.7m high, with a 2.8m-wide by 0.2–0.4m-deep internal ditch and traces of an external ditch (Fig. 6.29). The western end has a squared terminal, while the eastern end is more open close to the summit cairn.

The earthworks seem to have been built in stages, or through gang-working; the northern bank is larger than the southern, and there are deviations in size and shape, with a noticeable narrowing as the monument rises towards the summit. There are sections where the banks widen and narrow together, suggesting these variations were purposefully designed. There are six breaks in the bank, two of which have corresponding breaks in the ditches (Fig. 6.30). Both are positioned centrally on the southern earthwork. The varying slope within the cursus restricts internal visibility, but there are extensive views of the Baltinglass landscape from all parts of the interior. Conversely, the natural topography restricts visibility to the north, east and south, with the result that the summit cairn is not visible from inside the cursus despite abutting its eastern end. It has been observed that when standing at the centre of the cursus on the morning of the summer solstice (21st June), and looking towards the summit, the sun rises behind Keadeen Mountain to flood the interior with light.

LiDAR survey has identified up to four additional cursus monuments at Baltinglass. These include examples at Boleylug, Sruhaun, Ballinacrow Lower and Hughstown (see

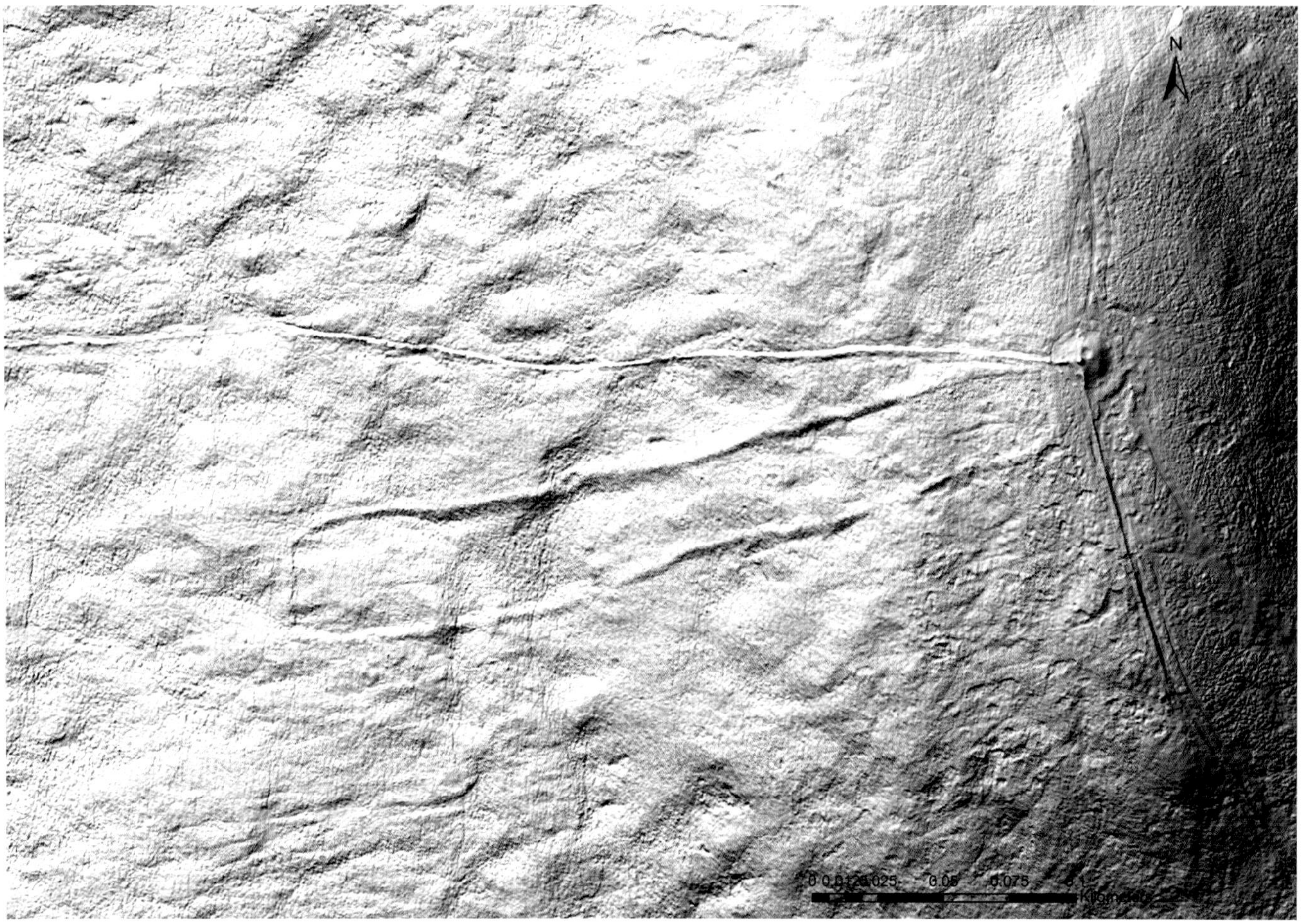

Fig. 6.29 Hillshade model of the Keadeen cursus, from LiDAR data.

Fig. 6.30). The Boleylug cursus is 98m from a tributary of the River Slaney, at the edge of a steep break of slope. It measures 113m long by 24m wide and rises 13m from the river on the western side towards the east. The eastern terminal is rounded; the western side is open. The LiDAR data shows two parallel banks, 7.2–9.3m in width, with no evidence of an entrance. The interior is notably sunken, restricting visibility to the north and east. The nearby river and the Neolithic enclosures of Rathcoran and Hughstown are highly visible, while one of the large cairns and another possible early enclosure on Kilranelagh Hill are in view on the eastern side. The cursus runs E/NE, orientated on a dip between two hillocks to the east. Within this dip, the sun rises at 7.21am on the Autumn equinox when looking along the axis of the cursus.

The cursus at Sruhaun has a similar landscape setting (Fig. 6.31). Positioned at the western base of Tuckmill Hill close to the River Slaney, its western end is truncated by modern housing. The eastern side survives as a 131m-long, 29.5m-wide pair of parallel banks, each up to 7.3m wide, with a slightly sunken interior. The cursus narrows to 22m at the east, where a sub-circular terminal is apparent. There are hints the earthwork crosses the River Slaney and terminates with another sub-circular terminal, potentially creating a 427m-long monument. This has an E/W orientation, rising 51m along its length. It seems to be orientated on the Pinnacle summit of Baltinglass Hill, with its Neolithic passage tomb and enclosure. While viewshed analysis indicates these features are not visible from the cursus, at 8.15am on the day of the Autumn equinox, the sun rises over Baltinglass Hill, breaking the crest of the hill in line with the long axis of the cursus, cairns and enclosure.

Another cursus in Ballinacrow Lower follows the line of a river terrace (Fig. 6.32). Again, there is a set of parallel banks, each up to 5.4m wide and placed 54.5m apart, with some indication the northern bank has an internal ditch (see

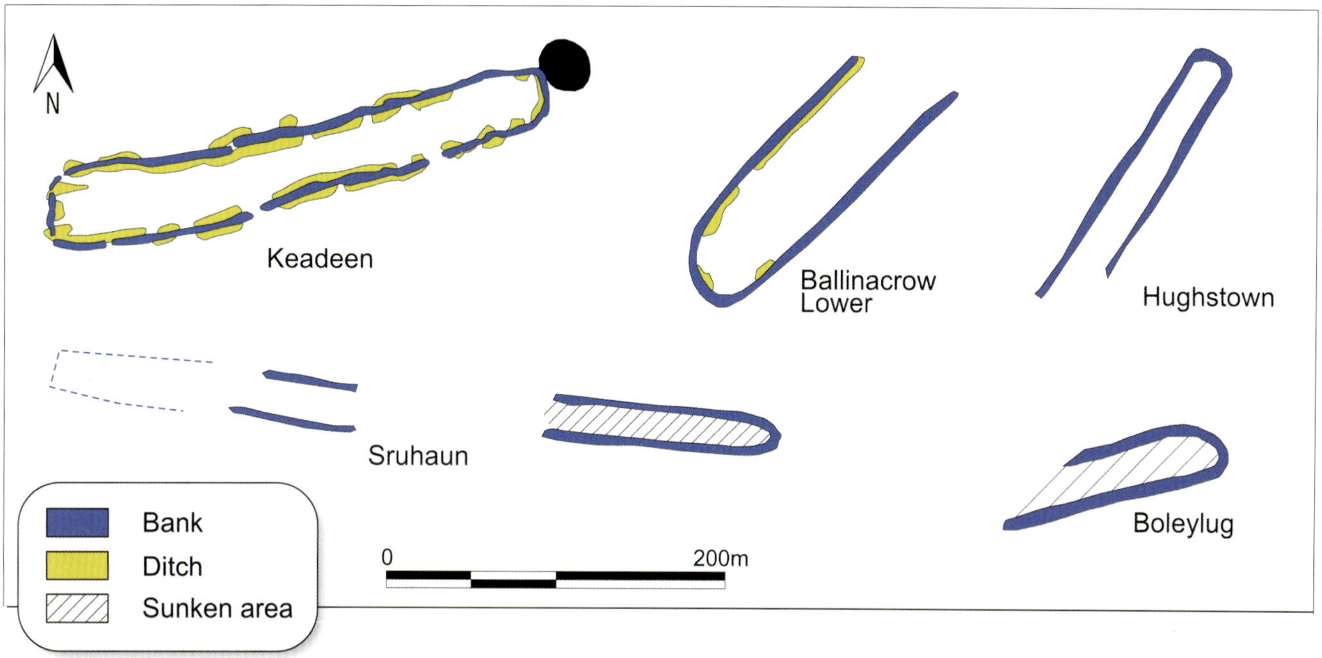

Fig. 6.30 Plan of the cursus monuments identified in the Baltinglass landscape.

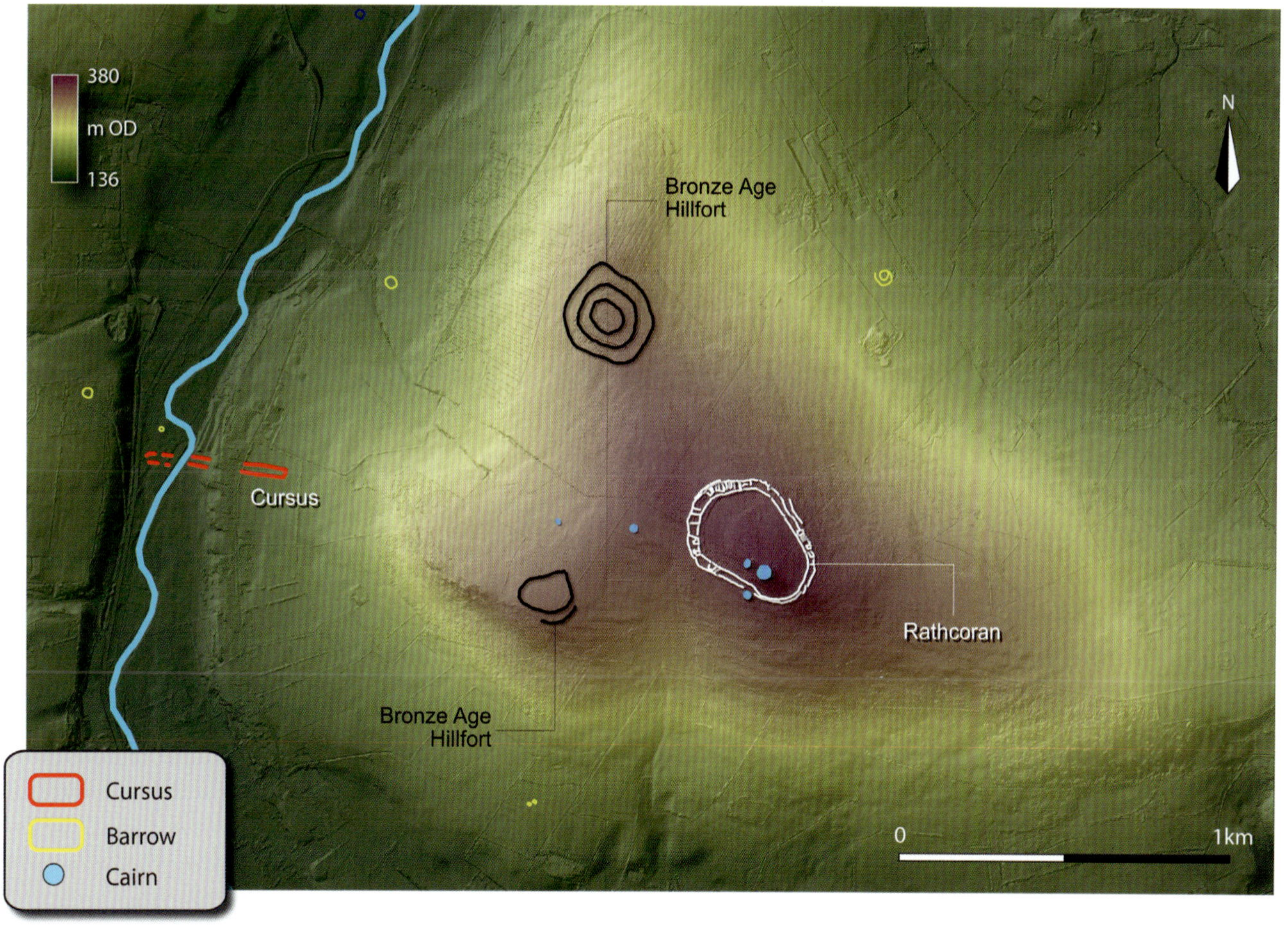

Fig. 6.31 Plan of the Sruhaun cursus complex.

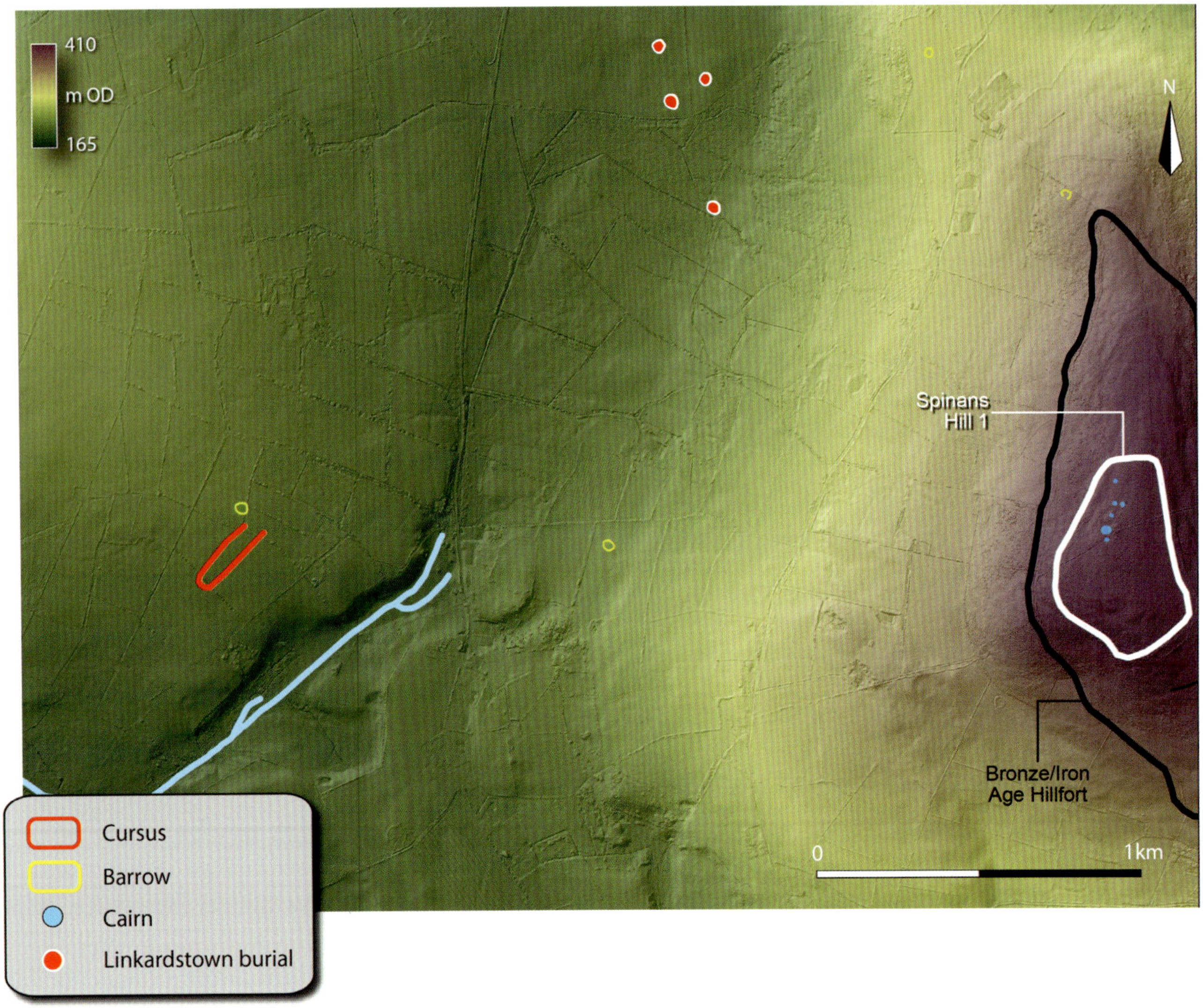

Fig. 6.32 Plan of the Ballinacrow Lower cursus complex.

Fig. 6.30). The south-western end of the cursus has a sub-circular terminal, where the axial banks narrow to 43.5m. Notably, the southern bank is straight, while the northern example is slightly curved. The cursus runs for 185m, rising 7.5m along its length. From this cursus, there is limited visibility of the Linkardstown burial site at Ballintruer More to the north-east. That burial ground comes into view as an observer reaches the north-eastern end of the cursus. On the morning of the Summer solstice, the sun rises in line with the long axis of this cursus over the Ballintruer More burial site, suggesting the latter was significant in the orientation of this linear earthwork.

A possible fifth cursus in this area was previously identified by the Archaeological Survey of Ireland, close to the southern side of the Early Neolithic enclosure at Hughstown (Fig. 6.33). This is recorded as a 171m-long by 29.8m-wide structure, created by two parallel banks each up to 5m in width (Figs 6.30 and 6.34). The cursus is orientated NE/SW, with its south-western end open and its north-eastern end defined by a squared terminal. This monument has since been planted with forestry. Close to this cursus there is a possible hut platform (KD036-026) of unknown date.

The potential cursus sites identified at Baltinglass are now the largest group known in Ireland, and this is the only location with more than two examples (see Newman 1999). In Britain, clusters are more common (Brophy 2016, 137). These large monuments represent massive investments of

Fig. 6.33 Photograph of Hughstown cursus complex (lower centre), July 1966 (reproduced with permission of the Cambridge Collection of Aerial Photography; © copyright reserved).

time, labour and resources on major construction projects that may have served to connect communities under a single, cohesive identity (Loveday 2015, 468). Whereas the function of cursus monuments is uncertain (Barber 2018), the Baltinglass sites seem to show a connection between the dead, major solar events and seasonal farming cycles. The rising of the sun over burial complexes during significant solar events may have symbolised the ascent of the dead into the heavens, their perceived rebirth and/or the blessing of the ancestors. The cursus may have physically demarcated the final route of the dead, the place where they left the land of the living and joined the ancestors beyond the visible horizon.

Barrows

A significant number of definite or possible ring-barrows have been identified in the Baltinglass landscape, through a combination of aerial photography, LiDAR and geophysical survey (Fig. 6.35). These monuments usually comprise an annular bank with internal ditch surrounding a flat space or mound, and there are many morphological variants (Newman 1997, 155–7). They were primarily used to inter the dead, and usually contain one or more cremations of high-status individuals; the burnt bone is generally placed in the central area, or occasionally the ditch. While many were built in the Bronze Age, there are some examples from the Neolithic, and ring-barrows were built through the Iron Age into the early medieval period (Waddell 1998). They can

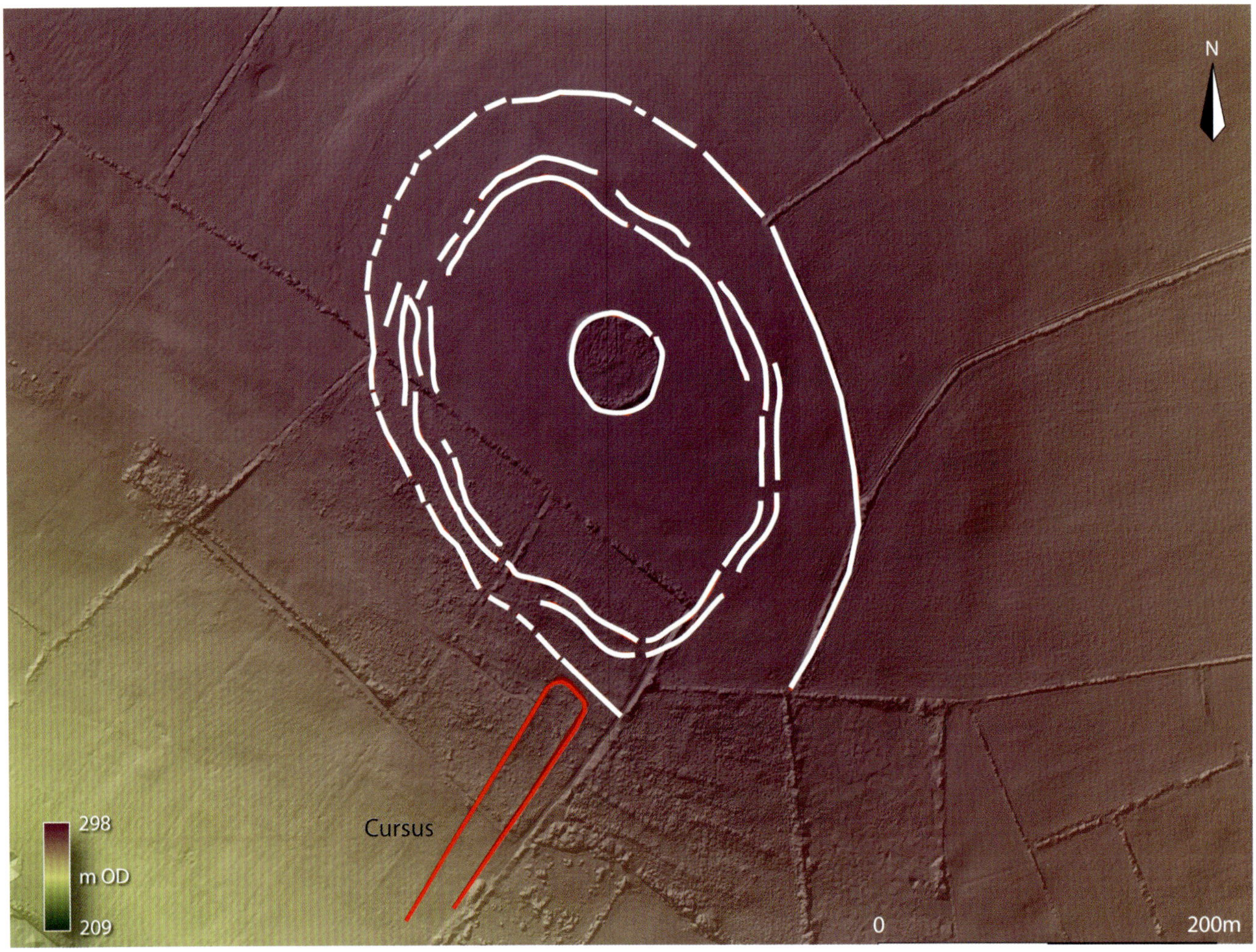

Fig. 6.34 Plan of possible cursus monument at Hughstown, based on Cambridge University aerial survey photograph, July 1966.

occur individually or in cemetery groups, with the latter often used over a long period. Excavation is required to date these monuments, as surface morphology is no guide to age.

As well as being ritual monuments honouring the dead, Woodward (2000) and Cooney (2009, 376–8) suggest ring-barrows also functioned as 'landscape monuments', with cemeteries arranged in certain ways to emphasise ancestral history and lineage. In many traditional societies, the knowledge of descent, genealogy, alliance and inheritance is an important form of legitimacy and power (Thomas 2007, 261). For Bronze Age elites, this 'access to origins', and the control of 'media' believed to be closely related to ancestry, would have been crucial to their rule (Kristiansen and Larsson 2005, 45). Groups of barrows could have been used to visibly express a society's rights to land or resources through patterns of actual or imagined lineage, which may have been particularly important at territorial margins.

This is suggested in different ways in the Baltinglass landscape, where a number of possible barrows are all in low-lying areas, either at the base of hills with hillforts or adjacent to streams and rivers (see Fig. 6.35). Clusters of barrows appear at the base of Baltinglass Hill, Tinoran Hill and Spinans Hill, whereas individual barrows or small groups of up to four are found near rivers and streams. The large group of unrecorded barrows at the south-eastern base of Baltinglass Hill occurs at an excellent access point to the summit, where the gradient of slope is least severe (O'Driscoll 2016). Other access routes outlined by Least-Cost-Path analysis (O'Driscoll 2016) to the west and north/north-west are close to smaller barrow groups. There are also a number of individual barrows and cist burials to the east and north-west. It seems the base of this hill was surrounded by numerous burial monuments, with clusters of visible barrows in areas that allowed access to the summit.

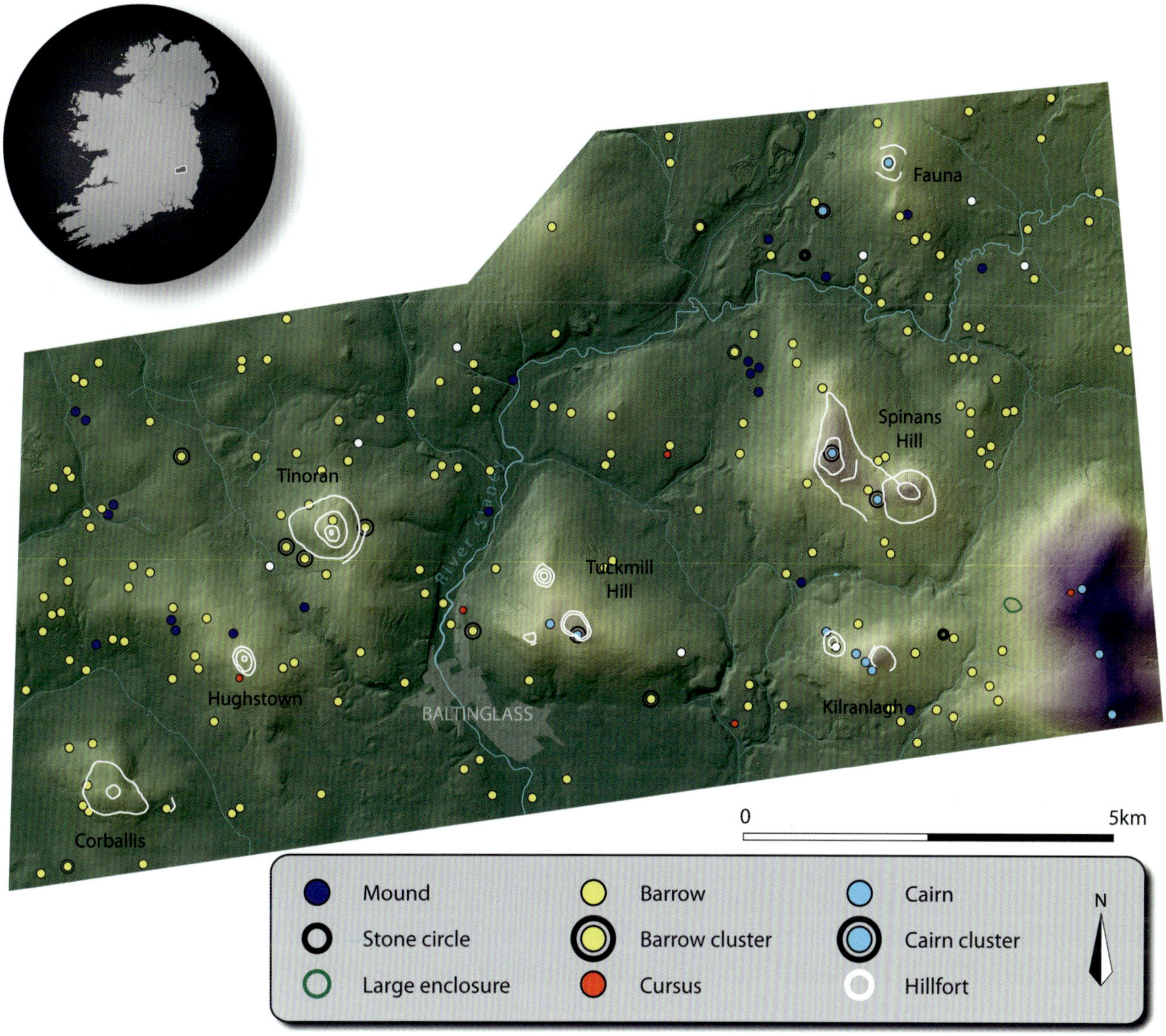

Fig. 6.35 Distribution of possible burial mounds and barrows, as well as other prehistoric ritual monuments, in the Baltinglass landscape.

This latter arrangement could be viewed as an attempt to force visitors to progress past burial monuments that emphasise the legitimacy of the community associated with the hill and its leaders, while the former could be a reserved effort to placate local hilltop deities, to ensure the fertility of the land and its people. A similar scenario could be argued for at Tinoran, where there is an exceptionally large ring-barrow (WI026-005) adjacent to the hillfort (see Fig. 5.30; also Fig. 8.7 below). Barrows and possible Linkardstown burial mounds have been identified near the north-western base of Spinans Hill, where the only obvious entrance to the massive Spinans Hill 2 contour fort is located.

There is also a notable concentration of barrows near rivers and streams in the Baltinglass area (see O'Driscoll 2016). These monuments to the dead may have been placed near territorial boundaries, to both physically and ritually demarcate a community's tribal ground. A number of researchers, including Grogan (2005b, 140), Mason (2013, 273) and Tilley (2010, 221), have suggested that barrows could have acted as significant territorial markers on or near important routeways. They may also have demarcated important places, an example being a newly discovered, exceptionally large ring-barrow, 72m in diameter, overlooking a large bog in Moneymore and Hartstown

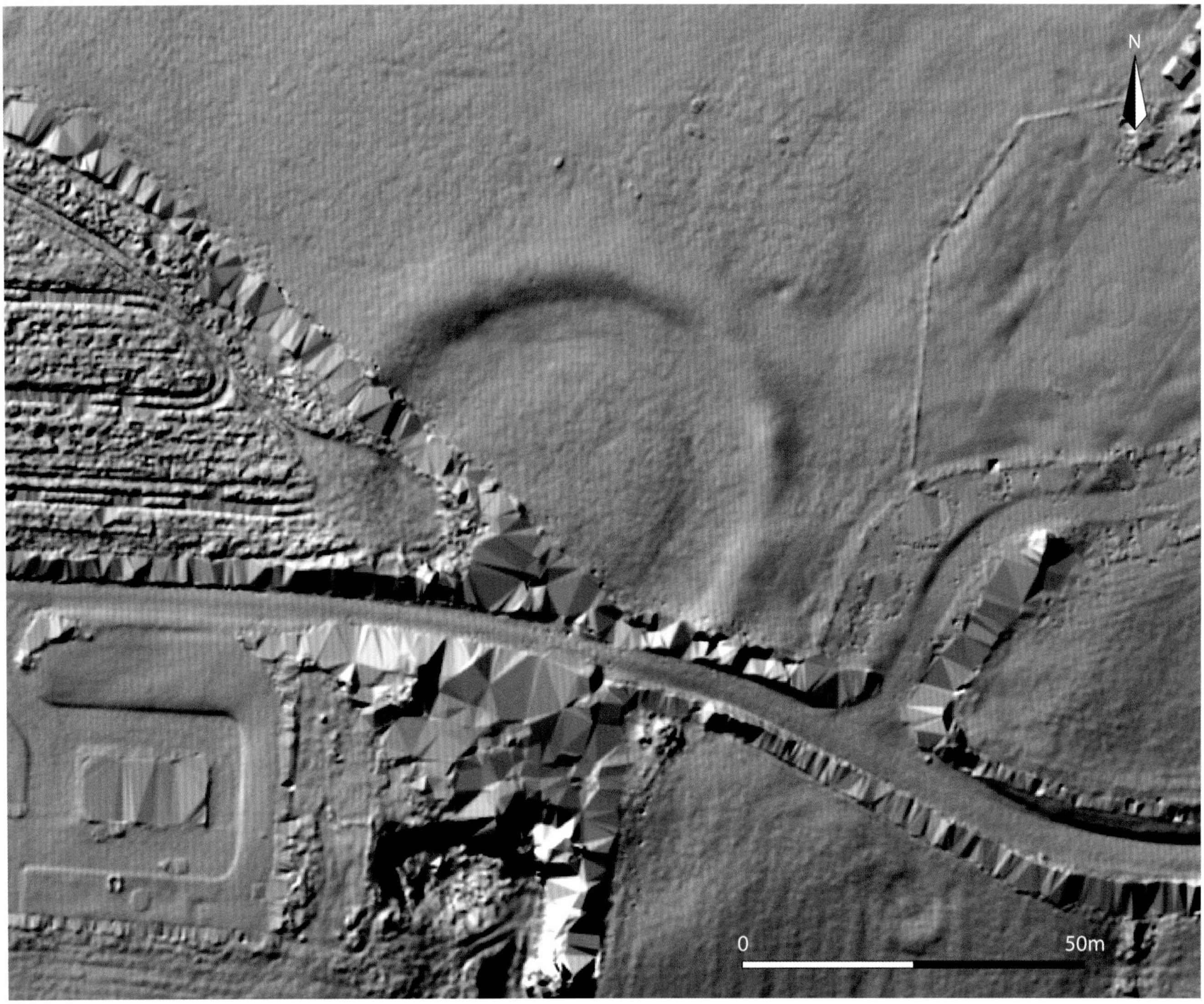

Fig. 6.36 Large, unrecorded ring-barrow in Knockarigg Hill townland, north of Tinoran hillfort.

townlands to the north of Tinoran (Fig. 6.36). Cunliffe (1991, 510) views natural settings, such as springs, streams and woodlands, as religious and ritual locations. The importance of rivers and bogs in later prehistory is also emphasised by the considerable number of prestige objects deposited at such locations. They are often interpreted as liminal places, where rituals of various types may have been conducted. The presence of an exceptionally large burial monument near such a location may imply its importance.

The 'power' of the ancestors played a significant role in the social and cosmological order of tribal societies (Waddell *et al.* 2009, 205). We could consider the positioning of barrows in the Baltinglass landscape as deliberate — helping to define territories, acting as physical and visible links to the past and reinforcing ancestral rights to land and resources by the people who inhabited these territories.

Early medieval ringforts

LiDAR survey has also significantly increased the number of recorded ringforts in the Baltinglass landscape (Fig. 6.37). These enclosed settlements mostly date to the early medieval period, with as many as 47,000 extant examples in Ireland (Stout 1997). Some 300 have been excavated (Comber 2008; O'Sullivan *et al.* 2008), confirming their construction and use from the fourth to the twelfth century AD. The majority were used by the average subsistence farmer, while

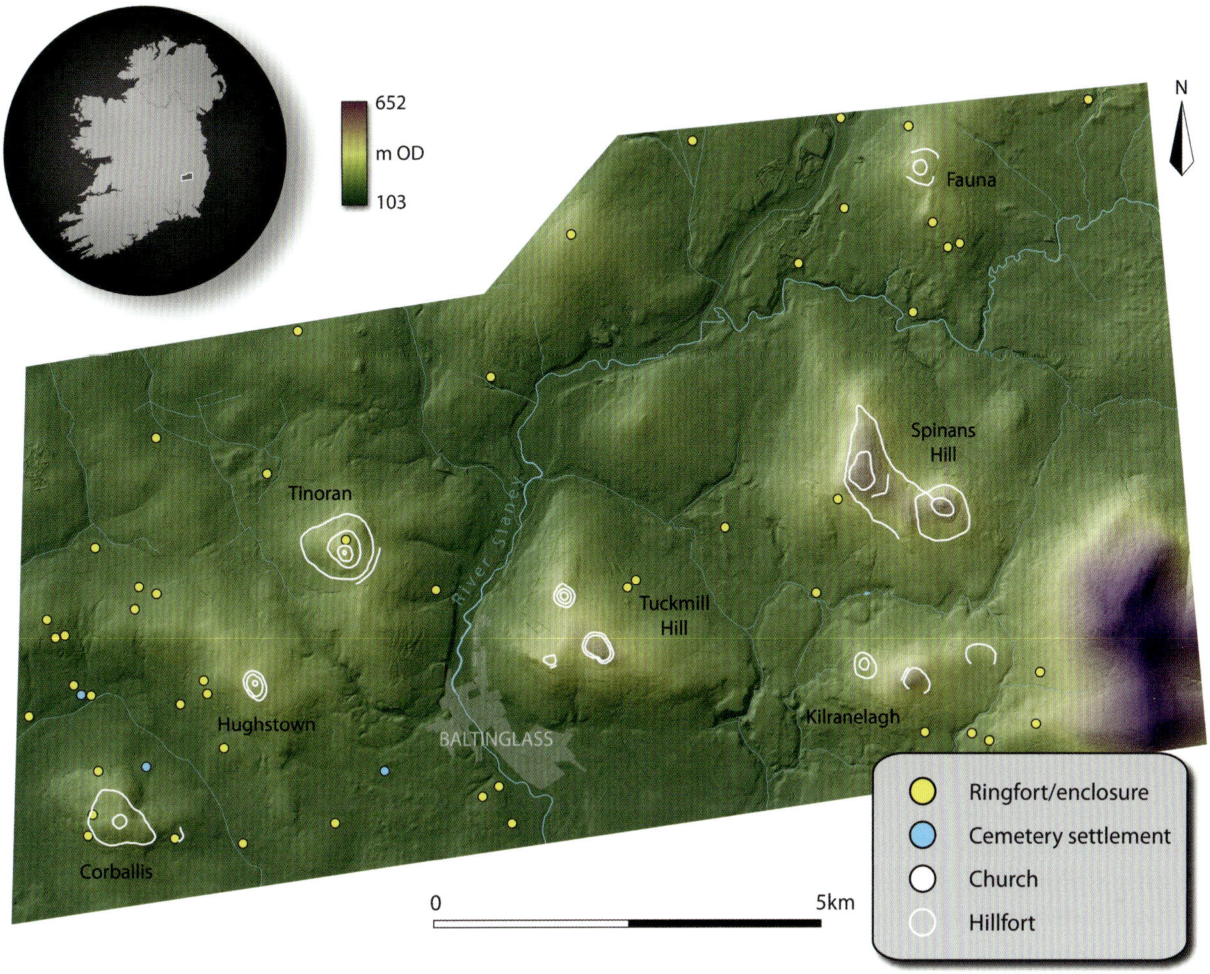

Fig. 6.37 Distribution of possible ringforts in the Baltinglass landscape.

larger multivallate examples, such as at Garranes, Co. Cork (O'Brien and Hogan 2021), were the residence of elites and high-status craftworkers.

No ringfort in the Baltinglass landscape has been excavated. Most are small, univallate enclosures, probably a protected family farmstead. One site that does stand out is a large, univallate ringfort in the townland of Rathbran, north of Baltinglass Hill. The enclosure is 73.6m in diameter, with a single, east-facing entrance. LiDAR survey and satellite photography have revealed a pair of 5.5m-wide banks extending from this entrance for a distance of 214m, towards the northern side of Spinans Hill. They form a rare, funnelled entrance to the ringfort that can only be paralleled on Iron Age royal centres such as Navan Fort and some cropmark sites in the central lowlands (Rassmann *et al.* 2022, 358). Such sites are more readily identified in Wales, where they are termed 'banjo enclosures' (Murphy *et al.* 2012). These typically date to the first centuries BC/AD and are sometimes associated with high-status occupants. Price (1949a, 121) had previously recognised the potential importance of this fort, linking the name of the townland (Rathbran – 'the fort of Bran') with the provincial king Brandub, who may have resided in the Baltinglass area (see Chapter 8).

CONCLUSIONS

While recent survey and excavation have provided valuable insights about the Baltinglass hillforts, this chapter shows how much more research is required to understand their cultural landscape setting. LiDAR survey has revealed a large number of new archaeological monuments, including several massive hilltop enclosures that have been obscured by commercial forestry, while adding significant new detail about previously recorded sites. These are only the monuments with visible traces on the surface; many more sites likely exist beneath the ground.

We now have a better understanding of the Spinans Hill complex and the massive 131ha fort of Spinans Hill 2. The LiDAR data reveals a substantial earthwork with very few entrance breaks, suggesting that this could have functioned as a defensive structure. This massive enclosure incorporates Brusselstown Ring at its south-eastern edge, and the relationship of their enclosing elements suggests the latter was built before Spinans Hill 2. How long before is a question that can only be answered through excavation. It is possible, however, that Brusselstown Ring, along with its dense concentration of hundreds of houses, formed an urban-like domestic centre that expanded to incorporate the entire hill. There is comparative evidence to place this complex either in the Late Bronze Age or at the end of the Iron Age, and to suggest potential links with the royal caput of Dún Bolg. There is, therefore, a pressing need for future excavation here.

Given that Early Neolithic enclosures in Ireland and Britain do not usually exceed 11ha or so, it is possible that the larger enclosures at Baltinglass date to the later prehistoric period. The newly discovered 41ha multiple-enclosure hillfort on Corballis Hill, and the 16ha site on Fauna Hill, may be Bronze Age hillforts. Again, this needs to be confirmed by excavation. The smaller hilltop enclosures at Kilranelagh may be earlier in date. The 7.76ha enclosure at the summit of the hill is associated with three large cairns, drawing comparisons with Rathcoran and its Neolithic passage tomb. More difficult to date is the 12.46ha site on the eastern spur of Kilranelagh. This potential site surrounds a ring-barrow and the embanked stone circle of Boleycarrigeen, suggestive of a Late Neolithic or Bronze Age date. It is difficult to assess the site, given the damage caused by commercial forestry. On the western slopes of Kilranelagh, a newly identified 6.64ha enclosure may be connected to an early monastic centre, mention of which is made in a number of medieval texts.

LiDAR, aerial and satellite imagery, along with targeted geophysical survey, demonstrate how new sites remain to be found on the hill slopes and lowlands of Baltinglass. As many as five possible cursus monuments have been identified, potentially the largest concentration of such monuments in Ireland. Other broadly contemporary monuments include a possible Linkardstown cemetery at Ballintruer More. Other burial monuments such as mounds and ring-barrows have been identified, found in low-lying settings, near rivers or at the base of important hills such as Tinoran or Tuckmill.

Furthermore, some unusually large enclosures have been identified in lowland settings at Baltinglass. Sites such as Rathmoon are interpreted as early medieval cemetery settlements, representing kin-based burial sites used for local assemblies. LiDAR has also significantly increased the number of potential ringforts at Baltinglass, emphasising the important early medieval component in this cultural landscape. More research is required to examine the significance of Baltinglass as an early medieval power centre in Leinster, a subject we will return to in Chapter 8.

7. SETTLEMENT AND ENVIRONMENT

Kevin Kearney

This chapter presents the results of a detailed palaeoecological study of Holocene vegetation change and human activity in the wider Baltinglass landscape. Palaeoecology is the study of long-term vegetation patterns and includes a range of palaeoenvironmental techniques used to investigate past changes in terrestrial environments. Pollen analysis, or palynology as it is termed, is one of the most established of those approaches. When preserved in anoxic environments, pollen grains provide a valuable insight into the kinds of vegetation that grew in a given location in the past, allowing the identification of plants to family, genus and even species level from distinct morphological characteristics. Palynology is frequently used to investigate the environmental context of archaeological sites in order to enhance their interpretation, particularly with respect to settlement, agriculture and woodland clearance (Mitchell 1954; Mitchel and Cooney 2004; Molloy and O'Connell 1995). Palaeoenvironmental studies have greatly enhanced our understanding of past human activity, allowing for a broader interpretation of the interaction of and interference by past peoples with their natural environment. It is possible through analysis of sub-fossil pollen specimens to enhance the picture created by the interpretation of material culture, and to infer the presence of human activity where there is no archaeological record.

Palynology samples contain a combination of locally and regionally derived pollen grains; the former coming from vegetation that would have grown close to the depositional basin, and the latter a homogenous representation of regional vegetation that is collected, carried and deposited by airflows. These differing origins are reflected in the types of pollen that are represented in different environments (Jacobson and Bradshaw 1981; Sugita 1994; 2007a; 2007b; Sugita *et al.* 1999). Typically, peatland sites contain three main pollen sources (Jacobson and Bradshaw 1981), beginning with plants growing on and around the sampling site, such as *Sphagnum* spp. (bog moss), Cyperaceae (sedges) and Ericaceae (heathers). The next source is extra-local plants growing in the vicinity of the sampling basin, such as *Corylus avellana*-type (hazel) and *Alnus* (alder). Finally, sources of regional pollen from vegetation growing in the wider landscape might include such trees as *Quercus* (oak) and *Pinus sylvestris* (Scots pine).

Taxon-specific factors also have a role in determining the representation of different vegetation in a pollen sample. First, entomophilous taxa (insect-pollinated) tend to be under-represented in the pollen record compared to anemophilous taxa (wind-pollinated), as the former produce less pollen of a type suitable for wind dispersal. Several key non-arboreal pollen (NAP) taxa, such as Asteraceae (daisies) and *Cerealia*-type, and certain arboreal taxa such as Maloideae (crab-apple/pear, etc.), are either insect- or self-pollinating (autogamous), and so are under-represented in palynological studies. An understanding of pollination methods, be they anemophilous, entomophilous or autogamous, is therefore of primary importance in palynlogical research, as is the varying rate of decrease of dispersed pollen grains. Moreover, an appreciation of the processes affecting deposition and preservation of different types of pollen assists in reconstructing local vegetation records.

Second, the amount of pollen produced differs between taxa, and this can influence their representation in the fossil record. For example, many arboreal taxa, such as Scots pine, are high pollen producers, whereas herbaceous taxa tend to be lower producers, therefore low representation of the latter may still be significant. Several environmental factors influence pollen productivity, including climate, vegetation patterning and structure, which in turn influences availability of light and location in relation to the taxon habitat range. Pollen transportation introduces further complexities; for example, dispersal of pollen released by understory plants will be slowed by standing vegetation, whereas pollen released higher in the canopy may travel greater distances in faster winds (Moore *et al.* 1991). Finally, as pollen grains are morphologically distinct, the size, shape and features can influence dispersal. For example, Scots pine pollen has two air bladders, which makes it more efficient for wind dispersal, thus increasing its representation in palynology samples. Pollen dispersed or carried in water may accumulate at considerable distances from point of origin, with serious implications for palynological interpretation.

Fig. 7.1 Aerial view of kettle bog at Holdenstown Upper, Baltinglass.

These factors can impact greatly on the relationship between pollen frequency and vegetation abundance at any particular site, with implications for an understanding of biodiversity.

POLLEN ANALYSIS AT HOLDENSTOWN UPPER

In May 2020, the author (KK) sampled a small kettle bog at Holdenstown Upper, approximately 5km south of Baltinglass (Fig. 7.1). A 3.10m-deep peat core was taken using a 0.5m-long Russian corer with a cylindrical diameter of 6cm (Fig. 7.2). Sub-sampling for pollen analysis was carried out at depth intervals of 2cm or 4cm. Sub-samples of 1cm^3 were prepared for pollen analyses following standard techniques, including potassium hydroxide (KOH) digestion, hydrofluoric acid (HF) treatment and acetylation (Moore *et al.* 1991). Pollen concentrations were established by adding a known concentration of *Lycopodium clavatum* spore (batch number 177745) to the samples before treatment (Stockmarr 1971). Pollen counts were made using a Leica DM 1000 LED microscope at ×400, ×800 and ×1000 magnification, under oil immersion for critical examination of pollen sculpture and measurement of pollen grains. A minimum pollen sum of 500 Total Land Pollen (TLP) grains, excluding spores and aquatics, was employed. Pollen grains were identified mainly using the key from Moore *et al.* (1991) and Bennett (1995), with reference to Fægri *et al.* (1989). Pollen and spore identification was made to the lowest taxonomic level possible using the available references and following the nomenclature of Stace (1997), with suggestions from Bennett *et al.* (1994). The programs TILIA and TILIA - GRAPH (Grimm 2013) were used to construct spreadsheets and pollen diagrams. Local pollen assemblage zones (LPAZ) were defined based on visible changes in the pollen record.

The designation '*cf*' in this study indicates the closest identification possible, but not an exact match, or that type material was not available to confirm the identification. *Cerealia*-type pollen (cereal) was distinguished from other Poaceae (grass) pollen based on the size of grain pore and annulus, with the results presented in a separate curve. Monoporate pollen grains of less than 37µm were placed in the Poaceae (non-cultivated grass) curve (cf. Moore *et al.* 1991). The difficulty in the separation of *Myrica gale* (sweet-

Fig. 7.2 Coring at Holdenstown Upper.

gale) and *Corylus avellana* (hazel) pollen resulted in these grains being classified as *Corylus avellana*-type (Edwards 1981). For the saccate grains of Scots pine, the individual air sacs were counted and subsequently divided by two, in order to estimate the number of grains.

Eight samples of organic sediment (peat) from this core were AMS-radiocarbon dated at Queen's University Belfast (Fig. 7.3). The results are presented as conventional radiocarbon ages (Stuiver and Polach 1977) and calibrated to calendrical years BC/AD using the published datasets, IntCal20, (Reimer *et al.* 2020) and the computer program OxCal v4.4 (Bronk Ramsey 2009a). The calibrated date ranges have been calculated using the maximum intercept method (Stuiver and Reimer 1986) and the graphical distribution of the calibrated dates are derived from the probability method (Stuiver and Reimer 1993). All radiocarbon dates are cited at 95.4% confidence, unless stated otherwise.

In order to refine the chronology of palynological features and extend the chronological framework to changes that fall between dated horizons, Bayesian analysis was applied to the modelling of these radiocarbon dates (Buck *et al.* 1992). The Bayesian approach has been widely discussed

Fig. 7.3 Radiocarbon dates from the Holdenstown Upper pollen core.

Depth	Dated material	Lab code	Radiocarbon date BP	95.4% (2 sigma) probability
100cm	Peat (humin fraction)	UBA-45676	2685±25	900–803 cal. BC
125cm	Peat (humin fraction)	UBA-45675	1776±33	cal. AD 214–373
150cm	Peat (humin fraction)	UBA-45061	3885±27	2466–2239 cal. BC
175cm	Peat (humin fraction)	UBA-45674	6192±36	5295–5030 cal. BC
200cm	Peat (humin fraction)	UBA-45673	6330±35	5371–5216 cal. BC
225cm	Peat (humin fraction)	UBA-45672	7177±37	6087–5926 cal. BC
250cm	Peat (humin fraction)	UBA-45060	5770±32	4711–4541 cal. BC
300cm	Peat (humin fraction)	UBA-45059	8746±38	7944–7606 cal. BC

in the literature (see, for example, Blaauw and Christen 2005; Blaauw *et al.* 2007a; 2007b; 2018; Bronk Ramsey 2008). The approach taken here uses the software OxCal v4.4 program (Bronk Ramsey 2009a), and the *P_Sequence* function (Bronk Ramsey 2008) was chosen to allow for a Poisson process, or a potentially random rate of sediment formation. The prior information for the deposition rate was defined as log_10(*k*/*k*_0) where k_0 = 1. This allows *k* to take any value from 0.01 to 100. This value used was estimated from the radiocarbon dates following the approach outlined in Blockley *et al.* (2007, 2008) The command *Outlier()* was used in OxCal (Bronk Ramsey 2009b) to identify any measurements that were statistically defined as outliers at a 0.05 probability (1 in 20 chance).

Results

Chronology

Two radiocarbon dates (UBA-45060 and UBA-45675) were identified as outliers (Fig. 7.4) and were excluded from an age-depth model created to provide a chronology for the sequence (after Bronk Ramsey 2008). The *P_Sequence* model (Fig. 7.5) has good agreement (Amodel = 99) and has been used to provide estimates for the boundaries between the local pollen assemblage zones (Fig. 7.6). The pollen sequence at Holdenstown Upper is estimated to span a period of *c.*9,300 years. Estimates derived from the age-depth model suggest an average deposition rate of 3cm/100 year (distribution not shown) between the upper and basal radiocarbon measurements, representing 34 years (distribution not shown) in every centimetre. While a relatively stable rate of accumulation is noted for much of the profile, this reduces considerably between 168–156cm, where an average deposition of 1.2cm/100 year is recorded, representing 81 years in every centimetre in that section of the profile.

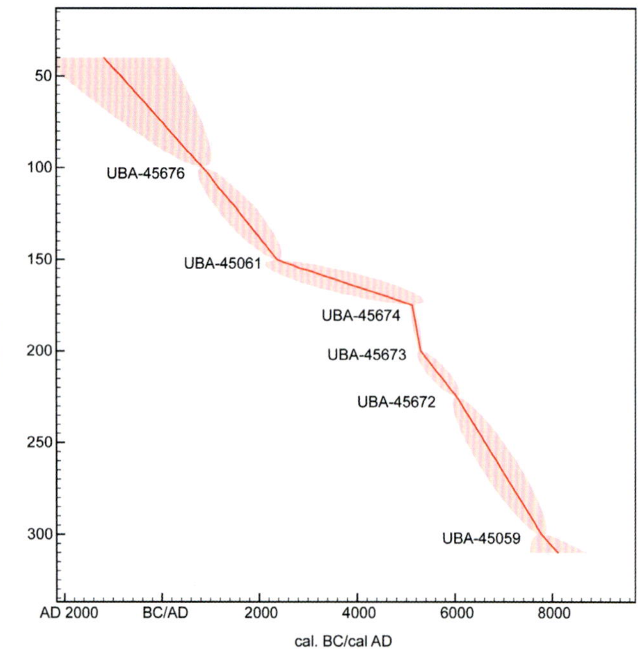

Fig. 7.5 Age-depth model of radiocarbon dates from Holdenstown Upper.

Pollen record

The pollen profile from Holdenstown Upper commences at *c.*8010 BC, with a dominance of arboreal pollen, primarily hazel, oak, birch and elm. Low levels of Scots pine are also noted (Fig. 7.7). Open grassland environments are restricted during LPAZ HU1, with only trace amounts of grasses, sedge, mugwort, daisies and meadowsweet recorded. This indicates a relatively closed woodland structure *c.*8065–6385 BC, which continues into LPAZ HU2 when alder becomes more prominent, at the expense of hazel, oak and birch. Low levels of non-arboreal pollen are again exhibited throughout this local pollen assemblage zone. Alder continues to increase

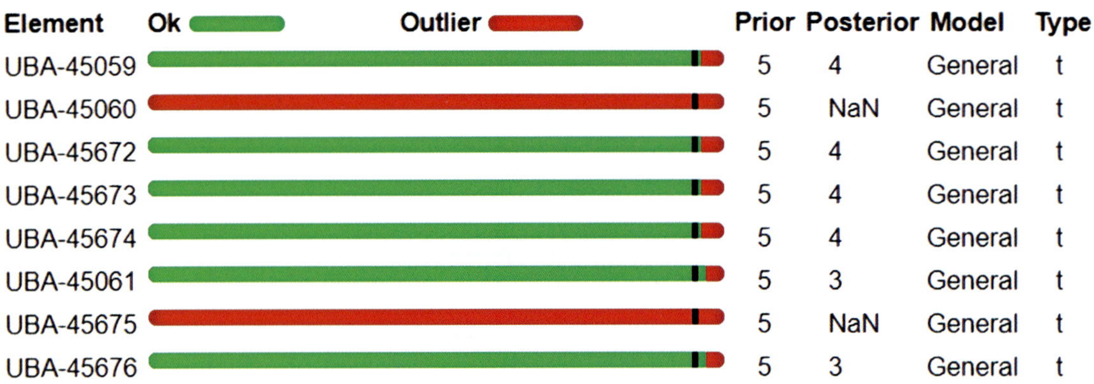

Fig. 7.4 Outlier analysis of radiocarbon dates from Holdenstown Upper.

Fig. 7.6 Results of pollen analysis, Holdenstown Upper.

LPAZ	Depth (top of LPAZ)	LPAZ date range	
HU11	50cm	AD 435–1240	Reduction in *Alnus* (*c*.30 to 20%), *Salix* (*c*.10 to 5%) and *Corylus* (*c*.40 to 20%). Major increase in NAP, primarily Poaceae (*c*.5 to 25%). Continuous presence of *Cerealia*-type (*c*.1–2%) and *Plantago lanceolata* (*c*.2–5%). *Artemisia, Rumex, Urtica, Trifolium, Plantago media/major,* Caryophyllaceae, Chenopodiaceae, Asteraceae, *Rumex* and *Filipendula* recorded. Peak in charcoal (*c*.25%).
HU10	54cm	160 BC–AD 435	High AP values, primarily *Corylus* (c.50%) and *Alnus* (c.40%). NAP values low, primarily Poaceae and Cyperaceae. Trace amounts of *Potentilla*, Asteraceae and *Filipendula*. Charcoal values fluctuate.
HU9	76cm	390–160 BC	Reduction in *Alnus* and *Salix*. Minor increase in NAP, primarily Poaceae (*c*.5 to 10%). *Cerealia*-type again recorded. Trace amounts of *Plantago lanceolata*, Asteraceae, *Rumex, Trifolium* and *Filipendula*. Charcoal values increase marginally.
HU8	84cm	970–390 BC	Dominated by AP, high values of *Corylus* (*c*.30–40%), *Quercus* (*c*.10%), *Alnus* (*c*.40–50%) and *Salix* (*c*.10–20%). NAP values greatly reduced. Charcoal values also low.
HU7	104cm	1410–970 BC	Minor increase in *Corylus* and *Quercus*. Continuously reducing NAP values (*c*.25 to 10%) across LPAZ. *Cerealia*-type again recorded. Continuous low presence of *Plantago lanceolata* (*c*.1%). Trace amounts of *Rumex, Trifolium, Plantago media/major,* Caryophyllaceae, Chenopodiaceae, Asteraceae, *Rumex* and *Filipendula* recorded. Charcoal values increase to *c*.20%.
HU6	118cm	1820–1410 BC	Reduction in *Corylus* and *Quercus*. Considerable increase in NAP values, primarily Poaceae (*c*.7 to 20%), and *Cerealia*-type recorded. Continuous presence of *Plantago lanceolata* (*c*.1–3%). Trace amounts of *Artemisia, Rumex, Trifolium, Plantago media/major,* Caryophyllaceae, Chenopodiaceae, Asteraceae, *Rumex* and *Filipendula* recorded. Charcoal values increase to *c*.15%.
HU5	132cm	3335–1820 BC	Dominated by AP. *Corylus* values increase to *c*.55%. *Ulmus* and *Pinus* recorded sporadically. NAP values increasing, primarily Poaceae and Cyperaceae. Charcoal values fluctuate (*c*.1–10%).
HU4	158cm	4195–3335 BC	Minor reduction in overall AP values, primarily *Alnus* (c.50 to 45%), and *Corylus* (c.35 to 30%). Considerable decline in *Ulmus* (*c*.10 to <1%). *Fraxinus* begins to appear continuously. NAP values increase but still very low; trace amounts of Poaceae, Cyperaceae, *Plantago lanceolata*, Chenopodiaceae, Asteraceae, *Rumex* and *Filipendula*. Charcoal values also low.
HU3	166cm	5950–4195 BC	Dominated by AP. *Alnus* values increase to *c*.55%, *Salix* also increases (*c*.7–15%). Reduction in *Corylus, Betula, Ulmus, Pinus* and *Quercus*. NAP values very low. Charcoal values also low.
HU2	222cm	6385–5950 BC	Dominated by AP. *Alnus* values increase across the LPAZ to *c*.20%, minor reduction in *Corylus, Betula* and *Quercus*. NAP values very low. Charcoal values increase marginally.
HU1	240cm	8065–6385 BC	Dominated by AP, high values of *Corylus* (*c*.40–50%), *Quercus* (*c*.25–35%), *Betula* (*c*.10–20%), *Ulmus* (*c*.10–15%) and *Pinus* (*c*.1–6%). Trace amounts of *Alnus* also recorded. NAP values very low, trace amounts of Poaceae, Cyperaceae, *Artemisia*, Asteraceae and *Filipendula*. Charcoal values also low.

in LPAZ HU3 (*c*.5950–4195 BC) at the expense of birch, oak, hazel and elm. That expansion, with an increased representation of willow, suggests the formation of carr woodland on wet ground close to the sampling site. Despite the reduction in birch, oak, hazel and elm, these trees continued to be major components of the woodland canopy, but were probably restricted to the drier mineral soils in the vicinity. The low levels of herbaceous taxa suggest that the local woodland remained undisturbed throughout this zone.

A minor reduction in woodland taxa is exhibited in LPAZ HU4 (*c*.4195–3335 BC), primarily through a collapse in elm values, although a minor reduction in alder and hazel is also exhibited. Herbaceous taxa increase marginally following the reduction in elm, with a small increase in grasses and the sporadic occurrence of light-demanding ruderal taxa such as ribwort plantain. This minor increase in non-arboreal pollen, in addition to continuing representation of ash, indicates a more open woodland canopy from *c*.3900 BC. A regeneration of local woodland occurs in LPAZ HU5 (*c*.3335–1820 BC), primarily with an expansion of hazel. Elm and Scots pine are only recorded sporadically in this zone and largely cease to be a component of the local vegetation thereafter. Values of herbaceous taxa are low at the start of LPAZ HU5, but begin to increase by *c*.1820 BC.

Greatly increased values of non-arboreal taxa are exhibited in LPAZ HU6 (*c*.1820–1410 BC), with grass expanding rapidly and ribwort plantain recorded

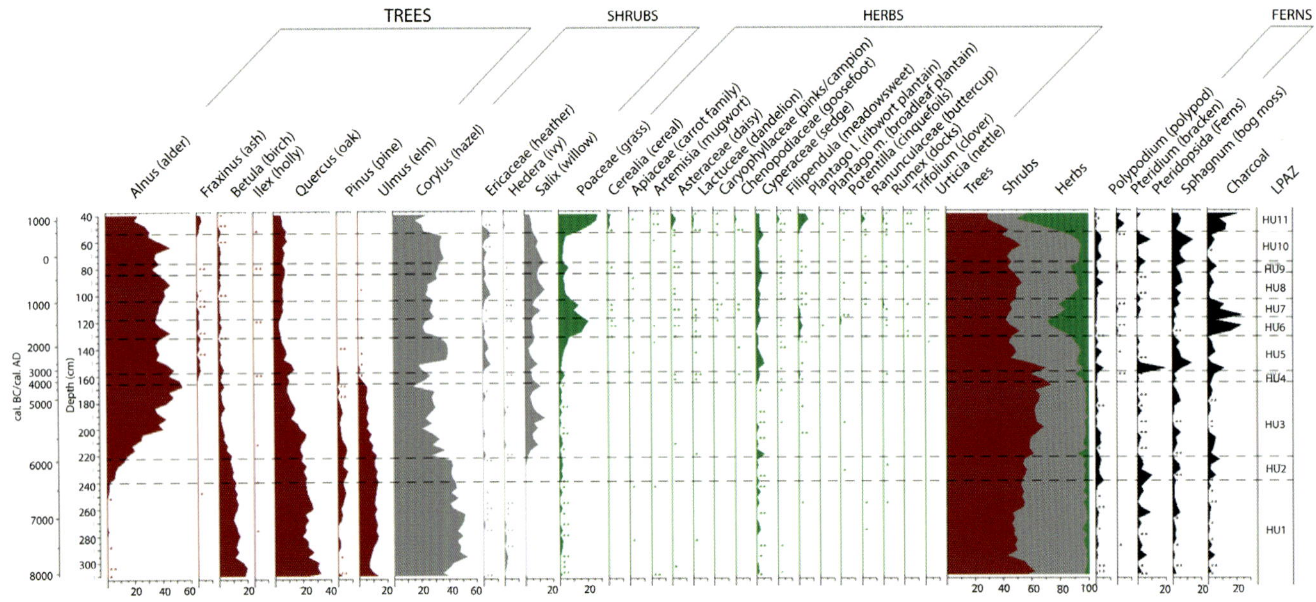

Fig. 7.7 Pollen diagram from Holdenstown Upper, Baltinglass.

continuously. The first record of cereal pollen is noted during LPAZ HU6, while docks, daisies, dandelions, clover, mugwort and goosefoot occur more regularly. The representation of micro-charcoal also increases considerably during this zone. A decrease in hazel and oak values *c.*1820–1410 BC coincides with an increase in herbaceous taxa, suggesting a reduction in woodland to create land suitable for arable and pastoral agriculture. A minor recovery of hazel and oak is exhibited during LPAZ HU7 (*c.*1410–970 BC). Herbaceous taxa are still strongly represented, and cereal pollen is again recorded, but both steadily and gradually decline across this zone, to indicate continued, but reducing, levels of arable and pastoral agriculture *c.*1410–970 BC.

Arboreal pollen values, especially hazel, oak, alder and willow continue to expand across LPAZ HU8 (*c.*970–390 BC), while levels of herbaceous taxa and micro-charcoal are greatly reduced. This would suggest a cessation, or at least major reduction, in human activity through LPAZ HU8. There are marginally increased levels of herbaceous taxa in LPAZ HU9 (*c.*390–160 BC), with cereal pollen again recorded and fluctuating charcoal values. A decrease in alder and willow suggests a reduction in woodland, with evidence of some arable and pastoral agriculture *c.*390–160 BC. Further woodland recovery is noted in LPAZ HU10 (*c.*160 BC–AD 435), when increased representation of hazel and alder is accompanied by low levels of herbaceous taxa and micro-charcoal. There is a major reduction in alder, willow and hazel in LPAZ HU11 (*c.*AD 435–1240), coinciding with a major increase in herbaceous taxa, primarily grasses. Cereal pollen and ribwort plantain are recorded continuously, while docks, daisies, dandelions, clover, mugwort and goosefoot occur more regularly. This, together with charcoal peaks, indicates considerable agricultural activity in the vicinity of Holdenstown Upper during LPAZ HU11.

EARLY HOLOCENE VEGETATION CHANGE

The pollen record from Holdenstown Upper spans much of the Holocene, from *c.*8070 BC to AD 1240. This provides insights into vegetational responses to ecological and anthropogenic conditions from the Early Mesolithic to the medieval period. A series of expansions and contractions of arboreal and herbaceous taxa are apparent over that long period. Some of these reflect human disturbance, characterised by increases in taxa indicative of open, pastoral environments and disturbed soils (especially ribwort plantain, grasses, docks, daisies, dandelions and occasional grains of cereal pollen suggesting arable agriculture), and falls in values of tree/shrub pollen showing contraction in wood/scrubland. Total tree and shrub pollen percentages rarely drop below 70% of total land pollen for the entire record, implying that although herbaceous taxa are probably underrepresented (Caseldine and Fyfe 2006), woodland/scrub cover was of greater extent than open ground, even during episodes of human impact and woodland clearance.

Episodes of intensified human activity seem to have impacted most on the populations of hazel and oak, with elm affected at some points, especially at the start of the Neolithic. The incidence of micro-charcoal, an indicator of the frequency of burning in the landscape around the site (probably mainly from domestic fires, but potentially from natural fires), closely track these phases, with increased values associated with rises in pollen taxa indicating human activity. Micro-charcoal falls noticeably during episodes of woodland recovery.

As the profile opens, oak, birch and elm are well established and constitute the main tall canopy trees in the Baltinglass landscape. Hazel is abundant, comprising a major component of the vegetation, probably as an understorey shrub. Scots pine may have existed in the landscape, although it is possible that the low pollen values recorded reflect long-distance transport from these trees growing on poorer soils elsewhere (Lageard *et al.* 1999; Pilcher *et al.* 1995). While the low values of Scots pine at Holdenstown Upper are comparable with other profiles from East Leinster and the Irish Midlands (Caseldine and Hatton 1996; Kearney *et al.* 2022; Selby *et al.* 2005), the tree was present at sites such as Kelly's Lough, Co. Wicklow (Leira *et al.* 2007) by 7450–7070 BC. This indicates that while Scots pine was not a major component of the local woodland at Holdenstown Upper, it was established at other sites in the region.

The early Holocene landscape at Holdenstown Upper was dominated by deciduous woodland. Low levels of non-arboreal taxa suggest that open environments were limited in the vicinity of the sampling site. Ivy appears in the pollen record from Holdenstown Upper continuously, although holly is absent. The occurrence of ivy and absence of holly is in general accord with evidence from elsewhere in Ireland (Jessen 1949; Singh and Smith 1973; O'Connell 1980; Kearney *et al.* 2022). The presence of ivy and true ferns probably represent epiphytes within the deciduous woodland, as seen at Lough Sheeauns, Co. Galway (Molloy and O'Connell 1991) and Lough Cullin, Co. Kilkenny (Kearney *et al.* 2022).

An increase in alder is recorded at Holdenstown Upper from *c.*6300 BC, a period marking the Boreal/Atlantic transition (Jessen 1949; Mitchell 1951). The pollen percentage values of alder suggest this tree had become established in the local landscape (Douda *et al.* 2014) and may signify an expansion of damp woodland at the edge of the sampling site. Alder was presumably colonising the wetter soils, leading to the formation of carr woodland, with a mixed elm-oak-hazel woodland on the drier mineral soils in the landscape. This is recorded in other palaeoenvironmental records from sites in eastern Ireland (Caseldine and Hatton 1996; Gearey *et al.* 2010; Kearney *et al.* 2022; Timpany 2009).

The Mesolithic period is represented in the Holdenstown Upper profile by the two earliest LPAZs, which indicate the local landscape was relatively closed during the Early Holocene. There is no evidence of woodland disturbance or Mesolithic anthropogenic activity in this record. The low values for non-arboreal pollen and ferns suggest the woodland around Holdenstown Upper had a rather closed structure, with limited open environments during the early Holocene. Periodic openings in this woodland allowed more shade intolerant taxa to flourish. Such openings probably did exist during the Mesolithic, but it is not possible to know if these were created by human activity or natural agency. While the former is proposed in some studies (for example Smith 1970; Simmons and Innes 1996; Innes *et al.* 2003; Warren *et al.* 2014), natural processes such as wind throw could create a similar pollen signal (Brown 1997). The potential role of storms in palaeoenvironmental records is often under-estimated, as high winds can have a significant impact on tree cover (Allen 1996; Blackburn *et al.* 1988; Denslow *et al.* 1998), allowing light-demanding ruderal taxa to become established in an manner similar to that resulting from anthropogenic woodland disturbance.

There were increased levels of micro-charcoal at Holdenstown Upper *c.*6300–5500 BC. The use of 'fire ecology' (Woodman 2015, 261) for woodland management during the Mesolithic has been suggested in other studies (Fossitt 1994; Mighall *et al.* 2008; Smith 1970), where increased micro charcoal representation coincided with vegetation change. This has been interpreted as deliberate attempts by Mesolithic foragers to create clearings to attract browsing animals, or to encourage growth of plant foods (Simmons and Innes 1996; Warren *et al.* 2014), or perhaps for social purposes (Davies *et al.* 2005). Issues relating to taphonomy, source area and the interpretation of sedimentary micro-charcoal remain for the reconstruction of fire history (Mooney and Tinner 2011), however, and so distinguishing anthropogenic burning and natural wildfires is problematic. The possibility that increased micro-charcoal levels at Holdenstown Upper represent some attempt to create or maintain natural open habitats seems unlikely, given the absence of large herbivores in Ireland (Woodman *et al.* 1997).

Elm Decline and Neolithic Human Activity

A reduction in elm, from *c.*10% to less than 1%, was noted at Holdenstown Upper from *c.*3900 BC. This represents the well-known 'Elm Decline' of the mid-Holocene in the region, occurring at a time when a low, but continuous, presence of light-demanding ash was expanding in woodland openings (O'Connell and Molloy 2001). The 'Elm Decline' is extensively used as a proxy chronological marker for the start of the Neolithic (O'Connell and Molloy 2001; Parker *et al.* 2002), as it often coincides with early farming activity (Whitehouse *et al.* 2014). This occurred at Holdenstown Upper around the same time as the 'fixed' date for the mid-Holocene 'Elm Decline' in Ireland, though this temporal synchroneity is debatable (Parker *et al.* 2002; Whitehouse *et al.* 2014; Kearney and Geary 2020). 'Elm Decline' pollen diagrams in Ireland frequently demonstrate evidence for woodland instability and/or early agricultural activity (see, for instance, Mitchell 1942; O'Connell 1980; O'Connell and Mollloy 1988; Molloy and O'Connell 1991; Fossitt 1994; Heery 1997; Connolly 1999; Brown, A.G. *et al.* 2005; Selby *et al.* 2005; Caseldine and Fyfe 2006; Molloy 2008; Ghilardi and O'Connell 2013; Molloy *et al.* 2014).

The apparent correlation between this 'event' and the adoption of Neolithic practices led to early suggestions of an anthropogenic cause for the 'Elm Decline' (e.g. Piggott 1954; Mitchell 1954; Troels-Smith 1960). Counter-arguments to this have been made by Rackham (1980) and Rowley-Conwy (1982), who questioned whether the scale and rapidity of the 'event' negated suggestions of an Early Neolithic anthropogenic cause. Over the years, many explanations have been offered, including climate change, soil deterioration, anthropogenic activity and pathogenic attack (Girling and Greig 1985; Girling 1988; Peglar and Birks 1993; Parker *et al.* 2002). Many of those theories were based on the supposed rapid and synchronous nature of the 'Elm Decline', which is now called into question (Whitehouse *et al.* 2014; Griffiths and Gearey 2017; Kearney and Gearey 2020). While there may be several contributing factors, it is possible that human activity contributed to reduction in elm at that time. At Holdenstown Upper, the latter was followed by a minor increase in indicators of open environments, with increased representation of grasses and ribwort plantain. Due to the slow accumulation rate at this section of the profile, however, the chronological relationship between the 'Elm Decline' and human activity is difficult to unpick.

There are increased values of non-arboreal pollen (to *c.*10%) at Holdenstown Upper from the Early Neolithic around 3600 BC, some 300 years after the initial decline in elm. This may indicate that the 'Elm Decline' was unrelated to human activity, although rising values for grass and trace values for anthropogenic indicators are co-eval with reductions in the presence of this tree. This might, however, also reflect open environments resulting from a loss of elm trees due to disease (Caseldine and Fyfe 2006). Evidence for woodland instability and/or early agricultural activity in post-'Elm Decline' contexts is found in other pollen records in Ireland (Caseldine and Fyfe 2006; Ghilardi and O'Connell 2013; Molloy *et al.* 2014). Some of these (O'Connell and Molloy 2001; Kearney and Gearey 2020) indicate an interval between the 'Elm Decline' and palynological evidence for human disturbance. Overall, this may refute an anthropogenic cause for the reduction in elm, although the chronological disparity could also reflect increased stimulation of arboreal pollen production resulting from openings to the woodland canopy (cf. Aaby 1986; Feeser and Dörfler 2014).

The Early Neolithic at Holdenstown Upper is marked by a minor increase in grass and the occasional presence of ribwort plantain from *c.*3600BC. Grass values increase to *c.*5%, while ribwort plantain (*c.*1%), daisies, dandelions, goosefoot and docks are recorded. This increase in herbaceous taxa is primarily at the expense of elm, but levels of oak and alder are also marginally reduced. During this period, there was a limited opening up of woodland and an expansion of open habitats, presumably relatively close to the sampling site. This occurred marginally later than the generally accepted date for the start of the Neolithic in Ireland (McSparron 2008; Cooney *et al.* 2011; McClatchie *et al.* 2014; Whitehouse *et al.* 2014; McLaughlin *et al.* 2016), but was broadly contemporary with the enclosures at Rathcoran or Hughstown. Due to the constrained chronology and reduced rates of pollen accumulation, however, it is possible Neolithic activity commenced earlier at Baltinglass than is recorded at Holdenstown Upper.

The palynological evidence from Holdenstown Upper

and many other studies in Ireland (Caseldine and Hatton 1996; Ghilardi and O'Connell 2013; Molloy and O'Connell 1987; O'Connell 1990; O'Connell and Molloy 2001; Pilcher and Smith 1979; Stolze 2012; Stolze and Monecke 2012; Stolze *et al.* 2013) suggests that the agricultural activity at this time was predominantly pastoral, with localised evidence of arable farming during the earliest stages of the Early Neolithic. No evidence of cereal cultivation is noted in the Holdenstown profile. Notwithstanding the issues relating to identification, cereal type pollen is the most important indicator of arable farming in a pollen record (cf. Behre 1981). Evidence from further south, at Lough Cullin and Newrath (site 34) in Co. Kilkenny (Timpany 2009), suggests that arable farming had assumed some importance in the region at this time. As reported elsewhere (Ghilardi and O'Connell 2013, Molloy and O'Connell 1987), fire does not appear to have played a role in the limited Neolithic woodland clearance at Holdenstown Upper.

Overall, the impact of Early Neolithic agriculture in Irish pollen records is rather variable (Kearney and Gearey 2020), possibly revealing that Early Neolithic agriculture was spatially heterogeneous (Whitehouse *et al.* 2014) with varying levels of intensity, while the relative proximity of activity to sampling sites would further attenuate the signal. Although Early Neolithic agriculture is recorded in pollen records across the region, some sites show little anthropogenic impact during this period, including Clara Bog, Co. Offaly (Connolly 1999; Crushell *et al.* 2008), Cornaher Lough, Co. Westmeath (Heery 1997), and Ballinderry Lough, Co. Offaly (O'Carroll 2012), with only a marginal increase in grass and sporadic occurrence of ribwort plantain noted at Kelly's Lough, Co. Wicklow (Leira *et al.* 2007). This suggests that early agriculture did not always have a substantial role in the regional landscape.

At Kelly's Lough, no evidence of Neolithic activity was noted after the 'Elm Decline', while at Lough Cullin, Co. Kilkenny (Kearney *et al.* 2022) unequivocal evidence for anthropogenic activity occurred after the reduction in elm. At Lough Cullin, Early Neolithic anthropogenic activity is indicated by a continuous presence of ribwort plantain and overall increased values for non-arboreal pollen (especially ruderal taxa indicative of agriculture) from *c.*3960 BC, some 220 years after the decline in elm. This would concur with other Irish pollen records (see, for example, Molloy and O'Connell 1987; O'Connell and Molloy 2001; Ghilardi and O'Connell 2013; Molloy *et al.* 2014), in which clear evidence of Early Neolithic human disturbance is exhibited. At Lough Cullin, increased representation of anthropogenic indicators, such as ribwort plantain, daisies, dandelions, buttercups, docks and pinks/carnations, strongly suggests an increase in open environments in the vicinity of the lake. This increase coincides with an overall reduction of arboreal pollen, especially oak and hazel, in addition to the previously mentioned decline in elm, to indicate a deliberate opening of the woodland canopy on drier mineral soils for the provision of agricultural land. This is further supported by the observed increased minerogenic in-wash into the lake, suggesting soil erosion possibly caused by deforestation. The increase in non-arboreal pollen, especially grasses and ribwort plantain, following the reduction in elm is also exhibited at other sites in the region, such as at Scragh Bog, Co. Westmeath (O'Connell 1980), Corlea 9, Co. Longford (Caseldine and Hatton 1996), the Bog of Cullen, Co. Tipperary (Molloy 2008), and further afield (see Pilcher and Smith 1979; Almgren 1989; Molloy and O'Connell 1991; 1995; 2004; O'Connell and Molloy 2001; Ahlberg *et al.* 2001; Ghilardi and O'Connell 2013; Chique *et al.* 2017; Spencer *et al.* 2020).

This phase of early agriculture was followed by woodland regeneration and a decline in anthropogenic indicators. The steady increase in arboreal pollen is likely to indicate the regeneration of woodland and the abandonment of farming in this part of Baltinglass. Despite the occasional occurrence of ribwort plantain, this marks the beginning of a less-intensive use of the landscape around Holdenstown Upper. What few open habitats had previously existed in the area were no longer present, and a human presence is not discernible in the pollen record. A similar pattern of re-afforestation is implied during the Middle Neolithic in other parts of Ireland (Chique *et al.* 2017; Ghilardi and O'Connell 2013; Kearney *et al.* 2022; Molloy *et al.* 2014). It has been suggested that the Middle Neolithic saw a reduction in human activity overall (Whitehouse *et al.* 2014). This is also indicated by the archaeological record, with the number of confirmed Middle Neolithic archaeological sites in the region, and across Ireland, significantly lower than those recorded in the preceding Early Neolithic (Whitehouse *et al.* 2014; McLaughlin *et al.* 2016).

Evidence for sustained human activity is also absent at Holdenstown Upper during the Late Neolithic and Chalcolithic periods, though some activity is noted in the wider region during the third millennium BC. At Lough Cullin, Co. Kilkenny ribwort plantain and other anthropogenic indicators again appear more frequently from

3040–2530 BC, while cereal pollen with accompanying ruderal taxa mugwort and broadleaf/hoary plantain are again recorded at 3330–2840 BC and 3050–2290 BC. This suggests that agricultural activity, both pastoral and arable, was once again widespread in southern and eastern Ireland following a long period when woodland regeneration and low human activity were typical of many pollen profiles. This resurgence of farming in the region during the Late Neolithic is also hinted at Clowanstown, Co. Meath (Gearey *et al.* 2010), where values of grass and ribwort plantain increase marginally during 2890–2690 BC (Gearey *et al.* 2010), and from other sites across the island (see for example Pilcher and Smith 1979; Fossitt 1994; Molloy and O'Connell 2004).

A reduction in Scots pine at Holdenstown Upper from *c.*3000 BC probably marked the beginnings of the 'Pine Decline' in the region. The decline of this tree species is well documented across much of Ireland, northern Scotland and England (for example by Bennett 1984; Bridge *et al.* 1990; Gear and Huntley 1991; Lageard *et al.* 1999; Mighall *et al.* 2004; Pilcher *et al.* 1995), although recent studies have confirmed its survival in some locations (McGeever and Mitchell 2016; Sassoon *et al.* 2021). Numerous competing hypotheses have been proposed for this decline in Scots pine, including anthropogenic activity (Dodson 1990; Tipping *et al.* 2008) and the spread of blanket peat connected to changing hydrological conditions (Bradshaw and Browne 1987). While the latter may have been significant for some local areas (Dodson 1990), palynological evidence is lacking on a regional scale (Dwyer and Mitchell 1997; Mighall *et al.* 2004). A combination of climate change, in particular increased precipitation, and the resulting increased surface wetness appears to be the most favoured causal factor (Birks 1975; Bennett 1984; McNally and Doyle 1984; Bradshaw and Browne 1987; Bridge *et al.* 1990; Anderson 1995; Lageard *et al.* 1999).

A study by Mighall *et al.* (2004) at Cadogan's Bog, Co. Cork suggests that a reduction in Scots pine coincided with a short-lived increase in wet-loving mire taxa. The authors argued that increased surface wetness, possibly resulting from increased precipitation, created conditions unsuitable for the growth of this tree. The study also identified a reduction in concentrations of phosphorus, potassium, magnesium, calcium, sodium, iron and zinc in association with this period of increased surface wetness. This would indicate that the mid-Holocene 'Pine Decline' at Cadogan's Bog was potentially caused by soil mineral deficiency and increased surface wetness, possibly due to climate change in the form of increased precipitation. At Holdenstown Upper, Scots pine was not a major component of the local vegetation, and there is no obvious explanation for its decline.

BRONZE AGE HILLFORTS AND ENVIRONMENT

A major landscape change in terms of vegetation and land use is recorded from *c.*1820 BC at Holdenstown Upper. A landscape dominated by woodland was transformed to a farmscape environment, where grasslands prevailed. Arboreal pollen fell dramatically, coinciding with a rise in herbaceous taxa, in particular grass and ribwort plantain. That woodland clearance was connected to an expansion of grasslands from *c.*1820 BC. The expansion of ribwort plantain, considered a classic anthropogenic indicator (Behre 1981), in combination with bracken and other ruderal taxa, indicates an expansion of extensive pasture in the surrounding area. Woodland clearance led to an increase in biodiversity and to species-rich grasslands that included dandelions, daisies, buttercups, docks and clovers. This vegetation pattern points to grazing close to the sampling site. In addition to pastoral farming, indicators for arable cultivation are also plentiful. Cereal pollen is recorded, and other pollen types considered to be weeds of disturbed soils/arable crops, such as goosefoot and mugwort, are also noted, albeit in low numbers. While pastoral farming predominated, arable cultivation also occurred on better, drier soils. Some of this tillage must have occurred close to the sampling site given the poor dispersal of cereal pollen and many of its associated weeds (Hall 1989). The reduction in overall arboreal pollen and increase in herbaceous taxa reveal significant scrub and woodland clearance connected to farming in the Baltinglass area from *c.*1820 BC, peaking at *c.*1450 BC.

At Holdenstown Upper, herbaceous taxa increase from *c.*8 % to *c.*25% between *c.*1820 BC and *c.*1450 BC. This is primarily represented by an increase in grass values to *c.*20%, and in ribwort plantain to *c.*2%, while mugwort, daisies, dandelions, pinks/carnations, goosefoot, docks and clover occur more regularly. Cereal pollen is recorded sporadically at *c.*1820 BC, *c.*1580 BC and again at *c.*1450 BC, while arable weeds such as goosefoot, broadleaf plantain and mugwort are also noted, indicating arable activity in the vicinity. Hazel and oak values decrease from *c.*45% and *c.*12% to *c.*28% and *c.*8% respectively, coinciding with an increase in herbaceous taxa to indicate a reduction in woodland in favour of land suitable for arable and pastoral agriculture *c.*1820–1450 BC. The representation of micro-charcoal increases from minimal levels to *c.*20% in this phase of woodland reduction. Whether this relates to woodland clearance by fire or general anthropogenic activity is uncertain (see above).

There is a similar picture at Lough Cullin in Co. Kilkenny (Kearney *et al.* 2022), which is characterised by limited open areas during the Early Bronze Age. This picture changes around the start of the Middle Bronze Age, with increases in ribwort plantain and the appearance of other anthropogenic indicators, including dandelions and docks, reflecting an expansion in open, pastoral environments. This seems to follow a brief period of reduced anthropogenic indicators and increases in hazel, and is in turn followed by a very pronounced increase in herbaceous taxa, especially grasses, and an associated decline in arboreal pollen, demonstrating a significant opening up of the woodland cover. The occurrence of a single grain of cereal pollen at 1380–1220 BC indicates arable farming. There are also reductions in alder, suggesting that carr woodland on wetter soils, probably close to the lake edges, was affected by clearance at that time.

A substantial expansion in farming activity is also recorded at Lough Muckno, Co. Monaghan during the Middle Bronze Age (Chique *et al.* 2017). This is most visible from *c.*1500 BC, with increased levels of herbaceous taxa and cereal pollen recorded almost continuously until *c.*800 BC. The intensity of agricultural activity decreases but is still at a considerable level during the Middle to Late Bronze Age, *c.*1300–1030 BC, and a period of lower activity occurs during the Late Bronze Age, *c.*1030–650 B.C. Evidence from Owenduff (Plunkett 2009) and Lough Doo (O' Connell 1990) in Co. Mayo indicates moderate levels of activity for the Early Bronze Age, with a considerable expansion of anthropogenic activity from *c.*1700 BC. The record from Loughnashade, near Navan Fort, Co. Armagh, indicates substantial clearance from the mid-fifteenth century BC (Weir 1993). This pattern seems to be replicated in the southern region of Ireland, with increased evidence of woodland clearance and agriculture at Mooghaun, Co. Clare (O'Connell *et al.* 2001; Molloy 2005) and Moyreen, Co. Limerick (Plunkett 1999) from the twelfth century BC.

Following a period of substantial impact at Holdenstown Upper during the Middle Bronze Age, human activity then seems to have decreased in two 'steps': an initial reduction, which may be described as a contraction, during the Middle and Late Bronze Age *c.*1410–970 BC, followed by a pronounced 'collapse' from *c.*970 BC, the Bronze Age to Iron Age transition. Human impact on this landscape seems to have reduced very significantly after *c.*970 BC, with little evidence of settlement *c.*970–390 BC (see below). Despite a gradual reduction in human activity at Holdenstown Upper between *c.*1450 and *c.*1100 BC, however, there is evidence of both pastoral and arable agriculture throughout that period. Comparison with data from other Irish pollen records indicates a broadly coherent pattern during the Early to Middle Bronze Age, of consistent and increasing woodland clearance and agriculture, followed by fluctuating human activity during the Late Bronze Age (Chique *et al.* 2017; Spencer *et al.* 2020; Stolze and Monecke, 2021).

At Holdenstown Upper, levels of herbaceous taxa decrease gradually, yet continuously, from *c.*25% at *c.*1410 BC, to *c.*12% by *c.*970 BC. Grass values decrease to *c.*8% and ribwort plantain to less than 1%, while other ruderal taxa such as mugwort, daisies, dandelions, pinks/carnations, goosefoot, docks and clover appear less frequently. Despite this gradual reduction, it appears that both pastoral and arable activity continued across the Middle to Late Bronze Age at Holdenstown Upper, as cereal pollen is recorded at *c.*1240 BC and *c.*1110 BC. What is apparent from the Holdenstown Upper pollen profile is that the early first millennium BC was a period of reduced settlement in the wider Baltinglass landscape.

In contrast to the situation at Holdenstown Upper, and indeed Lough Cullin and Lough Muckno, palynological evidence from other parts of Ireland reveals a widespread upsurge in agricultural activity corresponding to the onset of the Late Bronze Age (Ghilardi and O'Connell 2013; Molloy and O'Connell 2004; Overland and O'Connell 2008; Spencer *et al.* 2020). A link has been suggested between reduced archaeological visibility and palynological evidence for decline of pastoralism at the end of this period, possibly pointing to a consolidation of settlement and agriculture (Plunkett 2009). This pattern is paralleled by the changes in archaeological site distributions across the entire period (cf. Armit *et al.* 2013; Becker *et al.* 2017), with extensive landscape utilisation activity during the Late Bronze Age, followed by a marked contraction at the beginning of the Iron Age.

Certainly, the palynological record from Holdenstown Upper, Lough Cullin (Kearney *et al.* 2022) and Lough Muckno (Chique *et al.* 2017), where there was woodland regeneration at the end of the Bronze Age, supports this picture. In contrast to these peat deposits, however, palynological analysis of lake deposits at Loughnashade (Weir 1993) and Mooghaun (O'Connell *et al.* 2001; Molloy 2005) indicates an expansion of cereal pollen at that time. Plunkett (2009) suggests this may be due to the nature of cereal pollen dispersal, which is more likely to wash into lakes than transport to distant peat deposits. The presence of cereal pollen at certain sites in the vicinity of hillforts may represent a concentration of population and associated food production activity around centres of political power. Evidence from Loughnashade (Weir 1993) and Moyreen (Plunkett 2009) may also indicate a possible shift to a pastoral agrarian economy, implying a dispersal of settlement away from centralised locations and the abandonment of some areas of widespread past human activity.

Later settlement and environment

Woodland regeneration and a reduction in human activity is recorded at Holdenstown Upper from *c.*970 BC, spanning the Late Bronze Age/Iron Age transition into the mid first millennium BC. Grass values remain low at *c.*5%, while ribwort plantain, daisies, dandelions, pinks/carnations, meadowsweet and buttercups are only recorded sporadically. There is no evidence of cereal cultivation during that period. The regeneration of woodland is represented by an increase in alder and willow to *c.*42% and *c.*15% respectively, with hazel also expanding as the period progresses. The notable reduction in herbaceous taxa, in addition to an absence of cereal pollen, indicates reduced agricultural activity at Baltinglass during the Early Iron Age. The pollen profile from Holdenstown Upper reflects the general picture across Ireland (Mitchell and Ryan 1997), with a decline in arable activity and contraction of open pastures from the end of the Late Bronze Age.

The archaeological record suggests that the flourishing society of the Late Bronze Age declined significantly from the sixth century BC. The palynological evidence from Moyreen, Co. Limerick (Plunkett 2009), Beaghmore, Co. Tyrone (Pilcher 1969), Derryville, Co. Tipperary (Caseldine *et al.* 2005) and Cashelkeelty, Co. Kerry (Lynch 1981) supports this notion. The records from Ballynagilly, Co. Tyrone (Pilcher and Smith 1979), Lough Doo, Co. Mayo (O' Connell 1990) and the Céide Fields in Mayo (Molloy and O'Connell 2007), however, suggest that a highly dispersed pattern of settlement may account for the low level of activity at those sites (Plunkett 2009). There are also examples of increased human activity near established settlements, such as at Loughnashade (Weir 1993) and Mooghaun (Cody 1981; O'Connell *et al.* 2001; Molloy 2005), possibly reflecting some concentration of settlement in response to socio-political developments. Additionally, low levels of activity are exhibited at Lough Sheeauns, Co. Galway (Molloy and O'Connell 1991) and Essexford Lough, Co. Louth (Weir 1995) during the fourth century BC. Overall, the Bronze Age/Iron Age transition indicates a reduction of economic output, and also reduced pressure on the land in many, but not all, parts of Ireland. With a probable shift to pastoral agriculture from the Later Bronze Age it is unlikely that soil exhaustion accounts for this decline, which is better explained by socio-political instability and/or a collapse of trade networks.

There is evidence for renewed anthropogenic activity at Holdenstown Upper from *c.*300 BC to *c.*160 BC, when herbaceous taxa indicative of pastures/meadows increase to *c.*10%. This is primarily represented in increased levels of grass, to *c.*8%, and the occasional presence of ribwort plantain, daisies, docks and clover, while the presence of cereal pollen at *c.*260 BC indicates that arable farming was undertaken in the vicinity during the Middle Iron Age. Similar evidence of renewed activity during the Middle Iron Age was also noted at Lough Cullin, Co. Kilkenny, where there was a reduction in hazel-dominated woodland and a considerable increase in herbaceous taxa, especially grass, ribwort plantain and dandelions, from *c.*400 BC (Kearney *et al.* 2022). At Lough Muckno, Co. Monaghan (Chique *et al.* 2017) hazel scrub was cleared extensively from *c.*300 BC, coinciding with increased values of herbaceous taxa to indicate a considerable expansion of grasslands and pastoral habitats. The general picture from Holdenstown Upper would therefore mirror that of other regional pollen profiles, which exhibit a brief period of renewed agricultural activity during the Iron Age from *c.*300 BC.

The well-known 'Late Iron Age Lull' in Ireland (Mitchell and Ryan 1997) is clearly evident in the palaeoenvironmental record from Baltinglass from *c.*160 BC, when evidence of human impact on the landscape is low. Levels of herbaceous taxa decline to less than *c.*8%, while arboreal pollen values increase, primarily hazel to *c.*50% and alder to *c.*30%, indicating an almost complete cessation of human activity in the region during the Late Iron Age. This mirrors palaeoenvironmental records from other parts of Ireland, where arboreal taxa, especially hazel, increase in the pollen diagrams (Weir 1993; 1995; Mitchell and Ryan 1997; Overland and O'Connell 2008; Chique *et al.* 2017), indicating forest regeneration, a decline in arable activity and contraction of open pastures from the beginning of the Late Iron Age. The extent of woodland regeneration may indicate a collapse of the subsistence economy and a marked decline in population (Weir 1995), potentially resulting from environmental and climatic constraints (Baillie 1993; Baillie and Brown 2013). This view is tempered by recent research that reveals the 'Late Iron Age Lull' to have been a more time-transgressive phenomenon than previously observed, the onset of which varied considerably, *c.*200 BC–AD 200 (Coyle McClung 2013; Chique *et al.* 2017). The asynchronous nature of the 'lull' has led to suggestions that this reduction in activity represented a 'more gradual, socially-determined process involving both economic and political re-organisation' (Coyle McClung and Plunkett 2020, 154) rather than a climate-driven 'event'. Notwithstanding whether it was culturally or climatically driven, the increase in arboreal pollen recorded from *c.*160 BC at Holdenstown Upper falls within a broad timescale for a wider reduction in farming activity during the Late Iron Age in Ireland.

There is evidence of intense human activity in the Holdenstown Upper record from *c.*AD 500, marked by an unprecedented expansion of open habitats and an emphasis on cereal-crop cultivation. The widespread clearances of hazel scrub, oak and birch, and the accompanying expansion of grassland, indicate renewed focus on pastoral activity. Arboreal pollen falls to its lowest levels for the entire profile (*c.*50%), in particular hazel, which declines from *c.*40% at *c.*AD 435 to *c.*20% by *c.*AD 950. The considerable decline of alder, from *c.*30% to *c.*20%, and of willow from *c.*10% to *c.*5%, from *c.*AD 700, may point to agricultural expansion onto marginal land. This reduction in the woodland canopy coincides with increased levels of grass, to *c.*25%, and ribwort plantain, to *c.*7%, while mugwort, daisies, dandelions, buttercups, docks and clover are recorded continuously throughout this period. There is also a sudden expansion of arable farming from *c.*AD 500, beginning a period of intensive agricultural activity that continued uninterrupted until *c.*AD 1240, with evidence of both pastoral and arable farming.

At Lough Cullin, Co. Kilkenny (Kearney *et al.* 2022), human activity seems to have ceased almost completely during the Late Iron Age until *c.*AD 500, when there was a relatively abrupt resumption of agriculture, evidenced by an increase in the grass and ribwort plantain curve and reductions in hazel and oak. There is a marked increase in anthropogenic indicators, and cereal pollen is recorded almost continuously, indicating a significant expansion of arable cultivation locally. This substantial growth of agriculture during the early medieval period is reflected in many pollen records from the Midlands and north-eastern Ireland (see for example Chique *et al.* 2017; Selby *et al.* 2005). The scale of clearance at Holdenstown Upper suggests a major expansion of pastoral and arable activity during the early medieval period, with a rapid surge in human activity from *c.*AD 500. This picture is also reflected in the archaeological record nationally, where the prevalence of ringforts reflects a settlement pattern based on individual farmsteads and supports palynological evidence for increased farming from *c.*AD 500 (O'Sullivan *et al.* 2013).

SUMMARY

The Holdenstown Upper pollen sequence provides a nuanced and detailed palaeoenvironmental reconstruction of Holocene environmental and landscape change spanning the Mesolithic to the medieval period, from *c.*8065 BC to AD 1240. The pollen record reveals that a relatively closed woodland of hazel, oak, birch and elm dominated the local environment through the Early Holocene. The expansion of alder and willow from *c.*5950 BC suggests the formation of carr woodland close to the sampling site. Open grassland environments were restricted, with only trace amounts of grasses, sedge, mugwort, daisies and meadowsweet recorded, with no evidence of human impact *c.*8065–3600 BC.

A minor reduction in woodland taxa occurred at Holdenstown Upper *c.*4195–3335 BC, primarily with a collapse in elm values, as well as a minor reduction in alder and hazel. Herbaceous taxa increased marginally following the reduction in elm, with a small increase in grasses and the sporadic occurrence of light-demanding ruderal taxa, such as ribwort plantain, from *c.*3600 BC. A regeneration of the local woodland and the return of a dense woodland canopy occurred *c.*3335–1820 BC, after which pastoral and arable agriculture peaked during the Middle Bronze Age. A steady decline in herbaceous taxa *c.*1410–970 BC indicates continued, but reducing, levels of arable and pastoral agriculture during the Middle and Late Bronze Age.

Arboreal pollen values, especially hazel, oak, alder and willow, continued to expand at Holdenstown Upper during the Bronze Age to Iron Age transition, *c.*970–390 BC. Levels of herbaceous taxa and micro-charcoal were greatly reduced in the same period, which suggests a cessation, or at least a major reduction, in human activity. This was followed by low levels of activity until *c.*AD 435, after which there is evidence of intensive agricultural activity, probably associated with ringfort settlement in the Baltinglass lowlands

8. HILLFORTS AND EARLY BALTINGLASS

William O'Brien and James O'Driscoll

Our study now turns to the wider context of the Baltinglass hillforts, beginning with a broad chronological model of how this unique landscape developed over time. The Neolithic settlement of Baltinglass is then explored, in relation to the discovery of three large enclosures on its hills dating to the fourth millennium BC. This is followed by a look at the cultural landscape of Bronze Age hillforts in the same area during the later second millennium BC. The chapter concludes with a discussion of the place of hillforts in the later story of Baltinglass, from Iron Age to early medieval times.

A CHRONOLOGY OF HILLFORTS IN BALTINGLASS

The recent programme of archaeological excavation and radiocarbon dating at Baltinglass provides a picture of hillforts and hilltop enclosures at different times in later prehistory. The radiocarbon record now available from six excavated sites points to two distinct periods of construction. The first involved the building of large, multiple enclosures at Hughstown and Rathcoran, and probably the univallate enclosure at Spinans Hill 1, during the Early Neolithic, *c.*3700–3500 BC. This was followed two millennia or so later by the construction of Rathnagree hillfort and the Sruhaun enclosure on Baltinglass Hill during the Middle Bronze Age, *c.*1400–1100 BC. Tinoran hillfort was then built on a neighbouring hill in the early part of the Late Bronze Age, *c.*1100–1000 BC, with activity occurring there as late as the ninth century BC. There is no evidence that hillforts were built or occupied in Baltinglass after this period, though that picture may well change when other sites, including Brusselstown Ring, Kilranelagh and Spinans Hill 2, are eventually dated.

The history of these hillforts may have overlapped, where individual sites were occupied, or in some cases built, during the same period. This may be the case at the Early Neolithic enclosures at Spinans Hill 1, Rathcoran and Hughstown, located on the eastern, central and western sides of the complex respectively. Those three sites are different in form, which may reflect differences in use or in date of construction. Radiocarbon results suggest Rathnagree and Sruhaun were in contemporaneous use during the Middle Bronze Age. The difference in their design relates to function, with Sruhaun probably used as an animal enclosure by the occupants of Rathnagree hillfort. Tinoran hillfort is presently the only hillfort at Baltinglass known from the Late Bronze Age, though again that might change with the dating of Brusselstown Ring and other sites discussed in Chapter 6.

While further research is required on individual sites, it is possible to outline a chronology for the Baltinglass hillfort complex as a whole. Mitchell and Ryan (1997, 240) suggested that these large enclosures might be contemporary, representing defensive positions built by groups in competition with each other. This theory can now be dismissed, as radiocarbon dating confirms the six excavated sites were not contemporary. While their use may have overlapped, there is a clear separation in time between the Neolithic and later sites, and between the Middle Bronze Age enclosures on Baltinglass Hill and the Late Bronze Age hillfort at Tinoran. This makes it very unlikely the Baltinglass landscape was divided up into a series of small hillfort polities, but does allow for more than one hillfort group in this area at the same time, during both the Early/Middle Neolithic and the later Bronze Age.

Mitchell and Ryan proposed a second scenario whereby these hillforts were not contemporary, but were instead built by successive generations of the same community who moved their tribal centre from one hill to another across this landscape. This is certainly possible for sites from the same period, but cannot apply to the building of hillforts over three millennia (*c.*3700–800 BC), particularly when there was a break of some 2,000 years or so between the Neolithic and Bronze Age examples. A modified version of this model would see Hughstown, Rathcoran and Spinans Hill 1 occupied successively during the Early Neolithic, with a similar shift from Rathnagree and Sruhaun on Baltinglass Hill during the Middle Bronze Age to Tinoran on an adjacent hill in the Late Bronze Age.

This diachronic model has a geographical expression across the Baltinglass landscape, with distinct clusters of

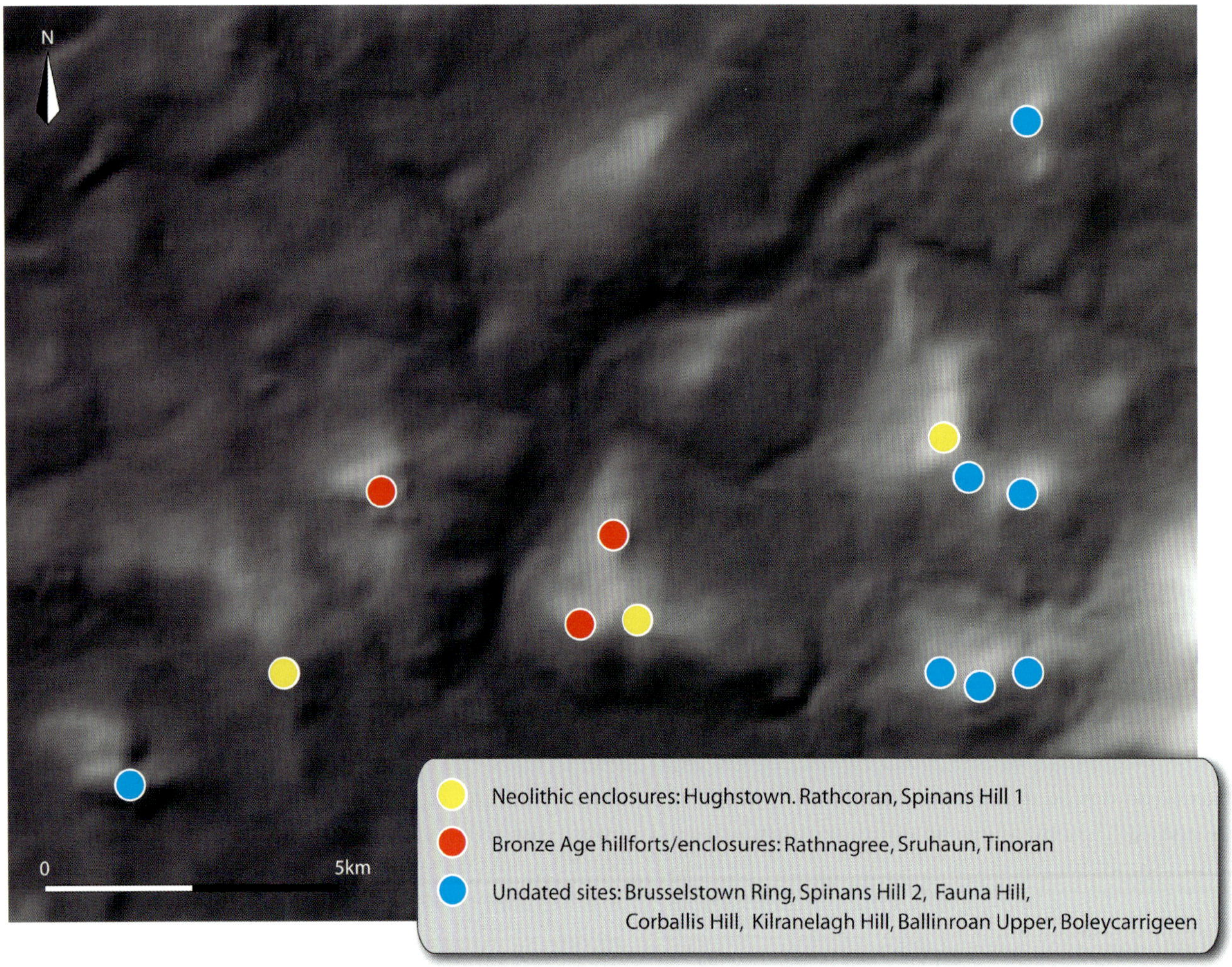

Fig. 8.1 Distribution of hillforts and hill enclosures in Baltinglass area.

hillforts and enclosures on three of its main hills (Fig. 8.1). Each of those locales has a separate Neolithic and Bronze Age component, as confirmed by recent radiocarbon dating. They include:

Carrigeen Hill/Tinoran Hill

The Early Neolithic hillfort of Hughstown and the Late Bronze Age hillfort of Tinoran are sited on opposing ridges on the western side of the Baltinglass complex.

Baltinglass Hill

The Early Neolithic hillfort of Rathcoran with its contemporary passage tomb is located on the summit of Baltinglass Hill, with Middle Bronze Age enclosures at Rathnagree and Sruhaun on its lower western slopes.

Spinans Hill

The Early Neolithic enclosure of Spinans Hill 1 on the eastern side of the complex is on the same ridge as Brusselstown Ring hillfort, which may be Bronze Age in date. The relationship of these two sites to the large Spinans Hill 2 enclosure is not known.

There may be a fourth cluster, with up to four large enclosures identified on Kilranelagh Hill. The chronology of those sites is not known as none has been excavated. They include a large enclosure (WI027-097) at the summit in Colvinstown Upper townland; a second example (WI027-098) at the northern side of the hill in Kilranelagh townland; and a recently identified site on the eastern shoulder of the hill in Boleycarrigeen townland. A large enclosure in Ballinroan Upper townland on the north-western slopes of Kilranelagh Hill may be part of an early medieval ecclesiastical site, but that also remains to be confirmed (see Chapter 6).

Much more excavation is required before the history of individual hillforts at Baltinglass is understood. In some instances this history may have been short-lived, while other enclosures may have experienced prolonged, multi-period occupation. There is, for example, no evidence that the Early Neolithic multiple enclosure at Hughstown was occupied during the Bronze Age. This contrasts with the Neolithic enclosure at Rathcoran, where there is evidence for some Bronze Age activity inside the enclosure (see Chapter 3). It is notable that none of the six excavated sites has evidence of post-Bronze Age occupation. While the innermost enclosures at Hughstown and Tinoran ('Round O') may be later in date, these are not typical ringforts (raths) of the early medieval period. There is still much to learn about the chronology of this hillfort landscape, particularly as there are seven sites that have not been dated (see Fig. 8.1).

BALTINGLASS IN THE AGE OF STONE

The earliest human presence in the Baltinglass area probably dates back to the eighth millennium BC. This was a time when Ireland was settled by small groups of foragers who had crossed the Irish Sea. Their numbers grew slowly, but steadily, across the island over the next four millennia or so, during a period known as the Mesolithic, notable for its distinctive stone stools and for the population's reliance on wild food resources, in particular from fishing. Mesolithic artifacts have been found in Wicklow, mostly along the coastline between Arklow and Wicklow town (Woodman 2015, fig. 9.5). This includes the discovery in 1932 of worked flint in a cave at St Bride's Head east of Wicklow town, and more recent finds in the Brittas Bay area (Stout 1989; 1994). There are no such examples from West Wicklow, but they are recorded in the adjacent counties of Carlow and Kildare, including a recent find of Late Mesolithic stone tools from eight sites on the M9 Carlow Bypass project (Woodman and Sternke 2015, figs 4.1 and 4.2).

Mesolithic sites or artifacts have not been discovered at Baltinglass or its immediate environs. This may be explained by poor visibility of archaeological remains in an area where little fieldwalking of ploughed fields has been undertaken to identify lithic scatters. There have been some discoveries, including three flakes of struck chert from Castleruddery Lower (National Museum of Ireland, NMI 2016: 106–8). Several pieces of struck flint were found in Boleycarrigeen townland, along with a possible thumb-nail scraper (NMI 2020: 30–32). These are not necessarily Mesolithic, as the working of flint and chert continued into the Bronze Age. There is evidence for this in the discovery of Neolithic worked flint, including scrapers and a javelin-head, in the 1934–6 excavation of Baltinglass passage tomb (Walshe 1941, figs 3, 6 and 7), and also in the recent excavation of Rathcoran (see Fig. 3.43).

First Farmers in Baltinglass

The first visible human impact on the Baltinglass landscape came with the arrival of the earliest farmers, *c.*3800–3700 BC. This was a period marked by the introduction of agriculture and a new way of life. The domestication of animals and the cultivation of crops first began in the Near East around 9000 BC. The knowledge of farming spread slowly across Europe, only reaching Ireland in the early fourth millennium BC. The practicalities were considerable, as neither the animals (cattle and sheep) nor cereals (wheat and barley) involved were native to Ireland. This required small groups of farmers to undertake hazardous sea crossings, most likely from southern Britain, and to engage peacefully or otherwise with the native Mesolithic population.

The adoption of farming provided a subsistence base for sustained population growth across Ireland during the fourth and third millennia BC. Farming required a more sedentary lifestyle and a relationship with the environment very different from that of the Mesolithic people. This is reflected in the construction of permanent farmsteads, where these farmers lived much of their lives in small village communities, as well as single-family settlements, dispersed across the landscape. Farming had a lasting impact on the Irish landscape, through the clearance of trees to create fields for cultivation and animal grazing. Pollen records obtained from lakes and peat bogs reveal the scale of this woodland clearance in many areas. For Baltinglass, the Holdenstown Upper study records a small increase in open grassland and a limited opening up of woodland *c.*3600 BC (see Chapter 7).

Many Neolithic settlements have been found in Ireland in recent decades in the course of road building, pipeline laying and other developments. Archaeological excavation at such sites has uncovered foundation traces of small farmhouses, mostly square or rectangular in plan, with walls of timber posts, planking, woven wattle and mud rendering, which supported wood-framed roofs covered by reed or cereal thatch. These houses often had storage and cooking facilities, represented by the presence of hearths, pits and floor deposits with animal bones and cereal grains. This sedentary farming life supported craft specialisation, including the first use of pottery and new methods of stone tool production. Raw materials, such as clay or hard rock, were obtained locally, but were also sourced from farther away through trade or social exchanges with other communities.

While the distinctive square/rectangular houses of the Early Neolithic in Ireland have not been found in Baltinglass, there have been few opportunities in local development archaeology to discover those sub-surface sites. In their absence, the enclosures at Rathcoran, Hughstown and Spinans Hill 1 indicate an important Early Neolithic settlement landscape at Baltinglass during the early to mid-fourth millennium BC. These large enclosures must have been connected to a wider farmscape in the wooded but fertile lowlands of the Slaney river catchment around Baltinglass. This is suggested by the discovery of polished stone axeheads in the area, which would have been used in forest clearance, woodworking and probably as weapons by local Neolithic communities. Examples of such finds were excavated from Baltinglass passage tomb (Walshe 1941, fig. 5; NMI E11:1) and the Rathcoran enclosure (see Chapter 3). A stone axe (NMI 1974:46) was found in ploughed land in Spinans Hill townland, on the southern slope of Brusselstown Ring, with another example recovered from Fortgranite (NMI 1935:22) 5km south-east of Baltinglass. Stone axes found within 10km of the town include examples from Deerpark (NMI record 1A/243/64), Fiddancoyle (NMI 1929:1344), Killamoat Upper (NMI 1934:10,859) and Rathgorragh Lower (NMI 1932:5602), all in the parish of Kiltegan, and another from Grangecon Upper (NMI P1954:8) in Ballynore parish to the north.

Neolithic ritual

The Neolithic period is notable for the first burial monuments built in the Irish landscape. The best known are megalithic chambered tombs, of which some 1,500 examples survive in regional concentrations across four main designs (portal tombs, court tombs and passage tombs, with wedge tombs as a later format). The building of these imposing monuments was central to the process of 'becoming Neolithic' and to the expression of religious belief. They also represent new social formations, very different from those of the people of Mesolithic society. The use of these sacred sites as temples and shrines was closely connected to the Neolithic farming way of life, invoking solar and other astronomical alignments to connect the seasons with fertility, the passage of human life and the Otherworld. These tombs contained the burials of important individuals who were part of segmentary societies that placed great emphasis on elders and ancestors. Some of these 'special dead' were also interred as single burials in caves, rock shelters and under mounds of the so-called Linkardstown type.

Neolithic funerary monuments were also built in the Baltinglass area during the fourth millennium BC. They include the passage tomb on Baltinglass Hill discussed in Chapter 3. This impressive, multi-phase monument was built and used *c.*3600–2900 BC, as place of religious ceremony for the interment of special dead. The tomb was a focal point in a local Neolithic landscape, its importance emphasised by its prominent position within the Rathcoran enclosure.

There are other cairns on the hills around Baltinglass, none of which has been excavated. Some may contain small passage tombs or other prehistoric burials, while others could be of later date. These include six examples inside the Spinans Hill 1 enclosure discussed in Chapter 4. To the north of Spinans Hill, there are three examples on a ridge at Castleruddery Upper. One of these (WI021-017001) is described as a cairn circle, consisting of an 11–13m-wide ring of contiguous granite boulders, with another cairn (WI021-017002) 12m to the south, and a third (WI021-017003) 140m to the north-east. At least four cairns (WI027-033, WI027-035, WI027-036 and WI027-037) are recorded on the western slopes of Kilranelagh Hill. These are 5–27m in diameter, with no features to indicate their age or significance.

To the east, four cairns are recorded on Keadeen Mountain (653m OD) and the adjacent Carrig Mountain (571m OD). These include a circular cairn (WI027-044) of horizontally laid stones, 20m in diameter, located near the summit of Keadeen (Fig. 8.2). This has been interpreted as a passage tomb (Herity 1974, 260), but that cannot be confirmed. There are three smaller cairns (WI027-045, WI027-059 and WI027-077) on the ridge connecting Keadeen south to Carrig Mountain, none of which has been excavated. There is also a linear earthwork (WI027-089) on the steep western slope of Keadeen, leading to the summit with its aforementioned cairn (WI027-044) at the north-eastern corner. This is a *c.*300m-long by 35m-wide rectangular enclosure, with 5m-wide stony banks on either

Fig. 8.2 Cairn on summit of Keadeen Mountain.

side and closing the western end. The structure has been interpreted as a Neolithic cursus or ceremonial avenue leading to a passage tomb (Corlett 2014a), which also remains to be confirmed.

Finally, the Ordnance Survey of the nineteenth century recorded the 'Remains of Cromlech' in Lathaleere townland, overlooking the River Slaney on the south-eastern side of Baltinglass town. This description often refers to a megalithic tomb, but there are no remains today apart from some large stones on an adjacent field boundary. The site (WI027-047) seems to have been destroyed *c.*1980, despite a preservation order having been in place since 1940. Liam Price made the following record of this lost monument:

> *The monument at Lathaleere, which is marked 'cromlech' on the O.S. map, looks like the ruined remains of another allée couverte, but until the monument is excavated nothing definite can be said. It was planted with trees about 25 years ago, and at present all one can see is a mound of grass and stones, about 2 feet high, of an oblong shape, 20 feet long and 13 feet wide, at each end of which there is a large granite boulder partly covered; in the centre there is a large flag-stone of shale sticking out of the ground at an angle: it is about 6 feet 3 inches long, and about 2 feet of its width is visible. At the south-western end of this flag is another smaller one, standing upright: it is 2 feet 3 inches wide, and 1 foot high above the ground. I was told locally that the large flag had previously stood on six support stones, but that these were blasted, and the flag fell to where it is now; but from the appearance of the monument I am inclined to think this story is an invention* (Price 1934/5, 35–6).

BALLINTRUER MORE

Another important Neolithic monument at Baltinglass is a now-destroyed burial mound at Ballintruer More, located

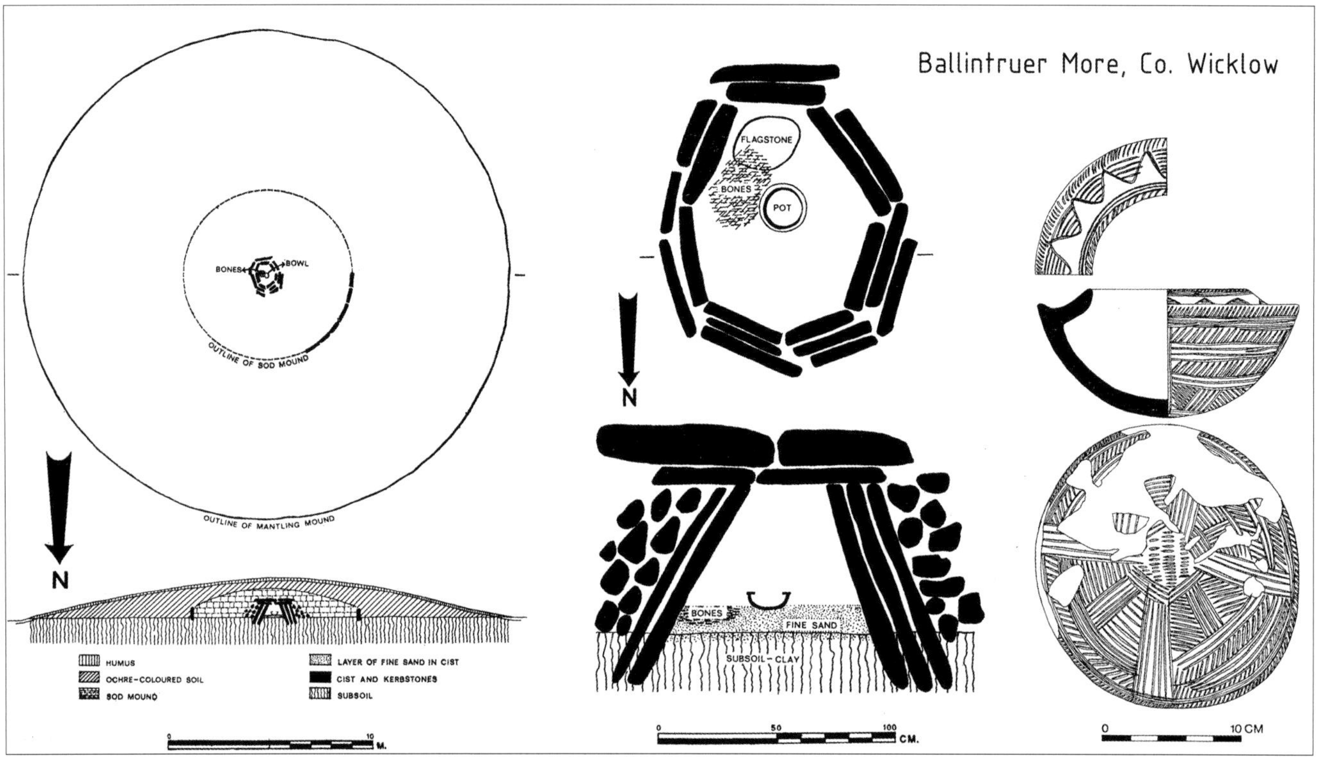

Fig. 8.3 Neolithic single burial at Ballintruer More 1 (after Raftery 1973).

1.4km north-west of the Spinans Hill 1 enclosure, 4km north/north-east of Rathcoran and 8km north-east of Hughstown. The site was discovered in 1970 during reclamation of the 'Moat Field' in the southern part of this townland. Rescue excavation by the National Museum of Ireland recorded a circular earthen mound, 24m in diameter, covering a central stone cist (Raftery, J. 1973). The latter had seven sides, each formed by two or three overlapping stones that leaned inwards to create a small structure on the old ground surface (Fig. 8.3). This cist was 0.95m by 0.73m at the base, narrowing to a 0.3m-wide opening at the top, which was closed by two flat stones overlain by two heavier examples. The side stones averaged 0.95m in length, with the lower 0.3m set into the subsoil. Smaller stones were packed against the exterior of the cist, which was then covered by a circular mound of turves, 8m in diameter and *c.*1m high, retained by a kerb of large stones. This sod mound, in turn, was overlain by a circular mound of sandy soil that extended 8m out from the stone kerb.

While the burial was much disturbed on discovery, the excavation was able to recover a single interment. The cist floor was covered by a 0.1m-thick layer of fine sand, in which a deposit of unburnt human bone was placed on the south-eastern side. This bone partly overlay a slightly concave slab, 0.26m by 0.24m, lying flat on subsoil beneath the sand. Osteological analysis identified the remains of a single adult, probably male, in what seems to have been a disarticulated burial. Several bones are missing or broken, suggesting the body was originally buried elsewhere before its reinterment here. Radiocarbon dating of this bone dates the burial to 3708–3374 BC (Brindley, Lanting and Mook 1983, 7).

The only artifact from the cist is a highly decorated, round-based pot (NMI 1970:36), found upright on the surface of the sand layer. This is a shallow vessel, 95–100mm in diameter and 90mm high, with a pronounced, concave shoulder. There is elaborate grooved decoration with hatched bands and triangles in a form of basketry pattern at the base (Fig. 8.3). This ceramic places Ballintruer More into a category of Neolithic single burials called Linkardstown Cists, found mostly in Leinster and North Munster (Ryan 1981). Their distinctive features include large, sub-megalithic cists with multiple inclined walling, built on the original ground surface and covered by a circular mound. These contain one, or occasionally two, unburnt burials accompanied by a highly decorated, round-based pot, but few other grave-goods. Examples with this distinctive pottery occur at Ardcrony, Co. Tipperary, Jerpoint West, Co. Kilkenny, as well as at Baunogenasraid and Linkardstown in Co. Carlow, closer to the Baltinglass discovery. Similar sites without pottery include Poulawack, Co. Clare and Knockmaree, Co. Dublin. Several of these monuments are radiocarbon dated to the Early Neolithic, *c.*3600–3300 BC (Brindley, Lanting and Mook 1983; Brindley and Lanting 1989/90).

There are other possible burials (WI021-087, -088 and -089) at Ballintruer More, located *c.*300m north of the Linkardstown Cist mound. Local information recorded by the Archaeological Survey of Ireland indicates a number of cists were uncovered there during land reclamation in recent years. These are visible now as cropmarks, but without excavation cannot be confirmed as burials in a possible Neolithic cemetery.

There is also a group of four unclassified barrows (WI021-054001, WI021-054002, WI021-054003 and WI021-054004) in Ballintruer More townland, on the southern side of the River Slaney, 500–600m north-west of the Linkardstown burial. All four are listed as levelled circular enclosures, 18–20m in diameter, each with an enclosing ditch. Also of interest is a low mound (WI021-091) recently discovered in Eadestown North townland at the north-western side of Spinans Hill. In the absence of excavation, it is not known whether any of these are Linkardstown burials, though the possibility remains of an Early Neolithic burial ground in the vicinity of Spinans Hill.

There are some discoveries of rock art in the Baltinglass area. This refers to human-made markings of prehistoric date on natural rock surfaces or large boulders. These petroglyphs, as they were previously termed, are found in several parts of Ireland and also in northern Britain and other places in Atlantic Europe (Bradley 1997). The largest concentrations are in Donegal and Kerry, with smaller regional groupings, including in south Leinster (Corlett 2014b), There are two examples of rock art at Baltinglass. A boulder with at least seven cup-and-ring marks (WI027-080) was discovered in the later nineteenth century at Barraderry East during the construction of an artificial lake. The stone is presently located at Humewood Castle. A large boulder with at least 16 cupmarks and two or three lines (WI027-100) is recorded in Spinans East townland. The Archaeological Survey of Ireland also recorded a boulder with a single cupmark (WI027-044001) at the base of the summit cairn (WI027-044) on Keadeen Mountain.

The chronology of rock art is contentious, often dated to the later Neolithic on the basis of stylistic influence from passage tomb art. An example of the latter is recorded at Baltinglass passage tomb (Walshe 1941, figs 8 and 9), which provides some local inspiration for this art. While independent dating is weak, rock art was probably created in different parts of Ireland throughout the third millennium BC, with the use of some motifs, notably cupmarks, surviving into the later Bronze Age. The meaning of rock art is equally enigmatic, with interpretations ranging from the practical (for example maps) to the numinous (such as solar religion).

THE BRONZE AGE IN BALTINGLASS

The adoption of metal (copper, bronze and gold) during the late third millennium BC led to a new phase of human settlement in Ireland. The Bronze Age (*c.*2100–700 BC) is one of the most archaeologically visible periods of Irish prehistory, with rich material culture (pottery, metalwork, etc.), and numerous ritual monuments of stone and earth, as well as thousands of burnt mounds (*fulachtaí fia*) and a growing number of settlement discoveries on road projects and as a result of other modern developments. The Bronze Age was an era of technological progress, as regional societies expanded their agricultural economies and developed extensive trade connections. New funerary customs reflect a concern with status and power relations, while mass production of weapons reveals an underlying warrior culture. Such militarism was an important background to the emergence of hillforts after *c.*1400 BC in Baltinglass and other parts of Ireland.

Settlement and farming

No Bronze Age house settlements are recorded in lowland areas around Baltinglass. The same reason that Neolithic sites have not been discovered applies, namely an absence of development archaeology to discover sub-surface evidence of habitation. While those lowland sites have not been identified, the building of large hillforts at Rathnagree and Tinoran indicates an important centre of later Bronze Age settlement at Baltinglass.

This is supported by the evidence from the Holdenstown Upper pollen study discussed in Chapter 7, which provides a proxy record of Bronze Age farming in the Baltinglass area. This study detected a major change in land use from *c.*1820 BC, when a woodland environment was transformed to one of open grassland. The expansion of that farmscape continued to *c.*1450 BC, after which there was a gradual reduction in human activity to *c.*1100 BC. There is evidence of both pastoral and arable agriculture during that Middle Bronze Age period, at a time when the occupants of Rathnagree hillfort were farming on Tuckmill Hill. The study also records an ongoing decline in farming activity from the tenth century BC, at a time when Tinoran hillfort was occupied.

As with the removal of Neolithic fields, trackways and settlements, the Bronze Age farmscape is not visible in the lowland farming environment of Baltinglass today. There are traces of earlier agriculture on higher ground, such as the stake fence and enclosure at Sruhaun on Baltinglass Hill examined in Chapter 5. Circular hut-sites are recorded on the upper slopes of the Keadeen and Carrig mountains (WI027-105 and WI027-084), and on the lower slopes of the former in Kelshabeg townland (WI027-041001). These have not been excavated and so cannot be dated. This is also the case for a group of structures on the lower western slopes of Keadeen (Corlett 2004). These include a sub-oval, stone-walled, enclosure (WI027-043001), 208m by 162m in extent, with the foundations of six stone huts (WI027-043003, -043006, -043007, -043008, -043009 and -043010) in the interior, and two others (WI027-0430-04 and -043005) close to the southern side. The presence of a 1.76m-high standing stone (WI027-043002) near the centre of the enclosure suggests this may be a prehistoric settlement, but that is not certain.

Burnt mounds or *fulachtaí fia* are another important indicator of later prehistoric settlement in many parts of Ireland (Hawkes 2018). The Archaeological Survey of Ireland lists 142 examples in Co. Wicklow, most of these in the eastern coastal region, where a significant number were discovered on road schemes and other developments. An example is a site at Kilnacarrig near Greystones, where excavation identified several burnt mounds with water troughs, dated to the early second millennium BC, along with finds of Bronze Age pottery and worked flint (Hayden 1994).

There are only a few recorded *fulachtaí fia* in the environs of Baltinglass. There are two examples in Rampere townland, 2.3km north-west of Rathnagree hillfort. These were discovered in 2005 during archaeological monitoring of a landfill site. Excavation exposed a burnt mound (WI021-085) overlying two troughs and three post-holes, with a radiocarbon date of 1607–1570 BC for one of several phases of activity. One of the troughs was sub-rectangular, 1.7m by 1.4m by 0.35m deep, and lined with stone slabs. A second burnt mound (WI021-086) was discovered 50m to the south-west, where a 6m-wide circular spread of burnt stone contained two pieces of struck flint, with two other flakes from the underlying surface (McQuade 2008, 420).

Recently, one of the present authors (AH) discovered a burnt mound adjacent to a small stream in Coolinarrig Upper townland, on the lower northern slopes of Tuckmill Hill (ITM 0688967, 0689631). This is an irregular mound, *c.*6m long by 4m wide by 0.8m high, with charcoal and fire-cracked stone exposed on the western side. A line of large boulders at the southern side of the mound may represent an ancient field wall.

Bronze Age metalwork

The first use of metal in Ireland occurred in the mid third millennium BC, when copper and gold metallurgy was introduced by the groups connected to the international Beaker culture. The first objects of copper-tin alloy date from *c.*2100–2000 BC, beginning a gradual transition to the Bronze Age in technological terms. There was a steady increase in the circulation of tin-bronze with the emergence of fully metal-using societies by 1500 BC, leading to an almost industrial scale of supply and consumption in the later Bronze Age. This transformed many aspects of daily life in Ireland, while the aesthetic side of these metals was a new medium of social expression. The supply of metal to regions lacking local sources was the basis for an enduring trade network in a range of commodities, both within Ireland and overseas. Control of metal production and circulation had important repercussions within society and contributed to the social changes that mark the later Bronze Age (O'Brien 2022).

There is a darker side to these innovations in the mass production of bronze weaponry across Ireland during the Middle and Late Bronze Age. This includes the only two items of Bronze Age metalwork recorded from the Baltinglass area. The first is a 116mm-long, side-looped, bronze spearhead (NMI 1959:604) found in the environs of the town (Lucas 1961, 82; Lineen 2016, no. 312). This has a slender, kite-shaped blade, attached to a 50mm-long socket with two side loops. There are no details about where or how this weapon was found. It is one of 44 bronze spearheads recorded from counties Wicklow, Carlow and Kildare, which include 30 looped examples of the Middle Bronze Age and 14 riveted examples of Late Bronze Age date (Lineen 2016). The majority are from Co. Kildare (21 looped and 11 riveted), with five spearheads from Carlow and seven from Wicklow. The latter include two examples from the Blessington area (Lineen 2016, nos 760 and 931), three from East Wicklow (nos 101, 925 and 1409) and an excavated example from Rathgall hillfort (no. 1668) in the south of the county.

The second bronze find from Baltinglass is an unlooped palstave of Middle Bronze Age date. This was found in a bog at Ballinclea townland in Donaghmore parish, *c.*5km north-east of Brusselstown Ring (NMI 1967:215). Palstaves are a type of bronze axehead, introduced in the Middle Bronze Age, on which flanges and a stop-ridge were used in a new method of hafting to a wooden handle. There are no other finds of Bronze Age metalwork from Baltinglass. The absence of swords is notable, with Eogan (1965) listing only one example from Co. Wicklow, while the county also has only a single rapier find (Burgess and Gerloff 1981). The closest finds to Baltinglass are eight bronze swords found *c.*1926–34 during dredging of the River Barrow. These include four from Co. Kildare, one from Co. Laois and three from Co. Carlow (Bourke 2001, 221–3; fig. 42). In general, the amount of later Bronze Age metalwork from Wicklow is sparse in comparison with other parts of Leinster. As an example, there are only four socketed bronze axeheads from Wicklow, found in eastern and northern parts of the county, with none close to Baltinglass. This is a small proportion of the 2,100 or so examples recorded from Ireland, approximately 900 of which have some find location (Eogan 2000).

There are only two hoards of Later Bronze Age metalwork from Wicklow. They include the find of a basal-looped spearhead, two socketed axeheads and a socketed knife from Kish near Arklow (Eogan 1983, no. 155). The second hoard consists of a socketed axehead and a gold penannular bracelet provenanced to 'Co. Wicklow'. Finds in counties close to Baltinglass include the hoard from Coolmanagh Upper, Co. Carlow, and four examples from Kildare, found at Bishopsland, Grange, Saintjohns and Tipper respectively (Eogan 1983*)*. Finally, there are very few Bronze Age gold finds from Wicklow. These include two possible penannular bracelets of uncertain provenance (Eogan 1994, 149, 152), and an penannular ring excavated at Rathgall hillfort (Raftery 1994; 2004).

Bronze Age funerary sites

The Early Bronze Age was marked by the adoption of new funerary practices in many parts of Ireland *c.*2200–1600 BC. This was a wider phenomenon across Europe during the early second millennium BC, connected to fundamental changes in society and the overt display of social hierarchy. In Ireland, the cremated or unburnt remains of important individuals were buried in individual pits, sometimes lined with stones to form cists. These single burials, as they have been termed, occur individually or in flat or mound cemeteries. They are often accompanied by so-called food vessel pottery of the Bowl and Vase traditions, as well as by small items of bronze and other grave-goods. This burial rite was replaced in the early second millennium BC by in-urned cremation using different styles of cinerary urn pottery.

Early Bronze Age burials from the Baltinglass area include a possible cemetery in the townland of Tuckmill Lower, located at the foot of Tuckmill Hill on its north-eastern side (Waddell 1990, 166). This was first recorded in 1969 when a cist (WI027-074) was destroyed during land reclamation. A search of the site revealed fragments of cremated bone and sherds of two pots of the Vase tradition. One of these (NMI 1969:735) had a bipartite profile with whipped cord ornament (Ó Ríordáin and Waddell 1993, 147, fig. 581), while the other vessel (NMI 1968: 736) was tripartite, with elaborate impressed and incised designs (Ó Ríordáin and Waddell 1993, fig. 444). This pottery can be broadly dated to 2020–1740 BC (Brindley 2007, table 69). There is local information that another grave with cremated bone (WI027-074001) was found *c.*1964 near that cist (Ó Ríordáin 1972, fn 8). There is also a record of a third burial at this location, discovered some time before 1934 (Price 1934/35, 46).

Early Bronze Age burials are also recorded on a low ridge in Kelshamore townland, 3km north of Brusselstown Ring. Two short, rectangular cists were discovered in 1950–1 during land clearance (Hartnett 1952, 153–61). The first of these (WI021-036) measured 0.95m by 0.58m by 0.5m deep, with slab walls and a paved floor. This contained cremated bone and a broken pot of the Bowl tradition (Ó Ríordáin and Waddell 1993, 145, fig. 225). A second grave (WI021-036001), 5.4m to the west, was also stone-built, measuring 0.7m by 0.2m, by 0.4m deep. The floor was covered by the cremated bones of an adult human, on which stood a pot of the Bowl tradition, along with a plano-convex flint knife (Waddell 1990, 162).

Fig. 8.4 *In the year 1785 Mr. Green has occasion to open a piece of ground near his house of Greenville, in the county of Wicklow. At the depth of six feet beneath the surface, the workmen discovered a small enclosure of eight flags; six of these formed its sides and two closed in the top and bottom. Within this was placed an earthen vase, containing a considerable quantity of ashes and calcined human bones ... A general tradition prevails, though without any precise authority for it, that the ground wherein this urn was found had formerly been a place of interment.* 'Account of an Ancient Urn found in the Parish of Kilranelagh, in the County of Wicklow' (Green 1787).

An Early Bronze Age burial is also recorded at Kilranelagh, though the exact location is not known (Waddell 1990, 163). This seems to have been a polygonal cist, recorded as 'a small enclosure of eight flags, six of these forming its sides, and two closed in the top and bottom', in which cremated bone and a vase urn (Fig. 8.4) were found (Green 1787; Price 1934/35, 47). This vessel is presently in the National Museum of Ireland (NMI 129:1289). This may be the burial mentioned by Liam Price on a visit to Kilranelagh in July 1951, when he noted the discovery of a 'Late Bronze Age urn' in that area (in Corlett and Weaver 2002, 540).

There is a record of a flat cemetery of 'several graves' found in 1787 in Saundersgrove townland, *c.*2.3km north of Rathnagree hillfort. These were possibly short cists that contained 'nothing but urns with ashes and burned bones' (Price 1934/5, 46; Waddell 1990, 166). This may be the 'ancient cemetery' mentioned by Lewis in his Baltinglass entry for the *Topographical Dictionary of Ireland* (Lewis 1837, vol. 1, 174). Human remains were found at a destroyed site (WI021-078) in demesne land south-west of Goldenfort House, in a townland of the same name. This is described as a circular platform, 30m in diameter by 1m high, with no other features. Human bones, including three skulls, were found during sand extraction in the early twentieth century (Harrington 1937, 127). There is an earlier record of a 'kistvaen with urn of rude pottery, in which were ashes, with a number of human bones scattered around', said to have been found in a circular earthwork at this location (Lewis 1837, vol. 1, 174). Liam Price also mentions the discovery of golden ornaments in the nineteenth century in the vicinity of Knockarigg ('Hill of the Kings'), from which the name Goldenfort is derived (1934/35, 57)

Another flat cemetery of the Early Bronze Age was uncovered in 1931, in Clonshannon townland on the northern side of Keadeen mountain, 3.6km east of Brusselstown Ring. Three cist burials (WI022-017) were excavated (Mahr and Price 1932). They include a polygonal cist containing the cremation of a young adult male covered by an inverted encrusted urn (Fig. 8.5). There are indications of another burial 0.6m to the south, where sherds of a vase urn and some cremated bone were found. Two other cist graves are recorded from the site. A 0.55m-square cist contained sherds of a vase and the burnt remains of an adult. A polygonal cist, 0.48m by 0.41m, held the cremation of a child covered by an inverted vase urn, accompanied by a biconical cup (Waddell 1990, 159–60). The dating of this pottery, together with radiocarbon results for the burials, indicates the cemetery was in use *c.*2140–1772 BC (Brindley 2007).

As with the Tuckmill Lower discovery, the full extent of the Clonshannon cemetery is not known. These burials with food vessel and urn pottery are evidence of a significant Early Bronze Age settlement at Baltinglass, *c.*2200–1700 BC. These are likely to be the graves of a local elite, buried in kin-based cemeteries, representing a social hierarchy whose descendants may have been central figures in the building of Rathnagree and Tinoran hillforts. There are similar burials elsewhere in Wicklow and surrounding counties (Waddell 1990, 159–66).

Fig. 8.5 Early Bronze Age burial at Clonshannon, Co. Wicklow (after Mahr and Price 1932).

Burials of the Middle and Late Bronze Age are less easily recognised, as they tend not have grave-goods or dateable pottery (see Grogan 2004). There is one confirmed example from Baltinglass, found in 2018 when excavation was undertaken in advance of development at Rathcoran House (St Joseph's Convent) in the town. One of the excavation trenches uncovered two post-holes joined by a slot and a cremation burial pit (WI027-106), all of which were sealed by large, sub-angular, flat stones. The cremation pit was 0.76m by 0.60m by 0.18m deep. It contained pyre material mixed with cremated human bone, identified as the remains of an adult and possible juvenile. Charcoal from the pit is radiocarbon dated to 1118–916 BC (Whitty 2021, 15–16).

Human remains recovered from a number of other sites in the Baltinglass area have not been dated, but are likely to be prehistoric. These include the discovery in the mid-1920s in Tuckmill Upper townland on the north-west lower slopes of Tuckmill Hill of a cist (WI027-008002) with an unburnt human burial. The cist was *c.*1.82m long, paved with stones and covered by a slab. It was found within a circular mound (WI027-008001), *c.*19m in diameter by 0.45m high (Price 1934/35, 46–7).

Also of interest is a destroyed barrow (WI026-006001) sited on a low ridge in the northern part of Rathmoon townland, *c.*1km west of Baltinglass town. Records show this circular earthen mound was *c.*20m in diameter and up to 4m high, with a possible eroded bank at the base (Price 1934/35, 47). The mound was levelled by agriculture in 1958, when a slab-covered cist, 0.8m by 0.45m by 0.5m deep was found, containing the cremations of three adult females, a new-born infant and a 6–8 year old child. (Fig. 8.6) A burnt, roughly leaf-shaped arrowhead of flint was found with these remains (Lucas 1960, 84–8). While there is no independent date for the burial, the arrowhead find suggests it could be Neolithic. Rathmoon mound is *c.*700m north-west of a levelled hilltop enclosure (WI026-009) in the same townland (see Chapter 6).

A number of other mounds of possible prehistoric age are recorded in the Baltinglass lowlands. These include two

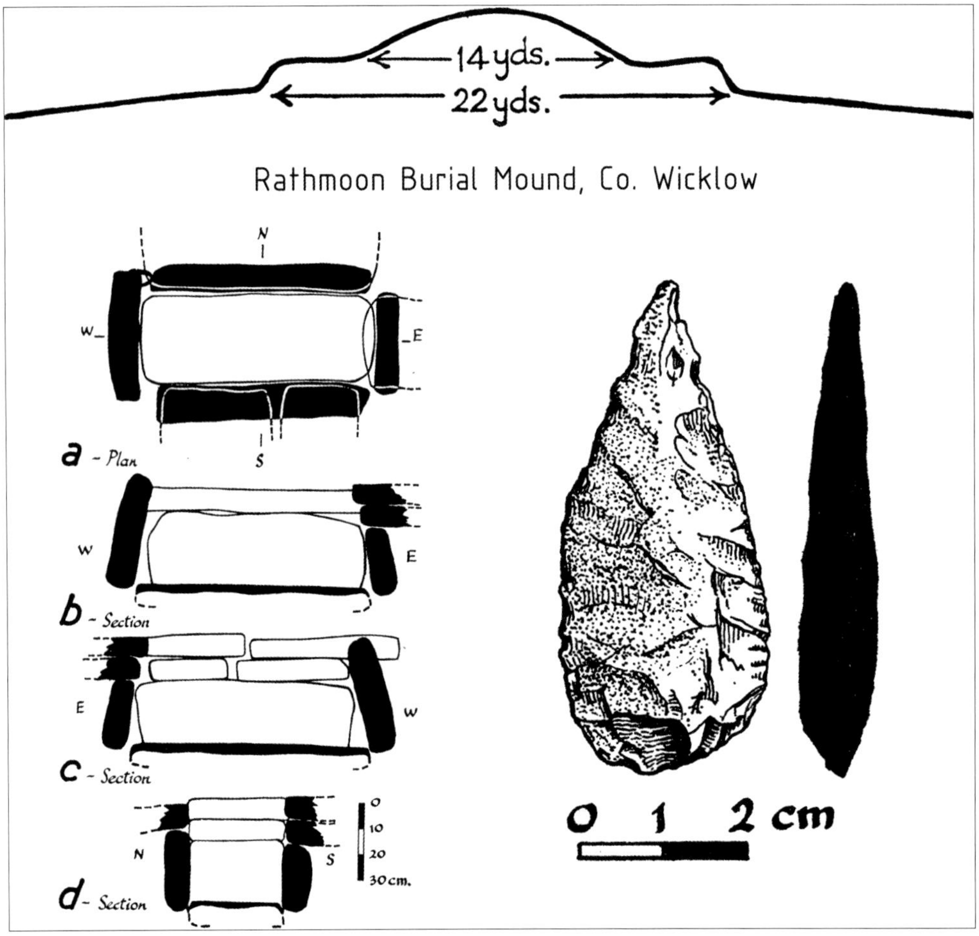

Fig. 8.6 Prehistoric burial at Rathmoon, Baltinglass (after Lucas 1960).

ploughed-out ring ditches (WI027-093 and WI027-094), each *c*.8m in diameter, visible as crop marks in Bawnoge townland, *c*.400 south of the town. These ring ditches are directly adjacent to a levelled D-shaped enclosure or a field (WI027-092), *c*.540m by 70m in extent, with a possible 8m-wide entrance on its northern side. Another ring ditch (WI027-095), *c*.5m in diameter, is 300m to the south in the same townland (information from: Archaeological Survey of Ireland).

There is a circular mound (WI027-006), *c*.50m in diameter by 2.4m high, in the north-eastern corner of Raheen townland adjacent to the River Slaney on the north-western side of Tuckmill Hill. Other possible ancient burial mounds include an example at Boleycarrigeen (WI027-040) on the eastern lower slopes of Kilranelagh Hill. This was recorded by Liam Price as a circular mound with a possible external ditch, and with a possible long cist in the centre (Price 1934/35, 40). There is a possible prehistoric mound (WI027-103) on the demesne lands of Kilranelagh House in Spinans East townland. Finally, there is an large ring-barrow (WI026-005) on the eastern slopes of Tinoran Hill, located outside the fourth enclosure of the hillfort. This monument has a low, domed interior surrounded by a 7m-wide shallow ditch with an external bank (Fig. 8.7; see also Fig. 5.30).

Standing stone monuments

A small number of single standing stones are recorded in the Baltinglass area, none of which is excavated or dated. These include three examples (WI027-086, -088 and -043002), 0.9–1.76m in height, on the lower western slopes of Keadeen. A 1.5m-high standing stone (WI026-011) on the south-eastern slopes of Tinoran Hill is located between the third and fourth enclosures of the hillfort. There is a 1.71m-high granite standing stone (WI021-079), aligned NE/SW in Eadestown North townland at the south-western foot of Spinans Hill, with a 2.1m-high standing stone (WI021-027) in the adjacent Ballintruer More townland.

There are two prehistoric stone circles in the Baltinglass area, neither of which has been excavated. The stone circle at Castleruddery Lower (WI021-032) is a National Monument

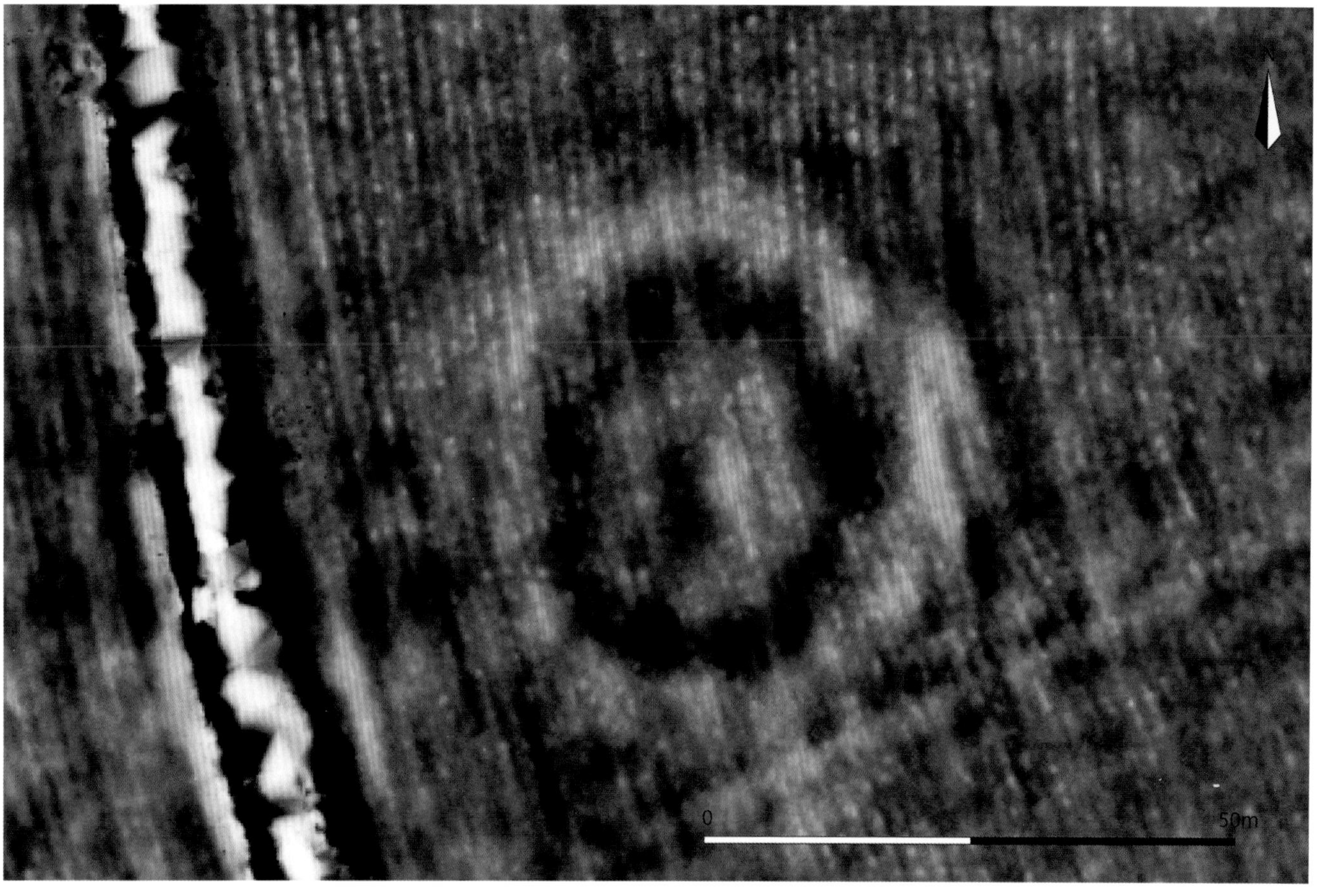

Fig. 8.7 LiDAR image of large levelled ring-barrow adjacent to eastern side of Tinoran hillfort.

in state ownership (Walshe 1931, 131–4; Leask 1945, 266–7, Burl 1976, Fig. 41; Condit and Corlett 2001). It consists of an embanked enclosure, *c.*40m in overall diameter and *c.*30m wide in the interior (Fig. 8.8). There is a 1.3m-wide entrance passage marked by two exceptionally large boulders of white quartz on the eastern side (Fig. 8.9). Both Walshe and Leask suggested some stones outside the entrance were part of an avenue leading to the monument. The enclosing bank is of earth and stone construction, 4–5m wide by *c.*1–1.2m high, with 29 large boulders and other smaller stones placed contiguously against its inner side (the Ordnance Survey *Name Book for Co. Wicklow c.*1838 mentions 42 large stones in the circle). The circle is largely intact on the northern side, but less so on the southern side. The site occurs centrally within a circular cropmark enclosure *c.*80m in diameter, possibly defined by a 4–5m-wide ditch. Between this and the earthen bank is a narrower cropmark, *c.*50m in diameter, defined by a trench or narrow ditch (Grogan and Hillery 1993).

The second stone circle (WI027-039) is located at Boleycarrigeen on a pass between Brusselstown Ring to the west and Keadeen Mountain to the east. Known locally as the 'Griddle Stones', this is a circular arrangement of eleven stones spaced 1.3–1.8m apart, with an internal diameter of *c.*12.5–13.5m (see Fig. 2.16). There may have been as many as 17 stones in the original circle (Ó Nualláin 1995, 11). The stones appear to rise in height, from 1.3m on the S/SW side to the tallest stones, measuring 1.4–1.88m, at the N/NE. The stones are placed on the inner edge of a 1.75–2m-wide earthen bank, less than 1m in height, with no indication of a ditch (Price 1934/35, 39–40, fig. 4; Burl 1995, 249, fig. 41c).

These are two examples of the many types of prehistoric stone circle in Ireland. There are two main groups: those from the Late Neolithic and Chalcolithic cultures of the third millennium BC, and stone cicles of the later Bronze Age built after 1500 BC. The latter include the axial stone circles of Cork and Kerry, such as at Drombeg in West Cork, and the distinctive stone circles of mid Ulster, including at Beaghmore and Copney in Co Tyrone. A small number of

Fig. 8.8 Castleruddery Lower stone circle, Co. Wicklow.

Fig. 8.9 Large white quartz boulders marking entrance to Castleruddery Lower stone circle.

stone circles is recorded in Leinster (Burl 1976, 232), of which the best-known is at Newgrange in Co. Meath. The three confirmed sites in Wicklow — Athgreany, Castleruddery and Boleycarrigeen — have not been excavated, so their chronology and cultural associations are unclear.

Castleruddery and Boleycarrigeen are variants of what is known as an embanked stone circle. Examples include the Nymphsfield group of monuments near Cong, Co. Mayo, and the impressive monument at Grange, Lough Gur, Co. Limerick, the largest stone circle in Ireland. Radiocarbon dating confirms the Grange circle was built *c.*2950–2850 BC, with the discovery there of Grooved Ware and Beaker pottery indicating continued use during the third millennium BC (Cleary 2015). While of different scale, the design of the Grange and Castleruddery monuments is similar, suggesting a similar early date for the Wicklow example. Boleycarrigeen is somewhat different, with spaced as opposed to contiguous stones inside an earthen bank. This is more likely to be of an early date than to parallel stone circle/ring barrow hybrids, such as those found in Cork (see O'Brien 2004), though this cannot be ruled out for Boleyarrigeen. The free-standing stone circle at Athgreany (Burl 1976, plate 26), 16km north-east of Baltinglass, may be of later date, but again this is speculation in the absence of excavation and scientific dating.

One interpretation is that Castleruddery and Boleycarrigeen represent significant settlement in the Baltinglass area during the third millennium BC. This was a time when the great Neolithic enclosures at Rathcoran, Hughstown and probably Spinans Hill were abandoned. It is possible the two stone circles held a special significance for the later Bronze Age hillfort communities of the area, as these monuments would have been a visible reminder on the landscape of ancient times

Finally, mention must also be made of the 'Gates of Heaven', an unusual arrangement of stones in the old graveyard at Kilranelagh (WI027-034001). While the burials there are mostly early modern in date, there is an unusual occurrence of two upright stones on either side of a flat stone. This has been suggested as the remains of a megalithic tomb, but may also represent gateposts between the inner and outer enclosure of the church. There is a local tradition of carrying a coffin between the upright stones to ensure passage to heaven for the deceased (Marsh 2007, 69).

Bronze Age Baltinglass: final thoughts

The Bronze Age was not just an age of technological progress, but also a time of important developments in the way society was organised, in terms of the daily lives of ordinary people, their religious beliefs and artistic expression. Many parts of Ireland were transformed during the second millennium BC, as population grew and agriculture expanded to create a managed landscape of field patterns and agricultural settlements. This period was also marked by the first significant settlement of uplands, with small-scale agricultural activity and also the building of hillforts as central places in larger political communities. The militarism of that period is expressed in the construction of these fortified settlements and in the large-scale production of bronze weaponry. That wider context for the Baltinglass hillforts will be explored in Chapter 9.

There is an obvious discrepancy between the presence of Bronze Age elites at Baltinglass, connected to at least two major hillforts, and an absence of contemporary settlement sites and material culture in its agricultural lowlands. This is to a great extent a problem of archaeological visibility. A paucity of Middle and Late Bronze Age metalwork, particularly weapons, can be explained in part by an absence of turf-cutting and river dredging in the area. As already noted, the evidence of houses, burnt mounds and other features of Bronze Age lowland settlement in Ireland depends on survival and discovery. This is particularly true for the Baltinglass landscape, where there has been intensive farming in recent centuries, and few local examples of development-led archaeology in recent times

Baltinglass should be viewed as part of a wider Bronze Age settlement landscape in eastern Ireland during the second millennium BC. This is evident in the large number of Early Bronze Age burials from Leinster and the growing number of Middle and Late Bronze Age sites uncovered by recent road, pipeline and other developments. For Wicklow, such developments have revealed extensive settlement along the eastern coastal margin. The picture from western parts of the county is less complete, but does align with similar discoveries in adjacent counties of Carlow, Laois and Kildare.

MYTH AND LEGEND

> 'Baltinglass or Beal-tine-glas, or the Fire of Beal's Mysteries, the fire being lighted by the Druids on the first of May and August in honour of the sun ...'
> *Ordnance Survey Name Book, 1838.*

Fig. 8.10 Quartz boulders on slopes of Kilranelagh Hill, the legendary *Bae Aife* of White Cow Hill (photograph courtesy Robert Hanbidge and Paul Carbery).

This brief review of the prehistory of Baltinglass has focused on the archaeology of built monuments, sub-surface sites and material culture. That physical record is only part of the early story of the place, and it is also important to connect with the mythologised landscape of Baltinglass, its many legends, and the way natural features were imbued with cultural meaning. This is a place believed by antiquaries to derive its name, Baal-Tin-Glas ('the pure fire of Baal'), from its significance as 'one of the principal seats of druidical worship' (Lewis 1837, 173). The scholar Liam Price recorded some of this place-lore in a study of local place-names. He recounts a story in *Agallamh na Senórach* in which Fionn mac Cumhaill engaged the Tuatha de Danann in battle, after which the latter raised a *lecht-lighi* (monumental cairn) to their dead, identified by some as the passage tomb on Baltinglass Hill (Price 1949a, 129). The Schools Folklore Collection of 1937–9 contains many stories of ancient raths and fairies and of the legendary Fionn Mac Cumhaill. There is an association with the Griddle Stones at Boleycarrigeen, and with Keadeen Mountain, where this legendary figure is supposed to have died (Drury 1905).

Kilranelagh seems to have been a place of great significance, and there is a legend connected to a guesthouse, or *bruiden*, for the warriors of Ireland at this location. Buchet's House was a 'cauldron of hospitality', with fifty warriors and fifty young women in their purple clothes dancing and singing to the melodies of fifty harps (Marsh 2007, 11–21). Liam Price also recounts the legend of *Bae Aife*, a mountain covered with white stones that look like white cows from afar. This is known as the place where the battle of Dún Bolg was fought in *c.* AD 587, in which Áed mac Ainmuirech, king of the Uí Neill, was killed by Brandub mac Eachach, king of the Uí Cheinnselaig and the Lagin. Price noted that Kilranelagh Hill was referred to as White Cow Hill in the Down Survey of 1655 (Price 1949a, 122–3). There is an unusual concentration of large, white, quartz boulders (WI027-099) in dense forestry in Colvinstown Upper townland, just below the summit of Kilranelagh Hill on the north-western side (Fig. 8.10). Price connected these with *Bae Aife* and identified the nearby hillfort of Brusselstown Ring as the legendary Dún Bolg, which brings us to the next part of the Baltinglass story.

EARLY MEDIEVAL BALTINGLASS

While the Baltinglass landscape is best known for its concentration of Early Neolithic and Bronze Age enclosures, there is also a significant early medieval element that has received less consideration (O'Driscoll and Gleeson 2019). Placenames like *domnach*, a toponym indicative of a conversion-period church, as well as newly identified cemetery settlements, a large burial mound possibly used for inauguration, and a number of ogham stones, are suggestive of a significant Late Iron Age to early medieval landscape, which evolved into an important royal complex by the sixth or seventh century AD. A core focus of this royal estate was Dún Bolg, a major fortification overlooking the Glen of Imaal that acted as the seat of the Uí Chennseláig and latterly the Uí Máil. Dún Bolg enjoys a rich historical tradition, featuring in saga literature such as *Fingal Rónáin* (tenth century AD) and the *Bórama Laigen* (eleventh century AD), as well as having occasional references in the Annals, reflecting the importance of this landscape and the dynasties that held it. Dún Bolg may have been as important a symbol of regional control for southern Leinster as Dún Ailinne was in Co. Kildare at the beginning of the Early Medieval period (O'Driscoll and Gleeson 2019).

Dún Bolg and the Central Midlands dynasties of ancient Leinster

The ancient province of Leinster occupied a unique place in the real and imagined structure of the medieval period (O'Brien 1962, 1–78; Smyth 1982, 8–13). By the fifth century AD, the province probably extended as far north as the River Boyne, encompassing the Hill of Tara, Co. Meath and much of the Midlands (Byrne 1973; Bhreathnach 2000; MacShamhráin 1996; Smyth 1974), as well as lands in northern Wales (Charles-Edwards 2000, 159; 2013, 176; Stokes 1892, 57). The province was ruled by several loosely confederated groups, although by the seventh century, the Uí Dunláinge and Uí Chennseláig had come to dominate much of the region. The rise of the former as a provincial power saw a focus emerge on Dún Ailinne and Óenach Carmain in east Kildare around the eighth century, representing the symbolic 'provincial' heart of Leinster (Swift 2006, 113; Gleeson and Ó Carragáin 2016, 77–9). However, historical sources reveal earlier regional centres of power, including Lyon's Hill, Killiney, Delgany and Naas in north-central Leinster. Further south, Dún Bolg would appear to have been a major fortress associated with the Uí Cheinnselaig and Uí Máil at the height of their respective powers. One of the most powerful septs of the Uí Cheinnselaig were the Uí Felmeda, who settled in the lands around Dún Bolg from the sixth century AD. During this period, the Uí Felmeda provided some of the Uí Cheinnselaig's most famous kings, including Brandub, his father, Eochu, his grandfather, Muiredach, and his great-grandfather, Óengus. Regardless of the accuracy of later synthetic histories, those sources emphasise the significance of the Baltinglass region at that time.

There are two important references to Dún Bolg in the Annals. The first recounts a major battle at the site *c.*AD 597, in which Brandub mac Eachach, head of the Uí Cheinnselaig and king of Leinster, defeated Áed mac Ainmuirech , king of the Uí Néill and perhaps king of Tara (AU 598.2; cf. AU 597.1 re: Dún Buchat; AI 600.2; 601.1; A. Tig. 596.2; cf. 599.1; AFM 594.1). A second major battle occurred at Dún Bolg around AD 870, again involving an Uí Néill king of Tara, Áed mac Níall, and the Osraige king, Cerball mac Dúngal (AU 870.2; AFM 868.15). This indicates that Dún Bolg continued as an important symbolic and political centre into the ninth century AD (Swift 2006, 15–22; Bhreathnach 2011, 135). Dún Bolg might also be identified as Bolg Lúatha in the historical sources (Smyth 1994, 79–80), also associated with dynastic kings and major conflicts involving the Uí Néill (AU 626.2; cf. A. Tig. 628.4) and with intra-provincial disputes with the Uí Faeláin sept of the Uí Dunláinge (AU 628.1). The AU reference suggests a battle for supremacy in central Leinster between rival emergent dynasties and implies that Dún Bolg held a regional to supra-regional importance at that time (O'Driscoll and Gleeson 2019). Bhreathnach (2000, 312) notes that early medieval kings were very much aware of the importance of such ceremonial sites during a period when nascent kingdoms were jostling for power.

Further historic references support a connection between Dún Bolg, the most powerful dynasts in sixth/seventh century Leinster, and the Uí Néill, who were the major antagonists of the Laigin in that period (Smyth 1982, 52; Clinton 2000, 275). Many of the aforementioned Uí Cheinnseláig kings also reigned as kings of Leinster and resided within or near Dún Bolg. The importance of this place meant that regardless of which dynasty held the fort, it continually drew the brunt of Uí Néill aggression, particularly during the sixth and seventh centuries.

It was not until the rise of the Uí Dúnlainge in the eighth century AD, when they began to dominate a nascent kingship of Leinster (Ó Cróinín 2005, 199), that there is a notable absence of references to Dún Bolg and a de-escalation of tensions between the Uí Néill and the Laigin. The Uí Dúnlainge kingship seems to have become a puppet institution sustained by the Uí Néill at this time. This assumption is supported by the fact that Uí Néill hostility quickly re-emerged when the Uí Máil gained provincial supremacy around AD 715, (Smyth 1994, 93), before the Uí Dúnlainge regained power and held it until the middle of the eleventh century (Clinton 2000, 277; Ó Cróinín 2005, 200). It is also at this point that we see Dún Ailinne and Óenach Carmain become important institutions in the Uí Dúnlainge's provincial hegemony (see Grabowski 1990, 35; Gleeson and Ó Carragáin 2016, 77–79, 94), places they seem to have annexed in the seventh and eighth centuries. This might imply that the idea of a province of Leinster focused on these two sites was a creation of Uí Dúnlainge propaganda (Gleeson and Ó Carragáin 2016, 77–9; 96). Indeed, the Uí Cheinnselaig and Uí Máil kings of Leinster do not appear to have coveted Dún Ailinne and Óenach Carmain, but instead fought for control of Dún Bolg and its environs. This suggests that Dún Bolg may have been as important as Carman and/or Dún Ailinne as a symbol of regional control for southern Leinster until the eighth century (O'Driscoll and Gleeson 2019).

While it appears that the Baltinglass area and much of northern Carlow and south-west Wicklow were under the control of the Uí Cheinnselaig by AD 500–650 (Smyth 1994, 80), there are indications by the middle of the seventh century that the Uí Máil had begun to test Uí Cheinnselaig power at Dún Bolg. By the beginning of the eighth century, they had annexed this territory (O'Driscoll and Gleeson 2019), as confirmed by the tenth century *Fingal Rónáin* saga, which focused on Dún Bolg and featured heroic members of the Uí Máil in central roles (Greene 1955; Smyth 1982, 52). Despite the Uí Chennseláig being *de facto* rulers of southern Leinster (with a base emerging at Ferns) during most of the period AD 700–1200, the Uí Máil seem to have held their position at Dún Bolg until at least the thirteenth century. The symbolic shift of provincial power to Dún Ailinne and Óenach Carmain in this period may have made Dún Bolg a less important strategic position for the Uí Chennseláig. Regardless, the Uí Máil controlled a large and important tract of east-central Leinster, and were a major influence in contemporary provincial politics (MacShamhráin 1996; MacCotter 2008, 131; 177–8; Price 1949b, 29–33). The dynasty's name is preserved in the placename Glen of Imaal (*Glinn Ua Máil*), and in their association with the church of Domnach Mór Ua Máil (Hogan 1910, 457).

Toponymy of the Dún Bolg landscape

It was Liam Price (1949a, 121) who first suggested that Dún Bolg may be the large hillfort of Brusselstown Ring. His interpretation is based on the topographical description of the site in the *Bórama Laigen* (Stokes 1892, 55–95), a saga recounting a major battle in the shadow of Dún Bolg that was also recorded in the Ulster Annals (AU 598.2). The cause of this battle was the killing of Cummascach, son of Áed mac Ainmuirech of the Uí Néill, by Brandub mac Eachach, the Uí Cheinnselaig king of Leinster. The story begins as Cummascach, on a royal tour, went to Brandub's house in Belach Conghlais (Baltinglass) and demanded the right to sleep with Brandub's wife. It is notable that the text specifically mentions Belach Conghlais, not only setting the conflict in this region, but also highlighting that the king of Leinster resided here. In retaliation, Brandub attempted to kill Cummascach, though the latter escaped and fled to nearby Móin Cummascaigh, near the *faitche* (an area of open space outside a high-status dwelling) of Cill Rannaireach (Kilranelagh). Here the *erenagh* of Cill Rannaireach killed Cummascach in return for gaining exemption from tribute for the monastic centre. In retribution, Áed mac Ainmuirech invaded Leinster the following year, continuing to Dún Bolg before setting up camp. After an unsuccessful attempt by Áedán of Glendalough (possibly of Kilranelagh, see Eyjólfsdóttir 2012, 49) to obtain a truce, Brandub devises a plan and pretends to provision the king's army and enters his camp hidden in baskets of food. After a prolonged battle, Áed mac Ainmuirech is killed and buried at Kilranelagh, further implying that the battle was fought nearby (Price 1949a, 123). This was a decisive victory for Brandub, which possibly helped to restore territories lost to the Southern Uí Néill in earlier decades (Byrne 1973, 142), or perhaps even re-established Laginian overlordship of the south-central midlands (O'Driscoll and Gleeson 2019).

Regardless of the veracity of these retrospective accounts, which were likely coloured by contemporary political and ideological agendas, the topographical details may prove useful, as the saga highlights sites of significance in the period of compilation. For example, the slain king Áed mac

Ainmuirech was reputedly buried at Kilranelagh, which Price (1949a, 121) suggests is an early tradition that he was killed nearby. Likewise, another key fort in the narrative is Dún Buchat, mentioned as the secret shelter to which Brandub sent his wife once the battle commenced. Price (1949a, 121) has argued that Dún Buchat was located near or at the *faitche* of Kilranelagh, possibly a levelled fort at the north-eastern base of Kilranelagh Hill (O'Driscoll and Gleeson 2019).

Brandub's *dún*, mentioned at the beginning of the saga, is differentiated from Dún Bolg, suggesting that the latter was considered a ceremonial centre rather than a place of residence. It is described as being located close to the River Slaney near Baltinglass. Price (1949a, 121) connected this description to a large univallate ringfort a few hundred metres from the river, in the townland of Gibraltar, 4km north of Baltinglass, which is described in more detail in Chapter 6. The unusual funnelled entrance on the eastern side of the fort may signify that this was an important, high-status residence. Notably, this funnel extends eastward, towards the suggested location of Dún Bolg on Spinans Hill. This may have been associated with ceremonial processions towards the hilltop complex, a feature found at many Iron Age/early medieval royal sites in Ireland (Newman 1998). Remarkably, this funnelled fort is the largest example of such a monument found in the parish of Rathbran, a land unit that may preserve the name of the famous sixth-century Leinster king, Brandub mac Eachach.

There is a concentration of multivallate ringforts near the modern town of Donard at the north-western entrance to the Glen of Imaal. This may indicate a significant concentration of high-status settlements associated with the royal residence of the Uí Máil (Clinton 2000, 281). As such, sites like Dún Bolg may represent central places for these polities rather than actual residences; likewise, royal sites such as Tara, Knockaulin or Rathcroghan seem to lack evidence of permanent residence within their core complexes.

Another site, Bun Aife, is also mentioned and distinguished from Kilranelagh and Dún Buchat in early sources. According to the *Bórama Laigen* (Stokes 1892, 83), the Uí Néill king sent part of his army south towards Bun Aife, with Brandub's men passing them when making their final attack. This suggests that Bun Aife was near the battlefield. Both Price (1949a, 121) and O'Driscoll and Gleeson (2019) have shown that Aife was the ancient name for Kilranelagh Hill, where three large enclosures have been identified.

A second major battle occurred at Dún Bolg around AD 870. The *Fragmentary Annals of Ireland* include an entry stating that Áed mac Níall, king of Ireland, marched into Leinster, plundering from Áth Cliath (Dublin) to Gabrán (Gowran Pass). Then Cerball mac Dúngal, king of Osraige, and Cennétig mac Gáerthíne, king of Loíches, came from the other side of Leinster, and did 'as much burning and plundering and killing as they could until they reached Dún Bolg, and they camped there' (Frag. A. 387). The Leinstermen rallied behind their king, Muiredach mac Brán, and attacked the enemy at Dún Bolg. A description of the battle records some of the army 'in the clefts of the rocks', which might correspond with the rocky outcrop over much of the south-east part of Spinans Hill/Brusselstown Ring.

Another prominent saga, *Fingal Rónáin*, firmly places the seat of Uí Máil power during the seventh century in west Wicklow, and more specifically, in the area around Kilranelagh and the neighbouring hills (Smyth 1994, 103). The fortress of Rónáin, identified as the king of Leinster, is located near 'The Cows of *Aife*' (Fig. 8.10), which accords well with the suggested location of Dún Bolg near Bun Aife.

Identifying Dún Bolg

It seems likely the concentration of prehistoric hillforts and enclosures at Baltinglass influenced the development of its early medieval landscape. This landscape association with ancient dynasties may be significant in the rise of Dún Bolg as an early medieval power centre. None of these hillforts has produced evidence of early medieval occupation, though the small enclosures at the centre of Hughstown and Tinoran might date to that period. Taking literary, genealogical and annalistic evidence into account, it seems likely the eastern side of the complex, specifically Spinans Hill and Kilranlagh, was a focus for early medieval activity. It is possible that Dún Bolg, being positioned to the north of Kilranlagh, was one of the three hillforts on Spinans Hill. Considering the relative chronology of these forts, the impressive size of Spinans Hill 2 and its prominence in the Glen of Imaal, O'Driscoll and Gleeson (2019) have argued this is the best candidate for Dún Bolg, though this needs to be confirmed by excavation and scientific dating.

Other Late Iron Age/early medieval royal centres and assembly places in Ireland often focus on large hilltop enclosures in prominent locations in their respective landscapes (Wailes 1982, 51; Newman 1998, 135; Gleeson 2014, 177; Gleeson 2017b). Some of these were re-used hillforts, including Clogher, Grianán of Aileach, Ballymount

Great and the Hill of Lloyd. In the early medieval period, hillforts like those of the Baltinglass group may have been seen as the physical manifestation of successful ancient dynasties who inscribed the landscape with massive and enduring fortifications. Early medieval elites may have attempted to re-imagine these forts as the physical monuments of known ancestors, in an attempt to affirm their place and power in contemporary society.

Kilranelagh also features prominently in early historical sources, which suggests the hill had a prolonged and complicated history of use. The western slopes are defined by a distinct flat terrace, where recent LiDAR survey identified three concentric earthworks enclosing an area of *c.*7ha. This encompasses Kilranelagh church (WI027-034001), graveyard (WI027-034002), St Brigit's Well (WI027-0340013) and early stone crosses (WI027-034004 and -034006). Considering the *cill* placename, the archaeological remains, and references in early sources, this is almost certainly a major early medieval ecclesiastical site, probably the Cill Rannaireach mentioned in *Bórama Laigen.*

Two other large enclosures have been identified on the central and eastern summits of Kilranelagh Hill. While the central example (WI027-097) is associated with several cairns and is more reminiscent of the Early Neolithic enclosure of Spinans Hill 1, the eastern site surrounds a stone circle (WI027-039) and barrow (WI027-040), as well as a badly weathered ogham stone (WI027-038002). The latter is one of three such commemorative stones of likely fourth- to seventh-century date in the wider Baltinglass area, the other examples being located at Ballylion Lower (WI021-081) and Knickeen (WI022-012). Outside the main group of ogham stones in the Co. Cork/Kerry/Waterford region, notable concentrations occur around important Iron Age/early medieval centres such as Freestone Hill, Co. Kilkenny; Rathcroghan, Co. Roscommon; the Hill of Tara and Raffin Fort in Co. Meath. The presence of ogham stones around Dún Bolg is therefore significant. Considering the connections between the name Aife and Kilranelagh outlined above, as well as the presence of an ogham stone, it is possible that the newly discovered enclosure on the eastern summit of Kilranelagh is the Bun Aife mentioned in the historic sources.

At the northern base of Kilranelagh, Price recorded a large enclosure (Corlett and Weaver 2002, 540), though this has not been identified in the LiDAR survey. Satellite imagery reveals an oval vegetation mark in that area, *c.*172m in diameter over 2.37ha. The enclosure and surroundings are overgrown, making further identification of features difficult. Price (1949a, 121) has argued that this enclosure is the Dún Buchat mentioned in the *Bórama Laigen.*

The Dún Bolg environs

While there are several candidates for the forts and other places mentioned in these historical sources, including Dún Bolg, Cill Rannaireach, Brandub's *dún*, Bun Aife and Dún Buchat, as well as a potential royal settlement for the Uí Máil near Donard, there are other monuments not referenced in the literature that hint at the importance of the area in this period. Of particular significance is the place-name Donaghmore, a large parish immediately north of Spinans Hill. From Domnach Mór ('Great Church'), the first element *domnach* signifies an early conversion-period church. Derived from the Latin *dominicum*, most scholars agree this was no longer an active toponym by around AD 600 (Flanagan 1984). Furthermore, *domnach* placenames normally signify that the ecclesiastical site in question was the principal church of a defined geographical area or of a discrete kindred or dynasty (such as the Uí Máil). In addition, these sites are often found in proximity to early royal estates and assembly places (Gleeson 2015, 43; 2017a, 79). Gleeson (2017a, 79) has argued that assembly places and practices were a focus of missionary activity, stating that at least 39 of some 118 assembly landscapes known in Ireland are specifically associated with these *domnach* churches. In this instance, the church at Donaghmore is strategically located at the entrance to the Glen of Imaal, visible to, and just beyond, the northern edge of Spinans Hill 2. It is one of only three *domnach* sites known in counties Carlow, Kildare and Wicklow.

Research has highlighted how royal centres often occur near other important places, such as early churches, royal inauguration places, assembly complexes and ancient burial cemeteries (Smyth 1982, 27–8; Gleeson 2015, 43–5). Some of these sites can be identified in the Baltinglass area. Approximately 1.5km to the west of Donaghmore church, a large sub-circular mound in Castleruddery Lower townland, misclassified as an enclosure (WI021-026), is located close to the River Slaney, in a location highly visible from Spinans Hill. The mound is in a natural hollow and measures 50.37m (east–west) by 49.2m (north–south), with a maximum height of 2.07m (Fig. 8.11). There is no evidence for enclosing elements at the base of the mound, though a 12m-wide berm suggests it may have been built with soil scraped from the adjacent ground. The summit is partly

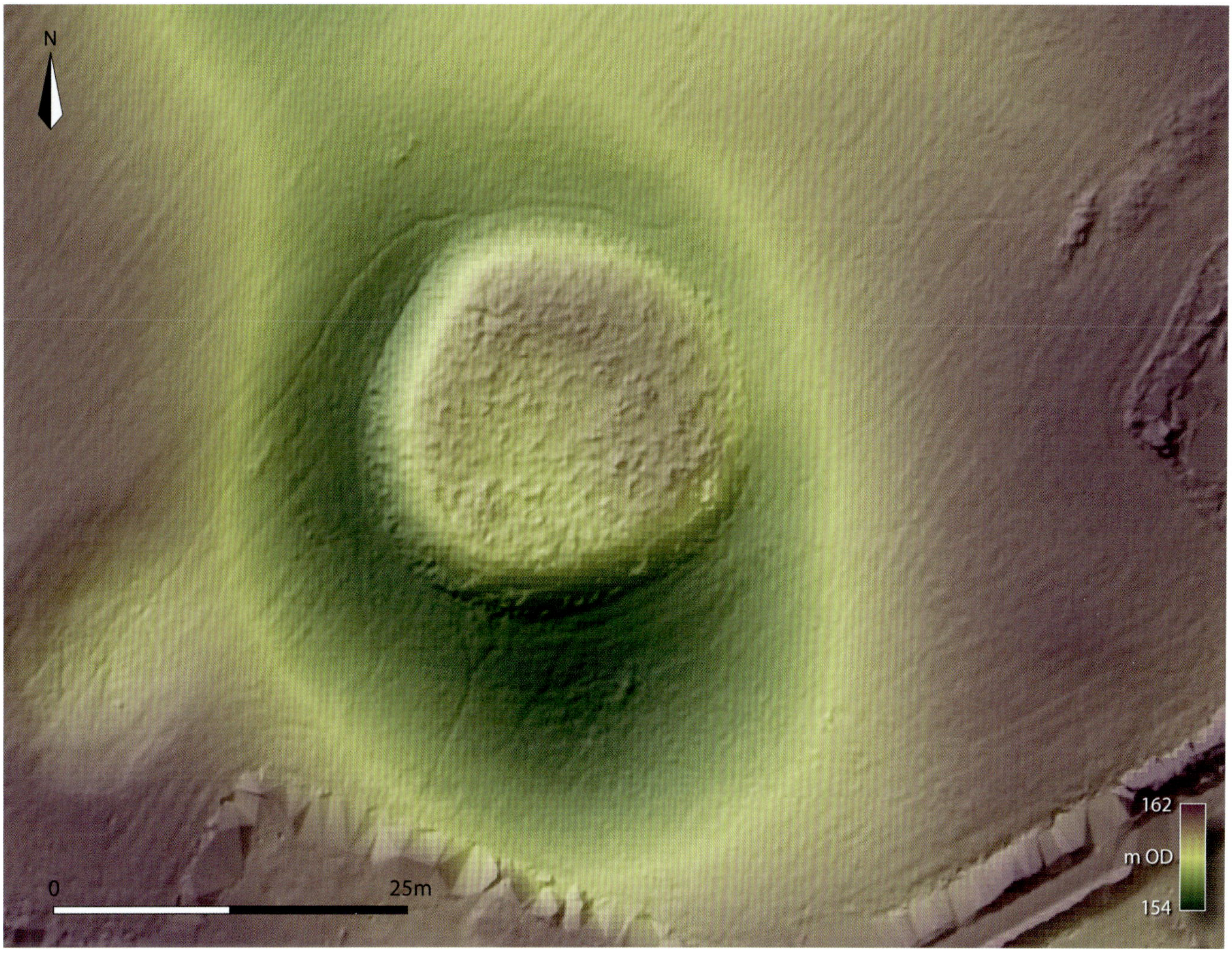

Fig. 8.11 Hillshade model of Castleruddery Lower mound, Co. Wicklow, derived from LiDAR data.

dished and slopes to the south, which broadly corresponds with the surrounding topography. The edge of the mound is steep and there is no obvious ramp or entrance. This mound could be a raised rath, though the absence of any form of enclosing element makes this unlikely. It is also possible that this is a burial and/or inauguration mound. The landscape setting is similar to that of Magh Adhair, Co. Clare, the inauguration site of the Dál Cais, also located in a hollow prone to flooding.

There are several prehistoric monuments in the vicinity of the mound at Castleruddery Lower. These include an embanked stone circle (WI021-032), 450m to the east (see Fig. 8.8), of a type that may date to the Late Neolithic (Cleary and O'Driscoll 2014, 32). There are several cairns in the same area, with a cluster of large barrows, a standing stone and possible Linkardstown burials 1.3km to the south (see Chapter 6). As noted previously, several barrows are recorded in the Baltinglass area, including some exceptionally large examples. This, along with the large number of prehistoric cairns in the area, represents a significant ancient burial complex. Bradley (2002, 47) argues that the past in contemporary society was particularly important during periods when new regions were settled and new relationships formed between people and the land. This was particularly important in the early period of conversion, when ancestry played a significant role in the social and cosmological order of societies and the legitimisation of power (Semple 2013 1–6; 9; Waddell *et al.* 2009, 205; O'Driscoll 2016, 330). The mound at Castleruddery Lower may have been re-used in the early medieval period for

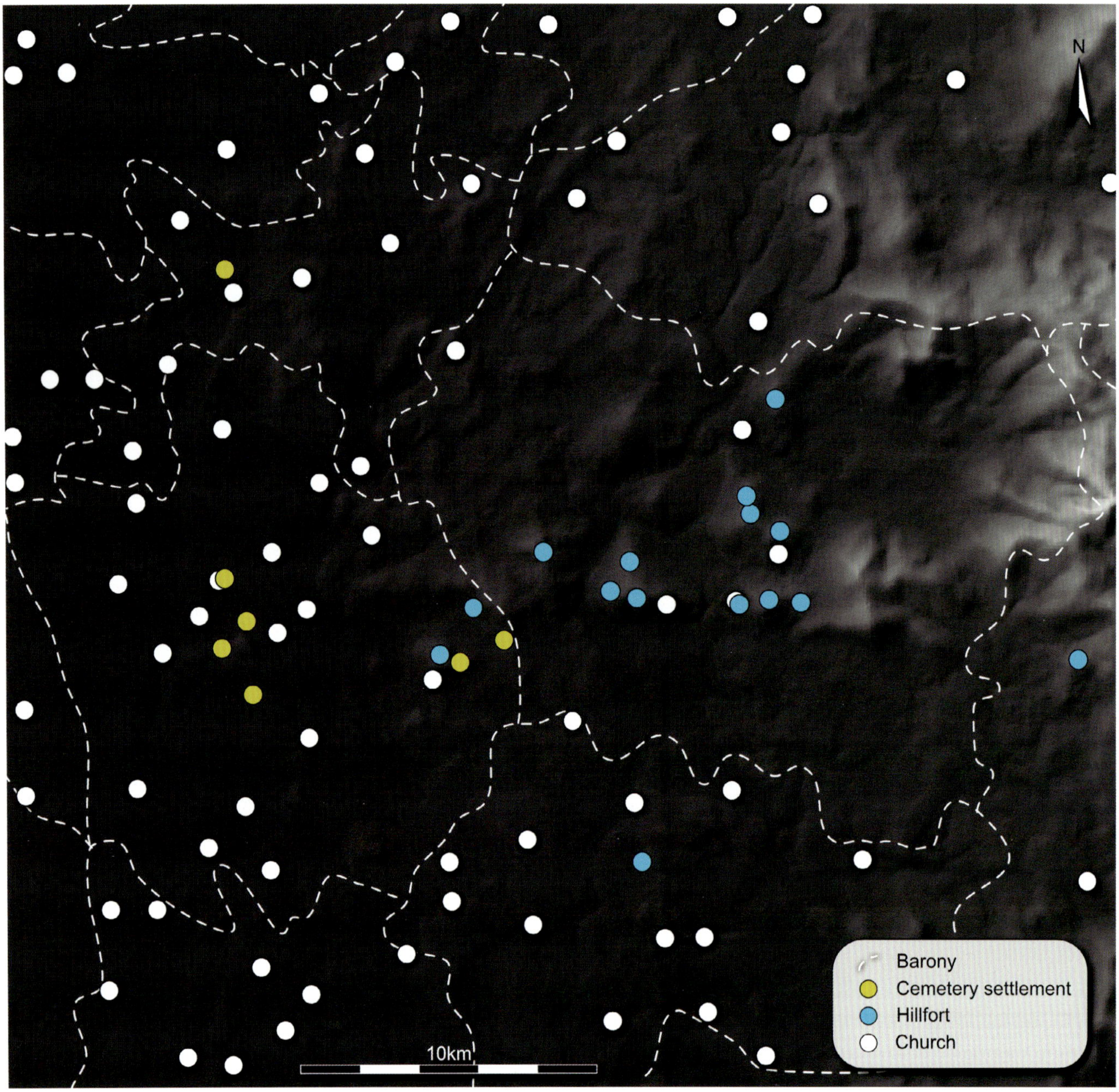

Fig. 8.12 Distribution of churches in respect of parish boundaries, highlighting a notable decrease in churches in Donaghmore parish.

ceremonial purposes. Such monuments, along with other ancient burial sites, were important in the inauguration rituals of medieval kingdoms (FitzPatrick 2004; Gleeson 2014, 182–3).

The Castleruddery Lower mound, the aforementioned early church site, as well as Spinans Hill (Dún Bolg) and much of the Glen of Imaal, are all within Donaghmore parish in the barony of Talbotstown Upper. Despite its large size, there are only four churches recorded in this parish, in contrast to a large number of churches sited just outside the parish boundary on all sides (Fig. 8.12). This pattern is also mirrored in a distribution of possible early medieval cemetery settlements. Might Donaghmore parish represent the approximate limits of a royal estate centred on Dún Bolg, with royal power limiting the presence of the church within this landscape? The possibility that Domnach Mór Ua Máil was an early, conversion-period royal foundation would support this assertion.

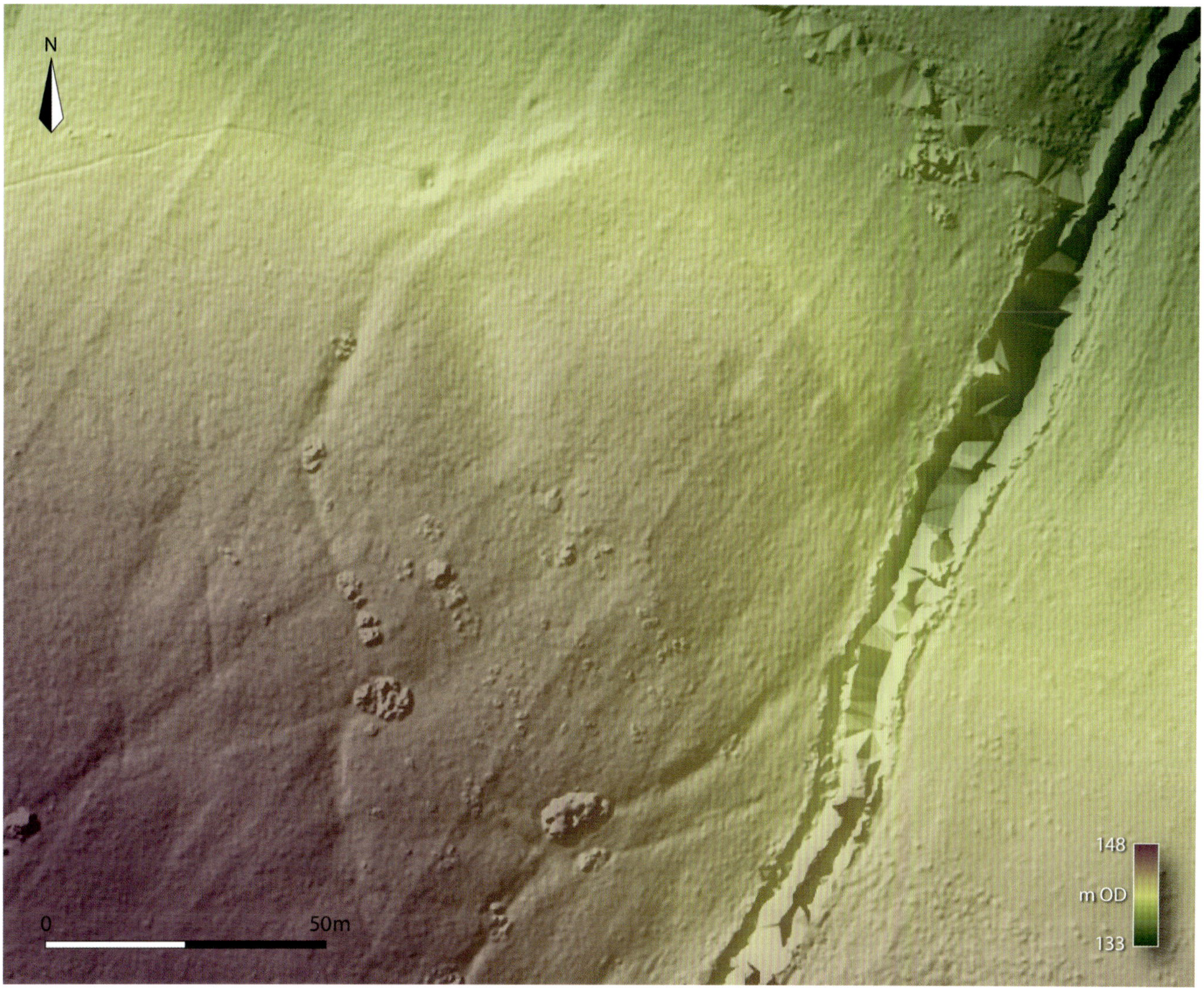

Fig. 8.13 Hillshade LiDAR model of Corballis cemetery settlement, Co. Kildare.

Rathmoon and other cemetery settlements

Further evidence of early medieval activity, and possibly assembly, can be found at possible cemetery settlements in this landscape. One of those sites is in Rathmoon townland, recorded as a large, levelled enclosure (WI026-009) at the flat south-eastern side of Carrigeen Hill, near a prehistoric burial mound (WI026-006001) that was destroyed in the 1960s. As discussed in Chapter 6, the site is depicted on Ordnance Survey historic maps as a univallate enclosure, though aerial and satellite imagery reveal a more complex system of somewhat concentric enclosing elements. This is imaged in magnetic gradiometry survey that shows a sub-oval enclosure, 160m (east–west) by 120m (north–south), with up to four widely spaced enclosing elements over 1.71ha. Recent LiDAR survey suggests the enclosure extended further to the north, where geophysical survey has not been undertaken.

Cemetery settlements are generally characterised by large, concentric, sub-circular or oval enclosures, with a burial ground in the central enclosure. Excavation at some sites has revealed activities such as craft-working, crop-processing and ceremonial feasting in the outer enclosures (O'Sullivan *et al.* 2008, 179; Ó Carragáin 2009, 135–7; 2010, 217). O'Sullivan *et al.* (2008, 179) noted these sites often lack a church, as well as having limited evidence for domestic structures. Gleeson (2015, 43) further argues that these sites were local community assembly and burial locations for specific kin groups within a *túath*. The chronology of these sites may vary, with Johnstown 1 in Co. Meath dating to the fourth to seventh century (McCormick and Murray 2007, 243–5) and Carrowkeel, Co. Dublin dating to the eighth to eleventh century (O'Sullivan 2007). O'Sullivan *et al.* (2008, 177) argue that the dating evidence does not indicate origins prior to the early medieval period, though they do observe some sites may be associated with prehistoric funerary monuments. There is little evidence these sites were founded after the eighth century, even if a number do remain in use until the eleventh century and later. Gleeson and Ó Carragáin (2016, 104) and Gleeson (2017b, 75) suggest the majority tend to cluster together near parish boundaries and within known assembly landscapes. Rathmoon fits this description, located as it is near the royal fortification of Dún Bolg, at the western edge of the parish boundary of Baltinglass abutting the county boundary dividing Wicklow, Carlow and Kildare.

While it seems reasonable to interpret Rathmoon as a cemetery settlement, the site is one of a cluster of large, multivallate, sub-oval enclosures in lowlying positions in the Baltinglass landscape. Just over 3km west of Rathmoon, a large oval enclosure, 1.05ha in extent, is marked on Ordnance Survey maps at the eastern base of Corballis Hill, at the edge of a parish and townland boundary (Fig. 8.13). This site may be similar to Rathmoon, but its significance remains to be clarified by geophysical survey and excavation.

The distribution of these sites is reminiscent of churches in the area, which are located beyond the edge of the parish of Donaghmore. Gleeson (2017b, 77) has noted a similar pattern at Óenach Carmain, Óenach Roigne and Óenach Maoinmaighe, the respective assemblies of the Laigin, Osraige and Uí Fhiachrach Aidne. In all cases a variety of early medieval burial complexes was located around the peripheries of those landscapes.

EARLY MEDIEVAL BALTINGLASS: FINAL THOUGHTS

The study of early medieval Irish royal landscapes has progressed significantly over the past few decades, developing from the investigation of royal sites, such as Navan Fort, Knockaulin, Rathcroghan and Tara (e.g. Waddell *et al.* 2009), to studies of regional kingdoms and dynasties that are perhaps more representative of governance and rulership as a whole (e.g. FitzPatrick 2004; Gleeson 2014; Lacey 2006; Warner 1988; Newman 1998). These sites have many features in common, and it does appear to be common to find a caput with nearby inauguration and assembly locations (Warner 1988, 53; Gleeson 2015, 33). We cannot be too rigid in applying such frameworks. The 'check-list' of archaeological criteria used by Wailes (1982) and Warner (1988) to identify royal landscapes seems less useful than the approach advocated by Newman (1998, 129) in which corroborating information, such as the location, scale and morphology of complexes with recognition of their 'special significance' in documentary sources, is given due prominence. A considerable problem in this regard is the documentary evidence, which is not always present or is perhaps too subjective to be reliable. Certainly there is a pressing need for more integrated, landscape-scale, interdisciplinary programmes of analysis.

This approach has identified the legendary Dún Bolg, an early medieval political centre in Leinster connected with the Uí Cheinnselaig and latterly the Uí Máil. There seems to be sufficient documentary and archaeological evidence to identify Dún Bolg with the forts on Spinans Hill, and possibly the Spinans Hill 2 enclosure. We can see that the royal landscape of Dún Bolg appears to have been demarcated by contemporary ritual or ecclesiastical sites, including an early *domnach* church, located in close proximity to a series of highly visible prehistoric monuments, ancient burial sites, ogham stones and early medieval cemeteries. Dún Bolg was probably the core focus for an assembly landscape of Uí Cheinnselaig and Uí Máil kings, as well as other sixth- to seventh-century kings who wished to rule south-central Leinster. While the *Bórama* saga may not reliably indicate the significance of Dún Bolg in the fifth to seventh century, it certainly attests to its long-term importance, implied by entries in the annals of the sixth and early seventh century, and in later sources. The identification of Dún Bolg in its wider cultural landscape reveals a major centre of power and supra-regional kingship in early medieval Ireland, for a time perhaps comparable in importance to the so-called provincial centres.

9. THE BALTINGLASS HILLFORTS IN CONTEXT

James O'Driscoll and William O'Brien

Having looked at their cultural landscape setting, we can now consider how the Baltinglass sites compare to other hillforts and hilltop enclosures in Ireland and abroad.

NEOLITHIC HILLFORTS IN IRELAND?

The radiocarbon results for Hughstown, Spinans Hill 1 and Rathcoran at Baltinglass add to a growing number of enclosures of Neolithic date discovered in Ireland (Sheridan 2001; Cooney 2002; Cooney *et al.* 2011). One of the first examples was excavated in 1937–51 at Lyles Hill, Co. Antrim, where Evans (1953) identified Neolithic occupation evidence that was initially linked to an earthen bank enclosure (Fig. 9.1). Subsequent excavation in 1987–8 dated this bank to the Bronze Age, but obtained dates of 3330–2920 BC and 2600–2350 BC respectively for two parallel palisades that may have surrounded the hill at different times during the Neolithic (Simpson and Gibson 1989, 215).

To the north of Lyles Hill in Antrim is Donegore Hill, where an oval area of 212m by 168m over 3.5ha is enclosed by two concentric lines of interrupted rock-cut ditches (Fig. 9.2). There is evidence of an inner palisade that held a timber fence at least 1.5m high. Excavation uncovered Neolithic pottery, worked flint and polished stone axeheads, in mostly plough-disturbed contexts, with little evidence of structures apart from some pits and stake-holes. There was prolonged occupation during the Early Neolithic *c.*3800–3500 BC, with some re-occupation during the Late Neolithic and Bronze Age (Mallory *et al.* 2011).

Donegore Hill has been compared to the Early Neolithic causewayed enclosures of southern Britain, as has a site in a lowland setting at Magheraboy, Co. Sligo (Danaher 2007). This circular enclosure is 150m by 130m in extent over 1.1ha, enclosed by a single, interrupted ditch, inside which there was a continuous palisade trench. There is evidence of prolonged use *c.*4000–3600 BC, possibly for ceremonial and special purposes, but not permanent residence.

Palisaded enclosures without accompanying banks or ditches are also known from Knowth, Co. Meath; Inisloughlin, Co. Antrim; Thornhill, Co. Derry and Tullahedy, Co. Tipperary (see Waddell 1998, 37–45). At Tullahedy, for example, a defended Neolithic settlement was discovered on an esker ridge, 5km south of Lough Derg. The original location was a promontory surrounded by a lake on two sides, with the landward approach protected by an oak palisade. The remains of three rectangular houses built with split oak planks were found, along with hearths, pits, broken pottery, stone tools and food waste connected to farming. The settlement was occupied by Neolithic farmers *c.*3700–3400 BC, at a location carefully chosen to protect its occupants (Cleary and Kelleher 2011).

There are a few examples, though not at Baltinglass, where Neolithic enclosures were re-built as hillforts in later periods. In 2013, a series of large enclosures and associated features were discovered by geophysical survey at Faughan Hill in County Meath. Subsequent excavation revealed the hill was encircled by a fenced enclosure, 250m in diameter over *c.*5.2ha, during the Middle Neolithic *c.*3635–3380 BC (Fig. 9.3). Some two millennia later, *c.*1280– 920 BC, during the Late Bronze Age, a substantial multiple enclosure (Class 2a) hillfort, *c.*400m in diameter, was built. There was further activity on this hill during the Early Iron Age *c.*800–520 BC, and also during the early medieval period when the location was significant in the political and territorial ambitions of the Uí Néill, as the reputed burial place of their most distinguished ancestor, Niall of the Nine Hostages (Dowling and Schot 2023).

The Hughstown enclosure at Baltinglass has features in common with excavated Neolithic enclosures in Ireland. These sites have obvious elements of protection, in the form of defensive lines created using wooden palisades with external ditches. There is also much variability in the design and use of these enclosures; some sites are more residential in character, while others seem to have special significance as ritual spaces. An example of the latter is the demarcation of a sacred mountain at Knocknarea, Co. Sligo, where the upper eastern slopes are cut off by a series of stone-built walls dated *c.*3350 BC (Bergh 2000; 2002). While there are many hut-sites on the summit, settlement there was probably connected to the special significance of a passage tomb cemetery, the focal monument of which is the massive

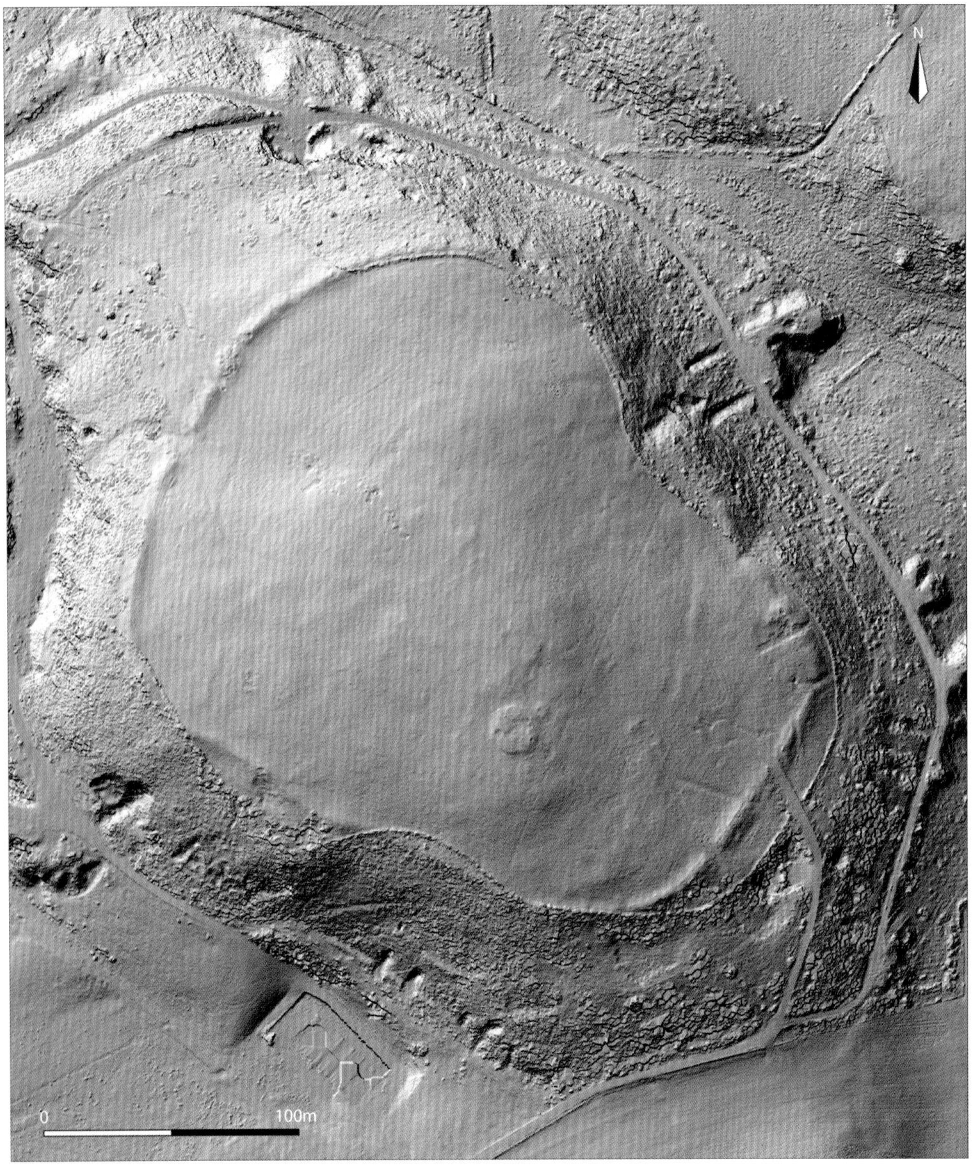

Fig. 9.1 Neolithic enclosure at Lyles Hill, Co. Antrim.

Queen Maeve's Grave (Fig. 9.4). The same may be true in Baltinglass for Rathcoran with its imposing passage tomb and, on a smaller scale, Spinans Hill 1 with its cairns.

These variations in size, design and landscape setting point to several traditions of enclosure in Neolithic Ireland (Sheridan 2001; Cooney 2002). There is also true of Neolithic enclosures in Britain and mainland Europe, where there are many variants in addition to causewayed enclosures (see below). Within the Baltinglass landscape, Hughstown has a different design than the Neolithic enclosures at Rathcoran and Spinans Hill 1. This may relate to the different use of these sites and their relative chronology. Hughstown may have been a protected residential settlement with no obvious ritual component, whereas the significance of Rathcoran and Spinans Hill 1 may lie with the passage tombs/burial mounds in those enclosures.

In terms of chronology, radiocarbon dates suggest the Hughstown enclosure was built between the thirty-seventh and thirty-sixth centuries BC. This overlaps with the so-called house horizon of the Early Neolithic II era (3720/3680–3640/3620 BC), known for its distinctive square or rectangular timber buildings (Cooney *et al.* 2011; Smyth 2014; McLaughlin *et al.* 2016). Rathcoran seems to have been built somewhat later, between the thirty-sixth and thirty-fourth centuries BC, broadly contemporary with the Faughan Hill enclosure during Middle Neolithic I, *c.*3640–3400 BC. Is it possible that Hughstown was in some way 'replaced' by Rathcoran in that period, in the same way that

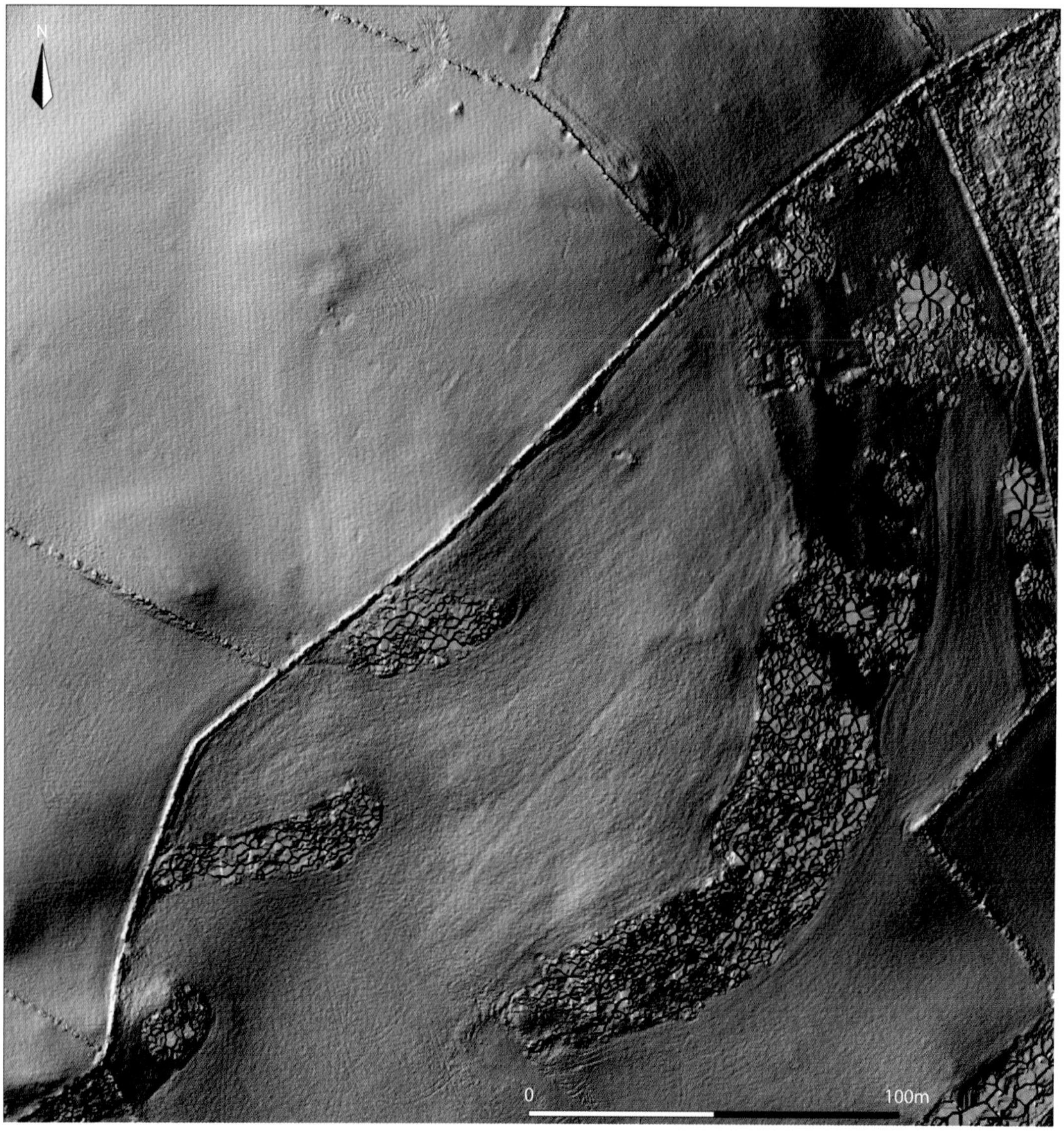

Fig. 9.2 Neolithic enclosure at Donegore Hill, Co. Antrim.

the occupation of Rathnagree was followed by activity at Tinoran hillfort during the Middle to Late Bronze Age transition? That would add to a picture of successively built hillforts at Baltinglass and a reluctance to re-use older enclosures, as occurred at Faughan Hill. It is important to stress, however, that much more excavation and radiocarbon dating is required to understand the history of these Baltinglass hillforts.

Neolithic war?

The results from Hughstown indicate the first hillforts in Ireland may have been large, multiple enclosures built by farming communities of the Early Neolithic, *c.*3700–3500 BC. The defensibility of those sites, combined with their economic and symbolic importance, meet many criteria of a hillfort. These sites were part of a wider phenomenon of enclosure of land, settlement and ritual space in the period. A connection with farming is relevant, as the creation of fields and animal enclosures was a feature of agricultural practice from early in the Neolithic. This had a broader significance in terms of the assertion of land ownership and territorial rights, which were also affirmed by the building of megalithic tombs and these enclosures.

The function of Neolithic enclosures in Ireland is much debated, with comparisons made to the causewayed enclosures in southern Britain that were used variously for assembly, trade and ceremonial purposes. Defence was also a consideration in the location and design of those sites;

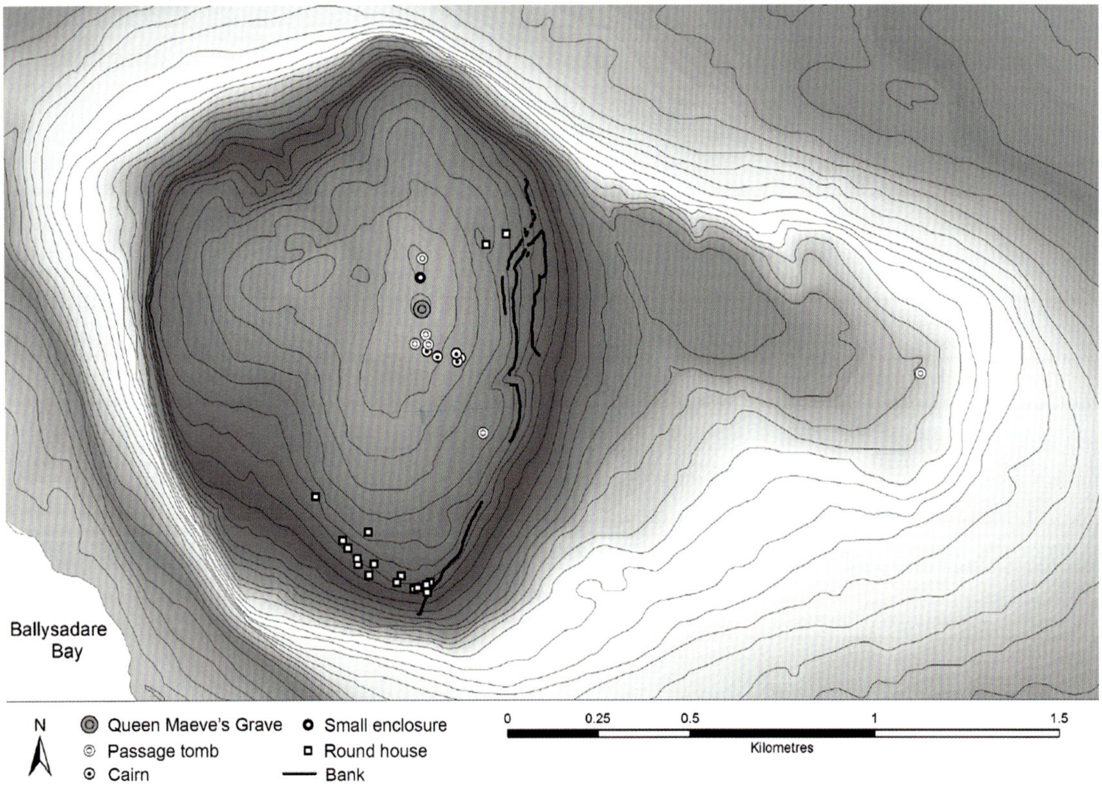

(Above) Fig. 9.3 Magnetic gradiometry survey showing multiple enclosures of Neolithic and Bronze Age date on Faughan Hill, Co. Meath (courtesy Ger Dowling and Roseanne Schot).

(Left) Fig. 9.4 Knocknarea Mountain in Co. Sligo, showing passage tomb cemetery and hut-sites on summit (320m OD), with banks on eastern upper slopes (courtesy John Waddell, after Bergh 2002).

effective barriers were created by a varying combination of ditches, banks, stone walls and timber palisades. Evidence of violent assault and destruction at many Neolithic enclosures in Britain will be discussed later in this chapter. While the transition to farming is often presented as peaceful, there is much evidence of conflict among early farming populations in Britain and continental Europe (Mercer 1999). The underlying causes are unknown, but probably had to do with control of resources and with various territorial disputes that arose among Neolithic groups and during their early dealings with the Mesolithic indigenes. The gradual expansion by Neolithic farming groups into Mesolithic hunting grounds would have been a source of tension, while the attraction for forager groups of food crops and domesticated animals, particularly cattle, should not be underestimated on an island with few game animals.

The protection of human life and property was certainly a major consideration in the design of the Hughstown enclosure. Design features there include the use of continuous (fourth enclosure) or interrupted ditches (possible second and third enclosures), timber palisades (second and third enclosures) and earthen banks (second, third and fourth enclosures). This emphasis on defence means the site should be regarded as a Neolithic hillfort, notwithstanding other uses and significance. The size and sub-division of the overall enclosure, and the availability of water (there are at least two natural springs on this hill today), suggests that the stockading and protection of cattle was an important part of its design. This is not to argue that such Neolithic hillforts were the same as their Bronze Age counterparts, as the historical and societal contexts were entirely different, but it does link the abundant evidence of conflict in the Neolithic world to the creation of enclosures that provided for protection of human life and property.

The record of Neolithic conflict in Ireland has been reviewed by Moore (2004) in respect of violent attacks on settlements and human skeletal evidence. There is evidence of archery assault and deliberate burning of a Neolithic house at Ballyharry, Co. Antrim, and the same at a palisaded settlement at Thornhill, Co. Derry. These are among a number of Neolithic settlements in Ireland destroyed by fire, though in other cases the evidence of violence is equivocal (Moore 2004, 143–8). The burning of a fence in the third enclosure at Hughstown may represent deliberate destruction, but there is no corroborating evidence, such as arrowhead concentrations or skeletal remains.

BRONZE AGE HILLFORTS IN IRELAND

While it is not known when the Neolithic enclosures at Baltinglass were abandoned, there is no evidence of occupation on those hills for the next 1,500 years or so. This changes around the fourteenth century BC, when similar enclosures with new military and political significance started to be built in this part of Wicklow and other parts of Ireland. The earliest of these date to the Bishopsland Phase of the Middle Bronze Age *c.*1400–1200 BC, and include Rathnagree at Baltinglass. Hillforts were built in increasing numbers during the Roscommon Phase (1150–1000 BC) of the Late Bronze Age, with some large examples, including Tinoran, occupied into the Dowris Phase to around 700 BC.

Many Bronze Age hillforts in Ireland have been excavated and so can provide important information on the likely significance of the Baltinglass sites. One of the best known is located only 16km south of Baltinglass, near Shillelagh village in south-west Wicklow.

Rathgall

As outlined in Chapter 1, our understanding of Bronze Age hillforts in Ireland began with the 1969–79 excavations conducted by Barry Raftery at Rathgall. This hillfort lies on a low-lying ridge and features four, concentric, circular enclosures over an area of 7.3ha (Fig. 9.5; see also Fig. 1.5). The innermost enclosure is a stone cashel of early medieval date, which overlies a complex sequence of late prehistoric activity (Raftery 1972, 1976). Radiocarbon dates place the primary occupation of this hillfort in the Middle to Late Bronze Age transition, *c.*1400–1000 BC. This is consistent with finds of metalwork of the Bishopsland and Roscommon phases (Becker 2010). While the hillfort defences are not closely dated, the Bronze Age occupation is likely to be contemporary with the middle and possibly the outer ramparts (Raftery and Becker forthcoming).

There is evidence of elite residence at Rathgall in the ceramic record and funerary deposits, and also in the presence of imported materials and specialist craftworking. The latter includes a workshop area, where excavation revealed several thousand fragments of clay moulds and crucibles used to produce bronze metalwork of high status, such as socketed spearheads, swords, chapes and possibly rapiers, palstaves and socketed axes, knives and razors, and pins (Raftery 1976; Becker 2010). Bronze finds include a socketed gouge, a tanged punch, part of an axehead, a spearhead, part of a sword, chain link and a perforated disc.

Fig. 9.5 Rathgall hillfort in south-west Wicklow.

There is also evidence of goldworking, including copper rings covered with gold foil (Warner 2014a). Rathgall produced a large collection of Bronze Age glass beads made in northern Italy, one of which has a gold mount. Other exotic finds include two amber beads, a bronze bar toggle of north European origin, and bracelets of imported jet or lignite. As the excavator concluded, 'the wealth of the occupants of Late Bronze Age Rathgall was considerable' (Raftery 1976, 346).

Other hillfort excavations

The Rathgall discovery was followed in 1987–95 by investigations at Haughey's Fort, located on a prominent hill 1km west of the Iron Age ceremonial enclosure at Navan Fort, Co. Armagh. This Bronze Age hillfort is mostly levelled, but originally comprised three concentric bank-and-ditch enclosures, with an overall size of 340m by 310m (Fig. 9.6). Excavation revealed a long duration of occupation, lasting from 1300 BC to 900 BC, with evidence of activity pre-dating the hillfort, as well as some Iron Age occupation (Mallory 1995; Mallory and Baban 2014). Radiocarbon dates for the infilling of the inner ditch suggest the defences may have been established in the twelfth century BC; this suggested date is supported by a dendro-date of 1166 BC for wood from the same context (Baillie and Brown 1998).

The excavation also uncovered evidence of on-site metallurgy in contexts dated 1150–950 BC. Evidence of the casting of bronze swords was discovered at the nearby Kings Stables, a votive pond believed to be connected with the occupants of Haughey's Fort (Lynn 1977). Also significant is the discovery in 2004 of the Tamlaght hoard near Haughey's Fort, which contains a bronze sword, a bronze ring and two bronze vessels of Central European type. One of these is a variant of the type Fuchstadt bowls found in the upper Rhine or lower Elbe region of Germany, while the

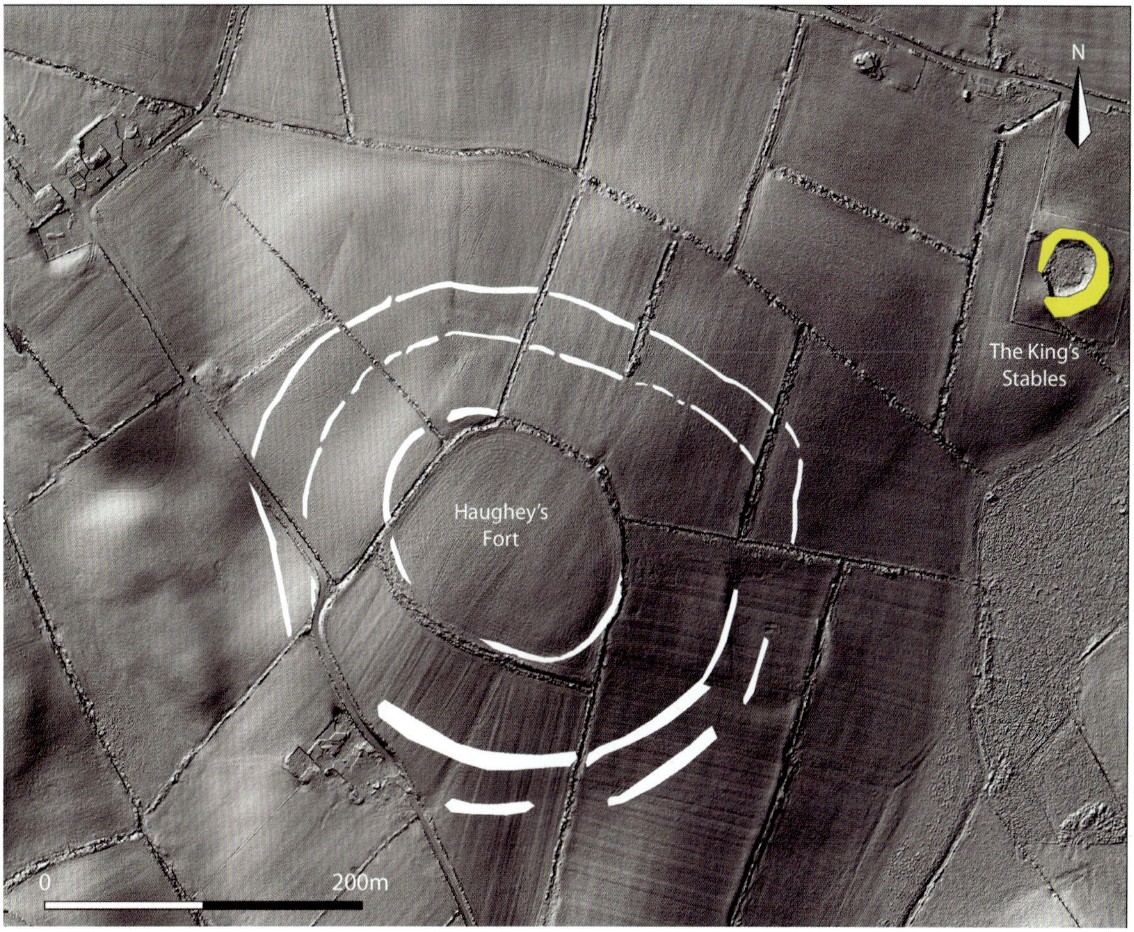

Fig. 9.6
Haughey's Fort, Co. Armagh, with location of a Bronze Age votive pond (King's Stables).

other is a type Jenisovice cup from the region of the middle Danube (Warner 2006). Both objects were imported to Ireland during the Hallstatt B1 phase in Central Europe, *c.*1050–950 BC. Neither type had been previously found in Atlantic Europe, and so they are significant finds in respect of the long-distance connections of Haughey's Fort (Mallory and Baban 2014, 26). These connections are also indicated by bronze metalwork found in this hillfort, namely a disc-head (sunflower) pin of possible West Baltic origin, and part of a handle of a bronze vessel that may be a native attempt to copy an imported Urnfield vessel (Brandherm 2014). There is also evidence of goldworking, in the form of fragments of gold sheet, foil, wire and casting residues (Warner 2014b). An Iberian-style gold neck ring of the same period was found in the vicinity of the hillfort (Warner 2013).

Our knowledge of Bronze Age hillforts expanded in the early 1990s, with archaeological excavations conducted by the Discovery Programme at Mooghaun, Co. Clare and Dún Aonghasa on Inis Mór, Co. Galway. The former is an impressive hillfort, comprised of three concentric stone walls over 11ha (Fig. 9.7). The excavator argued this hillfort was built as a single design, most probably 915–905 BC, preceded by activity around 925–915 BC, and with continued occupation to possibly 815 BC (Grogan 2005a, 240, fig. 7.10). Earlier activity at Mooghaun is possible, as there are radiocarbon results of 1125–918 BC for the middle enclosure, while charcoal under the outer bank is dated 1255–917 BC.

The chronology for Dún Aonghasa, located on the largest of the Aran Islands, is more complex (Cotter 2012, fig. 12.3). The innermost enclosure is an impressive citadel, spectacularly sited on an 87m-high vertical sea cliff (Fig. 9.8). This, together with the outer walls and a formidable *chevaux-de-frise* in stone, creates several layers of defence over an enclosed area of 5.7ha. Radiocarbon results indicate settlement on this cliff edge as early as 1300 BC, with the earliest phase of wall building around 1100 BC. The site was occupied to 800 BC, with further settlement well into the Iron Age when modifications may have been made to the enclosure walls (Warner, in Cotter 2012, 212–24).

The Dún Aonghasa excavation uncovered evidence of

Opposite page

(Above) Fig. 9.7 Late Bronze Age hillfort at Mooghaun, Co. Clare.

(Bottom) Fig. 9.8 Dún Aonghasa hillfort, Inis Mór, Co. Galway.

bronze workshops used to make a variety of weapons, tools and personal ornaments during the Dowris Phase of the Late Bronze Age. The mould evidence confirms the production of socketed spearheads, swords and socketed axeheads, as well as knives, plain and disc-headed pins, bracelets and stud bottoms. Approximately 40 items of bronze were recovered, including chisels, axes, blades, buffered rings, solid rings, hollow rings, pins, bracelets, along with fragments of sheet and cast bronze (Cotter 2012, 48–54). Seventeen pieces of amber, mostly beads, were also found. Scientific analysis confirms this amber is of Baltic origin, examples of which were also found at Haughey's Fort and Rathgall (Feeney-Johnson 2012). The presence of these exotic materials and imported objects, along with evidence of bronze casting and use of gold, testifies to the high status of these hillforts. The finds provide strong evidence of direct and indirect trade connections with mainland Europe during the Middle and Late Bronze Age.

There have been other discoveries of Bronze Age hillforts in recent years. A large Class 2 example with three enclosures was excavated in 2004–5 in advance of road construction at Rahally, Co. Galway (Mullins 2008). Radiocarbon dates for charcoal from the enclosing ditches returned dates of 994–827 BC, 790–520 BC and 1090–900 BC respectively. Pottery finds from the interior confirm that the site was occupied during the Late Bronze Age. A similar site to Rahally was recently investigated at Faughan Hill in Co. Meath. Excavations in 2017 identified four phases of activity, beginning with the construction of a fenced enclosure, with an estimated diameter of 350m, on the hill, *c.*3635–3380 BC. A large Class 2 hillfort was built there during the Late Bronze Age, *c.*1280–920 BC. This had three concentric enclosures, with rock-cut ditches that originally had internal banks (Dowling and Schot 2023).

Overall, the results from excavation at Rathgall, Haughey's Fort, Mooghaun, Dún Aonghasa, Rahally and Faughan Hill indicate the building and use of Class 2 hillforts during the Middle to Late Bronze Age transition, *c.*1300–1100 BC, continuing into the tenth and ninth centuries BC. These excavations highlight the problem of obtaining secure dates for the construction, modification and abandonment of hillfort defences. This was addressed in research undertaken by University College Cork on which this book is based, which examined the history of eight Bronze Age hillforts in southern Ireland (O'Brien 2017; O'Brien and O'Driscoll 2017). These include a large-scale investigation in mid Cork; sample excavation of Class 2 hillforts in counties Clare, Kerry, Limerick and Kilkenny; and excavation at Rathnagree, Sruhaun and Tinoran in Baltinglass.

Clashanimud, Co. Cork

This Class 2 hillfort is located on a prominent ridge (179m OD) in the hill and valley topography of mid Cork. Marked as 'Cashel Hillfort' on Ordnance Survey historic mapping, there are two concentric oval enclosures spaced *c.*48m apart, with an overall size of 350m by 250m over 8.8ha (Fig. 9.9). Excavation inside both enclosures did not uncover any evidence of occupation (O'Brien 2016). The outer enclosure has a perimeter of 1.04km, surrounded by a 4m-wide by 0.6–0.8m-high earthen bank with a stake fence, and an external V-shaped ditch, 2.85m wide by 1.7m deep. The inner enclosure is surrounded by a low bank of soil and broken rock obtained from an external ditch, with an outer stone facing and an internal wooden revetment (Fig. 9.10). A line of large post-holes, 1.5m apart along the axis of the bank, held upright posts that were secured by packing stones and the bank itself. An estimated 360 such posts of oak roundwood, each 4–5m long with a diameter of 0.2–0.3m, were used to build this palisade structure along a 0.8km-perimeter of the inner enclosure. The palisade was completed by the insertion of an estimated 3,000 smaller posts in foundation trenches between the main posts. The adjacent ditch had a U-shaped profile, 2.4m wide at the top and 0.65–1.4m wide at the base, with a central depth of 1.7–1.8m cut through subsoil into bedrock. The palisaded bank and ditch combined created a 6–7m-high barrier for the inner enclosure.

The entrance to the inner enclosure is located on the western side, where a 6m-wide causeway across the rock-cut ditch led to a 2.2m-wide stone-faced opening in the palisaded bank, with a wooden gate. The discovery of charcoal deposits, charred timbers, semi-vitrified stones and fire-reddened soil indicates that this entrance and the entire palisade of the inner enclosure were burned down in a deliberate act. Radiocarbon dates confirm these defences were built in or around the twelfth century BC, during the transition from the Middle to the Late Bronze Age. The outer enclosure was built *c.*1511–1089 BC, based on

Fig. 9.9 Late Bronze Age hillfort at Clashanimud, Co. Cork.

(Left) Fig. 9.10 Part-reconstruction of defences of inner enclosure, Clashanimud hillfort, Co. Cork.

radiocarbon dating of charcoal from beneath the bank and in the adjacent ditch. The palisade of the inner enclosure is dated 1258–1006 BC, while a radiocarbon date of 976–815 BC for charcoal from the adjacent ditch may place the burning of this hillfort to a century or two after it was built.

Glanbane, Co. Kerry

The second hillfort investigated in this project is located on a ridge (86m OD) at the eastern end of the Sliabh Mis mountains in West Kerry, with wide views across the Castleisland and Killarney lowlands. The site was levelled by agriculture in the late 1960s, with only low-relief indications of the enclosing elements visible today. Aerial photographs indicate two concentric enclosures, spaced 20–25m apart, each comprising a bank with external ditch (Fig. 9.11). This is confirmed by magnetic gradiometry survey, which shows the hillfort was originally sub-circular in plan, measuring 290m by 280m extending over 6.6 hectares, with an inner enclosure of 240m by 230m over 4.7ha (O'Brien, O'Driscoll

Fig. 9.11 Aerial view of levelled Late Bronze Age hillfort at Glanbane, Co. Kerry.

Fig. 9.12 Excavation of defences of inner enclosure at Glanbane hillfort, Co. Kerry, with reconstruction of bank facing.

and Hogan 2016). The magnetic survey indicates possible entrances on the north-eastern side, as well as foundation traces of possible post-built structures of substantial size in the centre of the hillfort.

In 2012 two trenches were excavated across both enclosing elements on the eastern side of the hillfort (Fig. 9.12; O'Brien and O'Driscoll 2017, 125–42). This confirmed the two enclosures were originally surrounded by a rock-cut ditch with a stone-faced internal bank. There is no evidence for a timber palisade or stake fence accompanying either bank. The defensive height of the inner enclosure (from base of ditch to top of bank) is estimated at 2.5–3m, while that of the outer enclosure is possibly 2m. The scale of construction is impressive over the entire extent of the hillfort. The perimeter of the inner enclosure is 790m, while that of the outer enclosure in 932m, amounting to 1.7km of artificial defences. The total estimate of rock extraction for both enclosure ditches at Glanbane is 2,644 tonnes, with an estimated 33,000 stones required to face the associated banks. Radiocarbon dating of charcoal from the ditch of the inner enclosure indicates the latter was built *c.*1118–927 BC, placing this hillfort in the Late Bronze Age.

Ballylin, Co. Limerick

This Class 2 hillfort is located near Ardagh village in West Limerick, on a prominent ridge (243m OD) off the eastern margin of the Mullaghareirk mountains, with wide views of the lowlands of central Limerick and the lower Shannon estuary. There are two concentric enclosures over an area of 21ha, each surrounded by two banks with an intervening ditch, visible today as low-relief features or vegetation patterns (Fig. 9.13). The outer hillfort enclosure measures

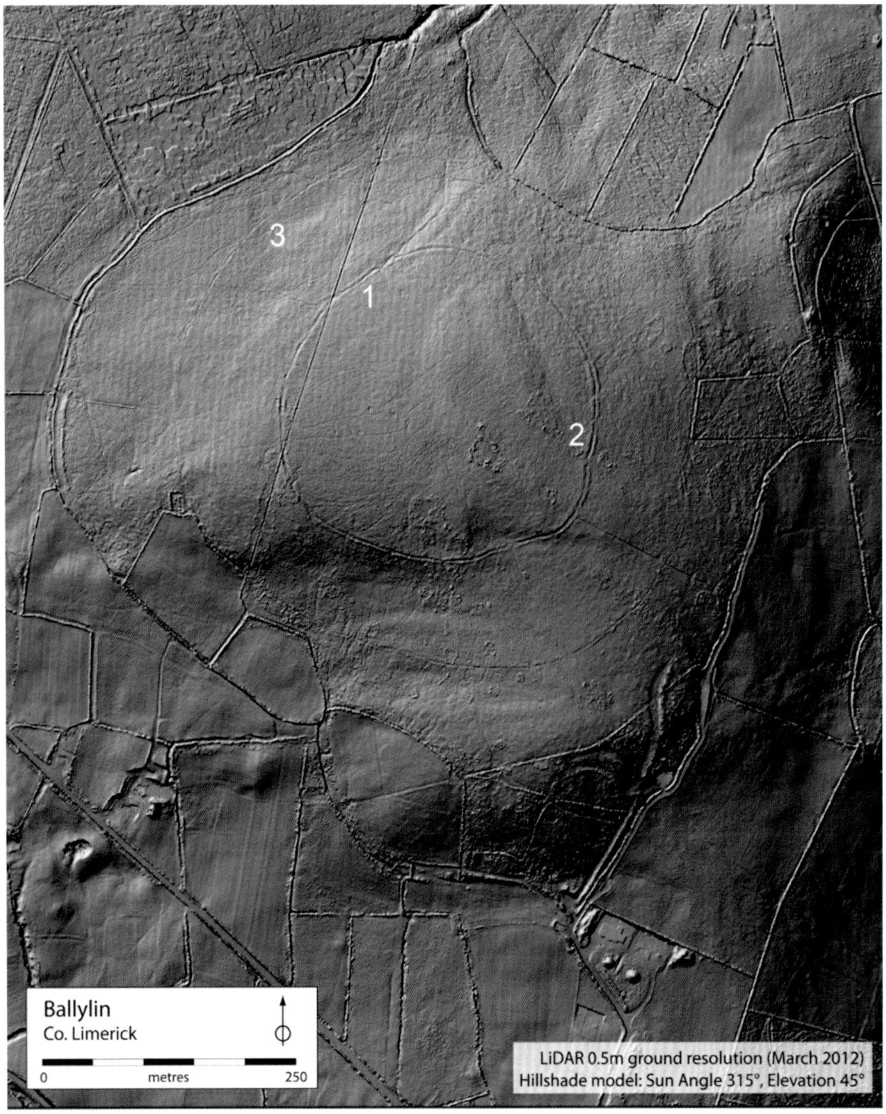

Fig. 9.13 LiDAR image of Late Bronze Age hillfort, Ballylin, Co. Limerick. 1) Inner enclosure; 2) Excavated entrance to inner enclosure; 3) Outer enclosure.

500m by 525m over an area of 13.5ha, while the inner enclosure is 300m by 315m over 7.5ha. Magnetic gradiometry over part of the inner enclosure did not reveal built structures, though detailed survey was not possible due to vegetation cover.

Sample excavation in 2012 examined the original entrance to the inner enclosure, as well as the defences of the outer enclosure (O'Brien, Hogan and O'Driscoll 2016; O'Brien and O'Driscoll 2017, 142–59). The latter comprised a shallow, soil-cut ditch with a low bank on either side. The inner enclosure was protected by a 3.5m-wide by 1m-deep ditch, from which soil and broken rock were piled on both sides to form low banks. The excavation examined a causewayed entrance to this enclosure, protected by a wooden gate represented by large post-holes placed 2.9m apart at an opening in the inner bank. Radiocarbon dating places the use of this entrance to 1368–979 BC, again placing this hillfort in the Late Bronze Age.

Fig. 9.14 Aerial photograph (top) and plan (bottom) of two enclosures at Late Bronze Age hillfort, Formoyle, Co. Clare.

Formoyle, Co. Clare

This hillfort overlooks the Broadford Gap, a broad valley that cuts across the hills of the Cratloe/Slieve Bernagh ridge to connect the Shannon basin with south east Clare. The enclosure lies on the summit of Formoyle Hill (242m OD) in the townlands of Formoyle Beg and Clooncorry More. There are two concentric enclosures 40–60m apart over an area of 6.4ha, each of which is surrounded by a low bank with an external ditch (Fig. 9.14). The inner enclosure is 200m by 145m, with a perimeter of 580m and an internal area of 2.57ha. The outer enclosure measures 315m by 230m, with a perimeter of 920m and an internal area of 3.85ha.

Excavation revealed the inner enclosure is surrounded by a 2.4m-wide by 0.65m-deep ditch, with a low, earthen bank on either side (O'Brien and O'Driscoll 2017, 159–76). A line of stake-holes spaced 0.5–

1.15m apart indicates a light stake fence on the inside of the inner bank. The outer enclosure was protected by a similar arrangement, with a low, earthen bank on either side of a 2.7m-wide by 0.7m-deep rock-cut ditch. A row of stake-holes on the inside of the inner bank originally held wooden stakes, some of which had been burnt. Radiocarbon dating indicates both enclosures were probably built in the eleventh century BC. There is no information on the occupation history of the site, with no indication of built structures from geophysical survey over part of the interior.

Toor More, Co. Kilkenny

This hillfort lies on the highest point (242m OD) of a ridge overlooking a broad expanse of lowland, 3km east of Ballyragget village in north-west Kilkenny. Geophysical survey indicates two concentric circular enclosures (Fig. 9.15), spaced approximately 105m apart over a total area of 8.94ha, with both enclosing elements visible today as low-relief banks (O'Brien, Hogan and O'Driscoll 2014–5; O'Brien and O'Driscoll 2017, 176–91). The inner enclosure is *c.*125m in diameter over an area of 1.72ha, while the outer enclosure is 290m wide over 7.22ha.

The inner enclosure was surrounded by a V-shaped ditch, 3.5m wide and 1.5m deep. Soil and broken rock from this ditch were piled on the inner side to create a low bank with a stone wall or revetment. There was a wooden palisade 1.4m inside this bank, where a line of upright posts in a slot trench was secured with packing stones (Fig. 9.16). This palisade was burnt down, with charred timbers found during excavation. The outer enclosure was surrounded by a V-shaped ditch, 2m wide by 1.22–1.45m deep. Soil and broken rock from this ditch were piled on the inside, to form a low bank on which there may have been a stone wall or revetment. A narrow slot 2.3m inside the bank held a line of wooden posts, 0.15m in diameter and spaced 0.1–0.15m apart. Charcoal deposits confirmed this fence was also burnt down. Radiocarbon dating confirms the timber fencing of both enclosures was built and destroyed some time during the twelfth or eleventh century BC. There is no evidence that the defences were re-built, or whether the hillfort was abandoned following this destruction event.

Combining the results of these excavations, it seems that multiple enclosure hillforts began to be built in Ireland during the Bishopsland Phase of the Middle Bronze Age, *c.*1400–1200 BC. The early dates for Rathnagree and Rathgall suggest that Wicklow was an important area in the emergence of the Bronze Age hillfort in Ireland. Hillfort construction increased during the twelfth and eleventh century BC, in the transition

Fig. 9.15 LiDAR (left) and magnetic gradiometry (right) images of two enclosures of Late Bronze Age hillfort, Toor More, Co. Kilkenny.

Fig. 9.16 Excavated defences of inner enclosure of Toor More hillfort, Co. Kilkenny. Post palisade on inner side of stone-faced bank with external ditch. Reconstruction of bank facing using original stones.

to the Roscommon Phase of the Late Bronze Age (1100–1000/900 BC). Examples include Ballylin, Clashanimud, Glanbane, Formoyle, Haughey's Fort, Toor More and Rahally, and also Tinoran at Baltinglass. Pollen records indicate the landscapes around many of these hillforts were the focus of concentrated population and farming activity at different times *c.*1400–1000 BC (Plunkett 2006; 2009). The same pattern is likely in the Baltinglass area, as suggested by the palynological results from Holdenstown Upper bog discussed in Chapter 7.

Hillforts and Bronze Age Society

While we know when Rathnagree and Tinoran were built, there is little information on the use and wider significance of these hillforts. The discovery of domestic pottery at both sites, as well as some hearths at Tinoran, is evidence of occupation, but this cannot be connected to activities within either hillfort. Geophysical survey was limited at both sites, because of vegetation cover. Some possible hut-sites have been identified, but these remain to be confirmed, and there is no certainty they date to when these hillforts were used. Large-scale excavation is required to understand the history of both hillforts and the various activities associated with their occupation.

The possibilities here are suggested by the discoveries at Rathgall, Haughey's Fort and Dún Aonghasa, where built structures were found with the material culture of elite residence. The evidence from other hillforts is more meagre, indicating different site histories and, in some cases, short-lived occupation. Clashanimud in Cork and Toor More in Kilkenny are examples of where large hillforts were destroyed by fire and abandoned soon after construction. Something similar occurred on Baltinglass Hill, where a palisaded hillfort at Rathnagree and a nearby fenced enclosure at Sruhaun were destroyed by fire, though unlike Clashanimud both were re-built. Various explanations can be advanced for this wanton destruction of such large enclosures, the most plausible being acts of war.

Recent research has considered how warfare was an important factor in the rise of hillfort chiefdoms in Middle and Late Bronze Age Ireland (O'Brien and O'Driscoll 2017; O'Brien 2018). The militarism of those centuries is well known from the enormous output of specialised bronze weapons, notably swords, spearheads and shields. The scale of conflict, particularly during the twelfth and eleventh century BC, moved beyond the local and personal, to opposing political forces on a regional level. This type of warfare was both a consequence and a driver of more complex political systems. Various explanations have been advanced to explain this instability, from foreign invasion to environmental change, population pressure and food shortages. A review of pollen records in Ireland, however, identified no evidence of a crisis in agriculture caused by climate change around the twelfth century BC, nor any connection to the building of hillforts as a response to such pressures (Plunkett 2006; 2009).

These conflicts were probably rooted in the aggressive expansion of hillfort chiefdoms and the aggrandisement of their elites, whose competing ambitions included control of trade (O'Brien 2022). Specific issues connected to personal honour could be a pretext for war, but most conflicts probably had wider political and economic objectives. The martial culture of that period was connected to the emergence of simple and complex chiefdoms with hierarchical power structures, controlled by leaders with aggrandising tendencies. These societies had a strong organisational capacity, with large populations and a level of economic power required to engage in large-scale military conflicts. Most important, this was a culture with values that promoted aggressive competition and warrior status.

This is also reflected in the location of Bronze Age hillforts, selected to create imposing strongholds in the landscape. Rarely built as mountain fortresses, they are found mostly on prominent hills overlooking large expanses of agricultural lowland. The siting in most instances was not suitable for refuge, as there were few lines of retreat from highly exposed locations. That said, their elevation and topography did present defenders with some tactical advantages, particularly the inland promontory and cliff-edge hillforts such as Knockdhu, Co. Antrim and Dún Aonghasa, Co. Galway. This may have been a secondary consideration, however, as some hillforts occur in relatively low-lying locations, including such well-known examples as Haughey's Fort, Mooghaun and Rathgall.

The design of Class 2 hillforts suggests defence in depth, where a fortified inner enclosure in an elevated position was shielded by an outer perimeter. The defenders were afforded a certain level of protection from enemy weapons, and had a screen of manoeuvre that made it difficult for attackers to see how those defending the hillfort were deployed. These tactical advantages were weakened by the difficulty of defending a large perimeter, often extending to several kilometres. This would have been a major challenge at Tinoran, where the perimeter extended over several kilometres with many blind spots. Any active defence would have required the rapid deployment of defending forces to points of attack, though how that was managed in the case of the multiple-enclosure hillforts is unclear. This may not have been a major concern in the Bronze Age, where instead of massed infantry assault or siege warfare, for which there is no evidence, confrontations were on a smaller, less organised scale, with attack targeted on entrances and other points of weakness.

Given these considerations, it is likely these hillforts were not designed for passive defence, but rather were places that projected military power and political dominance over a wide landscape. Physical defences are often quite slight, a good example being the low earthworks at Ballylin and Formoyle. Others are more formidable, such as the stone walling at Dún Aonghasa, or the 6–7m-high palisaded earthwork of the inner enclosure at Clashanimud, Co. Cork. Different methods of construction were used, as illustrated by the two examples at Baltinglass. The Period 1 hillfort at Rathnagree had a stout timber palisade with stone footing, whereas the second and third enclosures at Tinoran were surrounded by ramparts of dumped stone; there were bank-and-ditch earthworks at Rathnagree (middle enclosure, Period 2) and Tinoran (fourth enclosure). The defensive potential of these enclosures was not only based on these physical barriers, combined with topography, but also on the active force of defenders. The number of warriors, their experience, fighting spirit and motivation, and the quality of command, would have been critical in the defence of any hillfort, which also served as mustering locations for offensive warfare.

The multiple-enclosure design of Rathnagree and Tinoran suggests some separation of activities within these Class 2 hillforts. One possibility is that the outer enclosure(s) was used for stockading livestock, with the innermost enclosure fortified for human protection. This is supported by excavation evidence for residential occupation in the innermost enclosure at Dún Aonghasa, Haughey's Fort and Rathgall. With raiding likely to have been a feature of Bronze Age warfare, an ability to protect large herds of cattle at short notice may have been a significant concern in the design of these hillforts.

While layered defence may explain the design of the Class 2 hillfort, there are also elements of display connected to the visual symbolism of the monument. The division of space created by the multiple enclosures may have been significant in terms of access and social division. These sites manifest authority and political power, as the permanent or occasional residence of a political elite and as places of assembly and ritual ceremony. Their physical construction was a powerful statement of allegiance and solidarity by related groups who came together for this purpose, an act of communal endeavour central to the symbolic construction of their polity.

The burning of Rathnagree

As the central places of regional power, hillforts were significant in the conflicts that erupted between the competing chiefdoms of Bronze Age Ireland. Recent investigations confirm some of these centres were deliberately burnt down. Excavation of their defences has revealed deposits of charcoal, charred timbers, burnt soil and vitrified stone, with strong magnetic signatures in geophysical survey today (O'Brien, O'Driscoll and Hogan 2018). The hillforts of Toor More and Clashanimud were probably abandoned after their destruction. In the case of Rathnagree, adjacent animal enclosures were also destroyed, as indicated by the burning of a stake fence of similar date at nearby Sruhaun. The occupation on that hill resumed soon afterwards, when the middle enclosure at Rathnagree was re-built with a substantial bank-and-ditch earthwork, and the Sruhaun fencing was replaced by an enclosure with a stone bank and internal ditches.

The destruction at Rathnagree involved a considerable effort, particularly to burn several kilometres of heavy post palisades at Clashanimud and Rathnagree. A significant amount of tinder and brushwood was required to ignite such heavy fencing, possibly assisted by the use of animal fat. As one commentator observed,

> *... the more extensive and systematic the destruction, the more likely it is to have been the product of punitive razing after capture, whereas more limited evidence of burning, especially where concentrated around the gates, may be indicative of tactical use of fire in an attack on the hillfort itself (Harding 2012, 187).*

The latter may also indicate that an attack was successfully repelled, particularly if there is no evidence of destruction in the interior of the hillfort.

The burning of the defences at Clashanimud, Rathnagree and Toor More along their entire perimeter points to punitive destruction after those hillforts were captured. This could be explained by an internal power struggle, but it is more likely a victorious faction would seek to appropriate the special significance these centres held for the exercise of power. That would also explain why they were targeted for destruction by rival chiefdoms, whose goal was political dominance rather than territorial conquest. The use of fire was a very visible way of communicating the subordination of a rival group, while an ability to create that destruction was no less impressive. Ralston (2006, 163) observed that the intense glow from a burning hillfort would have been a distinctly unnatural sight and a spectacular display of calculated destruction and power.

The twelfth and eleventh century BC was a period of political turmoil and economic recession in Ireland and many other parts of Europe. The hillfort wars of this Roscommon Phase had their origins in the preceding centuries of the Middle Bronze Age, when regional chiefdoms first emerged in Ireland. Hillforts were important central places in this new political landscape and as such were targeted in war, with severe consequences for individual sites. The evidence of destroyed hillforts, such as Clashanimud and Rathnagree, suggests these conflicts were short-lived and intense, part of the changing political landscape rather than an element of endemic war.

Hillforts continued to be built into the Dowris Phase of the Late Bronze Age (1000/900–700 BC). This was a period of economic prosperity, with expanded settlement across Ireland evidenced by the number of settlements and burnt mounds, the large amount of bronze and gold metalwork in circulation, and far-flung trade connections. Pollen records indicate intensified agriculture and land clearance in many areas, but also reduced farming in places, including Baltinglass. This may reflect a contraction of settlement to core territories in hillfort-dominated settlement landscapes (Plunkett 2009). There may have been a greater concentration of power after 1000 BC, connected to the consolidation, peaceful or otherwise, of smaller hillfort territories into supra-regional polities represented by centres such as Mooghaun and Dún Aonghasa in western Ireland. This is the period when Tinoran may have emerged as a major political centre in Leinster. The final collapse of these later hillfort chiefdoms occurred soon after the eighth century BC. The reasons remain unclear, but were more connected to internecine warfare than older ideas of Celtic invasions. What emerges in the Early Iron Age is a fragmented settlement landscape of smaller communities, which distinguishes Ireland from many parts of Europe during the mid-first millennium BC.

THE INTERNATIONAL PICTURE

We now consider prehistoric hillforts and enclosures in other parts of Europe, sites that may be comparable to the examples at Baltinglass. Overseas contacts, involving migration, trade and political exchanges, played an important role in the emergence of hillfort culture in prehistoric Ireland. Britain is of particular interest in terms of proximity and wider cultural connections, with comparable use of hillforts and hilltop enclosures during the earlier Neolithic and later Bronze Age, but also for evidence of important differences during the Iron Age. In that respect, Ireland was open to external influences while maintaining its own traditions around the building and role of hillforts in indigenous society.

Early Neolithic enclosures in Europe

The practice of enclosing hilltops was a recurring feature in many parts of Europe during the Neolithic period, particularly associated with the construction of the causewayed or interrupted ditch enclosure. These large sites began to be built in western France *c.*3800 BC (Burnez and Louboutin 2002, 21), while in Scandinavia they date to 3400–3200 BC, some 500 years after the introduction of the Neolithic way of life (Andersen 2002, 1). The Irish examples were built *c.*3700/3600–3300 BC, soon after the introduction of farming. The Baltinglass sites of that period, namely Hughstown and Rathcoran, and possibly Spinans Hill 1, compare to examples in Wales built *c.*3650–3400 BC (Davis and Sharples 2017). That was two centuries or so after causewayed enclosures were constructed in southern England, reflecting the time it took for ideas, cultures and people to spread (Whittle *et al.* 2011).

The geographical distribution of causewayed enclosures is diverse, reflecting the migratory patterns and cultural interactions of Neolithic communities. Notable concentrations exist in southern Britain (Whittle *et al.* 2011), Scandinavia (Andersen 2002), Western France (Burnez and Louboutin 2002) and Germany (Whittle 2014, 6), with individual sites found throughout north-west Europe. Sometimes they occur in large groups, as in the Marais Poitevin and Saintonge regions of western France, where nearly three hundred examples are known (Burnez and Louboutin 2002, 11). In total, however, there are fewer than 1,000 examples known, making them much less numerous than the estimated 30,000 Bronze and Iron Age hillforts in Europe (Ralston 2006).

Many of these Neolithic enclosures occur in local clusters. In Scandinavia, sites such as Bjerggård and Toftum are only 3.5km apart (Andersen 2002, 2), while Burnez and Louboutin (2002, 25) note a similar spacing of 3–4km between enclosure sites in western France. Clustering is also recorded in southern England (see Whittle *et al.* 2011), while it has been observed in Ireland at Donegore Hill, Co. Antrim (Cooney *et al.* 2011, 574), and now in Baltinglass. One explanation is that these sites were not contemporary. An ethnohistoric example here are the Māori Pā enclosures of the North Island of New Zealand. The indigenous Māori built large, earthen, bank-and-ditch enclosures from the fifteenth to nineteenth century AD (Harding 2012, 251; Fox 1976, 7). After the death of a chief, some of these were abandoned and a new Pā built close by, often within a few hundred metres (Armit 2007). The ritual nature of the abandonment explains why the older enclosure was not re-used (Armit 2007, 35).

Some causewayed enclosures are so well dated it is certain they were used at the same time. At Kingsborough, Kent, England, two contemporary enclosures are 300m apart on the same hill (Allen *et al.* 2008). Despite this proximity, each overlooks a distinct landscape not visible to the other. The material culture of both sites is distinct, with ceramic, fabrics and flint sources unique to each site, implying the enclosures related to two separate communities with different social and territorial identities (Allen *et al.* 2008, 309). In this instance, clustering may indicate a dense area of Early Neolithic populations, with contemporary communities who built enclosures that represented their central place in a developing social landscape. In essence, they became a physical representation of a new group identity. Andersen (2002, 8–9) suggests the two enclosures at Sarup, Denmark, were a microcosm of the disparate community spread out across the surrounding landscape. Each individual ditch segment may have been associated with a family, settlement, clan or a land unit — the whole site serving as a unifying symbol that embraced a large number of territories or settlements.

An important characteristic of these clusters is that individual enclosures are often morphologically dissimilar

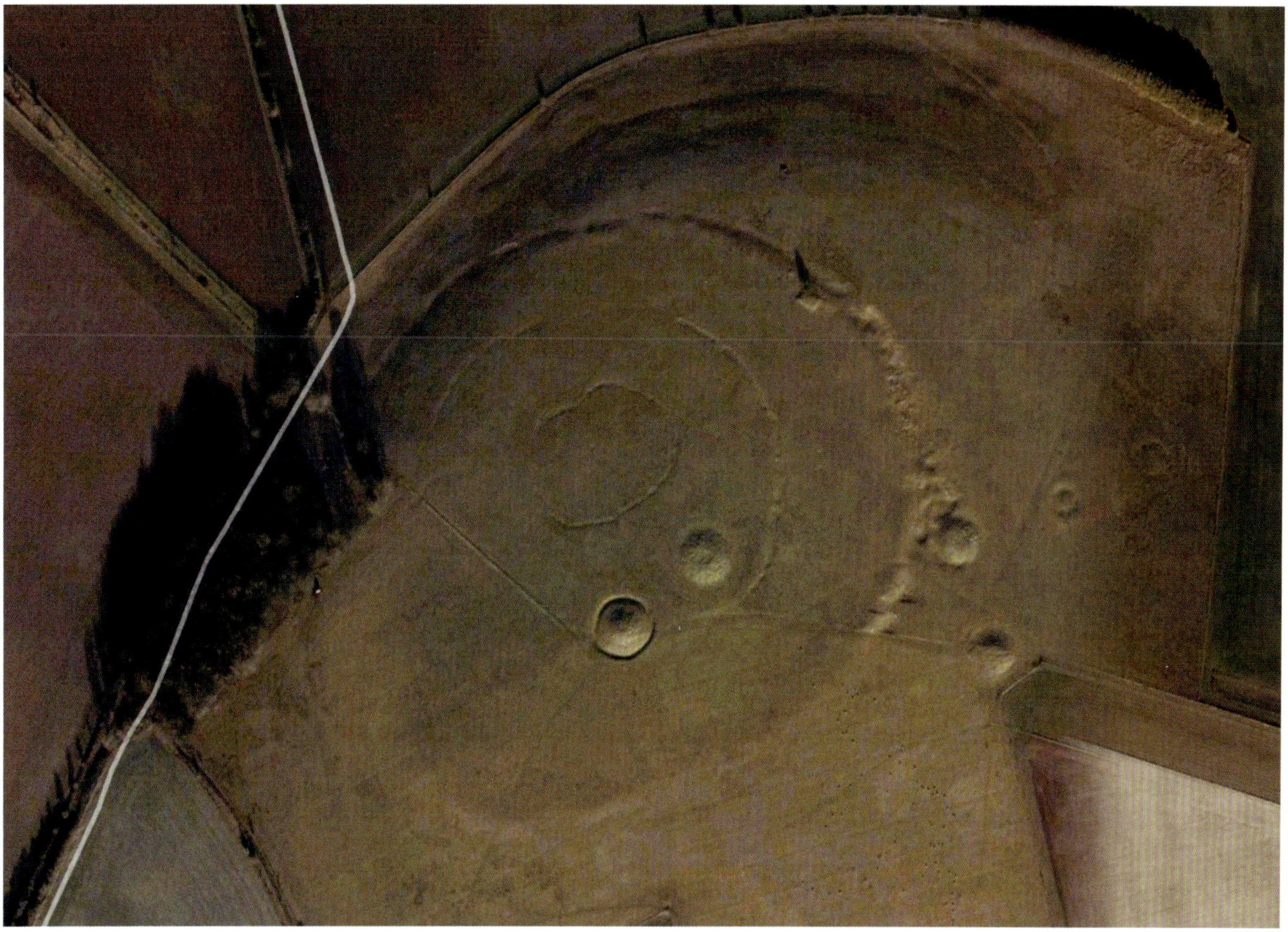

Fig. 9.17 Aerial image of the Windmill Hill causewayed enclosure in Wiltshire, showing the three lines of segmented ditches and monumental barrows. Source: Google Earth.

(Allen *et al.* 2008, 277), a feature also of the Baltinglass sites. This may have been a deliberate attempt by new communities to distinguish themselves from neighbouring groups. In West Sussex, England, for example, a cluster of Early Neolithic enclosures were built in very different ways. The 1ha-enclosure on Bury Hill had a single, continuous bank and ditch, while a nearby 7ha-enclosure, known as the Trundle, had multiple, widely spaced lines of segmented ditches, and a 2.8ha example at Barkhale was enclosed by two closely spaced, segmented ditches (see Whittle *et al.* 2011).

If some clusters do represent different contemporary communities, why did they build enclosures in such close proximity? Many of the Scandinavian sites lie close to wetlands, suggesting boundary locations in the landscape (Andersen 2002, 4). Evans *et al.* (1988, 82) argue these sites were positioned at the edge of territories, as symbolic or religious centres where trade with other communities took place. Evidence of trade is recorded at several excavated sites, including Carn Brea, Cornwall and Crickley Hill, Gloucestershire (Mercer 1980, 184). Environmental data from the causewayed enclosures at Maiden Castle, Dorset and Windmill Hill, Wiltshire (Fig. 9.17), suggests both sites were relatively isolated, located in marginal land away from areas of agriculture (Evans *et al.* 1988, 82; Smith 1984). These peripheral locations would have been ideal for inter-community trade, as outsiders could be kept isolated and conflicts contained away from settlement zones (Evans *et al.* 1988, 82).

This interpretation may explain the dearth of evidence for residential occupation. While few sites have seen extensive excavation, this was undertaken at two causewayed enclosures at Sarup in Denmark, where no buildings were found and only a small number of random pits and post-holes. There is a similar picture in western France (Burnez

Fig. 9.18 Aerial view of the Hambledon Hill causewayed enclosure in Dorset, visible as a cropmark.

and Louboutin 2002, 16). A notable exception may be the causewayed enclosure at Etton, Maxey, England, where an abundant number of pits were identified, some of which contained structured deposits of symbolic meaning, though again no built structures were found (Pryor 1998, 353).

Andersen (1997, 97; 2002, 4) observed that many Scandinavian enclosures are closely associated with monumental graves. Another example is the causewayed enclosure at Büdelsdorf, Germany, close to a cemetery of 14 graves (Bauch 1988). In some instances, human remains were deposited within the enclosure ditches, with many examples of this practice from western France (Burnez and Louboutin 2002, 19) and England (Whittle *et al.* 2011, 11). Andersen (2002, 8–9) argued that the human remains in the ditches at Sarup were temporary deposits, with the enclosures acting as a transitional zone from the land of the living to that of the dead. This would explain the absence of domestic buildings or occupation in these enclosures. A similar connection with monumental burials has been identified by Mercer (1980, 63), who argues that the causewayed enclosures were excarnation sites, used before the final deposition of disarticulated remains in graves. Hambledon Hill, Dorset is a good example (Fig. 9.18), producing a large amount of scattered human remains in the inner ditch, which could have been deposited there by chance after the natural dismemberment of the body nearby (Drewett 1977; Mercer 1980; 1988).

As well as the deposition of human remains, other 'structured' deposits of a ritual nature are recorded in many Neolithic enclosures. At Sarup, after an initial phase of natural infilling, 'special' layers and specifically selected finds were deposited in the ditches. These included deposits of organic material, charcoal, human remains and broken pottery, often carefully covered by a layer of stones (Andersen 2002, 5). At Markildegård, several vessels were placed on mats of birch bark (Sørensen 1995, 19). Other examples of deliberate deposition in ditches are recorded in western France. At Le Chaillot at La Jard in Charente-Maritime, a bundle of stone tools found with a pottery vessel containing a cardium shell was overlain by a sheep scapula (Burnez and Louboutin 2002, 19). Detailed excavation at the 2.5ha causewayed enclosure at Etton, Maxey, England, revealed the eastern arc of the segmented ditch had structured deposition of artefacts and animal bone and underwent repeated recutting and backfilling (Pryor 1998, 353–4; Whittle *et al.* 2011, 315). In contrast, the western arc of the ditch saw much less deposition, leading the excavator to propose a division of ritual space inside the enclosure. He suggested that the western side was used as a 'public' area for feasting, ritual slaughter and exchange of livestock, while the eastern side served as 'private' space for small-scale ceremonies such as funerals (Pryor 1998, 353–4).

In many instances, evidence of ritual deposition has been lost, either as a result of poor soil preservation or through continued ritual activities, such the re-cutting of ditches. The latter was a common element of the causewayed enclosures of western France (Burnez and Louboutin 2002, 16) and Scandinavia (Andersen 2002, 4). At the Sarup enclosures, various lengths of fencing seem to have linked the two lines of segmented ditches together, in a layout that has some similarities to Rathcoran. These may have been deliberately built to define areas of the segmented enclosures that 'belonged' to specific families and groups. Excavations at Haddenham, Cambridgeshire, revealed similar fence lines delimiting specific areas of the segmented ditch (Whittle *et al.* 2011, 275).

The position of many Early Neolithic enclosures in peripheral locations, their symbolic association with a group identity, their use as trading locations and transitional zones for the dead, led Heath (2009, 51) to conclude that causewayed enclosures became 'inevitable targets' that attracted the hostile intentions of rival communities seeking to remove and usurp their material wealth and social power. In sites where large-scale excavation has been undertaken, arrowheads and evidence for destruction point to conflict among early farming communities. For example, some 700 arrowheads were recovered at Carn Brea, Cornwall, many found within the enclosure wall (Mercer 2003). The discovery of an estimated 400 arrowheads and comprehensive burning of the enclosing elements at Crickley Hill, Gloucestershire, is convincing evidence of assault (Dixon 1976; 1988). The same is true of Hambledon Hill, where there were two phases of extensive burning and possible associated burials, along with arrowhead concentrations (Mercer 1980; Whittle *et al.* 2011, 717–18).

Whittle *et al.* (2011, 718) list five causewayed enclosures in Britain where extensive burning of enclosing elements was identified, with four of these sites providing evidence for violent assault. Geophysical survey at Hughstown shows that the site may have been partly destroyed by fire, and it would not be surprising if this was associated with a violent assault by a rival community. Such destruction remaining visible is reliant upon the incorporation of wooden elements into the structure, which was a common feature of enclosures in western France (Burnez and Louboutin 2002, 19) and parts of England (Whittle *et al.* 2011).

Despite the potential for attack, many Early Neolithic enclosures were unlikely to have been built as defensive strongholds. Not only would the many breaks in their perimeter have been difficult to defend, the banks and ditches of the enclosures themselves often varied greatly in size. At Sarup, for example, the ditches were only 0.3–2.5m in depth (Andersen 1997, 286); similar variation is seen in the enclosing elements at Rathcoran.

The construction of enclosures may have aroused social tension and precipitated attacks on rival enclosure complexes (Whittle *et al* 2011, 718). The act of destroying a rival community's central monument that may have materialised group cohesion and success would have been a strong declaration of resistance and power (O'Driscoll 2017b; O'Brien and O'Driscoll 2017). With many Neolithic enclosures used for trade, their destruction by a rival group had the strategic outcome of removing those communities from competitive exchange networks.

Bronze Age hillforts in Europe

The building of causewayed enclosures began to decline in western Europe around 3300 BC; in many cases this is because the focus of community effort shifted to other types of monumental architecture, such as passage tombs and cursus monuments. The construction of hilltop enclosures ceased in many parts of Europe until the end of the Early Bronze Age *c.*1800 BC (Harding 2006). At that time, 'true' hillforts emerged around the Alps (Della Casa 2013, 714; Jiráň *et al.* 2013, 791; Krause 2008, 65) and in small pockets throughout Europe like north-west Spain and Portugal (Pardo *et al.* 2009). They were typically built near natural resources or in areas that could control trade. In many cases, there is evidence of metalworking in these first Bronze Age hillforts.

Their emergence reflects cultural shifts towards more hierarchical societies and the rise of elites in many parts of Europe during the early second millennium BC. The new centres were more defensive in nature than the causewayed enclosures of the fourth millennium BC. Sites such as Bruszczewo in Poland, for example, were strategically sited on high ground, and in this particular instance protected by a massive 22m-wide, 4m-deep ditch with two internal palisades (Czebreszuk and Müller 2004; Müller and Czebreszuk 2010). This emphasis on defence is highlighted at Spišsky Štrvtok, Slovakia, where the large enclosure had a single entrance — reducing the number of defensive points — flanked on either side by two round towers (Gogâltan 2008, 52). That did not stop Spišsky Štrvtok from being attacked, as the site was burnt down, possibly by a rival group.

Many hillforts built in Europe during the Early Bronze Age were abandoned by *c.*1600 BC (Jockenhövel 1990, 219; 2013, 740). It would be three centuries or so before there was a resurgence in hillfort construction (Harding 2000, 298). It seems that hillforts were built in large numbers across temperate Europe *c.*1300–1000 BC (Primas 2002, 50). This is also the period when hillforts began to be built in Ireland, such as the examples at Rathnagree and Rathgall in Wicklow. Once again, hillforts of this period were often positioned in strategic locations overlooking natural routeways such as rivers or mountain passes. Some were linked with densely settled, fertile basins, such as Glauberg and Bliebeskopf in Germany. Here again, the parallels with Baltinglass are notable, in the location of Rathnagree and Tinoran overlooking the River Slaney. The later Bronze Age hillforts of Europe often have an unsophisticated layout, with simple entrance features (Jockenhövel 2013, 741; Härke 1979, 30; 166–7). There is evidence of dense internal settlement at some sites, which may indicate increasing population, though hillforts with strong fortifications can also show little evidence of occupation, an example being Thinsberg in northern Switzerland (Jockenhövel 2013, 741; Härke, 1979, 30).

There is evidence of a significant increase in violence and destruction at these later Bronze Age hillforts (Thorpe 2013, 240), with Harding (2001, 334) and Bogucki (2004, 88–9) suggesting that almost all examples in Central Europe were rapidly destroyed. Biskupin hillfort in Poland had three phases of Late Bronze Age settlement, each destroyed and rebuilt in rapid succession (Harding 2001, 335). Similarly, Velim hillfort in the Czech Republic was destroyed after a catastrophic fire associated with a violent assault that resulted in many deaths (Harding *et al.* 2007, 145). The ditch of the hillfort and isolated pits within the interior were haphazardly filled with human remains. Many had fatal wounds, as well as showing evidence of attempts at decapitation (Harding *et al.* 2007, 145). What pushed others to act in such a violent, destructive manner? Once again, the production and supply of metal may be significant. Thorpe (2013, 240) suggested that Velim may have been built to control trade; such competition often gave rise to conflict, with disastrous consequences for individual hillforts.

We see similar evidence for destruction and interpersonal violence at other hillforts. An example is at Heunischenburg, Germany (Abels 2002), where finds of bronze weapons and armour are indicative of military activity (Thorpe 2013, 240). An increase in the use of wooden defences at hillforts during this period (Primas 2002, 50) made fire an option in attacking sites. Härke (1979, 33) argued that destruction layers at many German hillforts indicate they were destroyed by fire. For example, a wooden palisade at the hillfort of Bernstorf shows signs of destruction (Moosauer and Bachmaier 2000), with similar evidence from hillforts at Bullenheimer Berg, Germany (Diemer 1995) and Limberg in Austria (Schindler 1968; 1974). There is comparable evidence from Ireland, at sites such as Clashinmud, Co. Cork; Toor More, Co. Kilkenny; and Rathnagree and Sruhaun in Baltinglass (O'Brien 2018; O'Brien, O'Driscoll and Hogan 2017). These highly visible acts of destruction may have represented an attack by a rival community, who attempted to destroy the central monument of an elite and effectively remove them from the competitive system of trade and exchange that was so prevalent throughout Europe at this time (O'Driscoll 2017a; O'Brien 2022).

As many hillforts in central Europe were important nodes in the supply of metal, access to raw material meant they were also centres for metalworking and specialised craft production. Excavation confirms that many hillforts in Portugal (Lull *et al.* 2013, 612), Germany (Härke 1979, 30), Austria (Jiráň *et al.* 2013, 792) and the Czech Republic (Jiráň *et* al. 2013, 792) were centres of craft and trade controlled by local elites (Vandkilde 2004, 32). Indeed, by the end of the Late Bronze Age, a significant amount of metal production seems to have taken place at fortified hilltop sites (Osgood and Monks 2000, 66). The distribution of artefacts at the massive 160ha hillfort of Várvölgy–Nagy-Lázhegy, Hungary, allowed the excavators to identify areas of bronze-working in the interior (Müller 2006, 191). Similarly, at Ormož, Slovenia, and Feudvar, Serbia, densely occupied interiors were given over to metal- and craftworkers, with domestic settlement found only outside the hillforts (Dular and Tomanič Jevremov 2010; Teržan 2013, 847).

Such deliberately planned layouts are exemplified at the French hillforts of Fort-Harrouard, Sorrel-Moussel; (Mohen and Bailloud 1987) and Saint-Pierre-en-Chastres,

Vieux-Moulin. The Late Bronze Age phases of both sites have produced large numbers of bronze objects, with evidence of metalworking in the form of mould and tuyère fragments, furnaces, metal-working tools and bronze ingots (Mohen and Bailloud 1987, 140). There is evidence of large-scale weapon production, possibly intended for export (Mohen and Bailloud 1987, 178). A total of 1,252 metal objects recovered at Fort-Harrouard allowed the excavators to identify specific areas of craft specialisation (Mohen and Bailloud 1987, 138). The absence of metalworking evidence at the Baltinglass sites is not surprising, given the limited amount of excavation undertaken and its focus on enclosing elements. Where large-scale excavation of Irish hillforts has been undertaken, evidence of specialist metalworking has been found, including at Haughey's Fort, Co. Armagh (Mallory and Baban 2014), Dun Aonghasa, Co. Galway (Cotter 2012) and Rathgall, Co. Wicklow (Raftery and Becker forthcoming).

While the hillfort emerged as a place of elite residence in Middle and Late Bronze Age Europe, even larger fortifications were being built in eastern Europe (Molloy *et al.* 2020). The size of enclosures such as Corneşti-Iarcuri in Romania is phenomenal, with four widely spaced enclosures over 1,722 hectares (Szentmiklosi *et al.* 2011, 819). This was no token enclosure either, with the inner defences comprised of an earthen bank retained by two palisades, outside of which was an 11m-wide by 4.7m-deep ditch (Szentmiklosi *et al.* 2011, 824). Excavation of the interior revealed a remarkable number of pits and houses, indicating a dense, urban-like settlement (Szentmiklosi *et al.* 2011, 830).

Late Bronze Age hillforts in Britain are still considered 'atypical' (Sharples 2010, 55), despite a growing number of discoveries (Campbell 2021). This new evidence suggests developments there partly reflect the situation in mainland Europe. There was a significant construction phase at the beginning of the Late Bronze Age, with the British sites following the characteristic morphological traits of their European counterparts — a simple layout, simple gap entrances and often slight defences that incorporated palisades (Lynch *et al.* 2000, 15). While there are a few examples, such as Cadbury Castle, Somerset, with continuous occupation through the first millennium BC (Tabor 2008, 74), most Bronze Age hillforts in Britain were abandoned around the ninth or eighth century BC.

Radiocarbon dating of Rams Hill in Berkshire, England, shows this hillfort was built and occupied at the beginning of the Late Bronze Age *c.*1200 BC, and went through various phases of refurbishment (all of which incorporated wooden elements) until it was abandoned around 1000 BC (Bradley and Ellison 1975; Needham and Ambers 1994, 231–5). Excavation at Taplow hillfort in Buckinghamshire revealed a similar chronology and use of wooden defences. This site was built around the eleventh century BC and continued through several phases of refurbishment until the ninth century BC (Allen *et al.* 2009, 119). The entrance at Taplow shows significant signs of burning, which the excavators have interpreted as evidence for an attack (Allen *et al.* 2009, 87). Other hillforts from this period are notable for their wooden defences. Sites such as Thwing in Yorkshire (Manby 2007), Springfield Lyons in Essex (Buckley and Hedges 1987) and the Breiddin hillfort in Wales (Musson 1991), often had double palisades. Earthen hillforts were also constructed, including at Camp Gardens, Stow-on-the-Wold (Parry 1999) and Fairfield, Stotfold (Webley *et al.* 2007).

In northern Britain, the earliest evidence for hillfort construction is *c.*1000 BC. Nine sites are now known from the Late Bronze Age, though only Eildon Hill North and Traprain Law in the Scottish Borders are reliably dated (Lock and Ralston 2022, 324). The 19ha-example at Eildon Hill North had up to five phases of construction, with as many as 500 house platforms, some of which have Late Bronze Age dates (Figs 9.19 and 9.20). Intensive reoccupation and refurbishment of the enclosing elements during the first to fourth century AD have somewhat obscured this early phase (Owen 1992; O'Driscoll and Noble forthcoming). A similar situation occurs at the well-known Traprain Law, a 16ha hillfort with Late Bronze Age and Roman Iron Age phases of occupation. Despite intermittent excavations over the last century, the sequence of rampart construction at this site is still unclear (Lock and Ralston 2022, 320). Feachem (1958) proposed four phases of enclosure, with Armit *et al.* (1999) dating one of these to 1000–800 BC (Armit *et al.* 2005, 3). Outside of this enclosure on the western side of the hill, excavations have produced a considerable assemblage of artefacts dating to *c.*950–700 BC (Burley 1955, 124; Armit *et al.* 2005, 3). These finds were probably associated with a contemporary settlement, with houses, paved areas and multiple hearths identified from this phase (Cree 1923, 201–06).

Iron Age and later hillforts in Europe

Following this major phase of Bronze Age construction, the hillfort phenomenon began to wane in many parts of Europe

(Above) Fig. 9.19 Aerial view of Eildon Hill North, Scottish Borders, showing the large outer enclosing elements of the hillfort under excavation.

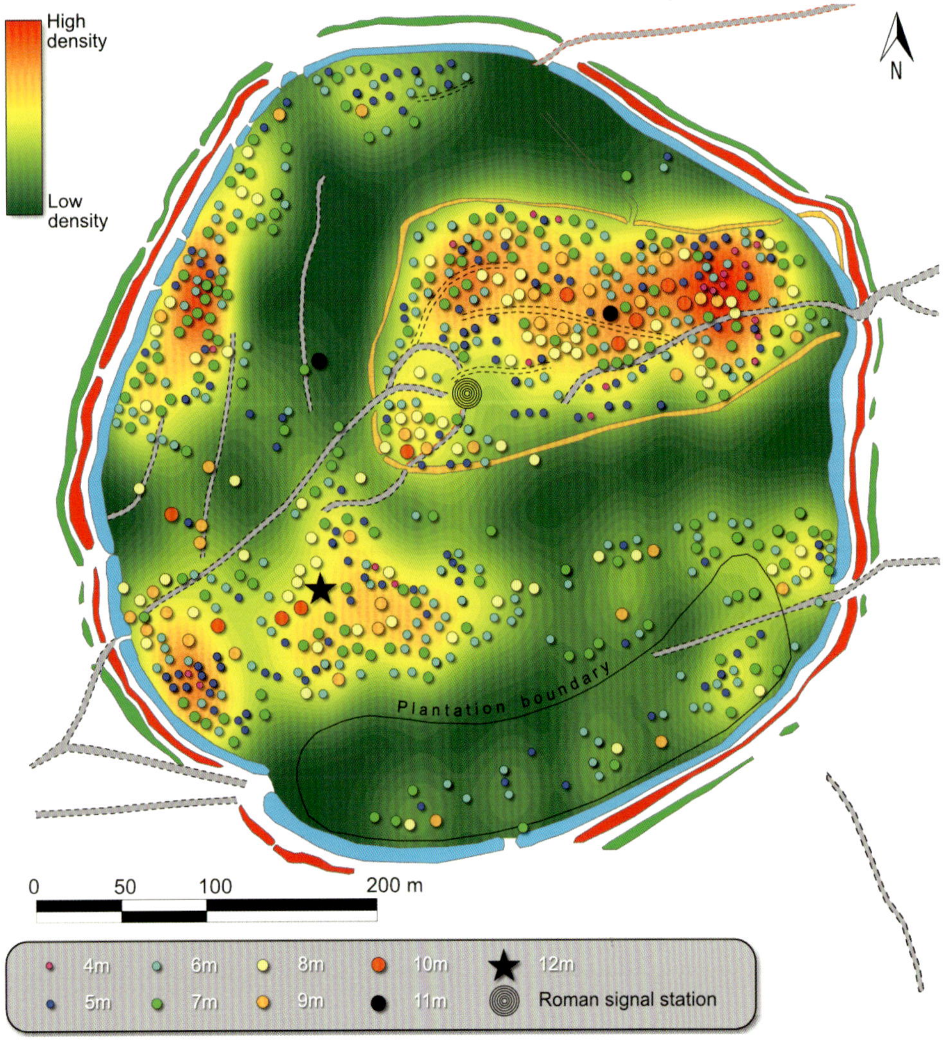

(Left) Fig. 9.20 Plan of Eildon Hill North, highlighting the distribution of internal house platforms in relation to the enclosing elements.

(Härke 1979, 261–3). This is true of southern Germany (Gerlach 1998; Rind 1999; Metzner-Nebelsick 2012, 425), north-west France (Delrieu 2013, 144) and eastern parts of Hungary and Slovakia (Matuz and Nováki 2002), where hillforts were abandoned by 800 BC. Other regions, however, notably Britain, north-east France, Belgium, parts of Germany and the Czech Republic, witnessed renewed construction of hillforts. On current evidence, it seems the Baltinglass sites and most other Irish hillforts are in the former category, with most abandoned by the eighth century BC.

These later hillforts in Europe are generally larger and less densely inhabited (Ralston 2006, 14). Well-dated hillforts, such as Biskupin in central Poland (Czebreszuk 2013, 782) and other examples in north-western Spain and Portugal (Pardo *et al.* 2009), were built and quickly abandoned in the eighth century BC (Harding and Razckowski 2010), possibly after direct assaults. Others were built slightly later, such as the iconic *Fürstensitze*, or 'princely seats' of the sixth century BC. These sites were associated with hierarchical communities presided over by an elite, and are found in an area stretching from Závist in Bohemia to the Heuneburg in southern Germany and Bourges in central France (Fernández-Götz *et al.* 2014). These are widely considered to represent the first examples of urbanisation in north-west Europe (Collis 2014; Fernández-Götz 2014, 30; Fernández-Götz and Ralston 2017, 259), though O'Driscoll (2023) has argued the large Bronze Age hillforts of Ireland could pre-date that phase of early urbanisation.

The Heuneburg in Baden-Wurttemberg, Germany is a well-known example of these later hillforts. Excavation uncovered evidence of elite occupation, supported by the discovery of richly furnished graves covered by massive earthen mounds near the hillfort (Fernández-Götz and Krausse 2012, 29). The latter was rebuilt or modified at least ten times after repeated attacks, with the original phase comprising a 5m-high wall of unfired mudbrick, with an external 14m-wide and 6m-deep, V-shaped ditch (Fernández-Götz and Krausse 2012, 30). The walls were further protected by forward-projecting, rectangular bastions, an architectural feature possibly derived from contact with the Mediterranean (Ralston 2006, 78; Fernández-Götz and Krausse 2012, 29). Outside those strong defences was a dense settlement over 100ha (Fernández-Götz and Krausse 2012, 31).

The Heuneburg was abandoned in the mid-fifth century BC, around the time when the 'princely seat' of Glauberg in south-west Germany was growing in importance (Fernández-Götz and Krausse 2012, 34). That hillfort was built in the early sixth century BC, in the form of a large, wood-laced stone bank constructed around a steep-sided, flat plateau. Excavation shows that the hillfort was destroyed by fire in the fifth century BC and quickly rebuilt. Here again, exceptionally furnished graves under massive earthen mounds indicate high-status occupation (Knipper *et al.* 2014). By the fourth century BC, Glauberg had largely been abandoned, along with many of the other 'princely seats' in Central Europe.

The development of the hillfort in Central Europe largely ceases with the enormous *oppida* that date from the second century BC to the first century AD. These large enclosures are distributed in a broad band from Hungary through temperate Europe, west to Atlantic France and north into southern England (Ralston 2006, 14). Manching oppidum in Bavaria, Germany, for example, is strategically located in a riverine plain overlooking important north–south routeways across the Danube and east–west overland routes (Krämer 2002, 63–5). The site comprises a bank with an outer face of dry-stone walling and wood, which surrounded an area of 380ha. Excavation revealed an impressive gate-house and intermittent areas of dense occupation within the interior (Krämer 2002, 66–70; Ralston 2006, 81). Industrial activity was also identified by an iron-working area, as was evidence for copper and bronze working (Krämer 2002, 71). The discovery of around 100 swords, 40 spearheads and iron shield bosses within the settlement may indicate Manching was destroyed by the Romans (Krämer 2002, 75–7).

While the building of hillforts generally declined in Europe during the Iron Age, this was not the case in Britain. There, hillforts re-emerged around 800–600 BC, represented by simple, curvilinear enclosures with two opposing entrances (Needham 2007; Sharples 2010, 116; Sharples 2010, 55). That period witnessed the first phases of construction at the well-known hillforts of Danebury and Maiden Castle, part of a 'hillfort dominated zone' that extended from the south-east coast of England to north Wales (see Cunliffe 1991, 312; 2013, 304). Excavation confirms that most of those hillforts were built during the sixth and fifth century BC (Cunliffe 2013, 304), at the same time that the 'princely seats' in mainland Europe were at the height of their power. Evidence of occupation varies considerably at these British sites. At one extreme, there are hillforts that show little trace of sustained use, while others were intensively occupied by a permanent population

Fig. 9.21 The massive banks and ditches of Hambledon Hill, Dorset, with the well-known hillfort of Hod Hill in the background.

(Cunliffe 2013, 305; Harding 2012, 206; Mytum 2013, 10).

Around 450–200 BC, the mobilisation of resources for boundary construction became the principal medium for elite competition in Britain (Sharples 2010, 120). This manifests in the evolution of some hillforts through the substantial enhancement of enclosing elements and the creation of complex entrance features. These 'developed hillforts' include Hambledon Hill (Fig. 9.21) and the well-known Maiden Castle in Dorset (Fig. 9.22). The first phase of the latter dates to around 600 BC, with a bank and external V-shaped ditch, up to 6.5m deep, enclosing an area of 6.47ha. Around 450 BC the enclosing elements were dramatically refurbished, and the hillfort was expanded to create a 45.28ha-enclosure (Sharples 1991, 63). The interior seems to have been densely occupied at that time. Analysis of the surrounding landscape indicates that contemporary settlements and hillforts were abandoned, with the population moving to the hillfort at Maiden Castle (Sharples 1991, 260). This trend is apparent elsewhere, including at Danebury hillfort in Hampshire, which expanded at a time when the nearby hillforts at Bury, Woolbury and Quarley Hill were abandoned (Cunliffe 2000, 166). This may be a sign of the increasing importance of these developed hillforts as centres for larger social units (Sharples 2010, 76; Cunliffe 2013, 306). By about the second century BC, occupation at Maiden Castle had evolved into a regular layout of streets and roundhouses. In the later part of the Iron Age, settlement may have been confined to the eastern half of the interior, with that regular layout replaced by a looser structure, before Maiden Castle was largely abandoned by the end of the first century AD (Sharples 1991).

In northern Britain, hillforts also continued to be built, but did not evolve into the 'developed' forts of southern England and Wales. Sites such as Broxmouth, East Lothian show a complex sequence of development that began *c.*640–570 BC and continued to expand and contract for another 800 years (Armit and McKenzie 2013). Recent work has shown that many of the hillforts in northern Britain were built *c.*400–200 BC (Noble *et al.* 2020).

By 100 BC, most British hillforts had been abandoned, and it becomes difficult to trace native settlements more generally (Fernández-Götz *et al.* 2020). The very few that remained in use, such as Traprain Law, are seen as exceptional (SCARF 2012, 57; Armit 1997, 129; 144). It is not until the middle of the first millennium AD, that we

Fig. 9.22 Iron Age hillfort at Maiden Castle, Dorset, in the summer heatwave of 2022.

again see an abrupt diffusion of enclosed settlements linked with the evolution of complex, highly stratified societies throughout Europe (Bhreathnach 2014; Evans 2014; Ó Cróinín 2005; Woolf 2007; Noble *et al.* 2013; Seaman and Sucharyna Thomas 2020).

Recent surveying and excavations in northern Britain have begun to fill this void. 'Atypical' sites like Eildon Hill North and Traprain Law have been joined by other massive, densely populated hillforts, such as Tap o' Noth, Aberdeenshire and East Lomond Hill, Fife, to reveal a major phase of centralisation during a period often portrayed as a 'Dark Age' (Reid 2023, 199). At Eildon Hill North, refurbishment of the Late Bronze Age enclosing elements was accompanied by re-use of old and building of new house platforms (Owen 1992; O'Driscoll and Noble forthcoming). Roman material of the first to fourth century AD indicates that the inhabitants of Eildon Hill North had strong links with the Roman Empire, and may have facilitated the occupation of the nearby Newstead Roman Fort. Excavations at Traprain Law by Curle and Cree (1921) uncovered stratified deposits of the first to fifth century AD overlying a Late Bronze Age phase of occupation. This was set within the 'Cruden Wall', a large, 12ha enclosure dated to the fifth century AD (Close-Brooks 1983). While the full extent of the occupation is not clear, the final phase shows a dense distribution of houses, pathways and streets. The considerable amount of Roman goods found suggests that the occupants of Traprain Law may have voluntarily submitted to Rome, with a treaty that provided the natives with protection and trade goods.

Trade with the invading Romans seems to be a characteristic feature of these massive, densely populated, native hillforts. At Tap o' Noth (Fig. 9.23), a large, 16ha, univallate, stone enclosure surrounded an urban-like settlement of more than 800 broadly contemporary house platforms, with streets and pathways branching through the interior (Noble and O'Driscoll forthcoming). Excavation of ten house platforms in this enclosure reveal these date from the second to sixth century AD, with the settlement at its peak when all of the houses were occupied contemporaneously in the fifth/sixth century AD. Crucible and mould fragments, bronze sheeting, glass beads, native and Roman pottery, Roman glass and a Roman tesserae — the first example of its type found in Scotland — were

Fig. 9.23 The 16ha stone rampart of Tap o' Noth, enclosing an estimated 800 house platforms, with the vitrified oblong fort on the summit under excavation.

recovered from these houses, indicating this was a complex native settlement with links to the Roman Empire.

These densely populated hillforts find close parallels in England and Wales, with sites such as Yeavering Bell, England (Miket 2013), or the spectacular Tre'r Ceiri hillfort, Wales (Hogg 1960, 1; Hopewell 1993), producing Roman material *c.*AD 150–400. While the picture is still tentative, we can envisage some very large hilltop communities of urban proportions at the apex of a complex settlement pattern. This is of interest in respect of the densely occupied Brusselstown Ring at Baltinglass, which may be the location of a Late Iron Age/early medieval caput known as Dún Bolg (O'Driscoll and Gleeson 2021).

It seems that large, densely populated hillforts were abandoned in Britain around the sixth century AD and replaced by smaller sites occupied by emerging regional kings. These sites, known as 'nuclear hillforts', occur throughout northern Britain and Wales. They are characterised by a complex hierarchical layout, with a series of enclosures defining descending terraces that surround a central, higher enclosure of seemingly greater significance (Noble and O'Driscoll 2019, 100). Excavations at sites such as Trusty's Hill in south-west Scotland (Toolis and Bowles 2017) suggest nuclear hillforts were built from the early sixth century AD, with other sites like Mither Tap, Aberdeenshire (Fig. 9.24) or Burghead, Moray, occupied until the ninth century AD. Excavations at Clatchard Craig (Close-Brooks 1983) and Burghead identified centres of high-status metalworking, which may be why those sites were attacked. Many examples have good archaeological and historical evidence for kingship, notably Dunadd, a major royal seat of the Dál Riata (Lane and Campbell 2000) mentioned in the *Annals of Ulster* in AD 741 as the place where King Áed Findliath died.

The evidence in Continental Europe for the continuation of hillfort construction and use is less clear once the oppida are abandoned. This may be a direct result of Roman control

Fig. 9.24 The rocky summit of Bennachie mountain, Aberdeenshire, crowned by the nuclear hillfort known as Mither Tap.

of native populations, who were encouraged to relocate to Roman towns in lowland areas. With the collapse of the Roman Empire at the end of the fifth century AD, however, we again see native populations 'retreat to hilltops' (Christie and Hodges 2016, 140). The use and re-use of hillforts and the development of castles and other types of 'strongholds' in mainland Europe becomes particularly widespread in the eighth to tenth century AD, when north-west Europe once again becomes dominated by enclosed communities (Christie and Herold 2016, xix).

SUMMARY

Hilltop enclosures began to be built in Europe during the Neolithic, spreading to Ireland and Baltinglass by around 3700/3600 BC, soon after farming was introduced by migrant groups from southern Britain, where causewayed enclosures were already established. These enclosures seem to have been built as a means to create a single group identity between a series of disparate farmers. They were built in marginal locations at the edges of territories, and in many cases several communities clustered in one area to facilitate trade and other exchanges. These marginal locations were places where ritual commemoration and burial of the dead took place, with the enclosures acting as spaces where individual families could have prepared the deceased for the otherworld. The Baltinglass sites also share this link with the dead, with both Rathcoran and Spinans Hill 1 enclosing passage tombs and burial cairns. These enclosures continued to be used until 3300/3200 BC, when it is possible other forms of monumental architecture, such as cursus monuments, became the focus of community building.

Following a hiatus of nearly 1,500 years, large hilltop enclosures start to reappear in Europe around 1800 BC. Although not uniform in distribution, the hillfort phenomenon flourished in three distinct phases: the Early

Bronze Age/Middle Bronze Age, the Middle Bronze Age/Late Bronze Age and the Late Bronze Age/Early Iron Age. It is interesting to note that construction of hillforts generally occurred at transition periods, possibly indicating that social upheaval may be a cause for their construction. The initial construction phase during the Early Bronze Age/Middle Bronze Age transition can be associated in Central Europe with control of copper sources and trade. During the Middle Bronze Age hilltop settlements were almost completely abandoned, and it is not until the Middle Bronze Age/Late Bronze Age transition that hillforts re-emerge, with an 'unprecedented' intensification in construction (Primas 2002, 50). This phase was much more dispersed than the Early Bronze Age hillfort horizon. The importance of controlling natural routeways and highly visible locales is an important feature of hillfort location during that period. This may be due to the increasing reliance on long-distance trading for high-status materials such as bronze. A notable increase in the evidence for violence and traces of destruction, as seen at Velim hillfort, may be an indication of increasing competition to control these routeways. A final construction phase occurs at the Late Bronze Age/Early Iron Age transition, although in more regionalised areas of the continent. Again, these are largely associated with natural routeways. This period also saw the emergence of the 'princely seat', a type of hillfort associated with the production of high-status goods and elite occupation.

In Britain, the hillfort phenomenon partly reflects the situation in mainland Europe, where a significant construction phase begins at the start of the Late Bronze Age. The hillfort tradition in Britain continues into the later part of the first century BC, however, when some were still being intensively occupied. Many of the British hillforts were built during 600–200 BC, in contrast to the situation in Continental Europe at that time, when a small number of 'princely seats' were being constructed and hillforts were largely abandoned. In mainland Europe, the hillfort phenomenon largely ceased with the construction of large enclosures known as *oppida*, dating to around the second and first century BC. In parts of Britain, however, evidence for the continued construction and occupation of large, densely populated hillforts during the first half of the first millennium AD is beginning to appear more frequently. These may represent some of the first 'urban-like' native centres in these regions. In northern Britain and Wales, a new type of fort linked with developing regional kingship, known as the 'nuclear hillfort', emerged with the abandonment of those centres. At the same period in Europe, there is a notable increase in the occupation of hilltops and the creation of a variety of fortifications, including what some might term 'hillfort'.

In many ways, the Early Neolithic enclosures and Bronze Age hillforts of Baltinglass reflect this picture from Britain and mainland Europe. The three Early Neolithic enclosures in Baltinglass were built around the same time as similar sites in Wales, though the Baltinglass sites seem larger. They share some morphological characteristics with other sites in Europe, such as the Sarup enclosures in Denmark. Rathnagree and Rathgall in Wicklow were two of the earliest hillforts in Ireland, part of the Middle/Late Bronze Age transition that Primas (2002) emphasised as the most intensive period of hillfort construction across Europe. The building and occupation of Tinoran during the Late Bronze Age occurred at a time when many hillforts in Europe were built and refortified (Primas 2002). The likely cessation of hillfort construction at Baltinglass may also reflect broader trends in Europe. The tentative identification of Spinans Hill 2 or Brusselstown Ring as the royal caput of Dún Bolg raises the possibility of renewed hillfort building during the Late Iron Age/early medieval period. While that remains to be confirmed, it fits well with the picture emerging from northern Britain and Wales, where large, densely populated hillforts involved in the production and procurement of tradable goods began to spring up. Unlike other parts of Europe, where there was a revival of hilltop fortification around the eighth to tenth century AD, however, there is little evidence for this at Baltinglass, though the region clearly retained its importance, as indicated by early medieval texts such as the *Bórama Laigen* and *Fingal Rónáin.*

10. A PREHISTORIC LANDSCAPE

William O'Brien

Hillforts were central to many important developments in society in late prehistoric Ireland. The earliest examples are arguably hill-top enclosures used by some farming communities during the mid-fourth millennium BC. Their protective design, combined with residential, economic and other uses, meet many criteria of a hillfort, even if they are generally not described as such. What distinguishes these Neolithic enclosures from later hillforts is their local significance as central places for small-scale segmentary societies.

Settlement enclosure on a larger scale would next occur in Ireland two millennia later, when hillforts emerged as power centres in regional chiefdom societies of the Middle and Late Bronze Age. Like many of their foreign counterparts, the Irish examples are generally connected to political authority, representing control of territory and a command of labour and other resources. The special character of structures and artifacts in some excavated hillforts is consistent with elite residence, the practice of specialist crafts and conspicuous consumption of sumptuary goods. The wealth of those societies is illustrated by the number of gold prestige objects in circulation in Ireland during the later Bronze Age (Eogan 1994). Those economies were underpinned by agriculture, with many Irish hillforts located in areas of good farmland. At an ideological level, these were important places of assembly and ceremony, and for the creation of group identity.

These prominent places were also an intimidating display of military power in the landscape, part of a political climate manifested in other types of protected settlement during the Middle and Late Bronze Age in Ireland. That concern with security is vible in mass production of specialised bronze weapons, including the sword, use of which was adopted around the twelfth century when hillforts began to be built in large numbers. This was an element of a new warrior culture with origins in mainland Europe, where there was a connection between hillforts and sword warfare during the later second millennium BC. Those developments eventually spread to Ireland in ways that did not involve invasion or large-scale movement of population. Trade connections were important, with hillforts playing an important role in the sourcing and re-distribution of bronze and the importation of gold and amber (O'Brien 2022). This was one factor in a new climate of territorial disputes and competition, whereby the ambitions of warlords led to periodic outbreaks of war, often with catastrophic consequences for individual hillforts.

'IRELAND'S HILLFORT CAPITAL'

The significance of the Baltinglass hillforts lies in the cultural and historical importance of individual sites and how they combine to create a unique archaeological landscape. Baltinglass has the largest concentration of prehistoric hillforts and hill-top enclosures in Ireland, representing a local palimpsest of significant Neolithic and Bronze Age settlement in south Leinster. When compared to other Irish hillforts, several of the Baltinglass sites are exceptional in their size and design. While not dated, Spinans Hill 2 (covering 131ha) is likely to be the largest prehistoric enclosure in Ireland (Fig. 10.1). This earthwork incorporates Brusselstown Ring on its south-eastern side, where two concentric enclosures extend over an area of 38ha. This is also one of the largest hillforts in Ireland, but remains undated. The same is true of several of the smaller hill enclosures at Baltinglass, including Boleycarrigeen (12.5ha), Kilranelagh Hill/Colvinstown Upper (7.8ha), Fauna Hill (2.5ha) and Corballis Hill (2.2ha).

The earliest dated examples at Baltinglass, namely Rathcoran (10.1ha) and Hughstown (8.2ha), are the two largest Neolithic enclosures in Ireland. Examples at Lyles Hill (7ha) and Donegore Hill (3.5ha), both in Co. Antrim; Magheraboy, Co. Sligo (1.1ha); and the recently excavated site at Faughan Hill, Co. Meath (c.5.2ha) are in comparison substantially smaller. Radiocarbon dating indicates that the occupation of Rathcoran and Hughstown c.3600–3400 BC overlapped, suggesting a substantial Neolithic settlement at Baltinglass. The relationship of those early farmers in Wicklow to other Neolithic core territories in eastern Ireland, including the Boyne Valley and the Loughcrew communities, needs to be explored.

Around 2,500 years later, the largest Bronze Age hillfort

Fig. 10.1 Western side of the massive Spinans Hill 2 earthwork, Baltinglass.

in Ireland was built at Baltinglass. The four definite enclosures on Tinoran Hill cover an area of 55.7ha, increasing to 84ha should a tentative fifth enclosure be confirmed. This greatly exceeds the next largest examples, namely Ballylin, Co. Limerick (21ha) and Mooghaun, Co. Clare (11ha). Other Bronze Age hillforts are significantly smaller, including Clashanimud, Co. Cork (8.8ha); Dún Aonghasa, Co. Galway (5.7ha); Formoyle, Co. Clare (6.4ha); Glanbane, Co. Kerry (6.6ha); Haughey's Fort, Co. Armagh (8.3ha); Rahally, Co. Galway (14ha); Rathgall, Co. Wicklow (7.3ha); and Toor More, Co. Kilkenny (7.2ha). Rathnagree hillfort (5.8ha) on Tuckmill Hill is more typical of those smaller Class 2 hillforts, which are still impressive monuments in distinctive landscape settings in their own right.

In terms of their cultural historical significance, these enclosures reveal how Baltinglass was a focus of settlement and political power at different times in prehistoric Ireland. The dating of Hughstown, Rathcoran and Spinans Hill 2 indicates a major Neolithic territory in south Leinster during the fourth millennium BC. Other elements of this settlement include the large, developed passage tomb on Baltinglass Hill and a likely Neolithic burial ground at Ballintruer More. While the house settlements of those first farmers have not been found, this is a problem of archaeological visibility in a landscape where there are few opportunities to discover sub-surface remains of such structures.

There were significant changes at Baltinglass during the third millennium BC, with no evidence of hill-top settlement. The embanked stone circles at Castleruddery and Boleycarrigeen may represent a local henge tradition, but this needs to be verified by excavation. The Early Bronze Age is the next visible phase of prehistoric settlement at Baltinglass, with evidence of several cemeteries containing food vessel and urn pottery. Those high-status burials indicate the presence of a hierarchical society *c.*2200–1600

BC, with local lineages whose descendants may have been connected to the building and use of Rathnagree hillfort, *c.*1400–1200 BC, and possibly Tinoran hillfort in later centuries. It is not known when Tinoran was abandoned, and whether the end of hillfort building at Baltinglass was connected to a 'collapse' of the local and wider Bronze Age world. The absence of Iron Age settlement at Baltinglass is partly due to lack of archaeological visibility; there is no excavation evidence for the reoccupation of the earlier hillforts in that period. Pollen evidence confirms the next major phase of settlement was in the early medieval period, when many ringforts were built in the Baltinglass lowlands. As discussed in Chapter 8, there is also a possibility that Dún Bolg, legendary seat of Uí Cheinnselaig and later the Uí Máil, was located on Spinans Hill in that period.

AN ARCHAEOLOGICAL LANDSCAPE

This concentration of hillforts and hill-top enclosures in south-west Wicklow is entirely unique in the Irish archaeological record, and there are few parallels elsewhere in Europe. While Irish hillforts do occur in pairs (see Fig. 1.3), there is no other clustering of sites comparable to the dozen or so large enclosures on the Baltinglass hills. Radiocarbon dating of six of the Baltinglass sites suggests they were not occupied contemporaneously, but at different times in the Neolithic and Bronze Age. This is an important record for the prehistory of Baltinglass, providing a strong basis for future research on other archaeological sites and monuments in the area.

While the focus tends to be on individual monuments, the Baltinglass hillforts are an important example of landscape archaeology — an approach that looks at the dynamic relationship between communities and the places they inhabited over time. A landscape perspective allows us to explore how people in the past related to the local worlds in which they lived, and how they invested their surroundings with cultural meaning through various symbolic processes connected to their sense of time and place, collective memories and cosmological understanding of the world. This was often expressed in physical form, such as the building of hillforts and other monuments. It also involved a mythologising of the landscape, whereby significance was attached to natural elements such as rivers and rock formations; an example in Baltinglass being the white quartz boulders of Bae Aife (see Fig. 8.10).

Because landscape is socially constituted, it has the potential to reflect social order and power relations. The study of the social landscapes of Iron Age and early medieval Ireland has long been dominated by research on power relations, focusing on 'royal sites' such as the Hill of Tara, Cruachain/Rathcroghan and Emain Macha/Navan Fort centres. The concentration of hillforts at Baltinglass also points to hierarchical social relations in a landscape of power, but this was also a landscape with many layers, where family, kin, community, gender and age relations were linked to land, dwellings and ceremonial places. One of the challenges for future research is to understand this wider cultural landscape of the Baltinglass hillforts and not just to focus on these sites in isolation.

THE FUTURE OF THE BALTINGLASS HILLFORTS?

This book provides information that will hopefully raise awareness of the historical and archaeological significance of the Baltinglass hillforts. While certain protections are in place, the survival of this unique landscape cannot be taken for granted. Many sites have been damaged over the centuries and face ongoing threats in the modern landscape. Some of those pressures are specific to the sheer size of hillforts, while others relate to how uplands are today viewed as marginal land with particular uses.

Given their size, it is not surprising that many Irish hillforts have been damaged or destroyed in the modern era. Their location generally means they are not impacted by large infrastructure projects such as road building and the laying of pipelines, with Rahally, Co. Galway being an exception. Smaller developments are, however, recorded at many sites, including the building of telecommunication masts (such as at Claragh, Co. Cork and Toor More, Co. Kilkenny); quarrying (at Clashanimud, Co. Cork and Faughan Hill, Co. Meath); and the creation of walking paths, memorials and other modern features.

A small number of hillforts are in low-lying areas of good agricultural potential, but most have an exposed position in upland terrain with poor soils. The impact of farming varies accordingly, with some sites having been totally or partially cleared for farm pasture (for example Glanbane, Co. Kerry; Formoyle, Co. Clare; Rahally, Co. Galway and Toor More, Co. Kilkenny). Many hillforts on higher elevations are no longer grazed, which can lead to animal burrowing and uncontrolled growth of bracken and shrub scrub, as seen at Clashanimud, Co. Cork and Ballylin, Co. Limerick. The ongoing decline in upland farming across Ireland has implications for the visibility of hillforts and other archaeological features. Without controlled animal grazing there is increased risk of hill fires; in addition, access can be difficult at overgrown hillforts, as is currently the case at Clashanimud in Co. Cork and Ballylin, Co. Limerick.

Several of the Baltinglass hillforts remain in a good state of preservation, notably Rathcoran, Spinans Hill 1 and Brusselstown Ring. Most, however, have been damaged at various times, including the present day. Three sites were entirely or partly levelled by agriculture by the nineteenth century: the Hughstown and Sruhaun enclosures, and parts of Tinoran hillfort. The land at Rathnagree and Spinans Hill is used for coarse grazing to the present day, resulting in no significant interference with the monuments apart from some trackways and boundary walls. None of these hillforts has been cultivated, with the possible exception of some large fields at Hughstown.

All known hillforts and hilltop enclosures in the Republic of Ireland and Northern Ireland are now registered as archaeological monuments. This affords a considerable degree of protection, with a requirement that landowners notify the relevant state authorities in advance of any proposed interference with those sites. Planning controls, preservation orders and a general prohibition on metal detecting offer further protection. While these controls have protected hillforts from developments such as wind farms, there are many instances where forestry, land reclamation and the placement of telecommunication masts have caused damage to these sites.

At present there are numerous legal and policy instruments that could provide adequate protection of upland archaeology in the Republic of Ireland. These include the recent enactment of the Historic and Archaeological Heritage and Miscellaneous Provisions Act (2023) to replace the National Monument Act (1930–2004). The latter provided for the protection of recorded sites and monuments, through the Sites and Monuments Record (SMR) and its statutory list of recorded monuments, the *Record of Monuments and Places* (RMP). A 1987 amendment to the National Monuments Act did allow for the protection of entire landscapes as 'archaeological areas', but was never fully implemented. There is no such provision in the new act, with the focus of protection now on individual monuments.

There is also a body of state and European Union directives on environmental protection, with potential to protect archaeology in upland landscapes. Some of these measures operate various EU agricultural grant schemes, so that farmers receiving payments must comply with environmental protection, including an undertaking not to damage recorded archaeological sites. Hillforts are also protected where they are located in areas of natural diversity, the most important of which in Ireland are designated Special Areas of Conservations (SACs).

Given these environmental protections, it is ironic that the major threat to hillforts in Ireland today comes from two elements central to state policy on climate change mitigation, namely wind farms and forestry. While the former have mostly been excluded from recorded hillforts in Ireland, their 'green' credentials mean that proposals for the construction of wind farms can reach such an advanced stage in the planning process to threaten individual archaeological sites. A good example is a case at Baltinglass, where in 2021 a developer applied for permission to construct five 165m-high wind turbines in the vicinity of Kilranelagh Hill, close to enclosures and other recorded monuments in the townlands of Colvinstown Upper and Boleycarrigeen. There was considerable local and wider concern around this proposal, with community action groups raising objections through the planning process. Wicklow County Council refused planning permission for the development, citing the importance of the Baltinglass hillfort landscape as a major concern. The developer appealed this decision to An Bord Pleanála, which also rejected the proposal, partly on grounds of visual impact and physical interference with archaeological sites.

Forestry and hillforts

Hillforts are particularly vulnerable to modern forestry, in the form of high-density planting of conifers on what is often regarded as marginal land (Fig. 10.2). Of 108 confirmed or possible hillforts in Ireland listed in a recent survey (O'Brien and O'Driscoll 2017), 20% have been seriously impacted by forestry, with many others affected by trees having been planted very close to the monument. The worst cases involve clearance, deep ploughing and planting/re-planting across all or most of the hillfort interior, with further damage caused by machine harvesting and the placement of trackways. This has occurred at the Class 1 hillforts of Coolagad and Downshill in Co. Wicklow, and Knockadigeen, Co. Tipperary, as well as the Class 2 hillforts of Ballincurra and Curraghadobbin in Co. Tipperary, Cumber Lower and Ballymacmurragh in Co. Offaly, and

Fig. 10.2 Aerial view of Spinans Hill with recent forestry, showing location of the prehistoric enclosures of (1) Spinans Hill 1; (2) Spinans Hill 2; (3) Brusselstown Ring.

Mooghaun, Co. Clare, among many others.

Today, approximately 809,000 hectares, or 11.6% of land, in the Republic of Ireland is under forestry. Of the total forest area, 31% is broad-leaved forest; 69% is conifer forest, dominated by Sitka spruce monoculture. Ireland's forest cover remains low by European standards, and there is a target to reach 18% of land area under forestry by 2027 through the planting of 8,000 hectares of new forest each year. Approximately half of forests in Ireland are in public ownership, mainly managed by a state-owned forestry company, as well as in National Parks and Nature Reserves. There is an ongoing push to increase the amount of private forestry, supported by state grants; farmers represent most of an estimated 23,500 owners of forestry today. The decline of hill farming across Ireland has contributed to afforestation of upland areas, in some instances accompanied by wind farms. Current policy is to expand the forest cover on public and private land in a manner that will deliver lasting benefits for climate change, biodiversity, water quality, wood production, economic development, employment and quality of life. Climate change is the new driver of state forestry policy, identified as one of the most effective land-use changes that can contribute to achieving Ireland's carbon emission targets.

Fig. 10.3 Conifer plantation encroaching on western side of Rathnagree hillfort, Tuckmill Hill.

These priorities are outlined in a policy statement, Ireland Forest Strategy 2023–30, a 57-page document that makes no reference to the potential impact of large-scale afforestation on cultural heritage, or on the measures needed to protect archaeological sites and monuments. This follows decades of state policy in which economic priorities took precedence over protection of cultural heritage. While EU policy requires forestry programmes to undertake environmental impact assessments (EIA), the Irish state has historically set the area threshold very high. For many years the practice of project splitting, whereby large areas of upland were planted in adjoining blocks below EIA-threshold size, meant that archaeological assessment was rarely carried out in Irish forestry plantations. While that practice has been curbed, land holdings up to 50 hectares may be forested today without the need for an EIA. Unlike wind farms and other developments, forestry in Ireland does not require planning permission, but rather a licence issued by a state authority promoting forestry. No archaeological assessment needs to be carried out unless there is a recorded monument in the plantation area.

The problem with desk-based assessment is that much of the archaeology of Irish uplands is not necessarily recorded in the *Record of Monuments and Places*. This database was established by field inspection of archaeological sites and monuments marked on Ordnance Survey historic mapping. The latter has minimal detail for terrain over 200m OD, which is why many ancient field patterns and settlement features are not recorded. The absence of a recorded monument means there is often no basis to initiate archaeological assessment of proposed forestry developments, a situation not helped by the small number of state archaeologists available to monitor forestry developments in Ireland.

This failure to maintain archaeological oversight of forestry over many years is illustrated by what has occurred

Fig. 10.4 Aerial view of stone wall built in 1936 around the passage tomb on the Pinnacle summit of Baltinglass Hill.

in 'Ireland's hillfort capital'. Eight of thirteen hillforts/hilltop enclosures in the Baltinglass landscape are covered entirely or in part by commercial conifer plantation, with active planting and harvesting at many of those locations today (Fig. 10.3). These include the sites at Ballinroan Upper, Boleycarrigeen, Corballis, Fauna Hill, Kilranelagh, Rathnagree, Spinans Hill 2 and Tinoran, all of which are listed in the *Record of Monuments and Places* for Co. Wicklow. The damage in some instances is confined to part of the monument (Rathnagree, Ballinroan Upper and Spinans Hill 2), but blanket destruction has occurred at Boleycarrigeen, Corballis, Kilranelagh, Fauna Hill and Tinoran (see Fig. 5.29).

The legal responsibility for protection of this cultural heritage lies with the state, which needs to be more proactive around the devastating impact forestry can have on archaeological landscapes. This is particularly important when the state is the largest developer of forestry in Ireland. Future forestry policy should be based on the principle that all new and renewed plantations in upland areas require archaeological assessment on the ground, and not only where there are known recorded monuments. While it may not be financially feasible to adopt the high standards of mitigation applied in road and pipeline archaeology, neither is a minimalist approach acceptable just because the planting of trees has wider benefits. Some of these benefits are in fact increasingly being questioned in respect of the impact of conifer monoculture on biodiversity, the environment and local communities.

Public presentation and heritage initiatives

The protection of hillforts in Ireland can be enhanced by public awareness of their historical importance. These impressive monuments have considerable potential for heritage tourism, as illustrated by the number of visitors drawn to the Dún Aonghasa, Mooghaun and Rathgall hillforts every year, and to 'royal sites' such as Tara, Cruachain and Dún Ailinne. All of those monuments are either owned by the state or are in its guardianship, allowing public access and presentation to be managed by the Office of Public Works. There are 25 so-called National Monuments in Co. Wicklow, including Baltinglass Abbey and the stone circle and motte at Castleruddery, all three of which are state properties. The passage tomb and Rathcoran hillfort on Baltinglass Hill are both in guardianship, while Rathgall hillfort to the south of Baltinglass is owned by the state.

None of the Baltinglass hillforts has formal access arrangements, walks, signage or information panels. With the exception of Rathcoran, where this could be done, the other sites remain in private ownership. Landowners are generally encouraging of public access, but this needs to be supported by the state for insurance, safety and other reasons in landscapes that are farmed today. The size of hillforts, their multiple ownership and perceived maintenance costs tends to discourage central government and local authorities from acquiring these monuments. As shown by the example of Dún Aonghasa, Mooghaun and Rathgall, however, such initiatives can happen with political will and local support, to the long-term benefit of the communities concerned.

A number of site-specific conservation measures might be taken to protect hillforts in the Baltinglass area. Among these would be the prohibition of wind farms and telecommunication masts within appropriate constraint zones around these hills. Forestry might be removed at some sites, notably Rathnagree and Tinoran, and a restriction could be placed on further planting on Spinans Hill. Where access can be secured by ownership or agreement with landowners, walkways, signage and information panels might be created at the most important hillforts. These site presentations could form part of a new Baltinglass Hillfort Trail, to connect with other public walkways in West Wicklow; in addition to history, tourism and education, these upland locations have a growing amenity value as walking trails, and they can also have a value as nature reserves.

An exciting initiative would be to restore the passage tomb cairn on Baltinglass Hill. A century or so ago, Lord Walter FitzGerald photographed 'a huge carn, or prehistoric sepulchral monument, consisting of a vast pile of stones and boulders' at the so-called Pinnacle on the eastern summit (see Fig. 3.46). Excavation in 1934–6 led to the removal of this cairn to expose the various burial chambers in the passage tomb. On concluding this work, 'the cairn was not replaced, as it was considered desirable that the chambers should remain open to inspection rather than be filled up and covered again with stones. A retaining wall of dry stone was built round the monument outside the outer ring of kerb stones to prevent its being interfered with by animals grazing on the mountain' (Walshe 1941, 229).

While the intention there was to expose the burial chambers to public view and protect the monument from grazing animals, it would have been better to restore the cairn to its original appearance. The massive wall built with this stone has the appearance of an early medieval stone fort ('cashel'), easily confused with Rathcoran hillfort on the same hill (Fig. 10.4). The restoration of the cairn could be done in such a way as to leave the chambers visible, at least in part. This would restore an impressive feature to the Baltinglass skyline, comparable to another great passage tomb in Wicklow, that on the summit of Seefin near Blessington. The project would bring national and wider attention to Baltinglass, creating support for other heritage initiatives at these hillforts.

While it is hoped that some of the Baltinglass hillforts may be acquired as National Monuments at some stage, it is worth considering their international profile as a possible World Heritage Site. The latter are places of cultural and/or natural heritage designated by UNESCO to be of outstanding universal value to humanity. At present there are only two World Heritage properties in the Republic of Ireland, namely Brú na Bóinne in Co. Meath and Sceilg Mhichíl in Co. Kerry. The state maintains a Tentative List of other heritage sites considered suitable for nomination, which since 2022 includes the Royal Sites of Ireland, namely Dún Ailinne, Uisneach, Rock of Cashel, Rathcroghan and the Hill of Tara. While the Baltinglass hillforts may not be comparable to those regional centres in historical or legendary terms, they do deserve special consideration as one of the most distinctive hillfort landscapes in Europe.

Appendix 1

Radiocarbon dates (47) for Baltinglass hillforts (calibration after OxCal v.4.2.4). Ten dates for Baltinglass passage tomb are included for comparison (after Schulting *et al.* 2017, table 1).

Site	Sample No.	Material	Trench	Context	Lab No.	^{14}C BP	Calibration
Rathcoran	RN2017-013	Charcoal (Hazel)	T1	Pre-bank charcoal spread (C.26)	UBA-35423	4705±32 BP	3626–3372 BC
	RN2017-009	Charcoal (Oak)	T1	Charred oak post (C.17) on oxidised bank (C.13)	UBA-35422	4905±32 BP	3767–3637 BC
	RN2017-006	Charcoal (Hazel)	T1	Silt/charcoal deposit (C.14) at top of oxidised bank (C.13)	UBA-46474	4761±25 BP	3635–3385 BC
	RN2017-004	Charcoal (Oak)	T1	Charcoal flecked silt (C.11) from base of revetment (C.12)	UBA-46457	4865±26 BP	3706–3537 BC
	RN2021-104	Charred grain (Emmer wheat)	T7 (T1 ex)	Charcoal layer (C.182), inner ditch (C.186)	UBA-46472	4620±25 BP	3508–3351 BC
	RN2021-106	Charcoal (Hazel)	T7 (T1 ex)	Charcoal-enriched clay (C.180), inner ditch (C.186)	UBA-46471	4737±31 BP	3633–3378 BC
	RN2021-107	Charred nutshell (Hazel)	T7 (T1 ex)	Backfilled subsoil (C181), inner ditch (C.186)	UBA-46473	4613±32 BP	3515–3198 BC
	RN2018-021	Charcoal (Hazel)	T2	Charcoal deposit from pre-bank layer (C.150)	UBA-39424	4807±29 BP	3643–3528 BC
	RN2018-016	Charcoal (Hazel)	T2	Lump charcoal at the top of bank (C.36)	UBA-39423	2898±25 BP	1202–1007 BC
	RN2019-044	Charcoal (Elm)	T3	Charcoal from old ground surface (C.90), pre bank	UBA-46459	5069±26 BP	3954–3796 BC
	RN2019-039	Charcoal (Hazel)	T3	Charcoal-flecked silt (C.84) on inside of bank	UBA-46458	4775±26 BP	3636–3521 BC
	RN2019-042	Charcoal (Alder)	T3	Charcoal deposit (C.87), base of ditch (C.89)	UBA-42444	4738±37 BP	3634–3378 BC
	RN2019-040	Charcoal (Hazel)	T3	Charcoal from middle fill (C.74) of ditch (C.89)	UBA-46460	4825±26 BP	3650–3528 BC
	RN2019-055	Charcoal (Hazel)	T4	Lump charcoal from fill (C.113) of pit (C.119)	UBA-46463	4925±26 BP	3768–3643 BC
	RN2019-056	Charcoal (Willow)	T4	Lump charcoal from fill (C.115) of pit (C.123)	UBA-42443	4537±37 BP	3368–3101 BC
	RN2019-051	Charcoal (Hazel)	T4	Lump charcoal from grey silt (C.106) of central area	UBA-46461	2882±32 BP	1200–933 BC
	RN2020-069	Charcoal (Hazel)	T5	Charcoal from basal fill (C.161) of quarry pit (C.165)	UBA-46465	4476±25 BP	3339–3031 BC
	RN2020-063	Charcoal (Hazel)	T5	Grey silt (C.155) from top of quarry pit (C.165)	UBA-46469	3649±30 BP	2136–1935 BC
	RN2020-073	Charcoal (Hazel)	T5	Hearth deposit (C.163), top of quarry ditch (C.165)	UBA-46466	3482±29 BP	1887–1698 BC
	RN2020-059	Charcoal (Hazel)	T5	Fill (C.95) of pit (C.173), cutting through hearth (C.163)	UBA-46467	3438±23 BP	1876–1639 BC
	RN2020-067	Charcoal (Oak)	T5	Charcoal layer (C.160), beneath radial bank	UBA-46464	5336±27 BP	4317–4052 BC

Site	Sample No.	Material	Trench	Context	Lab No.	^{14}C BP	Calibration
Baltinglass passage tomb	E11:61-1	Human bone	–	Outside Chamber II	UBA-14754	4726±41	3635–3376 BC
	E11:61-2	Human bone	–	Outside Chamber II	UBA-14755	4879±29	3706–3637 BC
	E11:62-1	Human bone	–	Chamber II	UBA-14756	4310±25	3011–2887 BC
	E11:62-2	Human bone	–	Chamber II	UBA-14757	4441±32	3331–2931 BC
	E11:64-1	Human bone	–	Chamber III	UBA-14758	4885±30	3710–3637 BC
	E11:64-2	Human bone	–	Chamber III	UBA-14759	5031±25	3946–3715 BC
	E11:58-1	Human bone	–	Chamber III	UBA-14753	289±24	AD 1514–1660
	E11:181-1	Charred Wheat grain	–	Under cairn	UBA-14811	4718±26	3632–3376 BC
	E11:181-2	Charred Wheat grain	–	Under cairn	UBA-14812	4729±37	3635–3377 BC
	E11:182	Charred Hazelnut shell	–	Under cairn	UBA-23040	4693±36	3630–3370 BC
Hughstown	HT2015-01	Charcoal (Alder)	1	Sediment (Context 33) at base of ditch of second enclosure	GrA-64434	4815±35	3661–3521 BC
	HT2015-02	Charcoal (Willow)	1	Upper fill (Context 16) of slot trench (Context 25) inside bank of second enclosure	GrA-64437	4825±35	3694–3523 BC
	HT2015-03	Charcoal (Alder)	1	Fill (Context 12) of small pit (Context 13) inside bank of second enclosure	GrA-64436	4850±35	3704–3533 BC
	HT2016-01	Charcoal (Alder)	2	Basal fill (Context 56) of slot trench (C.61) of third enclosure	GrA-67382	4725±35	3635–3376 BC
	HT2016-02	Charcoal (Willow)	2	Basal fill (Context 56) of slot trench (C.61) of third enclosure	GrA-67383	4690±35	3629–3369 BC
	HT2016-03	Charcoal (Alder)	2	Lower fill (Context 53) of ditch (C.55) of third enclosure	GrA-67384	4710±35	3632–3373 BC
	HT2016-04	Charcoal (no id)	3	Ditch sediment (Context 46) of fourth enclosure	GrA-67385	4730±40	3636–3376 BC
	HT2016-05	Charcoal (Holly)	3	Lower fill (Context 47), from west side of ditch (C.48) of fourth enclosure	GrA-67386	4685±35	3627–3369 BC
Spinans Hill 1	SH2016-01	Charcoal (Alder)	1	Dark brown silt (C.06) on top of lower stones of bank	GrA-67387	4835±35	3697–3527 BC
	SH2016-02	Charcoal (Alder)	1	Old ground surface (C.07) under bank	GrA-67389	4835±35	3697–3527 BC
	SH2016-03	Peat	1	Overlying collapsed stones, inner side of bank	GrA-67391	102.13 ± 0.35	Modern peat

Site	Sample No.	Material	Trench	Context	Lab No.	^{14}C BP	Calibration
Rathnagree	RNG2014-01	Charcoal (Ash)	1	Burnt timber (C.08) next to palisade posts	GrA-60925	3045 ± 40	1414–1135 BC
	RNG2014-02	Charcoal (Oak sapwood)	1	Basal fill (C.16) of posthole (C.18)	GrA-60927	3055 ± 40	1417–1213 BC
	RNG2014-03	Charcoal (Hazel)	2	Burnt spread (C.30) under Period 2 bank	GrA-60929	3050 ± 40	1417–1208 BC
	RNG2014-04	Charcoal (no id)	2	Stake-hole (C.57) under Period 2 bank	GrA-60930	3015 ± 40	1395–1126 BC
	RNG2014-05	Charcoal (Oak sapwood)	3	Burnt timber (C.61) next to palisade posts	GrA-60931	3020 ± 40	1397–1128 BC
	RNG2014-06	Charcoal (Oak sapwood)	3	Fill (C.65) of post-hole (C.67)	GrA-60932	3035 ± 40	1411–1131 BC
	RNG2014-07	Charcoal (Hazel twig)	2	Burnt spread (C.30) under Period 2 bank	GrA-63007	3240 ± 35	1535–1450 BC
	RNG2014-08	Pot residue	2	Base of Period 2 ditch	GrA-63008	3170 ± 35	1495–1415 BC
Sruhaun	SR2015-01	Charcoal (Oak sapwood)	1	Burnt layer under bank	GrA-64430	3030 ± 35	1375–1225 BC
	SR2015-02	Peat	1	Base of inner ditch	GrA-64432	126.73 ± 0.39	1959–1982 AD
Tinoran	TN2015-01	Charcoal (Oak sapwood)	1	Fill (C.17) of ditch of second enclosure	GrA-64438	2600±30	826–763 BC
	TN2015-02	Burnt bone	2	Hearth (C.34) inside bank of third enclosure	GrA-64571	2685±30	899–803 BC
	TN2015-03	Burnt bone	2	Hearth (C.40) inside bank of third enclosure	GrA-64572	2640±30	893–786 BC
	TN2015-04	Charcoal (Oak sapwood)	2	Layer (C.36) under bank of third enclosure	GrA-64439	2865±35	1188–923 BC
	TN2015-05	Pot residue	2	Layer (C.36) inside bank of third enclosure	GrA-64440	2905±35	1214–1001 BC

REFERENCES

AI: *Annals of Inishfallen*, CELT database: https://celt.ucc.ie//published/T100004/index.html [last accessed 7th April 2020].

AFM: *Annals of the Four Masters*, CELT database https://celt.ucc.ie/published/T100005A/ [last accessed 25th June 2020].

A. Tig.: *Annals of Tigernach*, CELT database https://celt.ucc.ie/published/T100002A/index.html [last accessed 25th June 2020].

AU: *Annals of Ulster*, CELT database: https://celt.ucc.ie//published/T100001A/index.html [last accessed 22nd November 2019].

CS: *Chronicon Scotorum* CELT database: https://celt.ucc.ie//published/G100016/index.html [last accessed 29th June 2020].

Frag. A.: *Fragmentary Annals*, CELT database: https://celt.ucc.ie//published/T100017/ [last accessed 22nd November 2019].

M: Annals of the Four Masters, CELT database: https://celt.ucc.ie//published/T100005B/index.html [last accessed 7th April 2020].

T: Annals of Tighernach, CELT database: https://celt.ucc.ie/published/T100002A/index.html [last accessed 7th April 2020].

Aaby, B. 1986. Trees as anthropogenic indicators in regional pollen diagrams from eastern Denmark. In Behre, K. (ed.), *Anthropogenic indicators in pollen diagrams*, 73–93. Rotterdam, Balkema.

Abels, B. 2002. *Die Heunischenburg bei Kronach. Eine späturnenfelderzeitliche Befestigung*. Regensburg, Univ.-Verl.

Ahlberg, K., Almgren, E., Wright Jr, H. and Ito, E. 2001. Holocene stable-isotope stratigraphy at Lough Gur, County Limerick, Western Ireland. *The Holocene* 11, 367–72.

Allen, J.R.L. 1996. Windblown trees as a palaeoclimate indicator: regional consistency of a mid-Holocene wind field. *Palaeogeography, Palaeoclimatology, Palaeoecology* 144, 175–81.

Allen, M., Leivers, M., Ellis, C., Stevens, S., Clelland, S., *et al.* 2008. Neolithic causewayed enclosures and later prehistoric farming: duality, imposition and the role of predecessors at Kingsborough, Isle of Sheppey, Kent, UK. *Proceedings of the Prehistoric Society* 74, 235–322.

Allen, T. Hayden, C. and Lamdin-Whymark, H. 2009. *From Bronze Age enclosure to Anglo-Saxon settlement: archaeological excavations at Taplow Hillfort, Buckinghamshire*. Oxford, Oxford University School of Archaeology.

Almgren, E. 1989. Woodland establishment, expansion, and regression in association with prehistoric and later human settlements around Lough Gur, Co. Limerick, Ireland. Unpublished PhD thesis, University of Minnesota.

Anderson, D. 1995. *An abrupt mid-Holocene decline of* Pinus sylvestris *in Glen Torridon, north-west Scotland: implications for palaeoclimatic change*. Oxford, School of Geography, University of Oxford.

Andersen, N. 1997. *The Sarup enclosures. The Funnel Beaker culture of the Sarup site including two causewayed camps compared to the contemporary settlements in the area and other European cultures*. Sarup vol. 1. Århus, Jutland Archaeological Publications XXXIII.

Andersen, N. 2002. Neolithic enclosures of Scandinavia. In Varndell, G. and Topping, P. (eds), *Enclosures in Neolithic Europe*, 1–10. Oxford, Oxbow Books.

Armit, I. 1997. *Celtic Scotland*. Edinburgh, Birlinn Press.

Armit, I. 2007. Hillforts at war: from Maiden Castle to Taniwaha Pā. *Proceedings of the Prehistoric Society* 73, 25–38.

Armit, I. and McKenzie, J. 2013. *An inherited place: Broxmouth Hillfort and the south-east Scottish Iron Age*. Edinburgh, Society of Antiquaries of Scotland.

Armit, I., Dunwell, A., and Hunter, F. 1999. Traprain Law (Prestonkirk parish), Neolithic axehead; Iron Age and medieval occupation. *Discovery Excavation Scotland 1999*, 30–31.

Armit, I., Dunwell, A., Hunter, F. and Nelis, E. 2005. Traprain Law: archaeology from the ashes. *PAST: Newsletter of the Prehistoric Society* 49, 1–4.

Armit, I., Swindles, G.T. and Becker, K. 2013. From dates

to demography in later prehistoric Ireland? Experimental approaches to the meta-analysis of large ^{14}C data-sets. *Journal of Archaeological Science* 40, 433–38.

Ashe FitzGerald, M. 2000. *Thomas Johnson Westropp: an Irish antiquary.* Dublin, Department of Archaeology, University College Dublin.

Avery, M. 1976. Hillforts of the British Isles: a student's introduction. In Harding, D. (ed.), *Hillforts: later prehistoric earthworks in Britain and Ireland,* 1–58. London, Routledge.

Baillie, M. 1993. Dark ages and dendrochronology. *Emania* 11, 5–12.

Baillie, M. and Brown, D. 1998.The dendro-date from Haughey's Fort. *Emania* 17, 45–6.

Baillie, M. and Brown, D. 2013. A chronological framework for the period from 208 BC to AD 600. *Emania* 21, 59–71.

Barber, M. 2018. *Prehistoric avenues and alignments: introduction to heritage assets.* Swindon, Historic England.

Bauch, W. 1988. Eine nachbestattung von Borgstedt, kreis Rendsburg-Echernförde. *Offa*, Band 45, 43–73.

Becker, K. 2010. *Rathgall, Co. Wicklow.* Archaeology Ireland Heritage Guide 51. Dublin, Wordwell.

Becker, K., Armit, I. and Swindles, G. 2017. New perspectives on the Irish Iron Age: the impact of NRA development on our understanding of later prehistory. In Stanley, M. (ed.), *Stories of our past,* 85–100. Bray, Wordwell.

Behre, K.E. 1981. The interpretation of anthropogenic indicators in pollen diagrams. *Pollen et Spores* 23, 225–45.

Bennett, K.D. 1984. The post-glacial history of *Pinus sylvestris* in the British Isles. *Quaternary Science Reviews* 3, 133–55.

Bennett, K.D. 1995. Pollen catalogue of the British Isles. Available online: http://chrono.qub.ac.uk/pollen/pc-intro.html [last accessed 11 January 2024].

Bennett, K., Whittington, G. and Edwards, K. 1994. Recent plant nomenclature changes and pollen morphology in the British Isles. *Quaternary Newsletter* 73, 1–6.

Bergh, S. 2000. Transforming Knocknarea. *Archaeology Ireland* 14 (2), 14–18.

Bergh, S. 2002. Knocknarea: the ultimate monument. Megaliths and mountains in Neolithic Cúil Irra, northwest Ireland. In Scarre, C. (ed.), *Monuments and landscape in Atlantic Europe,* 139–51. London, Routledge.

Bergh, S. 2015. Where worlds meet. Two Irish prehistoric mountain-top 'villages'. In Moscatelli, U. and Stagno, A. (eds), *Archaeology of Europe's mountain areas,* 21–44. Fermo, University of Macerata.

Bhreathnach, E. 2000. Kings, the kingship of Leinster and the regal poems of *laídshenchas Laigen*: a reflection on dynastic politics in Leinster, 650–1150 AD. In Smyth, A. (ed.), *Seanchas: studies in early and medieval Irish archaeology, history and literature in honour of Francis J. Byrne,* 299–312. Dublin, Four Courts Press.

Bhreathnach, E. 2011. Transforming kingship and cult: the royal provincial ceremonial capitals in the early medieval period. In Schot, R., Newman, C. and Bhreathnach, E. (eds), *Landscapes of cult and kingship,* 126–48. Dublin, Four Courts Press.

Bhreathnach, E. 2014. *Ireland in the medieval world AD 400–1000.* Dublin, Four Courts Press.

Birks, H.H. 1975. Studies in vegetational history of Scotland IV. Pine stumps in Scottish blanket peats. *Philosophical Transactions of the Royal Society of London, Series B (Biological Sciences)* 270, 181–226.

Blaauw, M. and Christen J.A. 2005. Radiocarbon peat chronologies and environmental change. *Journal of the Royal Statistical Society: Series C (Applied Statistics)* 54, 805–16.

Blaauw, M., Bakker, R, Christen, J.A., Hall, V. and van der Plicht, J. 2007a. A Bayesian framework for age modeling of radiocarbon-dated peat deposits: case studies from the Netherlands. *Radiocarbon* 49, 357–67.

Blaauw, M, Christen, J.A., Mauquoy, D., van der Plicht, J. and Bennett, K.D. 2007b. Testing the timing of radiocarbon-dated events between proxy archives. *The Holocene* 17, 283–88.

Blaauw, M., Christen, J.A., Bennett, K.D., and Reimer, P.J. 2018. Double the dates and go for Bayes: impacts of model choice, dating density and quality on chronologies. *Quaternary Science Reviews* 188, 58–66.

Blackburn, P., Petty, J.A. and Miller, K.F. 1988. An assessment of the static and dynamic factors involved in windthrow. *Forestry* 61, 1, 29–43.

Blockley, S.P.E., Blaauw, M., Bronk Ramsey, C. and van der Plicht, J. 2007. Building and testing age models for radiocarbon dates in Late-Glacial and Early Holocene sediments. *Quaternary Science Reviews* 26, 1915–26.

Blockley, S.P.E., Ramsey, C.B., Lane, C.S. and Lotter, A.F. 2008. Improved age modelling approaches as exemplified by the revised chronology for the Central European varved lake Soppensee. *Quaternary Science Reviews* 27, 61–71.

Bogucki, P. 2004. Late Bronze Age urnfields of Central Europe. In Bogucki, P. and Crabtree, P. (eds), *Ancient Europe: 8000 BC–AD 1000. Encyclopedia of the Barbarian World*, 86–91. New York, Charles Scribner and Sons.

Bourke, L. 2001. *Crossing the Rubicon. Bronze Age metalwork from Irish rivers*. Bronze Age Studies 5. Galway, Department of Archaeology, National University of Ireland, Galway.

Bradley, R. 1997. *Rock art and the prehistory of Atlantic Europe*. London, Routledge.

Bradley, R. 2002. *The past in prehistoric societies*. London, Routledge.

Bradley, R. and Ellison, A. 1975. *Rams Hill: a Bronze Age defended enclosure and its Landscape*. British Archaeological Report 19. Oxford, Archaeopress.

Bradshaw, R.H.W. and Browne, P. 1987. Changing patterns in the post-glacial distribution of *Pinus sylvestris* in Ireland. *Journal of Biogeography* 14, 237–48.

Brandherm, D. 2014. Late Bronze Age casting debris and other base metal finds from Haughey's Fort. *Emania* 22, 59–68.

Bridge, M.C., Haggart, B.A. and Lowe, J.J. 1990. The history and palaeoclimatic significance of subfossil remains of *Pinus sylvestris* in blanket peats from Scotland. *Journal of Ecology* 78, 77–99.

Brindley, A. 2007. *The dating of food vessels and urns in Ireland*. Bronze Age Studies 7. Galway, Department of Archaeology, National University of Ireland, Galway.

Brindley, A.L. and Lanting, J.N. 1989/1990b. Radiocarbon dates for Neolithic single burials. *Journal of Irish Archaeology* 5, 1–7.

Brindley, A.L., Lanting, J.N. and Mook, W.G. 1983. Radiocarbon dates from the Neolithic burials at Ballintruer More, Co. Wicklow and Ardcrony, Co. Tipperary. *Journal of Irish Archaeology* 1, 1–9.

Bronk Ramsey, C. 2008. Deposition models for chronological records. *Quaternary Science Reviews* 27, 42–60.

Bronk Ramsey, C. 2009a. Bayesian analysis of radiocarbon dates. *Radiocarbon* 51, 337–60.

Bronk Ramsey, C. 2009b. Dealing with outliers and offsets in radiocarbon dating. *Radiocarbon* 51, 1023–45.

Brophy, K. 2016. *Reading between the lines: the Neolithic cursus monuments of Scotland*. London, Routledge.

Brown, A.G., Hatton, J., O'Brien, C.E., Selby, K.A., Langdon, *et al.* 2005. Vegetation, landscape and human activity in midland Ireland: mire and lake records from the Lough Kinale–Derragh Lough area, Central Ireland. *Vegetation History and Archaeobotany* 14, 81–98.

Brown, G., Field, D. and McOmish, D. 2005. *The Avebury landscape. Aspects of the field archaeology of the Marlborough Downs*. Oxford, Oxbow Books.

Brown, T. 1997. Clearances and clearings: deforestation in Mesolithic/Neolithic Britain. *Oxford Journal of Archaeology* 16, 133–46.

Brück, J. and Fontijn, D. 2013. The myth of the chief: prestige goods, power, and personhood in the European Bronze Age. In Fokkens, H. and Harding, A (eds), *Oxford handbook of the European Bronze Age*, 197–215. Oxford, Oxford University Press.

Buck, C.E., Litton, C.D. and Smith, A.F.M. 1992. Calibration of radiocarbon results related to archaeological events. *Journal of Archaeological Science* 19, 497–512.

Buckley, D. and Hedges, J. 1987. *The Bronze Age and Saxon settlements at Springfield Lyons, Essex: an interim report*. Essex, Essex County Council.

Burgess, C. and Gerloff, S. 1981. *The dirks and rapiers of Great Britain and Ireland*. Munich. Prähistorische Bronzefunde, abteilung IV, Band 7. Stuttgart, Franz Steiner Verlag.

Burl, A. 1976. *The stone circles of the British Isles*. New Haven, Yale University Press.

Burley, E. 1955. A catalogue and survey of the metal-work from Traprain Law. *Proceedings of the Society of Antiquaries of Scotland* 89, 118–226.

Burnez, C. and Louboutin, C. 2002. The causewayed enclosures of western-central France from the beginning of the fourth to the end of the third millennium. In Varndell, G. and Topping, P. (eds), *Enclosures in Neolithic Europe*, 11–27. Oxford, Oxbow Books.

Byrne, F. 1973. *Irish kings and high-kings*. Dublin, Four Courts Press.

Campbell, L. 2021. The origins of British hillforts: a comparative study of Late Bronze Age hillfort origins in the Atlantic West. Unpublished PhD Thesis, University of Liverpool.

Carey, A. 2002. Excavations at Knockacarrigeen Hill,

Tuam, Co. Galway. *Journal of the Galway Archaeological and Historical Society* 54, 55–71.

Caseldine, C. and Fyfe, R. 2006. A modelling approach to locating and characterising elm decline/landnam landscapes. *Quaternary Science Reviews* 25, 632–44.

Caseldine, C. and Hatton, J. 1996. Early land clearance and wooden trackway construction in the third and fourth millennia BC at Corlea, Co. Longford. *Biology and Environment: Proceedings of the Royal Irish Academy* 96B, 11–19.

Caseldine, C., Hatton, J. and Gearey, B. 2005. Pollen and palaeohydrological analysis. In Gowen, M., O'Neill, J. and Philips, M. (eds), *The Lisheen Mine archaeological project, 1996–98*, 83–136. Bray, Wordwell.

Charles-Edwards, T.M. 2000. *Early Christian Ireland.* Cambridge, Cambridge University Press.

Charles-Edwards, T.M. 2013. *Wales and the Britons, 350–1064 AD*. Cambridge, Cambridge University Press.

Chique, C., Molloy, K. and Potito, A. 2017. Mid-Late Holocene vegetational history and land-use dynamics in County Monaghan, Northeastern Ireland—the palynological record of Lough Muckno. *Journal of the North Atlantic* 32, 1–24.

Christie, N. and Herold, H. (eds.), *Fortified settlements in early medieval Europe*. Oxford, Oxbow Books.

Christie, N. and Hodges, R. 2016. Anxious abbots? Questions of monastic security and insecurity in early medieval Europe. In Christie, N. and Herold, H. (eds), *Fortified settlements in early medieval Europe*, 139–57. Oxford, Oxbow Books.

Cleary, K. 2007. Irish Bronze Age settlements: spatial organisation and the deposition of material culture. Unpublished PhD thesis, University College Cork.

Cleary, R.M. 1995. Late Bronze Age settlement and prehistoric burials, Lough Gur, Co. Limerick. *Proceedings of the Royal Irish Academy* 95C, 1–92.

Cleary, R.M. 2000. The potter's craft in prehistoric Ireland. In Desmond, A. *et al.* (eds), *New agendas in Irish prehistory*, 119–34. Dublin, Wordwell.

Cleary, R.M. 2003. Enclosed Late Bronze Age habitation site and boundary wall at Lough Gur, Co. Limerick. *Proceedings of the Royal Irish Academy* 103C, 97–189.

Cleary, R.M. 2008. The pottery from Site A. In M. Doody, *The Ballyhoura Hills project*, 259–303. Discovery Programme Monograph 7. Bray, Wordwell.

Cleary, R.M. 2012. Pottery. In C. Cotter, *The western stone forts project: excavations at Dún Aonghasa and Dún Eoghanachta* (vol. 2), 8–26. Discovery Programme Monograph. Dublin, Wordwell.

Cleary, R.M. 2015. Excavation at Grange stone circle (B), Lough Gur, Co. Limerick, and a review of the dating. *Journal of Irish Archaeology* 24, 51–77.

Cleary, R.M. 2018. *The archaeology of Lough Gur.* Dublin, Wordwell.

Cleary, R.M. and Kelleher, H. 2011. *Archaeological excavations at Tullahedy, County Tipperary*. Cork, Collins Press.

Cleary, R.M. and O'Driscoll, J. 2014. Archaeological remains and geophysical surveys at Lough Gur and Grange stone circle. In Dalton, C. and O'Carroll, E. (eds), *Irish Quaternary Association Field Guide 32*, 31–44. Dublin, Irish Quaternary Association.

Clinton, M. 2000. Settlement patterns in the early historic kingdom of Leinster (seventh to mid twelfth century). In Smyth, A. (ed.), *Seanchas: studies in early and medieval Irish archaeology, history and literature in honour of Francis J. Byrne*, 275–98. Dublin, Four Courts Press.

Close-Brooks, J. 1983. Dr Bersu's excavations at Traprain Law, 1947. In O'Connor, A. and Clarke, D. (eds), *From the Stone Age to the 'Forty-Five'. Studies presented to R.B.K. Stevenson, Former Keeper, National Museum of Antiquaries of Scotland*, 206–23. Edinburgh, RCAHMS.

Cody, E. 1981. A hillfort at Ballylin, Co. Limerick, with a note on Mooghaun, Co. Clare. *Journal of the Royal Society of Antiquaries of Ireland* 111, 70–80.

Collis, J. 2014. Urbanisation in temperate Europe in the Iron Age: Mediterranean influence or indigenous? In Fernández-Götz, M. Wendling, H. and Winger, K. (eds), *Paths to complexity: centralisation and urbanisation in Iron Age Europe*, 15–23. Oxford, Oxbow Books.

Comber, M. 2008. *The economy of the ringfort and contemporary settlement in early medieval Ireland.* British Archaeological Reports S1173. Oxford, Archaeopress.

Condit, T. 1992. Ireland's hillfort capital: Baltinglass, Co. Wicklow. *Archaeology Ireland* 6 (3), 16–20.

Condit, T. 1998. Observations of the Baltinglass hillfort complex. In Corlett, C. and O'Sullivan, A. (eds), *Wicklow Archaeology and History* vol. 1, 9–25.

Condit, T. and Buckley, V. 1998. The Doon of Drumsna: an Iron Age frontier fortification in Connacht. *Archaeology Ireland Heritage Guide* 1. Bray, Wordwell.

Condit, T. and Corlett, C. 2001. The stone circle at Castleruddery Lower. *Archaeology Ireland Heritage*

Guide 13. Bray, Wordwell.

Connolly, A. 1999. The palaeoecology of Clara Bog, County Offaly. Unpublished PhD thesis, Trinity College, Dublin.

Conway, M. 2000. Mount Offaly, Cabinteely: early medieval and enclosed cemetery. In Bennett, I. (ed.), *Excavations 1998: summary accounts of archaeological excavations in Ireland*, 36–7. Dublin, Wordwell.

Cooney, G. 1981. A saddle quern from Baltinglass Hill, County Wicklow. *Journal of the Royal Society of Antiquaries of Ireland* 111, 102–6.

Cooney, G. 2002. From Lilliput to Brobdingnag: the traditions of enclosure in the Irish Neolithic. In Varndell, G. and Topping, P. (eds), *Enclosure in Neolithic Europe*, 69–82. Oxford, Oxbow.

Cooney, G. 2009. Tracing lines across landscapes: corporality and history in later prehistoric Ireland. In Cooney, G., Becker, K., Coles, J., Ryan, M. and Sievers, S. (eds), *Relics of Old Decency. archaeological studies in later prehistory: a Festschrift for Barry Raftery*, 375–88. Dublin, Wordwell.

Cooney, G., Bayliss, A., Healy, F., Whittle, A., Danaher, E., *et al.* 2011. Ireland. In Whittle, A., Bayliss, A. and Healy, F. (eds), *Gathering time: dating the Early Neolithic enclosures of southern Britain and Ireland*, 562–669. Oxford, Oxbow.

Corlett, C. 2004. A prehistoric enclosure at Keadeen, Co. Wicklow. *Journal of the Royal Society of Antiquaries of Ireland* 134, 80–90.

Corlett, C. 2014a. Some cursus monuments in south Leinster. *Archaeology Ireland* 28 (2), 20–25.

Corlett, C. 2014b. *Inscribing the landscape: the rock art of south Leinster*. Dublin, Wordwell.

Corlett, C. and Weaver, M. 2002. *The Liam Price notebooks: the placenames, antiquities and topography of County Wicklow* (2 vols). Dublin, Department of Arts, Heritage and the Gaeltacht.

Cotter, C. 2012. *The western stone forts project: excavations at Dún Aonghasa and Dún Eoghanachta* (2 vols). Dublin, Wordwell.

Coyle McClung, L. 2013. The Late Iron Age Lull—not so Late Iron Age after all! *Emania* 21, 73–83.

Coyle McClung, L. and Plunkett, G. 2020. Cultural change and the climate record in final prehistoric and early medieval Ireland. *Proceedings of the Royal Irish Academy* 120C, 129–58.

Cree, J. 1923. Account of the excavations on Traprain Law during the summer of 1922. *Proceedings of the Antiquaries of Scotland* 57, 180–226.

Cree, J. and Curle, A. 1922. Account of the excavations on Traprain Law during the summer of 1921. *Proceedings of the Society of Antiquaries of Scotland* 56, 189–259.

Crushell, P., Connolly, A., Schouten, M. and Mitchell, F.J.G. 2008. The changing landscape of Clara Bog: the history of an Irish raised bog. *Irish Geography* 41, 89–111.

Cunliffe, B. 1991. *Iron Age communities in Britain* (3rd edition). London, Routledge.

Cunliffe, B. 2000. *The Danebury environs programme: the prehistory of a Wessex landscape,* Vol. 1, *Introduction.* Oxford, English Heritage and Oxford University Committee for Archaeology.

Cunliffe, B. 2006. Understanding hillforts: have we progressed? In Payne, A., Corney, M. and Cunliffe, B., *The Wessex Hillfort project: extensive survey of hillfort interiors in central southern England*, 151–62. London, English Heritage.

Cunliffe, B. 2013. *Britain begins*. Oxford, Oxford University Press.

Curle, A. and Cree, J. 1921. Account of the excavations on Traprain Law during the summer of 1920. *Proceedings of the Antiquaries of Scotland* 55, 153–206.

Czebreszuk, J. 2013. The Bronze Age in the Polish lands. In Fokkens, H. and Harding, A. (eds), *Oxford handbook of the European Bronze Age*, 767–86. Oxford, Oxford University Press.

Czebreszuk, C. and Müller, J. (eds.), 2004. *Bruszczewo. Ausgrabungen und Forschungen in einer prähistorischen Siedlungskammer Grosspolens/Badania mikroregionu z terenu Wielkopolski. Band/Tom I. Forschungsstand – Erste Ergebnisse – Das östliche Feuchtbodenareal/Stan badán – Pierwsze wyniki – Wschodnia, torfowa część stanowiska.* Poznań-Kiel-Rahden (Westf.), Verlag Marie Leidorf.

Danaher, E. 2007. *Monumental beginnings: the archaeology of the N4 Sligo Inner Relief Road*. Dublin, National Roads Authority.

Davies, P., Robb, J.G. and Ladbrook, D. 2005. Woodland clearance in the Mesolithic: the social aspects. *Antiquity* 79, 280–88.

Davis, O. and Sharples, N. 2017. Early Neolithic enclosures in Wales: a review of the evidence in light of recent discoveries at Caerau, Cardiff. *The Antiquaries Journal* 97, 1–26.

Davis, S. and Moore, C. 2024. *Excavations at Tlachtga,*

Hill of Ward, Co. Meath. Oxford, Oxbow.

Della Casa, P. 2013. Switzerland and the central Alps. In Fokkens, H. and Harding, A. (eds), *Oxford handbook of the European Bronze Age*, 706–22. Oxford, Oxford University Press.

Delrieu, F. 2013. Chronologie et statut des sites fortifiés de hauteur au Bronze final et au 1er Fer ancien dans le Nord-Ouestd e la France (Haute-Normandie, Basse-Normandie et Bretagne). In Krause, S., Colin, A., Gruel, K., Ralston, I. and Dechezleprêtre, T. (eds), *L'âge du Fer en Europe, mélanges offerts à Olivier Buchsenschutz*, 131–46. Mémoires 32. Pessac, Ausonius Editions.

Denslow, J.S., Ellison, A.M. and Sanford, R.E. 1998. Treefall gap size effects on above- and below-ground processes in a tropical wet forest. *Journal of Ecology* 86, 597–609.

Diemer, G. 1995. *Der Bullenheimer Berg und seine Stellung im Siedlungsgefüge der Urnenfelderkultur Mainfrankens*. Materialhefte zur Bayerischen Vorgeschichte A 70. Kallmünz/Opf.: Lassleben.

Dixon, P. 1976. Crickley Hill, 1969–1972. In Harding, D. (ed.), *Hillforts: later prehistoric earthworks in Britain and Ireland*, 162–75. London, Academic Press.

Dixon, P. 1988. The Neolithic settlements on Crickley Hill. In Burgess, C., Topping, P., Mordant, C. and Maddison, C. (eds), *Enclosures and defences in the Neolithic of Western Europe*, 75–89. British Archaeological Reports 403. Oxford, Archaeopress.

Dixon, P. 1994. *Crickley Hill:* Vol. 1. *The hillfort defences*. Nottingham, Crickley Hill Trust and Department of Archaeology, University Of Nottingham.

Dodson, J.R. 1990. The Holocene vegetation of a prehistorically inhabited valley, Dingle Peninsula, Co. Kerry. *Proceedings of the Royal Irish Academy* 90B, 151–74.

Doody, M. 2008. *The Ballyhoura Hills project*. Dublin, Wordwell.

Douda, J., Doudova, J., Drasnarova, A., Kunes, P., Hadincova, V., *et al.* 2014. Migration patterns of subgenus *Alnus* in Europe since the last glacial maximum: a systematic review. *PLoS One* 9. Available online:https://journals.plos.org/plosone/article?id=10.1371/journal.pone.0088709 [last accessed 2 June 2024].

Dowling, G. and Schot, R. 2023. Gathering ground: unearthing 3000 years of prehistory at Faughan Hill, eastern Ireland. *Proceedings of the Prehistoric Society* 89, 1–44.

Drewett, P. 1977. The excavation of a Neolithic causewayed enclosure on Offham Hill, East Sussex. *Proceedings of the Prehistoric Society* 43, 201–41.

Drury, C. 1905. County Wicklow archaeological notes around Kiltegan. *Journal of the Kildare Archaeological Society* 4 (5), 352–8.

Dular, J. and Tomanič Jevremov, M. 2010. *Ormož. Utrjeno naselje iz pozne bronaste in starejše železne dobe*. Opera Instituti Archaeologici Sloveniae 18. Ljubljana, Založba ZRC.

Dunne, L. and Bartlett, T. 2009. Knockanacuig/Lohercannan hillfort. In Bennett, I. (ed.), *Excavations 2006*, 226–7. Dublin, Wordwell.

Dunne, J., Gillard, T. and Evershed, R.P. 2021. Organic residue analysis of an Early Neolithic vessel from Rathcoran, Co. Wicklow. Unpublished report prepared for Alan Hawkes, Rathcoran Hillfort Project. Organic Geochemistry Unit, School of Chemistry, University of Bristol.

Dwyer, R.B. and Mitchell, F.J.G. 1997. Investigation of the environmental impact of remote volcanic activity on north Mayo, Ireland, during the mid-Holocene. *The Holocene* 7, 113–18.

Edwards, K.J. 1981. The separation of *Corylus* and *Myrica* pollen in modern and fossil samples. *Pollen et Spores* 23, 205–18.

Eogan, G. 1965. *Catalogue of Irish bronze swords*. Dublin, Stationery Office.

Eogan, G. 1983. *The hoards of the Irish Later Bronze Age*. Dublin, University College Dublin.

Eogan, G. 1994. *The accomplished art: gold and gold-working in Britain and Ireland during the Bronze Age. Oxford,* Oxbow.

Eogan, G. 2000. *The socketed bronze axes in Ireland*. Prähistorische Bronzefunde 9, 22. Stuttgart, Franz Steiner Verlag.

Evans, E. 1953. *Lyles Hill: a Late Neolithic site in County Antrim*. Archaeological Research Publications 2. Belfast, Her Majesty's Stationery Office.

Evans, J., Rouse, A. and Sharples, N. 1988. The landscape setting of causewayed camps: recent work on the Maiden Castle enclosure. In Barrett, J. and Kinnes, I. (eds), *The archaeology of context in the Neolithic and Bronze Age: recent trends*, 73–84. Sheffield, University of Sheffield.

Evans, N. 2014. *A historical introduction to the Northern*

Picts. Aberdeen, University of Aberdeen.

Eyjólfsdóttir, E. 2012. The Bóruma: the poetry and the hagiography in the Book of Leinster. Unpublished PhD Thesis, University of Glasgow.

Fægri, K., Iversen, J., Kaland, P. and Krywinski, K. 1989. *Textbook of pollen analysis*. Chichester, Wiley.

Feachem, R. 1958. The fortifications of Traprain Law. *Proceedings of the Society of Antiquaries of Scotland* 89, 284–9.

Feachem, R. 1971. Unfinished hill-forts. In Jesson, M. and Hill, D. (eds), *The Iron Age and its hill-forts: papers presented to Sir Mortimer Wheeler*, 19–39. Southampton, Millbrook Press.

Feeney-Johnson, C. 2012. Amber beads. In Cotter, C. *The western stone forts project: excavations at Dún Aonghasa and Dún Eoghanachta* (vol 2), 93–98. Dublin, Wordwell.

Feeser, I. and Dörfler, W. 2014. The glade effect: vegetation openness and structure and their influences on arboreal pollen production and the reconstruction of anthropogenic forest opening. *Anthropocene* 8, 92–100.

Fernándes-Götz, M. 2014. Understanding the Heuneburg: a biographical approach. In M. Fernández-Götz, Wendling, H. and Winger, K. (eds), *Paths to complexity: centralisation and urbanisation in Iron Age Europe*, 24–34. Oxford, Oxbow Books.

Fernández-Götz, M. and Krausse, D. 2012. Heuneburg: first city north of the Alps. *Current Archaeology* 55, 28–34.

Fernándes-Götz, M. and Ralston, I. 2017. The complexity and fragility of Early Iron Age urbanism in west-central temperate Europe. *Journal of World Prehistory* 30, 259–79.

Fernándes-Götz, M., Wendling, H. and Winger, K. 2014. Introduction: new perspectives on Iron Age urbanisation. In Fernández-Götz, M., Wendling, H. and Winger, K. (eds), *Paths to complexity: centralisation and urbanisation in Iron Age Europe*, 2–14. Oxford, Oxbow Books.

Fernándes-Götz, M., Maschek, D. and Roymans, N. 2020. The dark side of the empire: Roman expansionism between object agency and predatory regime. *Antiquity* 94 (378), 1630–39.

FitzGerald, W. 1908a. Baltinglass Hill. *Journal of the Kildare Archaeological Society* 5, 352–3.

FitzGerald, W. 1908b. Baltinglass Abbey, its possessions, and their post-Reformation proprietors. *Journal of the County Kildare Archaeological Society* 6, 378–414.

FitzPatrick, E. 2004. *Royal inauguration in Gaelic Ireland, c.1100–1600: a cultural landscape study*. Woodbridge. Boydell Press.

Flanagan, D. 1984. The Christian impact on Early Ireland: place-name evidence. In Ní Chatháin, P. and Richter, M. (eds), *Ireland and Europe: the early church*, 25–52. Stuttgart. Stuttgart University Press.

Flood, R. 2009. Aspects of the Irish hillfort: a reappraisal in light of recent research in the Upper Slaney Valley. Unpublished MLitt thesis. University College Dublin.

Fossitt, J. 1994. Late-glacial and Holocene vegetational history of western Donegal, Ireland. *Biology and Environment: Proceedings of the Royal Irish Academy* 94B, 1–31.

Fox, A. 1976. *Prehistoric Māori fortifications in the North Island of New Zealand*. New Zealand Archaeological Association Monograph 6. Auckland, Longman Paul.

Gear, A.J. and Huntley, B. 1991. Rapid changes in the range limits of Scots pine 4000 years ago. *Science* 251, 544–7.

Gearey, B., Hopla, E.J. and Marshall, P. 2010. Palynological analyses of deposits from Clowanstown I, Kilmainham 1c and Lismullin I: M3 Clonee to north of Kells motorway scheme. Final report, volume 2: Appendices. Unpublished report, Birmingham Archaeo-Environmental on behalf of Archaeology Consultancy Services Ltd for Meath County Council and the National Roads Authority.

Gerlach, S. 1998. Urnenfelderzeitliche Höhensiedlungen Nordbayerns in ihrem siedlungsgeschichtlichen Zusammenhang. In Schmotz, K. (ed.), *Vorträge des 16. Niederbayerischen Archäologentages* 125–56. Rahden/Westf., Verlag Marie Leidorf.

Ghilardi, B. and O'Connell, M. 2013. Fine-resolution pollen-analytical study of Holocene woodland dynamics and land use in north Sligo, Ireland. *Boreas* 42, 623–49.

Ginn, V. and Rathbone, S. 2011. *Corrstown: a coastal community. Excavations of a Bronze Age village in Northern Ireland*. Oxford, Oxbow.

Girling, M.A. 1988. The bark beetle *Scolytus scolytus* (*Fabricius*) and the possible role of elm disease in the early Neolithic. In Jones, M. (ed.), *Archaeology and the flora of the British Isles*, 34–38. Oxford University Committee for Archaeology Monograph 14. Oxford, Oxford University Press.

Girling, M.A. and Greig, J. 1985. A first fossil record for

Scolytus scolytus (*F.*) (elm bark beetle): its occurrence in elm decline deposits from London and the implications for Neolithic elm disease. *Journal of Archaeological Science* 12, 347–51.

Gleeson, P. 2014. Assembly and elite culture in late Antique Europe: a case study of Óenach Clochair. *Journal of Irish Archaeology* 23, 171–87.

Gleeson, P. 2015. Kingdoms, communities and *óenaig*: Irish assembly practices in a northwest European context. *Journal of the North Atlantic* 8, 33–51.

Gleeson, P. 2017a. Luigne Breg and the origins of the Uí Néill. *Proceedings of the Prehistoric Society* 117C, 1–35.

Gleeson, P. 2017b. Gathering the nations: towards an archaeology of assembly in Early Medieval Ireland. In Beglane, F. (ed.), *Gatherings: past and present*, 72–85. British Archaeological Reports International Series 2832. Oxford, Archaeopress.

Gleeson, P. and Ó Carragáin, T. 2016. Conversion and consolidation in Leinster's royal heartland. In Ó Carragáin, T. and Turner, S. (eds), *Making Christian landscapes in Atlantic Europe: conversion and consolidation in the Early Middle* Ages, 75–108. Cork. Cork University Press,.

Gogâltan, F. 2008. Fortified Bronze Age Tell settlements in the Carpathian Basin. A general overview. In Czebreszuk, J., Kadrow, S. and Müller, J. (eds), *Defensive structures from Central Europe to the Aegean in the 3rd and 2nd millenium BC*, 39–56. Poznań, Wydawnictwo Poznańskie.

Grabowski, K. 1990. The historical overview of Dún Ailinne. *Emania* 8, 32–6.

Green, T. 1787. Account of an ancient urn found in the parish of Kilranelagh in the County of Wicklow. *Transactions of the Royal Irish Academy* 1, 161–2.

Greene, D. 1955. *Fingal Rónáin and other stories.* Medieval and Modern Irish Series 16. Dublin, Dublin Institute for Advanced Studies.

Griffiths, S. and Gearey, B. 2017. The Mesolithic–Neolithic transition and the chronology of the 'Elm decline' from Yorkshire and Humberside, United Kingdom. *Radiocarbon* 59, 1321–45.

Grimm, E.C. 2013. *Tilia and TGView*. Springfield, Illinois State Museum.

Grogan, E. 2004. Middle Bronze Age burial traditions in Ireland. In Roche, H., Grogan, E., Bradley, J., Coles, J. and Raftery, B. (eds), *From megaliths to metals: essays in honour of George Eogan*, 61–71. Oxford, Oxbow.

Grogan, E. 2005a. *The North Munster project.* Volume 1*: The late prehistoric landscape of south-east Clare.* Dublin, Wordwell.

Grogan, E. 2005b. *The North Munster project.* Volume 2: *The prehistoric landscape of North Munster.* Dublin, Wordwell.

Grogan, E. 2021. The prehistoric pottery from Rathcoran Hillfort, Co. Wicklow (2020 season). Unpublished report prepared for Alan Hawkes, Rathcoran Hillfort Project.

Grogan, E. 2022. The prehistoric pottery from Rathcoran Hillfort, Co. Wicklow (2021 season). Unpublished report prepared for Alan Hawkes, Rathcoran Hillfort Project.

Grogan, E. and Daly, A. 2005. Excavations at Clenagh, Co. Clare. In Grogan, E., *The North Munster Project.* Volume 1: *The late prehistoric landscape of south-east Clare*, 247–63. Dublin, Wordwell.

Grogan, E. and Hillery 1993. *A guide to the archaeology of County Wicklow*. Wicklow. Wicklow County Tourism Ltd.

Grogan, E. and Kilfeather, A. 1997. *Archaeological inventory of County Wicklow*. Dublin, The Stationery Office.

Grogan, E. and Roche, H. 2009. Clay and fire: the development and distribution of pottery traditions in prehistoric Ireland. In M. Stanley, E. Danagher and J. Eogan (eds), *Creative minds: production, manufacture and invention in ancient Ireland*, 27–45. Dublin, National Roads Authority.

Hall, V.A. 1989. Study of the modern pollen rain from a reconstructed 19th-century farm. *Irish Naturalists' Journal* 23, 82–92.

Halliday, S. 1985. Unenclosed upland settlement in the east and south-east of Scotland. In Spratt, D. and Burgess, C. (eds), *Upland settlement in Britain—the second millennium BC and after*, 231–52. British Archaeological Reports 143. Oxford, Archaeopress.

Harding, A. 2000. *European societies in the Bronze Age*. Cambridge, Cambridge University Press.

Harding, A. 2001. Reformation in Barbarian Europe. In Cunliffe, B. (ed.), *Oxford illustrated history of prehistoric Europe*, 304–35. Oxford. Oxford University Press.

Harding, A. 2006. Enclosing and excluding in Bronze Age Europe. In Harding, A. Sievers, S. and Venclová, N. (eds), *Enclosing the past: inside and outside in prehistory*, 97–115. Sheffield, Collis Publications.

Harding, A. and Razckowski, W. 2010. Living in the lake in the Iron Age: new results from aerial photographs, geophysical survey and dendrochronology on sites of Biskupin type. *Antiquity* 84, 386–404.

Harding, A., Šumberová, R., Outram, A. and Knüsel, C. 2007. *Velim: violence and death in Bronze Age Bohemia: the results of fieldwork 1992–95, with a consideration of peri-mortem trauma and deposition in the Bronze Age.* Prague, Prague Institute of Archaeology.

Harding, D.W. 2012. *Iron Age hillforts in Britain and beyond.* Oxford, Oxford University Press.

Härke, H. 1979. *Settlement types and patterns in the West Hallstatt province.* Oxford, Archaeopress.

Harrington, M. 1937. Finds of skulls in Goldenfort, Co. Wicklow. *Journal of the Royal Society of Antiquaries of Ireland* 7, 127.

Hartnett, P. 1952. Bronze Age burials in Co. Wicklow. *Journal of the Royal Society of Antiquaries of Ireland* 82, 153–62.

Hawkes, A. 2018. *The archaeology of prehistoric burnt mounds in Ireland.* Oxford, Archaeopress.

Hayden, A. 1994. 230: Kilnacarrig. In Bennett, I. (ed.), *Excavations 1993. Summary accounts of archaeological excavations in Ireland*, 80. Bray, Wordwell.

Heath, J. 2009. *Warfare in prehistoric Britain.* Gloucestershire, Amberley Publishing.

Heery, A. 1997. The vegetation history of two small lakes sites adjacent to eskers in Central Ireland. *Quaternary Newsletter*, 33–36.

Herity, M. 1974. *Irish passage graves.* Dublin, Irish University Press.

Hogan, E. 1910. *Onomasticon Goedelicum.* Dublin, Four Courts Press.

Hogg, A. 1960. Garn Boduan and Tre'r Ceiri, excavations at two Caernarvonshire hill-forts. *Archaeological Journal* 117, 1–39.

Hogg, A., 1975. *Hillforts of Britain.* London, Hart-Davis.

Holland, C. 2003. *The Irish landscape: a scenery to celebrate.* Edinburgh, Dunedin Academic Press.

Hopewell, D. 1993. Tre'r Ceiri conservation project. *Archaeology in Wales* 33, 49–50.

Innes, J.B., Blackford, J.J. and Rowley-Conwy, P. 2003. The start of the Mesolithic–Neolithic transition in north-west Europe—the palynological contribution. *Antiquity* 77, 297.

Jackson, P., Parkes, M. and Simms, M. 2010. *Geology of Ireland: county by county.* Dublin, Trinity College Dublin.

Jacobson, G.L. and Bradshaw, R.H.W. 1981. The selection of sites for paleovegetational studies. *Quaternary Research* 16, 80–96.

Jessen, K. 1949. Studies in Late Quaternary deposits and flora-history of Ireland. *Proceedings of the Royal Irish Academy* 52B, 85–290.

Jiráň, L., Salaš, M. and Krenn-Leeb, A. 2013. The Czech lands and Austria in the Bronze Age. In Fokkens, H. and Harding, A. (eds), *Oxford handbook of the European Bronze* Age, 785–812. Oxford, Oxford University Press.

Jockenhövel, A. 1990. Bronzezeitlicher Burgenbau in Mitteleuropa: Untersuchungen zur Struktur Frühmetallzeitlicher Gesellschaften, 209–28. *Orientalisch-Ägäische Einflüsse in der Europäischen Bronzezeit, Bd.* 15. Bonn, Tiberius Bader (Hrsg).

Jockenhövel, A. 2013. Germany in the Bronze Age. In Fokkens, H. and Harding, A. (eds), *Oxford handbook of the European Bronze Age*, 723–45. Oxford, Oxford University Press.

Johnston, S. and Wailes, B. 2007. *Dún Ailinne: excavations at the Irish royal site, 1968–1975.* Philadelphia, University of Pennsylvania Museum of Archaeology and Anthropology.

Kearney, K. and Gearey, B. 2020. The Elm Decline is dead! Long live declines in elm: revisiting the chronology of the Elm Decline in Ireland and its association with the Mesolithic/Neolithic transition. *Environmental Archaeology: the Journal of Human Palaeoecology.* Available online: https://doi.org/10.1080/14614103.2020.1721694 [last accessed 2 June 2024].

Kearney, K., Gearey, B., Hegarty, S., Richer, R., Ferreira, C., *et al.* 2022. A multi-proxy Holocene palaeoenvironmental record of climate change and prehistoric human activity from Lough Cullin, southeast Ireland. *The Holocene* 32 (4), 262–79.

Knipper, C., Meyer, C., Jacobi, F., Roth, C., Fecher, M., *et al.* 2014. Social differentiation and land use at an Early Iron Age 'princely seat': bioarchaeological investigations at the Glauberg (Germany). *Journal of Archaeological Science* 41, 818–35.

Krämer , W. 2002. The *oppidum* of Manching: *Antiquity* 34 (135), 1960. In Carr, G. and Stoddart, S. (eds), *Celts from Antiquity: Antiquity papers 2*, 63–77. Cambridge, Antiquities Publications Ltd.

Krause, R. 2008. Bronze Age hillforts in the Alps. In

Czebreszuk, J., Kadrow, S. and Müller (eds), *Defensive structures from Central Europe to the Aegean in the 3rd and 2nd millennium BC*, 65–84. Poznań, Wydawnictwo Poznańskie.

Kristiansen, K. 1999. The emergence of warrior aristocracies in later European prehistory and their long-term history. In Carman, J. and Harding, A. (eds), *Ancient warfare*, 175–89. Stroud, The History Press.

Kristiansen, K. and Larsson, T. 2005. *The rise of Bronze Age society: travels, transmissions and transformations*. Cambridge, Cambridge University Press.

Lacey, B. 2006. *Cenél Conaill and the Donegal kingdoms AD 500–800.* Dublin, Four Courts Press.

Lageard, J.G.A., Chambers, F.M. and Thomas, P.A. 1999. Climatic significance of the marginalization of Scots pine (*Pinus sylvestris L.*) *c.*2508 BC at White Moss, south Cheshire, UK. *The Holocene* 9, 321–31.

Lane, A. and Cambell, E. 2000. *Dunadd: an early Dalriadic capital.* Cardiff, Cardiff Studies in Archaeology.

Last. J. (ed.) 2022. *Marking place: new perspectives on Early Neolithic enclosures*. Oxford, Oxbow Books.

Leask, H.G. 1945. Stone circle, Castleruddery, Co. Wicklow. *Journal of the Royal Society of Antiquaries of Ireland* 75, 266–7.

Leira, M., Cole, E.E. and Mitchell, F.J.G. 2007. Long term impacts of atmospheric deposition and peat erosion on an oligotrophic lake in eastern Ireland. *Journal of Paleolimnology* 38, 49–71.

Lewis, S. 1837. *A topographical dictionary of Ireland* (2 vols). Dublin, S. Lewis and Co.

Lineen, J. 2016. Spearheads in the landscape: a contextual analysis. MPhil thesis, Department of Archaeology, University College Cork. Available online: www.academia.edu/33591964/Spearheads_in_the_Landscape_a_Contextual_Analysis [last accessed 2 June 2024].

Lock, G. 2011. Hillforts, emotional metaphors and the good life: a response to Armit. *Proceedings of the Prehistoric Society* 77, 355–62.

Lock, G. and Ralston, I. 2022. *Atlas of the hillforts of Britain and Ireland.* Edinburgh, Edinburgh University Press.

Logue, P. 2003. Excavation at Thornhill, Co. Londonderry. In Armit, I., Murphy, E., Neilis, E. and Simpson, D. (eds), *Neolithic settlement in Ireland and Western Britain*, 149–55. Oxford, Oxbow.

Loveday, R. 2015. Religious routine and pilgrimage in the British Isles. In Fowler, C., Harding, J. and Hofmann, D. (eds), *Oxford handbook of Neolithic Europe*, 463–79. Oxford, Oxford University Press.

Lucas, A.T. 1960. Burial mound at Rathmoon, Co. Wicklow. *Journal of the Royal Society of Antiquaries of Ireland* 90, 84–8.

Lucas, A.T. 1961. National Museum of Ireland archaeological acquisitions in the year 1959. *Journal of the Royal Society of Antiquaries of Ireland* 91, 68–107.

Lucas, A.T. 1971. National Museum of Ireland archaeological acquisitions in the year 1968. *Journal of the Royal Society of Antiquaries of Ireland* 101, 184–244.

Lucas, A.T. 1989. *Cattle in ancient Ireland.* Suffolk, Boethius Press.

Lull, V., Micó, R., Rihuete Herrada, R. and Risch, R. 2013. Bronze Age Iberia. In Fokkens, H. and Harding, A. (eds), *Oxford handbook of the European Bronze Age*, 594–616. Oxford, Oxford University Press.

Lynch, A. 1981. *Man and environment in S.W. Ireland.* British Archaeological Reports (British series) 85. Oxford, Archaeopress.

Lynch, E. 2019. The prehistoric pottery from Rathcoran, Co. Wicklow (2019 season). Unpublished report prepared for Alan Hawkes, Rathcoran Hillfort Project.

Lynch, F., Aldhouse-Green, S. and Davis, J. 2000. *Prehistoric Wales.* Gloucestershire, Sutton Publishing.

Lynn, C. 1977. Trial excavations at the King's Stables, Tray townland, County Armagh. *Ulster Journal of Archaeology* 40, 42–62.

Lynn, C. 2003. *Navan Fort: archaeology and myth.* Bray, Wordwell.

Lyons, S. 2022. Charcoal and plant macrofossil analysis, Rathcoran hillfort. Unpublished report prepared for Alan Hawkes, Rathcoran Hillfort Project.

Macalister, R.A.S. 1928. *The archaeology of Ireland.* London, Methuen.

Macalister, R.A.S. 1945. *Corpus inscriptionum insularum Celticarum.* Dublin, The Stationery Office.

MacCotter, P. 2008. *Medieval Ireland: territorial, political and economic divisions.* Dublin, Four Courts Press.

MacDonald, P. 2016. Excavations at Knock Dhu promontory fort, Ballyhackett, Co. Antrim, 2008. *Emania* 23, 33–52.

MacShamhráin, A. 1996. *Church and polity in pre-Norman Ireland: the case of Glendalough.* Maynooth Monographs 7. Maynooth. An Sagart.

McClatchie, M., Bogaard, A., Colledge, S., Whitehouse,

N.J., Schulting, R.J., *et al.* 2014. Neolithic farming in north-western Europe: archaeobotanical evidence from Ireland. *Journal of Archaeological Science* 51, 206–15.

McCormick, F. and Murray, E. 2007. *Knowth and the zooarchaeology of Early Christian Ireland. Excavations at Knowth 3.* Dublin, Royal Irish Academy.

McCorry, M. 1997. Coarse ware pottery from Phase 3. In Waterman, D.M., *Excavations at Navan Fort 1961–71, County Armagh*, 72–79. Belfast, The Stationery Office.

McGeever, A.H. and Mitchell, F.J.G. 2016. Re-defining the natural range of Scots Pine *(Pinus sylvestris L.)*: a newly discovered microrefugium in western Ireland. *Journal of Biogeography* 43, 2199–208.

McLaughlin, T.R., Whitehouse, N.J., Schulting, R.J., McClatchie, M., Barratt, P. and Bogaard, A. 2016. The changing face of Neolithic and Bronze Age Ireland: a big data approach to the settlement and burial records. *Journal of World Prehistory* 29, 117–53.

McNally, A. and Doyle, G.J. 1984. A study of subfossil pine layers in a raised bog complex in the Irish midlands: 1. Palaeowoodland extent and dynamics. 2. Seral relationships and floristics. *Proceedings of the Royal Irish Academy* 84B, 57–70.

McNeary. R. 2014. LiDAR investigation of Knockdhu promontory and its environs, County Antrim. *Archaeological Prospection* 21, 263–76.

McQuade. M. 2008. Rampere burnt mounds, Co. Wicklow. In Bennett, I. (ed.), *Excavations 2005*, 420. Dublin, Wordwell.

McSparron, C. 2008. Have you no homes to go to? Neolithic housing. *Archaeology Ireland* 22, 18–21.

Mahr, A. and Price, L. 1932. Excavations of urn burials at Clonshannon, Imaal, Co. Wicklow. *Journal of the Royal Society of Antiquaries of Ireland* 62, 75–90.

Mallory, J.P. 1995. Haughey's Fort and the Navan Complex in the Late Bronze Age. In Waddell, J. and Shee Twohig, E. (eds), *Ireland in the Bronze Age*, 73–86. Dublin, The Stationery Office.

Mallory, J.P. 2000. Excavations of the Navan Ditch. *Emania* 18, 21–36.

Mallory, J.P. and Baban, G. 2014. Excavations in Haughey's Fort East. *Emania* 22, 13–32.

Mallory, J.P., Nelis, E. and Hartwell, B. 2011. *Excavations on Donegore Hill, Co. Antrim.* Dublin, Wordwell.

Manby, T. 2007. Continuity of monumental traditions into the late Bronze Age? Henges to ring-forts, and shrines. In Burgess, C., Topping, P. and Lynch, F. (eds), *Beyond Stonehenge: essays on the Bronze Age in honour of Colin Burgess*, 403–24. Oxford, Oxbow Books.

Marsh, R. 2007. *Tales of the Wicklow hills: 2000 years of history, myth, legend and local stories.* New York, Syracuse University Press.

Mason, P. 2013. The power and the glory: hillforts, ironworking and the monumental landscape in the Early Iron Age of central and south eastern Slovenia. In Gheorghiu, D. and Nash, G. (eds), *Place as material culture: objects, geographies and the construction of time*, 258–76. Newcastle, Cambridge Scholars Publishing.

Matuz, E. and Nováki, G. 2002. *Spätbronzezeitliche, früheisenzeitliche Erdwälle in Nordungarn. Inventaria praehistorica Hungariae* 10. Budapest, Magyar Nemzeti Múzeum.

Mercer, R. 1980. *Hambledon Hill: a Neolithic landscape.* Edinburgh, Edinburgh University Press.

Mercer, R. 1981. The excavations of a late Neolithic henge type enclosure at Balfarg, Markinch, Fife, Scotland. *Proceedings of the Society of Antiquaries of Scotland* 111, 63–171.

Mercer, R. 1988. Hambledon Hill, Dorset, England. In Burgess, C., Topping, P., Mordant, C. and Maddison, C. (eds), *Enclosures and defences in the Neolithic of Western Europe*, 89–107. British Archaeological Reports 403. Oxford, Archaeopress.

Mercer, R. 1999. The origins of warfare in the British Isles, In Carman, J. and Harding, A. (eds), *Ancient warfare: archaeological perspectives*, 143–56. Stroud, The History Press.

Mercer, R. 2003. The early farming settlement of south-west England. In Armit, I., Murphy, E., Nelis, E. and Simpson, D. (eds), *Neolithic settlement in Ireland and Western Britain*, 56–70. Oxford, Oxbow Books..

Mercer, R. and Tipping, R. 1994. The prehistory of soil erosion in the northern and eastern Cheviot Hills, Anglo-Scottish Borders. In Foster, S. and Smout, T. (eds), *The history of soils and field systems*, 1–24. Aberdeen, Scottish Cultural Press.

Metzner-Nebelsick, C. 2012. Social transition and spatial organisation: the problem of the Early Iron Age occupation of the strongholds in Northeast Hungary. In Anreiter, P., Bánffy, E., Bartosiewicz, L., Meid, W. and Metzner-Nebelsick, C. (eds), *Archaeological, cultural and linguistic heritage: Festschrift for Erzsébet Jerem in honor of her 70th birthday*, 425–48. Vienna,

Innsbrucker Beiträge zur Kulturwissenschaft.

Mighall, T.M., Lageard, J.G.A., Chambers, F.M., Field, M.H. and Mahi, P. 2004. Mineral deficiency and the presence of *Pinus sylvestris* on mires during the mid- to late Holocene: palaeoecological data from Cadogan's Bog, Mizen Peninsula, Co. Cork, south-west Ireland. *The Holocene* 14, 95–109.

Mighall, T., Timpany, S., Blackford, J., Innes, J., O'Brien, C., *et al.* 2008. Vegetation change during the Mesolithic and Neolithic on the Mizen Peninsula, Co. Cork, south-west Ireland. *Vegetation History and Archaeobotany* 17, 617–28.

Miket, R. 2013. Understanding British/Anglo-Saxon continuity at Gefrin: Brian Hope-Taylor's excavations on Yeavering Bell. *Archaeologia Aeliana* 5 (42), 133–60.

Mitchell, F.J.G. and Cooney, T. 2004. Vegetation history in the Killarney Valley. In O'Brien, W. *Ross Island: mining, metal and society in Early Ireland*, 481–92. Bronze Age Studies 6. Galway, National University of Ireland Galway.

Mitchell, G.F. 1942. A composite pollen diagram from Co. Meath, Ireland. *New Phytologist* 41, 257–61.

Mitchell, G.F. 1951. Studies in Irish Quaternary deposits: No.7. *Proceedings of the Royal Irish Academy* 53B, 111–206.

Mitchell, G.F. 1954. Post-Boreal pollen-diagrams from Irish raised bog. Studies in Irish Quaternary deposits: No. 11. *Proceedings of the Royal Irish Academy* 57B, 185–251.

Mitchell, G.F. and Ryan, M. 1997. *Reading the Irish landscape* (3rd edition). Dublin, Country House.

Mohen, J. and Bailloud, G. 1987. *La vie quotidienne: les fouilles du Fort-Harrouard. Collection L'âge du Bronze en France*, 4; Picard, J. (ed.). France, Éditions Picard.

Molloy, B., Jovanović, D., Bruyère, C., Marić, M., Bulatović, J., *et al.* 2020. A new Bronze Age mega-fort in southeastern Europe: recent archaeological investigations at Gradište Iđoš and their regional significance. *Journal of Field Archaeology* 45 (4), 293–314.

Molloy, K. 2005. Holocene vegetation and land-use history at Mooghaun, south-east Clare, with particular reference to the Bronze Age. In Grogan, E. *The North Munster project.* Volume 1: *The later prehistoric landscape of south-east Clare*, 255–87. Bray, Wordwell.

Molloy, K. 2008. Palaeoenvironments. In Doody, M. (ed.), *The Ballyhoura Hills project*, 23–30. Bray, Wordwell.

Molloy, K. and O'Connell, M. 1987. The nature of the vegetational changes at about 5000 B.P. with particular reference to the Elm Decline: fresh evidence from Connemara, Western Ireland. *New Phytologist* 107, 203–20.

Molloy, K. and O'Connell, M. 1991. Palaeoecological investigations towards the reconstruction of woodland and land-use history at Lough Sheeauns, Connemara, western Ireland. *Review of Palaeobotany and Palynology* 67, 75–113.

Molloy, K. and O'Connell, M. 1995. Palaeoecological investigations towards the reconstruction of environment and land-use changes during prehistory at Céide Fields, western Ireland. *Probleme der Küstenforschung im südlichen Nordseegebiet* 23, 187–225.

Molloy, K. and O'Connell, M. 2004. Holocene vegetation and land-use dynamics in the karstic environment of Inis Oírr, Aran Islands, western Ireland: pollen analytical evidence evaluated in light of the archaeological record. *Quaternary International* 113, 41–64.

Molloy, K. and O'Connell, M. 2007. Fresh insights into long-term environmental change on the Aran Islands based on palaeoecological investigations of lake sediments from Inis Oírr. *Journal of the Galway Archaeological and Historical Society* 59, 1–17.

Molloy, K., Feeser, I. and O'Connell, M. 2014. A pollen profile from Ballinphuill bog: vegetation and land-use history. In McKeon, J. and O'Sullivan, J. (eds), *The quiet landscape: archaeological and palaeoecological investigations on the M6 Galway to Ballinasloe motorway scheme* (on CD-ROM: /documents/3/Pollen-analysis-Ballinphuil-bog.pdf). NRA Scheme Monographs 15. Dublin, National Roads Authority.

Mooney, S. and Tinner, W. 2011. The analysis of charcoal in peat and organic sediments. *Mires Peat* 7, 1–18.

Moore, D.G. 2004. Hostilities in Early Neolithic Ireland: trouble with the new neighbours. The evidence from Ballyharry, County Antrim. In Gibson, A. and Sheridan, A. (eds), *From sickles to circles: Britain and Ireland at the time of Stonehenge*, 142–54. Tempus, Stroud.

Moore, P., Webb, J. and Collinson, M. 1991. *Pollen analysis* (2nd edition). Oxford, Blackwell Scientific.

Moosauer, M. and Bachmaier, T. 2000. *Bernstorf. Die Versunkene Stadt Uas Der Bronzezeit.* Stuttgart, University of Stuttgart.

Müller, R. 2006. A Várvölgy-Nagy-Lázhegyen feltárt későbronzkori magaslati településrészlet szerkezete. *Zalai Muzeum* 15, 189–201.

Müller, J. and Czebreszuk, C. 2010. Bruszczewo und Łęki Male—Ein frühbronzezeitliches Machtzentrum in Großpolen. In Meller, H. and Bertemes, F. (eds), *Der Griff nach den Sternen: Internationales Symposium in Halle (Saale) 16.–21. Februar 2005*, 381–96. Halle, Tagungen des Landesmuseums für Vorgeschichte Halle.

Mullins, G. 2008. Three thousand years of human activity at Rahally, Co. Galway. In O'Sullivan, J. and Stanley, M. *Roads, rediscovery and research: proceedings of a public seminar on archaeological discoveries on National Road Schemes, August 2007*, 25–35. Dublin, National Roads Authority.

Murphy, K., Mytum, H., Austin, L., Caseldine, A., Griffiths, C., *et al.* 2012. Iron Age enclosed settlements in west Wales. *Proceedings of the Prehistoric Society* 78, 263–313.

Musson, C. 1991. *The Breiddin Hillfort: a later prehistoric settlement in the Welsh Marshes.* London, Council for British Archaeology.

Mytum, H. 2013. *Monumentality in later prehistory: building and rebuilding Castell Henllys hillfort.* New York, Springer.

Neary, P. 2004. Archaeological excavations at Common of Lloyds, Co. Meath. Unpublished report prepared for Neary Archaeology Ltd.

Needham, S. 2007. 800 BC, the great divide. In Haselgrove, C. and Pope, R. (eds), *The Earlier Iron Age in Britain and the near continent*, 39–63. Oxford, Oxbow Books.

Needham, S. and Ambers, J. 1994. Redating Rams Hill and reconsidering Bronze Age enclosure. *Proceedings of the Prehistoric Society* 60, 225–43.

Newman, C. 1997. *Tara: an archaeological survey.* Bray, Wordwell.

Newman, C. 1998. Reflections on the making of a 'royal site' in early Ireland. *World Archaeology* 30, 127–41.

Newman, C. 1999. Notes on four cursus-like monuments in Co. Meath, Ireland. In Barclay, A. and Harding, J. (eds), *Pathways and ceremonies: the cursus monuments of Britain and Ireland*, 141–7. Oxford, Oxbow.

Noble, G. and O'Driscoll, J. 2019. Fortified settlement in early medieval Northern Britain and Ireland. In Lock, G. and Ralston, I. (eds), *Hillforts: Britain, Ireland and the nearer continent*, 97–116. Oxford, Archaeopress.

Noble, G. and O'Driscoll, J. forthcoming. Excavation at Tap o'Noth, Aberdeenshire and the Late Roman Iron Age urban-like centres of Northern Britain.

Noble, G., Gondek, M., Cambell, E. and Cook, M. 2013. Between prehistory and history: the archaeological detection of social change among the Picts. *Antiquity* 87, 1136–50.

Noble, G., O'Driscoll, J., MacIver, C., Masson-MacLean, E. and Sveinbjarnarson, O. 2020. New dates for enclosed sites in north-east Scotland: results of excavations by the Northern Picts project. *Society of Antiquaries of Scotland* 149, 165–96.

O'Brien, M.A. 1962. *Corpus genealogiarum Hiberniae.* Dublin, Dublin Institute for Advanced Studies.

O'Brien, W. 2004. (Con)fusion of tradition? The circle henge in Ireland. In Gibson, A. and Sheridan, A. (eds), *From sickles to circles: Britain and Ireland in the time of Stonehenge*, 323–38. Stroud, Tempus.

O'Brien, W. 2016. Clashanimud and the Bronze Age hillforts of Munster. *Emania* 23, 5–30.

O'Brien, W. 2017. The development of the hillfort in prehistoric Ireland. *Proceedings of the Royal Irish Academy* 117C, 1–59.

O'Brien, W. 2018. Hillforts and warfare in Bronze Age Ireland. In Hansen, S, and Krause, R. (eds), *Bronze Age Hillforts between the Taunus and Carpathian mountains*, 243–64. Proceedings of the 1st International LOEWE conference (Frankfurt 2016). Bonn, Verlag Dr. Rudolf Habelt GmbH.

O'Brien, W. 2022. Trade and the hillfort chiefdoms of Bronze Age Ireland. In Kristiansen, K. *et al.* (eds), *Trade before civilisation: long-distance exchange and the rise of social complexity*, 230–50. Proceedings of the Gothenberg 2016 conference. Cambridge, Cambridge University Press.

O'Brien, W. and Hogan, N. 2021. *Garranes: an early medieval royal site in south-west Ireland.* Oxford, Archaeopress.

O'Brien, W. and O'Driscoll J. 2017. *Hillforts, warfare and society in Bronze Age Ireland.* Oxford, Archaeopress.

O'Brien, W., Hogan, N. and O'Driscoll, J. 2014–5. Archaeological investigations at Toor More (Corrandhu) hillfort, Co. Kilkenny. *Journal of The Royal Society of Antiquaries of Ireland* 144 (5), 7–26.

O'Brien, W., Hogan, N. and O'Driscoll, J. 2016. Archaeological investigations at Ballylin hillfort, Co. Limerick. *North Munster Antiquarian Journal* 56, 1–26.

O'Brien, W., O'Driscoll, J. and Hogan, N. 2016. Glanbane hillfort and the Bronze Age in Kerry. *Journal of the Kerry Archaeological and Historical Society* 16, 77–105.

O'Brien, W. O'Driscoll J. and Hogan, N. 2018. Warfare and the burning of hillforts in Bronze Age Ireland. In Fernández-Götz, M. and Roymans, N. (eds), *Conflict archaeology: materialities of collective violence from prehistory to late antiquity*, 47–60. London, Routledge.

Ó Carragáin, T. 2009. Cemetery settlements and local churches in pre-Viking Ireland in light of comparisons with England and Wales. In Graham-Campbell, J. and Ryan, M. (eds), *Irish/Anglo-Saxon relations before the Vikings*, 239–61. Proceedings of the British Academy 157. Oxford, Oxford University Press.

Ó Carragáin, T. 2010. From family cemeteries to community cemeteries in Viking Age Ireland? In Corlett, C. and Potterton, M. (eds), *Death and burial in early medieval Ireland in light of recent archaeological excavations*, 217–26. Dublin, Wordwell.

O'Carroll, E. 2012. Quantifying woodland resource usage in the Irish midlands using archaeological and palaeoecological techniques. Unpublished PhD thesis, Trinity College, Dublin.

O'Connell, M. 1980. The developmental history of Scragh Bog, Co. Westmeath and the vegetational history of its hinterland. *New Phytologist* 85, 301–19.

O'Connell, M. 1990. Early land use in north-east County Mayo: the palaeoecological evidence. *Proceedings of the Royal Irish Academy* 90C, 259–79.

O'Connell, M. and Molloy, K. 1988. Post-glacial landscape evolution in Connemara, western Ireland with particular reference to woodland history. In Birks, H.H., Birks, H.J.B., Kaland, P.E. and Moe, D. (eds), *The cultural landscape: past, present and future*, 487–514. Cambridge, Cambridge University Press.

O'Connell, M. and Molloy, K. 2001. Farming and woodland dynamics in Ireland during the Neolithic. *Proceedings of the Royal Irish Academy* 101B, 99–128.

O'Connell, M., Molloy, K. and McMahon, H. 2001. Reconstructing prehistoric farming activity and human impact at a fine spatial resolution: palaeoecological investigations at Mooghaun, Co. Clare, western Ireland. In Schauer, P. (ed.), *Beiträge zur Siedlungsarchäologie und zum Landschaftswande,* 161–86. Regensburger, Beiträge zur Prähistorischen Archäologie.

Ó Cróinín, D. (ed.) 2005. *A new history of Ireland:* vol. 1 *Prehistoric and Early Ireland.* Oxford, Oxford University Press.

O'Donnell, L., 2007. Environmental archaeology: identifying patterns of exploitation in the Bronze Age. In Grogan, E., O'Donnell, L. and Johnson, P., *The Bronze Age landscapes of the Pipeline to the West*, 27–101. Bray, Wordwell.

O'Donnell, L., 2011. People and woodlands: an investigation of charcoal remains as indicators of cultural selection and local environment in Bronze Age Ireland. Unpublished PhD Thesis, University College Dublin.

O'Donovan, J. 1839. *Ordnance Survey letters.* Dublin, Royal Irish Academy.

O'Driscoll, J. 2016. The Baltinglass landscape and the hillforts of Bronze Age Ireland. Unpublished PhD Thesis, University College Cork. Available online: https://cora.ucc.ie/handle/10468/3532 [last accessed 8 June 2024].

O'Driscoll, J. 2017a. A multi-layered model for Bronze Age hillforts in Ireland and Europe. *Journal of Irish Archaeology* 26, 77–100.

O'Driscoll, J. 2017b. Hillforts in prehistoric Ireland: a costly display of power? *World Archaeology* 49 (3), 1–20.

O'Driscoll, J. 2017c. Ireland's 'hillfort capital' revisited. *Archaeology Ireland* 31 (4), 30–34.

O'Driscoll, J. 2023. Head for the hills: nucleated hilltop settlement in the Irish Bronze Age. *Journal of World Prehistory* 36, 1–47.

O'Driscoll, J. and Becker, K. 2022. Rathgall: piecing together the mosaic of a later prehistoric landscape. *Archaeology Ireland* 36 (4), 30–35.

O'Driscoll, J. and Gleeson, P. 2021. Locating historical Dún Bolg and the early medieval landscape of Baltinglass, Co. Wicklow. *Proceedings of the Royal Irish Academy* 121C, 91–124.

O'Driscoll, J. and Noble, G. forthcoming. Excavations at Eildon Hill North, Scotland: a Late Bronze Age and Late Roman Iron Age hillfort.

Ó Floinn, R. 2000. Freestone Hill, Co. Kilkenny: a re-assessment. In Smyth, A. (ed.), *Seanachas: studies in Early and Medieval Irish archaeology, history and literature in honour of Francis J. Byrne*, 12–29. Dublin, Four Courts Press.

O'Kelly, M.J. 1951. An Early Bronze Age ringfort at Carrigillihy, Co. Cork. *Journal of the Cork Historical and Archaeological Society* 51, 78–84.

O'Kelly, M.J. 1956. Review of Evans, E. 1953. Lyles Hill: a Late Neolithic site in County Antrim. *Journal of the Royal Society of Antiquaries of Ireland* 86, 113–15.

Ó Nualláin, S. 1995. *Stone circles in Ireland.* Dublin, Country House.

Ó Ríordáin, B. 1972. Prehistoric burials and pottery. *Journal of the Royal Society of Antiquaries of Ireland* 102, 234–9.

Ó Ríordáin, B. and Waddell, J. 1993. *The funerary bowls and vases of the Irish Bronze Age.* Galway, Galway University Press for the National Museum of Ireland.

Ó Ríordáin, S.P. 1954. Lough Gur excavations: Neolithic and Bronze Age houses on Knockadoon. *Proceedings of the Royal Irish Academy* 56C, 297–459.

O'Sullivan, A., McCormick, F., Kerr, T and Harney, L. 2008. *Early Medieval Ireland: archaeological excavations 1930–2004. EMAP Report 2.1.* Available online: www.ucd.ie/t4cms/emap_report_2_1_complete.pdf [last accessed September 2010].

O'Sullivan, A., McCormick, F., Kerr, T. and Harney, L. 2013. *Early Medieval Ireland, AD 400–1100: the evidence from archaeological excavations.* Dublin, Royal Irish Academy.

O'Sullivan, J. 2007. The quiet landscape: archaeological discoveries on a road scheme in east Galway. In McKeon, J. and O'Sullivan, J. (eds), *The quiet landscape*, 81–100. Dublin, National Roads Authority.

O'Toole, P. 1890. *History of the Clan O'Tool and other Leinster septs.* Dublin, Gill and Son.

Orpen, G. 1911. Rathgall, County Wicklow. *Journal of the Royal Society of Antiquaries of Ireland* 1 (2), 138–50.

Orpen, G. 1916. Dún Galion and the 'Dunum' of Ptolemy. *Proceedings of the Royal Irish Academy* 32, 41–57.

Osgood, R. and Monks, S. 2000. *Bronze Age warfare.* Stroud, The History Press.

Oswald, D., Dyer, C. and Barber, M. 2001. *The creation of monuments: Neolithic causewayed enclosures in the British Isles.* Swindon, English Heritage.

Overland, A. and O'Connell, M. 2008. Fine-spatial palaeoecological investigations towards reconstructing late Holocene environmental change, landscape evolution and farming activity in Barrees, Beara peninsula, southwestern Ireland. *Journal of the North Atlantic* 1, 37–73.

Owen, O. 1992. Eildon Hill North, Roxburgh, Borders. In Rideout, J., Owen, O. and Halpin, E. *Hillforts of Southern Scotland*, 21–71. Dundee, Burns and Harris.

Pardo, J., Rey Castiñeira, J., Picón Platas, I., Abad Vidal, E. and Marín Suárez, C. 2009. Radiocarbon and chronology of the Iron Age hillforts of Northwestern Iberia. In Karl, R. and Leskovar, J. (eds), *Interpretierte Eisenzeiten. Fallstudien, Methoden, Theorie. Tagungsbeiträge der 3 Linzer Gespräche zur interpretativen Eisenzeitarchäologie*, 81–98. Studien zur Kulturgeschichte von Oberösterreich, 22. Linz, Oberösterreichischen Landesmuseum, .

Parker, A.G., Goudie, A.S., Anderson, D.E., Robinson, M.A. and Bonsall, C. 2002. A review of the mid-Holocene elm decline in the British Isles. *Progress in Physical Geography* 26, 1–45.

Parkes, M., Meehan, R., Gallagher, V., Hennessy, R. and Gatley, S. 2022. *Glaciers, glens and granite.* Wicklow, Wicklow County Council.

Parry, C. 1999. Excavations at Camp Gardens, Stow-on-the-Wold, Gloucestershire. *Transactions of the Bristol and Gloucestershire Archaeological Society* 117, 75–87.

Peglar, S.M. and Birks, H.J.B. 1993. The mid-Holocene Ulmus fall at Diss Mere, South-East England—disease and human impact? *Vegetation History and Archaeobotany* 2, 61–8.

Petrie, G. and O'Malley, D.J.S. 1972. Aspects of George Petrie: an essay on military architecture in Ireland previous to the English invasion. *Proceedings of the Royal Irish Academy* 72C, 219–69.

Piggott, S. 1954. *Neolithic cultures of the British Isles.* Cambridge, Cambridge University Press.

Pilcher, J.R. 1969. Archaeology, palaeoecology, and ^{14}C dating of the Beaghmore stone circle site. *Ulster Journal of Archaeology* 32, 73–91.

Pilcher, J.R., Baillie, M.G.L., Brown, D.M., McCormack, F.G., McSweeney, P.B. and McLawrence, A.S. 1995. Dendrochronology of subfossil pine in the north of Ireland. *Journal of Ecology* 83, 665–71.

Pilcher, J.R. and Smith, A.G. 1979. Palaeoecological Investigations at Ballynagilly: a Neolithic and Bronze Age settlement in County Tyrone, Northern Ireland. *Philosophical Transactions of the Royal Society of London. Series B, Biological Sciences* 286, 345–69.

Plunkett, G. 1999. Environmental change in the Late Bronze Age in Ireland (1200–600 cal. BC). Unpublished PhD thesis, Queen's University, Belfast.

Plunkett, G. 2006. Hekla 3, environmental downturn and Irish Late Bronze Age hillfort connections revisited.

Emania 20, 62–7.

Plunkett, G. 2009. Land-use patterns and cultural change in the Middle to Late Bronze Age in Ireland: inferences from the pollen record. *Vegetation History and Archaeobotany* 18, 273–95.

Price, L. 1934/35. The ages of stone and bronze in Co. Wicklow. *Proceedings of the Royal Irish Academy* 42C, 31–64.

Price, L. 1949a. *The place-names of Co. Wicklow III–the barony of Talbotstown Upper*. Dublin, Dublin Institute for Advanced Studies.

Price, L. 1949b. Place-name study as applied to history. *Journal of the Royal Society of Antiquaries of Ireland* 79 (1), 26–38.

Primas, M. 2002. Taking the high ground: continental hill-forts in Bronze Age contexts. *Proceedings of the Prehistoric Society* 68, 41–59.

Proudfoot, B. 1954. Excavations at the Cathedral Hill, Downpatrick, Co. Down, 1953. *Ulster Journal of Archaeology* 89, 97–102.

Proudfoot, B. 1955. Excavations at Cathedral Hill, Downpatrick, Co. Down: preliminary report on excavations in 1954. *Ulster Journal of Archaeology* 90, 57–72.

Pryor, F. 1998. *Etton: excavations at a Neolithic causewayed enclosure near Maxey, Cambrideshire, 1982–7*. London, English Heritage.

Rackham, O. 1980. *Ancient woodland: its history, vegetation and uses in England*. London, Edward Arnold.

Raftery, B. 1969. Freestone Hill, Co. Kilkenny: an Iron Age hillfort and Bronze Age cairn. *Proceedings of the Royal Irish Academy* 68C, 1–108.

Raftery, B. 1970a. The Rathgall hillfort, Co. Wicklow. *Antiquity* 44, 51–4.

Raftery, B. 1970b. A decorated strap-end from Rathgall, Co. Wicklow. *Journal Royal Society of Antiquaries of Ireland* 100, 200–11.

Raftery, B. 1971. Rathgall, Co. Wicklow: 1970 excavations. *Antiquity* 45, 296–8.

Raftery, B. 1972. Irish hill-forts. In Thomas, C. (ed.), *The Iron Age in the Irish Sea province*, 37–58. Research Report 9. London, Council for British Archaeology.

Raftery, B. 1973. Rathgall: a late Bronze Age burial in Ireland. *Antiquity* 47, 293–5.

Raftery, B. 1976. Rathgall and Irish hillfort problems. In Harding, D.W. (ed.), *Hillforts. Later prehistoric earthworks in Britain and Ireland*, 339–57. London, Academic Press.

Raftery, B. 1994. *Pagan Celtic Ireland*. London, Thames and Hudson.

Raftery, B. 2004. Pit 119, Rathgall, Co. Wicklow. In Roche, H., Grogan, E., Bradley, J., Coles, J. and Raftery, B. (eds), *From megaliths to metals*, 83–90. Oxford, Oxbow.

Raftery, B. and Becker, K. forthcoming. *A hillfort through time: excavations at Rathgall, Co. Wicklow*. Dublin, Wordwell.

Raftery, J. 1973. A Neolithic burial mound at Ballintruer More, Co. Wicklow. *Journal of the Royal Society of Antiquaries of Ireland* 103, 214–19.

Ralston, I, 2006. *Celtic fortifications*. Stroud, Tempus Publishing.

Rassmann, K., Scholz, R., Vob, H., Ó Drisceoil, C. and Cahill Wilson, J. 2022. Following in the footsteps of Gerhard Bersu at Freestone Hill and Stonyford, Co. Kilkenny. New contributions from magnetic surveys. Digging Bersu. Ein Europäischer Archäologe. *Bericht der Römisch-Germanischen Kommission*, Bd. 100 2019(2022), 335–66.

Rathbone, S. 2013. A consideration of villages in Neolithic and Bronze Age Britain and Ireland. *Proceedings of the Prehistoric Society* 79, 39–60.

Reid, J. 2023. *The eagle and the bear*. Edinburgh, Birlinn.

Reimer, P.J., Austin, W.E., Bard, E., Bayliss, A., Blackwell, P.G., *et al.* 2020. The INTCAL20 Northern Hemisphere radiocarbon age calibration curve (0– 55 cal kBP). *Radiocarbon* 62, 725–57.

Revell, M. 2023. The lithics from Rathcoran hillfort (2019–2021 seasons). Unpublished report prepared for Alan Hawkes, Rathcoran Hillfort Project.

Rind, M. 1999. *Der Frauenberg oberhalb Kloster Weltenburg. I: Höhenbefestigungen der Bronze- und Urnenfelderzeit.* Regensburger Beiträge zur Prähistorischen Archäologie 6. Bonn, Rudolf Habelt Verlag.

Roche, H. 2002. Excavations at Ráith na Ríg, Tara, Co. Meath, 1997. *Discovery Programme Reports* 6, 19–165.

Rowley-Conwy, P. 1982. Forest grazing and clearance in temperate Europe with special reference to Denmark: an archaeological view. In Bell, M. and Limbrey, S. (eds), *Archaeological aspects of woodland ecology*, 57–74. British Archaeological Reports. Oxford, Archaeopress.

Ryan, M.F. 1981. Poulawack, Co. Clare: the affinities of the central burial structure. In Ó Corráin, D. (ed.),

Irish antiquity. Essays and studies presented to Professor O'Kelly. Cork, Tower Books.

Sassoon, D., Fletcher, W.J., Hotchkiss, A., Owen, F. and Feng, L. 2021. Scots pine (*Pinus sylvestris*) dynamics in the Welsh Marches during the mid to late-Holocene. *The Holocene* 31, 1033–46.

SCARF (Scottish Archaeological Research Framework) 2012. *The Roman presence*. Edinburgh, Society of Antiquaries Scotland.

Schindler, R. 1968. *Studien Zum Vorgeschichtlichen Siedlungs- und Befestigungswesen des Sarrlandes*. Trier, Paulinus-Verlag.

Schindler, R. 1974. Hallstättische Höhenburgen im Saar- und Moselraum. In Chropovsky. B. (ed.), *Symposium zum Problemen der jüngeren Hallstattzeit in Mitteleuropa*, 435–46. Bratislava, Archäologisches Institut der slowakischen Akademie der Wissenschaften.

Schulting, R., McClatchie, M., Sheridan, A., McLaughlin, R., Barratt, P. and Whitehouse, N. 2017. Radiocarbon dating of a multi-phase passage tomb on Baltinglass Hill, Co. Wicklow, Ireland. *Proceedings of the Prehistoric Society* 83, 305–23.

Seaman, A. and Sucharyna Thomas, L. 2020. Hillforts and power in the British Post-Roman west: a GIS analysis of Dinas Powys. *European Journal of Archaeology* 23 (4), 547–66.

Selby, K.A., O'Brien, C.E., Brown, A.G. and Stuijts, I. 2005. A multi-proxy study of Holocene lake development, lake settlement and vegetation history in central Ireland. *Journal of Quaternary Science* 20, 147–68.

Semple, S. 2013. *Perceptions of the prehistoric in Anglo-Saxon England: ritual, religion and rulership*. Oxford. Oxford University Press.

Sharpe, S. 2018. The lithics from Rathcoran hillfort (2018 season). Unpublished report prepared for Alan Hawkes, Rathcoran Hillfort Project.

Sharples, N. 1991. *Maiden Castle: excavations and field survey 1985–1986*. English Heritage Archaeological Monographs. Swindon, English Heritage.

Sharples, N. 2007. Building communities and creating identities in the first millennium BC. In Haselgrove, C. and Pope, R. (eds), *The Earlier Iron Age in Britain and the near continent*, 174–84. Oxford, Oxbow Books.

Sharples, N. 2010. *Social relations in Later prehistory. Wessex in the first millennium BC*. Oxford, Oxford University Press.

Sheridan, A. 2001. Donegore Hill and other Irish Neolithic enclosures: a view from outside. In Darvill, T. and Thomas, J. (eds), *Neolithic enclosures in Atlantic Northwest Europe*, 171–80. Oxford, Oxbow.

Simmons, I.G. and Innes, J.B. 1996. Disturbance phases in the Mid-Holocene vegetation at North Gill, North York Moors: form and process. *Journal of Archaeological Science* 23, 183–91.

Simpson, D.D.A. and Gibson, A. 1989. Lyles Hill. *Current Archaeology* 114, 214–5.

Singh, G. and Smith, A.G. 1973. Post-glacial vegetational history and relative land- and sea-level changes in Lecale, Co. Down. *Proceedings of the Royal Irish Academy* 73B, 1–51.

Sleeman, A., McConnell, B. and Gately, S. 2004. *Understanding earth processes, rocks and the geological history of Ireland*. Dublin, Geological Survey of Ireland.

Smith, A.G. 1970. The influence of Mesolithic and Neolithic man on British vegetation. In Walker, D. and West, R.G. (eds), *Studies in the vegetational history of the British Isles*, 81–96. Cambridge, Cambridge University Press.

Smith, R. 1984. The ecology of Neolithic farming systems as exemplified by the Avebury region of Wiltshire. *Proceedings of the Prehistoric Society* 50, 99–120.

Smyth, A.P. 1974. The Húi Néill and the Leinstermen in the Annals of Ulster, 431–516 AD. *Études Celtiques* 14, 121–43.

Smyth, A. 1982. *Celtic Leinster: towards an historical geography of early Irish civilization AD 500–1600*. Dublin, Irish Academic Press.

Smyth, A. 1994. Kings, saints and sagas. In Hannigan, K. and William, N. (eds.), *Wicklow, history and society: interdisciplinary essays on the history of an Irish county*, 41–112. Dublin. Geography Publications.

Smyth, J. 2014. *Settlement in Neolithic Ireland: new discoveries on the edge of Europe*. Prehistoric Society Research Paper 6. Oxford, The Prehistoric Society.

Sørensen, P. 1995. Markildegård. En tidligneolitisk samlingsplads. *Kulturhistoriske Studier, Sydsjællands Museum*, 13–45.

Spencer, D.E., Molloy, K., Potito, A. and Jones, C. 2020. New insights into Late Bronze Age settlement and farming activity in the southern Burren, western Ireland. *Vegetation History and Archaeobotany* 29, 339–56.

Stace, C. 1997. *New Flora of the British Isles* (2nd edn).

Cambridge, Cambridge University Press.
Stockmarr, J. 1971. Tablets with spores used in absolute pollen analysis. *Pollen et Spores* 13, 615–21.
Stokes, W. (ed and trans) 1892. The Bóroma. *Revue Celtique* 13, 31–124, 299–300.
Stolze, S. 2012. High-resolution palaeoecological data from the Carrowkeel area, western Ireland: landscape change and human settlement dynamics during the fourth millennium BC. *Quaternary International* 279–80, 470.
Stolze, S. and Monecke, T. 2021. Neolithic land-use dynamics in northwest Ireland: Multi-proxy evidence from Lough Arrow, County Sligo. *Vegetation History and Archaeobotany* 30, 423–43.
Stolze, S., Muscheler, R., Dörfler, W. and Nelle, O. 2013. Solar influence on climate variability and human development during the Neolithic: evidence from a high-resolution multi-proxy record from Templevanny Lough, County Sligo, Ireland. *Quaternary Science Reviews* 67, 138–59.
Stout, G. 1989. The archaeology of county Wicklow. *Archaeology Ireland* 3 (4), 126–31.
Stout, G. 1994. Wicklow's prehistoric landscape. In Hannigan, K. and Nolan W. (eds), *Wicklow history and society*, 1–40. Dublin, Geography Publications.
Stout, G. and Stout, M. 2008. *Excavation of a secular cemetery at Knowth Site M, Co. Meath and related sites in North Leinster*. Bray, Wordwell.
Stout, M. 1997. *The Irish ringfort*. Dublin, Four Courts Press.
Stuiver, M. and Polach, H.A. 1977. Reporting of ^{14}C data. *Radiocarbon* 19, 355–63.
Stuiver, M. and Reimer, P.J. 1986. A computer program for radiocarbon age calculation. *Radiocarbon* 28 (2B), 1022–30.
Stuiver, M. and Reimer, P.J. 1993. Extended ^{14}C database and revised CALIB 3.0 14C age calibration program. *Radiocarbon* 35, 215–30.
Sugita, S. 1994. Pollen representation of vegetation in Quaternary sediments: theory and method in patchy vegetation. *Journal of Ecology* 82, 881–97.
Sugita, S. 2007a. Theory of quantitative reconstruction of vegetation. I: Pollen from large sites REVEALS regional vegetation composition. *The Holocene* 17 (2), 229–41.
Sugita, S. 2007b. Theory of quantitative reconstruction of vegetation. II: All you need is LOVE. *The Holocene* 17 (2), 243–57.
Sugita, S., Gaillard, M.-J. and Broström, A. 1999. Landscape openness and pollen records: a simulation approach. *The Holocene* 9, 409–21.
Szentmiklosi, A., Heeb, B., Heeb, J., Harding, A., Krause, R. and Becker, H. 2011. Corneşti-Iarcuri—a Bronze Age town in the Romanian Banat? *Antiquity* 85, 819–38.
Swift, C. 2006. Brigid, Patrick, and the kings of Kildare, A.D. 640–850. In Nolan, W. and McGrath, T. (eds), *Kildare: history and society*, 97–128. Dublin, Geography Publications.
Tabor, R. 2008. *Cadbury Castle: the hillfort and landscapes*. Stroud, The History Press.
Teržan, B. 2013. The western Balkans in the Bronze Age. In Fokkens, H. and Harding, A. (eds), *Oxford handbook of the European Bronze Age*, 837–63. Oxford, Oxford University Press.
Thomas, J. 2007. *Place and memory: excavations at the Pict's Knowe, Holywood and Holm Farm, Dumfries and Galloway, 1994–8*. Oxford, Oxbow Books.
Thorpe, N. 2013. Warfare in the European Bronze Age. In Fokkens, H. and Harding, A. (eds), *Oxford handbook of the European Bronze Age*, 235–47. Oxford, Oxford University Press.
Tilley, C. 2010. *Interpreting landscapes: geologies, topographies and identities*. London, Routledge.
Timpany, S. 2009. Appendix 9: Palaeoenvironmental analyses report, Site 34, Newrath Townland, Co. Kilkenny. N25 Waterford Bypass, Contract 3. Final Report on archaeological investigations at Site 34 in the townland of Newrath, Co Kilkenny. Unpublished excavation report, Headland Archaeology on behalf of Kilkenny County Council and the National Roads Authority.
Tipping, R., Ashmore, P., Davies, A.L., Haggart, B.A., Moir, A., *et al.* 2008. Prehistoric *Pinus* woodland dynamics in an upland landscape in northern Scotland: the roles of climate change and human impact. *Vegetation History and Archaeobotany* 17, 251–67.
Toolis, R. and Bowles, C. 2017. *The lost Dark Age kingdom of Rheged: the discovery of a royal stronghold at Trusty's Hill, Galloway*. Oxford, Oxbow Books.
Troels-Smith, J. 1960. Ivy, mistletoe and elm climate indicators—fodder plants: a contribution to the interpretation of the pollen zone border VII-VIII. *Danmarks Geologiske Undersøgelse II*, Series IV, 1–32.
Vandkilde, H. 2004. Spîšský Ŝtvrtok. In Bogucki, P. and Crabtree, P. (eds), *Ancient Europe: 8000 BC–AD 1000*.

Encyclopaedia of the Barbarian World, 30–33. New York, Charles Scribner's Sons.

Waddell, J. 1990. *The Bronze Age burials of Ireland*. Galway, Galway University Press.

Waddell, J. 1998. (revised 2022). *The prehistoric archaeology of Ireland*. Dublin, Wordwell.

Waddell, J., Fenwick, J. and Barton, K. 2009. *Rathcroghan: archaeological and geophysical survey in a ritual landscape*. Dublin, Wordwell.

Wailes, B. 1982. The Irish royal sites in history and archaeology. *Cambridge Medieval Celtic Studies* 3, 1–29.

Wailes, B. 1990. Dún Ailinne: a summary excavation report. *Emania* 7, 10–21.

Walshe, P.T. 1931. The antiquities of the Dunlavin-Donard district. *Journal of the Royal Society of Antiquaries of Ireland* 61, 113–41.

Walshe, P. 1941. The excavation of a burial cairn on Baltinglass Hill, Co. Wicklow. *Proceedings of the Royal Irish Academy* 56, 221–36.

Warner, R. 1988. The archaeology of early historic Irish kingship. In O'Driscoll, S.T. and Nieke, M. (eds), *Power and politics in Early Medieval Britain and Ireland*, 47–68. Edinburgh. Edinburgh University Press.

Warner, R. 2000. Keeping out the Otherworld: the internal ditch at Navan and other Iron Age 'hengiform' enclosures. *Emania* 18, 39–44.

Warner, R, 2006. The Tamlaght hoard and the Creeveroe axe: two new finds of Late Bronze Age date from near Navan, County Armagh. *Emania* 20, 20–28.

Warner, R. 2009. Clogher in late prehistory. In Cooney, G., Becker, K., Coles, J., Ryan, M. and Sievers, S. (eds), *Relics of Old Decency: archaeological studies in later prehistory*, 507–18. Dublin, Wordwell.

Warner, R. 2013. A lost, Iberian-style, Bronze Age gold neck-ring from near Navan, Co. Armagh. *Emania* 21, 36–9.

Warner, R. 2014a. The gold ornaments from Rathgall: the analytical evidence for their date and the sources of their gold. *Journal of Irish Archaeology* 23, 143–55.

Warner, R. 2014b. The gold fragments from Haughey's Fort, Co. Armagh: description and XRF analysis. *Emania* 22, 69–76.

Warren, G., Davis, S., McClatchie, M. and Sands, R. 2014. The potential role of humans in structuring the wooded landscapes of Mesolithic Ireland: a review of data and discussion of approaches. *Vegetation History and Archaeobotany* 23, 629–46.

Webley, L., Timby, J. and Wilson, M. 2007. *Fairfield Park, Stotfold, Bedfordshire: later prehistoric settlement in the Eastern Chilterns*. Bedfordshire Archaeology Monograph 7. Oxford, Bedfordshire Archaeology.

Weir, D. 1993. Dark Ages and the pollen record. *Emania* 11, 21–30.

Weir, D. 1995. A palynological study of landscape and agricultural development in County Louth from the second millennium BC to the first millennium AD. *Discovery Programme Reports* 2. Dublin, Royal Irish Academy.

Westropp, T.J. 1902. The ancient forts of Ireland: being a contribution towards our knowledge of their types, affinities and structural features. *Transactions of the Royal Irish Academy* 31, 579–730.

Westropp, T.J. 1911. Prehistoric remains (forts and dolmens) in the Burren, Co. Clare (continued). *Journal of the Royal Society of Antiquaries of Ireland* 41, 343–67.

Whitehouse, N.J., Schulting, R.J., McClatchie, M., Barratt, P., McLaughlin, *et al.* 2014. Neolithic agriculture on the European western frontier: the boom and bust of early farming in Ireland. *Journal of Archaeological Science* 51, 181–205.

Whittle, A. 2014. The times and timings of enclosures. In de Valera, A. (ed.), *Recent prehistoric enclosures and funerary practices in Europe*, 1–12. British Archaeological Reports 2676. Oxford, Archaeopress.

Whittle, A., Bayliss, A. and Healy, F. 2011. *Gathering time: dating the Early Neolithic enclosures of Southern Britain and Ireland*. Oxford, Oxbow Books.

Whittow, J. 1975. *Geology and scenery in Ireland*. London, Penguin.

Whitty, Y. 2021. Final Report. Baltinglass East License 18E0686. Unpublished report, De Faoite Archaeology, Tinahely, Co. Wicklow.

Williams, M. and Harper, D. 1999. *The making of Ireland: landscapes in geology*. London, Immel Publishing.

Woodman, P.C. 2015. *Ireland's first settlers, time and the Mesolithic*. Oxford, Oxbow Books.

Woodman, P.C., McCarthy, M. and Monaghan, N. 1997. The Irish Quaternary fauna project. *Quaternary Science Reviews* 16, 129–59.

Woodman, P.C. and Sternke, F. 2015. Hunter-gathers in Mesolithic Carlow. In Bolger, T., Moloney, C. and Shiels, D. (eds), *A journey along the Carlow Bypass. The archaeology of the M9 Carlow Bypass*. NRA Monograph 16. Dublin, National Roads Authority.

Woodward, A. 2000. *British barrows: a matter of life and death*. Stroud, Tempus.
Woolf, A. 2007. *From Pictland to Alba, 789–1070*. Edinburgh, Edinburgh University Press.

INDEX